Fourth Edition

Understanding Human Differences

Multicultural Education for a Diverse America

Kent L. Koppelman

Professor Emeritus, University of Wisconsin—La Crosse

Boston   Columbus   Indianapolis   New York   San Francisco   Upper Saddle River
Amsterdam   Cape Town   Dubai   London   Madrid   Milan   Munich   Paris   Montreal   Toronto
Delhi   Mexico City   Sao Paulo   Sydney   Hong Kong   Seoul   Singapore   Taipei   Tokyo

Dedicated To
Burt Altman and Dick Rasmussen
Who demonstrated the meaning of the word "good"
to precede the nouns: colleague, mentor, friend,
and human being.

Executive Editor: Linda Bishop
Senior Development Editor: Max Effenson Chuck
Editorial Assistant: Laura Marengi
Senior Marketing Manager: Darcy Betts
Production Editor: Paula Carroll
Editorial Production Service: Cenveo Publisher Services
Manufacturing Buyer: Megan Cochran
Interior Design and Electronic Composition: Cenveo Publisher Services
Cover Designer: Laura Gardner

10 9 8 7 6 5 4 3 2 1

www.pearsonhighered.com

ISBN 10: 0-13-282489-2
ISBN 13: 978-0-13-282489-7

Contents

CHAPTER 6 Religion and Oppression: The Struggle for Religious Freedom 135

SECTION 4 The Challenge of Diversity to American Institutions 314

Preface

Why Do We Need to Understand Diversity?

Americans live in the most racially, ethnically, and socially diverse country on earth. Yet too often we live, work, and play as if our own social, gender, or religious group is the only one that matters. To enjoy the advantages of our national diversity, it is necessary that Americans seek as many facts and consider as many issues as possible to enhance their ability to interact effectively with individuals from diverse groups. This book is not a collection of essays providing multiple perspectives on diversity—there are many books that already do that; instead, this book uses research to examine problems, perceptions, misperceptions, and the potential benefits of the diversity that exists in the United States. Understanding diversity is obviously a prerequisite for becoming an individual who values the diversity in American society.

If we are to value and respect the diversity represented by different groups in the United States, we can begin by learning how to value and respect opinions that differ from our own. It is not necessary to agree with everything a person might say, but it is necessary that when we disagree, we are able to express disagreement based upon a consideration of all available information and within a context of mutual respect.

The issues this book addresses are not new: Human beings have struggled with them in one form or another for centuries, as illustrated by the quotations from individuals of different eras that appear in each chapter. The quotations are not placed randomly in the text, but near a section of text that relates to each one. For example, near the section in Chapter 2 addressing the confusion about positive prejudices and explaining why prejudices are always negative, the quotation by Charles Lamb suggests that prejudices involve "likings and dislikings." Because Lamb was a respected writer of his era, his confusion about some prejudices being positive was not based on a lack

of education or intellectual ability, but instead illustrates how ancient this misperception is.

Since the first edition of *Understanding Human Differences* was published, the rights of various minority groups in the United States have become common topics for debate. For example, the term *marriage* has now become a legislative and judicial football, and American perceptions about how we differ from one another have changed in many ways. Students used to come to diversity classes oblivious of the issues, but that is less likely now, even though many diversity topics are still misunderstood.

New to This Edition

Two specific goals for this edition were to include content that had been absent in previous editions such as stereotype threat, racial profiling, racial disparities in school suspensions, and zero tolerance policies, and to expand the content on critical issues such as cyberbullying, white privilege, racial disparities in incarceration rates, implicit and explicit forms of ageism, and diversity issues for digital media.

As with any new edition, care has been taken to update statistics and sources and to find more current examples of issues, and this edition has expanded the number of examples pertaining to issues in K–12 schools. With regard to specific additions of content, the fourth edition of *Understanding Human Differences* includes a substantial expansion of information on the following:

- Explains confirmation bias and provides examples of its influence on human perception and behavior
- Describes actions at the U.S./Mexican border in response to nativist demands
- Discusses consequences of the anti-ethnic studies law in Arizona
- Provides a brief history of the medical exploitation of African American patients

- Explains long-term effects of preschool education
- Describes Matthew Shepard's murder and its influence on the expansion of the federal hate crimes law
- Discusses how one community confronted racism in their election process
- Describes the "mosque at ground zero" controversy
- Examines successful conflict resolution programs in preK–12 schools
- Expands the discussion of homelessness by addressing issues related to the education of homeless children
- Explains the rights of students with disabilities mandated by *Honig v. Doe*
- Describes increased deportations of illegal immigrants and provides additional content on contributions of legal and illegal immigrants
- Discusses the repeal of the military's "Don't Ask, Don't Tell" policy
- Examines recent research on charter schools
- Addresses four problems in implementing culturally responsive teaching
- Provides updated and expanded content on sexual harassment in K–12 schools and in the workplace
- Examines the influence of attendance at middle-class schools on the learning of low-income students
- Describes strategies for analyzing how people with a disability are included in school textbooks and curricular materials
- Discusses how other educational reform movements such as teacher collaboration and community schools are consistent with multicultural education goals

Students should benefit from exploring all of these issues because each is relevant to the society we live in now and the future society that these students may influence. The first step in problem solving is to understand why a problem exists and how it is perpetuated; with that understanding, a person or a community, or a state or a nation can implement solutions to address root causes of persistent problems. Consistent with this book's first three editions, the additional content offers information to understand problems or issues in society in order to find solutions, or in some cases

to describe solutions that have been proposed or implemented.

Inquiry Approach/Organization

Chapter narratives in this book are presented in an inquiry format. After a brief introduction, each chapter consists of related questions with responses based on research from a variety of disciplines and on author expertise. As references illustrate, information for this book has been collected from studies in a broad array of behavioral sciences, including education, psychology, sociology, anthropology, history, science, and literature. Although sources cited are from relatively recent publications, some older sources are also included either because they are still highly regarded in the field or simply because an author expressed a conclusion replicated by other research but not stated with as much clarity.

Section 1 focuses on individuals and interpersonal relationships. Chapter 1 defines terms essential for discussing diversity issues: Being able to make clear distinctions between terms such as *bias, prejudice,* and *bigotry* is critical for a conversation about problems related to individual and group differences. Chapter 1 also introduces the concept of *values.* The values promoted by a particular culture shape the values, beliefs, and actions of individuals living within that culture. Our cultural values define who we are and what we think is important; they shape the ideals that we embrace.

Section 1 also examines issues affecting all individuals, especially those living in a diverse society: the causes of prejudice, how it is learned, and the impact of prejudice; communication, conflict, moral reasoning, and conflict resolution.

Section 2 provides a historical context to illustrate how cultural biases were reflected in our evolving society. This context must be understood prior to examining the issues in Section 3, which describes intergroup relations in our diverse society. Section 2 also describes the foundations of oppression as observed in early interactions between the first European colonizers of America who created a new nation and the unceasing flood of immigrants coming to that nation. The attitudes of descendants of immigrants toward each successive wave of new immigrants reveal the difficulty of sustaining the ideal of America as a land of opportunity and freedom. Anti-immigrant sentiment was especially antagonistic toward immigrants of color, requiring an examination of the historical experiences of each of the four major racial groups. Anti-immigrant sentiment was also directed against new arrivals because of their religion, and eventually came to include blatantly anti-Catholic and anti-Semitic attitudes.

The final chapter in Section 2 reviews the development of alternative perspectives as expressed by Americans on immigrants and the diversity produced by immigration, including the idea (or ideal) of pluralism, also called *cultural pluralism*. The rationale for promoting pluralism in a diverse society is examined as well as the strategies that can be used to promote pluralism.

Section 3 describes various ways in which specific minority groups have been oppressed in our society. The description of relations between dominant and subordinate groups includes an analysis of current cultural, individual, and institutional behaviors. Examples illustrate cultural biases against certain groups; individual prejudices, myths, and stereotypes believed by members of the dominant group about members of subordinate groups; and institutional policies and practices that benefit dominant group members but disadvantage subordinate group members.

Section 4 discusses changes that have already occurred in various institutions in the United States, reflecting a shift toward pluralism. This final section describes efforts that will move individual attitudes and institutional practices toward an acceptance of pluralism as the most appropriate response of a diverse society. The final chapter includes implications for future changes as the United States struggles with the challenges inherent in its status as the most diverse society in the world.

Discussion Exercises

To assist in the examination of serious ethical questions, exercises for group discussion are provided at the end of each chapter. Based on specific issues, activities encourage readers to reflect on and discuss aspects of issues that involve ethical or moral dilemmas. The exercises are not designed to manipulate readers into finding a "politically correct"

solution; rather, they enable students to hear the variety of responses from others and appreciate the complexity of individual, institutional, and cultural issues in America today.

The Conceptual Framework for This Book

Understanding human differences is an ongoing challenge. Initially, scholars focused on *individual attitudes and behaviors*; later, they described the influence of *cultural expectations* in shaping individual attitudes. Finally, scholars addressed *institutional policies and practices* in which either discrimination was intentional against minority groups or it was an unintentional outcome. Vega (1978) describes a conceptual framework incorporating these three elements to understand human differences and the oppression of minority groups by dominant groups. This conceptual framework provides the basis for the organization of this book as we examine individual attitudes and actions, the evolution of cultural biases, and the establishment of discriminatory institutional practices (see Figure F.1).

FIGURE F.1 A Conceptual Framework for the Study of Intergroup Relations

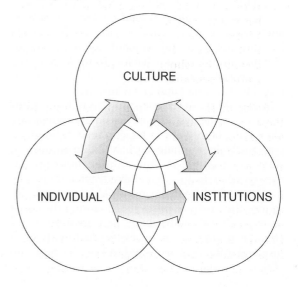

To understand human differences, Vega's conceptual framework allows us to analyze American cultural, individual, and institutional behaviors. In exploring culture, the objective is to describe *cultural norms and standards*. What images are associated with the ideal? Any culture associates particular images with the ideal woman, the ideal man, and the ideal family. For many Americans, those images are primarily white middle-class people living in a nuclear family. Norms and standards are powerful determinants of individual expectations and behaviors, represented by the arrow pointing from culture to individual. Once we understand norms and standards, we can begin to understand what is meant by *cultural biases*. In a multicultural society, cultural biases can be detrimental to minority groups whose norms or standards do not conform to those of the dominant culture.

Once we understand the influence of culture on individuals, we can analyze *individual beliefs, attitudes, values, opinions, actions, and inactions*; sometimes what a person chooses *not* to do reveals as much as his or her actions. Although individuals are influenced by their cultural norms and standards, the Vega conceptual framework portrays that arrow as double headed, meaning that when significant numbers of individuals accept cultural norms, express their agreement, and behave in accordance with them, the cultural norms and standards are reinforced. Any analysis of individual behavior must include the influence of prejudice on an individual's choices.

Finally, we analyze *institutional practices, policies*, and *standard operating procedures* that are influenced by cultural norms and standards as well as by individual attitudes and behavior. To the extent that they reflect cultural norms and standards as well as individual attitudes and behaviors, institutions also reinforce them. To relate institutions to human differences, the analysis must focus on discrimination, identifying both ways in which the institution intentionally discriminates against certain groups and ways in which the institution unintentionally advantages certain groups and disadvantages others.

Although the Vega conceptual framework describes the intricate relationship among the three areas—cultural, individual, and institutional—chapter narratives of necessity deal with each discretely. Readers are asked to keep in mind the double-headed arrows signifying that all three areas are interlocked to create the following relationships:

1. Cultural norms and standards influence and are reinforced by individual attitudes and behaviors and institutional policies and procedures.
2. Individual attitudes and behaviors influence and are reinforced by cultural norms and standards and by institutional policies and procedures.
3. Institutional policies and procedures influence and are reinforced by cultural norms and standards and individual attitudes and beliefs.

Before concluding this explanation of Vega's conceptual framework, consider this example to illustrate how interreliant culture is with individual and institutional behaviors. Although many forms of family exist in the United States, our cultural bias is for the nuclear family (the norm). Influenced by this cultural bias, Americans tend to form nuclear families. Even when people with a cultural tradition of extended families immigrate to the United States, they tend to form nuclear families within a few generations, sometimes reversing convention with elderly parents receiving care in nursing homes rather than at home.

American institutions have encouraged the formation of nuclear families because they are more able to relocate in an age in which mobility of workers is highly desirable. In an analysis of discrimination, problems may emerge for minority subcultures that value extended families if they maintain that value rather than adjust to the cultural norm. As this example illustrates, Vega's conceptual framework helps clarify the complexity of intergroup relations by describing the related factors involved in the oppression of minority groups by a dominant group.

The four sections of this book also relate to the conceptual framework. The first section focuses on the *Individual* by exploring personal values, interpersonal communication, and the way an individual develops negative attitudes toward other people based on perceptions of group identity (leading to bias, stereotypes, prejudice, and negative behavior toward members of these groups). Section 2 focuses on *Culture* by examining the pattern of historical responses in American society toward immigration and the increased racial and religious diversity that has always been a consequence of this immigration. The final chapter of this section describes how those who are pluralism advocates are engaged in efforts to reject this historical pattern of discrimination, but as the following section illustrates, discrimination remains a problem in our society. Section 3 describes interrelationships among culture, individuals, and institutions to produce discrimination based on race, gender, social class, sexual orientation, and disability, with institutional issues being a major focus of this section. Finally, Section 4 addresses changes that have been implemented to reduce levels of individual prejudice and institutional discrimination, focusing on major institutions in our society such as K–12 schools, the federal government, higher education, business, the media, and the military; their pluralistic policies and practices are designed to benefit from the diversity that exists in our society. This conceptual framework helps us to appreciate the changes that are occurring, but also the ongoing issues that illustrate how much farther we have to go.

The Intent of This Book

The information provided in this book is intended to challenge readers to think and talk about issues that each of us must consider as citizens in a multicultural society; this book is not necessarily intended to change reader values, but to challenge attitudes based on incomplete or erroneous information (see Chapter 1 for a description of the difference between *values* and *attitudes*). Diversity brings benefit as well as challenge, but the surest way to enjoy the benefits is to meet the challenges with a firm foundation of knowledge and insight that is based on research from all behavioral sciences. Once students have read this textbook, the primary goal will be realized if they have gained a better understanding of the issues addressed. Whether or not that is accompanied by changes in attitudes is up to each individual, but there is an Attitude Inventory in the Instructor's Manual that accompanies this text, and your instructor may ask

for your cooperation in taking this inventory before, during, or on completion of the course.

The intent of this book is to clarify our understanding of human differences and the role they play in interpersonal and intergroup relations. The Vega conceptual framework allows us to recognize how the interlocking circles of cultural biases, individual attitudes and actions, and institutional policies and practices have produced inequities that continue to polarize many Americans and that all too often prevent Americans from achieving ideals first expressed over two centuries ago when dreamers imagined a radical new concept, a nation where each person would be given the freedom to be whoever he or she wanted to be.

Student Outcomes

To illustrate some desired outcomes, the following statements were written by students enrolled in a class using this book after the course was completed:

> "If you had asked me whether I needed to know more (about diversity) at the beginning of the semester, I probably would have said no. . . . Now my views have changed. . . . I have been challenged to think about many issues and differences in society."

> "I don't hear jokes with the same lightness that I did before this course. Too many jokes are at the expense of the race, ability, poverty, gender, or orientation of someone else."

> "I am better able to consider the needs and situations of others in what I say and how I behave around others. Thanks. As I enter my profession, how I have changed my behavior . . . is a good career move!"

> "I have learned a lot about myself and I have come to a better understanding of prejudice and white privilege."

> "I did not fully understand that (as a white person) I have the odds in my favor when looking for housing, employment, or even shopping in a store. It is a strange feeling to know that I have an advantage over someone else simply because of what I was when I was born."

Supplements

Specific ancillaries accompany this text providing digitized instructional support and easy access to this content.

Instructor's Resource Center

The Instructor's Resource Center at http://www .pearsonhighered.com has a variety of course resources available in downloadable, digital format—all in one location.

As a registered faculty member, you can access and download pass code-protected instructional resource files, assessments, course-management content, and other premium online content directly to your computer.

Digital resources available for the fourth edition of *Understanding Human Differences: Multicultural Education for a Diverse America* include the following:

- A Test Bank of multiple choice and essay questions.
- PowerPoint presentations specifically designed for each chapter.
- Chapter-by-chapter materials, including discussion questions, content objectives, exercises, and suggested readings.
- Attitude inventory and instructions for its potential use.

To access these instructional resources, go to http://www.pearsonhighered.com and click on the Instructor option. You'll find the Instructor's Resource Center option in the top navigation bar. There you will be able to log in or complete a one-time registration for a user name and password. If you have any questions regarding this process or the materials available online, please contact your local Pearson sales representative.

Online TestGen

The computerized test bank software, Test Gen (0132824892), allows instructors to create and customize exams for classroom testing and for other specialized delivery options, such as over a local area network or on the Web. A test bank typically contains a large set of test items, organized by chapter and ready for your use in creating a test, based on the associated textbook material. The tests can be downloaded in the following formats:

- TestGen Testbank file—PC
- TestGen Testbank file—MAC
- TestGen Testbank—*Blackboard 9*
- TestGen Testbank—*Blackboard CE/Vista (WebCT)*
- *Angel* Test Bank
- *D2L* Test Bank
- *Moodle* Test Bank
- *Sakai* Test Bank

Acknowledgments

I want to thank Greg Wegner for his assistance in researching and writing on Ageism in Chapter 9. I also want to thank Robin DiAngelo for her assistance in researching and writing the new material for Individual and Cultural Racism in Chapter 8, and for updating the information on Culturally Responsive Teaching in Chapter 13. I also want to extend a special thanks to Jan Koppelman for her assistance on numerous aspects of revising this textbook and improving both content and illustrations. I am most grateful to my editors, Kelly Villella Canton, Linda Bishop, and Paula Carroll, for their wise counsel and assistance, and thanks to Associate Editor Anne Whittaker for all of her help. In addition I am especially appreciative of the work done by my copyeditor Kathy Smith who has worked so diligently on every edition of this book since the first one. Thanks also to the reviewers for this edition: John Barrera, University of St. Thomas; Kriss Ferluga, Davenport University; Zachariah Z. Gaye, Jackson State University; Sherry A. Green, Georgia Highlands College; and Doreszell "DC" Nash, Florida State College at Jacksonville.

Understanding Human Differences

Individual Attitudes and Interpersonal Relations

S ection 1 examines individual human differences. From the beginning, we human beings have been social animals; indeed, interpersonal relationships are the bedrock of our social nature. How we perceive and react to others is a complex combination of values, attitudes, beliefs, assumptions, and behaviors, including our communication skills.

Chapter 1 explores individual values in terms of our cultural context. We can be expected to share certain dominant cultural values, but we need to understand how individuals learn values in families and communities, and also how those values affect our individual behavior. The chapter also provides definitions for a number of important terms and concepts such as *race, ethnicity,*

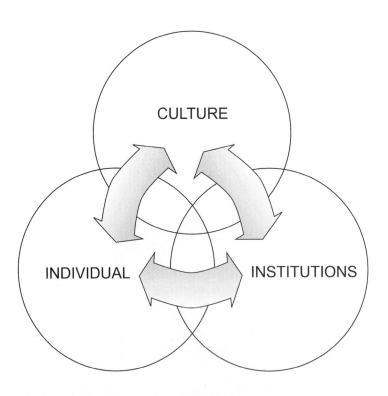

nationality, and *minority group.* Minority groups are often labeled, so this chapter explains how formal and informal labels are used to define and demean groups of people. It is essential to have shared meanings of important terms and concepts and to be aware of the influence of labels in order to understand human differences and perceptions of those differences.

The word *prejudice* is often confused with other terms, so Chapter 2 explains distinctions between important and related terms: *bias, stereotype, prejudice, bigotry,* and *discrimination.* Prejudice is not innate—it is learned—and this chapter describes how everyday language reflects and teaches negative attitudes toward groups of people. Although prejudice can lead to discrimination, other theories explaining discrimination also are discussed. The chapter concludes by describing factors that promote prejudice in our society and the rationalizations that people employ to avoid identifying and confronting their prejudices.

Chapter 2 shows how perceptions of, or reactions to, human differences may result in negative behaviors creating conflict; however, conflict does not have to be a destructive force. Chapter 3 investigates interpersonal communication, beginning with an analysis of misperceptions about communication. With the help of a communication model, the chapter explains elements of communication, the origins of interpersonal conflict, and certain attitudes that promote conflict resolution. The chapter concludes with an explanation of how human beings develop moral reasoning and takes a look at the role of moral reasoning in conflict resolution.

Understanding Ourselves and Others: Clarifying Values and Language

"I have striven not to laugh at human actions, not to weep at them, nor to hate them, but to understand them."

Baruch Spinoza (1632–1677)

"May you live in interesting times" is a Chinese curse. It implies that life is easier and more enjoyable when nothing out of the ordinary or controversial happens. As Americans in this complex, multicultural society, we certainly live in interesting times. Is it the best of times or the worst of times? Like the question about whether the glass is half empty or half full, the answer is the same: It's a personal decision. We can choose to be engaged in the challenges and opportunities of diversity issues, or we can retreat and resign ourselves to an attitude of indifference or even despair. Because America is not only a diverse society but also a democratic one, we have the freedom to choose our perceptions, assumptions, and behaviors.

If we take Spinoza's quote seriously, we need to understand all kinds of diversity—including opinions, appearances, values, and beliefs—as well as the categories of race, ethnicity, social class, gender, sexual orientation, and disability. The study of human diversity obviously requires an examination of social groups that encounter discrimination. However, in addition to focusing on the sociocultural differences among groups, we must also acknowledge the importance of individual differences. Each of us wants to be recognized as an individual. Our experiences are affected by multiple factors, including whether we are white or a person of color; female or male; from a low-, middle-, or upper-income family; or from a rural, suburban, or urban home. Each person's opinion offers a unique perspective that only the individual

expressing it can fully understand. The task for us as listeners is to understand as best as we can the ideas, values, and beliefs articulated by the individuals we encounter.

What is the difference between beliefs and values?

Kniker (1977) suggests that **beliefs** are inferences about reality that take one of three forms: descriptive, evaluative, or prescriptive. A *descriptive belief* is exemplified by those who argued that the world was not flat but round because they observed boats sailing off to the horizon and recognized that the hulls disappear while sails are still visible. An *evaluative belief* is illustrated by Winston Churchill's conclusion about democracy based on his reading of history: He understood why some called democracy the worst form of government, but he found it to be better than all other forms of government that had been attempted thus far. An example of a *prescriptive belief* would be the recommendation that students take a role in creating classroom rules because research showed that students who help create rules are more likely to be cooperative and abide by them. All beliefs are predispositions to types of action. Rokeach asserts that a cluster of related beliefs creates an **attitude**; he defines **values** as "combinations of attitudes which generate action or deliberate choice to avoid action" (Kniker, 1977, p. 33).

The Role of Values in Human Differences

Rokeach is saying that values determine our choices: Values are the foundation for actions we choose to take—or to avoid (see Figure 1.1). What value do Americans place on wealth? For some, money and possessions are the primary measures of success. They admire others who are rich and successful, and they define their own worth by their income and wealth. For others, money is not a priority. Their main concern is to make enough money to support a comfortable lifestyle, however they choose to define it. There are also people who believe the biblical caution that love of money is "the root of all evil," and refuse to let wealth play an important role in their choices. Their behavior is a reflection of their values. While serving as vice president to John Adams, Thomas Jefferson was once turned away from a prominent hotel because his clothes were soiled and he had no servants with him. After the proprietor was told whom he had refused, he sent word to Jefferson, offering him any room in the hotel. Having been accepted into another hotel, Jefferson sent a reply politely refusing the offer of a room, noting that if the hotel proprietor did not have a room for a "dirty farmer," then he must not have a room for the vice president either (Botkin, 1957).

What is the relationship between a person's values and behaviors?

America has a history of social commentary on the role of values in people's lives, and scholars engage in research examining the relationship between expressed values and behavior. Searching for consistent patterns in values research is challenging. However, one theme from social critics has been repeatedly supported by research and case study: There is a consistent inconsistency between what we say we value and our actual behavior (Aronson, 2008; Lefkowitz, 1997; Myrdal, 1944; Terry, Hogg, & Duck, 1999).

The tendency for Americans to say we believe in a certain value and then engage in contradictory behavior is a curious and yet consistent pattern. Contradictory behavior by human beings has been criticized and even ridiculed by essayists, novelists, and observers of American society. In 1938, the Carnegie Foundation invited Swedish social

---

FIGURE 1.1 The Relationship of Values, Beliefs, Attitudes, and Choices

From Charles R. Kniker, *You and values education.* Published by Allyn & Bacon/Merrill Education, Boston, MA. Copyright © 1977. Reprinted and Electronically reproduced by permission of Pearson Education, Inc., Upper Saddle River, NJ.

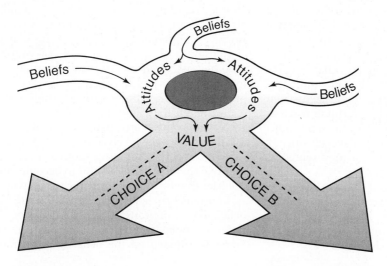

economist Gunnar Myrdal to the United States to conduct a study on the "American Negro Problem." Myrdal (1944) went far beyond a study of racial relations: He attempted to identify and understand the core values of American society.

In his analysis of Myrdal's research, Risberg (1978) identified nine values that Americans perceived as defining their culture:

1. Worth and dignity of the individual
2. Equality
3. Inalienable rights to life, liberty, property, and the pursuit of happiness
4. Rights to freedom of speech, press, religion, assembly, and private association
5. Consent of the governed
6. Majority rule
7. Rule of law
8. Due process of law
9. Community and national welfare. (pp. 5–6)

These identified core values seem to be accurate, especially if we compare American culture to other cultures. For example, many nations around the world put great emphasis on the collective good, but in the United States we tend to focus on personal worth and to reward individual achievements. Expectations of equality and of having "inalienable rights" are expressed in founding documents such as the Declaration of Independence, and our various freedoms are guaranteed by the Bill of Rights to the U.S. Constitution. Our representative form of democracy is based on the assumption that local, state, and national governments will be elected by the majority, with an expectation that they will rule with the consent of the governed for the welfare of the community, state, and nation. Finally, being ruled by laws and being given a chance to resolve issues by making our case in court (due process) was established to protect our citizens from the whims of the wealthy and powerful (a reaction to oppressive behavior from aristocrats and monarchs in the past). These values have historically defined America as a society, and they represent beliefs that all Americans share.

Despite the consensus about them, Myrdal observed that all of the values were regularly contradicted by American behavior. He provided examples from his observations, primarily based on race relations, to illustrate his conclusion.

What inconsistencies exist between American values and American behaviors?

Although Americans have always tended to emphasize individuality, American society quite consistently has demanded conformity. We Americans always seem to be uncomfortable with differences, often minimizing or ignoring them. In the turbulent era of the 1960s, many young people protested the Vietnam War, challenging authorities on college campuses and elsewhere in American society. Young men and women defied traditional gender roles in their choice of lifestyles and music, but most Americans did not celebrate this youth counterculture as an expression of individuality; instead, many denounced their behavior. Families were sundered and social critics predicted the downfall of American values. The protests passed, and expectations that Americans should conform have continued.

> The primal principle of democracy is the worth and dignity of the individual.
>
> Edward Bellamy (1850–1898)

The influence of peers on individual behavior illustrates the seductive power of conformity. Social psychologists studying the influence of peer pressure have reported that people in groups engage in behaviors they would not undertake as individuals (Aronson, 2008; Haag, 2000; Terry, Hogg, & Duck, 1999). According to LeBon (1968), when individuals congregate, the group "presents new characteristics very different from those of the individuals composing it" (p. 27). In a study of young men who had assaulted homosexuals, Franklin (2000) found that many of the men she interviewed expressed tolerant attitudes toward homosexuality even though they admitted that when they were with friends, they participated in verbal or physical assaults on people perceived to be gay. When questioned, 35% said they were motivated by a desire to prove their "toughness" and to become closer to the friends who engaged in antigay behavior.

Contradictory behavior also is illustrated in the belief that Americans value equality. The Declaration of Independence proclaims that the United States is founded on the belief that "all men are created equal," and yet the man who wrote that statement owned slaves. During World War II, boxing champions Joe Louis and Sugar Ray Robinson signed up for military service. At a bus stop in Alabama, a military policeman insisted that the two "colored soldiers" move to the rear of the station. When they refused, they were arrested. After an officer had reprimanded them, Louis responded, "Sir, I'm a soldier like any other American soldier. I don't want to be pushed to the back because I'm a Negro" (Mead, 1985, p. 231). Although racial inequality has diminished to some degree in the United States, the gap between the wealthy and the poor has become greater than ever. A chairman of the board for the First National Bank of Chicago admitted that it was difficult to defend an economic system that permitted such a wide disparity of income as existed in the United States (Terkel, 1980, p. 23).

The United States also was founded on the rule of law and the belief in a justice system that would be fair to everyone, yet people with wealth and status are routinely able to circumvent this ideal. The view that our courts favor those who can afford the best lawyers is widely recognized and is often portrayed in films and on television. Despite the contradiction, Americans continue to believe that justice can prevail in a courtroom and they are resentful of cases where they believe it has not. For example, Claus von Bülow was a man of wealth and status who was tried and convicted for attempting to murder his wife. He subsequently hired the famous defense attorney Alan Dershowitz, who identified a legal technicality that necessitated a new trial for his client. At the retrial, the jury acquitted von Bülow of attempted murder (Wright, 1983). No one except von Bülow knows if he is guilty or innocent; however, there are poor people in prison today because they could not afford to hire a lawyer as skilled as Alan Dershowitz.

> The law, in its majestic equality, forbids the rich as well as the poor to sleep under bridges, to beg in the streets, and to steal bread.
>
> Anatole France (1844–1924)

What Myrdal observed and reported in the 1940s continues to be true today: Americans behave inconsistently and engage in actions that contradict their expressed values. Myrdal's observations reinforced what American social critics had been saying for many years and what research and case studies have documented since the 1940s. These observations require some explanation, and it seems logical to begin by examining how people choose their values.

Are values individually chosen or are we taught to accept certain values?

The way American values are taught plays a major role in our acceptance of them. Individuals, subcultures, and institutions are involved in teaching values; parents, teachers, peers, clergy, relatives, and youth counselors are just a few examples. By studying how individuals and organizations in America teach values to children and youth, Raths, Harmin, and Simon (1978) identified seven traditional approaches.

A first way to teach values is to (1) *set an example*. Parents and teachers are supposed to be role models for children and youth. Young people are also told to emulate various individuals—from historical leaders to contemporary athletes—whose achievements are attributed to practicing certain values. In similar fashion, schools and other organizations use (2) *rules and regulations* to promote certain behaviors in children and youth (and adults) that represent important values. Learning punctuality is considered important enough that teachers send children to the principal's office for a tardy pass if they are late for class. This example is especially interesting because the child securing the tardy pass from the principal is kept away from the classroom for additional time while the other children engage in some kind of learning activity, which is supposedly the primary purpose for requiring students to attend school.

Another approach is to (3) *persuade or convince* others to accept certain values. Respectful discussions with reasonable arguments can be an effective means of convincing someone that the values being espoused are appropriate for living a good life. Related to this is (4) an *appeal to conscience* in which a parent or teacher may challenge a child or youth who seems to advocate an inappropriate value or belief. This approach is illustrated when a teacher responds to a student making an inappropriate comment by saying, "You don't really believe that, do you?" The point of such questions is not to give the student a chance to explain or defend what he or she said, but to produce a subtle and insistent form of moral pressure intended to coerce the student into rejecting an unacceptable point of view.

Parents often teach values by offering (5) *limited choices*. By limiting choices, parents intend to manipulate children into making acceptable decisions. If a mother values cooperation and tells her children that family members should share in household duties, what can she do if one of her children refuses? She asks one child to wash dishes twice a week, but the child hates to wash dishes and refuses. The mother might say, "Either you agree to wash dishes twice a week or you will not be allowed to play with your friends after school." The child is restricted to two options in the hope that he or she will choose to do the dishes, reinforcing the mother's original objective of wanting her children to learn the value of sharing domestic responsibilities.

Organizations have employed the approach of (6) *inspiring people* to embrace certain values, often by sponsoring a "retreat" with inspirational or motivational speakers or a social function where the combination of speakers, films, and activities is designed to have emotional or spiritual impact. Although religious groups employ this approach, corporations sponsor such events to inspire employees to work harder to achieve personal or group goals, and in doing so, contribute to the achievement of organizational goals.

Some religious groups and secular organizations emphasize (7) *religious or cultural dogma* to teach values. To accept beliefs without questioning them is to be **dogmatic.** If a Christian with dogmatic beliefs were questioned, he or she might say "That's what the Bible says," or, similarly, a dogmatic Muslim might say "This is what it says in the Qu'ran," even though for centuries people have interpreted the teachings of Jesus and Muhammad in different ways. Even early Christians held widely divergent views on the meanings of the life and words of Jesus (Pagels, 2006). Dogmatic beliefs stifle debate by emphasizing tradition: "This is what we have always believed."

Dogmatic beliefs also can be found in a secular context. When someone questions a value based on cultural beliefs, a dogmatic response might be "We've always done it this way." The appeal to tradition in opposing change has been employed in such controversies as using Native American mascots for school sports teams and including the Confederate flag in the official flags of some southern states. Only in 2003 did Georgia change its state flag to remove the confederate symbol.

> When people are free to do as they please they usually imitate each other.
>
> Eric Hoffer (1902–1983)

Understanding how values are taught provides some insight in answering the question about why people consistently behave in ways that contradict their expressed values. Each of the seven traditional approaches to teaching values seems to be based on a common assumption, and that assumption might explain the inconsistencies.

How does the way values are taught explain the inconsistency between values and behavior?

What do the seven traditional approaches to teaching values have in common? They are all based on an assumption that certain prescribed values are to be taught, and that the individuals being instructed should accept them. The person teaching values—the teacher, parent, scout leader, minister, priest, rabbi, imam, or employer—knows what values are appropriate. The goal is to persuade the student, child, parishioner, or worker to accept those values. In actuality, each approach is a form of **indoctrination**, where the intent is to dictate cultural values that must be accepted rather than assist people in deciding what is right and wrong (see Figure 1.2).

This assumption shared by all seven traditional approaches to teaching values in America caused Raths et al. (1978) to question whether all approaches were primarily successful in convincing people to say the right thing, yet not do the right

FIGURE 1.2

Often found in public school textbooks, illustrations such as this one suggest that Native Americans and colonists had a peaceful, harmonious relationship, but the reality was one of consistent conflict as Indians were pushed off their lands and forced to move westward.

Source: "The First Thanksgiving," painting by Jean Leon Gerome Ferris (1863–1930). Library of Congress, Prints and Photographs Division (LC-D416-90423).

thing. If this is true, there are important implications for how values should be taught. It is neither ethical nor prudent to teach values that are advocated but not practiced in our everyday lives. This teaches hypocrisy, not values. If the goal of teaching is to help learners understand what they genuinely believe and choose values to incorporate into their behavior, then those who teach must recognize the limitations of coercing children and youth to feign acceptance of prescribed values. For Americans to behave consistently with our expressed values, we must demonstrate authentic commitment to them.

Why should anyone be concerned about inconsistencies between values and behavior?

If we understand our values and consistently act on them, it is more likely that our choices will reflect our highest ideals. We are constantly confronted with ethical dilemmas that challenge our values and require us to make moral choices. A *New York Times* reporter interviewed a national sales manager for Wachovia who was living in an upper-middle-class suburb of Atlanta—a homogeneous community where everyone was of the same race and social class, and even shared similar opinions on a variety of issues. At his corporate worksite, the manager said the importance of diversity was emphasized: "At work, diversity is one of the biggest things we work on" (Kilborn, 2005, p. 157). Yet in his private life, the manager admitted that he and his suburban neighbors were "never challenged" to learn about other groups, so they did not. The contrast between what happens at work and what takes place at home represents an inconsistency that could call into question the sincerity of the manager's commitment to diversity.

Another example of inconsistency that came up during the interview was when the sales manager said that his family attended church and Bible Study classes. Because they were secure in their own comforts, the manager admitted that he and his family didn't give much thought to other "economic groups"—to families living in poverty. As a contrast, there is the example of Bono, lead singer for the rock group U2, who has used his position and wealth to lobby for human rights. Accepting an NAACP Image Award in 2007 for his work on poverty issues and the AIDS crisis in Africa, Bono identified Martin Luther King, Jr., as someone who inspired him, and he went on to say:

> The poor are where God lives. God is in the slums, in the cardboard boxes where the poor play house. God is where the opportunity is lost and lives are shattered. God is with the mother who has infected her child with a virus that will take both their lives. God is under the rubble in the cries we hear during wartime. God, my friends, is with the poor. God is with us if we are with them. This is not a burden. This is an adventure. (Gamber, 2007, p. 37)

Should parents rather than schools teach values to children?

The question of who should teach values is a rhetorical one. Both parents and schools in America are expected to contribute to the development of children's value systems. We constantly encounter people who reveal their values in everyday words and actions. Teachers model their values regardless of whether they consciously choose to do so. The question is not whether values should be taught, but how they should be taught.

Of the many approaches Kniker (1977) identified for teaching values, the most effective allow children and youth opportunity for discussion and debate, employing activities that stimulate them to think about their beliefs, hear other perspectives, and consider what effect different decisions could have for others as well as themselves. Discussing values, related behaviors, and possible consequences exposes young people to perspectives of others; evaluating arguments about values from their peers can help them decide which ones seem more attractive, compelling, and meaningful. In the process, they learn not only what values are important to them, but also how to accept people with values different from their own.

As adults, we do not tend to make decisions about values at a particular point in time and then never change our minds. Our values are based on beliefs and attitudes that change frequently, resulting in an ongoing process in which decisions are made and reevaluated throughout our lives. Culture, geographical location, parents, and life experiences influence each person's decisions. Each individual must determine what he or she believes is best, and the cumulative decisions individuals make influence the evolution of our society (Bellah, Madsen, Sullivan, Swidler, & Tipton, 1991; Lappe, 1989; Zinn, 1990). School classrooms are part of this journey. Teachers must present students with moral dilemmas and trust that when our children and youth are given the freedom to choose, they will be capable of making ethical decisions.

> Consciously we teach what we know; unconsciously we teach who we are.
>
> Don Hamachek (contemporary)

What problems can interfere with making ethical decisions?

One of the main problems in making ethical decisions about human differences is confusion concerning the language employed to address those differences. Many essential words or phrases are either unfamiliar terms or common terms with a history of misuse. Confused language often reflects the discomfort people feel toward sensitive issues. For example, the word *racism* did not appear in most English dictionaries until the 1960s. As the civil rights movement gained momentum and attracted considerable attention from the media and people across America, we could no longer avoid using the term. Similarly, the word *sexism* did not appear in dictionaries until the early 1970s, as the women's movement became increasingly successful at bringing issues concerning the treatment of women to public attention (Miller & Swift, 2000).

Using inaccurate or ambiguous language creates problems when we are addressing sensitive, uncomfortable issues. To be coherent and meaningful in our discussion of human differences, we must clarify our vocabulary and agree to specific appropriate meanings for significant words and concepts.

> How often misused words generate misleading thoughts.
>
> Herbert Spencer (1820–1903)

Defining Terms Related to Human Differences

One would expect that consultation with any scholarly authority would provide definitions for a term such as *prejudice*, but the scholarly world is not free from confusion. Some textbooks have defined *prejudice* as a prejudgment that could be either positive or negative; this definition confuses prejudice with *bias*, a feeling in favor of—or opposed to—anything or anyone. *Stereotypes* always refer to people, and also can be positive or negative. As with stereotypes, prejudice always refers to people, but prejudice is always negative.

This chapter includes a series of definitions intended to clarify terms referring to human differences. Definitions throughout the text are based on the work of scholars from various fields in the behavioral sciences, including racial and ethnic studies, women's studies, education, sociology, and anthropology. Unless cited, definitions reflect

a distillation of common themes identified in several scholarly sources (Andrzejewski, 1996; Feagin & Feagin, 2008; Herdt, 1997; Levin & Levin, 1982; Schaefer, 2008; Simpson & Yinger, 1985). The following series of definitions makes distinctions and indicates relationships between the terms.

Bias A preference or inclination, favorable or unfavorable, that inhibits impartial judgment.

Stereotype A positive or negative trait or traits ascribed to a certain group and to most members of that group.

Prejudice A negative attitude toward a group and persons perceived to be members of that group; being predisposed to behave negatively toward members of a group.

Bigotry Extreme negative attitudes leading to hatred of a group and persons regarded as members of the group.

Discrimination Actions or practices carried out by a member or members of dominant groups or their representatives that have a differential and negative impact on a member or members of subordinate groups.

Notice that each of the first four terms just listed represents attitudes of greater intensity than the previous one. Regarding bias and stereotypes, attitudes can be either positive or negative and can influence a person's perceptions of a person or group. Having a *bias* related to a group creates an inclination to favor or dislike an individual from that group. (See Table 1.1.) *Stereotyping* a group indicates an expectation that most members of the group will behave in certain positive or negative ways. No positive option exists for prejudice or bigotry because of the greater intensity of these attitudes. *Prejudices* are negative attitudes based on a prejudgment of a group; *bigotry* involves hatred and represents a harsher form of prejudgment against a person or group. Note that whereas bias, stereotype, prejudice, and bigotry relate to attitudes, discrimination refers to actions taken that demonstrate negative attitudes. A person can have a bias, a stereotype, or a prejudice, or even be a bigot and still not engage in any kind of negative or positive behavior. Unless an individual's attitudes are publicly expressed, others may not be aware of them. Discrimination can be seen and documented, and it can cause physical and emotional harm.

TABLE 1.1 Examples of Bias

The following selection comes from a list of 27 biases

1. **Family Bias:** Believing information from family members without seeking for evidence to support the accuracy of their information.
2. **Attractiveness Bias:** Believing information provided by attractive people.
3. **Confirmation Bias:** Believing information that reinforces beliefs already held and ignoring information that contradicts these beliefs.
4. **Self-Serving Bias:** Believing information that is beneficial to self-interest and goals.
5. **In-Group Bias:** Believing information from people who are members of our group (e.g., friends, co-workers, racial or ethnic group, etc.).
6. **Expectancy Bias:** When looking for information (or even conducting research), the tendency to pursue information and draw conclusions that reinforce our beliefs.
7. **Pleasure Bias:** Assuming that pleasant experiences offer greater insights for strengthening one's beliefs more than unpleasant experiences.
8. **Perceptual Bias:** Assuming that one's own perceptions and experience of reality reveal objective truths to confirm one's beliefs.
9. **Perseverance Bias:** Perpetuating one's beliefs even after encountering information that contradicts those beliefs.
10. **Uncertainty Bias:** Because people tend to be uncomfortable with ambiguity, they prefer to choose to believe or disbelieve information rather than remain uncertain.

Source: Adapted from Newburg and Waldman (2006), *Why We Believe What We Believe*. Free Press.

How do negative attitudes develop?

We learn various biases, stereotypes, and prejudices as we grow up. We can be biased in favor of or against certain kinds of foods, categories of books, styles of clothing, or types of personalities. Bias can affect decisions about what we eat, read, or wear; it can influence our choice of friends. A stereotype assumes that individuals possess certain human traits simply because they are members of a particular group. Some traits are regarded as positive—such as blacks have rhythm, Asians are good in math—and other traits are viewed as negative—certain groups are lazy, shiftless, dishonest, or violent. Although negative stereotypes are regarded as unacceptable, many people accept positive stereotypes. The problem with positive stereotypes is that they cause us to have specific expectations for individuals and groups even though we have little or no evidence for these assumptions. A positive stereotype may sabotage the process of forming a realistic and accurate perception of an individual, as is illustrated in the following example.

During a coffee break at a Midwestern university, three Asian American women employed by a student services office reminisced about their undergraduate days. They complained about how difficult math classes had been and laughed as they recalled some of their coping strategies. The student services director, an African American, walked into the room, overheard what they were saying, and interrupted their discussion to chastise them for "putting yourselves down." He said they should stop. He also said he was disappointed in them and departed.

After the director left, the three women initially were too surprised to speak. Once they started talking, they realized they were angry because his comments suggested that he assumed they all had good math skills and were not being honest when discussing their lack of math ability. The women had thought the director viewed them as individuals, and they were angry and hurt when they realized that he had allowed a stereotype to distort his perception of them. They were especially upset because they had not expected a person of color to believe in a stereotype—even a positive one about the math abilities of Asians—but apparently he did.

One of the ways that positive or negative stereotypes are reinforced is a result of confirmation bias. Newberg and Waldman (2006) describe *confirmation bias* as the tendency to accept information reinforcing one's beliefs while ignoring information contradicting those beliefs. It is a bias with a long history in human attitudes and behavior. In 1620, philosopher Francis Bacon observed: "the human understanding, once it has adopted an opinion, collects any instances that confirm it, and though the contrary instances may be more numerous and more weighty, it either does not notice them or else rejects them, in order that the opinion will remain unshaken" (Mlodinow, 2008, p. 189).

How does confirmation bias influence people, and can it be overcome?

Confirmation bias not only causes people to look for evidence that reinforces their views, it also causes them to interpret ambiguous information in a way that strengthens their preconceived notions. The latter is especially disturbing since accurate information about most issues is likely to have some degree of ambiguity that should stimulate critical thinking and perhaps lead to new insights, but confirmation bias pushes people along well-worn paths, diminishing their ability to think critically and solve problems effectively. Mlodinow (2008) cites a study in which some subjects supported the death penalty and some did not. All subjects were given a packet of research in which half of the studies supported the death penalty as a deterrent to crime and half refuted this claim. Subjects were instructed on the weaknesses of each study, but in the end, the subjects who had held opinions about the death penalty prior to being given the research said that reading these studies had reinforced their views. Mlodinow concluded that the subjects did not gain a deeper or more complex understanding of the issue; instead, "the data polarized the group" (p. 190).

Aronson (2008) described a study suggesting how confirmation bias could be used to achieve a positive outcome. Subjects were given a bogus personality test and then half were randomly identified as either "open-minded" or "closed-minded." Almost all of the subjects accepted these identifications as accurate. They were then given two controversial issues and asked to comment on both. The students identified as "closed-minded" articulated one point of view on each issue, whereas the "open-minded" subjects tended to make comments that reflected both sides of the issues. This suggests that if schools and other institutions engaged students in learning activities to promote being "open-minded," students could be taught to be aware of and take into account the influence of confirmation bias. Mlodinow (2008) also recommends that we teach students to search just as actively for information that contradicts their views as they do for evidence that supports them. Teaching science offers an opportunity to reinforce an open-minded approach because scientists are taught to question their assumptions, beliefs, and theories; this approach could be used in other disciplines as well.

If the influence of confirmation bias is reduced, the power and pervasiveness of stereotypes should also be diminished. On the other hand, negative attitudes reinforced by confirmation bias can strengthen prejudices, which are always negative, and may result in negative behavior. If a person engages in negative actions toward a group, this usually reinforces his or her negative attitudes about that group. If left unchallenged, prejudice can transform an individual into a bigot whose hatred of others could even lead to violence. Prejudice and bigotry toward others are usually based on human differences such as race, ethnicity, or nationality.

What are the differences among race, ethnicity, and nationality?

Race is not a scientific concept but a social reality dictated by the color of one's skin, even though skin color as a basis for human categorization is absurd. African Americans are identified as black, yet the skin color for many African Americans is more accurately described as brown. Contrary to the racist term "redskin," the skin color for Native

Americans is not red. Yellow is an inaccurate description of skin color for those of Asian heritage. At an elementary school in Minneapolis, young children created a poster with the title "The Human Rainbow." The first band of their rainbow was colored with a light brown crayon, making a very pale brown band, and each band above it was a slightly darker shade of brown until the outer band, which was colored in such a dark brown color that it almost looked black. The children had created a realistic way of representing and understanding the effect of melanin on the color of human skin.

The concept of race is both easy and difficult to discuss. Most Americans believe they know the meaning of the term, yet we have no specific set of racial categories acceptable to the scientific community. In 1758, Carolus Linnaeus proposed the first racial classifications based largely on human geographical origins, but as Gould (2002) pointed out, J. F. Blumenbach has usually been credited as the originator of racial categories. It was Blumenbach who created the term *Caucasian*, and his taxonomy established a racial hierarchy with white people on top. This would be the foundation for much "scientific" theory and research in the eighteenth and early nineteenth centuries. In the 1930s, scientists such as anthropologist Franz Boas challenged theories describing a hierarchy of races (Gosset, 1997). In 1937, American historian Jacques Barzun bluntly denounced the spuriousness of race as a legitimate scientific concept:

> [Racial classifications] come and go and return, for the urge to divide mankind into fixed types and races is evidently endless. Each attempt only illustrates anew how race-groupings have been shaped not by nature but by the mode of thought or the stage of mechanical efficiency that mankind valued at the moment. The history of these attempts confirms . . . that race-theories occur in the minds of men for an ulterior purpose. (1965, p. 196)

> In claiming the unity of the human race we resist the unsavory assumption of higher and lower races.
>
> Alexander von Humboldt (1769–1859)

The series of paintings on "Caste" from the Spanish colonial era (see Figure 1.3) supports Barzun's point about the historical effort to find ways to divide and label human beings. Current research on the human genome emphasizes human similarities rather than differences. According to this research, every woman living today has the mitochondrial DNA of a single woman who lived approximately 150,000 years ago, and every man living today has the Y chromosome of a single man who lived approximately 59,000 years ago (Wade, 2006). Scientists involved in this research report that 85% of human genetic variation occurs within groups and only 15% of human genetic variation occurs between groups. And yet, as Olson (2002) acknowledges, "societies have built elaborate systems of privilege and control around these miniscule genetic differences" (p. 69).

Although race is based on perceptions of physical differences, **ethnicity** is based on cultural differences (Jones, 1997). Ethnicity refers to the historic origins of an individual's family. For immigrants to the United States, ethnicity identifies their country of origin or that from which their ancestors came— Poland, Mexico, China, Italy, Cuba, Ethiopia, Russia, or Iran, for example. For those whose ancestors emigrated from different countries of origin, ethnicity can represent a choice about personal identity based on culture. As Dalton (2008) explains it,

> [Ethnicity] describes that aspect of our heritage that provides us with a mother tongue and that shapes our values, our worldview, our family structure, our rituals, the foods we eat, our mating behavior, our music—in short, much of our daily lives. (p. 16)

Most Americans identify more than one ethnic group as part of their heritage, and for that reason ethnicity may have little meaning because of a lack of strong cultural identification with one of those groups. Some of us with multiple ethnic heritages may claim a stronger cultural affinity with one of the groups. A person may be a mixture of Irish, German, and Swedish ancestry and yet, perhaps because her surname is Irish or because Irish traditions were more strongly promoted in her family, she identifies most strongly with being Irish (Banks, 1994).

For Native Americans, ethnicity generally refers to tribal affiliation: Apache, Kwakiutl, Cherokee,

FIGURE 1.3 Eighteenth-Century Paintings of "Castas"

A series of Mexican paintings from the eighteenth century identifies categories of people (such as Indian, Spanish, or African) and names the children of mixed marriages. For example, the child of a Spanish and African couple is a Mulatto, and the child of a Spanish and Mulatto couple is a Morisco. In these three paintings, the artist illustrates how descendants of a Spanish and Indian couple can regain status as a white person. The child of the Spanish and Indian couple is a Mestizo, the child of a Spanish and Mestizo couple is a Castiza, and the child of a Spanish and Castiza couple is considered Spanish.

Source: De Espanol, y India, na ce Mestiza (190.1996.1), De Espanol, y Mestiza, Castiza (190.1996.3), and De Espanol, y Castiza, Espanol (1990.1996.2), c. 1775, Francisco Clapera, Frederick and Jan Mayer Collection, Denver Art Museum.

Seminole, Mohawk, Hopi, or Lakota. For most African Americans, ethnic identity was obliterated by the experience of slavery, making it practically impossible to trace one's heritage to a specific tribal group such as Hausa, Ibo, or Tsutsi. The introduction of the term "African American" in the 1980s was intended to provide an "ethnic" label for black people as distinct from race (Dalton, 2008). Because of the unique preservation of his oral family history, Alex Haley (1976) was able to reconnect with his ethnic group as described in the book *Roots*.

Nationality refers to the nation in which one has citizenship. To ask people about their nationality is to ask where they reside or what nation is identified on their passport. People curious about someone's ethnic heritage often ask, "What is your nationality?" instead of "What is your ethnic background?" Being asked about one's nationality may be considered quite insulting because it implies that the questioner does not perceive the other person

as American but as belonging to another country (see Figure 1.4). What do the terms *race, ethnicity,* and *nationality* have in common? They each refer to people considered to represent minority groups in the United States.

What are minority groups and why are they called minority groups?

The term **minority group** does not necessarily imply anything about the *number* of people in the group; however, it does imply something about their power. Minority group members possess limited power compared to members of a dominant group. It is possible for a minority group to be larger than a dominant group because it is the group's lack of power that defines it. When the white minority held power in South Africa, black South Africans were the majority in terms of numbers, but they were considered a minority group

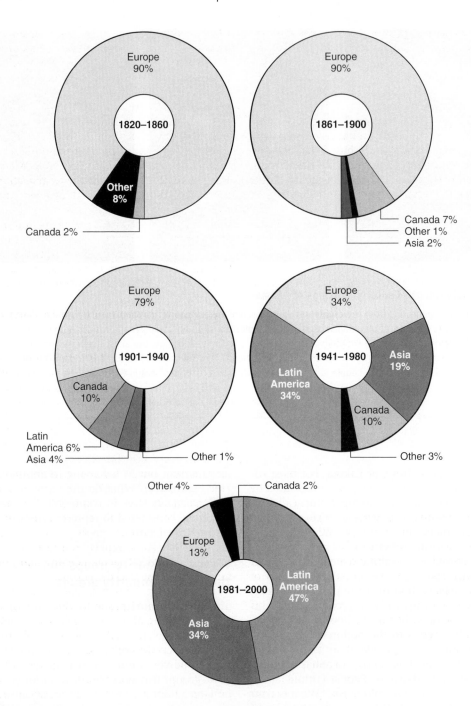

FIGURE 1.4 Nationalities of Ethnic Immigrants to America

Source: Schaefer, R.T. *Racial and ethnic groups*, 10th Edition. Copyright © 2006, p. 101. Reprinted and Electronically reproduced by permission of Pearson Education, Inc., Upper Saddle River, NJ.

because they lacked power under the racist system of apartheid. Women in the United States are included as a minority in affirmative action plans and equity proposals even though they are numerically the majority because historically they have not held as much power as have men.

A person in a minority group must overcome obstacles—handicapping conditions—related to her or his group identification based on such factors as race, ethnicity, gender, sexual orientation, socioeconomic status, religion, or disability. Some people refer to minority groups and diversity as if the two terms are synonymous, but **diversity** refers to the presence of human beings with perceived or actual differences based on a variety of human characteristics. Diversity exists both in classrooms having no minorities and in classrooms where all students are African American; too often, these differences can result in some children being stigmatized and marginalized by other children. The concept of diversity includes minority groups as well as groups identified according to differences based on age, marital status, parental status, educational status, geographic location, physical characteristics, and other factors that influence individual personality and behavior. As Banks (2006) has noted, it is imperative to recognize the interactions of all these variables in order to understand individual behavior.

How have minority groups been perceived by the majority?

The majority group has created derogatory names for members of minority groups. When a dominant group has the power to label a subordinate group, others will consistently associate that label with individuals from the subordinate group. The power to label results in the power to define the people in a group, not only for the dominant group, but sometimes for the members of the labeled group as well. In recognition of the power of such labels, many groups have engaged in efforts to label themselves in a positive way. In the 1960s, many in the group that the majority had labeled "colored people" or "Negroes" rejected the majority group's names and chose to call themselves "blacks." This was accompanied by calls for "black power" and claims that "Black is beautiful." Many black people continue to prefer that designation

because they believe it makes a positive contribution to an individual's sense of identity. Since the 1980s, "African American" has also become a popular choice among black people and others as a positive label for this group.

When a majority group has the power to label and define those belonging to a minority group, they also can control subordinate group members, obviously by limiting their opportunities, but sometimes in more subtle ways as well. Macedo and Bartoleme (2001) compare the term *migrant*, which most often labels Latinos seeking economic opportunity in the United States, with the term *settlers*, which is used to designate English and other Europeans immigrating to America to improve their economic opportunities. Reactions to the two terms are significantly different, even though both terms describe people engaged in a similar quest.

How have labels been used to define and control subordinate groups?

The idea that the power to label equals the power to define, which equals the power to control, was illustrated by the 2007 media coverage of the incident at Virginia Polytechnic Institute in which South Korean student Seung-Chi Ho killed 32 students and wounded 25 others before taking his own life. The media reported Cho's history of mental illness and that he was hospitalized for a time, but the coverage never mentioned that Cho's violence was unusual for the 46% of American adults diagnosed with some form of mental illness at some point in their lives (Friedman, 2008). Perhaps the failure to report lack of violence from mentally ill people reflects the history of various forms of American media labeling and portraying mentally ill people as dangerous.

In American films, mentally ill characters are often presented as prone to violent acts, whether in classic films like Alfred Hitchcock's *Psycho* or in numerous low-budget "slasher" films. In addition, the news media tends to report incidents of violence when mentally ill people are responsible: A 2005 survey of 70 major U.S. newspapers found that almost 40% of the stories on mentally ill people emphasized how dangerous they are, and yet research indicates that mentally ill people are responsible for only 3–5% of the violence in the United States (Friedman, 2008). Since studies have found that drinking alcohol increases violent behavior, Friedman concludes: "You have far more to fear from an intoxicated businessman in a suit than from a homeless man muttering on the street corner" (2008, p. A3). This overemphasis on violent behavior and the lack of information on the reality of mental illness, including information about people who have achieved success despite having a mental disorder, has caused many Americans to accept the label and to stereotype mentally ill people as dangerous and violent. For this reason, many Americans believe that mentally ill people should not receive outpatient care, but be institutionalized for their own protection and for the protection of society.

Labels related to mental illness are official, formal, bureaucratic terms; others are informal and societal—terms used or heard by people in everyday life. The existence of **derisive labels**—terms reflecting a sense of contempt or ridicule based on factors such as race, class, disability, sexual orientation, and gender—and their variety suggest the extent to which prejudices exist. Words such as *nigger, spic, chink, buck,* and *squaw* represent only a few of the racist terms in English. Wessler (2001) described the observations of elementary educators who have heard children using such labels, especially during recess where children may feel they have more freedom to express themselves. Stephan (1999) insists that reducing prejudice requires that teachers help children become aware of the tendency to attach negative labels to others. After all, such words can be heard on the playgrounds of America, and some, for example, the word *squaw,* even show up in instructional materials such as maps, textbooks, or activities.

One theory of the origin of the word *squaw* is that it derives from a French word meaning vagina and was used by early French trappers to indicate that they wanted sex, usually followed by an offer to pay or barter something (Chavers, 1997). Other linguists claim that squaw has a more neutral origin, merely referring to a woman, but as Green (1975) demonstrated, its use has been consistently negative. The word *squaw* can still be found in elementary school materials and in names for lakes and other geographic sites around the United States.

Because they objected to the term, high school students in Minnesota successfully lobbied the state legislature to change the names of state geographical sites containing "squaw," yet at least one white community in Minnesota, Squaw Lake, refused to change. Chavers (1977) reports that students have lobbied other state legislatures to delete squaw in geographic sites or town names because the word is offensive and insulting to Native American women.

The power of labels was the focus of a study that asked subjects to supervise groups whose task was to make a collective decision on various issues (Zimbardo, 2007). The "supervisor" listened to the group's conversation from an adjacent room, and was asked to evaluate the group's decision-making process using criteria provided that was supposed to describe good decision making. If the group made a bad decision, the supervisor was supposed to give them an electric shock ranging from a mild shock at level one to the maximum level of ten. No one was actually shocked, but supervisors heard a recording that simulated people being shocked.

The researcher was interested in how supervisors would be affected by overhearing labels ascribed to a group. The subjects "overheard" the researcher talking to his assistant over the intercom, describing the group that the subject was asked to supervise as an "animalistic, rotten bunch" or as a "perceptive, thoughtful group"; another group was not labeled either positively or negatively. Supervisors tended to give minimal shocks to all groups after the first trial, but as the experiment went on and groups continued to make bad decisions, the "punishments" chosen for the groups began to diverge. Supervisors tended to shock the group labeled "animalistic" with more intensity and they increased the shock level on subsequent decision-making exercises, whereas those teams labeled positively were given the smallest amount of shock and the neutral group fell in between. The study suggested that labels can enhance or diminish the human qualities we ascribe to others, and when human qualities are diminished, our concerns about not harming an individual or group may also be diminished.

What is the impact of labels on individuals who are labeled?

Wright (1998) believes that young children are only minimally aware of skin color and are often unaware of race. Asked what color she was, a three-year-old black girl wearing a pink and blue dress responded, "I'm pink and blue. What color are you?" At about the age of four, children begin to understand that skin color is permanent, yet they do not regard it as negative. At five years of age, children are likely to become more interested in differences of skin color and may ask teachers many questions; they also begin to be aware of race and societal attitudes about racial differences. However, true racial awareness does not tend to become a significant issue until children are eight or nine years old. Because of children's growing awareness of skin color and racial attitudes, teachers must consciously confront name-calling and other forms of prejudice in their classrooms and on the playground.

Racist name calling usually involves blatant, ugly words that carry harshly negative connotations: *coon, jungle bunny, gook, greaser, wetback, timber nigger*. What impact does it have on a child to hear such words? Some members of a subordinate group may believe and internalize myths, stereotypes, and prejudices expressed about their group. Even for those who do not internalize the negative messages, being called derisive names, especially by other children, has an impact. Anthropologist Jamake Highwater, who identified as a Native American, recalled the impact of the derisive terms he heard as a child:

> At first, the words had no meaning to me. Even when I was told their meaning, I couldn't easily grasp why they were supposed to be shameful. . . . [They] were whispered in the classroom and remorselessly shouted when adults were not around. On the playground. In the locker room. In the darkness of the balcony at Saturday movie matinees. Those were the words that filled my childhood. . . . They were words that aroused a sense of power and self-aggrandizement for those who shouted them; they brought shame and humiliation in those at whom they were shouted. (1997, pp. 24–25)

Highwater believes that *derisives,* derogatory terms, damage individuals in the dominant group as well as those in minority groups because derisive language creates boundaries. Derisive terms define the oppressor as superior and the oppressed as inferior. Herbst (1997) agrees that such terms create suspicion, fear, and contempt in members of dominant groups and arouse frustration and anger in individuals from minority groups. Some groups have tried to take over certain words, to "own" them and reshape them to make them less hurtful. African Americans, especially urban blacks, have taken the word *nigger* for their own purposes, as can be heard in their rap music (Kennedy, 2002). Gay men and lesbians, especially young people, are using the word *queer* as a generic term for the gay community, and courses in queer studies have sprung up on college campuses in an attempt to change formal, bureaucratic language (Jagose, 1996).

How are negative bureaucratic terms as harmful as social derisive terms?

When we think of derisive terms, we usually think of informal, social labels. Derisive terms for social class, such as *hillbilly* or *redneck*, often have a regional origin but may become widespread as in *white trash*, a term that evolved into a variety of forms including *trailer park trash*. Yet some argue that the most harmful derisive terms for low-income people come from formal sources such as government reports and scholarly studies; these terms include *culturally deprived, culturally disadvantaged, welfare households,* and *inner-city residents*. What images do such terms suggest? Derisive bureaucratic terms are powerful purveyors of negative images primarily because they have the sanction of authority behind them.

In addition to negative images, derisive bureaucratic terms send a negative message. Being labeled *culturally deprived* represents a form of blaming the victim. What group are we talking about? What do they lack? The term *cultural deprivation* suggests that poor people lack an ability to appreciate arts and humanities; it does not acknowledge the reality that they are economically deprived and need financial assistance for such things as job training, employment, and better health care. Using such a label implies that a deficiency in cultural qualities or values is the cause of their problems.

People with disabilities are labeled with derisive social and bureaucratic terms. Linton (1998) argues that when children tell "moron jokes" or insult others by calling them *retard, dummy,* or *cripple,* they are asserting a claim to normalcy and rejecting those with a disability. In a bureaucratic setting, the term *handicapped* labels people as deviant. Since the 1950s, people with disabilities have objected to the term *handicapped* and have successfully lobbied to have it removed from common bureaucratic usage. Phrases such as *the retarded* or *the disabled* are also derisive bureaucratic terms because they isolate one adjective for a disabled person and make it a noun to label the group. According to Charlton (1998), people with disabilities object to being labeled with such adjectives because "their humanity is stripped away and the person is obliterated, only to be left with the condition—disability" (p. 54).

> One may no more live in the world without picking up the moral prejudices of the world than one will be able to go to Hell without perspiring.
>
> H. L. Mencken (1880–1956)

To understand what Charlton means, imagine a person who is bold and energetic, impish yet compassionate, and now add *disabled* to the description. If the last adjective is singled out and made a noun, that word defines the person. This is how a term like *the disabled* distorts and diminishes people with a disability. Nondisabled people in America have viewed people with disabilities as unable to care for themselves and institutionalized them, justifying this by claiming that it was "for their own good." The history of institutionalizing people with disabilities illustrates the power of labels to control the quality of life for a labeled group.

How has our society responded to social problems experienced by minority groups?

Ryan (1976) described two radically different approaches involved in addressing social problems. The **exceptionalistic perspective** focuses on individuals; it perceives all problems as local, unique, exclusive, and unpredictable. Because problems are viewed as a consequence of individual defect, accident, or unfortunate circumstance, proposed remedies must be tailored to fit each individual case that is an "exception" to the general situation. A criticism of this approach is that it treats only symptoms of problems and not causes; exceptionalistic remedies have been derided as "Band-Aid solutions" that alleviate but do not solve problems.

Ryan describes an alternative approach, a **universalistic perspective** that views social problems as systemic, beginning in fundamental social structures within a community or a society. Because social structures are inevitably imperfect and inequitable, the problems that emerge are predictable and preventable because they do not stem from a situation unique to one individual but rather from conditions common to many. The universalistic perspective emphasizes engaging in research to collect and analyze data and to identify patterns that predict certain outcomes. Once patterns and root causes are identified, appropriate solutions can be created and implemented through public action, institutional policy, or legislation. Research takes time, so the universalistic approach has been criticized because it does not address the immediate consequences of particular problems or assist people who are currently suffering.

To illustrate the difference between exceptionalistic and universalistic perspectives, Ryan describes two responses to the problem of smallpox. An exceptionalistic approach would be to provide smallpox victims with medical care to help them recover; a universalistic approach would first demand legislation to fund inoculation of the population to prevent the disease from spreading. The contrast is similar to a metaphor from Kilbourne (1999) about bodies floating down a river and ambulances being called to rescue the drowning people. Although rescuing people from the river is important, it is also important to send someone upstream to investigate why people are falling in (p. 30).

These metaphors illustrate a need for both approaches. While people are engaged in studying problems, help must be provided to those who are suffering right now. If everyone goes upstream to discover why people are falling into the river, no one is left to save those who are drowning; if everyone stays downstream to rescue drowning people, the cause of the problem will never be found. Neither perspective can be neglected in the efforts employed to solve social problems.

AFTERWORD

The chapter began by discussing diversity and individuality. Holding differing values is part of both diversity and individuality. The values we choose are influenced by our membership in groups defined by such factors as race, ethnicity, gender, and social class; however, the ultimate decision to embrace certain values is up to the individual. Almost everyone holds some values similar to those of their parents, and almost everyone holds some values different from those of their parents. We share some values with friends, yet we hold some values that are different, too. Values, and the attitudes and beliefs that determine them, are part of the landscape of human differences. But beliefs and attitudes change as we learn more information that helps us to understand and appreciate diversity. For those interested in exploring their own attitudes concerning diversity issues, an Attitude Inventory is available on the MyEducationLab web site (www.myeducationlab.com). Respond to the statements now, and when you have finished reading this book, you may want to return to the Attitude Inventory and respond to the statements about these issues again.

> Freedom is the right to choose; the right to create for yourself the alternatives of choice. Without the possibility of choice and the exercise of choice, human beings are not human but instruments, things.
>
> Archibald MacLeish (1892–1982)

Language is the primary tool we use to pursue understanding. When we use language that labels a group of people, we create misunderstanding. It is important to observe and evaluate the behaviors of others, but we will never understand them without interacting with them or reading what they have written. Confusing or ambiguous language is like a smudge on the lens of a microscope; it prevents us from having a clear understanding of our subject. This chapter has tried to clarify some confusing terms so that our view is not distorted as we begin our study of human differences.

When Jewish author Isaac Bashevis Singer was asked if he believed people had free will, he replied, "Of course we have free will, we have no choice." As citizens of a democracy, we have many choices. As human beings living in a diverse society surrounded by a multitude of global cultures, trying to understand human differences would seem to be a necessary choice. For every reader who has already made that choice, this book offers insights and information to enhance your understanding. For readers who have not made that choice, this book may help to create an understanding of why the choice is necessary. But it is still each person's choice to make; as Singer said, we have no choice about that.

TERMS AND DEFINITIONS

Attitude A cluster of particular related beliefs, values, and opinions

Beliefs Inferences a person makes about reality that take one of three forms: descriptive, evaluative, or prescriptive

Bias A preference or inclination, favorable or unfavorable, that inhibits impartial judgment

Bigotry Extreme negative attitudes leading to hatred of a group and persons regarded as members of the group

Confirmation bias Believing information that reinforces beliefs already held and ignoring information that contradicts these beliefs

Derisive labels Names that reflect attitudes of contempt or ridicule for individuals in the group being named

Discrimination Actions or practices carried out by a member or members of dominant groups or their representatives that have a differential and negative impact on a member or members of subordinate groups

Diversity The presence of human beings with perceived or actual differences based on a variety of human characteristics

Dogmatic To accept beliefs one has been taught without questioning them

Ethnicity Identification of an individual according to his or her national origin and/or distinctive cultural patterns

Exceptionalistic perspective Views social problems as private, local, unique, exclusive, and unpredictable, a consequence of individual defect, accident, or unfortunate circumstance, which requires that all proposed remedies be tailored to fit each individual case

Indoctrination Instruction whose purpose is to force the learner to accept a set of values or beliefs, to adopt a particular ideology or perspective

Minority group A subordinate group whose members have significantly less power to control their own lives than do members of a dominant, or majority, group

Nationality Refers to the nation in which an individual has citizenship status

Prejudice A negative attitude toward a group and persons perceived to be members of that group; being predisposed to behave negatively toward members of a group

Race A social concept with no scientific basis that categorizes people according to obvious physical differences such as skin color

Stereotype A positive or negative trait or traits ascribed to a certain group and to most members of that group

Universalistic perspective Views social problems as public, national, general, inclusive, and predictable; a consequence of imperfect and inequitable social arrangements that require research to identify their patterns and causes so that remedial institutional action can be taken to eliminate these problems and prevent them from reoccurring

Values Combinations of attitudes that generate action or the deliberate choice to avoid action

DISCUSSION EXERCISES

Discussion exercises are provided in which groups of three to five students can delve deeper into the content presented in the chapter.

Clarification Exercise—My Values: What I Believe

Directions: Create personal responses to each of the ten items below. Share your responses individually with several others and listen to their responses to those same items.

1. How would you describe the way your parents raised you? If you choose to have children, will you raise them the same way your parents raised you? Explain.

2. If there were several experts who would guarantee that they could help you gain a certain ability that you do not currently have, what ability would you choose? Why would you prefer to have that particular ability over any other?

3. How much influence do your friends have concerning the choices you make? If you had made a decision to do something that was a little risky, but several friends found out and they all called you to urge you not to do it, would you follow through on your decision or would you follow your friends' advice? Explain.

4. Do you value experiences over possessions? Upon graduating from college, what if a wealthy relative offered to pay for a trip anywhere in the world or to give you an expensive gift (e.g., a new car) that you have wanted for a long time? Which option would you choose and why would you choose that option?

5. An eccentric multimillionaire approaches you and says he wants to give you money. He will either give you $100,000 to spend on yourself any way you want, or he will give you $1 million if you will anonymously distribute it to strangers. If you choose the first option, what would you spend the money on? If you choose the second option, on what basis would you give money to strangers (i.e., what would be your criteria)?

6. Can you think of anything that has happened to you that was beyond your control and had an impact on your life? What was that event, and how did it change you? Given that such events happen to most people, how much control do you think that you (or anyone else) have over the course of your life?

7. After getting married, you and your spouse have your first child. Even as a toddler you child shows signs of incredible intelligence, and it becomes clear that you will be raising a child much more intelligent than you are. How would you feel about that? When your second child is born, it soon becomes clear that this child has health problems and learning difficulties. How would you feel about raising that child?

8. It is early in your career and you have a job that you really enjoy, working with people that you really like, that pays enough for you to maintain a middle-class lifestyle. You are offered a job that will not be as enjoyable, and you will be competing with your co-workers, but the salary is twice what you currently make and may go even higher. Would you keep the job you enjoy or take the job with the higher salary? Explain.

9. You are walking to your car in a parking lot and a stranger comes up and asks for a dollar to catch a bus home, explaining that he has lost his wallet. Would you give him the money? Explain. The next day a rather unkempt stranger approaches you in that same parking lot and says he has lost his job and his home and is living on the streets; then he asks you for a dollar for food. Would you give him the money? Explain.

10. When America enters the next (twenty-second) century, do you think our nation will be a better place to live than it is today or worse? Explain.

Selected and adapted from Gregory Stock, *The Book of Questions* (1987) and *The Kid's Book of Questions* (1988) (New York: Workman Publishing).

Intergroup Exercise—A Mutual Support Dilemma

Directions: Examine the case situation explained below. Discuss it with those in your assigned group. Respond to each of the questions. Then, explain your group position to the class.

The Story of Mary and Luke: A Mutual Support Dilemma

Mary and Luke were married during their senior year in college. After their graduation, Mary took a secretarial job in the registrar's office of the university where Luke was attending graduate school. Mary worked for five years while Luke completed his doctoral degree. Their first and only child was born the second of the five years and Mary missed only two months of work at that time.

Luke has now been offered an assistant professorship at a prominent eastern school and is eager to accept it. Mary has applied and been accepted into graduate school at the University of Chicago. She is eager to accept the assistantship that she has been offered.

Mary argues that Luke should give her the chance for an education now that he has completed his. She also reminds him that he has been offered a job at the Chicago Junior College. Luke says that he intends to take the job in the east and that Mary can find someplace out there to go to school.

If Mary refuses to follow him, Luke promises to file for a divorce and seek custody of their three-year-old daughter.

Questions for discussion:

1. What would you do if you were Mary?
2. What advice do you have for Luke?
3. How could this situation be handled so that neither Mary nor Luke loses?
4. Does your group agree that either Mary or Luke loses?

REFERENCES

Andrzejewski, J. (Ed.). (1996). Definitions for understanding oppression and social justice. *Oppression and social justice: Critical frameworks.* Boston, MA: Pearson Custom Publishing.

Aronson, E. (2008). *The social animal* (10th ed.). New York, NY: Worth Publishers.

Banks, J.A. (1994). The complex nature of ethnic groups in modern society. In *Multiethnic education: Theory and practice* (3rd ed.). Boston, MA: Allyn & Bacon.

Banks, J.A. (2006). Multicultural education: Characteristics and goals. In J.A. Banks & C.A. McGee Banks (Eds.), *Multicultural education: Issues and perspectives* (6th ed.). New York, NY: Wiley.

Barzun, J. (1965). *Race: A study in superstition* (rev. ed.). New York, NY: Harper & Row.

Bellah, R., Madsen, R., Sullivan, W., Swidler, A., & Tipton, S. (1991). *The good society*. New York, NY: Vintage.

Botkin, B.A. (1957). *A treasury of American anecdotes*. New York, NY: Bonanza Books.

Charlton, J.I. (1998). *Nothing about us without us*. Berkeley: University of California Press.

Chavers, D. (1997). Doing away with the "S" word. *Indian Country Today, 16*(37), 5.

Dalton, H. (2008). Failing to see. In P. Rothenberg (Ed.), *White privilege: Essential readings on the other side of racism* (3rd ed.). New York, NY: Worth.

Feagin, J., & Feagin, C. (2008). Basic concepts in the study of racial and ethnic relations. In *Racial and ethnic relations* (8th ed.). Upper Saddle River, NJ: Prentice Hall.

Franklin, K. (2000). Anti-gay behaviors among young adults. *Journal of Interpersonal Violence, 15*, 339–363.

Friedman, R.A. (2008, July/August). Media and madness. *The American Prospect, 19*(7), A2–A4.

Gamber, F. (2007, March/April). Stars come out for NAACP Image Awards. *The Crisis, 114*(2), 36–37.

Gosset, T.F. (1997). *Race: The history of an idea in America*. Dallas, TX: Southern Methodist University Press.

Gould, S.J. (2002). The geometer of race. In *I have landed: The end of a beginning in natural history* (pp. 356–366). New York, NY: Harmony Books.

Green, R. (1975). The Pocohontas perplex: Images of Indian women in American cultures. *Massachusetts Review, 16*, 698–714.

Haag, P. (2000). *Voices of a generation: Teenage girls report about their lives today*. New York, NY: Marlow.

Haley, A. (1976). *Roots*. Garden City, NY: Doubleday.

Herbst, P. (1997). Ethnic epithets in society. In *The color of words: An encyclopedic dictionary of ethnic bias in the United States* (pp. 255–259). Yarmouth, ME: Intercultural Press.

Herdt, G. (1997). *Same sex, different cultures: Exploring gay and lesbian lives*. Boulder, CO: Westview.

Highwater, J. (1997). *The mythology of transgression: Homosexuality as metaphor*. New York, NY: Oxford University Press.

Jagose, A. (1996). *Queer theory: An introduction*. Washington Square, NY: New York University Press.

Jones, J. (1997). *Prejudice and racism* (2nd ed.). New York, NY: McGraw-Hill.

Kennedy, R. (2002). *Nigger: The strange career of a troublesome word*. New York, NY: Pantheon Books.

Kilborn, P.T. (2005). The five-bedroom, six-figure rootless life. In *Class matters* (correspondents of the *New York Times*) (pp. 146–165). New York, NY: Times Books.

Kilbourne, J. (1999). *Deadly persuasion: Why women and girls must fight the addictive power of advertising*. New York, NY: The Free Press.

Kniker, C.R. (1977). *You and values education*. Columbus, OH: Charles E. Merrill.

Lappe, F.M. (1989). *Rediscovering America's values*. New York, NY: Ballantine.

LeBon, G. (1968). The mind of crowds. In R. Evans (Ed.), *Readings in collective behavior* (pp. 10–21). Chicago: Rand McNally.

Lefkowitz, B. (1997). *Our guys: The Glen Ridge rape and the secret life of the perfect suburb*. Berkeley: University of California Press.

Levin, J., & Levin, W. (1982). *The functions of discrimination and prejudice* (2nd ed.). New York, NY: Harper & Row.

Linton, S. (1998). Reassigning meaning. In *Claiming disability: Knowledge and identity* (pp. 8–33). New York, NY: New York University Press.

Macedo, D., & Bartolome, L.I. (2001). *Dancing with bigotry: Beyond the politics of tolerance*. New York, NY: Palgrave.

Mead, C. (1985). *Champion: Joe Louis—black hero in white America*. New York, NY: Charles Scribner.

Miller, C., & Swift, K. (2000). *Words and women*. San Jose, CA: iUniverse.

Mlodinow, L. (2008). *The drunkard's walk: How randomness rules our lives*. New York, NY: Vintage Books.

Myrdal, G. (1944). *An American dilemma: The Negro problem and modern democracy*. New York, NY: Harper & Row.

Newberg, A., & Waldman, M.R. (2006). *Why we believe what we believe: Uncovering our biological needs for meaning, spirituality, and truth*. New York, NY: Free Press.

Olson, S. (2002). *Mapping human history: Discovering the past through our genes*. Boston, MA: Houghton Mifflin.

Pagels, E. (2006). *The Gnostic gospels*. London, England: Phoenix.

Raths, L., Harmin, M., & Simon, S. (1978). *Values and teaching: Working with values in the classroom* (2nd ed.). Columbus, OH: Charles E. Merrill.

Risberg, D.F. (1978, June 18). *Framework and foundations: Setting the stage and establishing norms*. Paper presented at the first annual National Conference on Human Relations, Minneapolis, MN.

Ryan, W. (1976). *Blaming the victim* (2nd ed.). New York, NY: Vintage.

Schaefer, R.T. (2008). *Racial and ethnic groups* (11th ed.). Upper Saddle River, NJ: Pearson.

Simpson, G.E., & Yinger, J.M. (1985). *Racial and cultural minorities: An analysis of prejudice and discrimination* (5th ed.). New York, NY: Plenum.

Stephan, W. (1999). *Reducing prejudice and stereotyping in schools*. New York, NY: Teachers College Press.

Terkel, S. (1980). *American dreams: Lost and found*. New York, NY: Ballantine.

Terry, D., Hogg, M., & Duck, J. (1999). Group membership, social identity, and attitudes. In D. Abrams & M. Hogg (Eds.), *Social identity and social cognition* (pp. 280–314). Malden, MA: Blackwell.

Wade, N. (2006). *Before the dawn: Recovering the lost history of our ancestors*. New York, NY: The Penguin Press.

Wessler, S.L. (2001, January). Sticks and stones. *Educational Leadership, 58*(4), 28–33.

Wright, M.A. (1998). *I'm chocolate, you're vanilla: Raising healthy black and biracial children in a race-conscious world*. San Francisco, CA: Jossey-Bass.

Wright, W. (1983). *The Von Bulow affair*. New York, NY: Delacorte.

Zimbardo, P. (2007). *The Lucifer effect: Understanding how good people turn evil*. New York, NY: Random House.

Zinn, H. (1990). *Declarations of independence: Cross-examining American ideology*. New York, NY: HarperCollins.

Chapter 2

Understanding Prejudice and Its Causes

"No one has ever been born a Negro hater, a Jew hater, or any other kind of hater. Nature refuses to be involved in such suicidal practices."

Harry Bridges (1900–1990)

No credible studies have concluded that prejudice is part of human nature, an innate outcome of being human. In fact, Hauser (2006) cited a study reporting that during their first hours of life, babies will cry if they hear other babies crying. One developmental psychologist explained this phenomenon as a "rudimentary form of empathy" (p. 193). The evidence supports the claim that prejudice, as Bridges suggests, must be learned. It is also important to remember that prejudice is an attitude, not an action. Whether you are looking at definitions in a dictionary or reading scholarly writing, you will inevitably encounter puzzling uses of the term *prejudice*. Some people describe prejudice as a hatred of others, but hatred is bigotry. Based on their study of world cultures, anthropologists have argued that people everywhere in the world have prejudices, yet they do not claim that hatred—or bigotry—is widespread.

Confusion, not clarification, is caused by a definition suggesting that prejudice is synonymous with bigotry. Such a definition may cause many of us to deny that we are prejudiced: A bigot hates, and we are certain we don't hate anyone. In addition, we deny the pervasiveness of prejudice because we don't observe widespread hatred in the world; thus confusing prejudice with bigotry creates misunderstanding about the nature and extent of prejudice.

Conceptions and Misconceptions of Prejudice

What are examples of misconceptions about prejudice?

We confuse prejudice with bias, stereotypes, and bigotry. As defined in Chapter 1, bias is a mildly positive or negative feeling about someone or something; and to stereotype is to associate positive or negative traits with a group of people. **Prejudice** is a stronger feeling, but it is always negative, and it always refers to a group of people. Prejudice predisposes us to behave negatively toward certain people because of a group to which they belong. And when prejudice reaches the intensity of hatred, it becomes bigotry.

Some dictionaries define *prejudice* as the process of forming opinions without looking at relevant facts, yet people with prejudices may examine relevant facts and simply interpret them to confirm their prejudices. Other definitions describe prejudice as being irrational, implying that those we acknowledge as rational could not possibly be prejudiced. The problem here is that rational people also hold prejudices; we know this from reading what they wrote. Aristotle claimed that a woman was an inferior man. Abraham Lincoln believed black people were intellectually inferior to white people. Carroll (2001) quoted Martin Luther warning German Christians, "do not doubt that next to the devil you have no enemy more cruel, more venomous and virulent, than a true Jew" (p. 368). However, their prejudices did not deter any of these men from achieving significant improvements in human rights.

It is easy to view ancient racist or sexist attitudes as patently absurd and to denounce them, yet often we do not acknowledge current widespread prejudices that future generations may find just as incongruous. In fifty or one hundred years, what will people think about today's programs for the poor in the United States? Or how people with disabilities were so often isolated or ignored? Or how gay men and lesbians were condemned by so many people?

How widespread is prejudice?

Although this book focuses on attitudes in the United States, prejudices are not limited to one country or one race. People living in nations around the world possess negative attitudes toward others within their own borders or close to them. Prejudices have been ignored, promoted, or tolerated, but rarely challenged. When prejudice has been challenged, the case often has become a cause célèbre, as when Emile Zola published "J'accuse," an essay denouncing anti-Semitism in France's prosecution of Alfred Dreyfus for treason (Bredin, 2008). Persistence of prejudice was illustrated by Jean-Paul Sartre's 1945 description of French anti-Semitic attitudes as Jews returned to France following World War II, even though French people were aware of the existence of Nazi concentration camps and of the genocide against the Jews.

> There are, in every age, new errors to be rectified, and new prejudices to be opposed.
>
> Samuel Johnson (1709–1784)

Today, nations around the world are being forced to confront historic prejudices because of economic globalization and population migrations that have created major demographic changes.

Some responses to immigration have revealed the persistence of historic prejudices. In the opening paragraph of their book on prejudice and discrimination, Simpson and Yinger (1985) describe this phenomenon:

> Western European nations discovered that "guest workers," whom they have employed by the millions, are something more than cogs in an economic machine.

And, for example,

> England, with a steady migration of people from India, Pakistan, Bangladesh, Africa, and the West Indies, found herself faced with problems of a color bar and passed an unprecedented law limiting immigration. Pressures against persons of Indian descent in the new nations of East Africa not only reshaped intergroup relations in those lands but influenced Britain's restrictive immigration policy. (p. 3)

As long as people lived in relative isolation from others, prejudice against those who were far away was not necessarily harmful. In a global economy requiring functional and respectful relationships among nations, prejudice can be a destructive force both in the world and in individual societies, especially diverse societies (Gioseffi, 1993). Language is an important source for understanding a culture because analyzing language reveals a culture's assumptions, beliefs, values, and priorities, as well as examples of prejudice. Some countries are now addressing their historic prejudices by changing or eliminating media images and language that have promoted negative attitudes, especially toward racial or ethnic groups.

How are prejudices reflected in American media?

To understand how prejudices are transmitted in our culture, we need only observe some of the prevalent images of racial or cultural groups in society. As Giroux (1998) said,

> My concern with such representations . . . lies not in deciding whether they are "good" or "bad" but in analyzing them in relation to the pedagogical work they are doing. That is, what knowledge, values, and pleasures do such representations invite or exclude? (p. 27)

Look for magazine advertisements that depict Native Americans, Asian Americans, or Hispanic Americans. Why is it that most advertisements seem to use African American models to reflect diversity? If people of color are included in advertisements, why are they often featured in ways that reflect historic stereotypes? Native Americans are almost never portrayed as contemporary people but as nineteenth-century warriors; Asian Americans are often shown working at computers or in math-related professions; Mexican Americans are presented as gardeners or servants. Problems of omission and stereotyping affect other groups as well: People with disabilities are invisible, blue-collar workers are usually stereotyped, if they appear at all, and women appear frequently in advertisements as sex objects to sell products. Still, we typically don't recognize these advertisements as stereotypes because these images are so familiar that they seem not to be stereotypes at all, but rather to portray reality. This is one reason so many white Americans do not understand why Native Americans are offended by the use of Indian mascots for sports teams. (See Figure 2.1.)

Media portrayals of Muslim Americans represent the most recent example of pervasive stereotyping.

Although anti-Muslim attitudes in the United States have a long history, Ansari (2004) insists that ever since the 1979 Iranian hostage crisis, the media has focused on activities of militant Muslims. Since then, media portrayals have often presented Muslims as "irrational, undemocratic (and) opposed to equality, freedom, and peace" (Khan, 2004, p. 100). According to McCloud (2006), the stereotype of Muslims as evil terrorists existed prior to 9/11, but such representations in the media have increased, and these portrayals have most likely contributed to the results reported in a 2004 opinion poll, where 25% of Americans said they had negative attitudes about Muslims and 50% supported the federal government restricting the civil liberties of Muslim Americans (Barrett, 2007). McCloud (2004) concluded that American media "have declared Islam and Muslims as violent, irrational, and anti-modern" (p. 79).

Although the media bears some responsibility for reinforcing a variety of stereotypes, there are other sources that foster negative attitudes. One reason many Americans may not even recognize portrayals of certain groups as stereotypical is that the prejudices are embedded in our language.

FIGURE 2.1

Source: John Branch, *San Antonio Express-News.*

What examples of prejudice exist in our language?

One pattern observed in the English language has been called the **black/white syndrome**. Scholars report that this language pattern emerged in English long before the British knew that people described as black were living in Africa (Moore, 2006). Although the pattern likely originated in biblical language referring to Satan, evil, and hell as black or dark, it has been argued that a consistently negative pattern for references to black affected British perceptions of Africans and that negative connotations for blackness were readily applied to all dark-skinned people they encountered. A negative pattern for *black* has persisted in the English language, as can be seen in familiar phrases: black deed, black day, black hearted, black mass, black magic, the Black Death, black thoughts, black looks, and blacklist. Such words and phrases illustrate the point made by linguist Skuttnab-Kangas (2000), "Dominant groups keep a monopoly of defining others, and it is their labels we see in dictionaries" (p. 154).

Skuttnab-Kangas also argues that labeling others includes "the power to define oneself" by not having to accept the definitions others have for your group. It should not be surprising that references to "white" in the English language follow a consistently positive pattern: telling little white lies, having a white wedding, cheering white knights (in shining armor), indicating approval by saying "that's really white of you," and even engaging in white-collar crime (perceived as less harmful than other crimes). Some authors have exploited the pervasive black/white pattern by deliberately using white as a negative term, invoking images of sterility, death, or evil to shock readers with unexpected associations. Robert Frost employed this reversal in some of his poems, and it was no accident that Herman Melville chose to make Moby Dick, the symbol of evil in Ahab's obsession, a white whale.

Sometimes prejudice is not obvious, as in the expression, "Where there's a will there's a way." At first glance, this expression seems nothing more than an attempt to encourage children and youth to try hard, but it has another meaning: If all that it takes to be successful is to have the will to succeed, then those people who are not successful are at fault for their failure because they just didn't "try" hard enough. This belief leads to blaming the victim, providing an ethical escape for middle-class people. After all, if they were successful because they worked hard, then someone who is poor must not have worked hard enough, perhaps because they are lazy or incompetent.

Such stereotypes for "the poor" reinforce the conclusion that poor people are responsible for their poverty and thus the rest of us are under no obligation to help them. Other stereotypes may be revealed in expressions. When people negotiate with the seller on the price of a product they might say, "I Jewed him down," alluding to an old stereotype. Parents and teachers have been overheard telling children to stop behaving "like a bunch of wild Indians." Teenagers who say, "That's so gay" do not intend it as a compliment. Boys are still ridiculed by comments such as "he throws like a girl" or "he's a sissy." Children are no longer limited to the term *sissy*. Today, even elementary children can be heard calling one another a *faggot*. They may not be certain what the word means, but they know it is a negative term (Wessler, 2001).

> You can tell the ideals of a nation by its advertisements.
>
> Norman Douglas (1868–1952)

And then there are jokes based on racial, ethnic, gender, or other prejudices. When we complain that these jokes aren't funny, we are likely to be told we don't have a sense of humor: "It was a joke!" Just a joke. Although people are more careful today about telling racist jokes, sexist jokes are frequently told at work and in school. Perhaps the numerous examples of sexist words and phrases in our language make it easier to express sexist attitudes publicly.

How does gender prejudice in our language promote sexist attitudes?

Unlike many other languages, English does not have a neutral pronoun that includes both men and women, so the word *he* is used to refer to someone of indeterminate gender. *Man* has traditionally been used in words or phrases where the referent could be female (even though there are neutral nouns such as *human* and *people*). Some people continue to insist that *man* is generic when used in words such as *businessman, chairman, congressman, fireman, layman, mailman, policeman, salesman, spokesman,* and *statesman,* but studies do not support the claim. Arliss (1991) described studies using subjects ranging from elementary children to adults; all concluded that generic language invoked mental images of males.

In a study reported by Miller and Swift (2000) involving 500 junior high students, one group of students received instructions to draw pictures of "early man" engaged in various activities and to give each person drawn a name (so researchers could be certain that a man or woman was the subject of the drawing). The majority of students of both sexes tended to draw only males for every activity identified except the one representing infant care, and even for that activity, 49% of boys drew a male image. A second group of students was instructed to draw pictures of "early people" engaged in the same activities and to give each human figure drawn a name; once again, the majority of the humans drawn by both sexes were male. It is possible that the phrase *early people* sounded strange and that many students translated it as "cave men" and drew male pictures. The third group of students was asked to draw pictures of "early men and early women," once again giving names to human figures. Only in this group did the figures drawn by students include a significant number of female images, but even with these instructions, some students of both sexes drew only male figures.

> I am, in plainer words, a bundle of prejudices—made up of likings and dislikings.
>
> Charles Lamb (1775–1834)

What sexist terms for men could be considered derisive?

Although a plethora of derisive terms exist for women, derisive language directed at men often sends a mixed message. It may be intended as an insult to call a man a *prick* or a *bastard*, but it can also be interpreted as the speaker being envious of the man's power or position. Men may feel that

they have to be tough, ruthless, and relentless if they are going to be successful in a "dog eat dog world"; such language could be regarded as a compliment to a man's prowess, his masculinity.

In American English, unambiguously derisive terms for men often accuse a man of being feminine. No little boy wants to be called a *sissy*; no man wants to be called a *wimp* or a *pussy*. Although a man may not like being called a name that implies he acts like a woman, according to Baker (1981), it is even more insulting to be called a name suggesting that a woman controls him, that he's *pussy whipped*. Men often use such language in a joking manner, but the message is serious.

That it is an insult for a man to be compared to a woman was illustrated by an incident at a summer festival. The dunking booth was not open yet, but a man and his son were getting it ready. Three young men came up to the booth and volunteered to be dunked. The man thanked them but said he had all the volunteers he needed. Animated by the alcohol they had consumed, the three of them badgered the man for several minutes before they gave up. As they walked away, the man at the booth said, "Good-bye, girls!" One of the young men turned around quickly and shouted, "What the fuck did you call me?" The vehemence of the young man's response was both surprising and disturbing as he came storming back. Even though the father had his son next to him, the young man was prepared to use violence to defend his manhood against such a degrading insult.

A mother and daughter were standing nearby in a line for face painting. Having observed this confrontation, the mother shouted sarcastically to the young man, "Oh, what a terrible thing to be called!" He looked over at the face-painting line, and other mothers standing with their daughters shouted similar comments. As the young man looked at them, his face betrayed his confusion. His body had swelled up with anger, but now it seemed to deflate. His shoulders drooped and his expression became almost sheepish. As he approached the man at the dunking booth, he was still angry, but not to the point of engaging in violence. After a brief conversation, a security officer arrived and escorted the young man away. Considering the hostility aroused by such a flippant remark, one has to wonder about the attitudes males are being taught concerning women. Is it possible for a man to hate the idea of being called a female and not subconsciously hate women as well?

Aren't some prejudices positive?

Some people misuse the term *prejudice* by saying they are prejudiced *for* something, but a prejudice is always a negative attitude. A milder attitude of liking or disliking anything or anyone is a bias; however, the concept of prejudice involves learning to fear and mistrust other groups of people, and to strengthen negative attitudes we have been taught about them. Once we learn to be prejudiced against a certain group, we tend to behave in negative ways toward others who appear to be members of that group. Negative behavior is discrimination: We no longer merely hold a negative attitude—we have acted on that attitude. To prevent such negative consequences of prejudice, it is necessary to unlearn whatever prejudices we have been taught, but that is more difficult than it sounds because there are powerful factors motivating people to persist in maintaining their prejudices.

The Perpetuation of Prejudice

People want to be successful and will try to promote their own self-interests. When members of one group believe that individuals from another group are becoming more successful than they are, they may become angry at those individuals—even hostile toward the entire group—and rationalize that an advantage other than talent or skill is responsible for that individual's or group's success. Resentment from economic competition for good jobs with high salaries and status fosters prejudice. Because humans are intelligent enough to identify these various causes of prejudice, it seems logical to assume that people should be able to recognize that they have prejudices and attempt to eliminate them.

How are prejudices perpetuated?

A major factor in the perpetuation of prejudice is the tendency to rationalize prejudices and the negative behaviors prejudices promote. As Gioseffi (1993) has noted, this not only affects individuals but also is an international phenomenon: "Just as individuals will rationalize their hostile behaviors . . . so nations do also" (p. xvii). Vega (1978) described rationalizations as taking three forms: denial, victim-blaming, and avoidance. To unlearn our prejudices and develop effective ways of confronting prejudices expressed by others, we need to recognize these rationalizations so we can make an appropriate response when they are expressed.

Denial rationalizations. In making **denial rationalizations**, we refuse to recognize that there are problems in our society resulting from prejudices and discrimination. Such claims are astonishing in their ignorance, yet they continue to be made. In response to assertions of racism, the most common denial rationalization is the reverse discrimination argument claiming that women and minorities receive the best jobs because of affirmative action programs. Is there any truth to this claim?

According to population demographics, women now comprise almost half of the workforce; another 10% consists of men of color, which means that white men constitute about 40% of the workforce (Daft, 2003). A job paying an annual salary of $50,000 or more is a criterion to identify which jobs involve some degree of authority, status, and decision-making power. How many of these jobs are in the hands of white men? It would be consistent with their proportion of the workforce if white men held slightly less than half of these jobs, yet according to the U.S. Bureau of Labor Statistics (2001), white men hold over three fourths of these positions, about twice as many as the percentage of white men in the workforce. Claims that white men are unfairly discriminated against as a result of affirmative action policies thus appear to be inaccurate (see Table 2.1).

The most common denial rationalization related to sexism is the "natural" argument, which denies gender discrimination, claiming that it is natural for women to do some things better than men, and for men to do some things better than women. This denial rationalization is offered as an explanation for why men and women have historically held certain types of jobs. The argument does not explain the difference between the skills of a tailor (predominantly men) compared to a seamstress (predominantly women) to justify the differences in their compensations. Nor does it explain why construction workers (mostly men)

TABLE 2.1 Annual Incomes of Full-Time Workers in the United States

Race/Gender	Median Weekly Earnings	
	2004	2011
White males	$732 (100%)	$856 (100%)
Black males	$569 (77.7%)	$653 (76.3%)
Hispanic males	$480 (65.6%)	$571 (66.7%)
White females	$584 (79.8%)	$703 (82.1%)
Black females	$505 (69.9%)	$595 (69.5%)
Hispanic females	$419 (57.2%)	$518 (60.5%)

Source: U.S. Bureau of Labor Statistics, 2012.

should be compensated at a greater rate than college-educated social workers (mostly women). Historically, women have been paid less than men for doing the same work, and occupations dominated by women still receive lower wages than occupations dominated by men (U.S. Bureau of Labor Statistics, 2001). This is the reality, but denial rationalizations have little to do with reality.

The most subtle denial rationalization is personal denial illustrated by the man who says, "How can I be sexist? I love women! I married a woman. I have daughters." This seems a reasonable statement: A man denying he has gender prejudices does not appear to deny the existence of widespread prejudice against women—but the statement actually does imply a more sweeping denial. Psychologically, most people feel they are normal, average people. If a person denies being prejudiced, he or she is actually denying that most other normal, average people are prejudiced as well. The real meaning of such a statement is that the speaker does not believe prejudice and discrimination are serious problems in society. If the person making this denial rationalization argues this point, he or she might resort to victim-blaming responses because the two are closely related.

> Prejudice blinds, ignorance retards, indifference deafens, hate amputates. In this way do some people disable their souls.
>
> Mary Robinson (1944–)

Victim-blaming rationalizations.   People employing **victim-blaming rationalizations** reject the notion that prejudice and discrimination are problems in society, even though they admit that problems exist. The problems they identify, however, are typically deficiencies or flaws in members of minority groups (Ryan, 1976). Victim blamers focus on the group being harmed by societal prejudices and insist that society doesn't need to change: The group needs to change. Victim blamers urge individuals to stop being so sensitive or so pushy, to work harder, and to quit complaining. Group members are told they are responsible for whatever problems they must overcome. Ironically, some victim blamers do not hold themselves responsible for their own failures, but instead blame the environment or other factors. In a study of college students who took an intelligence test, participants tended to explain the poor performance of others as an indication of inferior intellectual ability, but if *they* performed poorly, they were more likely to view the results as a consequence of the level of difficulty of the test (Aronson, 2008).

Victim blaming often occurs among people who want to believe in a just world. In one study, subjects observed two people working equally hard at a task. By a random decision, researchers gave one of the workers a significant reward when the task was completed; the other worker received nothing. When asked to rate how hard the two people had worked, the subjects tended to describe the person who received nothing as not working as hard as the person receiving the reward.

Aronson (2008) concluded his analysis of this study by suggesting that "we find it frightening to think about living in a world where people, through no fault of their own, can be deprived of what they deserve or need" (p. 323).

People who engage in victim-blaming rationalizations often go beyond blame to propose solutions. By defining the problem as a deficiency existing in the victimized group, every solution proposed by a victim blamer involves what victims need to do because they are the problem. The rest of us need do nothing. Rape is increasing on college campuses? That's a woman's problem, so what women need to do is to wear less provocative clothing, avoid going out late at night, and learn to defend themselves by taking martial arts classes or carrying pepper spray. What to do about the rapist isn't addressed. Because victim blamers offer solutions, it is easy to confuse victim blaming with some avoidance rationalizations.

Avoidance rationalizations.   Unlike people who employ denial and victim blaming rationalizations, those who promote **avoidance rationalizations** recognize the problems in society as stemming from prejudice and discrimination. This is a significant departure from the previous rationalizations. Even though a person making avoidance rationalizations admits there are problems, he or she will not address them and will rationalize a reason to avoid them. Ways to avoid confronting issues include offering a solution that addresses only part of a problem or suggesting a false solution that does not address the problem at all.

If college administrators decide to confront prejudice by requiring students to take an ethnic studies course, that requirement will address a small part of the problems caused by racial prejudice and discrimination. Learning more about ethnic groups is a good idea, but if colleges are serious about actively opposing racism and improving race relations, administration and faculty must recruit diverse students, hire diverse faculty, and promote cultural diversity through workshops and seminars both on campus and in the community.

A false solution that does not address the problems of sexism at all is the proposal that "sexism would just disappear if we didn't pay so much attention to it." Problems created by sexism did not suddenly appear and they won't disappear unless

people engage in actions to confront, challenge, and change sexist attitudes, policies, and laws. The only way any society can solve problems and improve conditions is to analyze a problem, create appropriate solutions, implement the solutions that seem most likely to be effective, and, after time passes, assess the impact of these solutions.

Another form of avoidance rationalization involves making an argument that distracts attention from the issue or question being discussed. Imagine a group of people discussing efforts that could be made to increase social justice in our society. Suddenly someone says, "You're being too idealistic. We are never going to solve this problem because we're never going to have a utopia." The speaker was not arguing for the creation of a utopia, a perfect society, but for ways to improve society. By making the reasonable statement that utopias are not possible, the speaker has shifted the focus of the conversation to a different topic that avoids the issue. It is not realistic to believe that it is possible to create a perfect society, but it is possible—in fact, essential—to believe that any society can be improved.

In a discussion about the need for child-care centers at work sites, someone might say, "I support the idea, but it takes time; it's not going to happen overnight." A reasonable response, except what has been achieved if the discussion ends with that comment? To implement any solution successfully, it is necessary to clarify what is entailed: What needs to be done? Who will do what? Which actions should be taken next month? What can we expect in the next six months? Who will determine whether the solution is working, and how will progress be assessed? Saying a solution takes time may be true, but it is still necessary to discuss what must be done to implement it. To avoid that discussion is to sidestep dealing with the problem. Problems are not solved by talk or the passage of time but by taking some kind of action.

Conservatives are often accused of engaging in denial and victim-blaming rationalizations. Their solutions tend to concentrate on perceived flaws in victims of prejudice rather than addressing the prejudice and discrimination that create many of these difficult circumstances. On the other hand, liberals are more likely to be criticized for engaging in avoidance rationalizations in which they acknowledge and express sympathy for the problems faced by oppressed groups, but never do anything to address the causes of these problems. As long as significant numbers of individuals continue to employ such rationalizations, Americans are not likely to perceive or confront causes or consequences of the persistent inequities stemming from prejudices based on race, gender, and other human differences.

Causes and Consequences of Prejudice

Considerable research has been conducted addressing the question of how individuals become prejudiced. Some studies suggest that elitist attitudes foster prejudice. **Elitism** is the belief that the most able people succeed in society and form a natural aristocracy, whereas the least able enjoy the least success because they are flawed in some way or lack the necessary qualities to be successful. This condescending attitude promotes the belief that those in the lower levels of society deserve to be where they are and that successful people have earned their place in society. Unsuccessful people are often held responsible for their failure. Elitist attitudes are a major factor in studies based on social dominance theory (Howard, 2006; Stephan, 1999).

The eugenics movement beginning in the late 1800s argued that an individual's genetic inheritance determined his or her fate and that environment played little or no role in human development (Selden, 2006). Based on this argument, proponents of the eugenics movement in the United States were promoting elitist attitudes. Selden quotes American biologist George W. Hunter, author of several biology textbooks widely used in schools between 1914 and 1941, who expressed this elitist attitude clearly:

> Those of low grade intelligence would do little better under the most favorable conditions possible, while those of superior intelligence will make good no matter what handicaps they are given. (p. 75)

Other studies suggest a link between prejudice and attitudes about power. Some people express a **zero-sum** attitude, a highly competitive orientation toward power based on the assumption that the personal gains of one individual mean a loss

for someone else; therefore, to share power is regarded as having less power. According to Levin and Levin (1982), an individual with a zero-sum orientation toward power tends to be a person with strong prejudices. Thurow (2001) has described the adverse consequences for society when a zero-sum orientation is prevalent. Studies also suggest that people with authoritarian personalities tend to be more prejudiced, although other studies refute the idea (Farley, 2005). Some have even proposed that prejudice is innate, but there are no scientific studies to support that claim.

> Everyone is a prisoner of his own experiences. No one can eliminate prejudices—just recognize them.
>
> Edward R. Murrow (1908–1965)

To be as pervasive and persistent as it has been, prejudice must serve some purpose and offer some benefit to individuals or to society.

What are the major causes promoting the development of prejudice?

Having reviewed research concerning causes of prejudice, Levin and Levin (1982) identified four primary causes, and within these causes, functions of prejudice that sustain it. The four causes include (1) personal frustration, (2) uncertainty about a person based on lack of knowledge or experience with the group to which they belong, (3) threat to one's self-esteem, and (4) competition among individuals in our society to achieve their goals in relation to status, wealth, and power.

How does frustration cause prejudice?

The frustration-aggression hypothesis maintains that as frustration builds, it leads to aggressive action. Frustration causes tension to increase until a person chooses to act on the frustration to alleviate the tension. Jones (1997) and others have called this the "scapegoat phenomenon." The word **scapegoat** derives from an ancient Hebrew custom described in Leviticus 16: 20–22, where each year the Hebrew people reflected on their sins during days of atonement. At the end of that time, a spiritual leader would stand before them with a goat, lay his hands on the goat's head, and recite a list of the people's sins, transferring the sins of the people to the goat—which was then set free. In modern America, the term generally refers to blaming a person or group for problems they did not cause.

When we take aggressive action—from verbal abuse to physical violence—we inevitably cause harm to others. Because most individuals define themselves as "good" according to some criteria, they will usually find a way to rationalize their actions as being good or at least justified. When southerners lynched black people in the late nineteenth and early twentieth centuries, they justified their actions by insisting that all blacks were lazy, lustful, or liars. Using the Kafkaesque reasoning that all blacks were guilty and therefore it didn't matter what crime a black person was accused of committing, they executed victims with no regard for whether that specific black person was guilty of a crime.

Ironically, data from some studies have shown that aggressive action may not alleviate frustration, but instead may exacerbate it. In one study, two groups of subjects were asked to allow medical technicians to take physical measurements of their bodies. After taking the measurements, the technicians made derogatory comments intended to make the subjects angry. One group was taken to the technician's "supervisor" if they wanted to complain; the other group was not. The researchers thought that members of the group being allowed to "vent" their anger would feel less hostile toward the technician afterward, yet those who were given the opportunity to complain reported stronger feelings of hostility than the subjects who were not allowed to complain (Aronson, 2008). The findings suggest that identifying a scapegoat on which to vent one's frustration does not solve a person's problems, and it may make matters worse.

The implication that finding a scapegoat does not solve problems is illustrated in domestic abuse cases. When a man takes out his frustrations by abusing his partner, he has to justify his actions. It is common for men arrested for domestic abuse to explain their behavior by saying, "She made me do it," or "She kept nagging and wouldn't shut up." This not only depicts the man as a victim (the suffering husband), but also reinforces the stereotype of nagging wives, providing the husband with an excuse for assaulting the woman he once claimed to love. As violence escalates with each domestic abuse complaint from the same home, it is obvious that blaming one's spouse or partner doesn't solve the problem; it may possibly cause the abuser to become more violent toward those interfering with his actions.

Because of the high rates of injury and death to police officers responding to domestic abuse cases, many American cities, counties, and states require officers to file abuse charges directly, even over the objections of the one abused. Courts often mandate counseling for abusers to address and understand how gender prejudices and stereotypes created negative attitudes leading to abuse, and to teach abusive men effective, nonviolent strategies for managing anger. The role of gender stereotypes in contributing to domestic abuse illustrates another major cause of prejudice—uncertainty.

What do stereotypes have to do with uncertainty and how do they cause prejudice?

Most of us only have knowledge of the groups to which we belong; often we do not know much about other groups. In the United States, schools have historically implemented curricula reflecting perspectives, contributions, and experiences of the dominant (white) group, and many of our neighborhoods still tend to be segregated by race or social class. The result is that people from different racial and ethnic groups have few opportunities to learn about one another. Because of our lack of accurate information, we may believe in stereotypes as a way to convince ourselves that we know about certain groups. (See Figure 2.2.) Our stereotypes can be reinforced by images or information contained in such media as advertisements, textbooks, and films.

For an example of ignorance promoting prejudice, how many Americans know that Muslims have been in the United States from colonial times because many slaves brought to America from West Africa were Muslim? The evidence is in the names that "read like a Who's Who of traditional Muslim names"—Bullaly (Bilali), Mahomet (Muhammad), Walley (Wali), and Sambo meant "second son" to Muslim Fulbe people (Abdo, 2006, p. 66).

FIGURE 2.2

This drawing has been used for research and in classrooms. One person is shown this picture and whispers a description of the entire scene to another person, who then whispers the description to another person until each person in the room has heard it. The last person is asked to describe the scene to everyone. Typically, the person describes a poorly dressed black man with a weapon preparing to attack a well-dressed white man, thus illustrating the power of racial stereotypes.

While Americans tend to stereotype all Arabs as Muslims, the majority of Arabs immigrating to the United States in the late nineteenth century were Christians. Another stereotype is that Muslims have only lived in urban areas. How many Americans know that in the 1920s a small group of Muslims settled in Ross, South Dakota, and built the first mosque in the United States, or that the oldest continuously functioning mosque is in Cedar Rapids, Iowa (Abdo, 2006)?

Even if they don't know this history, how many Americans know that Muslim Americans today own over 200,000 businesses and that there are over 2,000 mosques in the United States (Ansari, 2004)? How many Americans know that Muslim American adults are better educated than the average American (59% have college degrees compared to 27% of other Americans) and wealthier (a median annual income of $60,000 compared to the national median annual income of $50,000) (Barrett, 2007)? Muslims have done what America expects of immigrants. But, unaware of this information, and surrounded by stereotypes and the media's focus on Islamic terrorists, how many Americans harbor negative views of both the Islamic faith and Muslims? According to a 2004 survey by the Pew Forum on Religion and Public Life, nearly 50% of Americans perceived the Islamic faith as more likely to promote violence than other religions (a percentage that doubled compared to the results of a similar survey conducted two years earlier) and nearly 40% expressed a negative view of Muslims (Abdo, 2006).

People have long known that stereotypes skew an individual's perception of a group, but more recently scholars have reported that being aware of the stereotypes for your group can adversely affect members of a group. This is called a **stereotype threat**, which Aronson (2008) defines as "the apprehension experienced by members of a minority group that they might behave in a manner that confirms an existing cultural stereotype" (p. 437). Such apprehensions can contribute to feelings of anxiety and poor performance.

Ariely (2008) described a study in which Asian American women were divided into two groups and administered the same math exam. Prior to receiving the exam, one group was asked numerous questions related to their gender, and the other group was asked numerous questions related to their race. The second group performed much better than the first group on the math test, suggesting that stereotypes about women being deficient in math and Asians excelling at math may have influenced their performance. Other studies have reported similar results, including one study of white male engineering students who had almost perfect math scores on the SAT tests. These white males were randomly divided into two groups, and prior to being given a challenging math test, one group was told that the test would measure their math abilities, whereas the other group was told that the purpose of the study was to understand why Asians appear to be superior to all others in their math ability. The second group had much lower scores on the math exam than the first group (Aronson, 2008).

When a person actually encounters individuals of a different race, ethnicity, or social class, selective perception of the behaviors of those individuals often reinforces his or her stereotypes. Stephan (1999) reported on one study where subjects were presented with equal amounts of positive and negative information about a group to which they belonged (in-group) and a group to which they did not belong (out-group). Subjects tended to recall more positive information about the in-group and more negative information about the out-group. According to Stephan, negative attitudes in our memory tend to increase over time.

Selective perception was illustrated in another study in which two groups of subjects viewed consecutive videotapes: The first videotape was of a fourth-grade girl playing with friends, and the second videotape was of the same girl taking an oral test in school in which she answered some difficult questions correctly but missed some easy questions. Although the second videotape was the same for both groups, the first videotape shown to one group was the girl playing in a low-income neighborhood, and the first videotape shown to the other group was the girl playing in a high-income neighborhood. After watching both videotapes, subjects were asked to judge the girl's academic abilities. Those who saw her playing in the low-income neighborhood rated her academic ability lower than those who saw her playing in the more affluent neighborhood. Whether the subjects focused more on the girl's correct or incorrect answers appeared to have been influenced by the neighborhood in which they believed she lived and stereotypes associated with affluence and poverty (Aronson, 2008).

Researchers have also shown that becoming more knowledgeable about others helps people overcome stereotypical perceptions. In a psychiatric hospital with an all-white staff, patients acting violently were either taken to a "time-out room" or subjected to the harsher penalty of being put in a straitjacket and sedated. In the first month of a research study, both black and white patients were admitted. Although the black patients admitted were diagnosed as being less violent than the whites, they were four times more likely to be put in a straitjacket and sedated by the staff if they became violent. The discrepancy in the white staff's use of restraints suggests that they believed in the stereotype that black people were more prone to violence. As they became better acquainted with the patients, the staff responded to violent incidents with more equal use of restraints for both black and white patients (Aronson, 2008). Stereotypes that portray a group as being prone to violence, lazy, or less intelligent can influence a person's behavior; stereotypes can also play a part in a person's self-esteem being threatened, which is another major cause of prejudice identified in research.

> Sometimes (prejudice) is like a hair across your cheek. You can't see it, you can't find it with your fingers, but you keep brushing at it because the feel of it is irritating.
>
> Marian Anderson (1897–1993)

How does threat to self-esteem cause prejudice?

In the United States, people are encouraged to develop self-esteem by comparing themselves with others. We do so by grades in school, music contests, debates in speech, and athletic competitions. But what happens when positive self-esteem is achieved by developing feelings of superiority to someone else? Or when we achieve our sense of superiority by projecting our feelings of inferiority onto another person or group? If we believe in the innate superiority of our group compared to other groups, then we believe we are better than anyone who is a member of the inferior group. If members of an inferior group become successful, their achievements threaten those whose self-esteem was based on feelings of group superiority and their condescending attitude unconsciously turns into prejudice.

People of color confront the issue of self-esteem based on race as a cause of prejudice when they encounter white people whose self-esteem is threatened by their achievements or success. The first African American to teach at Harvard University Law School commented,

> You have to simultaneously function on a high level and try not to upset those whose racial equilibrium is thrown off when they recognize that you are not incompetent, not mediocre, and don't fit the long accepted notions about persons of color that serve as unrecognized but important components of their self-esteem. (Bell, 2002, pp. 66–67)

When we possess this kind of self-esteem, we are insecure and easily threatened. Coleman (2007) argued that people perceiving others as inferior "are more likely to identify and maintain negative stereotypes about members of stigmatized groups" (p. 222).

Studies suggest that part of the self-esteem for many men derives just from being male. In Michigan, over a thousand children wrote essays about what their lives would be like if they were the opposite gender. Although almost half the girls found many positive things to say about being male, 95% of the boys could find nothing positive to say about being female (Sadker & Sadker, 1994). Similar attitudes appear among adults. In their research on self-esteem, Martinez and Dukes (1991) reported

that males displayed higher self-esteem than did females, and that white males had the highest self-esteem of all groups.

When male self-esteem derives from perceiving one's gender as superior, it is easily threatened by women's achievements. American men often rationalize female achievements by attributing women's success to reasons other than competence. Their rationalizations may be characterized by resentment or anger, which intensifies the prejudice that created the initial illusion of superiority. If a woman receives the promotion a man wanted, he might complain that she is "sleeping her way to the top." Because self-esteem based on a belief in gender superiority is an illusion, it is ultimately inadequate because the individual has done nothing to earn it. Fearing that an "inferior" person might receive rewards the "superior" individual desires is related to the fourth primary cause of prejudice: competition for status, wealth, and power.

How does competition for status, wealth, and power cause prejudice?

There is evidence that competition fosters prejudicial attitudes. Jones (1997) described a study at a summer camp where Boy Scouts were given time to become acquainted and to develop friendships before being divided into two groups and housed in separate bunkhouses. The groups were divided so that approximately two thirds of each boy's friends were in the other bunkhouse. The two groups were encouraged to play a series of competitive games such as tug-of-war, football, and baseball. Boys who had liked each other began to intensely dislike each other and to engage in name-calling. Although there was solidarity within groups, friendships that had been established with boys from the other group no longer existed. After competitive games were concluded, researchers brought the boys together, but animosity remained until the boys were given tasks that required them to cooperate with each other. Working together to achieve a common goal reduced the hostility and resulted in the boys again making friendships with individuals from the other group. From this study we can argue how important it is, in schools and at work sites, to promote collaborative efforts among students or workers so that they not only complete necessary tasks, but build better relationships between individuals from diverse groups. This may be one of the most effective ways to reduce both prejudice and the kinds of discriminatory practices that stem from prejudice such as racial profiling.

What is racial profiling?

Racial profiling occurs when authorities assume that members of certain racial or ethnic groups are more likely to engage in criminal activity—anything from selling drugs to acts of terrorism. For many years African Americans have complained about being disproportionately stopped by police for no reason, or for what police insisted was a "routine" traffic stop. Blacks referred to this as being guilty of the crime of "Driving While Black" (DWB). But DWB is no longer the only form of racial profiling. Muslims have reported being similarly singled out by airport authorities for FWM ("Flying While Muslim"). A poll of American Muslims reported that they were encountering increased racial profiling in airports, and they were also being subjected to "extra surveillance" by the federal government (Niebuhr, 2008). Federal and state funding of anti-terrorism training for local police has contributed to racial profiling of Muslims. Stalcup and Craze (2011) observed specific trainers reinforcing anti-Muslim stereotypes and presenting false statements about Islamic beliefs including the attribution of extremist beliefs to mainstream Muslims. Critics argue that racial profiling is not only discriminatory, but an ineffective approach to curbing terrorism; yet few Americans are likely to object to racial profiling of Muslims because of their negative attitudes toward Islam. According to a 2009 poll, almost half of Americans had an "unfavorable opinion of Islam," and a 2010 Pew Research Center survey found 35% of Americans believing that Islam encouraged its followers to engage in violence, while 28% thought that American Muslims felt sympathetic toward Al Qaeda (Steinback, 2011).

In addition, the controversy over illegal immigration has led to racial profiling of Latinos by some law enforcement officials. This was exacerbated by Arizona's passage of a harsh immigration law that allows police officers to detain an individual on a suspicion that the person is an undocumented worker. With the passage of SB 1070, Latinos in Arizona can be forced to produce papers proving that they are U.S. citizens or legal immigrants, and without such papers they could be arrested and incarcerated. At a naturalization ceremony in the Rose Garden, President Obama warned that the Arizona law could potentially "undermine basic notions that we cherish as Americans, as well as the trust between police and our communities that is so crucial to keeping us safe" (Archibold, 2010, p. 1). Unfortunately, a majority of Americans appear to support the controversial law. In a 2010 poll of more than 1,000 Americans, 61% said they approved of the Arizona law. This approval spanned political parties with 49% of Democrats, 80% of Republicans, and 54% of Independents supporting the law (Tolev, 2010). Arizona's law should increase the pressure on federal lawmakers to pass some kind of immigration reform, but a divided Congress seems unwilling to address this critical issue. Meanwhile, Latino organizations and advocacy groups are monitoring police activities in Arizona to make sure that the rights of American citizens and legal immigrants are not abused by those charged with enforcing this law.

What other forms of discrimination are a consequence of prejudice?

With regard to discriminatory actions, Allport (1979) identified five negative behaviors caused by prejudice: (1) *verbal abuse* against others that occurs among friends or results in name-calling directed at others from a particular group. Name-calling can escalate into (2) *physical assaults*. The victim doesn't even have to be a member of the despised group to be assaulted; anyone could be a victim by being perceived as one of "them." When a large group of ethnic Hmong from Southeast Asia settled in a Wisconsin community of 50,000 people, some local citizens did not accept them. A Japanese foreign exchange student who attended a college in that community was severely beaten by a white man in the mistaken belief that his victim was Hmong. Another common example of violence based on misperceptions is heterosexual men who have been physically assaulted because they were perceived to be gay.

If prejudice evolves into bigotry, one's hatred can lead to (3) *extreme violence*, including the desire to commit murder. Such behavior is now called a "hate crime." In 1982, two Detroit men lost their jobs at an automobile factory and believed it was related to the popularity of imported Japanese cars. When they encountered Vincent Chin, a Chinese American, they mistakenly thought he was Japanese. Motivated by hatred and rage, they brutally murdered him. If homicidal rage spreads, it might lead to the extreme form of violence called **genocide**—the systematic and deliberate extermination of a nationality or a racial or ethnic group (Feagin & Feagin, 2008). A person can play a passive role that still supports genocide. After World War II, most Germans (also Poles, Austrians, and others) claimed they didn't know that six million Jews were killed in concentration camps; persuasive evidence has been gathered to argue that they knew but were not concerned enough to do anything about it (Goldhagen, 2002).

In contrast to confrontational negative behavior stemming from prejudice and bigotry, a more passive negative response to prejudice is to avoid members of other groups. We do this by (4) *limiting our interactions* with people from racial or ethnic groups other than our own. Measuring attitudes about avoiding others was the focus of research by Bogardus; this study used a Social Distance Scale in which people encounter a list of racial, ethnic, and religious groups and are asked to rank them in order of preference (Schaefer, 2008). People consistently reveal a preference for those groups most like their own, and they have less regard for people from groups they perceive as least like themselves.

Another way to avoid certain groups is (5) to *engage in or condone discrimination* in such areas as education, employment, and housing. To illustrate this behavior, consider how people choose what sort of neighborhood they want to live in. In the 1960s, when courts ordered urban school districts to desegregate, many school administrators responded by busing students to different schools, a controversial solution that caused massive movement of white families from urban neighborhoods to racially segregated suburbs, the **white flight** phenomenon (see Figure 2.3). Despite the passage of the 1968 National Fair Housing Act, studies have documented the preference of most white Americans to live in racially segregated neighborhoods (Farley, 2005; Massey, 2001). As Massey noted, the Fair Housing Act "theoretically put an end to housing discrimination; however, residential segregation proved to be remarkably persistent" (p. 424).

Is prejudice the main cause of discrimination in society?

For years we believed that discrimination was caused by prejudice; therefore, the way to reduce discrimination was to reduce prejudice. Efforts were made in schools and in popular culture to address and reduce prejudice, and they produced positive results. For many years, research reported a significant decrease in prejudice; however, studies did not find a significant decrease in discrimination (Astor, 1997). Based on efforts by scholars seeking alternative explanations, Feagin and Feagin (1986) described three theories of discrimination: the interest theory, the internal colonialism theory, and the institutionalized discrimination theory, all of which identify historic and contemporary forces responsible for inequities being perpetuated without the involvement of prejudice.

How does the interest theory explain discrimination?

The **interest theory** describes discrimination resulting from people protecting their power and privilege. Instead of being motivated by prejudice, people discriminate against individuals from subordinate groups because of self-interest. For example, white men may object to affirmative action programs not because of their prejudice but from fear of policies that might reduce their opportunities to be hired, retained, or promoted. Homeowners might persuade neighbors not to sell their home to a family of color because they are worried about what will happen to property values. Discrimination is a function of protecting one's interests; this is similar to the internal colonialism theory.

How is self-interest involved in the internal colonialism theory?

The **internal colonialism theory** of discrimination is an analysis of how privilege was created in the United States when the dominant group— white male Europeans—exploited subordinate groups to assume control of America's resources: land from American Indians, unpaid labor by African slaves, and wages and property of wives.

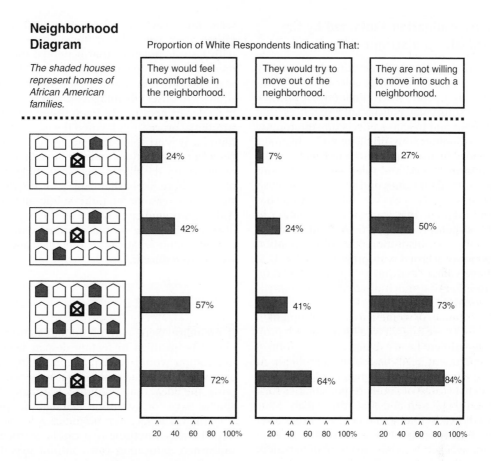

Neighborhood Diagram

The shaded houses represent homes of African American families.

Proportion of White Respondents Indicating That:

| They would feel uncomfortable in the neighborhood. | They would try to move out of the neighborhood. | They are not willing to move into such a neighborhood. |

FIGURE 2.3 Neighborhood Preference of White Respondents

In a study cited by Farley (2005), subjects were shown diagrams of neighborhoods consisting of 15 homes with an X on the home in the center of the neighborhood indicating the subject's home. Each shaded home represented an African American family. White respondents were asked: How comfortable would they feel in each neighborhood? If they were uncomfortable, would they leave? Would they move to such a neighborhood? The percentage not willing to live in those neighborhoods were only a fifth or a third of homeowners were African Americans illustrates attitudes that produced white flight.

Furthermore, by gaining control over resources and exploiting them to their advantage, certain white male Europeans achieved positions that provided them access to technological developments and control of industrial developments in the United States, including military technology. Once they are in a position of power, people will do whatever they can to maintain their advantage and stay in power.

Although initially established by force, unequal distribution and control of economic and political resources eventually became institutionalized. The theory of internal colonialism asserts that continued domination of nonwhites and women by white men is maintained by the way that institutions function in the United States. Internal colonialism theory creates the foundation on which the theory of institutionalized discrimination was built.

How is discrimination explained by the institutionalized discrimination theory?

The **institutionalized discrimination theory** accepts the history of internal colonialism but focuses on contemporary discrimination. This theory describes institutional policies and practices that have different and negative effects on subordinate groups. It examines how privilege and advantage are embedded in an organization's norms, its regulations, informal rules, and roles—social positions with their attendant duties and rights. An analysis based on this theory seeks to understand mechanisms and methods that lead to discrimination in institutional policies and practices. Similar to the other two theories, institutionalized discrimination theory is not concerned with prejudice (what U.S. courts have called "evil intent") but is based on the assumption that much discrimination today is unintentional.

When a number of women in city government in an urban area were interviewed for a research project, one department head explained how a group of female department heads had solved a problem. At the end of a workday, the women tended to leave immediately because of family responsibilities such as picking up children and preparing meals. Male department heads tended to meet for a drink after work once or twice a week, and to play golf together on weekends while women department heads spent that time with their families. At meetings in which they had to make decisions about funding for programs, female department heads were frustrated by their inability to be as effective as their male counterparts in supporting each other.

The women understood why the men had an advantage. Because of their social activities, male department heads knew more about each other's departments, so they could make informed arguments in support of each other's programs. To create a similar advantage for themselves, the women started meeting together one evening every month (child care provided) to talk about their programs and needs and to prepare for debates on funding priorities. As a result of their efforts, a greater amount of funding was distributed to departments headed by women (Koppelman, 1994).

The institutionalized discrimination theory provides a realistic basis for understanding discrimination: The actions of the male department heads were not based on a prejudice against women; rather, they were doing their job in accordance with historic practices that benefited their departments. The women understood that the solution was not to berate the men but rather to devise a strategy to offset advantages already established for male department heads. Even though informal institutional procedures favored the men, the women found a way to "play the game" more effectively. Discriminatory actions can still be a direct result of prejudice on the part of people making decisions, but it is more likely that causes for discrimination stem from reasons far more subtle and complex. Although prejudice may not be the main cause of discrimination, we should continue with research to understand what causes prejudice and do what we can to reduce it.

AFTERWORD

If prejudice were part of human nature, people would be justified in feeling despair because the implication would be that human beings eventually will destroy each other. But no evidence supports the idea that prejudice is innate. Instead, studies have consistently concluded that prejudice is learned. The fact that prejudice is learned offers hope because anything that can be learned can be unlearned. Education can confront negative attitudes both in the media and in our language to help students unlearn prejudices they have been taught, and also understand why it is in everyone's best interest not to act on prejudices.

> [There is a] strangely irrational notion that there is something in the very flow of time that will inevitably cure all ills. Actually time is neutral. It can be used either destructively or constructively.
>
> Martin Luther King, Jr. (1929–1968)

In their study of brain research, Newberg and Waldman (2006) found that people could "interrupt" prejudicial beliefs and stereotypes and generate new ideas, and that these new ideas "can alter the neural circuitry that governs how we behave and what we believe. Our beliefs . . . aren't necessarily static. They can change; we can change them" (p. 9).

Prejudice can be reduced by accurate information, by formal and informal learning, and by establishing equitable workplace policies and practices. Prejudices can also be unlearned by friends challenging one another's negative attitudes. Even though some people may not be able to give up their prejudices, they do not have to act on them. It is not inevitable that our prejudices control us. When we can identify our prejudices and understand how we learned them, we can choose to limit their influence on our behavior. We can control them instead of letting them control us.

When we make positive choices, we affirm the basis for having hope for the future. Positive choices that individuals have made throughout history have resulted in genuine human progress. If our society is to benefit from its diversity, it will be because enough Americans have chosen to regard diversity as an asset and to confront their prejudices. Those who make such positive choices today will shape the nature of the society in which our children and their children must live.

TERMS AND DEFINITIONS

Avoidance rationalization A response to a social problem—such as injustice toward a minority group—that acknowledges the existence of a problem but avoids confronting the problem by offering partial or false solutions or by using arguments that do not address the situation as in "Yes, but you should have seen how bad it was last year."

Black/white syndrome A pattern in the English language consisting of negative meanings for phrases including the word *black* and positive meanings for phrases including the word *white*

Denial rationalization A response to a social problem—such as injustice toward a minority group—that does not acknowledge the existence of a problem but insists instead that no injustice has occurred as in "That's not discrimination, men have always been the boss; it's just the way things are meant to be."

Elitism The belief that the best people ascend to a place of superiority in society and represent a natural aristocracy, whereas those who are not successful are viewed as lacking the necessary qualities to be successful within society

Genocide The deliberate and systematic extermination of a particular nationality, or racial, ethnic, or minority group

Institutionalized discrimination theory Institutional policies and practices that have differential and negative effects on subordinate groups in a society

Interest theory People engaging or acquiescing in discriminatory actions based on a desire to protect their power or privilege

Internal colonialism theory Explains contemporary discrimination as the maintenance of inequities resulting from historic exploitation of subordinate groups by the dominant group

Prejudice A negative attitude toward a group and anyone perceived to be a member of that group; a predisposition to negative behavior toward members of a group

Racial profiling People in authority taking actions against members of racial or ethnic groups based on assumptions that these groups are more likely to engage in criminal activity

Scapegoat An individual or a group of people blamed for another person's problems or difficulties; identifying a scapegoat is often employed to justify one's taking a negative action against that individual or group

Stereotype threat The apprehension experienced by members of a minority group that they might behave in a manner that confirms an existing cultural stereotype

Victim-blaming rationalization A response to a social problem—such as injustice toward a minority group—that identifies the problem as a deficiency in the minority group and not a societal problem, as in "If poor people want to escape poverty they just have to be willing to work harder."

White flight The migration of white families from an urban to a suburban location because of court rulings to desegregate urban schools

Zero sum An orientation toward power and resources based on assumptions of scarcity, as when struggling to achieve goals, one person gains at the expense of another. The belief that sharing power means a reduction of power

DISCUSSION EXERCISES

Clarification Exercise—Rationalizations: Victim-Blame, Denial, and Avoidance

Directions: This exercise provides everyday statements we might hear; each one is a specific kind of rationalization. Based on the text and on your group discussion, identify the statements below according to one of the three types of rationalizations. First, select which passages would most likely represent an avoidance of a problem. Then select those in which the speaker employs a denial rationalization—that the problem either does not exist or that the speaker is suggesting "That's just the way things are." Finally, locate victim-blame statements in which a specific person or group is being charged with its own downfall or problem.

Rationalizations for Our Prejudices

Directions: Decide whether the following statements represent a denial of the problem (D), a victim-blame that it is the speaker's problem (D/VB), or an avoidance of the problem (A).

_____ 1. Women and minorities are getting everything their way. They are taking away our jobs and pretty soon they are going to take over everything.

_____ 2. What we have here, basically, is a failure to communicate. We must develop better programs in interpersonal communications to address this issue.

_____ 3. This is the way these people want to live. You can't change poor people; they can't help the way they are.

_____ 4. We must move with deliberation on these issues. Real change takes time. We have to educate people.

_____ 5. All those women on welfare have it made. All they do is stay home and make babies while the rest of us have to work and pay taxes to support them.

_____ 6. I can't figure out what to call all these people. Why can't we all just be human instead of black, Chicano, Latino, Native American, or Asian American?

_____ 7. Indians are their own worst enemy. They should stop fighting among themselves and get together on whatever it is they really want.

_____ 8. If blacks want to make it in our society, they are going to have to get rid of those dreadlocks and other weird hairstyles, the baggy clothes, funny handshakes, and they better start speaking better English.

_____ 9. Yes, but in the old days, race and sex discrimination were much worse. And even today, women and minorities are much better off in this country than anywhere else in the world.

_____ 10. Women are just too sensitive about sexism. They need to look at these things less emotionally and much more rationally.

_____ 11. We need more programs in African American studies, Latino studies, Native American studies, and Asian American studies to learn about all the contributions these groups have made to our society.

_____ 12. Feminists are pushing too hard for the changes that they demand. They are hurting themselves more than they are helping.

_____ 13. I understand that some people face more difficulties than others, but this is a free country and I believe that anybody who is willing to work hard enough can be successful.

Follow-Up: Select any two from each of the three categories—D, VB, and A—and rewrite them to be the fourth kind of statement—those without rationalization. Explain why you chose to rewrite them as you did.

Exercise—The Liver Transplant Problem

Background: Today, the only medical procedure available to save the lives of persons suffering from diseases of the liver is an organ transplant. Unfortunately, there are not enough livers to take care of all cases now, and there will not be enough in the near future to save the lives of all those in need.

Your Role: The decision about which people can be saved must be made on criteria other than medical criteria. Your hospital has decided that the best way to select persons for a transplant is by setting up a volunteer citizens panel to make the decisions. You are on the panel and receive a Profile Sheet of applicants for transplants (see the table). Doctors have screened all patients, and all have equal prognosis for medical success.

Problem: There is a liver available for one person on the list. All those not served will die. The availability of other livers cannot be anticipated, although if other livers become available, additional persons on the list could receive transplants.

Directions: Your panel must make a unanimous decision regarding the person to be the liver recipient. A lottery violates institutional ethics and is not an acceptable strategy. As you deliberate, discuss your values and consider those of others related to the process being utilized and the criteria that you propose:

1. The criteria you develop for choosing the recipient.
2. Why you believe that the person you chose best fits your criteria.
3. How your panel arrives at a single selection of a recipient.

Please see the next page for more detailed notes about the recipients.

Liver Transplant Recipient Profile Sheet

Code	Age	Race	Sex	Marital Status	Religious Affiliation	Children	Occupation
A	24	Black	M	Married	Muslim	None	Postal worker
B	45	White	M	Married	Atheist	2	Executive
C	39	Asian American	F	Divorced	Buddhist	None	Medical Doctor
D	40	White	F	Married	Jew	3	Housewife
E	23	Black	M	Unmarried	Episcopal	None	PhD student
F	40	White	F	Unmarried	Pentecostal	9	Welfare Mother
G	28	Native American	M	Unmarried	Native	3	Seasonal Worker
H	30	Latina	F	Married	Catholic	7	Housewife
I	19	White	M	Unmarried	Baptist	None	Special Student

Notes about Recipients:
  A. Devotes time to volunteer work for black organizations
  B. Possible candidate for U.S. Senate
  C. College physician and feminist speaker
  D. Active in local synagogue and charitable activities
  E. Middle states chair of a gay rights task force
  F. Advocate and organizer of welfare mothers
  G. State chair, Indian Treaty Rights Organization
  H. Blind and physically disabled
  I. Cognitively disabled

REFERENCES

Abdo, G. (2006). *Mecca and Main Street: Muslim life in America after 9/11.* Oxford, England: Oxford University Press.

Allport, G. (1979). *The nature of prejudice.* Reading, MA: Addison-Wesley.

Ansari, Z.I. (2004). Islam among African Americans: An overview. In Z.H. Buhhari, S.S. Nyang, M. Ahmad, & J.C. Esposito (Eds.), *Muslims' place in the American public square* (pp. 222–267). Walnut Creek, CA: Altamira Press.

Archibold, R.C. (2010, April 23). Arizona enacts stringent law on immigration. *The New York Times* (www.nytimes.com/2010/04/us/politics/24immig .html)

Ariely, D. (2008). *Predictably irrational: The hidden forces that shape our decisions.* New York, NY: Harper-Collins.

Arliss, L.P. (1991). *Gender communication.* Englewood Cliffs, NJ: Prentice Hall.

Aronson, E. (2008). *The social animal* (10th ed.). New York, NY: Worth Publishers.

Astor, C. (1997, August). Gallup poll: Progress in black/white relations, but race is still an issue. USIA electronic journal, *U.S. Society & Values, 2*(3), 19–212.

Baker, R. (1981). "Pricks" and "chicks": A plea for persons. In M. Vetterling-Braggin (Ed.), *Sexist language: A modern philosophical analysis* (pp. 161–182). Lanham, MD: Littlefield, Adams.

Barrett, P.M. (2007). *American Islam: The struggle for the soul of a religion.* New York, NY: Farrar, Straus and Giroux.

Bell, D. (2002). *Ethical ambition: Living a life of meaning and worth.* New York, NY: Bloomsbury.

Bredin, J. (2008*). The affair: The case of Alfred Dreyfus.* Bethesda, MD: Gryphon Editions.

Carroll, J. (2001). *Constantine's sword: The church and the Jews, a history.* Boston, MA: Houghton Mifflin.

Coleman, L.M. (2007). Stigma. In L. Davis (Ed.), *The disability studies reader* (2nd ed., pp. 216–233). New York, NY: Routledge.

Daft, R.L. (2003). Managing diverse employees. *Management* (6th ed., pp. 436–468). Versailles, KY: Thompson Southwestern.

Farley, J. (2005). *Majority-minority relations* (5th ed.). Upper Saddle River, NJ: Prentice Hall.

Feagin, J., & Feagin, C. (1986). *Discrimination American style* (2nd ed.). Malabar, FL: Krieger.

Feagin, J., & Feagin, C.B. (2008). Glossary. *Racial and ethnic relations* (8th ed.). Upper Saddle River, NJ: Prentice Hall.

Gioseffi, D. (Ed.). (1993). *On prejudice: A global perspective.* New York, NY: Anchor.

Giroux, H. (1998). *Channel surfing: Racism, the media, and the destruction of today's youth.* New York, NY: St. Martin's.

Goldhagen, D.J. (2002). *Hitler's willing executioners: Ordinary Germans and the Holocaust* (2nd ed.) New York, NY: Knopf.

Hauser, M.D. (2006). *Moral minds: The nature of right and wrong.* New York, NY: Ecco.

Howard, G.R. (2006). *We can't teach what we don't know: White teachers, multiracial schools* (2nd ed.) New York, NY: Teachers College Press.

Jones, J. (1997). *Prejudice and racism* (2nd ed.). New York, NY: McGraw Hill.

Khan, M.A.M. (2004). Living on borderlines: Islam beyond the clash and dialogue of civilization. In Z.H. Buhhari, S.S. Nyang, M. Ahmad, & J.C. Esposito (Eds.), *Muslims' place in the American public square* (pp. 84–113). Walnut Creek, CA: Altamira Press.

Koppelman, K. (1994). *Race and gender equity in urban America: The efforts of six cities to define the issues and provide solutions.* Paper presented at the national conference of the Renaissance Group in San Antonio on October 15, 1994.

Levin, J., & Levin, W. (1982). *The functions of discrimination and prejudice* (2nd ed., p. 202). New York, NY: Harper & Row.

Martinez, R., & Dukes, R.L. (1991, March). Ethnic and gender differences in self-esteem. *Youth & Society, 22*(3), 318–339.

Massey, D.S. (2001, January). Residential segregation and neighborhood conditions in U.S. metropolitan areas. In N. Smelser, W. Wilson, & F. Mitchell (Eds.), *America becoming: Racial trends and their consequences.* (ERIC Document Reproduction Service No. ED449286)

McCloud, A.B. (2004). Conceptual discourse: Living as a Muslim in a pluralistic society. In Z.H. Buhhari, S.S. Nyang, M. Ahmad, & J.C. Esposito (Eds.), *Muslims' place in the American public square* (pp. 73–83). Walnut Creek, CA: Altamira Press.

McCloud, A.B. (2006). *Transnational Muslims in American society.* Gainesville, FL: University of Florida Press.

Miller, C., & Swift, K. (2000). *Words and women.* San Jose, CA: iUniverse.

Moore, R.B. (2006). Racism in the English language. In K. Rosenblum & T. Travis (Eds.), *The meaning of difference: American constructions of race, sex and gender, social class, and sexual orientation* (4th ed., pp. 451–459). Boston, MA: McGraw-Hill.

Newberg, A., & Waldman, M.R. (2006). *Why we believe what we believe: Uncovering our biological needs for meaning, spirituality, and truth*. New York, NY: Free Press.

Niebuhr, G. (2008). *Beyond tolerance: Searching for interfaith understanding in America*. New York, NY: Viking.

Ryan, W. (1976). *Blaming the victim* (2nd ed.). New York, NY: Vintage Books.

Sadker, D., & Sadker, M. (1994). *Failing at fairness: How America's schools cheat girls*. New York, NY: Charles Scribner.

Sartre, J.P. (1995). *Anti-Semite and Jew*. New York, NY: Schocken.

Schaefer, R.T. (2008). *Racial and ethnic groups* (11th ed.). Upper Saddle River, NJ: Pearson.

Selden, S. (2006). *Inheriting shame: The story of eugenics and racism in America*. New York, NY: Teachers College Press.

Simpson, G.E., & Yinger, J.M. (1985). *Racial and cultural minorities: An analysis of prejudice and discrimination* (5th ed.). New York, NY: Plenum.

Skuttnab-Kangas, T. (2000). *Linguistic genocide in education—or worldwide diversity and human rights?* Mahwah, NJ: Erlbaum.

Stalcup, M., & Craze, J. (2011, March/April). How we train our cops to fear Islam. *Washington Monthly, 43*(3/4), 20–28.

Steinback, R. (2011, Summer). The jihad against Islam. *Intelligence Report, 142,* 15–20.

Stephan, W. (1999). *Reducing prejudice and stereotyping in schools*. New York, NY: Teachers College Press.

Thurow, L. (2001). *The zero-sum society*. New York, NY: Penguin.

Tolev, M. (2010, May 12). Poll: Americans back Arizona's illegal immigrants law. *McClatchy Newspapers* (www.mcclatchydc.com/94050/most-Americans-approve-of-Arizonas.html).

U.S. Bureau of the Census. (2008). Statistical abstract of the United States. Retrieved October 15, 2008, from http://www.census.gov/compendia/statab.

U.S. Bureau of Labor Statistics. (2001). Chapter 1: Counting minorities: A brief history and a look at the future. *Report on the American workforce*. Washington, DC: U.S. Department of Labor. Retrieved December 20, 2008, from http://www.bls.gov/opub.

U.S. Bureau of Labor Statistics. (2012). Labor force statistics from the current population survey. Retrieved on April 2, 2012, from www.bls.gov/cps/cpsaat37.htm.

Vega, F. (1978). *The effect of human and intergroup relations education on the race/sex attitudes of education majors*. Unpublished doctoral dissertation, University of Minnesota, Minneapolis.

Wessler, S.L. (2001). Sticks and stones. *Educational Leadership, 58*(4), 28–33.

Chapter 3

Communication, Conflict, and Conflict Resolution

"If I were to summarize the single most important principle I have learned in the field of interpersonal relations it would be this: Seek first to understand, then to be understood."

Stephen Covey (1932–)

Communication seems simple. One person talks, and other people listen to understand what the speaker is saying; when the first person stops talking, another person responds, perhaps to agree or disagree with the first speaker. Nothing seems complicated here, so why are there misunderstandings that so often lead to conflicts among individuals, groups, organizations, and nations? One answer was suggested in the 1960s film *Cool Hand Luke*, in which Paul Newman as Luke, an inmate, keeps breaking the warden's rules. As he prepares to punish Luke once again, the warden says, "What we have here is a failure to communicate." Actually it's not that Luke doesn't understand the rules; the problem is he doesn't respect the rules, so he violates them. By referring to a failure in communication, the warden means that Luke has not demonstrated his understanding that he must conform to the rules.

Communication and Conflict

In communication, more is going on than speaking, listening, and comprehending one another's words. Understanding communication requires some knowledge of the purpose served by that communication and what attitudes support it. Spitzberg (2008) reported that we interact with other people 70% of the time we are awake. Communicating effectively is an asset in one's personal and professional life, especially when conflicts occur.

And conflicts are likely to be resolved only if those people involved communicate effectively.

What is an appropriate definition of communication?

Most people assume that the term *communicate* refers to interpersonal communication, but mass media represent another form of communication. Kougl (1997) offers a practical definition of **interpersonal communication**: "A dynamic process of interaction between people in which they assign meaning to each other's verbal and nonverbal behavior" (p. 7). Two features of this definition provide clues about how communication can lead to conflict: *assigning meaning* and *nonverbal behavior*.

How does assigning meaning lead to conflict?

We not only listen to words; we also make assumptions about what the other person means. If our assumptions are accurate, there is no problem, but if they are not, the result is likely to be a misinterpretation of the message.

When interaction occurs between members of different groups, individuals may interpret the meaning of a statement in terms of the perceived influence of stereotypes or prejudices. An example of assigning meanings to statements that result in conflict occurred during a college ethnic studies class discussion of offensive words, phrases, and images based on ethnic and racial differences. An Asian American college student described his visit to a local middle school. As soon as he entered the building, he saw a few white male students put their fingers next to their eyes and pull their skin to create a "slant- eyed" look, and they began talking with a stereotypical Asian accent. The Asian American college student was appalled that these middle school students would taunt a visitor to their school with such blatant stereotypes, but another college student said this did not necessarily reflect their prejudice, just their immaturity. He argued that students at that age, especially boys, tend to be very insecure and they make fun of everyone and everything to get attention.

An American Indian student disagreed, saying that when he was in middle school and high school he heard a lot of students talking in terms of stereotypes. That was one of the reasons he was opposed to using Indians as mascots for sports teams because such images reinforced stereotypes for American Indians. A white woman in the class who was a nontraditional student said she didn't think there was anything wrong with Indian mascots because they had an Indian mascot at her high school and she felt that it was used to honor Indian people. That led to the following dialogue among the white female (WF), American Indian (AI), and Asian American (AA) students:

AI: How am I supposed to be honored by an image like the Cleveland Indians mascot? These things are caricatures, cartoon figures! Even images that try to be respectable are just "noble savage" stereotypes that do not realistically depict real Indian people today . . . or at any time actually.

WF: Well, I suppose if you look at something long enough you can always find something to be offended about.

AA: Hold on, wait a minute! Are you saying that the problem is just in his head? That some people just make up stuff to be offended about but there's really nothing offensive there, nothing going on?

WF: No, no, I'm not saying that. I just meant that . . . like with the Indian mascots . . . I don't think anyone intends to offend anyone, but some people are offended.

AA: But you seem to be saying that the problem isn't real; that it's only a problem because of the way some Indian people look at this issue.

AI: Yeah, it sounds like you don't think Indian mascots are stereotypes, and if we would just stop saying they were, then there'd be no problem.

AA: Isn't that just another example of what we've talked about before? . . . You know, blaming the victim?

WF: But that's not what I'm saying!

AA: Maybe not, but that's what it sounds like, and if we keep talking like that, then no one will ever confront the stereotypes that kids have learned about Asians or Indians or Blacks or any other group. It's not about immaturity or good intentions. It's about what people are doing, you know, it's about certain behaviors that should be confronted, especially in schools, and how to go about doing that.

The white woman continued to defend her position, but she was frustrated that she could not seem to get the other students to understand what she was saying—yet they felt they understood her meaning all too well. They perceived that she was

> The meanings of words are not in the words; they are in us.
>
> S. I. Hayakawa (1906–1992)

denying the problem of stereotypes affecting white people's perceptions of people of color; they also believed that she blamed people of color for being offended about things that were never meant to be offensive. The white woman wanted to emphasize intent, but the other two students were focused on the consequences for people of color no matter what was intended. From this example, it is easy to see how conflicts can arise from the meanings assigned to verbal statements. Regardless of what a speaker intended to say, people will make assumptions and interpretations about the meaning of that person's statements. When the meaning assigned to a speaker's words becomes significantly different from what was intended, a conflict is likely to occur. Similarly, nonverbal communication can also lead to conflict based on an interpretation of the meaning of a nonverbal message.

How does nonverbal communication lead to conflict?

Hecht and DeVito (2008) define **nonverbal communication** as "all the messages other than words that people exchange" (p. 4). Estimates of how much meaning is taken from interpretations of nonverbal communication have been as high as 93%, although Burgoon (2002) estimated that 60% to 65% is more realistic. Children don't tend to find as much meaning from nonverbal behavior as do adults; still, parents and teachers must be conscious of their nonverbal cues, especially when they express disapproval or take disciplinary action. For a child to understand what adults mean, messages must not be contradicted or confused by nonverbal messages (Kougl, 1997).

Disciplinary action may be required in response to a child's unacceptable behavior—perhaps the child is teasing or taunting other children. The adult says, "Teasing is bad. It hurts people's feelings. It may make them angry and it certainly makes me angry. You must stop doing this or no one will like you and no one will want to play with you." The message is clear and provides good reasons, including self-interest, for the child to change his or her behavior. However, if this message is accompanied by angry looks, a loud voice, and gestures such as the adult pointing or jabbing a finger at the child, the good advice may get lost. The message the child gets is not that the behavior is bad but that "I'm bad" or "She hates me." (See Figure 3.1.)

FIGURE 3.1

According to Ekman (2003), expressions of contempt and disgust are often used to indicate hatred of another. Prior studies have indicated that expressions of hatred and anger are often confused. In these two photographs from Ekman's research, one expression represents contempt and the other is anger. Try to identify the emotion represented in each facial expression. (For the answer see the Ekman annotation in the References at the end of the chapter.)

Source: Used by permission of Paul Ekman.

Children receiving this message are not likely to change their behavior, but to persist in it, either as a way of rebelling against the adult who has made this negative comment about them or as a self-fulfilling prophecy: "She says I'm bad so I might as well be bad." Being told that certain behavior is unacceptable implicitly offers a child the power to choose. Children may not think they can change who they are, but they know they can change their behavior. If they hear an adult make a negative judgment about who they are, they can do nothing about that. Conflicts arising from such misinterpretations of nonverbal messages also occur among adults.

The need to assign meaning and the influence of nonverbal messages address two misconceptions about communication: (1) that communication simply means telling people something and (2) that communication is a verbal process to transmit messages using only words. Teachers who are committed to being good communicators understand the need to seek constant feedback from students to ensure that the knowledge they impart is being understood. Postman and Weingartner (1987) criticized educators for taking an "inoculation approach" in which teachers communicate information to students as if inoculating them against ignorance. When grades on tests reveal that students didn't retain much information, often the teacher's reaction is similar to that of a physician who doesn't understand why a vaccine had no effect when she knows she injected it. In discussing classroom communication, Kougl (1997) emphasized that teaching is not just talking; it involves more than words, as is true of all communication.

> Communication is something so simple and so difficult that we can never put it into simple words.
>
> T. S. Matthews (1901–1991)

What are other misconceptions about communication?

Of the many misconceptions about communication identified by Stone, Singletary, and Richmond (1999), the following five examples are especially important to recognize:

Communication is a natural human ability.
Communication is a good thing and should be encouraged.
Communication will solve all our problems.
Communications can break down.
Communication competence is equal to communication effectiveness. (pp. 56–61)

Communication is a natural human ability. In a longitudinal study of three communities in the Piedmont Plateau region of the Carolinas, Heath (2006) described the way children learned communication skills and how skills varied depending on the way the children had been taught. Heath found that low-income white parents taught language to children by reading storybooks with a moral for each tale. Parental communication style was didactic and authoritarian; their children memorized Bible verses, learned strict rules for right and wrong, and were severely punished for lying. When the children went to school, they did well initially because the learning activities and communication styles of teachers were similar to what they had experienced at home. The children obeyed teachers, looked for a single meaning— the moral—of a story, and memorized material as required.

As the children from low-income white families progressed through elementary school, however, they encountered activities requiring critical thinking and creativity. They had trouble making up stories because it seemed like lying. They struggled to make sense of stories with multiple meanings and to identify and analyze different perspectives for strengths and weaknesses. Their life experiences had not prepared them for reading, thinking, and communicating at any level of complexity. As they approached middle school their grades declined, as did their confidence. The majority never achieved academic competence in school, and some dropped out before finishing high school.

Heath described the language learning of black children from low-income homes as a more creative process where children listened to adults tell stories that often had no particular moral point; these stories related what had happened at work or in the neighborhood or gossip about "crooked politicians . . . or wayward choir leaders" (p. 168). Adults often told stories with a basis in fact, but with embellishment. When the stories got too far removed from reality, the teller was accused of "talkin' junk." In addition to hearing stories, boys developed language skills to respond to teasing based on "feigned hostility, disrespect and aggressive behavior" while girls became proficient in language by making up songs when skipping rope (p. 85). Both boys and girls practiced telling stories and, like adults, learned to embellish their stories with fictional details.

Black children from low-income homes came to school with highly creative communication skills, but they did not do well in the early elementary classes because they were not as adept at memorization or sticking to the facts. They saw many meanings to a story other than the simple moral the teacher wanted. As the students struggled with their assignments and growing feelings of inadequacy, they lost confidence in themselves as learners. When they finally encountered the more creative and complex learning activities later in elementary school, they were not successful because they had given up on the possibility of success.

Heath noted that the children who succeeded in school at all levels were from middle-class homes, black as well as white, where their parents had read to them and had asked for didactic meanings of stories but also encouraged engagement in creative and analytical activity. A parent might read a story and then ask, "Would you have liked to go fishing with Little Bear? What do you think you would have caught?" (p. 250). Middle-class children came to school with a range of communication and language skills: They were successful at memorization and didactic activities during early elementary years; they were also able to adjust to activities emphasizing creativity or critical thinking in later years. Heath's research demonstrated that learning to communicate is not a natural human ability but rather is a product of the cultural and social context one experiences as a child.

Communication is a good thing and should be encouraged.   Communication is a tool, and tools can be employed for good or bad purposes. Hitler used oratorical skills to arouse feelings of Aryan superiority and to deepen the anti-Semitic prejudices of Germans into a hatred that condoned

> Think like an active person; act like a thoughtful person.
>
> Henri Bergson (1859–1941)

persecution and execution. Martin Luther King, Jr., employed his oratorical skills to urge non-violent resistance to oppression, warning his followers not to hate oppressors but to focus on the cause of justice. With any communication it is essential to ascertain the speaker's purpose and then determine whether that purpose is a good one. As Skuttnab-Kangas (2000) says, language is "a tool for domination (or) a tool for change and self-determination" (p. 134).

It is also important to recognize when additional communication is not necessary—when the time has come to take action. Martin Luther King, Jr., deplored the "paralysis of analysis" as when people continue to talk about problems without ever doing anything. Of course it is essential to be thoughtful before acting, taking time to consider alternatives and consequences before deciding on a course of action, but there comes a time when one must stop analyzing every possible outcome and take action. After taking action, it is important to consider the consequences to determine whether to continue or choose another tactic. It is what Freire (2004) meant by the term **praxis**—taking action to address injustice and then reflecting on the effectiveness of the actions taken as the person or group continues their activities.

Communication will solve all our problems. Communication has the potential to solve problems, but it also has the potential to create them. In a speech to college students, poet Maya Angelou noted that whenever anyone asks, "Can I be brutally honest?" she always says "No" because she does not want to encourage anyone to do anything brutally. Whether information is accurate or inaccurate, truthful or distorted, if communication is delivered brutally it will be hurtful, and hurting people will create problems rather than solve them. We can communicate honestly without being brutal; we can show respect and sensitivity to the feelings of any person or group we encounter.

Ironically, some communication addresses problems with no intent of solving them. Berne (2004) described such interaction as playing "games." In the "Ain't It Awful" game, two people talk about a problem, not to solve it but to affirm each other's perceptions, sometimes at the expense of another. Imagine two teachers discussing a student. One describes Danny's misbehavior; the other responds with a similar story about something Danny did in her class, and they continue to exchange stories. The teachers are not trying to understand the boy's behavior to help him; instead, each is telling the other, "You and I are all right. Danny is the problem." When their conversation ends, both teachers walk away believing they are not to blame, nor are they obligated to do anything to help Danny. Their communication has not solved Danny's problem, but it has made them feel better.

Another game Berne has described is "Yes, but . . .," where one person comes to another asking for advice but actually wanting something else. For example, Luis is a teenager who is having problems with his parents. He goes to his best friend for advice. His friend suggests several strategies, and each time Luis says either (a) he tried that (or something similar) and it didn't work, or (b) he thought about doing that but explains why the suggestion wouldn't work. After the friend has exhausted all possible strategies he can think of, he may say something like, "Well I don't know what else to tell you. I don't know what else you can do." At this point, Luis walks away saying, "That's okay." The friend may be frustrated that he could not help solve the problem, but for Luis, the point of the conversation was to hear that he had done everything he could and there was nothing more for him to do. Now he can say the problem is not his responsibility; it is up to his parents. Both "Ain't It Awful" and "Yes, but . . ." involve a "solution" only in the sense that someone gets what he or she wants from the interaction, but the communication is not intended to solve the problem.

Communications can break down. Most of us have used this particular misconception about communication to justify ongoing conflicts. Rebellious teenagers say their parents don't understand them; husbands and wives complain that their partners don't appreciate them; workers may go on strike claiming that management isn't bargaining in

> Information voids will be filled by rumors and speculation unless they are preempted by open, credible, and trustworthy communication.
>
> Jean Keffler (Contemporary)

good faith. In such cases, we may rationalize that our conflict cannot be resolved because communication has broken down. When machines break, they stop; however, communication cannot break down because it never stops, even if people stop talking to each other. Their communication could be hearsay or it could be nonverbal; it could consist of interpretations by one person about perceived decisions and actions of another.

Communication occurs because one person wants or needs to know what the other is thinking about or doing; a person may make decisions to do (or not to do) something based on assumptions about someone else. One person may decide not to attend a Christmas party so that a co-worker will know he is still angry with her, or he may decide to attend the party but not speak to or make eye contact with her. In an extreme example, Dylan Klebold and Eric Harris had stopped responding to the taunts of some classmates and endured the verbal abuse at Columbine High School in silence, but when they went home, they left written and videotaped records of their repressed rage and their plans for revenge (Brown & Merritt, 2006). Communication can be ineffective or effective, but it does not stop. If verbal exchange ceases, communication in some other form—whether words or actions—will replace it.

Communication competence is equal to communication effectiveness. This is a misconception few college students should believe because almost every college student is familiar with professors who are knowledgeable about their subject matter but ineffective at communicating that knowledge. We are competent to communicate on a topic if we have sufficient knowledge of it; however, possessing knowledge does not mean that we can communicate it in a way that is easily comprehended.

A major function of teacher education programs consists of preparing people to be effective

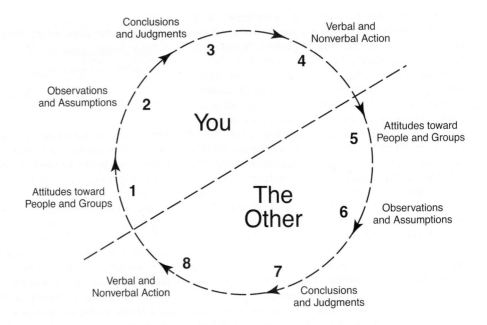

Figure 3.2 The Circular Model of Communication

at organizing and communicating information. Whether they are lecturing or using alternative means of delivering information, teachers must understand what studies have concluded about effective ways of helping people learn. To assess how effectively they deliver information, teachers must also evaluate how well students learn. Tests and other forms of assessment may measure student learning; more importantly, however, they reveal how effectively the teacher communicated.

Except for those in teacher education, most college professors learn how to communicate from mentors or self-study. Many professors have acquired the skills to become good teachers, yet the misconception that communication competence equals communication effectiveness is often the basis for student complaints that they aren't learning because a professor is incompetent. Professors may have **communication competence** because they have the necessary knowledge and may even have published articles and books on their specialty, yet they may not display **communication effectiveness** because they lack the appropriate skills to communicate effectively in a classroom.

How does effective communication occur?

Numerous excellent models have been developed that examine the communication process and analyze communication to ascertain why misunderstandings occur (Narula, 2006; Stone et al., 1999). The following model describes four factors involved in interpersonal communication. Each instance of a person interacting with another is influenced by these four cumulative factors (see Figure 3.2).

A Circular Model of Communication

1. Attitudes toward people or groups
2. Observations and assumptions
3. Conclusions and judgments
4. Verbal and nonverbal action

First, the communication process is grounded in an individual's *attitudes toward people or groups*. All people develop a general attitude about their interactions with others. Some of us are trusting, others are suspicious; some are willing to share ideas, others are reserved; some are motivated by dominance and control, others function with an egalitarian view. Our attitudes may change based on our relationship with the individuals involved in our interactions. Our interactions with family are different than they are with strangers. We communicate differently within same-gender groups than in mixed groups or with people of the opposite gender. Our behavior is different with others of our own race or ethnic group as opposed to being in mixed groups or with individuals from another race or ethnic group. Having prejudices or stereotypes about a particular minority group will certainly influence our interactions with a member of that group.

Second, our *observations and assumptions* about another person shape the communication between us before anything is said. Our initial reaction may be friendly and accepting, aloof and suspicious, or even hostile and rejecting, depending on the appearance of the other person and sometimes on which behaviors we choose to observe—a phenomenon known as **selective perception**. If an individual believes a stereotype about someone from a certain group, that stereotype is likely to be reinforced by selective perceptions.

How do our observations influence our assumptions? What if a person were introduced to a long-haired young white male who was dressed in torn overalls and wore a red bandana around his head? Based on observation, one might assume that the young man has rejected our materialistic society by imitating college students from the 1960s who questioned authority figures and rebelled against middle-class values, conformity, and the Vietnam War. These observations and assumptions are now taken to the next level.

The third step, *conclusions and judgments*, refers to the values and beliefs we employ to draw conclusions or to judge others. In the example of the young man with long hair, various people observing him and making reasonable assumptions could come to different conclusions. One person may have been in college in the 1960s and remember it as an exciting time that had a profound influence on his life. His initial reaction may be a positive conclusion: "That young man reminds me of myself when I was his age." Conversely, someone who was taught to respect authority and appreciate the material comforts of our society and whose goal is to acquire those material comforts may make a negative judgment, perhaps generating additional assumptions about the young man

smoking marijuana or using other illegal drugs. Prejudice and negative stereotypes lead to negative assumptions, which result in a negative judgment of another person.

The fourth and final step in the process is *verbal and nonverbal action*. When individuals meet, one person will say or do something to initiate interaction. Doing something might be as simple as smiling or frowning, making eye contact with the other or looking away. Nonverbal behavior employing such body language can initiate communication as much as words, often just as powerfully.

What does this communication model suggest about conflict resolution?

If conflict occurs during interaction, how can we resolve it? Our most common response is to focus on the action taken, on the words or behavior that initiated the conflict. For example, elementary teachers often witness conflict during recess in which one child insults or hurts another. Some teachers respond by making the perpetrator apologize: The problem was the child's action, so the teacher forces the child to take another action to offset the first. This response focuses on the symptoms of the conflict and not the cause, so it is not likely to result in a resolution. Because the child may not feel genuinely sorry, what is learned from such an apology is a lesson in hypocrisy—being forced to say something that is not true.

Effective conflict resolution rejects superficial attention to actions and analyzes other factors to identify probable causes of the conflict. As Schramm (1973) stated, "The full significance of acts of communication is seldom on the surface" (p. 23). For this reason, most strategies for resolving conflicts are intended to get past surface meanings: Expressing "I" messages (Gordon, 2000); engaging in transactional analysis (Harris, 2004); using empathy to promote understanding (Rogers, 1995); and negotiating "Win/Win" strategies (Jandt, 1985). This communication model (Figure 3.2) requires individuals to assess each other's attitudes, to question their own assumptions, to refrain from making judgments, and to be aware of the messages in their nonverbal communication. Still, any approach may be ineffective if the people involved do not accept the value of the process or techniques that are employed.

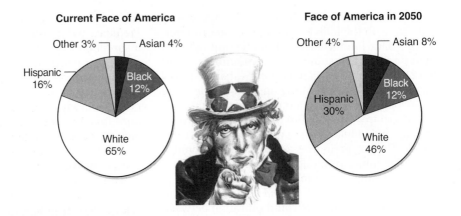

Current Face of America

Other 3% — ┐   ┌ — Asian 4%

Hispanic 16%

Black 12%

White 65%

Face of America in 2050

Other 4% — ┐   ┌ — Asian 8%

Black 12%

Hispanic 30%

White 46%

FIGURE 3.3 United States: Present and Future

As ethnic diversity increases in the United States, being aware of cultural differences will become increasingly important.

Source: Uncle Sam image, courtesy Library of Congress. Data from U.S. Census.

How can attitudes toward people or groups create conflict?

When people involved in interpersonal communication identify themselves—or are identified by others—as part of a specific group (such as by race or ethnicity), individual attitudes can be significantly influenced. In a multicultural society such as the United States, it is probable that people, especially in urban areas, will interact with others who are different by race, ethnicity, nationality, or religion (see Figure 3.3). How much the cultures of different nationalities or people of different racial or ethnic groups affect communication will depend on the level of cultural awareness that the person has.

What are the levels of cultural awareness?

Kimmel (2006) identified levels of cultural awareness:

Cultural chauvinism   Belief that one's culture is the best, superior to all other cultures; feeling no need to learn about other cultures.

Tolerance   Awareness of cultural differences, recognition that differences stem from the country of origin for that person (or his or her ancestors); no judgment of cultural differences as inferior, simply as different ways of thinking or behaving.

Minimalization   Minimizing cultural differences by emphasizing a universality of human needs and behaviors as a means of creating a stronger sense of relationship or connectedness with culturally different people.

Understanding   Recognizing that reality is shaped by culture and that each person's reality is different from that of a person from a different culture; having no judgment of different cultural realities; accepting and respecting cultural differences (cultural relativism).

Communication conflicts occur readily between people at the cultural chauvinism level, and they also may occur at the tolerance and minimalization levels. Only when people understand cultural differences and practice cultural relativism is it likely that conflicts between people from different cultures can be avoided or resolved.

Culture, Communication Style, and Conflict

Differences in cultural norms can cause misunderstanding and conflict. In the United States, business executives usually engage in minimal personal conversation before discussing a proposal at a group

> The test of a first rate intelligence is the ability to hold two opposed ideas in the mind at the same time, and still retain the ability to function.
>
> F. Scott Fitzgerald (1896–1940)

meeting. In some other cultures, communication is commonly expected to focus first on personal matters—questions about the person's health, family, or interests—before business is discussed. Ismail (2001) stressed how the global marketplace requires business executives to be knowledgeable about and employ appropriate communication strategies concerning use of direct speech, acceptable levels of informality, attitudes about time, and expressions of emotion in order to negotiate successfully with people from other cultures.

What are some communication style differences that are based on culture?

In the United States, it has become acceptable to take a direct approach to conflict resolution, with each party openly expressing their concerns. In other cultures, people are expected to show sensitivity to the feelings of others by taking an indirect approach to resolving conflicts. In some cultures, people tend to speak in a linear progression, going from one idea to the next, but in other cultures, people digress, often telling stories or anecdotes to illustrate their point. Cultures also reflect differences in nonverbal behavior. In Arab cultures, people tend to stand much closer in conversation than do Americans. In the United States, men greet one another with a firm handshake; in France, anything other than a quick handshake is considered rude; in Ecuador, greeting a person without offering one's hand is a sign of special respect. In the United States, the forefinger to thumb gesture means "okay"; in France, it signifies that something is worthless; and in Brazil, the gesture is considered obscene (Jandt, 2003).

Differences in communication styles have also been identified in subcultures in the United States. Kochman (1981) described how black and white children learn to express aggression. For most middle-class white people, aggressive language is viewed as a harbinger of aggressive behavior. "Fighting words"

are words that may provoke a physical confrontation (Meltzoff, 2007). Most white children learn to repress aggressive feelings and maintain a calm demeanor even though they may be furious. If they begin using language aggressively, it is likely that a fight is imminent. For some black males, however, words can be used aggressively without a conflict. Foster (1986) described how urban black male children may taunt one another in a playground game known by different names including "sounding" or "playing the dozens." Situations may become intense and emotional; however, a fight will only occur if a child gives an obvious signal such as making a fist to indicate that he is angry.

The contrast between the reactions of black and white people to aggressive language can lead to misunderstanding. Imagine two black children still playing the insult game as they come back to their classroom after recess. The teacher tries to intervene, but the boys continue to insult each other. A black teacher may recognize the childhood game and firmly tell them to stop, but a white teacher may perceive the boys as engaged in a hostile quarrel and order them to the principal's office. If the principal asks them why they were sent, they are likely to say they don't know. When the principal says their teacher saw them fighting, they will vigorously deny it, insisting that they were just teasing each other. Because the teacher has made this "false accusation," they might think she doesn't like them and become hostile to her in return.

Kochman (1981) describes another difference in communication styles concerning the conduct of arguments. White people are encouraged to present unbiased, objective arguments, but black people tend to accept the existence of bias and are skeptical of claims of objectivity. Although white people have been taught to argue in a calm, dispassionate manner, people in many black communities defend their beliefs passionately. In debates, black people do not expect impersonal or dispassionate arguments and

> Misunderstandings and inertia cause perhaps more to go wrong in this world than slyness and evil intent.
>
> Johann Wolfgang von Goethe (1749–1832)

may distrust people who are not passionate. Expressing ideas passionately during an argument is regarded as a measure of sincerity. In white society, the norm in debating issues is to repress emotions because they are believed to interfere with keeping an open mind. For many white Americans, arguing passionately seems confrontational; they think it exacerbates conflict and makes consensus less likely.

The potential for misunderstanding about how arguments are conducted was revealed in a televised program showing academics discussing racial issues in which a white professor misperceived a black professor based on his communication style. The black professor was making an eloquent and passionate argument. The white professor sitting beside him appeared uncomfortable, yet displayed no emotion. As the black professor paused before concluding, the white professor remarked in a defensive tone of voice but without facial expression, "Well you don't have to be so angry." Startled by the interruption, the black professor looked over at his white colleague and said, "Excuse me, you are mistaking intensity for anger."

In describing communication style differences, the intent is not to find fault with any group or person, nor is it to say that one communication style is better than the other. It is important to understand that communication styles are influenced by cultural heritage; we should not make assumptions about others based on their communication style. If a conflict occurs in a group whose members are different races or cultures, individuals in the group must articulate their perceptions about the cause of the conflict to see if everyone has a similar perception. Understanding our perceptions of others provides a basis for resolving cultural misunderstandings and conflicts. Meanwhile, research suggests that differences in communication styles create misunderstandings between men and women as well.

How does gender influence communication styles?

Communication differences based on gender are said to originate in differences in the way boys and girls are socialized. Traditionally, Americans have encouraged boys to be aggressive and girls to be nice; this has been documented in studies of children's play activities. American boys tend to play outdoors, typically in competitive games that require groups and involve aggressive behavior; they resolve disputes by engaging in debates in which everyone participates. In contrast, girls tend to play indoor types of games in small groups or with a friend; these games involve conversation and collaboration, and a quarrel will usually disrupt the game (Dow & Wood, 2006; Honig, 2006).

Gender differences persist even as children leave childhood behind. Some scholars believe that male aggressiveness in conversation is revealed in studies showing that men interrupt women more than women interrupt men (Dow & Wood, 2006), but Tannen (1994) argued that it is simplistic to say such behavior is always a dominance issue. Reviewing communication research on gender differences, Burgoon (2002) reported that women are more competent than men at giving and understanding nonverbal messages. Grumet (2008) found that women tend to have more eye contact than men and to pay more attention to their conversational partner.

Differences in degree of eye contact and face-to-face interaction often reflect differences in the way women and men express intimacy. Tannen (2007) described differences in male and female communication styles originating in childhood and continuing into adult years. In one study with subjects ranging from children to young adults, two people of the same age and gender were taken to a room, seated in chairs placed side by side, and asked to talk about a serious topic. The younger boys had trouble with the task; they didn't move the chairs, did not make eye contact, and spent much of their time shifting restlessly and talking about not wanting to talk. Males of all ages would sit in the chairs in their original position with minimal face-to-face interaction. At all age levels, female partners either moved the chairs or positioned themselves to face each other; they began talking immediately on a serious topic as requested.

High school boys express intimacy through aggressive behavior. Pushing, shoving, even punching each other is an indication of a close friendship. As adults, men transform aggressive physical behavior into aggressive verbal behavior. For example, American men are careful about expressing disagreement with someone they don't know very well, but they bluntly disagree with and even use sarcasm with a close friend. It is a sign of intimacy and trust when men don't have to "pull their punches" with each other.

From childhood through adulthood, American women tend to express intimacy by engaging in face-to-face interactions and expressing concern for the other person's feelings. For most, outright disagreement is regarded as a threat to intimacy and a lack of sensitivity or respect. When a woman disagrees with another woman, she will often begin by saying something positive or something they agree on, and then address the issue about which they disagree. The difference in male and female communication styles creates opportunities for misunderstanding. If a man and a woman have an intimate relationship and discuss an issue on which they disagree, he may make direct, honest comments because he feels so close to her, but she may interpret his harsh comments as insensitive, disrespectful, and even contemptuous of her opinions.

With such an emphasis on competition and aggression, boys become men who directly express wants, needs, or demands. With such an emphasis on cooperating, being nice, and caring about how others might feel, girls become women who are concerned about not imposing their wants or demands, preferring consensus. A man might attempt to convince someone to do what he wants, but a woman is more likely to ascertain whether the other person is interested in doing what she wants to do. Tannen (2007) argues that this difference may be a basis for historic gender stereotypes that have contributed to misunderstandings and conflict: men perceiving women as devious and cunning, and women perceiving men as arrogant and intimidating.

How do gender differences in communication styles lead to misunderstanding and conflict?

Imagine a woman coming home from work, greeting her husband, and then remembering, "Oh John, I meant to stop at the store and pick up a few things, but I am so tired I forgot to do it. This has been such a rotten day." She is indirectly asking him to go to the store for her, yet he may not get the message. Even if he tries to be sympathetic—"I'm sorry to hear that"—she will be upset if he doesn't offer to go to the store. If he wanted her to go to the store he would ask her directly; he needs to understand that her socialization and her communication style does not allow her to make demands as he would.

In a similar example, after leaving early for a long trip, a couple has been driving all morning on the interstate and it's almost noon. She sees a sign advertising a restaurant she likes at the next exit, points it out to him, and says, "Would you like to stop there and get something to eat?" He hears her comment not as an indirect request, but as a genuine question. He wants to drive for another hour before stopping to eat, so he says "No" and drives on. When he realizes that she is upset, they discuss the reason, and he criticizes her for not stating explicitly what she wanted. She thinks he should be able to understand that she did tell him in a manner that took account of his feelings. She believes that she has been sensitive and he has not. He believes she was being dishonest while he was being straightforward with her.

The reason for identifying gender differences is not to blame men or women, nor to say that one communication style is better than another. It is important to recognize the diverse ways people communicate so that differences in communication styles do not result in conflict. Knowing the influence on communication style of such factors as gender or culture provides a basis for preventing misunderstandings. If people recognize problems as possibly stemming from a difference in communication styles, they can modify their interaction to communicate more effectively (Jandt, 2003; Prince, 2004).

Conflict Resolution

Sometimes resolving conflicts seems hopeless. Groups have been in conflict for centuries; individuals take unresolved conflicts to their graves. Obviously, conflict resolution is not easy, and most people approach conflict with apprehension. In a study by McCorkle and Mills (1992), every metaphor chosen by participants to describe conflict was negative, often involving feelings of helplessness and of being an innocent victim.

Because K–12 schools are an environment for children and youth with adult supervision, we would expect to find less conflict, and yet studies find that considerable conflict occurs there. According to Wessler (2003), these conflicts usually stem from human differences such as race, mental disability, sexual orientation, and gender. Sexual orientation alone appears to result in many instances of harassment and conflict. According to an NMHA survey, students who were both gay and straight reported 20 or more incidences a day of hearing slurs and insults that were directed at their peers who were openly gay or simply perceived as gay. One third of the gay students in that survey had been threatened or actually injured at school in the previous 12 months (Roberts Jr., 2006). Garrett (2003) cites research documenting the consequences of harassment and conflicts between students:

10% of students drop out of school
20% of students avoid going to restrooms during the school day
54% of students say it would be easy for them to get a gun
30% of students have heard a peer threaten to kill someone
25% of students know a peer who has brought a gun to school (p. 12)

Because they are aware of student conflicts, school leaders have been especially concerned about making sure that students do not bring guns or other weapons to school, and it was this concern that resulted in the implementation of zero tolerance policies in many schools, especially urban schools.

What does "zero tolerance" mean and has it been effective in schools?

Although initially intended to keep weapons out of schools, **zero tolerance** eventually emerged as a school discipline policy that punished "both non-violent behaviors that are perceived to be disruptive and weapons and drug related infractions of school discipline codes" (Robbins, 2008, p. 5). Critics argued that such policies presumed students' guilt and made them have to prove their innocence or face such consequences as suspension or expulsion from school. The phrase "perceived to be disruptive" is a major reason for the failure of zero tolerance to prevent conflicts and provide a safe school environment. On more than one occasion, elementary school children were suspended simply for bringing Tylenol or Advil to school. Cornell (2004) describes reasons for student suspensions:

- A five-year-old boy found a razor blade at his bus stop, brought it to school, and gave it to his teacher.

- A six-year-old boy brought to school a two-inch knife and bottle opener that he had received at Toys for Tots.
- A ten-year-old boy brought to school a one-inch plastic toy pistol from his G.I. Joe action figure.
- A seventeen-year-old boy was expelled for shooting a paper clip with a rubber band.

Robbins (2008) argued that enforcing zero tolerance policies in such a "non-reflective" manner had resulted in a negative impact on school climate. Brownstein (2009) agreed, noting that suspensions and expulsions nationally had nearly doubled since zero tolerance policies were implemented. Further, the suspensions and expulsions contributed to an increase in school dropout rates, a decrease in student morale, and lower academic achievement. Brownstein also cited a survey by the Department of Education's Office of Civil Rights, which found that children with cognitive disabilities were more likely to be suspended or expelled than their peers who did not have disabilities, and African American students were three times more likely to be suspended or expelled as white students. Based on his review of zero tolerance policies, Robbins (2008) concluded that they had failed to reduce conflict and make schools safer, but instead had produced "intolerance, alienation, exclusion and the denial of educational opportunity" (p. 17).

With so much conflict occurring, how can conflicts be resolved?

Many schools have implemented conflict resolution programs, often including peer mediation, in an effort to give students the tools to resolve conflicts. Although studies of such programs have produced mixed results, these findings may simply reflect the quality of the programs being evaluated. Nation (2007) described a study of three elementary schools that implemented a peer-focused conflict resolution program that produced a dramatic reduction in the children's physically aggressive behaviors. The Peaceful Kids program trained teachers and staff to teach and model conflict resolution skills to preschool children in Boston, Dallas, and Los Angeles. After one year, program evaluations reported increased student self-control, increased cooperation among students, and significant decreases in student acts of aggression and student withdrawal behaviors (Coleman & Fisher-Yokida, 2008).

There is also evidence that conflict resolution programs may be effective with older students. Dillon (2004) described a program that taught conflict resolution skills to 225 students (primarily students of color) twice a week for five weeks. At the end of the five weeks, student acts of aggression had diminished significantly, as had the number of physical fights between students. Coleman and Fisher-Yokida (2008) describe a project at a New York City high school that implemented cooperative learning strategies and conflict resolution training. After two years, the program evaluation reported improved relationships between students, an increased ability among students to handle conflicts effectively, and students feeling an increased sense of control over their lives. Further, students reported an increased sense of self-esteem as well as improvement in their academic performance. These examples demonstrate that conflict resolution programs have the potential to produce positive outcomes for students, but to be successful, the conflict resolution approach must be designed not only to teach particular skills but also to cultivate and reinforce certain values that are essential for conflict resolution.

What values and skills are necessary for conflict resolution to be effective?

Conflict offers opportunity for constructive change, if all parties are prepared to make concessions and to establish a context conducive to resolution. Deutsch (2006) identified values that participants must share if they want to resolve conflict: fallibility, equality, reciprocity, and nonviolence.

Fallibility refers to accepting the possibility of being wrong. In conflict, people are customarily presented with evidence and arguments. However, presenting evidence will not help resolve a conflict if participants refuse to acknowledge that their position could be wrong. During deliberations in a jury room, the foreman of a jury said he believed the defendant was guilty and that he would not change his mind. Another jury member pointed out that such an attitude violated the jury process that requires discussing and debating evidence, listening to arguments with an open mind, and changing one's mind if justified by the weight of evidence or arguments. Although still

believing the defendant guilty, the foreman admitted the jury member was right, and he agreed to listen with an open mind. Ultimately he changed his mind.

Equality refers to the belief that every human being, regardless of status, occupation, or wealth, deserves to be treated respectfully, with consideration for his or her values, beliefs, and behavior. It is an acknowledgment that every human life has value and that no one should be treated unjustly. In another jury trial, some members of the jury began to criticize the testimony of two overweight and casually dressed female witnesses, based on their appearance rather than on what they said. Another juror chastised them for their negative attitudes and argued that if the jury was to render a just verdict, they should focus on the evidence the women presented, not on how they looked. Other jurors agreed.

Reciprocity means that participants in a conflict must behave toward others with the same sense of fairness and attentiveness that they would want for themselves—a restatement of the golden rule that appears as an ethical principle in practically all cultures, or as modified by Confucius: "Do not do to others what you would not like yourself" (Waley, 1938, p. 162). Apparently Confucius believed one

> The man who strikes first admits that his ideas have given out.
>
> Chinese Proverb

did not have to be good to others as long as no harm was done to them. Either way, the feeling of reciprocity is essential for participants in a conflict if they hope to negotiate a resolution to it.

To value *nonviolence* is to believe that the only genuine solutions are peaceful ones. As Deutsch explained in his fourth shared value, coercing others into accepting an imposed solution winds a long and tragic path through human history marked by brutality and blood, civil and global wars, leaving little evidence that solutions imposed by the strong on the weak are effective—or lasting—solutions.

In the context of the four shared values proposed by Deutsch, conflict need not be a destructive event; it can be a constructive opportunity. But to achieve a positive outcome from a conflict will depend on individuals having not only appropriate values, but the necessary skills to engage constructively in discussing issues with others when everyone is not in agreement.

Johnson, Johnson, and Tjosvold (2006) identified effective negotiation strategies to engage in what they termed **skilled disagreement**. Their first strategy for engaging in skilled disagreement is similar to what the jury member described in the fallibility anecdote: that all parties (1) agree to emphasize rationality, seek the best possible answer based on the available evidence and arguments, and are willing to change their position when justified by the evidence. Another strategy is that participants (2) agree that criticizing an idea is not criticizing those who propose the idea—that their worth as human beings is separate from their ideas.

It is also important that participants (3) make a conscious commitment to encourage others to contribute to discussion and to listen thoughtfully to the contributions they make. To ensure the process is effective, it is helpful when participants (4) restate ideas if they're not clear on what was said so that everyone understands the issue from all perspectives being presented. Finally, it is essential that participants (5) remember that the problem and any recommended solution will affect everyone; they must not be focused on winning a debate but upon arriving at a collaborative solution everyone can support. These conflict resolution skills are not difficult to learn, and many educators say they can and should be taught in schools, even to young children. Based on her review of research, Garrett (2003) argues that "Conflict resolution skills . . . learned by all students will help to change a school's atmosphere" (p. 135). By teaching these skills, educators may foster the development of not only cognitive abilities but also moral reasoning abilities.

How do people develop moral reasoning abilities?

Marc Hauser, Director of the Cognitive Evolutionary Laboratory at Harvard, argues that the human ability to engage in moral reasoning stems from an innate moral framework analogous to the linguistic framework described by Noam Chomsky and others that allows individuals to learn language. Based on cross-cultural research, Hauser (2006) claims that a shared moral framework explains the common human responses to moral dilemmas. Although there are differing theories regarding the development of moral reasoning, research based on the theory formulated by William Perry (1999) has found that this theory more accurately describes the moral reasoning engaged in by people of different ages, from different cultures or subcultures, and from both genders (Belenky, Clinchy, Goldberger, & Tarulle, 1997; King & Kitchener, 1994). Using this theory, teachers can provide students with moral dilemmas and controversial issues, then analyze student discussions and engage students with questions to challenge and strengthen their moral reasoning.

Perry's theory is based on the assumption that changes in moral reasoning are related to cognitive development: Increased cognitive ability allows individuals the possibility of increasing the complexity of their moral reasoning. Although there are nine developmental positions in Perry's continuum, as an introduction to the theory, it is sufficient to understand two major areas Perry has identified—dualism and relativism—and the mental shift that occurs within each: A dualistic thinker transitions into multiplicity, a relativistic thinker transitions into making commitments (see Figure 3.4).

Dualism.   All human beings begin as dualistic thinkers when confronted with moral decisions; children tend to operate simplistically with absolute categories of right and wrong. In dualism, every moral issue is a question of either/or: Either it's right or it's wrong, it's true or it's false, it's good or it's bad. This is also called "black and white" thinking because there are no "shades of gray" for dualistic thinkers. To be dualistic is to believe that what is true must be regarded as an absolute truth: It has always been and will always be true. Newberg and Waldman (2006) say that brain research offers a biological explanation for dualistic thinking: "The brain tends to reduce cause-and-effect cognition into dualistic scenarios because they are an easy, neurologically efficient way to make sense of the world" (p. 88).

Believing in absolutes is challenged when a person is confronted with problems that don't lend

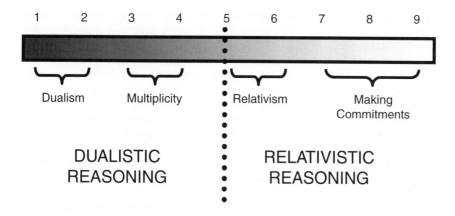

FIGURE 3.4 A Continuum of Moral Reasoning

Source: Perry W. (1970). *Forms of Intellectual and Ethical Development in the College Years: A Scheme.*
New York: Holt, Rinehart & Winston.

themselves to the either/or style of thinking. A popular moral dilemma exercise is to ask people what they would have done if they were hiding Jews in the early 1940s and Gestapo officers came to their home to ask if they knew the whereabouts of any Jews. For the person who believes "honesty is the best policy," this is a difficult question to answer. Another problem with dualistic thinking is that the cognitive process of simplification and generalization inevitably leads to stereotyping others because the process does not consider individual differences. As studies have reported, the "'us-versus-them' mentality can be easily converted into racism" (Newberg & Waldman, 2006, p. 89). Complex issues that challenge dualistic thinking may not present themselves until a student enters high school or college, but when students confront such issues, they often feel compelled to move away from rigid dualistic thinking and engage in the kind of moral reasoning called *multiplicity*.

Multiplicity. The perspective of **multiplicity** recognizes the difficulty of knowing "the right answer" in every situation. When the right answer is not obvious, the only recourse is for the individual to examine various opinions or multiple perspectives without being certain which one is right. Each person must consider the different perspectives and decide which one seems best. This is

not satisfying for people at the multiplicity position because they are still influenced by dualistic thinking. They would prefer to know the answer or the truth in a given situation, and often complain that all we have are opinions. Because of the influence of dualistic thinking, people at a multiplicity position

> The question should never be who is right, but what is right.
>
> Glenn Gardiner (Contemporary)

still believe the truth can be known and will be known some day, but for the moment, they reluctantly accept that they do not have the answer for a number of issues.

Relativism.   When people move beyond multiplicity to relativism, they tend to exhibit a change in attitude from reluctantly accepting the existence of multiple perspectives to becoming intrigued by the idea that each person must decide what is right. **Relativism** is based on the assumptions that there are no absolute truths, and that truth is relative, a concept reflected in the familiar phrases: "One man's meat is another man's poison" and "One person's treasure is another person's junk." The relativist is stimulated by differences of opinions, is interested in debates, and may enjoy playing the devil's advocate in a discussion by articulating arguments and ideas to defend a particular perspective without really believing in it.

Relativism requires an individual to be comfortable with ambiguity and not demand specific answers that are right for everyone. Many people are uncomfortable living in a world where they have to accept many points of view without regarding any of them as the right one. The difficulty of accepting such ambiguity causes some people to "retreat" (as Perry calls it) by resuming a dualistic thinking process. Other people who never progress beyond relativistic thinking sometimes adopt a cynical attitude toward life because relativistic thinking does not often result in becoming passionate about or personally invested in any issue or cause. However, some people who have also felt a sense of dissatisfaction with relativism's moral ambiguity have identified questions they wanted answered and are engaged deliberately in efforts to find their own answers.

Commitment.   Relativistic thinkers who continue to develop their moral reasoning are attracted to the idea of making **commitments** to certain personal truths, ideals, or causes that seem to give meaning to their lives. Most people need to believe in something and to feel a sense of satisfaction that their belief enhances the quality of their lives. Commitments may include being active in a political party or joining a church, an advocacy group, or some other organization. A commitment may result in volunteer work or influence a person's career decision. Whatever the choice, it is made from among many alternatives and the individual makes the commitment because it reflects his or her values.

Once people make commitments, they often become advocates for that particular cause or perspective. Because commitment is made in the context of relativistic thinking, people who reflect this perspective do not advocate like dualistic thinkers whose arguments are based on a sense of certainty. Relativistic thinkers may emphasize the sense of satisfaction they feel that their commitment provides a stronger sense of meaning and purpose in their lives, and they invite others to join them. In contrast, when dualistic thinkers advocate for truths

they believe are absolute, they tend to view those who agree with them as right and those who disagree as wrong. There is no other option. When people at the commitment level argue on behalf of their commitments, they do not tend to judge those who agree or disagree. They recognize that it is an individual's obligation to make his or her own choices, and they respect the person's right to choose. Someone at the commitment level does not reject relativism and its view of reality as ambiguous, but this person does recognize the satisfaction that may be gained by making commitments to provide a sense of meaning and purpose to his or her life. Being able to respect individual choice is not only important for moral reasoning, it is also essential for engaging in successful conflict resolution.

AFTERWORD

Even if we say exactly what we want to say, we can never assume that the meaning is heard and understood in the way we intend. Miscommunication happens when people do not check with others to ensure that they were understood. When misunderstandings are not clarified at the time they

> Wrongdoing can only be avoided if those who are not wronged feel the same indignation at it as those who are.
>
> Solon (640–558 BCE)

occur, they can cause people to become antagonistic toward others, thereby laying the foundation for an eventual conflict.

Some efforts to reduce conflict in schools have been successful, and there is much to be learned from them. In elementary classrooms, teachers must emphasize respect and nonviolence in their work with students. At the middle and high school levels, schools can empower students to intervene in conflicts by sponsoring workshops and providing other opportunities to develop mediation skills. At all levels it is important for students to work in groups and to have other experiences (e.g., peer tutoring) where they become better acquainted. According to Garrett (2003), studies have reported a reduction of conflict in schools in which children and youth have more opportunities to get to know each other.

Conflict resolution is not easy, yet it's better than coping with unresolved conflict. It is in everyone's interest to embrace the values that make conflict resolution possible and to practice communication strategies necessary for engaging in skilled disagreement. Conflict—from intimate disagreements between husbands and wives to global disputes among nations—is inevitable. The resolution of conflicts, however, is not inevitable. Teachers must challenge and enhance the moral reasoning abilities of our children and youth, and all of us must choose to engage in and be committed to the process of conflict resolution. The quality of individual lives and the quality of life for communities and for countries depends on the willingness of people to choose to resolve conflicts rather than hopelessly perpetuate them.

People must also recognize that there is no one best way to engage in moral reasoning. Although Hauser (2006) insisted that human beings share a common moral framework, he also found that different moral systems have emerged in different cultures. Based on his study of the differing systems, he concluded: "I favor a pluralistic position, one that recognizes different moral systems, and sees adherence to a single system as oppressive" (p. 425). By respecting and being open to diverse moral systems, human beings can lay the foundation for resolving conflicts and strengthening relationships between individuals (and nations) representing diverse cultures.

TERMS AND DEFINITIONS

Commitment Moral reasoning in a relativist context that recognizes the importance of becoming actively committed to certain personal truths to strengthen and deepen the meaningfulness of one's life experiences

Communication competence Having sufficient knowledge of a subject to communicate accurate information about that subject

Communication effectiveness Having the skills to communicate information in order to be easily understood

Cultural chauvinism An attitude that one's culture is the best, superior to other cultures

Dualism Moral reasoning involving a belief in absolute truths and unambiguous categories of right and wrong behavior; also called "either/or reasoning"

Interpersonal communication A dynamic process of interaction between people in which they assign meaning to each other's verbal and nonverbal behavior (Kougl, 1997)

Minimalization An attitude about other cultures that reduces the importance of cultural differences and emphasizes the universality of human needs and behaviors to create a stronger sense of relationship with all people

Multiplicity Moral reasoning in a dualistic context recognizing that it isn't possible to know what is the right behavior in certain situations, in which case opinions from multiple perspectives must be examined; a person can't be confident of the final decision in such instances because he or she can't be certain of having made the right choice

Nonverbal communication Those messages other than words that people exchange, also called "nonverbal behavior" or "nonverbal messaging"

Praxis Taking action to address injustice and then reflecting on the effectiveness of the actions taken as the person or group continues their activities

Relativism Moral reasoning that rejects absolute truth and is based on the assumptions that all truth is relative and that determining the right behavior depends on the individual and the situation

Selective perception Paying attention to behaviors of another person that reinforce our expectations for that person

Skilled disagreement Strategies that have been proven effective in achieving a successful resolution to conflicts

Tolerance Awareness of cultural differences without judging cultures as superior or inferior

Understanding Recognizing that culture shapes individual reality including acceptance of and respect for cultural differences

Zero tolerance A school discipline policy initially focused on preventing students from bringing weapons and drugs to school but later broadened to include punishments for "disruptive behavior"

DISCUSSION EXERCISES

Exercise 1: Statements Illustrating Perry's Continuum

Directions: Conversations can be categorized according to Perry's concepts. Identify each of the following statements according to the four broad areas in Perry's continuum of moral development. You will find three examples from each area. Record your answers as (a) dualism, (b) multiplicity, (c) relativism, or (d) commitment.

Statements Illustrating Perry's Continuum

_____ 1. In areas where even the experts disagree, everyone has a right to his own opinion. I mean, if answers aren't given, like in lots of things, then it has to be just anyone's opinion.

_____ 2. Understanding another point of view, especially a contrary one, helps me understand my own point of view. So trying to see through the other person's eyes helps my own understanding of the issue.

_____ 3. I came here from a small town in the Midwest where everyone believed the same things and everyone is, like, Methodist and Republican. But here, there is a variety of Protestants and Catholics and a Chinese boy who follows the teaching of Confucius. . . . Some people are quite disturbing; they say they're atheists, but I don't think they are.

_____ 4. I'm not sure how to make any decision at all. When you are here and having the issues thrust at you and reading about the people who pushed their thought to the absolute limit and seeing how that did not result in an all-encompassing answer . . ., you begin to have respect for how great their thought could be even though it did fall short.

_____ 5. The science lectures are all right. They sort of say the facts, but when you get to a humanities course, they are awful! The lecturer is just reading things into the book that were never meant to be there.

_____ 6. This place is full of bull. If you turn in a speech or a paper that is well written, whether it has one single fact in it or not is beside the point. . . . So you sit down and write a paper in an hour, just because you know that whatever it is isn't going to make any difference to anyone.

_____ 7. I get frustrated in class when the teacher only looks at things from her point of view. There are other ideas to consider. What is important to me is trying to understand and evaluate ideas and to come up with my own. I dislike discussions in which everyone just voices an opinion without backing it up. What good are opinions unless you put them to the test?

_____ 8. When I have an idea about something and it differs from the way another person is thinking about it, I will usually try to look at it from that person's point of view, see how they could say that, why they think they are right, why it makes sense.

_____ 9. In science you don't really want to say that something is true. We're dealing with a model and models are always simpler than the real world, which is more complex than anything we can create. We simplify so we can work with it. When we try to describe things, we leave out the truth because we are oversimplifying.

_____ 10. About the only thing I guess I would say to a prospective student is that if you come to this college, you had better do everything you are supposed to do and then you will be all right. That's just about all.

_____ 11. As soon as someone tells me his point of view, I immediately start arguing in my head the opposite point of view. When someone is saying something, I can't help turning it upside down.

_____ 12. I can't really say that one opinion is better than another. It depends on your beliefs. I am the type of person who would never tell someone that their opinion is wrong. If they have searched, well, even if they haven't searched, if they just believe it, that's cool for them.

Exercise 2: Words and Phrases That Hurt

Directions: Our conversations carry implications that reflect personal understanding, values, or beliefs. The 10 statements here contain implications that can offend others. Considering who the communicants are, why might the statements have been made in the first place? What are the implications in each? How does the context in which each is spoken make it offensive or hurtful?

1. A white person to a black person: "We must have law and order."
2. In a discussion of inequitable school funding, a suburban parent to an inner city parent: "You can make your schools as good as ours."
3. A Korean American to a black acquaintance: "You're different from most blacks."
4. A white employer announcing the intention of integrating the workplace: "Of course, we will make sure we only hire a qualified minority applicant."
5. In a discussion of racial discrimination in America, a black person to a Japanese American: "Asians have done well in America; you shouldn't have anything to complain about."
6. A white person to a Chicano: "I don't understand what you people want."
7. A white person to a black person: "Our old neighborhood used to be good when I was a kid, but it's gone downhill since it was integrated."
8. A Chinese American to a black person: "The death of Martin Luther King was a terrible loss to your race."
9. A black Christian to a Jew: "Oh, you're Jewish? I didn't realize you were Jewish—you sure don't act like one."
10. A white person to a Native American: "I think your people have made great progress."

REFERENCES

Belenky, M.F., Clinchy, B.M., Goldberger, N.R., & Tarulle, J.M. (1997). *Women's ways of knowing: The development of self, voice, and mind.* New York, NY: Basic Books.

Berne, E. (2004). *Games people play: The psychology of human relationships.* New York, NY: Ballantine. (Originally published in 1964)

Brown, B., & Merritt, R. (2002). *No easy answers: The truth behind death at Columbine.* New York, NY: Lantern Books.

Brownstein, R. (2009). Pushed out. *Teaching Tolerance,* Issue 36, pp. 58–61.

Burgoon, J.K. (2002). Nonverbal signals. In M. Knapp & G. Miller (Eds.), *Handbook of interpersonal communication* (3rd ed., pp. 344–390). Beverly Hills, CA: Sage.

Coleman, P.T., & Fisher-Yokida, B. (2008). Conflict resolution can be taught at all educational levels. In *Conflict resolution: Opposing viewpoints* (pp. 22–32). Detroit, MI: Greenhaven Press.

Cornell, D.G. (2004). Student threat assessment. In E.R. Gerler, Jr. (Ed.) *Handbook of school violence* (pp. 165–214). New York, NY: The Haworth Reference Press.

Deutsch, M. (2006). Cooperation and competition. In M. Deutsch, P. Coleman, & E.C. Marcus (Eds.), *The handbook of conflict resolution* (2nd ed., pp. 21–40). San Francisco, CA: Jossey-Bass.

Dillon, M. (2004). Lessons from the field: Balancing comprehensiveness and feasibility in peer mediation programs. In E.R. Gerler, Jr. (Ed.) *Handbook of school violence* (pp. 115–135). New York, NY: The Haworth Reference Press.

Dow, B.J., & Wood, J.T. (2006). *The SAGE handbook of gender and communication.* Thousand Oaks, CA: Sage Publications.

Ekman, P. (2003). *Emotions revealed: Recognizing faces and feelings to improve communication and emotional life.* New York, NY: Times Books.

Foster, H.L. (1986). *Ribbin', jivin', and playin' the dozens* (2nd ed.). Cambridge, MA: Ballinger. [In Figure 3.1 the picture on the left was anger; on the right, contempt.]

Freire, P. (2000). *Pedagogy of the oppressed.* New York, NY: Continuum. (Originally published in 1970)

Garrett, A.G. (2003). *Bullying in American schools: Causes, preventions, interventions.* Jefferson, NC: McFarland & Company, Inc.

Gordon, T. (2000). *Parent effectiveness training: The proven program for raising responsible children.* New York, NY: Crown.

Grumet, G.W. (2008). Eye contact: The core of interpersonal relatedness. In J. DeVito & M. Hecht (Eds.), *The nonverbal communication reader* (3rd ed., pp. 126–139). Long Grove, IL: Waveland.

Harris, T. (2004). *I'm OK—you're OK*. New York, NY: Morrow/Avon.

Hauser, M.D. (2006). *Moral minds: The nature of right and wrong*. New York, NY: Ecco.

Heath, S.B. (2006). *Ways with words*. Cambridge, UK: Cambridge University Press.

Hecht, M.L., & DeVito, J.A. (Eds.). (2008). Perspectives on defining and understanding nonverbal communication: Classic and contemporary readings. In *The nonverbal communication reader* (3rd ed., pp. 3–17). Long Grove, IL: Waveland.

Honig, A.S. (2006). Socio-cultural influences on gender-role behaviors in children's play. In D.P. Fromberg & D. Bergen (Eds.), *Play from birth to twelve and beyond: Contexts, perspectives, and meanings* (2nd ed., pp. 328–347). New York, NY: Routledge.

Ismail, N. (2001, September). *Communicating across cultures*. Victoria, BC: Pertinent Information. Available at http://pertinent.com/pertinfo/business/yaticom.html

Jandt, F.E. (1985). *Win-win negotiating: Turning conflict into agreement*. New York, NY: Wiley.

Jandt, F.E. (2003). *Intercultural communication: An introduction* (3rd ed.). Thousand Oaks, CA: Sage.

Johnson, D.W., Johnson, R.T., & Tjosvold, D. (2006). Constructive controversy: The value of intellectual opposition. In M. Deutsch, P. Coleman, & E.C. Marcus (Eds.), *The handbook of conflict resolution* (2nd ed., pp. 65–85). San Francisco, CA: Jossey-Bass.

Kimmel, P.R. (2006). Culture and conflict. In M. Deutsch, P. Coleman, & E.C. Marcus (Eds.), *The handbook of conflict resolution* (2nd ed., pp. 453–474). San Francisco, CA: Jossey-Bass.

King, P.M., & Kitchener, K.S. (1994). *Developing reflective judgment: Understanding and promoting intellectual growth and critical thinking in adolescents and adults*. San Francisco, CA: Jossey-Bass.

Kochman, T. (1981). *Black and white: Styles in conflict*. Chicago, IL: University of Chicago Press.

Kougl, K. (1997). *Communicating in the classroom*. Prospect Heights, IL: Waveland.

McCorkle, S., & Mills, J.L. (1992). Rowboat in a hurricane: Metaphors of interpersonal conflict management. *Communication Reports 5*(2), 57–67.

Meltzoff, N. (2007, Spring). Use another word. *Rethinking Schools 21*(3), 46–48.

Narula, U. (2006). *Handbook of communication models, perspectives and strategies*. New Delhi, India: Atlantic.

Nation, M. (2007). Empowering the victim: Interventions for children victimized by bullies. In J.E. Zins, M.J. Elias, and C.A. Maher (Eds.) *Bullying, victimization, and peer harassment: A handbook of prevention and intervention* (pp. 239–255). New York, NY: The Haworth Press.

Newberg, A., & Waldman, M.R. (2006). *Why we believe what we believe: Uncovering our biological needs for meaning, spirituality, and truth*. New York, NY: Free Press.

Perry, W.G., Jr. (1999). *Forms of intellectual and ethical development in the college years: A scheme*. San Francisco, CA: Jossey-Bass, Inc.

Postman, N., & Weingartner, C. (1987). *Teaching as a subversive activity*. New York, NY: Dell Publishing. (Originally published in 1969)

Prince, D.W. (2004). *Communicating across cultures*. Greensboro, NC: Center for Creative Leadership.

Robbins, C.G. (2008). *Expelling hope*. Albany, NY: SUNY Press.

Roberts, Jr., W.B. (2006). *Bullying from both sides: Strategic interventions for working with bullies and victims*. Thousand Oaks, CA: Corwin Press.

Rogers, C. (1995). *A way of being*. New York, NY: Mariner Books. (Originally published in 1980)

Schramm, W. (1973). *Men, messages, and media: A look at human communication*. New York, NY: Harper & Row.

Skuttnab-Kangas, T. (2000). *Linguistic genocide in education—or worldwide diversity and human rights?* Mahwah, NJ: Erlbaum.

Spitzberg, B.H. (2008). Perspectives on nonverbal communication skills. In J. DeVito & M. Hecht (Eds.), *The nonverbal communication reader* (3rd ed., pp. 18–22). Prospect Heights, IL: Waveland.

Stone, G., Singletary, M., & Richmond, V.P. (1999). *Clarifying communication theories: A hands-on approach*. Ames, IA: Iowa State University Press.

Tannen, D. (1994). *Gender and discourse*. New York, NY: Oxford University Press.

Tannen, D. (2007). *You just don't understand: Women and men in conversation*. New York, NY: Harper Collins. (Originally published in 1990)

Waley, A. (Ed.). (1938). *The analects of Confucius*. New York, NY: Vintage.

Wessler, S.L. (with W. Preble). (2003). *The respectful school: How educators and students can conquer hate and harassment*. Alexandria, VA: Association for Supervision and Curriculum Development.

Cultural Foundations of Oppression in the United States

Section 2 examines the history of oppression in the United States as experienced by immigrants who came to America in pursuit of the American dream. Immigrants encountered discomfort, rejection, and even persecution because they arrived as "foreigners" with different customs, traditions, attitudes, and beliefs. Immigrants of color also experienced oppression based on their race, and certain religions have been oppressed for their beliefs. The forms that this oppression have taken are identified in the definition of **oppression** provided in Andrzejewski (1996):

> Oppression exists when any entity (society, organization, group, or individual) intentionally or unintentionally distributes resources inequitably, refuses to share power, imposes ethnocentric culture, and/or maintains unresponsive and inflexible institutions toward another entity for its supposed benefit and rationalizes its actions by blaming or ignoring the victim. (p. 56)

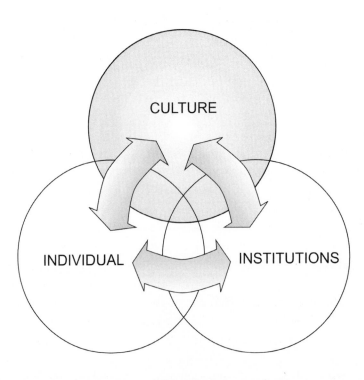

Chapter 4 describes how ethnic diversity of immigrants historically has been perceived as threatening to white supremacist attitudes of the majority group. Historic attempts have been made to curb immigration to America, especially of immigrants perceived as not being satisfactorily white enough, and to justify anti-immigration efforts through the early twentieth-century quasi science of eugenics. Because of the reform of immigration laws in 1965, ethnic diversity of immigrants has dramatically increased. The chapter examines issues stemming from this increased cultural and linguistic diversity, especially in our elementary and secondary schools. The chapter concludes with a description of anti-immigrant activities that underscores the persistence of these attitudes on the part of a significant percentage of the American population.

Chapter 5 describes negative attitudes and actions of Americans of European descent toward people of color in the United States, beginning with their conquest of American Indians and continuing with the importation of Africans as slaves, the rejection of Asian immigrants, and the exploitation of Spanish-speaking ethnic groups. The oppression of these groups took different forms, but the common denominator was that they were not white. The single factor of racial difference would sustain the oppression against individuals from these groups long past the period of time when they arrived as strangers in a strange land.

Chapter 6 focuses on the religious diversity of immigrants and the challenge that diversity has always represented to the creation of a free society. The religious diversity of people who settled in America eventually led to a shared conviction that religious differences should not be used to justify persecution, and the concept of religious freedom was included in the first amendment to the Constitution. Although members of different Protestant faiths began to accept one another as equals, Catholic, Jewish, and atheist immigrants were discriminated against. Although Catholics and Jews finally achieved a status as equals, the 1965 immigration reform resulted in an unprecedented increase in persons of other religions—such as Buddhists, Hindus, Muslims, and Sikhs. Once again the United States is being challenged to live up to its principle of providing religious freedom that acknowledges and accepts people from diverse faiths as equal partners in our religiously diverse nation.

In response to the cultural history just described, Chapter 7 provides insights and strategies for opposing efforts to perpetuate past oppression. The chapter begins by identifying four historical perspectives that describe individual reactions to racial, ethnic, and religious diversity in America. The most recent perspective, pluralism, emerged in the 1920s and is the only one that challenges this history of oppression by calling for Americans to recognize the value of diversity and the contributions diverse groups have made, and continue to make, to American society. The chapter provides a rationale for advocating for pluralism and strategies for pursuing social change. It is important to understand this foundation for change before moving on to Section 3, which describes the ongoing oppression of people from diverse groups. As readers learn about these issues and conflicts, they need to remember that change is possible and that even the worst problems can be overcome if people are united in their understanding of the causes of these problems. People also must be united in the vision of a more pluralistic future created by and for the incredibly diverse individuals living in the United States.

Chapter 4

Immigration and Oppression: The Assault on Cultural and Language Diversity

"We are all citizens of one world; we are all of one blood. To hate someone because he was born in another country, because he speaks a different language or because he takes a different view on a subject, is a great folly."

John Comenius (1592–1670)

As British colonists settled in America, they struggled with the issue of ethnic diversity because the need for more people to settle this new land conflicted with their **xenophobia**—the fear of or prejudice against people from other nations. There was no such struggle with racial diversity. As Kammen (1972) noted, European colonists came to America with racist notions of primitive Africans and savage Indians that justified enslaving them; seeds of white supremacy were sustained—and nurtured—on American soil. Ethnic diversity, however, was different. As the dominant ethnic group, British immigrants witnessed people from other European nations coming to the colonies, creating the difficult task of coexistence in a diverse community of immigrants. The challenge of devising an appropriate response to diversity has never been fully resolved. Instead, America has been enmeshed in an ongoing paradox of established immigrants fearing each wave of newcomers.

As the dominant ethnic group, how did British colonists react to diversity?

Part of the dilemma of ethnic diversity was the determination of British colonists to retain their identity. The French who settled to the north in Canada had readily adapted to Indian ways, especially with regard to economic practices such as trapping and through intermarriage with Native American women. The Spanish came as conquerors, but after their conquest, they still required Indian labor to sustain their control of conquered territory. Like the French, the Spanish borrowed cultural elements from conquered peoples, and intermarriages produced what would eventually be termed a new race: "La Raza."

Those who settled the English-speaking colonies tended to emigrate in family groups. Although some immigrants came to seek their fortune and return home, most came to establish permanent settlements. The British came as subjects of the English king, prepared to create an English colony as an extension of Britain. Although settlers occasionally used information gained from Indians about such things as edible plants and food preparation, their goal was to recreate as much of the Old World as was possible in the New World.

The problem with recreating the Old World was that it was not possible to make the colonies into a New England. In addition to British colonists (English, Scottish, and Irish), significant numbers of Dutch, German, and French colonists arrived, as well as small groups from other European countries and adventurers from parts of the world other than Europe. Germans in particular were as adamant as the English about maintaining their cultural heritage. They lived together in communities, spoke to each other in German, posted signs in German, imported books from Germany, and founded schools where their children were taught in German.

By the beginning of the eighteenth century, British colonial leaders became so alarmed by German behavior that some called for restrictions or exclusions of Germans from further immigration. Benjamin Franklin believed it was necessary to Anglicize the Germans because of the size of their population. As their numbers continued to grow, he feared that the Germans would "shortly be so numerous as to Germanize us instead of us Anglifying them" (Feagin, 1997, p. 18). Although Franklin obviously shared the desire of British colonists to Anglicize the colonies, he also recognized positive attributes of German immigrants and the contributions they were making to colonial development: "All that seems necessary is to distribute them more equally, mix them with the English, and establish English schools where they are now too thick settled" (Brands, 2000, p. 219).

Franklin was concerned with Anglicizing Germans and all immigrants who were not from Britain and, therefore, unfamiliar with British customs and language. In 1749, he sponsored the establishment of a school that included no foreign language instruction. His desire to Anglicize foreign colonists was also reflected in the views of President George Washington: "The more homogeneous our citizens can be made . . . the greater will be our prospect of permanent union" (Kammen, 1972, p. 74). Perhaps the desire for a more homogeneous citizenry was the reason the New American Congress passed a law in 1790 that limited citizenship in the United States to immigrants who were "white" persons. This early expression of xenophobia would lead to the growth of nativism in the United States.

> Law is a reflection and source of prejudice. It both enforces and suggests forms of bias.
>
> Diane Schulder (1937–)

Causes of Xenophobia and Nativism in the United States

Assimilation refers to a process in which immigrants adopt cultural traits from their host country and are absorbed into society (see Figure 4.1). British colonists preferred a homogeneous population of immigrants who could be assimilated into a dominant Anglo culture, but immigrants from other countries often demonstrated a persistent wish to maintain their own ethnic heritages. Their desires contributed to the development of xenophobia in response to the constant infusion of ethnicities among immigrants to America. When established immigrants, who considered themselves "natives," felt threatened by the many non-British immigrants in their midst, organizations based on nativist concerns would appear. Feagin and Feagin (1996) define **nativism** as "an anti-immigrant ideology that advocates the protection of native inhabitants of a country from [new or potential] immigrants who are seen as threatening or dangerous" (p. 503). Nativists have been the primary group engaging in the oppression of immigrants consistent with the definition of oppression (Andrzejewski, 1996) quoted in the section introduction.

Franklin's desire to Anglicize non-British immigrants and Washington's desire for a homogeneous population can be described as a benign form of nativism based on nationalistic concerns. Although nationalism represents one of the primary themes of nativist activities in the United States, two additional themes have characterized many nativist attitudes and actions: anti-Catholicism and anti-radicalism.

Nativism as anti-Catholicism

Although the religious beliefs of Benjamin Franklin, Thomas Jefferson, and other founders of the American republic were quite different from those of most Christians today, at its birth the United States was a nation strongly influenced by Protestant Christianity. The presence of Catholics had been tolerated throughout the colonial period, but by 1820, the 200,000 Catholics in the United States stimulated anti-Catholic sentiment, especially in

FIGURE 4.1 Assimilation Issues?

urban areas. (See Figure 4.2.) By 1850, there were almost two million Catholics in the United States; the Irish alone constituted 42% of that foreign-born population (Fuchs, 1990).

During George Washington's presidency, immigrants were required to be U.S. residents for a minimum of five years to be eligible for citizenship. The Nationalization Act signed by President John Adams changed the requirement to fourteen years of residency, but it was returned to five years after Thomas Jefferson became president. A nativist group calling itself "Native Americans" began forming in some of the larger cities; the party lobbied vigorously against immigrants becoming eligible for citizenship after five years. The Native American party insisted on a residency of twenty-one years before an immigrant was eligible for citizenship. Their main concern was voting, arguing that immigrants coming from nations governed by monarchs were not prepared to be self-governing. Since an immigrant came with:

all his foreign habits, prejudices and predilections . . . can it be believed that he can disburden himself so completely of these, and have so learned to fulfill

the duties of a citizen of the United States, in the very short term of five years? (Myers, 1960, p. 111)

At first, the Native American party encouraged people to welcome immigrants and only opposed their eligibility for citizenship after five years; however, by 1843, the movement had become hostile to continued immigration of both Irish and Catholics. In Philadelphia, the Native American party held a meeting in an Irish district of the city, initiating a confrontation between Protestants and Catholics; the violence that followed culminated in an angry mob setting fire to many buildings, and was reported in newspapers around the country. Federal troops were called in to restore order, which was no easy task, and peace prevailed for a little more than a month before mobs attacked a Catholic church and troops fired at the crowd to force them to disperse. Two more days of violence resulted in two soldiers being killed and twenty-six soldiers wounded.

Being confronted with such extreme violence was unusual, but American Catholics employed a number of strategies in response to anti-Catholic

FIGURE 4.2

A major factor in the anti-Catholic sentiment was the fear that Catholics would try to convert Protestants, especially children. The cartoonist, Thomas Nast, made Catholic bishops into alligators coming to U.S. shores, reflecting such fears.

activities. To avoid having their children subjected to anti-Catholic sentiments in public schools, Catholics created their own privately funded K–12 schools nationwide, eventually establishing Catholic colleges and universities as well. To counter anti-Catholic rhetoric in mainstream and Protestant newspapers, Catholics published their own newspapers. Hennesey (1985) described how Bishop John Hughes submitted several anti-Catholic articles to a Protestant newspaper under the name of "Cranmer," and then publicly announced that he was the author and that the articles included lies and distortions that the editors had not bothered to question or confirm. In addition, several Catholic organizations were founded in the 1800s, including the Knights of Columbus, which engaged in political activism but also provided centers for recreational activities and chapels for meditation and prayer. By the 1920s, church leaders adopted a different strategy, encouraging Catholics to become involved with "general reform groups in society and not limit their exertions to narrowly conceived partisan issues" (Hennesey, 1985, p. 247).

Nativism as anti-radicalism

Both anti-Catholicism and prejudice against the Irish fueled the nativism movement that flourished briefly in the 1850s, but the other negative sentiment contributing to the success of nativism was anti-radicalism. Most immigrants admitted to the United States in the first decades of the nineteenth century were overwhelmingly impoverished European laborers with minimal skills and little education. Some were sponsored by American capitalists to be contract laborers paid less than the wage native workers would accept. As new immigrant workers adapted to life in the United States, they came to realize how they were being exploited; many joined or helped create unions to demand better wages and benefits by engaging in strikes, marches, and protests. Nativists saw union actions as un-American, especially when the "foreigners" expressed socialist, anarchist, or other radical ideas. The antagonism toward what was regarded as radical activities by recent immigrants was clearly and frequently expressed on the editorial pages of urban newspapers (Higham, 1955):

> "Our National existence and . . . our National and social institutions are at stake."
> "These people are not Americans, but the very scum and offal of Europe."
> "There is no such thing as an American anarchist."
> "Europe's human and inhuman rubbish." (p. 55)

The first quotation illustrates the nationalism often expressed in nativist sentiments; the other quotations reveal hostility and a dehumanized view of the perceived "radicals." The un-American implication in each statement is central to the nativist perspective. Nativist concerns at that time also had to do with the decreasing amount of land available for immigrants in the Midwest and West; as a result, immigrants increasingly settled in urban areas. Because many immigrants were moving from southern and eastern Europe, land reformer Henry George commented, "What, in a few years more, are we to do for a dumping ground? Will it make our difficulty the less that our human garbage can vote?" (Higham, 1955, p. 42). The issue of immigrants becoming eligible for citizenship and voting continued to fuel individual xenophobia, and nativist political actions document a fear of the potential political power of incoming immigrants.

Nativism, Politics, and Social Change

The Native American party never gained political dominance, yet by the 1850s it had prepared the way for the rise of the "Know-Nothings," a somewhat secret movement whose members were told to respond to any question about the organization by saying that they knew nothing about it. Staunchly anti-immigrant and anti-Catholic, Know-Nothings were concerned with what they perceived as the growing political influence of Catholics; these fears were confirmed by President Franklin Pierce's appointment of a Catholic, James Campbell, to be the nation's attorney general.

How successful were the nativists in their political activities?

The Know-Nothings fielded candidates for the American Party, and in 1854 elected 9 governors, 8 (of 62) senators, and 104 (of 234) members of the House of Representatives (Myers, 1960). In the 1856 elections, Know-Nothing members used force and threats to keep immigrants from voting and encouraged election-day riots in Louisville, Kentucky, and St. Louis, Missouri. When the Whig Party refused to nominate Millard Fillmore for a second term as president, the American Party nominated him as their candidate. Despite the success of other American Party candidates, Fillmore received only eight electoral votes.

Reaction to the political success of the Know-Nothings was swift. In Congress a resolution was submitted, then voted down, condemning secret organizations and citing the Know-Nothings as a specific example. Political and religious leaders across the nation denounced the activities of the Know-Nothings, including the young political aspirant Abraham Lincoln, who wrote in a letter to a friend,

> As a nation we began by declaring that "all men are created equal." We now practically read it, "all men are created equal except Negroes." When the Know-Nothings obtain control, it will read: "All men are created equal except Negroes, foreigners, and Catholics." (Myers, 1960, p. 146)

Why did nativists fail to form a major political party?

The political success of nativism in the 1850s was brief because the issue of slavery began to take precedence over anti-Catholic prejudice and fears, and it divided the Know-Nothings. By the end of the Civil War, the Know-Nothings and the American Party were no longer a political force, although the nativist fears that fueled their activity persisted as a major influence in the United States. As the American people debated the issue of slavery, American capitalists continued to sponsor importation of labor from overseas to keep wages low and profits high.

Throughout U.S. history, a significant percentage of Americans consisted of recent immigrants or children of immigrants who appreciated the opportunities in America and vigorously opposed attempts by nativists to restrict immigration. Meanwhile, there was constant pressure from society to promote the **Americanization** of immigrants, and public schools carried out societal expectations by encouraging immigrants to abandon their heritage and conform to American ways (Pai & Adler, 2006). Nativist attitudes in the United States continued to wax and wane, with xenophobia historically balanced by those who believed in America as a place for oppressed people to achieve freedom and fortune.

The demand for Americanization of immigrants intensified in the late 1800s as the majority of immigrants were *not* northern Europeans—they were Greeks, Italians, Slavs, and Jews—people who did not conform to the Anglo ideal. Because of an economic downturn in the 1890s, nativism experienced a renewed popularity with American people;

> There is no room in this country for hyphenated Americans.
>
> Theodore Roosevelt (1858–1919)

then in the ebb and flow of xenophobia, nativist fears succumbed to a confidence inspired by the U.S. triumph in the Spanish-American War and by heroes such as Teddy Roosevelt. Although nativists never again succeeded in sponsoring an independent political party, events in the early twentieth century would establish the foundation for their greatest political triumphs.

What influenced twentieth-century nativist attitudes in America?

It seemed certain to most Americans that if the United States were going to become a dominant political and economic power in the world, immigrants would be needed in the labor market of its dynamic economy. But when World War I began, attitudes changed. Nativism surged again, driven by feelings of nationalism and anti-radicalism. German Americans were singled out for especially opprobrious treatment, and their loyalty to the United States was questioned. Rumors abounded that German Americans were spying for Germany.

Because German Americans insisted on maintaining their dual identity as Americans of German descent, people of influence such as Teddy Roosevelt admonished them by denouncing all immigrants who claimed a dual identity. German Americans were surprised by such criticisms. From colonial times they had maintained their culture, language, and traditions through separate schools, organizations, and newspapers. Because of their industriousness, efforts to preserve their German heritage had been tolerated by American society until World War I, when nativist individuals and organizations attacked German Americans for keeping themselves separate and not assimilating to an Anglo ideal.

During World War I, surging patriotism intensified the demand that immigrants be Americanized quickly. Although this nationalism was a less abrasive form of nativism, it became more virulent when reinforced by anti-radical attitudes. Radical organizations were attacked as un-American, especially radical unions like the International Workers of the World, the "Wobblies." Nativists accused certain immigrants of espousing ideas that were disloyal to the country and demanded their deportation.

German Americans were not the only targets of anti-American accusations. **Anti-Semitism**—having prejudices, stereotypes, or engaging in discrimination against Jews—increased with the success of the Russian Revolution in 1917. Jews were associated not only with communism, but also with international financiers who profited from the war. After World War I, nativists continued to complain that the Anglo ideal for America would disappear if diverse European ethnic groups continued to emigrate; however most Americans seemed to believe that those who came would eventually assimilate into the dominant culture.

By the 1920s, a revised perspective was being expressed. In settlement houses such as Hull House in Chicago, people providing social services began to appreciate the diversity of the immigrants. Social

> [America can have] a unity created by drawing out and composing into a harmonious whole the best, the most characteristic, which each contributing race and people has to offer.
>
> John Dewey (1859–1952)

activist Jane Addams, cofounder of Hull House, and University of Chicago philosopher John Dewey described the advantages of diverse cultures and the value of people maintaining their heritages while still learning, as Benjamin Franklin had recommended, the language and customs of American culture. Although resentment toward Germans slowly dissipated after the war, anti-Semitism persisted as part of a new development in xenophobic attitudes in the United States.

What new development affected xenophobic attitudes in the United States?

In 1899, William Z. Ripley, an economist from the Massachusetts Institute of Technology, published a so-called scientific study identifying and describing three European races: Teutonic, Alpine, and Mediterranean (Higham, 1955). Based on emerging theories about race, nativists argued that for U.S. citizenry to achieve unity, immigrants of the blue-eyed, blond-haired Teutonic type (also called "Nordic" or "Anglo Saxon") should be given preference. Senator Henry Cabot Lodge of Massachusetts

called for an end to all further immigration to the United States, and Teddy Roosevelt chastised Anglo Saxon women in America for contributing to the possibility of "race suicide" by not producing as many children as immigrant women (Brodkin, 2002). In the aftermath of World War I, pessimism about diverse groups being able to assimilate into an Anglo Saxon American culture fueled racist sentiments expressed in widely read books such as Lothrop Stoddard's *The Rising Tide of Color*. (See Figure 4.3.)

Madison Grant (1916/1970) provided the most influential expression of this pessimism in *The Passing of the Great Race, or the Racial Bias of European History*. Grant rejected the idea that immigrants with other than Nordic heritage could achieve the Anglo Saxon ideal; thus the "Great Race" of Anglo Saxons was doomed to disappear in America. Claiming that his ideas were grounded in the emerging science of genetics, Grant concluded that intermarriage between races produced degraded offspring who would revert to lower qualities contained in their parents' genes. Referring to Ripley's three European races, Grant stated, "The cross between any of the European races

---

FIGURE 4.3

This advertisement from a 1923 *Time* magazine warns its readers that the days of white supremacy may be numbered and urges white people who want to do something about it to read Stoddard's book, *The Rising Tide of Color*.

Three books by LOTHROP STODDARD

The Revolt Against Civilization

"The reason why this book has attracted such an extraordinary amount of attention is not far to seek. It is, so far as we know, the first successful attempt to present a scientific explanation of the world-wide epidemic of unrest that broke out during the Great War and still rages in both hemispheres."—*Saturday Evening Post*. $2.50

The New World of Islam

This book is *true*—current events are bearing it out in startling fashion. "He has presented, in compact and readable form, what did not exist before in any language: a short, concise account of the modern Mohammedan world and its reaction to the invasion of the West."—*Atlantic Monthly*.   With maps. $3.00

The Rising Tide of Color

White world supremacy is in danger. The world-wide ascendancy of the white race, apparently so unshakable, is in reality threatened by the colored races. This is a startling book, one for the reader who is able to stand up against the impact of new ideas. It is a clear, sharp warning to the whites, and an appeal for white solidarity.   With maps. $3.00

© *Bachrach*

LOTHROP STODDARD

From early manhood he has prepared himself, by wide travel and extensive study, to qualify as a true expert on world affairs. His is the mind of a trained observer who has received the soundest scientific training.

and a Jew is a Jew" (p. 16). Confirming Grant's assertion, the eugenics movement provided "scientific" evidence of the human degradation caused by miscegenation, and 30 states passed laws banning interracial marriage (Stubblefield, 2007). Many well-known and respected Americans such as automaker Henry Ford expressed beliefs consistent with Madison Grant's theories and the findings of eugenics, and racism—including anti-Semitism—was incorporated into traditional xenophobic attitudes.

How did racism affect nativist attitudes and actions?

Nativists used the new racist concern for preserving the nation's Anglo Saxon heritage to sound the alarm about the numbers of immigrants from southern and eastern Europe—80% of all U.S. immigrants from 1900 to 1910. Stanford University's Ellwood P. Cubberley echoed their concerns in his history of education textbook (1919):

> These Southern and Eastern Europeans were of a very different type from the North and West Europeans who preceded them. Largely illiterate, docile, lacking in initiative, and almost wholly without the Anglo-Saxon conceptions of righteousness, liberty, law, order, public decency, and government, their coming has served to dilute tremendously our national stock . . . our national life, for the past quarter of a century, has been afflicted with a serious case of racial indigestion. (p. 338)

Nativists triumphed in 1924 with the passage of an immigration law establishing quotas for immigrants based on country of origin. The quotas ensured that immigrants from northern Europe (the so-called Nordic type) would constitute the majority of U.S. immigrants, guidelines that remained largely unchanged for the next four decades. Although people of color were the primary targets of nativists, other groups were also affected by racist attitudes.

What groups were affected by the addition of racism to xenophobia?

This new racist form of nativism was directed not only against people of color, but also against white people perceived as not being white enough, which often meant that they did not share the

> We gave [immigrants] disparaging names: Micks, Sheenies, Krauts, Dagos, Wops . . . until [each group] became sound, solvent . . . whereupon each group joined the older boys and charged down on the newest ones. . . . Having suffered, one would have thought they might have pity on the newcomer, but they did not.
>
> John Steinbeck (1900–1969)

common prejudices of the white majority. This was especially observed in southern states. In 1898, debates at Louisiana's state constitutional convention focused on who would be denied the right to vote. Although blacks were the main targets, Italians were considered "as black as the blackest negro in existence" (Barrett & Roediger, 2002, p. 32). Because of such perceptions, some Italians were victims of southern violence in the nineteenth century. In Tallulah, Louisiana, five Sicilian immigrants owned businesses that served primarily black customers. Local whites resented the immigrant storekeepers because they treated black people as equals. Before long, the locals fabricated a quarrel over a goat and lynched the five Sicilians (Higham, 1955).

The idea of perceiving Italians, Irish, or others as separate races based on their national origins seems strange today; yet most Americans, including members of identified "races," accepted this designation. In the 1930s, an Irish campaign manager representing an Irish politician made the following speech at an Italian neighborhood meeting to ask the Italian men to vote for his candidate in the upcoming election:

> Maybe I'm the only Irishman here, but this is not a racial contest. You don't select your man because of his race. There are too many who cry him down because of that. But these people that sit behind closed doors and discriminate against a man because of his race have no place in American life. . .
>
> This district don't house men and women that vote only because of their racial strain. For the immigrants of your race and my race, I have no apology. In the time of need, we answered the call of our country. One of the largest quotas of men was sent out from this district. At that time there was no

FIGURE 4.4

Source: David Horsey © 2007. Tribune Media Services. Reprinted by permission.

discrimination because of a man's race, there was no turning men back for that reason. We sent out boys by the thousands in order that we might enjoy the blessings of free government. Here we never turn down a man because of his race or creed. (Whyte, 1955, p. 227)

The idea of national origin defining separate races declined as skin color became the primary determinant of racial identity, and racism would prolong the oppression of people of color beyond the time normally experienced by white ethnic groups. The experiences of the four major racial groups are the focus of Chapter 5.

As the civil rights movement gained momentum, allegations of racism were made in many areas. President John Kennedy admitted to inequities in immigration policies based on the 1924 law. Attorney General Robert Kennedy characteristically stated the issue more bluntly, "As we are working to remove the vestiges of racism from our public life, we cannot maintain racism as the cornerstone of our immigration laws" (Eck, 2001, p. 7). In 1965, Congress eliminated the racially biased National Origins Quotas by passing the Immigration and Nationality Act. Since then, the numbers of immigrants of color have increased dramatically, prompting a resurgence of nativism. The influx of illegal immigrants has also stirred anti-immigrant sentiments and created controversy even though individual and corporate employers are often dependent on them (see Figure 4.4).

The Paradox of Xenophobia and Nativism in a Nation of Immigrants

Daniels (2002) noted the absurdity among Americans to regard the people who first came to the United States as "colonists" or "settlers" and then to identify the people who came later as "immigrants."

Social observers such as author John Steinbeck (1966) have described how immigrants were initially reviled only to be accepted later: "the surges of the new restless, needy, and strong . . . were resisted, resented, and accepted only when a new and different wave came in" (p. 14). Part of being accepted involved the former immigrants expressing xenophobic sentiments against current immigrants. In fairness, Americans have not consistently expressed such sentiments; instead, Daniels (2002) has observed the following pattern:

> When most Americans are generally united and feel confident about their future, they seem to be more willing to share that future with foreigners; conversely, when they are divided and lack confidence in the future, nativism is more likely to triumph. (pp. 265–266)

As previously mentioned, nativists used the work of scholars and scientists within the growing ranks of the eugenics movement in support of their efforts to limit immigration. British scientist Francis Galton coined the term **eugenics** as "the study of agencies under social control that may improve or repair the racial qualities of future generations, either physically or mentally" (Lynn, 2001, p. 4). American scholars endorsing the eugenics movement were concerned about the perceived degeneration of mental abilities among Americans. Many believed there was a racial component to the problem represented by immigrants, whom they regarded as the primary cause of this decline of intelligence in America. As Stubblefield (2007) noted, many scholars believed that "White people were 'civilization builders,' while members of other races supposedly lacked the ability to produce civilization" (p. 163). Scholarly support for the eugenics movement would decline precipitously after the Nazis tainted it with their emphasis on race purification and their implementation of genocidal practices.

Although the eugenics movement in the United States never attracted a majority of academics, some in the eugenics camp were influential scholars: Robert Yerkes of Harvard (president of the American Psychological Association), Lewis Terman of Stanford, and Edward Thorndike from Teachers College, Columbia University (Selden, 2006). Because of their academic interests, Yerkes, Terman, and Thorndike were responsible for developing early

intelligence tests (see Table 4.1). When Henry Goddard implemented intelligence tests with the immigrants at Ellis Island, he reported that 80% were "feeble minded" (Brodkin, 2002).

Because some respected scholars supported it, the eugenics movement flourished from 1910 to 1940, shaping the content of biology textbooks, reinforcing popular views concerning white supremacy, and contributing to the growth of anti-immigrant attitudes. One legacy of the eugenics movement is the standardized testing used to measure academic achievement that students still take today—but testing is not the only legacy of the eugenics movement.

Established in 1937 to promote eugenics policies, the Pioneer Fund advocated the forcible removal of "American Negroes" to Africa. The first Pioneer Fund President, Harry Laughlin, wrote the Model Eugenical Sterilization Law, adopted by thirty states in the United States and Nazi Germany. Laughlin proposed that Adolf Hitler be given honorary membership in the American Eugenics Society. The Pioneer Fund continues to support scholars working on race-based IQ theories, including work employed in support of the controversial comments about race made in The Bell Curve (Herrnstein & Murray, 1994). The Pioneer Fund also supported a book by Lynn (2001) arguing in favor of eugenic principles, and has continued to be a major funding source for the English Only movement (Tatalovich, 1997).

How is the English Only movement an example of xenophobic behavior?

Nativists have always been critical of immigrants who maintain their native language. They lobbied for literacy tests primarily as a strategy to reduce immigration, but for almost two decades Congress rejected the idea. When Congress finally passed such legislation, both Democratic and Republican presidents vetoed these laws until 1917, when Congress passed this requirement over President Wilson's veto (Delgado, 1997). Nativist opposition to immigrants maintaining their native language was evident in their criticisms of German immigrants, and culminated during World War I with state and local laws that forbade public displays of signs with German words and banned the teaching of German in public schools. In some communities German textbooks were burned as an act of patriotism (Crawford, 2000). The percentage of students

TABLE 4.1 World War I Army Mental Tests

Alpha and Beta Tests developed by Psychologists Robert Yerkes, Louis Terman, and Henry Goddard assisted by Carl Campbell Brigham, Founder of Educational Testing Service (ETS)

These sample questions reveal how culturally biased and inappropriate the early tests of "intelligence" could be; yet such tests were used with immigrants to determine which ones were of acceptable intelligence and which were "feeble minded."

Sample questions:

1.	Seven-up is played with:	rackets	cards	pins	dice
2.	The Merino is a kind of:	horse	sheep	goat	cow
3.	Christy Mathewson is famous as a:	writer	artist	baseball player	comedian
4.	"There's a reason" is an "ad" for a:	drink	revolver	flour	cleanser
5.	Soap is made by:	B. T. Babbitt	Smith & Wesson	W. L. Douglas	Swift & Co.
6.	The Brooklyn Nationals are called the:	Giants	Orioles	Superbas	Indians
7.	The most prominent industry of Minneapolis is:	flour	packing	autos	brewing
8.	The forward pass is used in:	tennis	hockey	football	golf
9.	The Pierce Arrow car is made in:	Buffalo	Detroit	Toledo	Flint

Source: Owen, David. *None of the Above: The truth behind the SATs,* 1999, p. 176 and *History Matters* at: http://historymatters.gmu.edu/d/5293

taking German in U.S. high schools went from 25% in 1915 to 0.6% by 1922 (Baron, 2000). Today, **English Only** advocates demand that English be declared the "official language" of the United States, and they are working toward that goal on a state-by-state basis. English Only supporters claim that their desire to establish English as the official language of the United States is simply a response to the large number of immigrants who refuse to learn how to speak English.

The problem with this claim is the lack of supporting evidence. English Only proponents point to the existence of dual language street signs, billboards, and government brochures and to bilingual instruction in schools. They believe that the use of non-English languages, especially in bilingual instruction, legitimizes these languages and elevates their status as well as the status of those who speak these alternate languages. Yet studies do not indicate

a threat to the widespread use of English, reporting that well over 90% of U.S. residents speak English fluently (Crawford, 2000; Wiley, 2005). Critics of English Only activities argue that it is no coincidence that the current movement was initiated just 15 years after the 1965 immigration reform that resulted in the majority of U.S. immigrants being people of color, and there is some evidence of a xenophobic motivation behind English Only organizations. For example, Crawford (2000) reports on an investigation of US English, a major English Only organization, that found evidence of their real agenda: "determination to resist racial and cultural diversity in the United States" (p. 23). Baron (2000) argues that the history of such organizations "often masks racism and certainly fails to appreciate cultural difference" (p. 447). Latino immigrants appear to be the main targets; in a survey asking financial supporters of US English why they contributed to the organization, 42% of respondents agreed with the statement: "I wanted America to stand strong and not cave in to Hispanics who shouldn't be here" (Crawford, 2000, p. 24). Such attitudes support criticism that English Only activities disguise xenophobic attitudes by insisting that their goal is to promote assimilation by encouraging immigrants to learn English. Reviewing historic and current efforts to pass English Only legislation, Baron (2000) concludes: "no matter how idealistic or patriotic its claims . . . (it has) a long history of nativism, racism, and religious bigotry" (p. 451).

Immigrants have always tended to learn English out of necessity for economic and social well-being. Today, fewer than 14% of Americans speak a language other than English: Fewer than 6% of Americans speak no English (Wiley, 2005). Despite these facts, the English Only movement has been successful in promoting state legislation to establish English as the official language. Almost half the states have existing laws declaring English as the official language. Some laws are largely symbolic, no penalties are enforced, and there is no prohibition against teaching foreign languages or implementing and supporting bilingual programs. However, some state laws prohibit their governments from printing materials in other languages.

Spanish is the first language of the majority of immigrants, so English Only laws largely affect Latino immigrants, preventing many of them from being able to gain access to useful information. Such laws may also prevent legally eligible people from voting (Tatalovich, 1997). Whether symbolic or harmful, English Only laws reflect the xenophobic attitudes of many Americans against recent immigrants, especially people of color who are not fluent or literate in English upon their arrival. It is no coincidence that activities of English Only advocates surged following the passage of the 1965 Immigration and Nationality Act; by eliminating national origins as a consideration, this reform radically changed the demographics of those immigrating to the United States.

What changes in immigration have occurred since the passage of the Immigration and Nationality Act of 1965?

Prior to 1965, most U.S. immigrants were white and primarily European, but in the first three decades after this immigration reform was implemented, about 80% of immigrants were people of color coming from Central and South America, the Caribbean, and Asia (Roberts, 1997). In less than 50 years, the foreign-born population in the United States has increased from 10 million to 40 million, of which 10 million were Asian immigrants, but the largest group—20 million immigrants—came from Latin America, primarily Mexico (Ehrenhalt, 2009). As was true in previous years, most immigrants intended to remain in the United States. From 1970–2000, more than 20 million immigrants became permanent U.S. residents, and 3 million achieved this status even though they had initially entered the country illegally (Chavez, 2009). There are over 40 million Latinos in the United States representing 15% of the workforce, and they are expected to exceed 50 million people and constitute 18% of the workforce in 2018 (Pabst, 2011). Given such numbers, it should not be surprising that Latinos are beginning to have an increasing political influence in states where they are concentrated such as Florida, Virginia, California, and Texas. Further, demographers predict that people of color, especially Latinos, will continue to be the majority of immigrants in the future. From 2010 to 2050, the population of the United States is expected to increase by almost 150 million, and 82% of this increase will be people of color who immigrated after 2005 and their descendants. Since 2005, almost half of the babies born in the United States have had Spanish surnames (Davis, 2009). By 2050, it appears likely that over half (53%) of Americans will be people of color (Meacham, 2009). Some Americans have reacted to such predictions with fear and anxiety, and this has resulted in the perpetuation of nativist attitudes and activities.

What American nativist attitudes and actions are evident today?

A focal point for nativist activity is the 2,000-mile border between the United States and Mexico. In 1990, the United States built a steel wall on the border near San Diego. From the moment it was being constructed, the Mexican government declared the wall not only an insult, but a provocative act by the United States; some Mexicans referred to it as "the new Berlin Wall" (Nevins, 2010, p. 100). Even though the wall proved ineffective at curbing illegal entry into the United States, nativists continued to lobby for additional fencing along the border, and the George W. Bush administration responded. Since 2006, over 1,000 miles of fencing has been built at a cost of $3.5–$6.5 million per mile, with maintenance costs expected to reach $60 billion by 2035 (Henderson, 2011).

To monitor the extensive fence construction, additional Border Patrol agents have been hired and Congress has funded supplementary Border Patrol agents in response to the 9/11 tragedy to address concerns about terrorists gaining entry into the United States. Yet there has not been a similar change for those charged with the responsibility of monitoring people coming across the Canadian border. The concern about terrorists infiltrating the immigrant population to gain entry into the United States does not appear to be a significant problem. Department of Homeland Security (DHS) data from 2004–2006 revealed that DHS filed charges against slightly more than 814,000 immigrants, but only 12 immigrants were charged with any terrorist activity (0.0015% of all immigrants being charged). Of the 14 charges against the 12 immigrants, 6 charges were dropped and one was dismissed (Nevins, 2010). A much more significant issue has been the high turnover rate for the Border Patrol, much higher than police departments or other comparable law enforcement agencies. Nevins (2010) suggested that it is related to the nature of their work. Police officers pursue criminals and often provide assistance to citizens, but Border Patrol agents pursue unemployed people who are poor and need a job, and the people they arrest often include women and children.

The added fencing and increased Border Patrol presence does not appear to have addressed the concerns about immigrants entering the United States illegally. Nevins (2010) cited a 2005 study acknowledging that it was more difficult to cross the U.S./Mexican border, but the study went on to note that two thirds of those seeking illegal entry were still successful, and of the one third that were caught, 92%–97% of them persisted in their efforts to cross the border. Some have scaled the fence using ropes or ladders; others have dug tunnels under the fence. Nevins (2010) concluded: "The fence has done remarkably little to deter would-be border crossers" (p. 144). Similarly, Henderson (2011)

argued that the primary outcome of more fences and an increased number of Border Patrol agents has been to force people trying to enter the United States illegally to attempt to do this in more remote and dangerous areas. Further, one of the major factors frustrating this effort to control the border is the North American Free Trade Agreement (NAFTA). Because of NAFTA, approximately 222,000 vehicles cross the U.S./Mexican border every day, and of necessity, Border Patrol agents allow much of that traffic to pass uninspected. Another factor is the weakened global economy. In 2009, 700,000 workers in Mexico lost their jobs, so it was inevitable that many of them would pursue legal or illegal entry into the United States in an effort to find employment (Henderson, 2011).

Because Latinos comprise the majority of immigrants, the brunt of anti-immigrant backlash is largely directed at them, especially Mexicans in areas such as Southern California where the Mexican population is expected to increase by two thirds from 2000 to 2020. Scherer (2005) quotes one Southern Californian's reaction: "Migration from Mexico is the catalyst that's starting the demise of America" (p. 57). This is not an isolated opinion. According to a 2010 survey by the Pew Research Center, nearly half of Americans agreed with the statement that immigrants "threaten traditional American customs and values" and only 39% believed that immigrants "strengthen our country because of their hard work and talents" (Navarro, 2011, p. A18). Despite such negative attitudes, a number of U.S. communities have erected signs in English and Spanish announcing a site as a place to procure a day laborer, and many Americans hire Latino immigrants at these sites for minimal compensation with no apparent concern about whether they are in the country legally. (See Figure 4.5.)

Negative attitudes have fueled an increasing amount of anti-immigrant activity since the 1990s, primarily directed at Spanish-speaking immigrants. A significant part of this increased activity has come from an expanding number of nativist groups. Buchanan and Kim (2005) profiled twenty-one leaders of anti-immigrant groups and described evidence of overt racist behavior for many of them: One was a member of the Council of Conservative Citizens, a white pride group that opposes "race-mixing"; one had published numerous articles reflecting a white supremacist perspective;

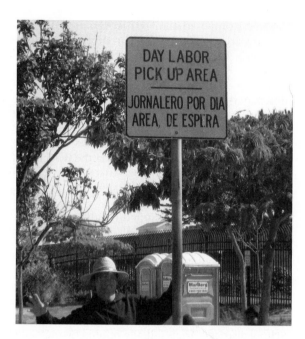

FIGURE 4.5

An immigrant waits to be hired at a day labor pickup site in Santa Barbara, California, an upscale oceanside community. Note the city posted sign sanctioning this site, and the portable toilets provided for day laborers who must wait here, sometimes for many hours, before being picked up for a job.

Kent Koppelman

the web site of another claimed that the Mexican government was plotting to take over the southwestern United States; and a group founded by one leader was identified as a hate group by the Southern Poverty Law Center, an organization that tracks activities of hate groups in the United States.

> We must get rid of fear; we cannot act at all till then. A man's acts are slavish, not true but specious, his very thoughts are false, he thinks as a slave and coward, till he have got fear under his feet.
>
> Thomas Carlyle (1795–1881)

Comments by many of these anti-immigrant leaders often reveal their prejudice, if not bigotry, especially toward illegal immigrants. Sherer (2005) quoted the leader of an Arizona anti-immigrant group who said that the United States "was being flooded with illegals, people that are substandard humans" (p. 57).

Certain talk show hosts on radio and cable television often echo the anti-immigrant sentiments disseminated by nativist groups, and there have been many instances where negative attitudes resulted in Latinos being victims of violence. In 2008, two white men from Brooklyn admitted attacking two brothers from Ecuador because they were Latinos, yet both were legal immigrants. One of the brothers died. In 2010, two Arkansas men rammed their pickup into a car carrying five Latino men, injuring all of them. In 2010, a white man in Arizona shot and killed his Latino neighbor after they argued about the state's controversial new immigration law; the victim was a third generation American. In 2011, a group of men attacked a Latino man at his home in Staten Island. They shouted anti-Mexican slurs and they took his money ($10) and beat him, shouting at him to "Go home" (Nelson & Steinback, 2011; Potok, 2011). The FBI has reported a 40% increase in hate crimes against Latinos from 2003 to 2007 (O'Grady, 2009), and in the most recent FBI report, almost 66% of all hate crimes were against Latinos, compared to less than 45% in 2003 (Huffington Post, 2011).

Anti-immigrant sentiments have been especially harsh toward undocumented workers, also referred to as illegal immigrants. Because of nativist rhetoric, many Americans assume that all undocumented workers entered the United States illegally, but at least 40% crossed the border legally with a visa, were hired for a job, and then remained after their visa expired (Levin & Rabrenovic, 2009). Employers often prefer to keep these workers, so they simply don't ask them if their visa has expired. Finding a job is the reason immigrants come to America, yet nativists have promoted a stereotype that illegal immigrants engage in a wide range of criminal activity, including violent crime. This stereotype has influenced American perceptions of legal as well as illegal immigrants, especially Latinos, and may have had an impact on those charged with enforcing immigration laws. A study of home raids by Immigration and Customs Enforcement (ICE) agents described "widespread misconduct" such as entering homes without permission, searching homes without warrants, and arresting people, including legal residents and citizens, based on an agent's perception of the person's limited proficiency in English (Nevins, 2010). Although legal residents and citizens have been arrested, in 2009, ICE reported over 33,000 undocumented workers held in detention facilities at a cost of $1.7 billion, yet the vast majority were nonviolent offenders. Crime statistics document that noncitizens living in the United States (both legal and illegal immigrants) are far less likely to be arrested for criminal activity than American citizens, and America's safest cities are those with large immigrant populations (Nevins, 2010).

Noncitizens have been increasingly incarcerated, and they now constitute one third of the federal prison population, in part because of an expansion of the criteria for deporting immigrants (Kretsedemas & Brotherton, 2008). Navarro (2011) found that deportations had nearly doubled in 2010 from what they were in 2005, and deportations often involve lasting harm to families. From 1998 to 2007, deportations separated more than a million individuals from their families, including children who were American citizens by birth. Many of these families were forced to accept the separation of a spouse or parent because keeping the family together required "uprooting their children from a community and lifestyle that is all (the children) have ever known" (Nevins, 2010, p. 187). In one case, shortly after a father was deported to Colombia, his 17-year-old son started his junior year in high school. The young man was so depressed over his father's absence that he committed suicide. When the father asked for permission to return simply to attend his son's funeral, the U.S. government denied his request (Nevins, 2010).

Despite the increased deportations, frustration among Americans continues to build because of the inability of the federal government to enact immigration reforms that address the problem of illegal immigration. Over 100 city governments debated proposals attempting to identify and arrest possible illegal immigrants, but a national study of immigration laws concluded that there was racial profiling in the enforcement of such laws, with people of Mexican descent being the primary targets (Kretsedemas, 2008). When the Arizona legislature debated a proposed immigration law, SB 1070, opponents argued that it would promote racial profiling; yet it became state law and similar bills were passed in Alabama and other states. Arizona's law made it a crime to be unable to produce immigration papers if police asked for them, and gave police the power to detain any person they believed might have entered the country illegally.

Arizona exceeded what other states have done when it also passed a bill outlawing the teaching of ethnic studies in schools. This Arizona law prohibited classes designed for a particular race or ethnic group, especially if the purpose was to promote ethnic solidarity. The State Superintendent of Schools, Tom Horne, defended the bill, arguing that such classes were racially segregated and fostered resentment toward white people (Cooper, 2010). In the Tucson School District, over half of the students are Latinos, and the district has developed a successful set of courses in Mexican American Studies, Native American Studies, and African American studies. School district officials initially refuted Horne's allegations, and the Director of the Mexican American Studies program claimed that enrollment in these classes had a positive effect on student academic achievement. In a statement released two days before Governor Brewer signed the bill into law, six human rights experts from the United Nations criticized the bill, advocating for the right of all people to learn about their cultural and linguistic heritage (Cooper, 2010).

In January of 2011, Arizona's new State Superintendent of Schools, John Huppenthal, ordered an audit of the ethnic studies courses at Tucson's Schools to ensure they were in compliance with the new ethnic studies law. In June, the audit report concluded that these courses did not violate the state law, went on to praise the academic success promoted by the ethnic studies program, and recommended that these courses be retained in the high school's core curriculum. Huppenthal ignored the audit and declared that the Tucson School District was in violation of the new state law and might lose $15 million of state funding. As students registered for classes for the fall 2011 semester, there were reports that the counselors assisting students were discouraging them from enrolling in ethnic studies classes, and that faculty teaching ethnic studies courses were being reassigned to teach other classes. Meanwhile, eleven

---

Spanglish?

Many commonly used words in American English are direct or slightly modified borrowings from the Spanish language. There are many place names that come from Spanish, including cities such as San Diego, Los Angeles, San Francisco, and Santa Fe, and states such as Arizona, California, Colorado, Florida, Montana, and Nevada. This list includes just a few of the many Spanish contributions to American English:

adios, adobe, amigo, bronco, burro, canyon, chili, cigar, coca, cola, coyote, guerrilla, hacienda, hombre, hurricane, lasso, loco, macho, mesquite, mosquito, padre, peon, pinto, plaza, poncho, ranch, rodeo, savvy, sombrero, vista

---

Tucson teachers have filed a lawsuit against the state, alleging that the ethnic studies law in unconstitutional (Bigger, 2011).

In response to such anti-immigrant hostility, Shorris (2001) argues that immigrants, especially illegal immigrants, make an important contribution to the U.S. economy by taking "the worst of jobs, the ugly work, the dangerous work, the backbreaking debilitating work, the jobs that even the jobless reject" (p. 272). Some of these jobs are extracting innards from slaughtered chickens on a conveyor belt; cultivating and harvesting mushrooms in damp caves; doing fieldwork as contract laborers (digging onions, picking beans, or harvesting other fruits and vegetables); skinning, gutting, and butchering animals at meatpacking plants; and working in manufacturing sweatshops for Third World wages. Despite complaints about illegal immigrants, it is not clear that Americans would be willing to pay the price, literally, if they were absent. (See Figure 4.4.) Scherer (2005) quotes one Arizona resident: "I don't want to pay five bucks for a can of string beans" (p. 56).

At the University of California, Los Angeles, the North American Integration and Development Center analyzed the work performed by 3 to 4 million undocumented workers in the United States. Their report stated that undocumented workers generated $154 billion toward America's gross domestic product, including $77 billion toward the state domestic product of California alone. Chavez (2009) cites a study reporting that 75% of illegal immigrants paid taxes, contributing $7 billion to Social Security and $1.5 billion to Medicare, and paying an indeterminate amount of money for sales taxes and other local taxes. Anti-immigrant leaders insist that illegal immigrants are receiving services such as welfare and health care that deplete limited resources of state and local governments. According to a University of California, Davis, study, however, the vast majority of undocumented workers do not enroll in government assistance programs because (1) they are not adequately fluent in English, (2) they are not aware of such programs, and (3) they are reluctant to ask for help for fear of being detained by authorities and deported (Ramos, 2002).

Another criticism directed at Spanish-speaking immigrants is that they aren't learning English fast enough and are changing American culture from Anglo to Spanish. Scherer (2005) quotes a Southern Californian arguing that where he lives has changed "literally overnight into a foreign country. The Fourth of July was not being celebrated but Cinco de Mayo was. All the billboards [were] in a foreign language" (p. 55). Although the Census Bureau reports that 78% of U.S. Latinos tend to speak in Spanish even if they can speak English, a study by HispanTelligence found that the number of Latinos fluent in both English and Spanish had increased to 63% (Grow, 2004). Ramos (2002) cites a University of Southern California research project reporting that 7 of 10 Latino children write and speak English fluently.

It is true that Latino children are more likely to maintain their native language than are other immigrant children, but that is consistent with past practices of immigrating groups. Germans, Italians, Norwegians, Chinese, Jews, and Japanese immigrants established schools, which children usually attend after public school, to maintain their native language and culture. It is also true that Latinos have changed U.S. society. It is easy to identify Latino influences on American music, entertainment, literature, business, scholarly activity, and even on the English language (see the box on page 85). Mexican cuisine can be found almost everywhere from fine restaurants to fast food; salsa recently surpassed ketchup as the most popular American condiment. Yet previous immigrant groups have also altered the culture by the influence of their native cuisine, language, and creativity. This does not mean that immigrants are not assimilating to American culture. Duke University professor Jacob Vigdon has proposed three different forms of assimilation: economic, cultural, and civic. *Economic assimilation* is measured by how quickly immigrants achieve middle class status; *cultural assimilation* is determined by how soon immigrants become fluent in English and begin to marry native-born partners; and *civic assimilation* relates to becoming naturalized, enlisting in the military, and being active in civic organizations. According to Vigdon's research, each form of assimilation develops independent of the others, and they are achieved in different ways among different ethnic groups (Ehrenhalt, 2009), and even as immigrants are becoming assimilated, they continue to make significant contributions to the American economy.

How do immigrants contribute to the American economy?

The anti-immigrant argument, directed primarily against Mexican Americans, is that they don't contribute to our economy but to the Mexican economy, because they tend to send much of their money home to families and relatives in Mexico. Ramos (2002) cites a study by the National Academy of Science finding that legal and illegal immigrants spend more than $10 billion each year within the U.S. economy. As they were becoming the largest minority group in the United States with almost 40 million people, Latinos' disposable income increased from 2001 to 2003 by about 30%, to a total of $652 billion (Grow, 2004). As this population continues to increase, so will their purchasing power, estimated to exceed $1 trillion by 2010. Latinos are currently about 13% of the U.S. population, and demographers predict that they will constitute 18% by 2030 and 22% by 2050 (Ramos, 2002).

Private sector businesses have started courting Latino consumers. Surveys report that Latinos tend to purchase high-quality brand-name products and maintain loyalty to those brands. Procter & Gamble spent $90 million in one year, 10% of its budget, on an advertising campaign targeting Latinos. Kroger Company, the nation's leading grocery store chain, spent almost $2 million creating a supermercado in a Houston neighborhood that had become 85% Latino. In addition, more Latinos are becoming entrepreneurs. According to the Internal Revenue Service, from 1988 to 2003, Latino entrepreneurs increased by 30% (Grow, 2004). Perhaps inspired by Cuban success, entrepreneurs from other Latino groups have discovered that their fluency in Spanish gives them an advantage in working with their counterparts in Central and South America. Despite this commercial success, most Americans still don't seem to appreciate the potential and immediate benefits of having a linguistically diverse citizenry.

The Value of Cultural and Linguistic Diversity

Cultural and linguistic diversity have evolved in human societies around the world, and each manifestation of a distinctive culture and language illustrates the complexity and richness of human creativity. Although human beings occupy the same planet, each language demonstrates how diverse groups interpreted and understood their world, and the differences between languages reveal that despite our similarities, human beings tend to see that world in distinctive ways. The four languages spoken by the most people in our global population are Mandarin Chinese (16%), English (8%), Spanish (5%), and Arabic (4%), but over 200 languages today are spoken by more than a million people (Skutnabb-Kangas, 2000). Taken together, these different worldviews provide a dynamic perspective on human beings accommodating to diverse environments.

Skutnabb-Kangas (2000) defines **linguistic diversity** as "the range of variation exhibited by human language" (p. 70), and she reports that there are between 6,500 and 10,000 languages throughout the world, as well as a number of different sign language systems. A more precise estimate is impossible because so many languages are disappearing. In the United States alone there used to be more than 300 indigenous languages, but only 175 still remain and many are becoming extinct. Linguists have identified 43 indigenous languages that are on the verge of extinction, and as for the rest, they are only confident that three indigenous languages will survive: Cree, Ojibway, and Inuktitut (Crawford, 2000). When 93-year-old Helen Sater died in a Canadian hospital in 1996, she was the last living person who was fluent in her native Tuscarora language (Skutnabb-Kangas, 2000). The Tuscarora were once part of the powerful alliance known as the Six Nations of the Iroquois Confederacy. With over 300 indigenous languages already present and with the arrival of people speaking diverse European languages, the history of North America should be regarded as an ongoing chronicle of communities that were multilingual as well as multicultural; yet Americans continue to be ambivalent about linguistic and cultural diversity. The reality of linguistic diversity in the United States today can best be appreciated by visiting our urban classrooms.

Do Americans support or oppose linguistic diversity?

According to Gort (2005), 25% of all K–12 students in the United States currently come from a home where a language other than English is spoken. Although more than three fourths of these students are Spanish-speaking, the following list includes other languages spoken by children in U.S. schools:

Southeast Asia: Hmong, Khmer, Lao, and Vietnamese
South Asia: Hindi, Punjabi, and Urdu
Asia: Cantonese, Japanese, Korean, Mandarin, and Russian
Europe: Armenian, French, Polish, Portuguese, and Serbo-Croatian
Other: Arabic, Haitian Creole, Tagalog, and Navajo

Continuing the pattern of using nationalistic justifications for nativist attitudes, some Americans argue that immigrants and their children should not be encouraged to maintain fluency in their native languages, but should instead focus on learning English and assimilating into American society. They often cite other countries such as Canada, the former Yugoslavia, India, or the former Soviet Union to illustrate their concern that social disruptions can occur when groups within a nation maintain their cultural and linguistic heritage, but as Baron (2000) has written, "where multilingualism has produced civil strife . . . (it) invariably occurs when minority-language rights are suppressed" (p. 451). Another argument against promoting bilingualism or multilingualism is based on the perception that it is normal for a nation's citizens to be monolingual, yet most individuals in the world today are either bilingual or multilingual. As Skutnabb-Kangas (2000) has noted, those of us who are monolingual are the abnormal ones.

A primary motivation for maintaining one's native language is to preserve one's sense of identity and ability to function within a linguistic community. The Latino parents that Villanueva (1997) interviewed were committed to helping their children become bilingual and bicultural so that the children could communicate with their grandparents and participate meaningfully in cultural celebrations in their community. In addition, an individual's identity is often grounded in his or her religious faith, and Skutnabb-Kangas (2000) has described the intimate relationship between language and religion. She reports that people who have learned to pray in their native language have established their sense of connection to their God in a way that often makes it difficult for them to pray in their second language. Despite these and many other reasons for maintaining one's native language, most immigrant families in the United States tend to learn English and eventually cease to be fluent in their native language.

Why do immigrant families tend to lose their native language?

In contrast to American fears concerning the failure of immigrants to learn English and assimilate into American culture, studies document a pattern of the loss of linguistic diversity in subsequent generations of immigrant families. In her review of this research, Gort (2005) concludes that fluency in the native language is usually lost by the third generation and cites some studies suggesting that the loss of language among U.S. immigrant families is accelerating rather than diminishing. Tse (2001) provides the following description to illustrate the typical pattern among immigrant families. Adult immigrants with or without children come to the United States and learn enough English to function in their daily lives while retaining fluency in their native language. They teach the native language to their children, but once these children begin attending K–12 schools, they learn English, speak English with their peers not only at school but in their community, and tend to prefer using English by the time they leave elementary school. When these children become adults and have children of their own, English is usually the only language spoken at home, resulting in grandchildren who are only able to talk to their grandparents in English.

Some Americans insist that this pattern does not accurately describe what is happening in the families of recent Latino immigrants, but Portes (2007) has reviewed studies of second generation Latino families in the United States reporting that 98% of the members of these families are fluent in English, whereas only 35% retain their fluency in Spanish. This loss of language is consistent across Western nations in which the dominant group (speaking English or French or German) demands that immigrants abandon their own language and heritage and adopt the language and cultural traditions of the dominant group. This can be most clearly seen in the education of immigrant children. After describing this form of assimilation that demands cultural and language conformity, Skutnabb-Kangas (2000) concludes: "This is the preferred Western strategy in the education of ethnic minority children. It amounts to linguistic genocide" (p. 174). Some educators in the United States and elsewhere have been sensitive to this issue and have advocated a different approach.

What alternative pedagogical strategy have American educators proposed?

American educators have advocated for bilingual education in an effort to preserve linguistic diversity in the United States; after some initial success, they have been losing ground over the past three decades. As part of the reform efforts of the 1960s, Congress overwhelmingly passed the Bilingual Education Act in 1968. To understand why bilingual education soon attracted critics, it is important to understand the rationale for the passage of this Act. The bill's chief sponsor offered the following argument to his Senate colleagues:

> It is not the purpose of this bill to create pockets of different languages throughout the country. It is the main purpose of the bill to bring millions of school children into the mainstream of American life and make them literate in the national language of the country in which they live: namely, English (Crawford, 2000, p. 88).

Ralph Yarborough (D-Texas) made this argument to convince his Senate colleagues that this bill would serve the needs of Mexican Americans like those in his district where adults with limited English skills were trying to find jobs while their children struggled to learn English. He portrayed the Bilingual Education Act as an anti-poverty program for a constituency he believed had largely been overlooked in other "Great Society" programs. This means that from the beginning, most politicians and Americans viewed bilingual education not as a way to achieve bilingualism but as a more effective means of encouraging assimilation. If students learned better by teaching them in Spanish, then some instruction could be delivered in Spanish so that students would not fall behind in their content learning. The assumption was that bilingual education was a transitional program that would temporarily maintain fluency in a native language until the student's English skills were sufficient to allow all of his or her instruction to be in English.

Many advocates for bilingual education disagreed with this interpretation, arguing that students had a right to maintain not only their native language but also their cultural heritage while they learned English and adapted to their new culture. These advocates were not opposed to assimilation, but they believed that it should be done in a more culturally pluralistic fashion. In the early 1970s, Massachusetts and several other states had to repeal their English Only laws to establish "transitional bilingual education," but these states and Americans across the country were disturbed when a nationwide study in the late 1970s reported that 86% of bilingual programs retained Spanish-speaking students after they had become fluent in English. This caused considerable consternation among those state and federal lawmakers who had believed that bilingual education programs would take a transitional approach (Crawford, 2000). In 1978, Congress voted to allow federal funds to be used only for "transitional" bilingual education programs. Lost in this controversy was another finding from the same study that half of all bilingual teachers were not proficient in the students' native languages, raising doubts about whether bilingual education programs could produce students who were genuinely fluent in their native language as well as English. In 1980, a report by the President's Commission on Foreign Language and International Studies encouraged advocates for bilingual education by stating: "The melting pot tradition that denigrates immigrants' maintenance of their skills to speak their native tongue still lingers, and unfortunately causes linguistic minorities (in the U.S.) to be ignored as a potential asset" (Tse, 2001, p. 51).

Even so, the nationwide study raised doubts that would continue to plague bilingual education programs, and early research did not diminish these doubts. Shorris (1992) described numerous conflicting studies that reported findings that were both supportive and critical of bilingual education. Increasingly, critics of bilingual education portrayed it as a language-maintenance program rather than as a way for children of immigrants to learn English and academic content more effectively. In the midst of this debate, the Reagan administration chose to promote and fund the implementation of English-only approaches to teaching students learning English as a second language (Crawford, 2000).

As the controversy continued, it became obvious that this was not simply an educational debate, but that there were social and political aspects as well. Advocates for bilingual education were interested in more than language learning; they argued for the value of teaching diverse "viewpoints, histories, sociopolitical realities and languages, and to promote the intrinsic worth of diversity in general" (Gort, 2005, p. 34). Opponents were adamant that such goals went beyond the original mandate of helping non-English-speaking students to learn English, and they also criticized bilingual programs for separating their students from students in the regular classes, isolating them from the kinds of interaction with their American peers that might enable their assimilation into American society. Critics of bilingual education were more successful in their efforts to persuade Americans that bilingual education programs were not working.

By the 1990s, many Americans perceived bilingual education as being more likely to promote students' maintenance of their native language and culture rather than their learning English and assimilating into American society, even though ongoing research began to make a stronger case for the efficacy of bilingual education programs. Salas (2006) cites a number of studies finding that students whose first language was not English achieved more academic progress in English when they also had instruction in their first language. Salas also referred to a review of research on bilingual education programs concluding that students in these programs "do as well as or better on standardized tests than students in comparison groups of English-learners in English-only programs" (p. 34). Still, the five million English language learners (ELLs) in K–12 public schools today are unlikely to be enrolled in bilingual programs because the federal Bilingual Education Act was not renewed in 2002, and, despite research supporting bilingual education, federal policies continue to emphasize English-only educational programs for ELLs.

Have research studies identified effective approaches to ELL instruction?

English-only programs have often involved a total immersion approach in which only English is spoken in the classroom, yet advocates for this approach can produce no credible studies to support it; instead, they usually offer anecdotal evidence. By contrast, there are numerous studies documenting the diverse outcomes achieved in bilingual education programs. Gort (2005) reviewed these studies and reported: ". . . a growing body of research points to the educational, social, and psychological benefits associated with educating bilingual learners in their native language as they develop skills in English" (p. 25). In 2006, the National Literacy Panel published its review of research on programs educating ELLs, and in that same year the Center for Research on Education, Diversity and Excellence published its review of these programs. Literacy expert Claude Goldenberg of Stanford University engaged in a meta-analysis of these two major reviews of literacy studies to determine what conclusions could be reached.

Goldenberg (2008) began by providing some demographic data: Of the five million ELLs in U.S. schools, 80% are Spanish-speaking. Approximately 60% of ELLs are receiving some form of English-only instruction. Test results reveal that ELLs tend to have low scores on measures of academic achievement, but there is no way of knowing if these low scores reflect poor content knowledge or the limitations of the students' proficiency in English because the tests taken by ELLs were in English. Although that question cannot be answered, Goldenberg (2008) reports that one of the major findings emerging from both studies was that "Teaching students to read in their first language promotes higher levels of reading achievement in English" (p. 14). Goldenberg also noted that this finding was consistent with four previous meta-analyses of research on ELLs. He emphasized the significance of this finding: "No other area in educational research with which I am familiar can claim five independent meta-analyses based on experimental studies, much less five that converge on the same finding" (p. 15). Further, both research reviews that Goldenberg analyzed reported that ELLs in bilingual education programs tended to develop sufficient literacy skills to be not only fluent in speaking two languages, but also fluent in reading and writing in both languages (i.e., not only bilingual but biliterate).

Why should educators be advocates for bilingual programs?

Tse (2001) suggests that American educators should refer to the report from the 1980 President's Commission on Foreign Language and International Studies, which stated: "Our vital interests are impaired by the fatuous notion that our competence in other languages is irrelevant" (p. 50). In addition, Gort (2005) argued that there is support for bilingual education in the No Child Left Behind Act of 2002 because it identified learning a foreign language as a "core academic subject" (p. 33). As the global economy becomes an increasingly important factor for our national economy, it is advantageous for the United States and any nation today to have citizens fluent in one or more languages other than their native language. There is evidence that this advantage has been apparent at the federal level for decades. Since 1946, when it was first established, the largest foreign language school in the United States has been the Defense Language Institute for military and government personnel.

Tse (2001) addresses the reason for establishing the Defense Language Institute in the first of her three arguments describing the advantages of increasing the number of bilingual or multilingual Americans. The first advantage is for diplomacy/security—having fluent speakers of the world's languages enables the United States to play a major role in global affairs and negotiate peaceful solutions to political conflicts. Bilingual Americans also strengthen our ability to gather credible intelligence with regard to issues affecting our national security. The second advantage is economic—because of globalization, businesses increasingly need employees who not only can speak another language, but also can understand the culture in which the language is spoken. Businesses that are able to navigate the linguistic and cultural terrain will be able to establish better relations with trading partners around the world. The third advantage is educational—promoting bilingualism in our children and youth will inevitably increase the numbers of college students majoring in a language, and that will likely result in increasing the numbers of bilingual students choosing to enroll in teacher training courses. For many years now, it has often been difficult for our K–12 schools to find teacher candidates who are both fluent in a language and have teaching certification.

For all of these reasons, educators who are advocates for bilingualism may be more successful today if they renew their efforts to implement bilingual education programs in our K–12 schools. There are also various forms of bilingual education approaches such as dual language (also known as two-way immersion) that have experienced great success with students and parents. Dual language programs pair ELLs with students who want to learn another language in the same classroom. A bilingual teacher may provide instruction in two languages and the students serve as resources for each other. In a program with Spanish-speaking students, the students learning Spanish use their ELL peers as language tutors, and ELLs use their partners to tutor them in English. The growing need in the United States and in the world for linguistic diversity and cultural competence should be a catalyst for a more pluralistic attitude toward diverse languages and cultures. If Americans develop greater respect for the linguistic and cultural diversity of immigrants to the United States, it could dispel some of the myths about immigrants that too many Americans still believe.

What myths about immigrants do many Americans believe?

Myths about "foreigners" who legally or illegally enter the United States have long fueled negative attitudes toward immigrants. Many Americans have expressed anti-immigrant sentiments openly, and immigrants and their children cannot help but hear them. As part of a longitudinal study, immigrant youth in high schools were asked what most Americans think about "people from my country"; 65% of their responses were negative—being stupid, lazy, thieves, and gangsters (Suarez-Orozco & Suarez-Orozco, 2001).

Although most myths about immigration refer to all immigrants, some refer specifically to immigrants with refugee status. According to the United Nations, a refugee is a person "unable or unwilling to return to his or her country because of a well-founded fear of persecution . . . based on race, religion, nationality, or membership in a particular social group or political party" (Pipher, 2002, p. 18). The myths highlighted in this chapter reveal current nativist attitudes about immigrants and refugees.

> **Myth #1:** Immigrants arrive ignorant, penniless, and with very little formal education and immediately have to go on welfare.

Macedo and Bartolomé (2001) record an example of this myth being expressed by a former president of Boston University complaining about the number of Cambodians in Massachusetts: "There has to be a welfare magnet going on here. . . . Why should Lowell be the Cambodian capital of America?" (p. 11). In fact, immigrants often have been professionals in their country of origin—doctors,

professors, and engineers. Although the figure varies each year, in 2007, 28% of U.S. immigrants had a college degree (Just the Facts, 2008). Still, even those arriving with college educations may take minimum wage jobs because institutions or professional organizations in the United States may not recognize their practices, skills, or degrees, forcing them to return to school to be certified in their profession or retrained in related fields. Despite obstacles of language and culture, the percentage of immigrants, including refugees, receiving welfare is approximately the same as native residents (Levinson, 2002). The statistics about modern immigrants to the United States document that they rarely become permanent recipients of public assistance.

Immigrants are consumers who pay rent and buy groceries and other products that help strengthen the economy. Most studies of the economic impact of immigrants report that they ultimately benefit local economies, even taking into account the services that may be required to assist them during their first few years in the country. With regard to undocumented immigrants, they are not eligible to receive most forms of public assistance beyond admitting their children to public schools or to the emergency room of a hospital, but they do pay taxes. The *New York Times* reported that illegal undocumented immigrants contribute approximately $7 billion each year to Social Security, and since they can never claim this money, it will be used to fund the benefits of other workers in the Social Security system (Scherr, 2008). Despite such contributions, many Americans express negative attitudes toward recent immigrants, especially the majority who are Spanish-speaking. Baron (2000) observes that some Americans appear to equate bilingualism with a lack of patriotism. Perhaps this was the basis for the animosity expressed by one caller to a Massachusetts radio talk show who referred to Spanish-speaking immigrants as "bilinguals" in a clearly derisive manner (Macedo & Bartolomé, 2001). It is ironic to see the ability to speak fluently in more than one language transformed into a racial slur.

> All the people like us are We. And everyone else is They.
>
> Rudyard Kipling (1865–1936)

> **Myth #2:** Immigrants cling to their culture, language, and traditions, and refuse to assimilate into the American "melting pot."

New immigrants have always maintained their cultural heritage, in part because their identity has been profoundly shaped by their native culture. When immigrant children become adults, they typically integrate their cultural heritage with American culture, producing a hybrid of traditions and values taken from both. As for learning English, it is not unusual to find that immigrants are multilingual when they arrive; often English is one of the languages they know.

Immigrants pay taxes, send children to schools, serve in the military, and are affected by local political decisions. Recent immigrants have demonstrated their desire to be actively engaged in our democratic society by participating in voter registration efforts and transporting voters to the polls for elections. Because the Constitution leaves the issue of voting qualifications up to the local government, some cities have responded by giving voting rights to immigrants who are not yet citizens. The assimilation of immigrants is further complicated by a backlog of those pursuing naturalization, a process that can take years if not decades before immigrants are granted legal permanent resident status, and the process has been delayed even further since the 9/11 tragedy (Wucker, 2003).

> **Myth #3:** The United States is taking more than its fair share of immigrants; other countries need to take more.

In many European countries, immigrants represent over 10% of the population. In Germany, this percentage is predicted to rise to 30% by 2030. The countries accepting more immigrants than the United States include Canada, Australia, Germany, and Switzerland (Ramos, 2002). The main difference between U.S. immigration and that of other countries is that more diverse groups are admitted to the United States than are accepted by other countries. Between 70% and 80% of immigrants around the world are refugees. The United States

accepts less than 1% of the refugees; several other countries admit a higher percentage. According to the 2000 Census, immigrants constituted 10% of the U.S. population, whereas in 1900, they constituted 15% (Passel & Edmonston, 1994; Pipher, 2002).

People who express concerns about excessive admission of immigrants to the United States often refer specifically to Mexicans, who constituted 25% of all legal immigrants in the 1990s, and an undetermined number of illegal immigrants. Current xenophobic attitudes have demanded restrictions on Mexican immigration and more money for border patrols to keep out illegal immigrants. Mexican immigration has not diminished, but increased border scrutiny has caused legal Mexican immigrants to stay in the United States rather than return home for fear they might not be allowed reentry: The number of those returning to Mexico plummeted in the 1990s. Although stricter border enforcement has not kept illegal immigrants from coming, it has resulted in three times as many deaths of those attempting to enter the United States (Massey, 2003).

> **Myth #4:** The main problem with U.S. immigration is the large number of illegal immigrants getting into the country.

Illegal immigrants make up 20% of the immigrant population and about 2% of the U.S. population. According to the U.S. Citizenship and Immigration Service, the number of illegal immigrants in the United States is relatively stable, increasing slightly since 1996 (USCIS, 2005). The popular image of illegal immigrants is that of Mexicans illegally crossing the border into the United States. In fact, over 41% of illegal immigrants in the United States entered legally, often recruited by employers, and only become illegal by remaining after their work visas expired.

The United States has a visa waiver program for residents of twenty-two selected countries, mostly in Western Europe, whose citizens can come to America for up to 90 days simply by purchasing a round-trip travel ticket. The Immigration and Naturalization Service (INS) reports that many people who come with such visas stay well beyond the 90-day limit, also becoming illegal aliens. According to the INS data, major abusers of the privilege come from France, Sweden, and Italy (Hernandez-Truyol, 1997). So why is it that only Mexicans are viewed as "illegals"? The stereotype of Mexicans sneaking across the U.S. border illustrates not only xenophobia, but racism.

Myth #5: Illegal immigrants are responsible for increased crime, disease, and terrorism in the United States.

This allegation appeared in a 34-page booklet on illegal immigration published by the American Legion and disseminated to its nearly three million members. It included the false assertion that illegal immigrants infected more than 7,000 Americans with leprosy, even though this myth had already been proven false through investigations by many sources, including the news program *60 Minutes* (Scherr, 2008). Further, the source for the claim that immigrants were bringing various diseases into the United States came from an article written by a lawyer with a history of anti-immigrant attitudes and no medical expertise. According to Scherr (2008), there is no medical research reporting an increase in the numbers of Americans with diseases stemming from the presence of immigrants.

Unlike the disease myth, the myth about immigrants engaging in criminal acts seemed to be supported by a *New York Times* article claiming that 21% of all crime in the United States was committed by undocumented workers; however, after the researcher making the claim was confronted with evidence of errors in his interpretation of the data, he corrected his calculations and reduced his estimate to 6.1% (Wilson, 2008). In addition, estimates of criminal behavior often come from data about people in prisons, and many immigrants are in prison for violating immigration laws, not for violent crimes. As Wilson (2008) reported, research on criminal activities over several decades has consistently concluded that: "Immigrants aren't a crime problem" (p. 21). Finally, with regard to the terrorism aspect of this myth, Scherr (2008) cites a 2005 study by the Nixon Center reporting that this allegation was patently false, concluding that ". . . not a single (terrorist) entered from Mexico" (p. 34).

Myth #6: Immigrants are taking jobs away from Americans.

For as long as there has been immigration, business owners have insisted and continue to insist that immigration is necessary to sustain U.S. economic growth. According to a Cato Institute study, immigrants do not increase joblessness, even in lowest-paid worker categories. A 2006 study found that states with large increases in immigration did not experience more unemployment for native-born workers (Scherr, 2008). Studies have also found that an influx of immigrant labor may create new jobs: One Los Angeles County study of a decade of immigration reported that Mexican immigrants created 78,000 new jobs (Cole, 1996). A 2005 study by the Kenan-Flagler Business School found that Hispanics accounted for 35% of the increase in the North Carolina workforce, and the increased number of Hispanic workers created 89,000 new jobs in the state (Wiggins, 2006).

As in the past, it is employers who are demanding immigrant labor for available jobs. In 1986, the U.S. government made it a crime for an employer to hire undocumented workers; now, many employers hire subcontractors to supply them with workers, thus placing the risk of arrest on the subcontractors for hiring undocumented workers. Unions have begun to accept the reality of immigrant labor and have been attempting to organize workers—especially laundry workers, janitors, hotel housekeepers, and waiters. These unions have become the main voice representing immigrant concerns (Massey, 2003).

A new and possibly growing problem may be the fault of businesses that urge opening immigration to more workers: the use of H1(b) visas and professional visas for entry into the United States. During the labor shortage of the 1990s, American companies increased their use of H1(b) visas to recruit qualified workers for vacant jobs, and there have been allegations of abuse concerning the use of these visas. Trade pacts signed by the Bush administration relaxed H1(b) rules to allow into the country additional thousands of workers from countries with whom the United States has free trade agreements. If this problem continues, immigration laws in the United States will likely be revised once again. Maintaining fairness in addressing the diversity and complexity of immigration issues in the American economy is an ongoing challenge, but the goal should be to provide opportunity to immigrants, no matter when they came to the United States.

AFTERWORD

This history of immigration demonstrates that there have been and still are diverse but clearly defined attitudes toward immigration on the part of American citizens, political leaders, and representatives of business and industry. Although entrenched workers sometimes resent the economic competition, our society has always benefited from the willing labor of immigrant workers. We have

> America, it would seem, is miraculously both singular and plural, organized and scattered, united and diffused.
>
> Henry Kariel (1924–)

also benefited from the cultural diversity represented by immigrants from so many different nations. Although some have complained that immigrants do not assimilate and have repeatedly insisted that immigrants should rid themselves of their old culture, history teaches us that there is no royal road for immigrants trying to adjust or adapt to a new culture; in reality, there are diverse pathways. Each immigrant may take a different route, but each will end at the same destination—becoming an American.

TERMS AND DEFINITIONS

Americanization The demand that immigrants to the United States reject their ethnic or cultural heritage and conform to American ways as defined by the dominant group

Anti-Semitism Having anti-Jewish prejudices or stereotypes, or engaging in discrimination against Jews

Assimilation A process whereby immigrants adopt cultural traits of the host country in order to be identified with that country and integrated into the immediate society

English Only A movement in various states demanding that legislatures make English the official language of the state, with the eventual goal of having the federal government make English the official language of the United States

Eugenics The study of agencies under social control that may improve or repair the racial qualities of future generations, either physically or mentally (Lynn, 2001)

Linguistic diversity The range of variation exhibited by human language (Skutnabb-Kangas, 2000)

Nativism An anti-immigrant ideology advocating the protection of "native" inhabitants of a country from new or potential immigrants who are viewed as threatening or dangerous (Feagin & Feagin, 1996)

Oppression When any entity (society, organization, group, or individual) intentionally or unintentionally distributes resources inequitably, refuses to share power, imposes ethnocentric culture, and/or maintains unresponsive and inflexible institutions toward another entity for its supposed benefit and rationalizes its actions by blaming or ignoring the victim (Andrzejewski, 1996)

Xenophobia Fear of or prejudice against people from other nations

DISCUSSION EXERCISES

Exercise #1 What I Know Is . . . What Do We Know about Hyphenated Americans?

Directions: In a society as diverse as that in many parts of the United States today, immigrant cultures are sometimes strongly demonstrated, as in those described here. After reading each item, explain what you know and how you tend to feel about the subcultural diversity illustrated within each category. If possible, explain what knowledge you have and/or the feelings you hold about those differences. Finally, attempt to explain any animosity or frustration that could result from experiencing those cultural differences.

1. Differences in social interaction:
   A. How loudly some racial or ethnic groups seem to talk in conversation.
   B. Direct eye contact between conversants is prohibited in some cultures.
   C. Some family sizes are large and seem to be happy living together, even in smaller spaces than actually needed.
   D. Physical contact in public between men and women is forbidden, and neither is walking together allowed.
2. Differences in dress:
   A. Women from a number of countries wear a traditional sari, many of them of exquisitely beautiful fabrics.
   B. The Sikh male turban is part of culture and religion.
   C. The burqua for Muslim women may be required by cultural and religious policy.
   D. Male Hasidic Jews wear black suits, hats, and payess (uncut sideburns).
3. Differences in cultural traditions:
   A. Preparing foods from many countries involves ingredients that are not familiar to many of us whose parents and grandparents have more thoroughly integrated customs and foods into a standard American fare.
   B. National celebrations such as Cinco de Mayo and Syttende Mai are often unknown to a majority of Americans, even though American

citizens with heritages from different countries work to keep their homeland traditions alive.
   C. The significant events of a culture can be observed through seasonal rituals, religious occasions, wedding ceremonies, and family activities and vary according to ethnicity, religion, and country, such as gathering for H'mong New Year and for funeral rites.

Exercise #2 The Immigration Letter to the Editor

Directions: This letter appeared in newspapers across the United States, each signed as if written locally. Discuss your understanding of its message, and then move to the Questions for Discussion. As you read, consider which of the four ethnic perspectives presented in this chapter is illustrated.

I am tired of this nation worrying about whether we are offending some individual or their culture. . . . I am not against immigration, nor do I hold a grudge against anyone who is seeking a better life by coming to America. Our population is almost entirely made up of descendants of immigrants. However, there are a few things that those who have recently come to our country, and apparently some born here, need to understand.

This idea of America being a multicultural community has served only to dilute our sovereignty and our national identity. As Americans, we have our own culture, our own society, our own language and our own lifestyle. This culture has been developed over centuries of struggles, trials, and victories by millions of men and women who have sought freedom.

We speak ENGLISH, not Spanish, Portuguese, Arabic, Chinese, Japanese, Russian or any other language. If you wish to become part of our society, learn the language! "In God We Trust" is our national motto. This is not some Christian, right wing, and political slogan. We adopted this motto because Christian men and women, based on Christian principles, founded this nation, and this is clearly documented. It is certainly appropriate to display it on the walls of our schools. If God offends you, then I suggest you consider another part of the world as your new home, because God is part of our culture.

We are happy with our culture and have no desire to change, and we really don't care how you did things where you came from. This is OUR COUNTRY, our land, and our lifestyle. Our First Amendment gives every citizen the right to express opinions and we will allow you every opportunity to do so. But once you are done complaining, whining, and griping about our pledge, our national motto, or our way of life, I highly encourage you to take advantage of one other great American freedom, THE RIGHT TO LEAVE.

God Bless America

Questions for Discussion

1. What do you think the writer means in saying that the view of America as a multicultural community "has served only to dilute our sovereignty and our national identity"?
2. Are large numbers of immigrants not learning English?
3. Should immigrants who are learning English be criticized for trying to maintain fluency in their native languages?
4. Are immigrants complaining about the use of "God" in the Pledge of Allegiance?
5. If "God is part of our culture," do you have to believe in God to be an American?
6. Who is intended to be included in the "We" of the last paragraph?
7. How could the letter be written to reflect any of the other ethnic perspectives?

REFERENCES

Andrzejewski, J. (1996). Definitions for understanding oppression and social justice. In J. Andrewski (Ed.), *Oppression and social justice: Critical frameworks* (5th ed., pp. 52–59). Needham, MA: Simon & Schuster.

Baron, D. (2000). English in a multicultural America. In K.E. Rosenblum & T.C. Travis (Eds.), *The meaning of difference: American constructions of race, sex and gender, social class, and sexual orientation* (pp. 445–451). Boston, MA: McGraw-Hill.

Barrett, J.R., & Roediger, D. (2002). How white people became white. In P. Rothenberg (Ed.), *White privilege: Essential readings on the other side of racism* (pp. 29–34). New York, NY: Worth.

Bigger, J. (2011, October 4). Arizona's dirty lessons: Is Tucson School District dismantling ethnic studies to appease Tea Party? Retrieved on October 4, 2011, from the *Huffington Post* at www.huffingtonpost .com/jeff-bigger/arizonas-dirty-lessons-is_b_921670.

Brands, H.W. (2000). *The first American: The life and times of Benjamin Franklin*. New York, NY: Doubleday.

Brodkin, K. (2002). How Jews became white folks. In P. Rothenberg (Ed.), *White privilege: Essential readings on the other side of racism* (pp. 35–48). New York, NY: Worth.

Buchanan, S., & Kim, T. (2005, Winter). The nativists. *Intelligence Report, 120,* 25–42.

Chavez, L. (2009). The realities of immigration. In W. Dvorak (Ed.) *Immigration in the United States* (pp. 40–49). New York, NY: The H. W. Wilson Company.

Cole, D. (1996). The new Know-Nothingism: Five myths about immigration. In J. Andrzejewski (Ed.), *Oppression and social justice: Critical frameworks* (5th ed., pp. 152–154). Needham, MA: Simon & Schuster.

Cooper, J.J. (2010, May 11). Arizona ethnic studies law signed by Governor Brewer, condemned by UN human rights experts. Retrieved on September 30, 2011, from *Huffington Post* at www.huffingtonpost .com/2010/05/12/arizona-ethnic-studies-la_n-572864.

Crawford, J. (2000). *At war with diversity: US language policy in an age of anxiety*. Clevedon, England: Multilingual Matters LTD.

Cubberley, E.P. (1919). *Public education in the United States*. Boston, MA: Houghton Mifflin.

Daniels, R. (2002). *Coming to America: A history of immigration and ethnicity in American life* (2nd ed.) New York, NY: Perennial (HarperCollins).

Davis, M. (2009, March/April). Editorial: Obama at Manassas. *New Left Review*, Vol. 56, pp. 5–40.

Delgado, R. (1997). Citizenship. In J.F. Perea (Ed.), *Immigrants out!: The new nativism and the anti-immigrant impulse in the United States* (pp. 318–323). New York, NY: New York University Press.

Eck, D.L. (2001). *A new religious America: How a "Christian Country" has become the world's most religiously diverse nation*. New York, NY: HarperCollins.

Ehrenhalt, A. (2009). Becoming us. In W. Dvorak (Ed.), *Immigration in the United States* (pp. 83–86). New York, NY: The H. W. Wilson Company.

Feagin, J. (1997). Old poison in new bottles: The deep roots of modern nativism. In J.F. Perea (Ed.), *Immigrants out!: The new nativism and the anti-immigrant impulse in the United States* (pp. 13–43). New York, NY: New York University Press.

Feagin, J., & Feagin, C. (1996). Basic concepts in the study of racial and ethnic relations. In *Racial and ethnic relations* (5th ed., pp. 6–26). Upper Saddle River, NJ: Prentice Hall.

Fuchs, L.H. (1990). *The American kaleidoscope: Race, ethnicity and the civic culture.* Hanover, NH: University Press of New England.

Goldenberg, C. (2008, Summer). Teaching English Language Learners. *American Educator, 32*(1), 8–23, 42–43.

Gort, M. (2005). Bilingual education: Good for U.S.? In T. Osborn (Ed.), *Language and cultural diversity in U.S. schools: Democratic principles in action* (pp. 25–37). Westport, CT: Praeger.

Grant, M. (1970). *The passing of the great race, or the racial basis of European history* (Rev. ed.). New York, NY: Arno Press. (Original work published 1916)

Grow, B. (2004, March 15). Is America ready? *Business Week,* pp. 58–70.

Henderson, T.J. (2011). *Beyond borders: A history of Mexican migration to the United States.* Chichester, U.K.: Wiley-Blackwell.

Hennesey, J. (1985). *American Catholics: A history of the Roman Catholic community in the United States.* New York, NY: Oxford University Press.

Hernandez-Truyol, B.E. (1997). Reconciling rights in collision: An international human rights strategy. In J.F. Perea (Ed.), *Immigrants out!: The new nativism and the anti-immigrant impulse in the United States* (pp. 254–276). New York, NY: New York University Press.

Herrnstein, R.J., & Murray, C. (1994). *The bell curve: Intelligence and class structure in American life.* New York, NY: Free Press.

Higham, J. (1955). *Strangers in the land: Patterns of American nativism, 1865–1925.* New Brunswick, NJ: Rutgers University Press.

Huffington Post. (2011). FBI hate crime statistics report finds higher percentages of anti-Latino hate crimes. Retrieved on Nov. 20, 2011, at www.huffingtonpost.com/2011/11/14.

Just the Facts. (2008, June). Immigrants and education. Retrieved on June 14, 2009, from the Public Policy Institute of California at www.ppic.org (Publications).

Kammen, M. (1972). *People of paradox: An inquiry concerning the origins of American civilization.* New York, NY: Vintage.

Kretsedemas, P. (2008). What does an undocumented immigrant look like?: Local enforcement and the new immigrant profiling. In D.C. Brotherton & P. Kretsedemas (Eds.), *Keeping out the other: A critical introduction to immigration enforcement today* (pp. 334–364). New York, NY: Columbia University Press.

Kretsedemas, P., & Brotherton, D.C. (2008). Open markets, militarized borders? In D.C. Brotherton & P. Kretsedemas (Eds.), *Keeping out the other: A critical introduction to immigration enforcement today* (pp. 1–25). New York, NY: Columbia University Press.

Levin, J., & Rabrenovic, G. (2009). Give us still your masses. In W. Dvorak (Ed.), *Immigration in the United States* (pp. 146–147). New York, NY: The H. W. Wilson Company.

Levinson, A. (2002). Immigrants and welfare use. Retrieved on May 15, 2009, from the Migration Policy Institute at www.migrationinformation.org/USFocus.

Lynn, R. (2001). *Eugenics: A reassessment.* Westport, CT: Prager.

Macedo, D., & Bartolomé, L.I. (2001). *Dancing with bigotry: Beyond the politics of tolerance.* New York, NY: Palgrave.

Massey, D.S. (2003). Closed-door policy. *American Prospect, 14*(7), 26–28.

Meacham J. (2009). Who are we now. In W. Dvorak (Ed.), *Immigration in the United States* (pp. 171–175). New York, NY: The H. W. Wilson Company.

Myers, G. (1960). *History of bigotry in the United States.* New York, NY: Capricorn.

Navarro, L. (2011, April). The melting pot. *The American Prospect, 22*(3), A18–A20.

Nelson, L., & Steinback, R. (2011, Fall). Undocumented immigrants targeted in propaganda, attacks. *Intelligence Report,* Issue 43, pp. 4–5.

Nevins, J. (2010). *Operation gatekeeper and beyond.* New York, NY: Routledge.

O'Grady, C. (2009, May). Hate speech, media activism and the first amendment. *Extra! 22*(5), 8–9.

Pabst, G. (2011, March 31). Report: Hispanic workforce growing. Retrieved on July 10, 2011, from the *Milwaukee Journal Sentinel* at www.jsonline.com/business/119034319.

Pai, Y., & Adler, S. (2006). Schooling as Americanization: 1600s–1970s. In *Cultural foundations of education* (4th ed., pp. 55–91). Upper Saddle River, NJ: Merrill Prentice Hall.

Passel, J., & Edmonston, B. (1994). Immigration and race: Recent trends in immigration to the U.S. In B. Edmonston & J. Passel (Eds.), *Immigration and ethnicity: The integration of America's newest arrivals* (pp. 31–71). Washington, DC: Urban Institute Press.

Pipher, M. (2002). *The middle of everywhere: The world's refugees come to our town.* New York, NY: Harcourt.

Portes, A. (2007, October). The fence to nowhere. *The American Prospect, 18*(10), 26–29.

Potok, M. (2011, Spring). Murder of Ecuadoran man dismissed with a shrug. *Intelligence Report*, Issue 141, pp. 10–11.

Ramos, J. (2002). *The other face of America.* New York, NY: Rayo.

Roberts, D. (1997). Who may give birth to citizens: Reproduction, eugenics, and immigration. In J.F. Perea (Ed.), *Immigrants out!: The new nativism and the anti-immigrant impulse in the United States* (pp. 205–219). New York, NY: New York University Press.

Salas, K.D. (2006). Defending bilingual education. *Rethinking Schools, 20*(3), 33–37.

Scherer, M. (2005). Scrimmage on the border. *Mother Jones, 30*(2), 50–57.

Scherr, S. (2008, Fall). Legionnaires' Disease. *Intelligence Report, 131*, 28–35.

Selden, S. (1999). *Inheriting shame: The story of eugenics and racism in America.* New York, NY: Teachers College Press.

Shorris, E. (2001). *Latinos: A biography of the people.* New York, NY: W.W. Norton.

Skutnabb-Kangas, T. (2000). *Linguistic genocide in education—or Worldwide diversity and human rights?* Mahwah, NJ: Lawrence Erlbaum Associates.

Steinbeck, J. (1966). *America and Americans.* New York, NY: Viking Press.

Stubblefield, A. (2007, Spring). "Beyond the pale": Tainted whiteness, cognitive disability, and eugenic sterilization. *Hypatia, 22*(2), 162–180.

Suarez-Orozco, C., & Suarez-Orozco, M. (2001). *Children of immigration.* Cambridge, MA: Harvard University Press.

Tatalovich, R. (1997). Official English as nativist backlash. In J.F. Perea (Ed.), *Immigrants out!: The new nativism and the anti-immigrant impulse in the United States* (pp. 78–102). New York, NY: New York University Press.

Tse, Lucy. (2001). *"Why Don't They Learn English?": Separating fact from fallacy in the U.S. language debate.* New York, NY: Teachers College Press.

United States Citizenship and Immigration Services (USCIS). (2005). Illegal Alien Resident Population. Retrieved July 5, 2006, from http://www.uscis.gov.

Villanueva, I. (1997). The voices of Chicano families: Life stories, maintaining bilingualism and cultural awareness. In M. Seller & L. Weis (Eds.), *Beyond Black and White: New faces and voices in U.S. schools* (pp. 61–79). Albany, NY: SUNY Press.

Whyte, W.F. (1955). *Street corner society: The social structure of an Italian slum.* Chicago, IL: The University of Chicago Press.

Wiggins, L.D.R. (2006). Will the immigration debate impact black employment? *The Crisis, 113*(3), 6–7.

Wiley, T.G. (2005). *Literacy and language diversity in the United States* (2nd ed.). Washington, DC, & McKinney, IL: Center for Applied Linguistics & Delta Systems.

Wilson, D.L. (2008, October). The illusion of immigrant criminality. *Extra! 21*(5), 21–22.

Wucker, M. (2003). Civics lessons from immigrants. *American Prospect, 14*(7), 45–46.

Chapter 5

Race and Oppression: The Experiences of People of Color in America

"Everyone likes to give as well as to receive. No one wishes only to receive all the time. We have taken much from your culture. I wish you had taken something from our culture for there were some good and beautiful things in it."

Chief Dan George (1899–1991)

The categorizing of human beings into racial groups has resulted in a history of racial oppression in America, beginning with the colonial period and continuing as rebellion against England created a new nation. Although all immigrants to the United States encountered obstacles and opposition, being perceived as white initially or eventually proved an enormous advantage. Whether they came voluntarily as immigrants or were brought involuntarily as slaves, people of color had to contend with blatant forms of oppression. Some of these experiences were similar for all groups, but other forms of oppression were unique to a particular group.

The quotation from Chief Dan George describes a problem for **indigenous people**, those who were established in the New World, in their encounter with European colonists. All immigrants of color would experience some version of this problem. Although perceived as different because of "race," the real difference that defined people of color was the different culture of each particular ethnic group. In rejecting them because of race, the majority also rejected the cultural gifts each group could have shared. The diversity created by people of color in the United States began with the American Indians, whose culture and knowledge were ignored first by the colonial settlers and later by the citizens of the new nation called the United States.

Native Americans

The Arawaks were one of more than 500 nations of indigenous people in the Americas when Columbus "discovered" a Caribbean island he called Hispaniola. Columbus created the pattern of oppression repeated by those who followed. After a brief period of peaceful relations, the Columbus party exploited the Arawaks and their natural resources. Columbus kidnapped a number of Arawaks to auction as slaves in Spain. When most of them died on the voyage back to Spain, Columbus looked for other ways to profit when he returned.

Columbus noticed gold jewelry worn by Arawaks, so he told them to bring him gold. They insisted that there was only a little gold on the island, but Columbus did not believe them. He demanded gold and warned them not to return without it. If any Arawaks came back empty-handed, Columbus had his men cut off their hands as punishment to intimidate the rest into complying (Zinn, 2003). By such brutal behavior, Columbus and his followers almost eradicated the Arawaks. Europeans eventually exterminated nearly half of the 500 nations of indigenous people in the Americas, and they very nearly eradicated the cultures of many of the nations that still remain today (Josephy, 2005).

What did Europeans learn from Native Americans?

English settlers in America tended to build on existing Indian settlements and walked on Indian paths, many of which eventually became the roads of the new nation. Benjamin Franklin studied the governance structure of the Iroquois League and borrowed heavily from it to create his "Albany Plan," the basis for the Articles of Confederation that was the first form of government implemented in the United States (Weatherford, 1988). Even though he borrowed ideas from the Iroquois League, Franklin's prejudice against Indians appears in a letter to James Parker:

> It would be a very strange Thing, if six Nations of ignorant Savages should be capable of forming a Scheme for such an Union and be able to execute it in such a Manner, as that it has subsisted for Ages, and appears indissoluble; and yet that a like Union should be impracticable for ten or a Dozen English Colonies, to whom it is more necessary. (Le May, 1987, p. 444)

Unlike Franklin, most colonists did not care to learn from Indians. Their ethnocentric goal was to establish the culture and traditions of their own European heritage in America. **Ethnocentrism** is the belief that one's own race, nation, or culture is superior to all others, as illustrated by colonial choices for settlement names. Dutch settlers called their town New Amsterdam until the English captured it and renamed it New York. Many settlements were named without even adding the term *new*, which can be seen by comparing city names on current maps of New England states with city names on maps of England. Williams (1954) described an example of ethnocentrism when English colonists called a bird a robin because it reminded them of an English robin. We still call this bird a robin today, but it's not an English robin, nor is it related to the English robin.

What did European settlers fail to learn from Native Americans?

If Europeans had been willing to listen, they could have learned much from Native Americans. The following five areas provide a few examples.

Foods and medicines. European settlers did not want to eat food initially unfamiliar to them such as potatoes, peanuts, corn, squash, tomatoes, peppers, and pumpkins. Later, these foods came to be exported around the world and had a major influence

> God teaches the birds to make nests, yet the nests of all birds are not alike.
>
> Duwamish Proverb

within countless nations. As Weatherford (1988) wrote, "It is difficult to imagine what Ireland would be today without the potato" (p. 64). Similarly, it is difficult to imagine what Italian food was like before the American tomato became part of its cuisine.

What's in a Name

Although the term *Native American* has become widely used, there is still not a consensus among native peoples about the generic term they prefer. Popular author Sherman Alexei is adamantly against the term, preferring to be called an American Indian. Some prefer to be called "indigenous people"; others are content with the traditional label of "Indian."

In this chapter, all of the terms are used to reflect this diversity of preferences. The only consensus among all of the indigenous people is their preference to be identified by their tribal affiliation such as Hopi, Apache, Sioux, Mohican, Kwakiutl, or Inuit. In conversations with individual American Indians, one would do well to follow Beverley Tatum's advice—ask the individual what his or her preference is, then use that term.

Europeans did not try to learn the indigenous people's knowledge of medicinal properties of plants. (See Figure 5.1.) For example, scurvy is a disease resulting from vitamin C deficiency, causing bleeding gums and fatigue; it often afflicted people voyaging on ships because fruit didn't last long at sea. Native Americans knew how to cure scurvy long before Europeans found a cure by noticing that German sailors on boats stocked with sauerkraut did not tend to get this illness (Weatherford, 1988). Suzuki and Knudtson (1992) estimate that 75% of prescription drugs derived from plants were discovered based on clues stemming from the healing practices of the indigenous peoples of the world. According to Harvard botanist Richard Schultes, every time a shaman dies, "it is as if a library had burned down" (Gell-Mann, 1994, p. 339).

Hygiene.   According to Spring (2001), European descriptions of Indians as "filthy savages" had nothing to do with hygiene but with their "seemingly unrepressed sexuality" (p. 10). American Indians practiced frequent bathing while Europeans did not. Europeans believed that exposing one's body to the air could cause colds and other health problems. Christian church leaders also disapproved of public bathing, fearing that nude people mingling in a public bath might inspire lust. Instead, throughout Europe, many, including the aristocracy, would dry-rub themselves with sand, ashes, or pumice stone. For the rich or royal, perfume disguised body odor. According to Smith (2001), England's Queen Elizabeth I took a bath once a month, and Spain's Queen Isabella proudly claimed that she had only taken two baths in her life: when she was born and when she was married. No wonder perfume was so expensive and so highly valued!

Governance and gender equality.   In 1642, Virginians met with a Cherokee delegation led by Cherokee leader Outacite to negotiate for a peaceful resolution of their recent conflicts. As he approached the colonial delegation, Outacite asked why he saw no women. Hearing that the colonists had brought no women, Outacite returned to his people saying he could not negotiate because the colonists did not have half of their people. Perdue (1998) also described a 1757 meeting of the South Carolina Governor's Council to which the noted Cherokee leader Attakullakulla had been invited. His first comment was to ask why no women were on the council. If Indian women owned property, it remained in their control regardless of marital

---

FIGURE 5.1 Kickapoo Sagwa Bottle

The use of Indian images on medicine bottles in the 1800s suggests that Americans were aware that Indians understood the medicinal value of plants. Instead of acquiring that knowledge, entrepreneurs created concoctions (usually including alcohol), put an image of an Indian on the bottle, and sold the bogus medicine to naive customers.

> Take only what you need and leave the land as you found it.
>
> Arapaho Proverb

status (White, 2001). Indian women belonging to the Iroquois League did not serve on the governing tribal council, but they selected the men who served (Woodward, 1988).

Childcare.   Europeans might also have benefited from learning childcare practices from American Indians. Children of European immigrants, like children in Europe, were expected to work on domestic chores at an early age. If they misbehaved, they were punished severely with beatings and whippings to teach them obedience to parental authority, just as parents had to be obedient to their superiors. Children were rarely shown overt affection and were allowed little freedom. By contrast, European observers of American Indian societies were surprised by the amount of freedom given to Indian boys and girls. Young children were not expected to assist their parents with farming, hunting, or household tasks. There were few restrictions on their activities as they became intimately familiar with their surroundings. Instead of punishing with straps or rods, Indian children were scolded and made to feel a sense of shame about misbehaving. The parents' goal was to promote a sense of personal pride and an independent, courageous spirit. They believed that threats and physical punishment would cause children to become passive and fearful (Mintz, 2004). European children who were captured and raised by Indians were called "white Indians." Even if offered a chance to return to their families, many of these children refused to leave. When "white Indian" children were returned to colonial society, most preferred to return to their Indian families. Benjamin Franklin addressed this phenomenon in 1753 (Mintz, 2004):

> When white persons of either sex have been taken prisoners young by the Indians, and lived awhile among them, tho' ransomed by their Friends, and treated with all imaginable tenderness to prevail with them to stay among the English, yet in a Short time they become disgusted with our manner of life . . . and take the first good Opportunity of escaping again into the woods, from whence there is no reclaiming them. (p. 8)

Ecology.   Native Americans have expressed the belief that human beings share a spiritual kinship with the natural world and are obligated to live in harmony with it. Suzuki and Knudtson (1992) cite a declaration by the Iroquois Confederacy deploring the destruction of forests by entrepreneurs, the depletion of wildlife by sports hunters and pesticides, the pollution of the air by factories, the pollution of water and poisoning of fish by industry and agribusiness, and the depositing of toxic wastes in chemical dumps across the country. The Iroquois declaration calls on people to preserve life around us, to "carry out our function as caretakers of the land" (pp. 240–241).

What relationships did colonists have with native people?

Instead of learning lessons from Native Americans, colonists practiced lessons already learned about conflict, conquest, and survival. Europeans usually began by being friendly toward Indians until they no longer needed them. For example, colonists at an early Connecticut settlement had good relations with the Pequot and Narragansett Indians until Fort Saybrook was built and stocked with munitions. The Pequots and Narragansetts did not understand why the fort was built. They had helped the settlers and signed treaties with them. Fortunes changed, however, when Narragansetts killed a colonist, John Oldham, in revenge for an unnamed outrage, probably holding him responsible for the outbreak of smallpox that took the lives of 700 of their people. With military might sufficient to ensure victory and Oldham's death as an excuse, General John Endecott was sent to Fort Saybrook to attack not only Narragansetts but also innocent Pequots. After initial skirmishes, some Pequots met with Lieutenant Lion Gardiner to determine if they could resume peaceful relations, but Gardiner was not willing to stop fighting. Having heard of Dutch brutality, the Pequots asked Gardiner if it was true that Europeans did not just kill warriors, but women and children. They expected him to deny such a harsh accusation; Gardiner replied, "they should see that hereafter" (Jennings, 1976, p. 212). They understood his meaning and returned to tell their people of this threat from their formerly friendly neighbors.

What was the main source of conflict between Europeans and Indians?

The primary contention between European colonists and Indians was about land ownership. In school, children are often taught that Columbus planted Spain's flag in the New World to claim the land for Spain, implying that Spanish and Indian representatives would resolve the competing claims either by negotiating a treaty or by warfare. Engaging in war based on claims to land was common in European history. Nations gained or lost inhabited land through conquest because only uninhabited land could be claimed, a principle identified as *vacuum domicilium* (Berkhofer, 2004).

Even in 1492, international law recognized the rights of indigenous people to own the land where they lived. Explorers were given charters to allow them to claim land under the legal principle of *terra nullius*, an ambiguous term suggesting lands without people, but interpreted as including land inhabited by a people not possessing religions and customs equal to that of Europeans.

When Columbus planted the Spanish flag, he was establishing the legal right for Spain to possess uninhabited land or to purchase the land if indigenous people had a legitimate claim to it. But most legal claims for land inhabited by Native Americans were not made under the principle of *vacuum domicilium* because natives made it clear that the land where they lived belonged to them collectively, and they belonged to the land. To resolve the ambiguity of making a *terra nullius* claim, European nations wanting to take possession of Indian land created a new concept called *occupatio bellica*, referring to peaceful seizure of land underutilized by the indigenous people. Although indigenous people might not agree with what was viewed as "underutilized," the principle allowed Europeans to take possession of land by peaceful means, such as by

> They made many promises, so many I can't remember, but they only kept one. They promised to take our land, and they took it.
>
> Red Cloud (1822–1909)

erecting crosses throughout the land marked with the royal seal or by bribing a few indigenous individuals to sign an agreement conceding the land.

Nomads were the exception. Defined as "pastoral people" wandering on the land and never staying in one place, **nomads** were not granted legal claim to land. In making land claims, colonists described indigenous people as "nomadic" because they would move their villages every few years because of soil depletion and decreasing crop productivity. After many years at another site, they might move again, eventually returning to a site abandoned decades before where the soil would now be replenished (Berkhofer, 2004). Such a pattern does not fit the definition of nomadic. Although Plains Indians, such as the Sioux or Cheyenne, were

nomadic and followed historic migratory patterns, most indigenous people lived in villages. If villagers resisted encroachment on their land, the result was often armed conflict ending with a treaty mandating the loss of land and Indian resettlement.

Why are Indian treaties still important today?

A **treaty** is a legal document negotiated between two (or more) sovereign nations involving terms of peace, trade, and other matters. Indian treaties document the cession of Indian lands to the U.S. government that were then made available for settlement. Land was also confiscated for resources. As described in Gedicks (1993), historian David Wrone has calculated that 19.5 million acres of land taken from just one indigenous group, the Chippewa, resulted in the United States gaining significant wealth. Besides taking possession of the land, the resources from the land included "100 billion board feet of timber; 150 billion tons of iron ore; 13.5 billion pounds of copper" (p. 51). Other resources taken from Indian land included water, ports, fish, fowl, and game, all contributing to a profitable tourism industry that has yielded considerable wealth to members of the dominant society who gained access as a result of treaties.

A treaty signed by an Indian nation and the United States was an agreement between sovereign nations. Treaties were written with provisions to be maintained in perpetuity, yet the U.S. government has violated virtually every treaty made with indigenous peoples, often during the lifetimes of those who signed the treaty (Josephy, 2005; Wilson, 1998). Yet treaties continue to be important documents because they affirm the status of Indian Sovereignty. Deloria (2001) described **Indian Sovereignty** as a principle affirming the legal right of Indian nations to define themselves on their own terms and to behave as unique cultural and legal entities.

Why were Native American treaties consistently violated?

When Indian treaties were signed, the land designated for indigenous people was often regarded as expendable; yet if the land became desirable, Indians were forced to surrender it. When settlers migrated to Wisconsin, Winnebago Indians were removed to Nebraska and Kansas. Many refused to leave and hid from authorities; others left but eventually returned (Bieder, 1995). As colonists and settlers demanded land, treaties with Indian nations were renegotiated, often forcefully.

The Cherokee possessed legal deeds to Georgia land where they had built homes and businesses. When ordered to go to Oklahoma territory, they took their case to the U.S. Supreme Court, which ruled in their favor; however, President Andrew Jackson refused to enforce the ruling. In 1838, he ordered federal troops to march the Cherokee to Oklahoma, a journey now called the Trail of Tears because of numerous deaths that occurred on the way (Wallace, 1993).

Because of treaties, several Indian nations were forced to occupy Oklahoma territory until white demands for cheap land led the United States to renegotiate the treaties, restricting Indians in Oklahoma to the least desirable land and allowing settlers to claim the rest. Americans had little interest in Indian land in Oklahoma—until oil was discovered. The treaty was renegotiated. Similarly, an 1868 Treaty of Fort Laramie declared that the Sioux would permanently retain lands sacred to them in the Black Hills—until gold was discovered. The treaty was renegotiated (Josephy, 2005; Wilson, 1998). This pattern has continued.

Many treaties signed over a century ago relegated Indians to small reservations but affirmed their right to hunt and fish on tribal lands beyond reservation boundaries. For native people, being able to hunt and fish on former tribal land was a critical concession that may have seemed an innocuous benefit to the other side when the treaty was signed. As hunting and fishing became profitable tourism activities, complaints that the treaties should be abrogated or renegotiated have increased. People promoting outdoor recreational activities have protested Indian hunting and fishing privileges, even though the treaties guarantee them. Indigenous people have responded by insisting on maintaining the treaties and respecting their rights as sovereign nations.

What are other contemporary issues affecting indigenous people?

Many schoolchildren are not taught about the multiplicity of Indian cultures that existed in early

America. The diversity among the more than 500 Indian nations encompassed political governance, economic structures, and cultural patterns. For example, diversity was apparent in Indian homes: the long houses of Northeastern woodland Indians such as the Wampanoag, the Pawnee earth homes later copied by Midwest pioneers as sod houses, the grass houses of the Wichita, the adobe houses of the Navajo, and the log houses of the Kwakiutl and other Northwestern Indians. Ask American children about Indian homes, and they will likely say Indians lived in "tepees." Instead of educating youth about Indian diversity, teachers have tended to promote a stereotype based on the Plains Indians, which is reinforced by the use of Indian mascots.

Many Native Americans and tribal councils have spoken out against Indian logos and mascots for sports teams, saying they are racist and offensive (Connolly, 2000). They have asked schools and colleges displaying such images to discontinue this practice. (See Figure 5.2.) Most sports fans say they don't see what is so offensive, insisting that mascots are meant to honor and show respect for Native Americans. But how can we "honor" a people in a manner that they find objectionable? We argue that Indian mascots honor a proud, fighting spirit; meanwhile we criticize or ignore Indians who proudly fight to eliminate the use of Indian mascots.

The response of non-Indians to Indian mascots illustrates how contemporary Indians are perceived. According to Berkhofer (2004), Americans tend to hold one of the following two images of Indians: the noble savages who lived long ago and were exterminated, or contemporary Indians who have lost their culture and been degraded by white

> All wars are civil wars because all men are brothers. . . . Each one owes infinitely more to the human race than to the particular country in which he was born.
>
> Francois Fenelon (1651–1715)

people's ways. Many school textbooks reinforce the former by presenting information about Native Americans only up to the nineteenth century;

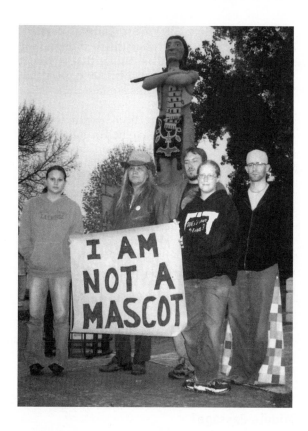

FIGURE 5.2

Photo courtesy of the author.

twentieth-century Indians don't appear at all. Students are left to assume that Native Americans lived long ago and then ceased to exist, except perhaps for a few living on reservations (Hawkins, 2005). Critics of American education charge that children and youth are not regularly taught about Indians living in urban areas or about current issues such as resistance by reservation Indians to the use of their land as sites for dumping toxic wastes or for other forms of environmental exploitation (Hendry, 2003).

One of the few facts about contemporary Indians that seems to be widely known is that they operate casinos, even though less than 1% of the total Native American population makes substantial revenue from gambling profits. If a state sanctions gambling activity, then by federal law it is legal for Native Americans living on reservations in that state to have gambling facilities. Although American Indians have been criticized for operating casinos, profits often have been employed to purchase land, build or improve schools, offer academic scholarships, support job-training programs, create jobs, and fund an array of projects intended to improve opportunities for Indian people and to perpetuate their culture.

Despite the financial gains from casinos on a few reservations, many living on reservations still confront consequences of their forced assimilation into the dominant society, including extremely high unemployment rates, low school completion rates, widespread domestic abuse, and considerable alcoholism. Tribal elders have witnessed the deterioration of cultural traditions and ancient beliefs, and they fear the survival of their people is in jeopardy. Despite the need for economic resources on reservations, many American Indians oppose corporate enterprises that have identified resources on reservation land and subsequently tried to purchase mineral or water rights (Gedicks, 1993; Matthiessen, 1993).

Legal action is a critical part of the ongoing struggle between indigenous people and the U.S. government. A recent class action suit accuses the Department of the Interior of mismanaging Indian lands and funds, denying Indian tribes an estimated $176 billion. The judge has delivered several rulings in favor of the Indian tribes. According to Whitty (2005), the U.S. government is continuing to appeal the case using resources at its disposal including "35 of the country's most expensive private law firms" (p. 58). This largest class action suit ever filed may eventually provide Native Americans with needed economic resources.

African Americans

The first Africans in the New World came not as slaves but as soldiers and explorers. Although we do not have individual names, records indicate that Africans came with Cortez and Pizarro in the early 1500s, that 30 Africans sailed with Balboa, and that 200 accompanied Alvarado to Quito. The names of a few black adventurers have survived. In the early sixteenth century, Estevanico (from Morocco) explored the American Southwest, preparing the way for later Spanish conquest.

In the late eighteenth century, Jean Baptist Point du Sable (from Haiti) came with French explorers and founded a permanent trading post in a settlement called Chicago (Painter, 2005).

The first Africans in the American colonies arrived in 1619. A Dutch ship traded twenty Africans to Jamestown settlers for food and water (Reiss, 1997). The seventeen men and three women were not slaves but indentured servants, able to gain their freedom after specified years of servitude. During the seventeenth century, 75% of American colonists came as servants, many of them indentured servants (Takaki, 1993), but Zinn (2003) argues that English colonists regarded African indentured servants as inferior to white servants and treated them accordingly.

How were the black indentured servants treated differently?

A few Africans were able to earn their freedom, and some had to resort to courts to free them from unwilling owners, but most were never free. A few free blacks bought property, even including slaves, but by the mid-1800s, the colonies were establishing different rules for white and black servants. Based on assumptions of black inferiority, Africans were often forced to accept permanent servitude status. A 1662 Virginia statute decreed that children born to a woman who was a permanent indentured servant must take her status (Reiss, 1997). Not surprisingly, 70% of Africans in Virginia at this time were permanent indentured servants (Takaki, 1993).

As southern agriculture gravitated toward large plantations for the export of crops, the use of slaves became increasingly attractive. Indian workers knew the region and easily escaped, and white indentured servants escaped and passed as free whites. Blacks could be easily identified, captured, and returned to their owners. Because England was already invested in the slave trade, exporting Africans to America was simply an expansion of an existing business. From the late 1500s to the early 1800s, more than 10 million Africans were brought to America.

Where and how did the British procure Africans?

In the sixteenth century, European traders had marveled at West African civilizations in Mali,

Timbuctu, and Ghana. By the seventeenth century, British merchants had established strong trade relations in West Africa, including the export of slaves (Smedley, 2007). Spivey (2003) says that 90% of all African Americans are descended from West African ancestors.

Historically, slaves have been victims of conquest. African slaves tended to be prisoners of war, and some were sentenced to slavery for crime or debt, but the removal of 15 to 18 million Africans to America, as Franklin and Moss (2000) have stated, was "one of the most far-reaching and drastic social revolutions in the annals of history" (p. 49).

> Until lions have their historians, tales of the hunt will always glorify the hunter.
>
> African proverb

Not all Africans sent to the New World arrived; a third are believed to have died during what is called the **Middle Passage**.

Why did so many Africans die during the Middle Passage?

Conditions on slave ships were horrendous. According to Reiss (1997), a full-grown man was allotted a space 6 feet long and 18 inches wide in the hold. Women and children were given even less. There was no room to sit up. Slaves were chained together and packed into the hold in a "spoon" position to maintain maximum space. Reiss quoted Lord Palmerston, "They had less room than a corpse in a coffin" (p. 34).

Enroute, slaves were fed twice a day and given buckets to relieve themselves; the buckets were seldom emptied and frequently overflowed. Many were unable to get to the buckets and soiled themselves where they lay. Not surprisingly, disease was a major cause of death, including typhoid, smallpox, yellow fever, and malaria (Painter, 2005).

Because bodies of the dead were tossed overboard, sharks routinely accompanied slave ships. As slaves were brought up on deck during the day, some took the opportunity to escape by leaping into the shark-infested waters. Scholars estimate that from 5 to 6 million Africans died during Middle

Passage, and some who survived the voyage were left permanently disabled (Reiss, 1997). As bad as conditions were on slave ships, slavery was even more brutal.

What was it like to be a slave?

Although slavery existed throughout all the colonies, it never led to the economic advantage in the North that it did on southern plantations where work was backbreaking and punishments severe. Working days were as long as 18 hours during harvest, with brief rest periods to eat. Overseers punished those who didn't appear to be working hard enough, usually by whipping. Other tasks included clearing land for planting, chopping wood, digging drains, or improving roads. At night, seven or eight slaves might be crowded into dirt-floor one-room cabins. Women worked with men, performed domestic chores, and often suffered sexual assault from masters and overseers. As former slave Harriet Jacobs (1861/1987) said, "Slavery is terrible for men, but it is far more terrible for women" (p. 77). But slavery enriched slave owners. A British visitor once asked future president James Madison how much profit he made from slaves. Madison replied that he only had to spend $12 to $13 annually for one slave who could produce almost $260 of profit each year (Zinn, 2003). Despite these huge profits, many people opposed slavery.

How did Africans resist the oppression of slavery?

African captives engaged in a range of activities in their resistance to slavery. Some cut off their toes or mutilated themselves in other ways so they would be less useful workers for their masters. In addition, some slaves murdered their masters; many slave owners lived in fear of being poisoned by their slave servants (Franklin & Moss, 2005). Some slaves learned to read and write either by tricking their masters into teaching them or by converting to Christianity and persuading their master to give them the literacy skills needed to read the Bible (Cornelius, 2000). They perceived competent literacy skills to be a useful tool to assist themselves and other slaves, as well as an important asset if they managed to escape from slavery.

When slaves converted to Christianity, their owners tried to use aspects of the faith to manipulate them into being more docile and obedient, but slaves usually resisted. For example, although white owners exhorted slaves to obey the commandment against stealing, slaves continued to steal. They justified their thefts by regarding their owners as hypocrites with no moral authority on this issue: White people were responsible for stealing Africans from their homeland and their families, and slave owners continued the offense by maintaining possession of this stolen property. The captive Africans also rejected many "moral" precepts emphasized by white ministers. Raboteau (2000) described a service for slave converts in which a white clergyman used a passage from the Apostle Paul in a sermon condemning slaves who ran away. During the sermon, the clergyman reported that, "one half of my audience deliberately rose up and walked off" (p. 31).

Why did blacks fight on the American side during the Revolutionary War?

When the war began, George Washington and his aides agreed that the Continental Army would not recruit blacks. Alexander Hamilton warned that if they did not, the British would (Chernow, 2004). In November 1775, Washington issued his policy against recruiting blacks, and British supporters quickly recruited slaves by promising emancipation for military service. Washington issued a new policy in December, permitting free blacks to serve in the Continental Army. Meanwhile, colonial militias were already recruiting slaves as well as free blacks. According to Franklin and Moss (2000), 5,000 of the 300,000 colonial troops were Africans, primarily free blacks from northern colonies. The bravery of black soldiers refuted the pervasive stereotypes, but their achievements were betrayed when the U.S. Constitution was drafted.

How did the U.S. Constitution address the issue of slavery?

Although slaves represented 20% of all Americans at this time, the word *slave* does not appear in the Constitution of the United States (Painter, 2005); instead, it refers to "unfree persons." Article II, section 9, states that "importation of such persons as any of the States now-existing shall think proper to admit, shall not be prohibited by Congress prior to the year 1808." In other words, in deference to southern plantation owners and businesses, the new nation had agreed to ignore the slave trade for twenty years; however, taxes were to be collected on imported slaves. Even northern states that had abolished slavery profited from the continued importation of slaves.

Another issue in drafting the Constitution concerned the question of whether slaves should count in determining political representation. With 300,000 slaves representing 40% of its population, Virginia wanted slaves counted, as did North and South Carolina with over 100,000 slaves in each state (Painter, 2005). The constitutional compromise was to count each slave as three fifths of a person, giving significant political power to southern states: Ten of the first fifteen American presidents were slaveholders. Nevertheless, anti-slavery organizations became increasingly influential.

Who opposed slavery and what did they do?

In 1775, Quakers organized the first anti-slavery society in Philadelphia; ten years later another was formed in New York. Anti-slavery societies soon formed throughout New England (Chernow, 2004). In 1777, Vermont abolished slavery in its state constitution, and in 1783, New Hampshire and Massachusetts did the same. In two decades, all northern states had abolished slavery or legislated a timeline for its extinction. Some organizations lobbied to end the slave trade and others wanted to deport slaves, but all agreed on the principle of abolishing slavery. When the twenty-year constitutional hiatus ended in 1808, anti-slavery groups successfully lobbied Congress to pass a law that prohibited importation of slaves to the United States. The law was primarily a moral victory because the American coast was too long and the U.S. Navy too small to stop the smuggling of slaves.

Africans, enslaved or free, adamantly opposed slavery. Thousands of slaves ran away and many successfully escaped. Former slaves Harriet Jacobs and Frederick Douglass gave speeches and wrote books denouncing slavery. In addition, between 1750 and 1860, there were an estimated 250 slave rebellions, each involving ten or more slaves (Zinn, 2003), and numerous smaller rebellions. In February of 1831,

a solar eclipse inspired perhaps the best-known rebellion. Nat Turner interpreted the eclipse as an omen, and six months later he led a slave rebellion that began with the killing of Turner's owner and family, and went on to result in the deaths of 60 other slave owners before the slaves were overpowered by federal troops (Franklin & Moss, 2005).

As early as the 1770s, free blacks petitioned colonial legislatures to emancipate slaves. Using the words of revolutionary leaders, they challenged whites to live up to their ideals of democracy and equality by making them a reality for all (Painter, 2005). The original draft of the Declaration of Independence denounced slavery as an "execrable" practice, but the Continental Congress deleted that particular passage at the insistence of southern slaveholders. Even the participation of blacks in the Revolutionary War did not resolve conflicting opinions about slavery. As the new nation began, slaves continued to oppose slavery, either through slave rebellions or by using the Underground Railroad to escape from slavery.

What was the Underground Railroad?

Named in the 1800s because of the popularity of steam railroads, the **Underground Railroad** existed as early as the late 1700s as a network of people helping slaves escape. Franklin and Moss (2000) quote a 1786 letter from George Washington complaining that one of his slaves escaped and went to Philadelphia where "a society of Quakers, formed for such purposes, have attempted to liberate (him)" (p. 205). By 1804, this informal network had become more organized and had established "stations" 10 to 20 miles apart for runaways to rest and eat after traveling all night. The organization eventually included over 3,000 people of all races (Painter, 2005). They had to be careful because helping slaves escape was a criminal activity, violating federal fugitive slave laws that compelled the return of any runaway slave.

Some slaves had a "conductor" to help them escape; one of the best known was Harriet Tubman, who made 19 trips and freed over 300 slaves. Plantation owners offered $40,000 to anyone who caught her, but they never did (Painter, 2005). Although it is impossible to determine how many slaves escaped using the Underground Railroad, one southern governor estimated that from 1810 to

1850 the South had lost 100,000 slaves worth $30 million (Franklin & Moss, 2000). Still, all enslaved Africans in America would not gain their freedom until the end of the Civil War.

Did slaves and free blacks fight for the Union during the Civil War?

Slaves supported the North during the Civil War by disrupting southern productivity. Many refused to work even though they were severely punished; others engaged in subversive tactics such as supplying information to approaching Union troops. When Union soldiers came near a plantation, slaves would abandon it. Early Union victories in western states liberated slaves, but the federal government had not allocated resources to assist them. In northern cities, relief societies formed to raise money for food, clothing, and shelter and provided some education and job training for newly freed blacks.

When the war began, free blacks offered to enlist, but once again they were rejected. Few people believed the conflict would last long, but when it did, the need for more soldiers intensified. In September of 1862, the **Emancipation Proclamation** freed blacks in rebellious states, but slave owners in Delaware and Kentucky kept slaves until the 13th Amendment was ratified. Issued in January 1863, the final version of the Emancipation Proclamation allowed free blacks to enlist in the army. Over 200,000 blacks enlisted. By August, 14 black regiments were trained and ready for service, with 20 more regiments in preparation (Franklin & Moss, 2000).

Black soldiers protested the Congressional Enlistment Act that established lower compensation for them. Two black regiments from Massachusetts refused their wages rather than be paid less than white soldiers. When the Massachusetts legislature offered them money to make up for the difference, the black soldiers refused that offer. They were fighting for the Union, and they insisted that the Union pay them fairly. In 1865, the War Department finally approved equal pay for black and white soldiers (Painter, 2005), even though it came too late for the 38,000 black soldiers who had died. For those who survived the war, the next task was to create a new society in the South that would include a significant number of free blacks.

Did blacks play a role in shaping the new South?

Black males (but not females) could vote and run for office, and sixteen were elected to the U.S. House of Representatives. There was one black governor (Louisiana), six black lieutenant governors, and over 600 blacks were elected to state legislatures and participated in drafting new state constitutions (Goldstone, 2011). In response, angry southern whites formed secret societies such as the Knights of the Ku Klux Klan to bribe or intimidate blacks and ostracize those whites who seemed to support the developing new social order. Many racist groups began to use violence to reestablish white supremacy in the South, usually engaging in activities at night.

Blacks who registered to vote were harassed; some were forced to leave their communities and some were lynched. In 1871, blacks elected to the South Carolina legislature were given fifteen days to resign. State laws prohibited such harassment, but even Union troops stationed throughout the South were ineffective to stop it. The U.S. Congress passed laws giving the president broad powers to punish anyone interfering with a citizen trying to vote. Hundreds were imprisoned, but violence persisted.

Throughout the 1870s, the Democratic Party, led by white southerners, elected majorities to state legislatures. Congress no longer required federal troops at all southern polling places during elections. By 1877 when President Harrison withdrew federal troops, efforts to re-establish white power accelerated. During the last two decades of the nineteenth century, the U.S. Supreme Court enacted rulings sanctioning Southern legislation that

> The basic race hatred in the United States is a matter of the educated and distinguished leaders of white civilization.
>
> W. E. B. Du Bois (1868–1963)

prevented blacks from voting, removed them from jury rolls, maintained their segregated schools, and required racial segregation in public transportation and public facilities (Goldstone, 2011). With these

Supreme Court decisions, the transformation to the "Jim Crow" South with complete racial segregation was concluded.

How did black citizens in the South respond to this transformation?

Southern blacks did not accept the threats and harassment passively, yet without support from the federal government or northern organizations, they did not have the resources to combat white supremacists. They regarded education as the best way to acquire resources and power on their own, but with minimal state funding for schools, educational opportunities were limited. As late as the 1890s, southern states supported segregated private schools, spending an average of less than $2 annually per student in public schools compared to the $20 per student provided in northern states (Lewis, 1993).

In 1881, Booker T. Washington came to Tuskegee Institute and created an educational approach that appealed to whites and many blacks. Washington wanted blacks to carve out a niche in the southern economy, and he knew that white people could accept black people doing agricultural, domestic, and factory work. Washington cultivated good relations with local leaders by having his students provide food and services to the community, and he promoted his school as a model for black education in the South. Eventually Washington attracted interest and funding from northern whites, many of whom were industrialists who wanted a better trained workforce in the South.

At the Atlanta Cotton Exposition of 1895, Washington declared that he believed black people would be willing to accept social inequality in exchange for economic opportunity. White politicians, business leaders, and the press claimed that Washington spoke for black Americans, but some blacks, notably W. E. B. Du Bois, believed black Americans deserved more.

What did Du Bois want for black Americans?

Based on his own experience as the first black graduate from Harvard, Du Bois felt that blacks could demonstrate academic ability if given an opportunity. Du Bois rejected the idea that social inequality for blacks was acceptable under any conditions. He supported vocational training for black students, but not for those who demonstrated academic ability. Du Bois's approach was overt and confrontational. Although Washington worked within the status quo, secretly donating money in support of legal efforts opposing racial segregation, Du Bois challenged the status quo, publicly denouncing all racial discrimination, as in the following statement (Lewis, 1993):

> Such discrimination is morally wrong, politically dangerous, and industrially wasteful and socially silly. It is the duty of whites to stop it, and to do so primarily for their own sakes. (p. 208)

In 1910, Du Bois helped found the **National Association for the Advancement of Colored People (NAACP)** and for twenty-five years he served as editor of its main publication, *The Crisis*. For eighteen years he hosted a conference on race problems at Atlanta University, and he helped found the American Negro Academy for black intellectuals. Throughout his life, Du Bois attacked racism and promoted racial equality in his research, reports, essays, and even fiction (Lewis, 2000).

What were black Americans doing to cope with race problems?

In the late 1800s, southern blacks began to migrate to northern cities, driven by economic need and persistent violence in the South, especially lynching. (See Figure 5.3.) For more than thirty years, Ida Wells-Barnett took a public stand against lynching, ignoring many death threats. In 1914, *The Crisis* published the names of 2,732 blacks lynched between 1885 and 1914, and the NAACP challenged Congress to pass anti-lynching laws (Lewis, 1993). According to Feagin and Feagin (2008), at least half of all lynchings were not recorded, so the total number is estimated to be over 6,000. The House of Representatives passed anti-lynching bills in 1922, 1937, and 1940, but southern senators blocked them. It was not until June 2005 that the Senate finally took a stand, voting to issue a public apology for its failure to pass an anti-lynching law.

Southern migration to the north was not dramatic until the twentieth century. According to Feagan and Feagin (2008), 90% of all black Americans still lived in the South in 1900. Migration

FIGURE 5.3

Cartoonist Albert Smith illustrated "The Reason" for blacks to migrate north in the 1920s.

what was going to happen—America was going on the greatest, gaudiest spree in history" (2005, p. 188). Prohibition drove drinking into the shadows of speakeasies. Jack Dempsey drew the first million-dollar gate in boxing. Babe Ruth became the highest paid baseball player in history. And in New York City, black people began a cultural and literary development called the *Harlem Renaissance*.

What was the Harlem Renaissance?

Whites came to Harlem in the 1920s to enjoy the clubs, the dancing, and the jazz, creating an open community where people from all races would dance to Duke Ellington at the Cotton Club or listen to Louis Armstrong at the Savoy. As Americans enjoyed a variety of new music, new dances, new artists, and new writers, Harlem contributed the novels of Jean Toomer, the poetry of Langston Hughes, and the creative works of many others who expressed the uniqueness of the black experience in America. Although it was a racially segregated community, Harlem was home to diverse black peoples including newly arrived southern blacks, Africans, and West Indians. Spivey (2003)

> Had it not been for our art and our culture, when all else was ripped from us, we would never have been able to survive as a people.
>
> Harry Belafonte (1927–)

increased significantly between 1914 and 1918 when World War I created labor shortages because so few Europeans immigrated. By the time the war ended, a million southern blacks had moved to northern cities. In addition, over 360,000 out of more than 2 million registered blacks served in World War I, and many returning southern black soldiers settled in northern cities (Franklin & Moss, 2000). In 1900, Chicago had 30,000 blacks; by 1920, it had over 109,000. By 1930, 2 million southern blacks had migrated to northern cities (Takaki, 1993).

As Americans welcomed war heroes from World War I, buried the dead, and cared for maimed and suffering veterans, they were ready for a new era. As F. Scott Fitzgerald said, "The uncertainties of 1919 were over—there seemed little doubt about

notes that this mix of people produced a new kind of black individual, quoting Alain Locke's description of how this "New Negro" emerged: "Each group has come with its own separate motives and its own special ends . . . but their greatest experience has been the finding of one another" (p. 165).

Was there a decrease in discrimination against blacks after World War I?

Many African Americans were upset that the U.S. military did not recognize the achievements of black soldiers during World War I. For more than six months, the black first battalion of the 369th infantry endured continuous fire while fighting in France. The French awarded the Croix de Guerre to the battalion, but the U.S. Army did not invite the first battalion (or any black units) to Paris for the victory parade in August 1918 (Lewis, 1993). Many black mothers received Gold Stars symbolizing the loss of a son, but when the French government invited American Gold Star mothers to France to honor them, the Army only paid for the white mothers. Black mothers who attended had to pay their own way (Painter, 2005).

The 1920s saw the rebirth of the Ku Klux Klan, reaching a peak of 5 million members in 1925. In 1921, a white mob in Tulsa, Oklahoma, set fire to all of the buildings in the black community and burned them to the ground. In 1923, whites also destroyed the black community of Rosewood, Florida. It is not surprising that the NAACP experienced dramatic growth at this time, expanding from 50 chapters to more than 500 between the two world wars (Woodward, 1966).

The 1920s were not "good times" for American farmers, especially black farmers in the South because two thirds of them did not own their own land (Painter, 2005). During the Great Depression, black farmers suffered even more than white farmers, with many being ejected from their land. As for black workers in northern cities, over twenty-six unions did not accept black members in 1930, and black unemployment was three to four times higher than that of whites (Feagin & Feagin, 2008).

In October 1933, 18% of blacks were receiving government assistance ("relief") compared to 10% for whites, and relief programs often provided black families less than than the amount given to whites (Takaki, 1993). In urban areas, some civic and religious organizations refused to serve black people in their soup kitchens. The best hope for black people seemed to be the nominee of the Democratic Party, Franklin Delano Roosevelt, but many black Republicans were still loyal to "the party of Lincoln." The "New Deal" would eventually convert most into Democrats.

Did the New Deal programs help black Americans?

Millions of black people benefited from New Deal programs, yet millions of others did not. The Social Security Act provided financial security for older Americans and the Fair Labor Standards Act established a minimum wage, but both excluded agricultural and domestic work—jobs largely held by blacks (Lui, 2004). Black union leader A. Philip Randolph threatened to organize a march on Washington until President Roosevelt issued Executive Order 8802 banning racial discrimination in defense industries and creating a Federal Employment Practice Commission. He was criticized, however, for appointing a white Mississippian to head the commission (Lewis, 2000).

Despite the president's mixed record, blacks appreciated the social activism of Eleanor Roosevelt and her close relationship with black activist Mary McLeod Bethune. In 1936, while heading the Division of Negro Affairs, Bethune helped create the Federal Council on Negro Affairs, an advisory group to the president consisting of thirty black professionals. Media soon referred to them as FDR's **Black Cabinet**. FDR appointed blacks to serve in the Federal Housing Authority, Department of the Interior, and other federal agencies; during this time black Americans increasingly changed their allegiance to the Democratic Party, but their participation in the nation's economic recovery was not meaningful until World War II began.

What gains did black Americans make during World War II?

With so many men enlisting in the military, including more than a million who were black, jobs were available for black men and women, especially in defense industries. Blacks in the military were selected for programs that had not been permitted before, such as the engineer corps, pilot training, and officer training. For the first time in its history, the Marine Corps recruited African Americans. When

> There is nothing quite so effective as a refusal to cooperate economically with the forces and institutions which perpetuate evil in our communities.
>
> Martin Luther King, Jr. (1929–1968)

the Navy restricted blacks to mess hall duties, they protested, and within a year they were given general assignments and included in officer training programs (Franklin & Moss, 2000). In 1948, President

Truman issued Executive Order 9981, officially de-segregating the U.S. Armed Forces.

What happened to African Americans after the war?

Americans seemed to regard the defeat of Nazi Germany as a victory over Nazi beliefs of racial superiority. By the war's end, half of the major unions had accepted black members (Feagin & Feagin, 2008). In business and industry however, the percentage of black men and women laid off during the postwar period was considerably higher than that for whites, suggesting a possible return to "business as usual" attitudes with regard to racial discrimination.

As the United Nations was being formed, W. E. B. Du Bois objected to its lack of representation for "750 million people, a third of mankind, [who] live in colonies" (Lewis, 2000, p. 504). People of color were engaged in a global struggle to free themselves from European domination. In 1947, Mahatma Gandhi's success in gaining India's independence from Britain encouraged African Americans who demanded their rights as citizens of the United States. Court cases involving transportation and education ruled against racial segregation, and in 1954, the **Brown v. Board of Education** decision overturned decades of legal discrimination based on race. It was a victory more in principle than in practice as segregation in America persisted; nevertheless, in the context of these national and global events, the civil rights movement was born, and Americans were challenged to recognize their prejudices and stereotypes. (See Figure 5.4.)

With more black people demanding their rights as American citizens, the response from southerners became more violent. In August 1955, a 14-year-old black youth from Chicago came to Mississippi to visit relatives. After Emmett Till showed a group of black friends a picture of a white girl he knew in Chicago, one of the boys dared him to go into the nearby store and talk to the white woman working there. After buying candy in the store, Emmett turned before leaving and said, "Bye, Baby." The woman's husband was out of town, but soon returned. It was shortly after midnight when he and two friends came to the home of Mose Wright where Till was staying and dragged the boy out of bed. They brutally murdered him and threw his body in the Tallahatchie River. When his corpse

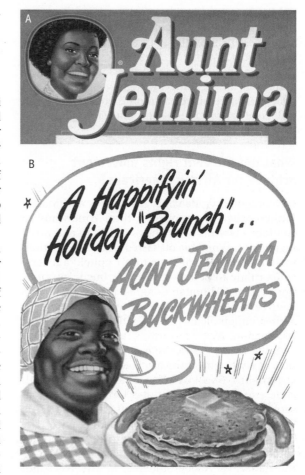

FIGURE 5.4

Despite the commercial advantage of maintaining a familiar face on one's product, Quaker Oats felt that the old image (B) of Aunt Jemima was too much of a stereotype and updated her image in the 1960s (A).

was found three days later, it was so badly mutilated that Mose Wright could only identify the boy by a ring on Emmett's finger (Williams, 1987).

Emmett's mother demanded an open casket at his funeral so that mourners could see what had been done to her son. Americans were shocked and revolted by the photographs of the boy's mangled face that appeared in newspapers across the nation. The three men responsible were arrested and brought to trial. Despite the courageous testimony of Mose Wright, who identified the accused men as the ones who took Emmett Till from his house, the all-white jury acquitted all three men of kidnapping and murder. People of all races across the nation expressed outrage at the violence and the injustice, and the civil rights movement grew in number and increased in resources as more people rose up to challenge racist attitudes and practices in America (Williams, 1987).

What did the civil rights movement achieve for African Americans?

In Montgomery, Alabama, Rosa Parks and Martin Luther King, Jr., inspired African Americans to conduct a boycott of city bus services to end racial segregation. The boycott lasted over a year; then in 1957, the U.S. Supreme Court upheld a federal court ruling to desegregate public bus transportation systems. Although Congress passed civil rights laws in 1957 and 1960, they were ineffective in addressing problems of segregation and racial discrimination.

In February 1960, as a practical demonstration of civil rights, four black college freshmen in Greensboro, North Carolina, entered a Woolworth store and deliberately sat at a lunch counter that served only whites. When refused service, the black students opened their textbooks and read. They eventually left, but they returned, and other students came with them. The idea spread across the nation as 70,000 students, mostly black but some white, staged more than 800 sit-ins in over 100 southern cities. As more than 4,000 students

were arrested, whites stayed away from lunch counters, and many would not shop in stores where sit-ins were occurring. The economic losses forced many businesses to begin offering services to blacks (Lomax, 1963).

Although Martin Luther King, Jr., encouraged nonviolent tactics, younger, radical black leaders encouraged black Americans to return violence for violence. The passionate oratory of Malcolm X may have predisposed some whites to be more comfortable listening to the peaceful rhetoric of change expressed by King and his followers. Even after Malcolm X ended his association with the extremist Nation of Islam to pursue a more authentic Islamic faith, he still insisted that black people should demand the same rights that white Americans enjoyed—not just civil rights but their human rights (Malcolm X, 2000):

> When you expand the civil-rights struggle to the level of human rights, you can then take the case of the black man in this country before the nation in the U.N.... You can take Uncle Sam before a world court.... Civil rights keeps you in his pocket. Civil rights means you're asking Uncle Sam to treat you right. Human rights are something you were born with. Human rights are your God-given rights. (p. 596)

Another militant voice came from the Black Panther Party founded in 1966 by Huey Newton and Bobby Seale. The Black Panthers attracted black youth, especially in urban areas. Despite the Panthers' sponsoring community service activities such as a free breakfast program for black children, they were viewed by white authorities as a paramilitary

A History of Medical Exploitation

Going back to the days of slavery, African Americans were subjected to painful medical experimentation. For example, Dr. James Sims performed numerous surgeries (without anesthesia) on slave women so that he could write a paper in 1852 about his perfected gynecological procedure, earning him the title of the "father of American gynecology." After the Civil War, physicians subjected black people, without their consent, to experimental surgeries and other medical procedures to learn from their mistakes prior to attempting the same procedures with white patients. In the 1930s, doctors at the

Tuskegee Institute lied to their control group of black men suffering from syphilis and gave them only aspirins, iron tonic, and vitamins instead of providing treatment so that they could observe the effects of syphilis as it progressed. When this scandal was finally revealed, causing President Clinton to issue a formal apology in 1997, it was the first time that such medical exploitation was publicly acknowledged. It also confirmed the suspicions of many African Americans that the medical establishment was more likely to view them as guinea pigs for research purposes rather than patients needing care.

In the twentieth century, African Americans have been subjected to experiments with radiation treatments without having the risks fully explained. Black men incarcerated in prisons have been infected with diseases so medical researchers could investigate the effect of untested, often toxic drugs. In the 1950s and 1960s, the CIA's MK-ULTRA project involved the release of disease-carrying mosquitoes into black communities in Florida and Georgia so that government scientists could assess if this was an effective tool for biological warfare. When African Americans go to health care facilities, they are less likely to receive aggressive treatment for serious health care problems, which is viewed as a contributing factor in higher mortality rates for blacks from heart attacks, liver disease, and cancer. Life expectancy for African Americans is nearly six years less than white Americans, and their deaths are often attributed to "common ailments that are more often prevented and treated among whites" (p. 3).

**From: *Medical Apartheid* (2006)
Harriet A. Washington**

organization. The FBI Counterintelligence program targeted its leaders for surveillance, and Panther members were subjected to police raids. Newton's 1967 arrest and imprisonment on murder charges weakened the Panthers, as did the violent assaults on party members that left 28 dead (Carson & Carson, 2000). By the mid-1970s, most of the Panther leaders either had been expelled from or had voluntarily left the organization.

Throughout the 1960s, the South was the primary scene for marches, protests, and demonstrations. In 1963 alone, the Department of Justice recorded over 1,400 events in three months (Zinn, 2003). As usual, the white response was immediate and violent, but this time some of the violence was recorded by a national press and witnessed by a national audience. The images of law enforcement officers using dogs, fire hoses, and clubs to assault unarmed black people left many white viewers appalled, yet even more violence took place. Mississippi civil rights leader Medgar Evers was shot and killed on his front porch. Four black children were killed by a secretly planted bomb in the basement of their Birmingham church, and Martin Luther King, Jr., was assassinated in Memphis.

Being white did not protect protestors from southern wrath. When Freedom Riders rode integrated buses to test southern compliance with desegregation laws, mobs attacked the buses, assaulting whites and blacks as local law enforcement and the FBI observed the violence but did nothing (Zinn, 2003). In Mississippi, authorities found the bodies of three young civil rights workers who had been murdered. During a Selma-to-Montgomery march in Alabama, a white minister was beaten to death, and a white housewife transporting marchers to Selma was shot and killed (Painter, 2005).

Amid this turmoil, Congress passed the Civil Rights Act of 1964 and the Voting Rights Act of 1965, forbidding discrimination in public accommodations, federally assisted programs, public facilities, education, and voting. In 1952, 20% of eligible southern blacks were registered to vote, but because of this legislation, 40% of eligible southern black voters were registered in 1964, and by 1968, 60% of blacks were registered, the same percentage as for whites (Zinn, 2003). Although some problems in the South were being addressed, the 1960s race riots in urban areas demonstrated that racial problems also existed in northern cities. The Kerner Commission's investigation of this outbreak of urban violence concluded that the major cause of the riots was the persistence of white racism. Naming the problem did not solve it, and discrimination against African Americans in the United States has persisted and continues to contradict our American ideals.

Asian Americans

The first Asian immigrants to the United States were from four villages in the Canton province of China. Arriving in 1850, they set the Chinese pattern of predominantly male migration to America with a ratio of 10 men for every 1 woman (Lowe, 2000). Chinese immigrants tended to be young and married, and were lured to California by the thought of finding gold and returning to China. San Francisco welcomed the new arrivals by inviting them to participate in California's statehood ceremonies, but by 1870, 63,000 Chinese immigrants had arrived, with more than 75% in California, representing 25% of the state's workforce (Fong, 2000). Chinese immigrants quickly became the targets of nativist sentiments expressed in slogans such as "California for Americans."

What actions did nativists initially take against the Chinese in America?

Nativists lobbied the California legislature for a tax on non-U.S. citizens who were mining for gold (Takaki, 1993). Although the tax penalized any immigrant, the passage of the "foreign miners" act was a major setback for the Chinese. Most had borrowed money and were expected to repay their debts on arriving in America. In addition to paying for their passage, they were expected to send money home to support their wives and families, and two thirds of them managed to earn enough money to take care of their financial obligations and return to China (Glenn & Yap, 2000). Because of the 1790 law restricting U.S. citizenship to

"whites only," there was little incentive to remain in the United States.

Why didn't Chinese men bring their wives and families?

In places like Singapore and Hawaii, Chinese men who chose to remain either married local women or sent for their wives, but neither option was possible in America. California law forbade interracial marriage, and entrepreneurs imported Chinese women to work as prostitutes. In 1870, the California legislature passed the Page Law to stop the immigration of Chinese prostitutes, but this resulted in the exclusion of almost all Chinese women. By 1890, the ratio of Chinese men to women was 26 to 1 (Fong, 2000).

Who employed Chinese immigrants?

Unable to mine for gold, many Chinese men found work as laborers on the western portion of the transcontinental railroad. Railroad owners paid the Chinese less than other workers and forced them to work during the winter of 1866, despite snowdrifts as high as 60 feet. They had to tunnel under the snow, digging shafts to allow for air so they could work. After that winter, Chinese workers went on strike for higher wages, only to be denounced by local newspapers and literally starved into submission when railroad owners cut off food supplies (Takaki, 1993). After the railroad was completed, most Chinese laborers returned to China, but some chose to stay, particularly in the area of San Francisco.

Wherever they settled, Chinese men continued to be paid low wages. In addition to agricultural jobs, they worked in factories or were employed as houseboys, gardeners, and cooks, and a few started small businesses. Starting a laundry was especially tempting because it required a small investment for equipment and minimal English skills. Being self-employed enabled them to avoid both exploitation by employers and competition with hostile white laborers.

What kind of hostile actions did the Chinese encounter?

The resentment of white laborers was not the only source of hostility; the white population in general

PACIFIC CHIVALRY.
Encouragement to Chinese Immigration.

© 1999 HARPWEEK®

FIGURE 5.5

Newspapers often expressed their hostility to Chinese immigrants in cartoons.

tended to perceive the Chinese as refusing to give up their "foreign" identity and become "Americanized." Some white men would occasionally target Chinese men who maintained traditions such as the "queue," a long single braid of hair worn down their back. (See Figure 5.5.) Chinese laborers complained of white men grabbing or even cutting off their queue. It wasn't long before such hostility escalated to violent confrontation.

The U.S. economy experienced a depression in the 1870s, yet the numbers of Chinese increased, and many were becoming visibly prosperous. Looking for a scapegoat, white politicians and labor leaders blamed economic problems on the Chinese, and newspapers published and disseminated their views. In 1871, mob violence resulted in the deaths of 21 Chinese men in Los Angeles; in

1885, 28 Chinese railroad workers were killed in Rock Springs, Wyoming (Fong, 2000; Wu, 1972). Although Chinese immigrants constituted less than 1% of the U.S. population in 1882, Congress passed the **Chinese Exclusion Act** to prohibit Chinese immigration for the next ten years; it was renewed for another ten years in 1892, and renewed indefinitely in 1902. The door to the "Gold Mountain" closed.

During another economic recession in the 1890s, unemployed white workers rioted, beating and shooting Chinese workers. Such violence often discouraged the Chinese from continuing to work as laborers, except for Chinese employers. The Chinese created their own communities in urban areas—Chinatowns—where they felt safe establishing businesses and homes, and less vulnerable

> If we believe absurdities we shall commit atrocities.
>
> Voltaire (1694–1778)

to white discrimination and violence. Chinese entrepreneurs often pooled their resources to start a business, and they would employ other Chinese. By 1890, the 6,400 Chinese workers employed in California laundries constituted 69% of all laundry employees in the state (Takaki, 1993).

Although they were willing to live in separate communities, most Chinese who remained in America were unwilling to be perceived as foreigners in the land. By 1924, Andrew Kan had lived and worked in the United States for over forty years, and he took his case to court to insist on his right to be an American citizen; the courts disagreed. Anti-Asian sentiment would intensify during World War II as the United States fought a Japanese enemy portrayed as treacherous and brutal.

How did Americans view the Japanese before World War II?

Initially, Japanese immigrants settled in Hawaii to work on plantations. By 1880, only 148 Japanese lived in the United States (Fong, 2000); however, 150,000 Japanese immigrated to the mainland between 1880 and 1908. By the 1920s, the Japanese population in America was twice as large as that of the Chinese (Zia, 2000). Unlike the Chinese, Japanese immigrants tended to include women. By 1920, women constituted 46% of the Japanese in Hawaii and 35% in California (Takaki, 1993). Based on their awareness of the hostility toward the male Chinese immigrants, Japanese government officials screened immigration applications to ensure that those approved included married couples, and they attempted to eliminate anyone who might engage in prostitution, gambling, or other vices that had been used to justify American anti-Chinese attitudes.

Despite these efforts, in 1905, California newspapers initiated a campaign against the **Yellow Peril** based on the belief that the Japanese, like the Chinese, could not or would not adopt the American culture (Feagin & Feagin, 2008). In reality, many

Japanese immigrants had assimilated and desired to become American citizens. In 1922, Takao Ozawa challenged the 1790 law restricting U.S. citizenship to white people. Ozawa had been educated in American schools, belonged to a Christian church, and spoke only English at home. Ozawa's argument to the U.S. Supreme Court was that he had done everything that any immigrant could be asked to do to assimilate into the culture, and the only thing that prevented his citizenship was his race. The Supreme Court said that was all that mattered, and rejected his appeal.

Before the Supreme Court made their decision, California legislators in both houses passed a resolution calling for the prohibition of further Japanese immigration. Responding to such nativist sentiment, President Theodore Roosevelt met with Japanese officials in 1908 and reached the **Gentleman's Agreement** that Japan would prohibit further immigration except for the close relatives of those already in the United States. Japanese immigrants could use this loophole until 1920 to bring family members—including "picture brides"—to join them in America.

What was a picture bride?

Japanese culture regarded marriage as an affair negotiated between families. In the **picture bride** system, matchmaking resulted from an exchange of photographs. Combining those who came with their husbands and those who came as picture brides, 60,000 Japanese women immigrated to America (including Hawaii) and gave birth to almost 30,000 children. These children, **Nisei**, were Americans by right of birth. Most Japanese immigrants still lived in Hawaii, constituting 40% of the population; they were less than 2% of California residents (Zia, 2000).

Where were Japanese immigrants employed?

The Japanese often worked in canneries and took a variety of jobs, but many worked as agricultural laborers, as they had done in Japan. Some began to contract for land, negotiating a share of the profits with the owner or guaranteeing a set price after the crop was sold. The owner provided seed and equipment, so with minimal investment and intense labor, Japanese farmers were able to be quite successful. Some saved enough money to secure a loan and lease or purchase land, giving them the opportunity for higher profits. By 1910, Japanese farmers in California owned or leased about 200,000 acres of land, producing almost all of the state's celery and snap beans, three quarters of the strawberries, and almost half of the onions and green peas (Takaki, 1993).

In 1913, California legislators passed the Alien Land Law to prohibit any immigrant ineligible for citizenship from owning land or leasing land for more than three years. Because their children, the Nisei, were American citizens, the Japanese leased or purchased land in their children's names; those who had no children paid other families for the right to use their children's names as their "land-lords" (Zia, 2000). This prompted the California legislature to pass a new Alien Land Law in 1920, prohibiting the use of children's names to lease or purchase land.

Japanese immigrants were disappointed that their success, their efforts to assimilate, and their children's citizenship status did not reduce hostility against them. Even when possessing a college diploma, their children were not likely to find work. Many returned to the family business, and those who were doctors or dentists tended to work in the Japanese communities (Takaki, 1993). Then World War II began, and Japan became America's enemy.

How did the war affect American attitudes toward Japanese families living in the United States?

Given the history of anti-Japanese sentiment, it is not surprising that rumors of spying and sabotage began circulating immediately. Japanese farmers were accused of planting flowers in a particular pattern to guide airplanes carrying bombs to their target (Feagin & Feagin, 2008). Fearing a broad anti-Asian backlash, many Asian-owned businesses posted signs saying that the owners were Asian but not Japanese. Some shops sold buttons that said, "I am Korean" or "I am Chinese" so Americans would not confuse them with Japanese (Koppelman, 2001).

What actions were taken against the Japanese during World War II?

Barely two months into the war, President Roosevelt issued Executive Order No. 9066 that was the basis for taking Japanese Americans from their communities and relocating them in federal "camps." Japanese families were given a week or less to sell property and possessions, packing what remained into their suitcases. More than 100,000 people, two thirds of them American citizens, lost almost everything as they were evacuated to ten federal camps. The path to these relocation camps was paved with widespread prejudices that were affirmed by political leaders at all levels of state and national government. (See Figure 5.6.)

Once at the camps, Japanese families were informed that the U.S. government required them to take a loyalty oath renouncing their allegiance to Japan. The Nisei were already American citizens, so this was not an issue for them, but for their parents, renouncing Japanese citizenship with no chance of becoming American citizens meant that they would become people without a country. When 4,600 of them refused to sign the oath, they were sent to federal prisons (Zia, 2000). Despite such treatment, 23,000 Japanese men joined the army to prove their loyalty. The army segregated its troops by race, and a Japanese American regiment, the 442nd, became the most highly decorated unit of the war. Yet, until the war's end, Japanese families continued to be kept in camps with barbed wire and armed soldiers. It is a tribute to the tenacity of Japanese Americans that so many were able to rebuild their lives and their finances after the war.

What other Asian immigrants faced anti-Asian attitudes?

Between 1907 and 1910, large numbers of Filipinos immigrated primarily to Hawaii as agricultural laborers. When the 1924 immigration law prohibited Asian entry into the United States, Filipinos immigrated, not as Asians but as "nationals" because the Philippines had become American territory after the Spanish-American War. Of the 45,000 who had entered the United States by 1930, most were young men who worked as agricultural workers or domestic servants. Filipinos tended to be active

FIGURE 5.6

The Japanese American relocation camps of World War II illustration the perception of these American citizens as "foreign." Rumors that there were spies from Japan circulating among them were enough to justify confiscating their property and keeping them behind barbed wire for the duration of the war.

Source: The Japanese American Citizens League.

> Almost all people have this potential for evil, which would be unleashed only under certain . . . social circumstances.
>
> Irish Chang (1968–2004)

Koreans first began immigrating to the United States in the early 1900s to work in agriculture or as domestic servants. Like other Asian immigrants, they encountered oppression. They were refused entrance into some restaurants, not allowed access to some public places, and restricted to racially segregated neighborhoods. Because Japan had conquered Korea in the late 1930s, Koreans hoped that the allies would defeat their historic enemy during World War II; instead, the U.S. government classified Koreans as "Japanese" during the war because Japan governed Korea (Feagin & Feagin, 2008).

After the war, the total ban on Asian immigration was slightly modified, but the number of Korean immigrants was minimal until the Korean War. Because the U.S. Army maintained a presence in South Korea, many American soldiers returned with Korean wives who were exempt from Asian immigration quotas. As with other Asian groups, the number of Koreans in America has increased dramatically since the Immigration Reform Act of 1965. There have also been significant increases in the numbers of other Southeast Asian immigrants such as Vietnamese, Cambodians, Laotians, and Hmong. Even though they have encountered prejudice, most refugees emigrated to escape violence in their native countries. Living safely with their families, they tend to be more optimistic about overcoming difficulties here (Pipher, 2002).

In the early 1900s, Sikh farmers were the first Asian Indian immigrants to America. Landowners employed them instead of Asians who had been targets of nativist outrage. In 1923, a Punjabi immigrant named Bhagat Singh Thind applied for U.S. citizenship using "scientific" race theories to prove he was white. Having cited race theories to deny citizenship to previous nonwhite applicants, the U.S. Supreme Court nevertheless chose to ignore "science" in this case, asserting that Thind was not white because they did not believe him to be white (Zia, 2000).

in labor unions, causing resentment among both white landowners and other laborers (Fong, 2000).

In 1934, Congress passed legislation restricting Filipino immigration to 50 people annually. Filipinos were prohibited from entering many professions and were declared ineligible for federal aid during the Great Depression. Yet, during World War II, the army recruited 30,000 Filipinos to fight the Japanese in the Philippines. Although Filipino soldiers were promised full citizenship, the promise was not kept until 1990, long after many had died (Feagin & Feagin, 2008).

Most Asian Indian immigration has occurred since 1965, with 80% of Indo-Americans being the first generation of immigrants. Yet Asian Indian immigration has involved significant numbers of people, producing an Indo-American population that is the fourth largest among all Asian groups (after Chinese, Japanese, and Filipinos). Asian Indians are notable for linguistic and religious diversity, and they are culturally diverse, more likely to identify with a province such as Bengal or Punjab than the country of India. Migrating Asian Indians often have academic qualifications in fields such as engineering, medicine, mathematics, and computer management. In one study of Asian immigrants employed as

> America has traveled and is still traveling a long, hard road . . . littered with persistent intolerance and bigotry. However, our progress as a nation has been marked by a succession of civil rights laws . . . (but) without proper enforcement, these laws are merely empty promises.
>
> Bill Lann Lee (1949–)

physicians, over half were Asian Indians (Kar et al., 2000). Their success has contributed to the "model minority" myth that has been used to counter claims of discrimination by other minority groups.

What is the model minority myth?

Beginning in the 1960s, white Americans praised Asian Americans as a **model minority** because they had overcome all obstacles and achieved success. People of color were told that if they were willing to work as hard as Asian Americans, they could be just as successful, and if they failed, it was their own fault. The model minority myth has created resentment among people of color, particularly African Americans, toward Asian Americans. Takaki (1993) suggests that this was the intent of those promoting the model minority myth: "Our society needs an Asian American 'model minority' in an era anxious about a growing black underclass" (p. 416). The model minority myth has often been criticized as a distraction that avoids the reality of ongoing discrimination against Asian Americans.

How does the model minority myth distort reality?

As a group, Asian Americans exist on both extremes of social status, but the model minority myth focuses on the upper extreme. Data that seems to document their financial success needs to be put in context. Asian Americans tend to live in urban areas of states where the cost of living is high, inflating salary data. One study said 60% of all Asian Americans lived in three states—Hawaii, California, and New York (Woo, 2000). Asian American incomes are also inflated because they are reported as household incomes. Although most American households consist of dual wage earners, Asian American households often have additional earners as well.

At the other extreme are Asian Americans working for low wages. In San Francisco, Asian American women constitute 80% of all garment workers, averaging 10 to 12 hours a day, 6 to 7 days a week (Louie, 2000). Their wages are low because they are competing against Third World workers who are hired by companies outsourcing jobs or establishing factories in other countries, making multiple incomes a necessity for many Asian American households. Although it is appropriate to celebrate the success of those who overcome oppression, the model minority myth actually harms Asian Americans, as Fong and Shinagawa (2000) have explained:

> [It] diverts attention away from serious social and economic problems that affect many segments of the Asian American population, detracts from both the subtle and overt racial discrimination encountered by Asian Americans, places undue pressure on young Asian Americans to succeed educationally and professionally, and fuels competition and resentment between Asian Americans and other groups. (p. 191)

Hispanic Americans/Latinos/as

There is no clear consensus on an appropriate term that includes all the diverse Spanish-speaking ethnic groups in the United States, but the immigration of Mexicans, Puerto Ricans, Cubans, Central Americans, and South Americans has created a need for an inclusive generic term. In 1980, the

U.S. Census Bureau suggested *Latino* as the generic term; however, some critics said that sounded like "Ladino," an ancient form of Castilian Spanish spoken by Spanish Jews. The Bureau chose *Hispanic*, a label rejected by many Spanish-speaking people as a contrived, bureaucratic term (Shorris, 2001). Although *Hispanic* seems to be the preferred term in the southeastern United States and Texas, it is rejected in many other places, including most of California and much of the Midwest. Given this lack of consensus, both *Hispanic* and *Latino* are used in this final section.

Which Spanish-speaking group was the first to come to the United States?

The Spanish established the first permanent U.S. settlements in 1565 at St. Augustine, Florida, and in 1598 at Santa Fe, New Mexico, yet rarely do American history books mention this. Historically, school textbooks have focused on the English settlements in 1607 at Jamestown, and in 1620 at Plymouth (Loewen, 2008). When the U.S. annexed Texas, Mexicans living there (Tejanos) found themselves in America; as the Tejanos like to say, "We didn't cross the border; the border crossed us" (Shorris, 2001, p. 37). After the Mexican-American War, Mexico signed the Treaty of Guadalupe Hidalgo, giving up a million square miles of land, half of its territory. Mexicans living in newly declared American territory were given six months to decide either to stay and become U.S. citizens or

> Poor Mexico, so far from God, so near to the United States.
>
> Porfirio Diaz (1830–1915)

to move to the redefined Mexico. Of the more than 82,000 Mexicans who had to choose, about 80,000 chose to stay (Duignan & Gann, 1998).

Article X of the treaty promised to honor the land claims of Mexicans who became citizens, but when the American Congress ratified the treaty, they rejected Article X. To reassure Mexico that the land titles and civil rights of Mexicans would be respected, American representatives presented a "Statement of Protocol" to the Mexican government with assurances that the U.S. government would not annul Mexican land grants and that these claims would be considered legitimate in American courts (Vento, 1998). That promise proved to be false.

Only a few **Anglos**, as Mexicans called white settlers, came to the new territory at first, but after gold was discovered in California, they flooded the land. Anglos settled on Mexican American land, refusing to move, and authorities took no action against the "squatters." When Anglos made legal claims to the land, Mexican Americans were forced to retain white lawyers to represent them because court proceedings were conducted in English. Although courts confirmed land grants for more than 2 million acres owned by Mexican Americans, they rejected Mexican American claims for almost 34 million acres (Vento, 1998). Even when the courts affirmed their claims, landowners often had to sell portions of their land to pay legal fees. Aggressive Anglo efforts soon created a society in former Mexican territory consisting of Anglo landowners and entrepreneurs and a pool of primarily Mexican laborers. What Shorris (2001) said of California was true for all of the former Mexican territory: "In less than a quarter of a century California changed from Spanish to Anglo" (p. 31); it was an enormous transfer of wealth and culture.

What was the experience like for Mexicans immigrating to the United States?

In the 1880s, Mexicans began crossing the border into the United States, recruited by American employers after the Chinese Exclusion Act was passed in 1882. Mexican immigrants tended to take jobs in agriculture, mining, and construction; they constituted 70% of workers laying track for the Southern Pacific and Santa Fe railroads. Although American businesses actively recruited them, many Anglos perceived Mexicans as inferior. Mexicans were refused admission to public places such as beaches and restaurants. Takaki (1993) quotes the wife of an Anglo rancher arguing that a Mexican "is not as good as a white man. God did not intend him to be; He would have made him white if He had" (p. 327). All members of Mexican families participated in agricultural work; child labor laws were not enforced. Experienced workers might make up to $1.50 per day compared to $4 to $5 a day earned by miners (Duignan & Gann, 1998).

Mexicans did not passively accept such exploitation. In 1903, Mexican and Japanese farm workers formed the Japanese-Mexican Labor Association (JMLA) and engaged in a strike to increase hourly wages. They were successful, but they couldn't survive without support from national labor organizations. They petitioned the American Federation of Labor (AFL) to accept JMLA members, but AFL president Samuel Gompers insisted that the JMLA would be granted a membership charter only if it excluded Asian members. The Mexicans refused to betray their Japanese co-workers, so the charter was not granted (Takaki, 1993). Although the JMLA did not survive, Mexican farm workers continued to strike and protest against low wages.

Because of the Gentleman's Agreement of 1908 and the restrictive 1924 immigration law, Mexico was regarded as an excellent source of cheap labor. By 1910, 222,000 Mexicans lived in the United States, some as far north as Montana. Many migrated to escape the violence of the Mexican Revolution from 1910 to about 1920. When the revolution was over, only 10% of Mexico's citizens were landowners, and the northern migration continued (Vento, 1998). By 1930, 90,000 Mexicans lived in Los Angeles, representing about 10% of the city's population. Smaller numbers settled in Denver, Pittsburgh, and St. Louis, and over 20,000 Mexicans lived in Chicago (Duignan & Gann, 1998). Only a small number of these immigrants applied for citizenship, perhaps because the proximity of Mexico made it easier to consider returning.

To promote Latino immigrants applying for citizenship, the **League of United Latin American Citizens (LULAC)** was formed in the 1920s. In addition to being American citizens, members promoted assimilation by encouraging the use of English and affirming the virtues of citizenship. Although criticized for its middle-class bias, for many years LULAC was the only Latino organization to have a national presence. LULAC worked to improve education for Latino students, to protest discrimination, and to promote civil rights for Hispanic Americans (Vento, 1998). LULAC also encouraged Latinos to become citizens so they would be less vulnerable to nativist activities. LULAC's efforts were only marginally successful, but World War II would cause a more significant change in American attitudes toward Mexican immigrants.

Why did attitudes toward Mexicans change during World War II?

When the United States entered the war, the government began negotiations for Mexicans to replace the workers who had joined the military and the Japanese workers who had been taken to relocation camps. The U.S. proposed a **Bracero Program**, *braceros* referring to contract laborers. The U.S. government offered transportation and jobs, and the Mexican government felt that this program would also provide Mexicans with an opportunity to learn about American agricultural practices. In 1942, the Bracero Program was implemented.

The U.S. government had guaranteed that Mexican workers would be paid the "prevailing wage" for their labor, but supervision of the program was inadequately funded, and many growers abused it by failing to pay the promised wages. In Texas, growers with a history of employing illegal immigrants continued to use them because they were less costly to hire. Although the Bracero Program was criticized on both sides of the border, it lasted well beyond World War II. When it ended in 1964, the program had issued almost 5 million contracts to Mexican workers (Vargas, 2000). In addition to the contribution of Mexican workers, more than 500,000 Spanish-speaking soldiers, primarily Mexican Americans, joined the American armed forces, the highest percentage of soldiers from any ethnic community (Takaki, 1993). Despite their willingness to fight for the country, many Latino soldiers encountered prejudice from fellow soldiers and in communities where they were stationed. One of the most publicized examples of anti-Latino prejudice was the **Zoot Suit Riots**.

What were the Zoot Suit Riots?

On June 3, 1943, eleven sailors on shore leave in Los Angeles claimed to have been attacked by a gang of Mexican youth. Local media often stereotyped young Mexicans in flamboyant "zoot suits" as criminals and gangsters. (See Figure 5.7.) On June 4, soldiers and sailors rented twenty taxicabs and cruised the barrio, attacking those who looked Latino, especially anyone wearing a zoot suit. At the Carmen Theater, sailors charged in and grabbed youth wearing zoot suits, ripping off their clothes and beating them severely. The police arrested

FIGURE 5.7 Zoot Suit

A soldier appears to be admiring a zoot suit, but servicemen would justify attacking Mexican American youth during the Zoot Suit Riots by claiming it was unpatriotic to wear zoot suits requiring so much cloth when cloth was being rationed because of the war.

Photograph by John Ferrel (1942). Library of Congress, Prints and Photographs Division.

I believe cruelty is the inability to assign the same feelings and values to another person that you harbor in yourself.

Carlos Fuentes (1928–2012)

several Mexican American youth, and the local media portrayed the sailors as heroes (Banks, 2003; Vento, 1998).

The following night sailors and soldiers marched into the barrio invading bars and businesses, destroying property and attacking patrons. Local police refused to charge them with destruction of private property or assault. On June 7, civilians and servicemen formed a mob of thousands, attacking anyone who looked Latino, including several Filipinos and blacks. Some were left naked and bleeding on the streets. Los Angeles police arrested 600 Mexican American youth. Eleanor Roosevelt declared in her newspaper column that the riots were the result of "long standing discrimination against

Mexicans" (Vento, 1998, p. 187). Los Angeles police and city government denied the accusation, but as they followed the events in the newspapers, Latinos, especially Latino soldiers, were angry that they were still not accepted in their adopted land.

Was it better for Latinos after the war?

Latino communities felt a great deal of pride in their returning veterans. Latino soldiers earned numerous bronze and silver stars given for bravery in battle, and seventeen Latino soldiers received the nation's highest military award—the Congressional Medal of Honor (Duignan & Gann, 1998). Because Latino soldiers had not been segregated and had served with white soldiers, some also rose to positions of command. As Shorris (2001) stated, "Men who had commanded Anglo troops in battle did not cringe before them in civilian life" (p. 97).

Although they had encountered difficulty getting home loans before the war, Latino soldiers now had their loan applications approved. The G.I. Bill allowed many to pursue college educations. These soldiers represented only a small portion of Latinos, but their experiences demonstrated that Latinos could receive equitable treatment. Yet the majority of Latinos still encountered prejudice and discrimination, even those who had served in the military. At Three Rivers, Texas, a funeral home director refused to bury Felix Longoria, a Mexican American who had been decorated for heroism in World War II. After Mexican Americans protested, Longoria was finally buried with military honors at Arlington National Cemetery (Shorris, 2001).

How did Mexican Americans respond to discrimination after the war?

Challenging racially segregated schools, Mexican Americans brought *Mendez v. Westminster School District* to California courts in 1946; the judge ruled it was unconstitutional to segregate Mexican American children. This case and others would create a legal context that helped the NAACP to bring *Brown v. Board of Education* to the Supreme Court in 1954. Recognizing the need for a legal organization similar to the NAACP, an attorney in San Antonio named Pete Tijerina persuaded the Ford Foundation to provide $2.2 million to establish the **Mexican American Legal Defense and Educational**

Fund (**MALDEF**). MALDEF continues to be involved in confronting discrimination and addressing civil rights issues affecting Mexican Americans.

To establish a fair wage for agricultural workers in California, Cesar Chavez assisted farm workers in creating a union. Chavez led a strike lasting from 1965 until 1970, resulting in a contract with one of the major growers. After another seven years of activism, the remaining growers agreed to pay farm workers standardized wages and benefits. Also in the 1960s, Reies Tijerina came to New Mexico in his quixotic pursuit of restitution for descendants of Mexicans who lost millions of acres of land they owned prior to the Treaty of Guadalupe Hidalgo (Tijerina, 1971). In Crystal City, Texas, Mexican Americans who were a large majority of the residents formed a third party called La Raza Unida and won control of the city council and the school board. They instituted bilingual education programs and hired numerous Mexican American administrators and teachers.

In 1957, El Paso citizens elected Raymond Telles to be the first Mexican American mayor in the United States. In 2005, Antonio Villaraigosa was the first Mexican American elected as mayor of Los Angeles. Political candidates in the Southwest, in urban areas, and in California eagerly court Mexican American voters. Mexican Americans have been elected to local, state, and national offices. Today, Mexican Americans are two thirds of all Latinos, the largest Spanish-speaking ethnic group in the United States, followed by Puerto Ricans and Cubans (Shorris, 2001). Unlike other Latino immigrants, however, Puerto Ricans came to America already claiming U.S. citizenship.

How did Puerto Ricans become citizens of the United States?

When Spanish ships arrived in 1493, they called the island San Juan Batista and the harbor Puerto Rico; over time the names reversed and the "rich port" of San Juan became the capital of the island of Puerto Rico (Fitzpatrick, 1971). The 70,000 Tainos inhabiting the island were almost exterminated, so Africans were imported to work as slaves. Because Spain mainly sent soldiers, marriages and relationships took place between Spaniards, Tainos, and Africans, producing the range of skin colors from light to dark that can be found among

Puerto Ricans today. In 1897, the Spanish government agreed to give Puerto Rico more autonomy, but the Spanish-American War made Puerto Rico a U.S. possession.

After almost twenty years of autocratic rule by the United States, Congress responded to Puerto Rican demands for more autonomy by passing the Jones Act in 1917. Puerto Ricans elected representatives to their two legislative bodies as well as a resident commissioner, but the U.S. president still appointed the governor and maintained veto power (Fitzpatrick, 1971). The Jones Act also provided the opportunity for Puerto Ricans to become U.S. citizens, giving them six months to make a decision. Although it made them eligible for military service, only 287 out of more than a million people rejected U.S. citizenship (Perez y Gonzalez, 2000).

> Come from where it may, racism divides.
>
> Jose Marti (1853–1895)

What effect did becoming part of the United States have on Puerto Rico?

When the United States assumed control, Puerto Rican farmers owned 93% of the farmland. By 1930, 60% of sugar beet production and almost all tobacco production came from farms with absentee owners, primarily American corporations. Although the United States built more roads and schools, the basis of the economy was transformed from small farms producing food to meet the local need to large farms hiring low-wage workers and exporting their products (Feagin & Feagin, 2008). Soon the island was not producing enough food for its own people, and malnutrition became common. Because of improved health care, Puerto Rico's population doubled by 1940, but jobs did not. Agriculture jobs paid as little as six cents an hour. By 1910, about 1,500 Puerto Ricans had come to America because of economic hardship, with a third of them living in Spanish Harlem in New York City (Duignan & Gann, 1998).

In the 1930s, Luis Marin formed the Popular Democratic Party (or "Populares") to address Puerto Rico's economic problems. The party sponsored legislation to limit the amount of land that absentee owners could control; land returned to the government was redistributed to small farmers, but two thirds of American corporations refused to cooperate with the law (Perez y Gonzalez, 2000). Puerto Ricans expressed their frustration by demanding more autonomy from the United States.

In 1949, the United States allowed Puerto Ricans to elect their own governor, and they elected Luis Marin. Three years later, Congress approved the proposed Puerto Rican Constitution, giving the island the status of a commonwealth. Although it now had more autonomy, Puerto Rico also had significant economic problems. After sixty years of American rule, more than 50% of the total national income went to 20% of the people, and there was persistent unemployment and underemployment (Duignan & Gann, 1998).

Governor Marin proposed an ambitious economic plan called **Operation Bootstrap** that offered incentives such as a large supply of cheap labor and tax exemptions for businesses moving to Puerto Rico. Many corporations took advantage of this offer. Throughout the 1950s and 1960s, Operation Bootstrap expanded the island's industrial base and created 140,000 manufacturing jobs. Personal income rose from an annual average of $118 in 1940 to $1,200 by 1970 (Perez y Gonzalez, 2000). Tourism increased, and Puerto Rico was called the "Showcase of the Americas," but economic problems persisted. With so much land being used for industry, the number of agricultural jobs decreased, resulting in unemployment rates as high as 10%. So much land was given over for industrial use that Puerto Rico had to import food. Corporate tax exemptions required Puerto Ricans to pay higher taxes to fund the necessary improvements in sewers, roads, electricity, and water (Feagin & Feagin, 2003).

For many Puerto Ricans, the primary economic benefit was the opportunity to earn enough money to migrate to the United States. By the 1980s, more than 900,000 were living in New York City alone, comprising about 12% of the city's population, and the 3 million Puerto Ricans living in the United States represented 11% of all Latinos. Approximately 60% of Puerto Ricans lived in either New York or New Jersey, but with unemployment rates as high as 23%, nearly 60% of these Puerto Rican families lived in poverty (Banks, 2009; Duignan & Gann, 1998).

How do the experiences of Puerto Ricans in the United States compare to those of other Latino groups?

Puerto Ricans have encountered many obstacles in the United States. The percentages of Puerto Ricans who are unemployed or on welfare have been higher than for other Latino groups. In part, the high unemployment rate is the result of a decline in unskilled and semiskilled jobs in the urban areas where they have settled. Puerto Rican children living in poverty have attended racially segregated urban schools without resources to provide the quality of education necessary for their students to compete for better paying jobs. One consequence of these economic and social problems is that Puerto Ricans have higher rates of drug use, drug addiction, and crime than other Latino groups. Single-parent families headed by women constitute a third of all Puerto Rican families, more than for any Latino group except Dominicans (Perez y Gonzalez, 2000). Shorris (2001) described the typical situation for many Puerto Ricans in New York City:

> Puerto Ricans work in marginal businesses; they have no unions, no benefits, nothing but the weekly paycheck, from which social security may or may not have been deducted and paid; when the marginal business goes broke after a few or even many years, . . . the loyal Puerto Rican employee is left with nothing. (p. 87)

Yet Puerto Ricans have succeeded in a variety of fields including literature, sports, politics, the arts, music, medicine, and more. For over forty years the Puerto Rican organization called Aspira has supported high school clubs to encourage Puerto Rican youth to graduate and go to college. Regardless of their success or failure, Puerto Ricans resent other Americans perceiving them as foreigners rather than regarding them as the fellow citizens that they are. If they migrate from Puerto Rico to a state, or from one state to another, Puerto Ricans should be viewed the same as a Minnesotan who moves to New York.

Today, the majority of Puerto Ricans living in the United States were born here. Puerto Ricans tend to be bilingual and bicultural, identifying themselves as Puerto Ricans but proud of their status as American citizens. Like other Latinos, they often speak Spanish at home, but young people are more likely to speak English to their peers (Perez y Gonzalez, 2000). Puerto Ricans encourage their youth to succeed, despite the difficulty of that goal. According to Shorris (2001), "Every Puerto Rican who survives and succeeds to any degree on the mainland is a miracle of love and will" (p. 144). Although they have not been as successful as other Latinos, especially Cubans, Puerto Ricans want to believe that such miracles are possible.

Why has the experience of Cubans been so different from that of Puerto Ricans?

The islands of Cuba and Puerto Rico have similar histories. Columbus and his men conquered the Taino Indians, inhabiting both islands and enslaving the residents. Yet by 1762, Cuba's capital city was twice the size of New York or Philadelphia; Havana was a port of such significance that the British captured the city and refused to give it back until Spain agreed to give up Florida in exchange. In addition to being a major trading center in the Caribbean, Cuba prospered because of its sugar production carried out by imported African slaves. By 1830, the combination of free and enslaved blacks was larger than the population of whites. By 1870, Cubans were trying to win independence from Spain; a few Cubans immigrated to the United States during the lengthy struggle that ended in 1898 when American troops prevailed in the Spanish-American War.

After four years of military rule, the United States agreed to make Cuba a sovereign nation, but the Platt amendment gave the United States the right to intervene in Cuba's affairs at any time to protect property and liberty in Cuba. For the next two decades, no Cuban who did not gain U.S. approval could be elected president nor stay in that office (Feagin & Feagin, 2008).

Even under American dominance, Cuba prospered; few Cubans immigrated to the United States until Fidel Castro's successful revolt against dictator Fulgencio Batista. After Castro announced that Cuba would be a communist nation, Cubans began leaving, most immigrating to Florida. The wealthiest Cubans left first. Those who followed in the 1960s were a heterogeneous group, but with a disproportionately high number of businessmen, professionals, and entrepreneurs. Many had been in the merchant navy; others were former government officials or were revolutionaries who were disillusioned with Castro (Duignan & Gann, 1998).

What happened to the Cubans who came to the United States?

A federally funded Cuban Refugee Program (CRP) was established to assist Cubans coming to Florida. CRP refugee centers provided resources rarely given to other immigrants (Portes & Bach, 1985). Cuban businessmen who had salvaged some of their wealth relied on traditional business methods called *socios* or *socioismo*, in which loans were approved not by an objective analysis but because the applicant was a friend. Cuban immigrants tended to be educated, and many had business experience. For the next two decades, Cubans used their resources to engage in business enterprises as well as to provide services such as grocery stores, legal assistance, and funeral homes for fellow Cubans. As Shorris (2001) stated, "The Cuban exiles, primarily middle- and upper middle-class, soon became middle- and upper middle-class again" (p. 67). Attracted by Cuban success in the United States and disenchanted with Castro's communism, more Cubans came.

The next wave of Cuban immigrants tended to be working-class people from urban areas (almost half from Havana alone). Many found work in businesses owned or managed by Cubans, where they tended to earn higher wages. By the mid-1980s, Cuban Americans were the majority in Dade County and in Miami. Although 40% of Cuban immigrants settled in Florida, they also settled in New York, New Jersey, and California (Duignan & Gann, 1998). A 1953 Cuban census identified 72% of Cubans as white, but the 1970 U.S. census identified 95% of Cubans living in the United States as white (Portes & Bach, 1985).

Compared to other major Latino groups in the United States, Cuban Americans have recorded the highest median household incomes. One reason for their success is that, similar to Asian American families, they tend to have multiple wage earners in a household. According to a study of Cuban immigration from 1960 to 1980, about two thirds of Cuban American wives worked outside the home, and 27% of these households had additional family members earning income. The presence of Cubans in Florida has attracted an increasing number of tourists and entrepreneurs from both Central and South America, providing additional business opportunities.

Although Cuban immigrants have traditionally viewed themselves as a people in exile, that view is not shared by Cuban American youth. According to Shorris (2001), "Older Cubans say they will return to Cuba as soon as Castro dies or is deposed. The younger generation is interested only in going back to visit" (p. 75). Their attitudes are similar to Mexican American and Puerto Rican youth, as well as other Latinos living in the United States.

What other Latino groups live in the United States?

Other Hispanic immigrant groups coming to the United States in the twentieth century included Dominicans, Central Americans, and South Americans. Since the 1960s, there has been a small but steady stream of immigrants from the Dominican Republic, surging in the early 1980s because of the global recession that drove down sugar prices, creating a huge foreign debt and an unemployment rate of 30%. By the time the crisis was over, 10% of Dominicans had immigrated, primarily to the United States, with 90% settling in New York City (Duignan & Gann, 1998).

Immigrants from Central America have usually come to the United States to escape political turmoil and violence in countries such as Guatemala, Honduras, Nicaragua, and El Salvador. To address their needs, the Central American Refugee Committee (CRECE) was established to provide food, temporary shelter, work, and legal assistance. CRECE food distribution centers raise money to purchase food wholesale, and they ask for small contributions from those taking food to help pay for the purchase of more food, making the centers a collaborative endeavor, not merely a charitable one (Shorris, 2001). As Central Americans have tended to settle in urban areas, CRECE has been a critical resource for them. So many Salvadorans have settled in Los Angeles that it has now become the second largest Salvadoran city after the nation's capitol of San Salvador.

Unlike Central Americans, who tend to come from impoverished areas, South American immigrants tend to have had the advantage of a good

education, with many having a doctoral degree. Some Chileans immigrated because of political repression, but few South Americans are refugees. Reasons for immigrating usually involve a desire for better jobs, higher salaries, and greater opportunity. Because they come with such resources, South Americans are reported to have the highest educational attainment and higher incomes than any other Spanish-speaking group in the United States (Duignan & Gann, 1998).

Why have many Americans objected to Latino immigration?

The primary motivation for all Latino immigrants is economic opportunity, but many have resorted to illegal means of gaining entry to the United States. Mexican Americans are the largest source of foreign labor in the United States, especially for manual labor jobs (Portes, 2007). Although the North American Free Trade Agreement that was implemented in the 1990s resulted in American industries building many factories just inside the Mexican border, Mexican workers have migrated to these border towns in huge numbers, creating a labor pool larger than the available jobs require. As a consequence, wages at these factories continue to be low, and many unemployed workers have crossed the border illegally to find work in the United States (Acuña, 2004).

In 1990, the U.S. Defense Department built an 11-mile fence along the Mexican border near San Diego as a strategy for keeping illegal drugs from being brought into the United States. This initiated a "militarization" of the Mexican border that has continued and has been extended to include denying entry to illegal immigrants (Acuña, 2004). Sociologist Douglas Massey argues that the border militarization has failed to stop the flow of drugs and has been equally ineffective at stopping illegal immigration. Militarizing the border has caused smuggling to become professionalized (Portes, 2007). Although professional smugglers are expensive, the odds of their being caught are reduced. By making the process of entering the United States more difficult, illegal immigrants tend to remain here, resulting in an outcome opposite to what people supporting border militarization wanted to achieve. Experts predict that the problem of undocumented workers will never be

> What the people want is very simple. They want an America as good as its promise.
>
> Barbara Jordan (1936–1996)

resolved until the U.S. government recognizes and facilitates historic patterns of cyclic immigrations for seasonal work between Mexico and the United States (Portes, 2007).

AFTERWORD

Human evolution is a story of survival, but once physical survival is assured, human beings create culture. The struggle to maintain one's culture while living in a new homeland with its own culture is no easy task, especially because physical and cultural differences have been used to create the concept of race. Race has then been used to divide human groups, creating subordinate races that are forced to struggle against a dominant race.

For the indigenous people in America, this struggle began when European colonists stepped on American shores. The roots of oppression expanded across the nation in the cultural and physical conflict that followed. The oppression eventually encompassed African slaves, Chinese and Japanese laborers, Mexican migrant workers, and other immigrants of color. This oppression was even directed against groups considered white today like Irish, Italian, and Slavic immigrants, but all European groups would eventually be offered the freedom and opportunity they sought in the United States while these continued to be denied to people of color.

Oppression based on race and related ethnic groups has been sustained by the descendants of the original European settlers, affecting people of color living in the United States and those who are coming with the same vision of freedom and opportunity that brought the first colonists. We are now a nation of nations with people from all over the world pursuing the happiness promised by a free society. If the United States is to be a pluralistic society embracing diverse groups, it must make sure that all people living in America are respected as part of our diverse national family.

By insisting on racial equality, Americans of color are simply demanding a chance to achieve the same American dream that has attracted so many immigrants to these shores. It is a dream not yet realized for far too many of them. In the poem "Let America be America Again," Langston Hughes (1994) speaks for all oppressed people who still pursue the American dream:

> America never was America to me,
> And yet I swear this oath—
> America will be! (p. 191)

TERMS AND DEFINITIONS

Anglos A term identifying white people who settled in Mexican territory, eventually becoming a generic term for white people

Black Cabinet The Federal Council on Negro Affairs, consisting of thirty black professionals, served as an advisory group to President Franklin Roosevelt

Bracero Program Initiated during World War II, this program continued to import Mexicans to work as manual laborers in the United States for twenty-two years

Brown v. Board of Education The 1954 Supreme Court decision overturning *Plessy v. Ferguson* by declaring racial segregation unconstitutional

Chinese Exclusion Act An 1882 law prohibiting Chinese immigration to the United States, renewed in 1892, and making exclusion permanent in 1902

Emancipation Proclamation Issued by President Lincoln to free slaves only in Confederate States and permitting free blacks to enlist in the Union Army

Ethnocentrism Believing one's race, nation, or culture is superior to all others; also individual actions or institutional practices based on that belief

Gentleman's Agreement The Japanese government assured the U.S. government it would issue no more passports (as of 1908) to Japanese workers except those already in the United States or their close relatives

Indian Sovereignty Legal rights of Indian nations, confirmed by treaties with the U.S. government, to define themselves and to act as unique cultural and legal entities.

Indigenous people A racial or ethnic group that is well established in an area before the arrival of a new group; a group that may be but does not need be native to the area in which it is established

League of United Latin American Citizens (LULAC) A national organization for members of Spanish-speaking ethnic groups who are American citizens that is dedicated to promoting the value of citizenship, protesting discrimination, and advocating for civil rights for Latinos

Mexican American Legal Defense Fund (MALDEF) An organization opposing discrimination and advocating for Mexican Americans' civil rights

Middle Passage The ocean crossing of slave ships resulting in the deaths of an estimated 5 to 6 million Africans being transported as slaves

Model minority The belief that Asian Americans have been successful because they have been willing to work hard, and that all other minorities could be just as successful if they emulated Asian American behavior

National Association for the Advancement of Colored People (NAACP) An organization opposing racism and advocating for black civil rights

Nisei The term for children of Japanese immigrants who were born in the United States and therefore possessed U.S. citizenship

Nomads A group of persons with no single fixed abode who move from place to place in search of food and water

Operation Bootstrap An economic plan for Puerto Rico during the 1950s and 1960s to boost its industrial base and create more manufacturing jobs

Picture bride A modification of the Japanese system for arranged marriages involving the exchange of photographs between families negotiating a marriage for Japanese men who had immigrated to the United States

Treaty A legal agreement between two or more nations involving terms of peace, trade, and other matters as agreed to by the negotiating parties

Underground Railroad An organization that established "stations" where runaway slaves could get food and rest as they escaped north to freedom

Yellow Peril The term for the belief that Chinese and Japanese immigrants could never be assimilated into American culture and therefore threatened the unity of American society

Zoot Suit Riots Several days of mob violence in 1942 in Los Angeles that demonstrated anti-Latino prejudice as U.S. servicemen (later joined by civilians) attacked Mexican American youth, especially targeting those wearing zoot suits

DISCUSSION EXERCISES

Exercise #1 Understanding Recollections of Larry Kobori Activity

Directions: Read to learn the feelings that Larry recounts having had about the incident that he describes. Then, respond to the Insight Builder Questions below.

Larry Kobori's School Story

When I was young I noticed I was a little different from my friends. My father told me I was Japanese and that I should never be ashamed of being Japanese. He has emphasized this for as long as I remember.

When I started school everything was perfect until the fourth grade. Some kids called me a "Chink." I told them I'm Japanese, not Chinese. If I was going to be called a dirty name, at least use the proper dirty name. My friends always told me to forget those kids, that those kids were stupid. I was glad to hear my friends say that.

After a while the fourth grade things straightened out. But in the seventh grade we started to read about World War I and World War II. I knew that in World War II Japan attacked Pearl Harbor. So I worked real hard on World War I. I answered every question I could. But when it came to World War II,

I never answered any questions. I would just slouch in my chair.

I guess I was feeling ashamed and embarrassed at the atrocities of Japan during World War II. But what I didn't understand was why the textbooks and the teacher glorified America's bombing of Hiroshima and Nagasaki. My teacher said thousands of civilians, including women and children, were killed by the atom bombs, thus making Japan surrender. She then added that the bombings had saved many American lives.

I then asked my teacher, "Wouldn't that be considered an atrocity since so many civilians died? That's the way you describe Japanese atrocities." I'll never forget the way she stared at me and said, "There's a difference." Today that episode is still clear as a bell. It's something that I've never forgotten.

My three years in high school were the best years. I felt that now I was really being accepted. I was the varsity scorekeeper for three years in football, basketball, and baseball. I couldn't compete on the high school level so I did what I could to help. I learned the plays and found myself getting to know the other guys much better. I was then encouraged to write sport stories in the local newspaper. When these stories came out the sophomores and juniors wanted me to help them. As a result I got to know quite a few of them.

Outside of class sometimes it was a different story. Traveling with the basketball team, some blacks called me a "Jap." Remembering my promise I turned around and was about to call the blacks "Niggers." I restrained myself because I was sure it would lead to a fight. The same thing happened when some Mexicans called me a "Jap." Once again I refrained from retaliating.

I'll never understand why those people called me a "Jap."

Insight Builder Questions

1. What are your impressions of Larry Kobori?
2. Do you think Larry Kobori's responses to the racial incidents were appropriate ways to deal with the discrimination that he experienced?
3. Regardless of whether you agree it was appropriate, what alternatives did Larry have?
4. Which of them would you recommend as the best strategy?

5. In your opinion, how should teachers present the Japanese role in World War II? The use of atomic bombs on Hiroshima and Nagasaki?
6. What conditions were favorable in his school experiences?
7. What conditions were not favorable?
8. Suggest a generalization about Americans and race today.

Exercise #2 College Racial Incidents Activity

Directions: The following case studies illustrate a variety of incidents that occurred. Imagine that you are a college counselor or residence hall assistant when the student of color in each incident comes to you to report what happened. What sort of advice would you give to this student? Explain why your advice represents the best course of action for the student to follow.

1. A Puerto Rican American, Jorge, interviewed for a graduate assistantship position. The director discussed the role and responsibility of the assistantship position and indicated that the primary responsibility would be to supervise outreach activities for Hispanic students who were not using available student services. The director believed that Jorge would be a good role model and could convince students to use services since there were biological factors resulting in some people being able to learn more and to be more intelligent than others. Noting Jorge's negative response, the director said he just wanted to be open and honest about his opinions.
2. When in the Marine Corps, Leonard, a Lakota Sioux, had been stationed in the United States and Germany. After serving three years, he returned to his reservation and enrolled in a nearby college. Visiting a sweat lodge, Leonard's friends and older members of the tribe shared stories of their ancestors. When Leonard had been a child, he remembered listening to his father telling stories about his great-grandfather; he had always enjoyed learning about his family history. Now Leonard realized, however, that the stories had no meaning for him, and he could not understand the importance that his tribe placed on talking about individuals who no longer existed. Leonard found himself in conflict with his family and friends. He considered dropping out of college to get a job to earn enough

money to leave and live elsewhere. But he knew there weren't many jobs for people with only a reservation high school diploma. Leonard became more depressed about the conflict he was experiencing and began to think that the only resolution was to drop out of college and reenlist for another full term.

3. Anthony, a Chinese American student transferring from community college to a four-year university, was invited to the new student orientation, where he met with his adviser. As he was leaving the adviser's office, the adviser said in a jovial and friendly tone of voice, "You know, the restaurant across the street sells the best wonton soup around." The more Anthony thought about it, the more upset he became.

4. Jessica, a 22-year-old Mexican American from central Illinois, left home to attend college in California. A few weeks into the semester she began to notice that the majority of the Hispanic students were able to speak both English and Spanish fluently. Although her parents spoke Spanish at home, they did not insist that their children become bilingual, so Jessica could understand Spanish if someone spoke to her, but she was not a fluent Spanish speaker. Jessica talked to the Chicano studies professor after class, who assured her that not all Mexican Americans share the same sociocultural experience, but that all people needed to understand and respect the values of others. He also suggested that if this situation continued to bother Jessica, she should consider seeing a counselor. In her English class, consisting primarily of white students, Jessica felt comfortable and relaxed; however, in a Chicano studies course, she felt out of place because she did not share the experiences of the other Hispanic students.

REFERENCES

Acuña, R. (2004). *Occupied America: A history of Chicanos* (5th ed.). New York, NY: Pearson Longman.

Banks, J.A. (2009). *Teaching strategies for ethnic studies* (8th ed.). Boston, MA: Allyn & Bacon.

Berkhofer, R., Jr. (2004). *The white man's Indian: Images of the American Indian from Columbus to the present.* New York, NY: Vintage Books.

Bieder, R.E. (1995). *Native American communities in Wisconsin, 1600–1960: A study of tradition and change.* Madison: University of Wisconsin Press.

Carson, C., & Carson, D.M. (2000). The Black Panther Party. In J. Birnbaum & C. Taylor (Eds.), *Civil rights since 1787: A reader on the black struggle* (pp. 618–620). New York, NY: New York University Press.

Chernow, R. (2004). *Alexander Hamilton.* New York, NY: Penguin Books.

Connolly, M.R. (2000, September/October). What's in a name?: A historical look at Native American-related nicknames and symbols at three U.S. universities. *Journal of Higher Education, 17*(5), 515–548.

Cornelius, J.D. (2000). Literacy, slavery, and religion. In J. Birnbaum & C. Taylor (Eds.), *Civil rights since 1787: A reader on the black struggle* (pp. 85–89). New York, NY: New York University Press.

Deloria, P. (2001). Sovereignty. In B. Ballantine & I. Ballantine (Eds.), *The Native Americans: An illustrated history.* North Dighton, MA: J. G. Press.

Duignan, P.J., & Gann, L.H. (1998). *The Spanish speakers in the United States: A history.* Lanham, MD: University Press of America.

Feagin, J., & Feagin, C.B. (2008). *Racial and ethnic relations* (8th ed.). Upper Saddle River, NJ: Pearson Prentice Hall.

Fitzgerald, F.S. (2005). Early success. In J.L. West (Ed.), *My lost city: Personal essays, 1920–1940* (pp. 184–192). Cambridge, UK: Cambridge University Press.

Fitzpatrick, J.P. (1971). *Puerto Rican Americans: The meaning of migration to the mainland.* Englewood Cliffs, NJ: Prentice Hall.

Fong, T.P. (2000). A brief history of Asians in America. In T.P. Fong & L.H. Shinagawa (Eds.), *Asian Americans: Experiences and perspectives* (pp. 13–30). Upper Saddle River, NJ: Prentice Hall.

Fong, T.P., & Shinagawa, L.H. (2000). Employment and occupation. In T.P. Fong & L.H. Shinagawa (Eds.), *Asian Americans: Experiences and perspectives* (pp. 191–192). Upper Saddle River, NJ: Prentice Hall.

Franklin, J.H., & Moss, A.A., Jr. (2000). *From slavery to freedom: A history of African Americans.* New York, NY: Alfred A. Knopf.

Gedicks, A. (1993). *The new resource wars: Native and environmental struggles against multinational corporations.* Boston, MA: South End Press.

Gell-Mann, M. (1994). *The quark and the jaguar: Adventures in the simple and the complex.* New York, NY: W.H. Freeman.

Glenn, E.N., & Yap, S.G.H. (2000). Chinese American families. In T.P. Fong & L.H. Shinagawa (Eds.), *Asian Americans: Experiences and perspectives* (pp. 277–292). Upper Saddle River, NJ: Prentice Hall.

Goldstone, L. (2011). *Inherently unequal: The betrayal of equal rights by the Supreme Court, 1865–1903.* New York, NY: Walker and Company.

Hawkins, J. (2005). Smoke signals, sitting bulls, and slot machines: A new stereotype of Native Americans? *Multicultural Perspectives, 7*(3), 51–54.

Hendry, J. (2003). Mining the sacred mountain: The clash between the Western dualistic framework and native American religions. *Multicultural Perspectives, 5*(1), 3–10.

Hughes, L. (1994). Let America be America again. In A. Rampersad & D. Roellel (Eds.), *The collected poems of Langston Hughes* (pp. 189–191). New York, NY: Alfred A. Knopf.

Jacobs, H.A. (1987). *Incidents in the life of a slave girl.* Cambridge, MA: Harvard University Press.

Jennings, F. (1976). *The invasion of America: Indians, colonialism, and the cant of conquest.* New York, NY: W.W. Norton.

Josephy, A., Jr. (2005). *500 nations: An illustrated history of North American Indians.* London: Pimlico.

Kar, S.B., Campbell, K., Jiminez, A., & Gupta, S.R. (2000). Invisible Americans: An exploration of Indo American quality of life. In T.P. Fong & E.H. Shinagawa (Eds.), *Asian Americans: Experiences and perspectives* (pp. 303–319). Upper Saddle River, NJ: Prentice Hall.

Koppelman, K. (2001). Was Orwell wrong? In *Values in the key of life: Making harmony in the human community* (pp. 57–63). Amityville, NY: Baywood.

Le May, J.L. (Ed.). (1987). *Benjamin Franklin: Writings* (pp. 442–446). New York, NY: Library of America.

Lewis, D.L. (1993). *W.E.B. Du Bois: Biography of a race, 1868–1919.* New York, NY: Henry Holt.

Lewis, D.L. (2000). *W.E.B. Du Bois: The fight for equality and the American century, 1919–1963.* New York, NY: Henry Holt.

Loewen, J. (2008). *Lies my teacher told me: Everything your American history textbook got wrong.* New York, NY: The New Press.

Lomax, L.E. (1963). *The Negro revolt.* New York, NY: Signet Books.

Louie, M.C. (2000). Immigrant Asian women in Bay Area garment sweatshops: "After sewing, laundry, cleaning and cooking, I have no breath left to sing." In T.P. Fong & L.H. Shinagawa (Eds.), *Asian Americans: Experiences and perspectives* (pp. 226–242). Upper Saddle River, NJ: Prentice Hall.

Lowe, L. (2000). Heterogeneity, hybridity, multiplicity: Marking Asian American difference. In T.P. Fong & L.H. Shinagawa (Eds.), *Asian Americans: Experiences and perspectives* (pp. 412–421). Upper Saddle River, NJ: Prentice Hall.

Lui, M. (2004). Doubly divided: The racial wealth gap. In C. Collins, A. Gluckman, M. Lui, B.L. Wright, & A. Scharf (Eds.), *The wealth inequality reader* (pp. 42–49). Cambridge, MA: Dollars & Sense.

Malcolm X. (2000). The ballot or the bullet. In J. Birnbaum & C. Taylor (Eds.), *Civil rights since 1787: A reader on the black struggle* (pp. 589–603). New York, NY: New York University Press.

Matthiessen, P. (1993). *Indian country.* New York: Penguin.

Mintz, S. (2004). *Huck's raft: A history of American childhood.* Cambridge, MA: Belknap Press of Harvard University Press.

Painter, N.I. (2005). *Creating Black Americans: African-American history and its meaning, 1619 to the present.* Oxford, England: Oxford University Press.

Perdue, T. (1998). *Cherokee women: Gender and culture change, 1700–1835.* Lincoln: University of Nebraska Press.

Perez y Gonzalez, M.E. (2000). *Puerto Ricans in the United States.* Westport, CT: Greenwood Press.

Pipher, M. (2002). *The middle of everywhere: The world's refugees come to our town.* New York, NY: Harcourt.

Portes, A. (2007, October). The fence to nowhere. *The American Prospect, 18*(10), 26–29.

Portes, A., & Bach, R.L. (1985). *Latin journey: Cuban and Mexican immigrants in the United States.* Berkeley, CA: University of California Press.

Raboteau, A. (2000). Slave religion, rebellion and docility. In J. Birnbaum & C. Taylor (Eds.), *Civil rights since 1787: A reader on the black struggle* (pp. 29–34). New York, NY: New York University Press.

Reiss, O. (1997). *Blacks in colonial America.* Jefferson, NC: McFarland.

Shorris, E. (2001). *Latinos: A biography of the people.* New York, NY: W.W. Norton.

Smedley, A. (2007). *The arrival of Africans and descent into slavery. Race in North America: Origin and evolution of a world view.* Boulder, CO: Westview.

Smith, V. (2001). Cleanliness. In P. Sterns (Ed.), *Encyclopedia of European social history: From 1350 to 2000* (Vol. 4, pp. 343–353). New York, NY: Scribner.

Spivey, D. (2003). *Fire from the soul: A history of the African-American struggle.* Durham, NC: Carolina Academic Press.

Spring, J. (2001). *Deculturalization and the struggle for equality: A brief history of the education of dominated cultures in the United States* (3rd ed.). Boston, MA: McGraw- Hill.

Suzuki, D., & Knudtson, P. (1992). *Wisdom of the elders: Honoring sacred native visions of nature.* New York, NY: Bantam Books.

Takaki, R. (1993). *A different mirror: A history of multicultural America.* Boston, MA: Little, Brown.

Tijerina, R. (1971). Reies Tijerina's letter from the Santa Fe jail. In W. Moquin & C. Van Doren (Eds.), *A documentary history of the Mexican Americans* (pp. 484–487). New York, NY: Bantam Books.

Vargas, Z. (2000). Citizen, immigrant, and foreign wage workers: The Chicana/o labor refrain in U.S. labor historiography. In R.I. Rochin & D.N. Valdes (Eds.), *Voices of a new Chicana/o history* (pp. 153–165). East Lansing: Michigan State University Press.

Vento, A.C. (1998). *Mestizo: The history, culture and politics of the Mexican and the Chicano.* Lanham, MD: University Press of America.

Wallace, A. (1993). *The long, bitter trail: Andrew Jackson and the Indians.* New York, NY: Hill & Wang.

Washington, H. A. (2006). *Medical Apartheid: The dark history of medical experimentation on black Americans from colonial times to the present.* New York, NY: Harlem Moon.

Weatherford, J. (1988). *Indian givers: How the Indians of the Americas transformed the world.* New York, NY: Fawcett.

White, R. (2001). Expansion and exodus. In B. Ballantine & I. Ballantine (Eds.), *The native Americans: An illustrated history.* North Dighton, MA: J. G. Press.

Whitty, J. (2005). Accounting coup. *Mother Jones, 30*(5), 57–63, 86.

Williams, J. (1987). *Eyes on the prize: America's civil rights years, 1954–1965.* New York, NY: Viking.

Williams, W.C. (1954). *The American background. Selected essays of William Carlos Williams* (pp. 134–161). New York, NY: Random House.

Wilson, J. (1998). *The earth shall weep: A history of native America.* New York, NY: Atlantic Monthly Press.

Woo, D. (2000). The inventing and reinventing of "model minorities": The cultural veil obscuring structural sources of inequality. In T.P. Fong & L.H. Shinagawa (Eds.), *Asian Americans: Experiences and perspectives.* Upper Saddle River, NJ: Prentice Hall.

Woodward, C.V. (1966). *The strange case of Jim Crow.* Oxford, England: Oxford University Press.

Woodward, G.S. (1988). *The Cherokees.* Norman: University of Oklahoma Press.

Wu, C. (Ed.). (1972). *"Chink!" A documentary history of anti-Chinese prejudice in America.* New York, NY: World Publishing.

Zia, H. (2000). *Asian American dreams: The emergence of an American people.* New York, NY: Farrar, Straus and Giroux.

Zinn, H. (2003). *A people's history of the United States.* New York, NY: HarperCollins.

Chapter 6

Religion and Oppression: The Struggle for Religious Freedom

"I wish you had a religion, Peter . . . Oh, I don't mean you have to be Orthodox, or believe in heaven and hell and purgatory and things. I just mean some religion. It doesn't matter what. Just to believe in something!"

Anne Frank (1929–1945)

The character of Anne Frank makes her comment about religion in *The Diary of Anne Frank*, a play based on the journal she kept while she was in hiding during World War II until the Nazis found her. Her story has frequently been used to introduce students to the horrors of the Holocaust. At the play's end, Anne's father reads her diary and the audience hears Anne say, "In spite of everything, I still believe that people are really good at heart" (Goodrich & Hackett, 1956). Both comments affirm the goodness of humanity, regardless of differences between people. Neither comment seems to be controversial, yet some Christians have demanded that children not read the play because the remark about religion suggests that all religions are equally valid. Usually those who complain believe that one religion, their religion, is the only true faith.

Religious Diversity in Colonial America

Americans have confronted religious controversy since early colonial times when immigrant groups arrived with an array of diverse beliefs and minority faiths contended with the power of a dominant faith to survive. Honoring the principle of religious **freedom/religious liberty**—the right to worship according to one's individual beliefs—has been an ongoing struggle in America, and the history of our efforts to achieve it is the focus of this chapter.

Although religious freedom does not deny an individual's right to disagree with the beliefs and practice of another religion, it does require acceptance of divergent beliefs, as long as they don't infringe on the rights of others. The constitutional separation of church and state principle was established to resolve the issues related to diverse faiths in America, and although the principle is appropriate, efforts to achieve religious liberty and the freedom to worship have been a source of dramatic conflict throughout American history.

How did the first colonists deal with religious diversity?

Puritans came to the New World to practice their religion freely, yet they had no intention of allowing others the same freedom. When Anne Hutchinson expressed religious sentiments contrary to Puritan teaching, she was excommunicated and then exiled in 1637. Roger Williams was exiled as well because he advocated respect for all religious faiths and for separation of church from state, a principle not inherent in either Puritan cultural heritage or that of other European immigrants. To reestablish Old World practices, dominant religious groups such as the Anglicans in Massachusetts expected their faith to be designated the **established church** of their colony and to be supported by an allotment of local tax dollars. Miller (1976) described this perspective: "The established religion with its educated ministers and stately rituals was an important element in creating or re-creating the world they left behind" (p. 26).

English colonists discovered that it was difficult to create an established church in the New World. Parishioners wishing to take care of their families could not afford to give their churches much financial support. Therefore, the need for support from colonial governments was greater than had been required in England, and this placed a significant fiscal burden on scarce colonial revenues. Furthermore, immigrants represented diverse faiths—Presbyterians, Quakers, Baptists—and were resentful when colonial tax revenues were expended to support a church to which they did not belong.

Religious resentment was mutual. Northern colony Puritans particularly disliked Quakers because of their ecstatic worship and their practice of allowing women to be church leaders. In Massachusetts, blasphemy laws were enacted to force Quakers out, threatening them with death if they returned. When they did return, authorities promptly arrested them; four Quakers were executed between 1659 and 1661. The executions stopped only because authorities in Britain were embarrassed, insisting that Quakers be sent to London for proper trials (Miller, 1976).

Most American colonies enacted blasphemy laws directed at those who did not belong to the colony's majority faith. *Blasphemy* was defined as an individual denying the truth and authority of the Bible. If anyone denied the divinity of Christ he could be executed or at least lose his property. Although violating blasphemy laws usually did not result in death, punishments could be quite severe, especially for freethinkers and atheists. According to a 1699 Maryland law, blasphemers, typically people who were using language that degraded Christ, the Apostles, or the Holy Trinity, were to be branded with a "B" for a first offense, have a hole burned through their tongue with a red-hot iron for a second offense, and have their property confiscated for a third offense. In a humanitarian gesture, some colonies allowed blasphemers to avoid punishment by publicly asking to be forgiven (Myers, 1960).

As colonies designated "established churches," blasphemy laws also required ministers from other churches to register as "dissenters" and agree to practice only after receiving colonial approval. Dissenting ministers sometimes refused to register and preached whenever they wished; however, there were consequences. In 1771, a sheriff accompanied by an Anglican minister disrupted a church service by arresting the Baptist minister, taking him to a nearby field and whipping him (Waldman, 2006). Being a minority faith, Baptist ministers were often arrested, sometimes with an effect opposite of what was intended. At one point when Baptist ministers were being aggressively pursued, arrested, and jailed for unauthorized preaching, the number of Baptist converts increased dramatically (Miller, 1976). Conversion efforts were customarily focused on those colonists who attended but were not members of a church or on those not attending a church—a majority in the colonies.

By 1775, more than 150 years since the first colonists arrived, approximately 10% of Americans were church members (Lippy, 1994). Although groups such as Puritans and Quakers came to the colonies to plant the seeds of faith in fertile ground, most immigrants came instead to escape physical destitution and moral despair. They hoped to achieve material success: to own their own land and to provide for their families. They wanted a better life on earth, not in heaven. Preachers from minority faiths focused on those who attended church with little enthusiasm or those who may have found a better material life but longed for satisfaction of spiritual needs. The competition for converts intensified the desire for religious freedom.

How did the colonies promote the concept of religious freedom?

Because of the influence of Roger Williams, William Penn, and Lord Baltimore, the colonies of Rhode Island, Pennsylvania, and Maryland declared religious freedom for those of any faith. Puritans regarded their faith as a "light to the world," so they often forced people to accept it. Williams argued that people could not develop true faith through coercion, and expressed the need for a "wall of separation between the garden of the church and the wilderness of the world" (Nord, 1995, p. 135).

With a Baptist majority in Rhode Island, the arrival of Quakers tested the colony's commitment to religious freedom. Williams personally disliked Quakers and attacked them in his writings, but general tolerance prevailed as religious freedom was maintained, attracting some intolerant Puritans and a small group of Jews settling in Newport. Quakerism eventually became the dominant religion in Rhode Island (Miller, 1976).

William Penn believed that God spoke directly to individuals through the conscience and that this was the basis for a commitment to religious freedom. Penn undertook deliberate efforts to bring to Pennsylvania people from diverse faiths: Anabaptists, Presbyterians, Puritans, Roman Catholics, and others who had no religious conviction. Pennsylvania was the first colony to experiment with the idea of denominational churches instead of an established church; no church received state assistance, nor did the state interfere in church affairs. Members of a denomination were not expected to withdraw from the world but to participate in it.

As might be expected, Pennsylvania's "holy experiment" was not without problems. Because Penn was a Quaker, Quakers had more government influence than other denominations, and for a time they functioned as an informal established church. Although Quaker dominance caused some friction, compared to other colonies, Pennsylvania and Rhode Island provided the clearest alternative to the Old World tradition of state support for an established church.

Founded by Lord Baltimore, Maryland was originally intended as a refuge for English Catholics.

> [If] Papists and Protestants, Jews and Turks, may be embarked in one ship . . . none of the Papists, Protestants, Jews or Turks [should] be forced to come to the ship's prayer or worship nor compelled from their own particular prayer or worship, if they practice any.
>
> Roger Williams (1603–1683)

The principle of religious freedom was self-serving because Catholics constituted a minority even among the first contingent settling Maryland, and Catholicism remained a minority faith throughout the colonial period. Still, Baltimore's commitment to religious tolerance attracted immigrants from diverse faiths. But Maryland's experiment was not successful: The Church of England became its established church in 1702. Because three other faiths—Anabaptists, Presbyterians, and Quakers—had more members, the Church of England was established on condition that religious tolerance would be maintained. Such tolerance was reserved for the currently residing religious groups; incoming Jews and Unitarians were not allowed to settle in Maryland at that time (Hudson, 1973).

How was the principle of religious freedom established in all the colonies?

As the mid-eighteenth century approached, a significant event (later termed the "Great Awakening") promoted the principle of religious freedom, beginning with ideas in the widely read writings of Jonathan Edwards and other New England ministers. Concerned about the "extraordinary dullness" of people's faith, Edwards challenged individuals to demonstrate personal commitment to their faith in their everyday lives, and he spoke of the necessity of faith being emotional as well as rational. Edwards argued that we can be told honey is sweet, but to taste honey results in a knowledge that is "direct, intuitive, certain, and rests upon experience that can be neither doubted nor denied" (Gaustad & Schmidt, 2002, p. 59). Edwards believed that such "knowledge" was the substance of genuine faith.

In 1740, English preacher George Whitefield presented his similar challenge to colonial people, with dramatic results. (See Figure 6.1.) Although Protestant ministers throughout the colonies invited him, Whitefield avoided churches, preferring to speak in open fields. His sermons stimulated people's emotions as much as their intellect, and audiences responded enthusiastically. Whitefield insisted that being a Christian was not about belonging to a particular church, but being committed to faith and demonstrating that commitment in everyday life. Ironically, his sermons resulted in a huge increase in church attendance and church members. Nord (1995) describes a sermon in

FIGURE 6.1

Whitefield's impact on colonial America is commemorated in this statue on the University of Pennsylvania campus.

Source: Photo courtesy of the author.

Philadelphia in which Whitefield looked up to the sky and shouted:

> Father Abraham, whom have you in heaven? Any Episcopalians? No! Any Presbyterians? No! Any Independents or Methodists? No, no, no! Who have you there? . . . We don't know those names here. All who are here are Christians . . . Then God help us to forget party names and become Christians in deed and truth. (p. 103)

The impact of the Great Awakening on religious freedom was that it denied the significance of differences between Protestant sects. Prior to the Great Awakening, Protestants belonged to one sect or another, each defining itself as the "true faith."

This **sectarian** view of Christianity gave way to a consensus about what it meant to be Christian: accepting others, doing good deeds, and ignoring theological controversy. The Great Awakening replaced a sectarian approach to Christianity with a **denominational** view based on the perception of a singular Protestant church that is called— denominated—by many different names such as Anglican, Lutheran, or Baptist. Although the denominational view united Protestants, Catholics were not included.

The Emerging Concept of Religious Freedom

In the mid-eighteenth century, Europeans were making significant discoveries based on scientific inquiry. Isaac Newton alone was responsible for discovering the principles of gravitation and light; he also developed differential calculus and even had time to invent the reflecting telescope. The dissemination of ideas and inventions during this era, eventually called "the Enlightenment," created an increased respect for science and a diminished belief in miracles and the supernatural. Some argued that religious truths, like scientific truths, would be discovered by human reason, not through divine revelation. This thinking led to the birth of **Deism**, a religious philosophy based on rationality that was devoid of mysticism. Deists acknowledged that God created the universe but insisted that human beings must use their intellects

> I do not believe in the creed professed by the Jewish church, by the Roman church, by the Greek church, by the Turkish church, by the Protestant church nor by any church that I know of. My own mind is my own church.
>
> Thomas Paine (1737–1809)

to understand the rational principles by which the universe functions. In response to the increased emphasis on rationality and the scientific method as the preferred means of ascertaining truth, many intellectuals rejected all religious faiths. Although some American colonists declared themselves **atheists**, denying the existence of God, the religious philosophy of Deism was more appealing than atheism to Christian intellectuals in the colonies.

What was the relationship between Deism and Christianity?

Deism dismissed much of what constituted traditional Christian beliefs. Deists believed God created the world and a system of natural laws that governed it. Although they believed that God would reward or punish the soul after death, they did not believe that God was an active force in the everyday world. Thomas Jefferson and Benjamin Franklin were among many who were attracted to Deism as a religious philosophy. Although Deists denied the divinity of Christ, they tended to admire his moral teachings; therefore, many Deists attended churches of various denominations while others never went to church. Although Deist views were not popular among the general public, the principles of Deism influenced several people who would write the documents that transformed the thirteen colonies into the United States of America. Curiously, these "enlightened" founders included little about religion in the Constitution.

Why was there so little reference to religion in the original Constitution?

Although the majority of men responsible for writing the U.S. Constitution were Protestant and of European descent, they chose to defy their European traditions and create the first secular

> The government of the United States of America is not in any sense founded on the Christian Religion.
>
> John Adams (1735–1826)

government. For centuries, the governments of most European nations claimed to derive their authority from God; therefore, the state had both the right and the responsibility to intrude into religious

issues and attempt to resolve religious controversies, usually in favor of a majority faith and against minority faiths. The Articles of Confederation had continued that tradition by referring to "the Great Governor of the World" (Jacoby, 2005, p. 30), but the authors of the U.S. Constitution cited "We the People" as the source of the government's power and authority, deliberately excluding any reference to God. When challenged to explain this omission, Alexander Hamilton's tongue-in-cheek response was "We forgot" (Chernow, 2004, p. 235).

They did not forget. When the delegates met in Philadelphia in 1787, they were well aware of the debate that had recently occurred in Virginia. In the early 1780s, Patrick Henry unsuccessfully lobbied to have Christianity declared Virginia's established religion. In 1784, he introduced a resolution calling for a tax on Virginians to promote Christianity but allowing them to designate their denomination or even a particular church as the recipient of their tax dollars. Those belonging to no church could contribute their taxes to a general education fund. This resolution gained wide support, even receiving George Washington's endorsement. On November 11, the Virginia legislature voted 47 to 32 in favor of the resolution, but the legislative session was dismissed shortly after this vote.

The opposition to this resolution and the legislation it called for was led by James Madison, soon to be a major contributor in drafting the U.S. Constitution. Madison saw the dangers inherent in enacting such legislation, and he wrote a pamphlet to describe them. Waldman (2006) cited Madison's major concern: "Who does not see that the same authority which can establish Christianity, in exclusion of all other Religions, may establish with the same ease any particular sect of Christians, in exclusion of all other Sects?" (p. 36). Madison's pamphlet was widely distributed and generated widespread support for his arguments. By the time the Virginia legislature reconvened, they were inundated with petitions and documents espousing staunch opposition to establishing Christianity as Virginia's state religion, some even coming from Christians—especially evangelical Christians.

Based on the previous passage of his resolution, Patrick Henry brought a bill to the Virginia legislature to establish Christianity as the state religion, but it was soundly defeated. Later, the legislators discussed Thomas Jefferson's "Statute for Religious Freedom," which they modified slightly before passing, making this legislation not only state law, but also a model for other states and for the first amendment that guaranteed religious freedom in the United States.

Why wasn't religious freedom guaranteed in the Constitution?

By the time of the Revolutionary War in 1776, four colonies had guaranteed the right of people to worship as they chose: Rhode Island, Pennsylvania, Delaware, and New Jersey. The Church of England remained the established church in other colonies; however, during the war one colony after another ceased providing church support. By the war's end, only Massachusetts, New Hampshire, Connecticut, and Virginia continued to have established churches. In 1786, the new nation was still struggling to function under its first constitution, entitled the Articles of Confederation, when the delegates met in Philadelphia to write the new Constitution. Especially after what had just transpired in Virginia, most of them did not question the issue of religious freedom, nor did they appear interested in debating it.

The delegates did debate other issues, however, such as which civil rights should be granted to those who were not Protestant. New Jersey's constitution stated that every officeholder had to be Protestant, a provision not revised until 1844. Some states required all those seeking public office to recite an oath that they had no allegiance to any foreign power—"ecclesiastic as well as civil" (Myers, 1960, p. 46). Of course, a devout Catholic could not take such an oath, which was the reason it was required. Some states merely demanded that an officeholder be a Christian; Maryland, which eventually permitted Jews to settle, stood alone as the only state that allowed Jews to vote and hold public office. Obviously, Jefferson's wall between church and state had yet to be built.

As they wrote the Constitution, the authors affirmed the principle of religious freedom by stating, "No religious Test shall ever be required as a Qualification to any Office or public Trust under the United States" (Article VI). When completed, this was the only reference to religion, and it was not widely supported. At the debate over ratifying

the Constitution in North Carolina, a minister protested that Article VI was "an invitation for Jews and pagans of every kind to come among us" (Jacoby, 2005, p. 30).

To secure consensus for the Constitution, the question of having an established church was left to each state. Because religious freedom was a well-established principle in most states, the authors may have thought there was no need to include such a statement until it became obvious that several amendments would be necessary before enough states would ratify the Constitution. Eck (2001) describes how Jefferson used the "Statute for Religious Freedom" he had written for Virginia's legislature in 1786 when he drafted the First Amendment's explicit guarantee of religious freedom.

Nord (1995) argued that much of the impetus for religious freedom stemmed from the Enlightenment belief that "natural reason, operating in a free culture, was the way to the truth" (p. 108). Yet most church leaders supported the First Amendment for similar reasons, especially evangelical Christians. They were concerned about separating church and state because they had already been persecuted and harassed. Evangelicals equated religious persecution with political persecution and insisted that Christ called for separating church and state in the statement: "render unto Caesar that which belongs to Caesar." Jefferson's letter espousing a "wall of separation between church and state" was written to Connecticut evangelicals who were pleased by his comments, saying to him in response, "Religion is at all times and places a matter between God and individuals" (Waldman, 2006, p. 38). Ministers such as Ezra Stiles believed that through competition, truth would prevail: "Here Deism will have its full chance; nor need libertines . . . complain of being overcome by any weapons but the gentle, powerful ones of argument and truth" (Hudson, 1973, p. 110).

Did the First Amendment establish religious freedom in the new nation?

Although the freedom to worship according to one's personal religious beliefs was guaranteed in the Bill of Rights, it was guaranteed in principle more than in practice. Of the two states still supporting an established church, Connecticut ended its tax subsidies to the Congregational Church in 1817, and Massachusetts did the same in 1833 (Myers, 1960). Yet having a minority faith could still affect one's political rights. As the Constitution was being ratified by the thirteen states, only three of them—Pennsylvania, Maryland, and Delaware—permitted Catholics to vote. Within five years of the Constitution's ratification, three more states—South Carolina, Georgia, and New York—granted the vote to its Catholic citizens, and eventually the remaining states did the same (Myers, 1960).

All states denied Jews the right to hold political office by requiring officeholders to take an oath that they believed in Jesus Christ, but in 1818, a Scottish Presbyterian named Thomas Kennedy introduced a bill to the Maryland legislature to end what he called this prejudice against Jews. Even though Kennedy was defeated in two subsequent elections, he continued to lobby for his bill, and after eight years it was approved, making Maryland the first state to grant full political rights to Jews (Niebuhr, 2008). Although their numbers were limited, Jews continued to encounter intolerance and a refusal to allow them to have political influence. Their political vulnerability was illustrated during the Civil War when General Ulysses S. Grant expelled Jews from areas he had reclaimed by military conquest for the United States; however, President Lincoln rescinded Grant's order (Miller, 1976). North Carolina granted civil rights to Jews in 1868; New Hampshire granted Jews the right to vote in 1876.

Was any group actively persecuted for their religious beliefs?

Religious freedom was violently denied to the followers of Mormonism, the Church of Jesus Christ of Latter-Day Saints, which was founded on the revelations of Joseph Smith in the early 1800s. After his *Book of Mormon* was published in 1830, Smith found followers captivated by his new vision of the past and his responses to major religious controversies of the day. He aroused animosity among traditional Christian denominations by his promotion of polygamy and other ideas deemed unconventional and unacceptable in American society. Smith's first church in Ohio was not welcomed, and when the members moved to Missouri, they were attacked and forced to leave, eventually settling in Nauvoo, Illinois. They lived there for only a few years before Smith was arrested and incarcerated at nearby Carthage, where a masked mob broke into his cell and shot and killed him. Miller (1976) declared, "The rise of Mormonism tested the American dedication to religious liberty, and the nation ultimately failed the test" (p. 111).

A Challenge to the Separation of Church and State

In 1810, Congress mandated Sunday mail service. Conservative Christian leaders lobbied aggressively against it, denouncing Sunday mail delivery as a sacrilege, but business leaders insisted on the necessity of uninterrupted mail. In 1828, the controversy came to the Senate Committee on the Post Office and Post Roads. Kentucky senator Richard M. Johnson, a war hero and devout Baptist, chaired the committee, yet in his report to Congress, he declared unequivocally that it would be unconstitutional for the federal government to engage in policy or practice that betrayed a preference for the Christian Sabbath. In the report, Johnson emphasized the history of religious persecution and intolerance that had created the need for a line separating church and state, and that "the line cannot be too strongly drawn" (Jacoby, 2005, p. 31). In the 1840s, the telegraph ended the reliance of business on daily mail service, but the principle of separation of church and state had been upheld.

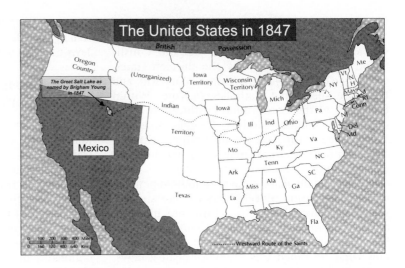

FIGURE 6.2 Mormon Trail Map

When Brigham Young was chosen to replace Smith, he was convinced that the Mormons would not be granted religious freedom anywhere in the United States, so he asked them to follow him "to a far distant region . . . where bigotry, intolerance, and insatiable oppression lose their power" (Gaustad & Schmidt, 2002, p. 178). In 1847, Young and his followers began an ambitious journey of a thousand miles, finally stopping to settle on land that belonged to Mexico. (See Figure 6.2.) One year later, as the Mexican-American War ended, the Great Salt Lake Valley where the Mormons had settled became part of the United States. Because there was no one close enough to persecute the Mormons, they successfully populated the territory of Utah and applied for statehood. Their application was denied six times until 1897, when they changed their state constitution to renounce polygamy (Kosmin & Lachman, 1993).

Religious freedom was also not extended to those who rejected religious beliefs. Atheists in Virginia could be arrested for publicly professing that God did not exist. In 1833, Abner Kneeland was arrested and incarcerated in Massachusetts for questioning the divinity of Jesus, his miracles, and his resurrection. Kneeland was convicted under the state's blasphemy law and sentenced to sixty days in jail; however, his conviction resulted in vigorous protests. Kneeland was the last person convicted of blasphemy in Massachusetts, although the law was not repealed for many years (Miller, 1976).

The Rise and Fall of Anti-Catholicism

In contrast to the slow but steady growth of members in Protestant churches, membership in the Catholic Church increased dramatically. By 1850, the number of Catholics in the United States had expanded from several hundred thousand to nearly 2 million. Between 1820 and 1865, of approximately 2 million Irish immigrants to the United States, over a million were Catholic (Kosmin & Lachman, 1993). Because of its assistance to Irish immigrants, the New York City political and labor organization known as Tammany Hall became a powerful force influencing the city and state of New York, which intensified anti-Catholic sentiments.

What was the impact of large numbers of Catholic immigrants?

Immigrants have almost always provoked hostility in some Americans, but the arrival of so many Catholics fueled Protestant fears and created an atmosphere of suspicion and distrust. Because the Catholic Church had persecuted, tortured, and even killed those who defied its authority in the past, Protestants believed that Catholics would not hesitate to employ any tactic that would convert Protestants to the Catholic faith. Several popular novels, including *The Awful Disclosures of Maria Monk,* described Protestant women being kidnapped and confined in underground cells in convents and subjected to unspeakable tortures.

Following a fistfight between laborers at a Charlestown, Massachusetts, convent and brickyard workmen, the workmen spread rumors that the convent had imprisoned a woman just as the novels suggested. Although published results of an investigation said there was no truth to the rumor, a mob gathered and set fire to the convent. No police or militia appeared. Ten fire engines responded to the call, but the fire brigades insisted they could

> We have just enough religion to make us hate, but not enough to make us love one another.
>
> Jonathan Swift (1667–1745)

not act without orders from a magistrate, so they watched as the convent was destroyed. A meeting of Protestants called by the mayor of Boston produced a formal statement denouncing the mob's actions, but the Catholic Church never received compensation for its losses (Myers, 1960).

Why was hostility directed against Catholics?

The 1830s and 1840s was the era of Native American and Know-Nothing parties promoting **anti-Catholicism** and anti-immigrant sentiments. The Know-Nothings dedicated themselves to reducing a perceived growth of Catholic power and influence. Anti-Catholic prejudices were also reflected in public school textbooks in which priests were depicted as living in luxury, oblivious to the poor and hungry, and the Catholic Church was described as the enemy of freedom and knowledge because of its history of religious persecution and its suppression of the Bible (Miller, 1976). It is not

surprising that at this time the Catholic Church felt compelled to create an alternative school system, increasing Protestant animosity toward Catholics.

Protestants were not opposed to separate schools for Catholics, but in 1840, Bishop Hughes of New York created controversy when he petitioned the New York Public Schools Society for funds to support Catholic schools. Hughes argued that separate schools for Catholic children had become necessary because of anti-Catholic materials in public schools. Protestants objected to using tax dollars to teach "Catholic dogma" and accused the bishop of trying to undermine public schools. Hughes provided excerpts from textbooks that ridiculed Catholicism, including one book in which the Catholic Church was accused of encouraging drunkenness to maintain its hold on church members who would reject the "Romish religion" if they could only think rationally (Myers, 1960). Although the New York Public Schools Society denied Hughes's petition for funds, they agreed to remove anti-Catholic content from textbooks and to exclude from school libraries books that clearly promoted anti-Catholic prejudice. Although this seemed to solve the problem in New York, growing anti-Catholic sentiment would lead to the shocking events of the Philadelphia Bible Riots.

What were the Philadelphia Bible Riots?

In 1844, the Philadelphia School Board approved the substitution of the Douay (Catholic) Bible for Catholic students when Bible reading was required. An anti-Catholic group called for a meeting in Kensington, an Irish Catholic district in Philadelphia, to protest the use of the Catholic Bible in public schools. The meeting provoked area residents, who attacked participants and forced the meeting to end. The leaders of the anti-Catholic group insisted on a second meeting in Kensington, which resulted in violence that left one person dead and fifty wounded.

The following day, a large crowd gathered to approve a resolution in support of teaching the Protestant version of the Bible in public schools. The meeting soon became uncontrollable, and when the mob heard shots fired from a nearby building, they set fire to that building and went on a rampage. Troops were called in, but before they could restore order, several homes had burned, eight men were dead, and sixteen were wounded. The night was quiet, and there was no further violence the next morning. Most of the soldiers withdrew.

By mid-afternoon, a Protestant mob gathered once again, setting fire to a Catholic Church and a nearby row of houses whose tenants were Irish. Troops were recalled, but before they arrived, the mob attacked another church. This time the police surrounded the church, but the mob drove them off with bricks and stones and set fire to that church and a Catholic school; then the fire spread to frame houses nearby. The troop commander summoned to Philadelphia declared martial law. Property losses from the riots included forty-five homes, two churches, and a school. Violence flared again a month later, and by the time the Philadelphia Bible Riots were finally over, 58 people had been killed and 140 wounded. The anti-Catholic group blamed the Irish for the deaths and injuries and even for the destruction of churches and homes in Irish neighborhoods (Myers, 1960; Ravitch, 1999).

People settling in frontier areas were initially more receptive to Catholics because of the need to attract more people and establish communities. In the early 1800s, there was a wave of migration to Kentucky, and Louisville was one of the early settlements. While Methodists built the first church in 1809, Catholic settlers constructed their church just two years later and the majority of donations were from members of the Methodist Church. As the number of Catholics increased, they needed a bigger church, and the celebration of the laying of the cornerstone took place in the Presbyterian Church with Protestants representing the majority of those attending the ceremony. Then came the surge of nativism in the 1850s. For the 1855 elections, Louisville newspapers endorsed a slate of anti-immigrant candidates, predicting dire consequences if they were not elected. On the day of the election, mobs assaulted Catholic voters and attacked Catholic property, with one church averting damage when the archbishop turned over the keys for the church to Louisville's mayor. Anti-Catholicism had come to the frontier (Niebuhr, 2008). Although anti-Catholic sentiment would remain strong for another decade, other issues and events would command the nation's attention.

What caused anti-Catholic sentiments in the United States to subside?

Nord (1995) concluded, "The politics of race and the Civil War put the politics of anti-Catholicism to rest" (pp. 73–74). Although the Great Awakening unified Protestant churches, they were split over the slavery issue. During the Civil War, Catholic soldiers fought and died as bravely as the Protestant soldiers beside them, and anti-Catholic sentiments declined. After the war, anti-Catholic prejudice still existed and flared up on occasion, yet it never reached the level that fostered the rise of the Native American and Know-Nothing parties. Another factor in the decline of anti-Catholic prejudice after the Civil War was that the Catholic Church was no longer the only serious opponent for Protestant churches. Religious diversity in the United States was about to increase dramatically.

How did religious diversity increase following the Civil War?

After the Civil War, immigration to the United States surpassed prewar levels. By 1900, there were 75 million Americans, 25 million of whom were foreign-born adults and their children. The number of Roman Catholics in the United States increased from 2 million in 1850 to 4 million in 1870, and to 12 million by 1900. Although Protestants continued to be the dominant group, a third of Americans who claimed church membership in 1920 were members of the Catholic Church (Hudson, 1973).

Catholic immigrants came from Germany, Ireland, Poland, Italy, and Czechoslovakia, and their ethnic diversity created tension within the church. Not only did they speak different languages, but also they had different traditions and customs related to their worship. The church's inability to resolve ethnic differences led to the creation of the Polish National Catholic Church in the 1890s and the Lithuanian National Catholic Church in 1914. Protestant churches faced similar challenges. The majority of Protestant immigrants were Lutherans whose diversity resulted in Finnish, Icelandic, Swedish, Danish, German, and Norwegian Lutheran churches. According to Hudson (1973), there were at least twenty-four different kinds of Lutheran churches by 1900.

Diversity also resulted from missionaries proselytizing Native Americans and former slaves. Minimal efforts to reach either group had been made prior to the Civil War because both groups had been perceived as heathen. The Great Awakening had generated some enthusiasm for seeking Indian converts, but Native Americans who accepted Christianity usually blended new beliefs with their old ones. Following the Civil War, the federal government banned many tribal religions and provided missionaries with funding to build schools for Indian children. Protestants often established off-reservation boarding schools, whereas Catholics tended to establish boarding schools and day schools on reservations (Hendry, 2003).

Although Christian ministers were willing to evangelize and recruit slaves into the faith, many slave owners were reluctant to have their captives converted. They approved of conversion only if ministers emphasized the need for the slaves to submit to both divine and earthly authorities with the promise of eternal life as their reward for enduring slavery in this life (Lippy, 1994). After the Civil War, Protestant missionaries actively recruited the 3.5 million newly freed slaves. Former slaves who were Christians no longer wanted to attend the churches their owners had forced them to attend, especially when the church members still expected former slaves to sit in the back seats. Separate churches for freedmen were established, the majority being Baptist with Methodists a distant second. By 1916, 43% of blacks were members of a church, a higher percentage than for the white population (Hudson, 1973).

As racial and ethnic groups added to the diversity, so did the creation of new faiths. Mary Baker Eddy responded to the growing importance of scientific research by founding Church of Christ, Scientist. Eddy spoke of an Eternal Mind as the source of life, and believed that disease was a consequence of mental error. Christian Scientists sought to overcome the illusions that have been the source of all human troubles (Lippy, 1994).

William Miller was abandoned by "Millerites" in 1844 when his prediction about Jesus returning did not come true. Many of his former followers turned to Ellen Harmon White, whose spiritual revelations included hygienic practices and dietary restrictions for the faithful to ensure the return of Jesus; White's followers became Seventh-Day Adventists.

Adding to the complexity of diverse faiths in the late nineteenth century was the fact that all immigrants were not simply Christian.

What non-Christian religions were included among immigrants?

Immigrants to the United States included members of non-Christian religious groups. On the West Coast, Buddhists among Chinese and Japanese immigrants established a Young Men's Buddhist Association in 1898. On the East Coast, 1.5 million Jews came to America between 1880 and 1905 to escape anti-Semitism in Russia, Poland, Rumania, and Austro-Hungary. Hudson (1973) cites an adviser to the czar predicting the consequences of new Russian policies: "One-third of the Jews will emigrate, one-third will be baptized, and one-third will starve" (p. 332).

Diversity increased within the Jewish community as well. In 1880, most of the 250,000 Jews in the United States were descendants of German-speaking Jews from central Europe affiliated with reform Judaism; Jews emigrating later from Eastern Europe were more likely to be orthodox than reform. According to Hudson (1973), more than 3 million Jews had immigrated by 1920, with orthodox Jews outnumbering reform Jews. The largest Jewish group, larger than the total number of all religious Jews combined, comprised those not affiliated with any synagogue; many of them were Zionists whose activity was more likely to be political than religious.

America also experienced an increase in people professing no religion. Darwin's theory of evolution and other scientific advances caused many people to question the validity of religious faith. English scientist Thomas Huxley declared himself an **agnostic**, believing that one could neither prove nor disprove the existence of God. Lawyer

> A believer is a bird in a cage; a freethinker is an eagle parting the clouds with tireless wing.
>
> Robert Ingersoll (1833–1899)

and orator Robert Ingersoll published *Why I Am an Agnostic* in 1896 and traveled across America questioning many aspects of Christianity. Still, some scholars reconciled Darwin's ideas with religion by believing in God, just not in specific denominational doctrines. The Christian majority reacted by punishing those who strayed from conventional beliefs as well as nonbelievers. In 1878, Alexander Winchell publicly rejected the Genesis version of creation, and Vanderbilt University trustees asked him to resign. When Winchell refused, they abolished his position. In 1886, James Woodrow was removed from his faculty position at Columbia Theological Seminary for advocating the possibility of reconciling Darwin's ideas with those of the Bible (Hudson, 1973).

Did increasing numbers of non-Christians cause anti-Catholic prejudice to diminish?

Although racial prejudice became more dominant than religious prejudice after the Civil War, a large Catholic immigration fueled anti-Catholic attitudes. Protestant leaders called for tolerance, yet others said tolerance meant a lack of religious commitment and an indifference to the true faith, and they urged Protestants not to give equal status to any other religion.

Forced to disband by federal troops during Reconstruction, the Ku Klux Klan was revived in 1915. In their efforts to promote and maintain white supremacy in the United States, the Klan employed tactics of intimidation including threats and violence. Although their primary targets were blacks and foreigners, as a Christian group, its members were also hostile to Catholics and Jews. Membership in the Klan increased every year for ten years, peaking at 2 million in 1925. (See Figure 6.3.) It fell to 100,000 by 1928. At a 1941 rally in Charleston, the Grand Dragon of North Carolina was heckled and booed by many of the 3,000 who attended (Myers, 1960). The last time the Klan's anti-Catholicism would be seen on the national stage was in the presidential election of 1928.

FIGURE 6.3

The Ku Klux Klan had its highest membership when the group sponsored this 1925 march in front of the nation's capitol.

Source: Library of Congress, Prints and Photographs Division.

How did the 1928 election demonstrate anti-Catholic prejudice?

The Democratic Party nominated Alfred E. Smith, the first Catholic to run for president. Some political and religious leaders hailed the nomination as evidence of growing religious tolerance; others saw it as a threat to the social order. The Klan and other anti-Catholic organizations insisted that the Vatican was directing Smith's campaign with a Jesuit committee assigned to persuade Protestants to ignore Smith's religion as an issue. Presbyterians were urged to vote for the Republican candidate. Methodists were urged to vote for the man who prayed the same way they did. Myers (1960) quoted an excerpt from an anti-Catholic magazine claiming that Smith would get not only the Catholic vote, but also "the Jew and Negro vote . . . gamblers, the red-light and dope-ring vote . . . the Jew-Jesuit movie gang (vote) who want sex films and Sunday shows to coin millions through the corruption of youth" (p. 268).

Although anti-Catholic prejudice contributed to Smith's defeat, it is not clear how large a role it played. Democrats were the minority party, the economy was doing well, and Republican candidate Herbert Hoover was widely respected. Despite the anti-Catholic assault, Smith received 40% of the vote, more than the Protestant Democratic candidates had received in the two previous elections (34% in 1920; 28% in 1924). Smith had a higher percentage of votes than a majority of Democrats running for Congress in that election (Hudson, 1973).

After Franklin Roosevelt was elected president in 1932, Catholic participation in national politics became common, and the question of whether a Catholic could be elected president was answered in 1960 when Americans chose John F. Kennedy. It is possible that Kennedy's election was not so much a measure of increased religious tolerance as it was an indication of what has been called the "Americanization of religion." Since World War II, attitudes of American Catholics gradually diverged from a strict recognition of Roman Catholic Church doctrine and more closely allied with attitudes of the Protestant majority. By the 1990s, polls documented Catholic attitudes as similar to Protestant attitudes on such issues as abortion, birth control, ordination of women, and marriage of priests (Kosmin & Lachman, 1993).

Anti-Semitism in America

In 1451, the King of Castile (Spain) endorsed a blood purity statute declaring that Jewish converts could not hold office in the Catholic Church. This was the beginning of the transformation of Jews being perceived in racial rather than religious terms, and that change was not restricted to Europe. In the 1870s, American public school textbooks referred to Jews as "a race," using traditional stereotypes of Jews as greedy, selfish, and manipulating. Jews were described as unethical entrepreneurs who tried to monopolize certain professions and as the devious power behind the throne in many European countries (Miller, 1976). In 1879, the term **anti-Semitism** was employed

> Anti-Semitism is a noxious weed that should be cut out. It has no place in America.
>
> William Howard Taft (1857–1930)

for the first time by a German journalist to express his opposition to the Jewish "race." In his essay, Wilhelm Marr made the paradoxical argument that although Jews were inferior to Aryans, they were a threat to Aryan world dominance (Carroll, 2001). Reacting against such stereotypes, one Jewish writer complained, "In the popular mind, the Jew is never judged as an individual, but as a specimen of a whole race whose members are identically of the same kind" (Eck, 2001, p. 303). All of this anti-Semitism culminated in the holocaust where the Nazis even arrested Jews who had converted to Christianity because "once born a Jew, always a Jew" (Wegner, 2002, p. 152).

From 1890 to 1914, Jews accounted for 10% of all immigrants. With increased numbers of Jews in America, anti-Semitism was at least as strong as earlier anti-Catholicism. Ironically, despite their experience of oppression, Catholics joined Protestants in vilifying Jews. In the popular press, Eck (2001) found Jews presented as undesirable aliens who could not assimilate because they were "incapable of grasping American ideals" (p. 50), although many Jews refuted the view by achieving extraordinary success, especially in higher education. As the number of Jews at Harvard escalated from 6% in 1908 to 22% in 1922, the president of Harvard proposed establishing a quota for the number of Jews Harvard would accept. Faculty rejected his plan, but Harvard still limited the number of Jews for many decades. Other colleges established quotas for Jewish enrollment at anywhere from 3% to 16% (Dinnerstein, 1994).

In what ways was anti-Semitism promoted?

Anti-Semitism had several popular advocates. In the 1920s, one was Henry Ford. In his role as publisher of a weekly newspaper, *The Dearborn Independent*, Ford printed the text of "The Protocols of the Elders of Zion," which documented the activities of a Jewish conspiracy plotting a revolution to undermine Christian civilization and establish Jewish supremacy throughout the world. Ford's popularity made it likely that his readers would take his warning seriously. In a poll taken in 1923, *Collier's* magazine reported that 260,000 people— over a third of those polled—endorsed Ford to run for president (Ribuffo, 1997).

Shortly after Ford published "Protocols," the document was exposed as a forgery concocted in the late 1890s by Russian loyalists supporting the czar. In response to this revelation and to a legal action for slander brought by a Jewish businessman, Ford wrote a letter of apology, promising not to publish anti-Semitic articles again, but the damage had been done. Ford ceased publishing his newspaper, yet he continued to maintain and express anti-Semitic attitudes. In 1938, Ford traveled to Germany to receive a medal from Adolf Hitler in honor of his anti-Semitic actions, and two years later in England during an interview with the *Manchester Guardian*, Ford insisted that "international Jewish bankers" caused World War II (Ribuffo, 1997).

In the 1930s, President Franklin Roosevelt invited many Jews into his cabinet, and over vigorous objections, he appointed a Jew to the Supreme Court, Felix Frankfurter. However, anti-Semitism found a spokesman in a priest named Charles Edward Coughlin. In his popular radio show, Father Coughlin attacked President Roosevelt, communists, and Jews. Although reprimanded for his attacks on the president, Coughlin was not criticized by church superiors for his anti-Semitism because he disguised it in anti-communist rhetoric (Myers, 1960).

In 1938, Coughlin revealed his anti-Semitic attitudes by reprinting "The Protocols of the Elders of Zion" despite the evidence of its forgery. Nineteen thousand people attended a gathering in Madison Square Garden where Coughlin gave a speech, surrounded by banners declaring "Smash Jewish Communism!" and "Stop Jewish Domination of Christian America!" Coughlin's use of rumor and distortions of fact to castigate Jews was challenged by Jewish groups, denounced by many Protestants, and contradicted by his embarrassed superiors in the church. He was forced to abandon his radio program in 1940, but for the next three years, young men belonging to his "Christian Frontier" organization roamed the streets in several large cities, affixing obscene materials to Jewish businesses or synagogues and even assaulting Jews they chanced to encounter (Myers, 1960). Anti-Semitism intensified during World War II. According to one poll, over half of Jewish soldiers in the armed forces had changed their names to generic American surnames to avoid anti-Semitic remarks

> [The Jew] always talks about the equality of all men, without regard of race or color. Those who are stupid begin to believe that.
>
> Adolf Hitler (1889–1945)

from other soldiers. By the end of the war, 58% of Americans agreed with the statement, "Jews have too much power in the United States" (Dinnerstein, 1994, p. 146).

What influence did the Holocaust have on American attitudes?

Learning about the horrors of the Holocaust changed American attitudes toward Jews after World War II. Many returning veterans deplored anti-Semitism and other prejudices they had witnessed. Hollywood produced films exposing the prejudice and bigotry of anti-Semitism in America, and one of them, *Gentleman's Agreement*, won the

Oscar for best picture in 1947. Editorials in many newspapers and magazine articles reinforced the idea that anti-Semitism was no longer acceptable in the United States. Although it was in the 1950s that "under God" was added to the Pledge of Allegiance and "In God We Trust" to U.S. currency to emphasize U.S. opposition to "godless communism," being a Catholic, Protestant, or Jew was less important than being someone who believed in the Judeo-Christian God (Fraser, 1999).

In his analysis of religion in America, *Protestant-Catholic-Jew*, sociologist Will Herberg (1955) wrote that Catholics and Jews reflected American attitudes as much as Protestants did. An "Americanization" of religion meant that each faith "regards itself as merely an alternative and variant form of being religious in the American way" (p. 278). Herberg admitted that the majority of Americans were still anti-Semitic, but they knew it was inappropriate to act on their feelings. *Look* magazine reported that Hitler had made anti-Semitism unequivocally disreputable. A series of polls in the 1950s reported Americans expressing increasingly positive attitudes toward Jews. Discrimination against Jews still occurred, especially in such prestigious professions as law and medicine, yet doors had opened, especially to colleges and universities. By 1965, *Time* magazine reported that "anti-Semitism is at an all time low," and that overt expressions of anti-Semitism were "out of fashion" (Dinnerstein, 1994, p. 171). However, a national immigration law was passed in 1965 that would challenge Americans with a new religious dilemma.

The Impact of Immigration Reform on Religious Diversity

The 1924 U.S. immigration law had prohibited Asian immigration, and strict quotas ensured that the majority of American immigrants would be white and Christian. When President Lyndon Johnson signed the Immigration and Nationality Act of 1965, not only did the racial makeup of incoming immigrants change dramatically, but their religious affiliation did as well. From 1960 to 1990, Asians constituted more than 5 million of 15 million immigrants to the United States, and from 1990 to 1999, the Asian population grew 43% to total almost 11 million people.

They increased the religious diversity within and outside of Christianity; among them were 4 million Buddhists and enough Korean Christians to form 2,000 congregations. Jainists have established 60 temples and centers, Sikhs have almost 250 gurdwaras, and more than a million Hindus have established 700 temples (Gaustad & Schmidt, 2002; Niebuhr, 2008). Nationwide, America can claim over 6 million Muslims, exceeding the number of Presbyterians and equaling the number of Jews (Eck, 2001). There are increasing numbers of children from diverse faiths: About 20% of students attending public school in the United States identify as "religious minorities" (Clark et al., 2002).

Although proportions of those representing different religions have changed, what has not changed is the importance of religion. According to Elshtain (2001), data from the 2000 census report that 90% of Americans believed in God and 70% were members of a church, synagogue, or mosque. To appreciate this variety of faiths, Americans must confront stereotypes. We often make assumptions about an individual's religion based on his or her ethnicity, although there is religious diversity within any religion. An old stereotype is that Irish Americans are Catholic, even though the majority of Irish Americans are not. Most Asian Americans are not Buddhist or Hindu but instead are Christian, as are most Arab Americans, and most American Muslims are not Arabs (Kosmin & Lachman, 1993).

How have Americans responded to the increasing religious diversity?

Unfortunately, recent immigrants continue to encounter prejudice as Americans persist in their past religious animosities and revert to learned stereotypes. Muslim Americans have received the brunt of these negative reactions, in part because they are the largest religious minority in America. With 6 million Muslims now residing in the United States, including 4 million who were born here, Muslims have now surpassed Jews to become the second largest religious group in the nation (McCloud, 2006). But the primary reason for Barrett (2007) reporting that 75% of Muslims have personally experienced or know someone who has encountered anti-Muslim behavior is related to the terrorist activities carried out by extremist members of the Muslim faith. Americans have used the terrorist activities of some Muslims to stereotype all Muslims, including American Muslims. This has especially troubling implications for education, as illustrated by a study assessing how much pre-service teachers knew about the Islamic faith. Taggar (2006) reported the study's finding that one third of the pre-service teachers associated Islam with such negative words as "enemy," "Bin Laden," "terrorist," and "oppression of women." Only 5% of the future teachers said they would make sure their students understood that all Muslims were not terrorists.

Some American Muslims accuse television news programs of perpetuating Muslim stereotypes. Abdo (2006) has argued that: "television news programs (portray) Muslims as the new enemy of the West" (p. 5). This was illustrated following the 1995 bombing of the Murrah Federal Building in Oklahoma City when television broadcasts suggested that it was a terrorist attack and that authorities were pursuing "Middle Eastern-looking" men; the backlash was immediate. Islamic centers across the nation were sites for drive-by shootings and bomb threats. Muslim students on college campuses were assaulted. Muslim parents kept their children home for fear they would be taunted or even assaulted in school.

What the media did not report was the presence of Muslim firefighters rescuing victims of the bombing, Muslim physicians working to save victims' lives, and individual Muslims and Muslim organizations donating money to help the families of the victims. Despite their efforts, Muslims were denied an opportunity to participate in the nationally televised memorial service featuring words of consolation from President Clinton and representatives of Catholic, Jewish, and Protestant faiths.

Similar to the reaction following the Oklahoma City incident, media coverage of the 1996 crash of TWA Flight 800 prompted many Americans to suspect that Muslim terrorists were responsible, despite the lack of any evidence to support their suspicions. According to Khan (2004), this was another example of American media promoting the "demonization of Islam . . . and the prejudice, hatred and intolerance it bred" (p. 100). Anti-Muslim behaviors have included arson at mosques in Minneapolis and Quincy, Massachusetts, and a shotgun attack on Muslims in Memphis.

Anti-Muslim activity increased after the destruction of New York City's World Trade Center on 9/11. More than 8,000 Muslim Americans and Arab Americans were immediately interrogated, and within a few weeks, approximately 1,200 were incarcerated. This action was called a "preventive detention"; the prisoners were held without charges, they were denied the opportunity to post a bond, and they were not allowed any contact with their families (Abdo, 2006). Two months later, 600 were still held in custody, yet the FBI eventually admitted that they had no evidence linking any of the people incarcerated to terrorist activities. Of the 82,000 Muslim immigrants who were eventually fingerprinted and interrogated under the Patriot Act, officials could only find enough evidence to declare 11 of them as "suspected" terrorists (Lee, 2004). Such actions caused McCloud (2006) to claim that no other religion has been treated in such fashion in the history of America. According to Nimer (2004), in the thirty days following 9/11, Muslims filed 1,700 complaints of harassment and hate crimes. One man drove his car through the plate glass doors of an Ohio mosque, a Texas mosque was firebombed, and mosques were vandalized in Tallahassee, Cleveland, and Seattle. The violence has not been restricted to Muslims; Buddhist and Hindu temples were vandalized in Boston, Houston, and Detroit. An Egyptian businessman who had resided in the United States for twenty years was shot and killed in his California store. He was a Christian.

Although Muslims are accused of terrorism and violence, McCloud (2004) notes that it was the American government that imprisoned Muslims who were not guilty of any crimes, and American individuals who attacked mosques and Muslims. In Tennessee, citizens of Murfreesboro protested the construction of a mosque in their community, and an arsonist damaged construction equipment at the site. In New York, a teenager fired a shotgun outside a mosque, and three days later several teenagers shouted obscenities outside the same mosque during Ramadan services and they assaulted one Muslim worshipper. Graffiti has been spray-painted on many mosques (see Figure 6.4), and in Texas, in addition to graffiti spray-painted on an Arlington mosque, the vandals started a fire that destroyed the mosque's playground equipment. In Florida, a pipe bomb exploded in a Jacksonville mosque injuring 60 people (*Intelligence Report*, 2010).

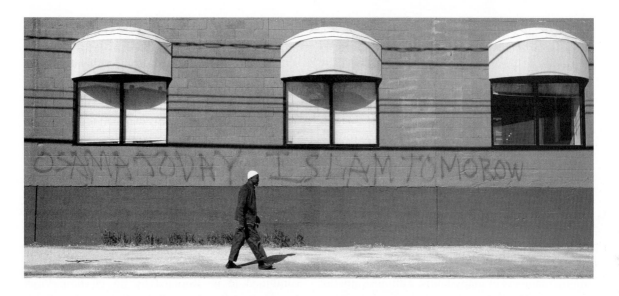

FIGURE 6.4 Mosque Graffiti

An American Muslim walks in front of a mosque that has been defaced by graffiti linking its worshippers with the terrorist Osama Bin Laden.

Source: Photograph by Gregory Rec, courtesy of the *Portland Press Herald.*

A national controversy erupted when New York Muslims announced the "Cordoba House" project to establish a mosque and community center a few blocks from the former site of the World Trade Center. Critics denounced the idea of a mosque at "Ground Zero," yet advocates pointed out that the building would not even be visible to someone standing at the memorial being built at Ground Zero. Critics argued that the proposed mosque was within a three-block radius of Ground Zero that they claimed was hallowed ground; yet advocates noted that within that three-block radius you could also find liquor stores, strip clubs, and pornography shops. Critics said "Cordoba House" was selected as the name in honor of a mosque built on the ruins of a former Christian church following the Muslim conquest of Spain; yet advocates explained that the name honors Cordoba for the tolerance that existed among Christians, Muslims, and Jews in that Spanish city over a thousand years ago (Rendall & Kane, 2010). Fortunately, the furor slowly began to diminish, efforts to create the mosque quietly continued, and on September 21, 2011, the Park 51 Islamic community center in Manhattan opened its doors without incident.

It is heartening that most Americans reject the violent discriminatory acts of bigots. Ever since 9/11, neighbors, churches, and community groups have offered sympathy and support to American Muslims. In Seattle, an ecumenical group created a program called "Watchful Eyes" to prevent or minimize anti-Muslim violence. In Denver, community volunteers stood with linked arms in a circle around a mosque to create a "ring of protection" against violence. In other cities, Christians and Jews helped to clean graffiti sprayed onto mosques and some purchased new signs or other items to replace those that were damaged or destroyed by vandals (Niebuhr, 2008). Despite these activities, Muslims continue to be victims of prejudice and violence. According to a 2007 Pew Research Center study, 15% of American Muslims reported being addressed with a racial slur and almost 25% had experienced discrimination. Further, over half said that it was more difficult to be a Muslim in America since 9/11 (Niebuhr, 2008). American Muslims have made numerous efforts to emphasize that Islam is a religion of peace and to distance themselves from terrorist activities. In 2005, the Islamic Society of North America disseminated a statement condemning extremism and violence, calling on all American Muslims to denounce such actions (Barrett, 2007), and every major Islamic organization in the United States has responded by issuing a statement condemning terrorist violence (Abdo, 2006). If Americans are not aware of this, it is probably because the American media has rarely reported these proclamations, especially the national media. In addition to denouncing terrorism, Muslims in the United States have recognized the importance of interacting with people to clarify beliefs and practices of the Islamic faith. Smith (2004) cites a Bagby survey of American Muslims reporting that 65% had participated in an interfaith activity.

As the United States has become home to believers from diverse faiths, some American individuals and organizations have engaged in activities to recognize this diversity and to promote interactions among members of many faiths. Administrators of the Mall of America in Minneapolis, the largest enclosed shopping facility in the United States, have created an interfaith group called the Mall Area Religious Council to promote interfaith dialogue and conversations between people of different religions and cultures. Is American interfaith support a harbinger of the future as business and community leaders come to terms with the implications of religious diversity? At a Whirlpool manufacturing

> The First Amendment has erected a wall between church and state. That wall must be kept high and impregnable.
>
> Justice Hugo Black (1886–1971)

plant in Nashville, Tennessee, a Muslim employee quit when he was refused permission to perform his midday prayers; those Muslim employees who remained prayed secretly. After a Muslim support group intervened, Whirlpool managers agreed to schedule afternoon coffee breaks to accommodate the Islamic prayer schedule (Eck, 2001).

In politics there have been some efforts to be inclusive of diverse faiths. Since 1991, Muslim and Hindu chaplains have joined Protestant, Catholic, and Jewish chaplains to provide invocations at the opening sessions of the House of Representatives

and Senate. But perhaps the most significant event occurred in 2006 when voters in a Minneapolis suburb made history by electing the first Muslim representative to Congress. Democrat Keith Ellison was a 43-year-old criminal defense attorney who had already served in the Minnesota state legislature. Ellison had converted to Islam while he was a college student, and he and his wife had four children. In addition to his public swearing into office ceremony, Ellison planned a private ceremony as well, a common practice among his colleagues. However, he created an immediate controversy when he announced that at the private ceremony he would take his oath on the Qur'an and not the Bible. In response to the controversy, Ellison chose a historic and indisputably American copy of the Qur'an—the one from Thomas Jefferson's personal library, housed in the Library of Congress. Yet some of Ellison's colleagues continued to be troubled by his election. Virgil Goode, Jr., a Republican from Virginia, wrote to his constituents expressing his concerns about the possibility of more Muslims being elected to Congress and demanding the kind of accommodation that Ellison had requested (Niebuhr, 2008).

Finally, many universities and colleges are promoting interfaith dialogue. Wellesley College developed a Multi-Faith Council, Chapman (CA) University created an All-Faiths Chapel, and Johns Hopkins University instituted an Interfaith and Community Service Center; in each, faiths as diverse as Baha'i, Buddhist, Christian, Jewish, Muslim, and Hindu may come to worship or to talk with members of other faiths. Interfaith discussions not only address commonalities between faiths, but also encourage honest dialogue concerning differences in beliefs (Eck, 2001). It is essential that students at colleges and universities engage in religious discussions because religious freedom requires an understanding of different faiths. Public and private educational institutions from elementary grades through high school must also play a critical role in fostering that understanding.

How have K–12 schools taught students about the concept of religious freedom?

The history of American education reveals a gradual secularization of public schools. Public schools in the United States originally did not teach about religious freedom; they reinforced Protestant beliefs, causing

Catholics and Jews to establish schools for their children in addition to or instead of public schools. History credits Horace Mann with shaping public schools in the United States, yet he was denounced as the "archenemy of the Christian church" for advocating that the Bible should be read—but not interpreted—in school because biblical interpretation should be a parental prerogative (McMillan, 1984, p. 85). When Bible reading was eliminated, *McGuffey's Reader* became the most popular public school textbook. It referred to God and used Protestant perspectives to deliver its moral lessons. Later revisions of *McGuffey* eliminated overt religious language but maintained a sermonizing tone. By 1870, most Protestants agreed that a sectarian religious perspective should not be presented in public schools, but felt that a nonsectarian Christian perspective was essential (Nord, 1995).

Starting in the 1940s, U.S. federal courts wrote several decisions related to the constitutional guarantee of religious freedom being enforced or contradicted in schools (see Table 6.1). The next sixty years of court rulings would challenge schools to eliminate their Christian bias and to become more **secular**, reflecting the civic culture and not promoting any religious perspective. U.S. courts have ruled that schools are forbidden to force students to say the Pledge of Allegiance, compel students to pray, begin the day with devotional reading from

TABLE 6.1 Court Rulings on Religion in Public Schools (a selection of significant cases)

1943	*West Virginia v. Barnette* (brought by a Jehovah's Witness family): No child can be forced to recite the Pledge of Allegiance.
1947	*Everson v. Board of Education:* Students attending parochial schools to be transported to their schools on buses provided for public school students.
1962	*Engel v. Vitale:* Students attending public schools could not be forced to recite state written prayers.
1963	*Abington Township v. Schempp:* Public schools could not insist that students recite the Lord's prayer or any prayer nor require "devotional Bible reading."
1968	*Epperson v. Arkansas:* An Arkansas law forbidding the teaching of Darwin's theory of evolution in school was ruled unconstitutional.
1971	*Lemon v. Kurtzman:* Established that the separation of church and state principle was not violated if the statute, policy, or practice under consideration: (1) had a secular legislative purpose; (2) did not foster excessive government entanglement with religion; or (3) neither advanced nor inhibited religion as its primary purpose.
1980	*Stone v. Graham:* A Kentucky law requiring a copy of the Ten Commandments posted in every public school classroom was declared unconstitutional.
1985	*Wallace v. Jaffree:* Since the intent of an Alabama law requiring a moment of silence was "to return prayer to the public schools," it was unconstitutional.
1987	*Edwards v. Aguillard:* Schools could not teach creationism as an alternative to evolutionary theory because creationism was based on religious beliefs and did not satisfy the criteria to constitute a scientific theory.
1990	*Westside Community Schools v. Mergens:* If a public school allows community groups to use its facilities, religious groups must have equal access.
1992	*Lee v. Weisman:* Schools could not include prayers offered by religious leaders (of any faith) at graduation ceremonies; if a school policy or practice has a coercive effect, it is unconstitutional.
2000	*Santa Fe School Independent School District v. Doe:* Student-led prayers at football games violated separation of church and state.

Source: The religious history of America: The heart of the American story from colonial times to today by E. Gaustad and L. Schmidt, 2002.

the Bible, have a minister, priest, or rabbi give a prayer at graduation, post the Ten Commandments in classrooms or hallways, or teach religion disguised as science—"creationism"—as a scientific alternative to evolutionary theory (Allen, 1996; Fraser, 1999; McMillan, 1984).

In 2002, the Ninth Circuit court created a controversy in *Newdow v. United States Congress* by ruling that the inclusion of the phrase "under God" meant the Pledge of Allegiance served a religious, not a secular, purpose. The court concluded that schools could not have students recite the pledge even if they are allowed to choose to not participate because the school setting is a coercive context that puts pressure on students to conform to the majority (Pauken, 2003).

How can public schools teach about religion in a way that respects all religions?

As federal and district courts ruled on what schools could not allow, they also provided guidelines for constitutional activities. Schools were encouraged to teach objectively about all religions, and even about the Bible. As Justice Clark wrote,

> It might well be said that one's education is not complete without a study of comparative religion or the history of religion and its relationship to the advancement of civilization. It certainly may be said that the Bible is worthy of study for its literary and historic qualities. (McMillan, 1984, p. 163)

Although schools cannot force students to pray, they cannot prevent a student from praying, as long as the prayer does not create a disruption. If students representing a religious group want to use school facilities, they have the same right of access as any community group.

Another action that schools can take is to permit the formation of a Secular Student Alliance (SSA). These groups are intended as a safe place for students who are atheists or agnostics or who have more questions than answers when it comes to religion. In the past, nonreligious students were not open about their beliefs for fear of being harassed or bullied, and this has happened to students who openly admitted a lack of faith. A 2006 Pew Research survey reported that Americans felt more antagonistic to atheists than to immigrants, Jews, Muslims, or lesbians and gay men (Lim, 2011). Youthful

nonbelievers have encountered hostility not only from students at school but sometimes from family members. In addition, some schools have refused to allow students to establish SSA groups, in violation of the 1984 law that requires schools receiving federal funds to allow the formation of such a group if the school sponsors other student groups. Ironically, this law was the result of intense lobbying by conservative Christians to ensure that schools would have to allow their children to form student groups. Many schools are already providing support for student nonbelievers. By 2009, about 143 SSA groups had been established, and in just two years that number had almost doubled (Lim, 2011). At SSA meetings, students discuss issues related to religion, but they also discuss politics and current events, and many have fundraising events for charities. More importantly, such student groups provide an affirmation of religious freedom by reminding students that faith is a choice and not an obligation, and all choices should be respected.

In 1999, the U.S. Department of Education sent comprehensive guidelines on issues related to religion in public schools to every public school in the nation. A committee of diverse religious and educational leaders had developed the guidelines that include legal assurances for recommended practices (al-Hibri, 2001). Teaching about religions has now been incorporated into national and state standards for teachers (Douglass, 2002); following the guidelines will ensure that schools address those standards by providing accurate information about fundamental beliefs of the world's major religions.

AFTERWORD

Although historically the Protestant majority in the United States vigorously, and at times even violently, resisted accepting other faiths, Protestants of all denominations accepted each other on equal terms and eventually accepted Catholics and Jews. Will the faiths of new immigrants—Hinduism, Buddhism, Islam, and other non-Christian religions—become acceptable to the dominant Judeo-Christian groups in America? Although U.S. courts have consistently upheld the principle of religious freedom, schools will also have an important role to play.

In the past, public schools promoted Protestantism and reinforced anti-Catholic and anti-Semitic attitudes. As schools became more secular, they engaged less in proselytizing and contributed to the resolution of conflicts among Protestants, Catholics, and Jews. Because current immigration has increased non-Christian religious diversity in the United States, it is important that public schools continue to affirm court decisions and use the guidelines offered by the Department of Education. Students need to learn more about other religions.

If the United States is to be successful as a religiously diverse society, it is essential that "the principal religious groups not only claim freedom for themselves, but affirm equal freedom

> We establish no religion in (America), we command no worship, we mandate no belief, nor will we ever. Church and state are, and must remain, separate. All are free to believe or not to believe, all are free to practice a faith or not, and those who believe are free, and should be free, to speak of and act on their belief.
>
> Ronald Reagan (1911–2004)

for others, whatever their beliefs may be" (Katz & Southerland, 1968, p. 269). As students learn about diverse religions, they may also come to appreciate why religious freedom was guaranteed in the Bill of Rights, and why it has been so difficult to achieve that ideal.

TERMS AND DEFINITIONS

Agnostic A belief that human beings cannot prove or disprove the existence of God

Anti-Catholicism Expressing stereotypes about or prejudices against Catholics or discriminating against Catholics

Anti-Semitism Having anti-Jewish prejudices or stereotypes, or engaging in discrimination against Jews

Atheism A belief that God does not exist

Deism A belief that God created the world and the system of natural laws that governed the world, but was not a presence (and did not play a role) in everyday life

Denominations A perspective on diverse Protestant faiths that views all of them as a singular Protestant church with different names (denominations)

Established church When one church is declared the official faith of a political unit (a colony or state) and tax revenues are used to fund this church

Religious freedom/religious liberty The right to worship in any church of one's choice consistent with that church's beliefs and practices

Sectarian A perspective on diverse Christian churches or sects in which an individual regards his or her own sect as the "true faith"

Secular The civic culture of a society not reflective of religious perspective

DISCUSSION EXERCISES

Exercise #1 Separation of Church and State Activity

Directions: Read the situation below and decide which requests for changing school policy from the following list will be implemented (Agree) and which requests for change will be rejected (Disagree). On completion of your group's consideration of the twelve proposed rule changes, compare your recommendations with those of other groups.

The Situation: It is December 5. As a citizen and parent, you have been publicly assigned to a select committee to examine a list of new school district policies that has been proposed by a group of Jewish parents. Twenty-five percent of the students in the district are Jewish, 15% have no religious affiliation, and 60% declare some sort of Christian affiliation.

Proposed District Policies: Breaks and Absences

1. Vacation breaks during the school year will be established without regard to religious holidays.
2. Jewish children will be excused when they are absent on Jewish holidays.

3. Jewish teachers will not be charged with personal leave when they are absent during Yom Kippur and Rosh Hashana.

Religious Holidays

4. No celebration of Christmas as part of the school curriculum.
5. No celebration of Hanukkah as part of the school curriculum.
6. No creche will be displayed in school.
7. No Christmas trees will be displayed in school.
8. No gift exchanges or Christmas parties in class.

Curricular and Extracurricular Activity

9. Impact of religious values on historic or current events and issues will be examined and discussed in the classroom.
10. Holocaust will be studied as part of the World War II unit and as part of the history of Western civilization.
11. No extracurricular activity will be scheduled on Friday evening.
12. No songs that refer to Jesus Christ will be sung in the winter music program.

Exercise #2 Religious Freedom in the United States: What Is Your Judgment?

Directions: The following list contains incidents that have actually occurred. Determine which items you believe violate the rights of people to behave in accordance with their chosen faith.

Religious Freedom in the United States

1. Should a Sikh be allowed to wear his turban on a hard-hat job even though it appears to be a violation of safety regulations?
2. Can a soldier who is a member of Wicca practice his or her religion on an army base?
3. Should Hindus be forced to build their temple with a "Spanish" architectural style that will match the other buildings in a Southern California community instead of building it based on their traditional temple architecture?
4. Because a Jainist student attends the high school, must the cafeteria staff clearly mark the contents of the meals prepared so that the student can be assured of eating only vegetables?

5. Can a Muslim woman teaching in a public school wear her traditional head covering in her classroom?
6. Should members of the Native American Church be allowed to ingest peyote because this drug has historically been part of their religious rituals?
7. Should a Florida city council allow members of the Santeria faith to engage in animal sacrifice because it is traditionally part of their religious practice?
8. Should a Sikh student come to school with the symbolic knife (kirpan) he is required to wear following his initiation?
9. Should Muslim employees be given time to perform obligatory prayers during the workday?
10. Do Seventh-Day Adventist or Jewish employees have the right to be excused from work on Saturday because it is their Sabbath?

REFERENCES

Abdo, G. (2006). *Mecca and Main Street: Muslim life in America after 9/11.* Oxford, England: Oxford University Press.

al-Hibri, A.Y. (2001). Standing at the precipice: Faith in the age of science and technology. In A. al-Hibri, J.B. Elshtain, and C.C. Haynes (Eds.), *Religion in American public life: Living with our deepest differences.* New York, NY: W.W. Norton.

Allen, R.S. (1996). *Without a prayer: Religious expression in public schools.* Amherst, NY: Prometheus.

Barrett, P.M. (2007). *American Islam: The struggle for the soul of a religion.* New York, NY: Farrar, Straus and Giroux.

Carroll, J. (2001). *Constantine's Sword: The church and the Jews, a history.* Boston, MA: Houghton Mifflin.

Chernow, R. (2004). *Alexander Hamilton.* New York, NY: Penguin Books.

Clark, C., Vargas, M.B., Schlosser, L., & Allmo, C. (2002, Winter). It's Not Just "Secret Santa" in December: Addressing educational and workplace climate issues linked to Christian privilege. *Multicultural Education*, pp. 53–58.

Dinnerstein, L. (1994). *Anti-Semitism in America.* New York, NY: Oxford.

Douglass, S. (2002). Teaching about religion. *Educational Leadership, 60*(2), 32–36.

Eck, D.L. (2001). *A new religious America: How a "Christian Country" has become the world's most religiously diverse nation.* New York, NY: HarperCollins.

Elshtain, J.B. (2001). Faith of our fathers and mothers: Religious belief and American democracy. In A. al-Hibri, J.B. Elshtain, & C.C. Haynes (Eds.), *Religion in American public life: Living with our deepest differences* (pp. 39–61). New York, NY: W.W. Norton.

Fraser, J.W. (1999). *Between church and state: Religion and public education in a multicultural America.* New York, NY: St. Martin's.

Gaustad, E., & Schmidt, L. (2002). *The religious history of America: The heart of the American story from colonial times to today.* New York, NY: HarperCollins.

Goodrich, F., & Hackett, A. (1956). *The diary of Anne Frank.* New York, NY: Random House.

Hendry, J. (2003). Mining the sacred mountain: The clash between the Western dualistic framework and Native American religions. *Multicultural Perspectives, 5*(1), 3–10.

Herberg, W. (1955). *Protestant-Catholic-Jew: An essay in American religious sociology.* Garden City, NY: Doubleday.

Hudson, W.S. (1973). *Religion in America: An historical account of the development of American religious life* (2nd ed.). New York, NY: Charles Scribner.

Intelligence Report (2010, Winter). Intelligence briefs: Ground zero battle may be stoking anti-Muslim violence. Issue 140, pp. 3–5.

Jacoby, S. (2005). Original intent. *Mother Jones, 30*(7), 29–31, 74.

Katz, W., & Southerland, H. (1968). Religious pluralism and the Supreme Court. In W. McLoughlin & R. Bellah (Eds.), *Religion in America* (pp. 269–281). Boston, MA: Beacon Press.

Khan, M.A.M. (2004). Living on borderlines: Islam beyond the clash and dialogue of civilization. In Z.H. Buhhari, S.S. Nyang, M. Ahmad, & J.C. Esposito (Eds.), *Muslims' place in the American public square* (pp. 84–113). Walnut Creek, CA: Altamira Press.

Kosmin, B.A., & Lachman, S.P. (1993). *One nation under God: Religion in contemporary American society.* New York, NY: Crown.

Lee, E. (2004). American gate keeping: Race and immigration law in the twentieth century. In N. Foner & G.M. Frederickson (Eds.), *Not just black and white: Historical and contemporary perspectives on immigration, race and ethnicity in the United States* (pp. 119–144). New York, NY: Russell Sage Foundation.

Lim, V. (2011, Fall). The unaffiliated unite. *Teaching Tolerance,* Issue 40, pp. 33–35.

Lippy, C.H. (1994). *Being religious, American style: A history of popular religiosity in the United States.* Westport, CT: Praeger.

McCloud, A.B. (2004). Conceptual discourse: Living as a Muslim in a pluralistic society. In Z.H. Buhhari, S.S. Nyang, M. Ahmad, & J.C. Esposito (Eds.), *Muslims' place in the American public square* (pp. 73–83). Walnut Creek, CA: Altamira Press.

McCloud, A.B. (2006). *Transnational Muslims in American society.* Gainesville: University of Florida Press.

McMillan, R.C. (1984). *Religion in the public schools: An introduction.* Macon, GA: Mercer University Press.

Miller, G.T. (1976). *Religious liberty in America: History and prospects.* Philadelphia, PA: Westminster.

Myers, G. (1960). *History of bigotry in the United States* (rev. ed.), G. Christman (Ed.). New York, NY: Capricorn.

Niebuhr, G. (2008). *Beyond tolerance: Searching for interfaith understanding in America.* New York, NY: Viking.

Nimer, M. (2004). Muslims in the American body politic. In Z.H. Buhhari, S.S. Nyang, M. Ahmad, & J.C. Esposito (Eds.), *Muslims' place in the American public square* (pp. 145–164). Walnut Creek, CA: Altamira Press.

Nord, W.A. (1995). *Religion and American education: Rethinking a national dilemma.* Chapel Hill: University of North Carolina Press.

Pauken, P. (2003, January). *I Pledge Allegiance to the Curriculum: The establishment clause and the legal balance between educational authority and individual rights.* Presented at the Hawai'i International Conference on Education, Honolulu.

Ravitch, F.S. (1999). *School prayer and discrimination: The civil rights of religious minorities and dissenters.* Boston, MA: Northeastern University Press.

Rendall, S., & Kane, A. (2010, October). The media's construction of the "Ground Zero Mosque." *Extra!* *23*(10), pp. 8–9.

Ribuffo, L.P. (1997). Henry Ford and the international Jew. In J. Sarna (Ed.), *The American Jewish experience* (2nd ed., pp. 201–218). New York, NY: Holmes & Meier.

Smith, J.I. (2004). Muslims as partners in interfaith encounter. In Z.H. Bukhari, S.S. Nyang, M. Ahmad, and J.L. Esposito (Eds.), *Muslims' place in the American public square* (pp. 165–197). Walnut Creek, CA: Altamira Press.

Taggar, S.V. (2006). Headscarves in the headlines! What does this mean for educators? *Multicultural Perspectives 8*(3), 3–10.

Waldman, S. (2006). The framers and the faithful. *Washington Monthly, 38*(4), 33–38.

Wegner, G.P. (2002). *Anti-Semitism and schooling under the Third Reich.* New York, NY: Routledge Falmer.

Chapter 7

Rejecting Oppressive Relationships: The Logic of Cultural Pluralism for a Diverse Society

"In the United States, we have the richest mix of ethnic groups, of racial groups, of global experience that the world has ever known and it is this richness of this mix that yields our incredible creativity and innovation. We have not even begun to experience the real potential of our fantastic human resource mix—our competitive edge in the global economy."

James Naisbitt (1929–)

James Naisbitt, author and respected consultant, provides corporate clients with analyses of data and trends to facilitate corporate decision making related to many pertinent social issues. In these remarks, Naisbitt is describing the possibilities for America because we have become the most diverse society in the world—and most demographic projections about the United States predict even greater diversity in the future. Because demographic changes have not yet occurred in many areas of the United States, it is possible for some people to have difficulty believing in these projections, but even if we focus on the present, the obvious changes in many states, especially in bellwether states such as California and Texas, make it impossible to ignore the reality of the change in the U.S. population toward increased diversity.

Diversity in the United States

In 2005, Texas became the fourth state to have more people of color in the state's population than white people (the others are New Mexico, Hawaii, and California). Hispanic Americans constitute the largest group among people of color in all of these states except Hawaii, where Asian Americans are the largest group. In six additional states, people of color represent approximately 40% or more of the population—Arizona, Florida, Georgia, Maryland, Mississippi, Nevada, New Jersey, and New York. And people of color are the majority of the population in the 100 largest cities in the United States (U.S. Census Bureau, 2010). White people have been the majority group in the United States since the founding of the nation, but demographers are saying that this is going to change before the end of the twenty-first century. As early as 2050, non-Hispanic whites will constitute only 53% of the U.S. population; white men will represent about 26% of the population and many of them will be retired, resulting in about half of the workforce consisting of people of color (Schaefer, 2008). For the social security system to continue to provide its promised benefits, people of color will need jobs that pay living wages. All Americans must care about diversity because in our complex, technological society we are already highly dependent on each other.

Based on data from the 2000 census, Pipher (2002) reported that one in ten people in the United States was born in another country and that one in five children in school is a child of recent immigrants. Historically, immigrants tended to settle in urban areas of a few states, primarily

New York, California, and Florida, but immigrants now live in smaller cities of all states. Pipher illustrates this point by observing that in a Lincoln, Nebraska, newspaper, "Our obituary column . . . is filled with Hrdvys, Andersens, Walenshenkskys, and Muellers. But the births column . . . has many Ali, Nguyen, and Martinez babies" (p. 6).

Demographers track movement of people in society, yet none can predict accurately what the mix of people will be in the future. Demographers tend to be conservative in their speculations, yet the harbingers of changes to come surround us. Pipher (2002) provides this example: Police in Nashville, Tennessee, have computers that explain laws and basic words for simple requests or demands in twenty languages in preparation for dealing effectively with the diverse groups within that city. Rather than debate demographic predictions, it is more useful to study the responses of the white majority population to the diverse population that has been a consistent part of U.S. history, and to understand which responses are favored by most members of minority groups. Further, we need to explore the rationale for collaboration as well as specific strategies for working together to promote changes that will accommodate and respect the needs and aspirations of both groups.

How have members of the majority responded to diverse groups?

In any society, there is often a group hierarchy where preferred groups occupying superior positions disregard groups that are devalued by that society. As we have already seen in previous chapters, the history of the United States reveals that the white majority has never been consistently respectful of the rights of diverse groups. Terry (1993) described the relationship of dominant and subordinate groups by using an "up/down" metaphor. To determine who is up or down in a society, one must discover which groups have the most wealth, status, and power, and which have the least. In the United States, a person becomes an "up" by belonging to these groups: white, male, middle or upper class, Christian, heterosexual, or nondisabled. A "down" belongs to one or more of these groups: people of color, female, lower class, non-Christian, homosexual, bisexual, transgender,

or disabled. Most individuals represent a mixture of memberships in these up or down groups.

With reference to his metaphor, Terry suggests that ups don't know much about downs, and they think they don't need to know about them because downs are not regarded as socially important. Such ignorance is one cause of prejudice as Eck (2001) noted when she described prejudice as "being down on something you're not up on" (p. 300). Ups do not compete with downs; they move in different circles. The only time ups become concerned about downs is when downs start getting "uppity" by challenging the power structure or the status quo by engaging in marches, demonstrations, or some other kind of protest about an issue. The response of ups is likely to be "What do these people want?" because they genuinely do not know. They are "dumb ups" when it comes to understanding issues affecting downs. By contrast, downs know a great deal about ups because they must; it is essential for their survival and for their success. To achieve whatever goals they have set for themselves, downs have to understand ups so that, as Terry says, they know what the ups are up to (pp. 194–196).

It is tempting to assume that if someone is a down in one category, that person will be more sensitive to downs in a category in which he or she functions as an up. Unfortunately it doesn't seem to work that way. When people are behaving as part of an up group, they tend to be "dumb ups." It's as if there are separate file folders; their experiences in one category stay in that file and don't influence other files. People living in poverty can be racist; people of color can be homophobic; gays and lesbians can be prejudiced against immigrants; immigrants can be sexist; women can be prejudiced against people with disabilities; and people with disabilities can be prejudiced against welfare recipients. Terry's "up/down" metaphor provides a useful way of thinking about the complexity involved in a society that includes diverse minority groups.

When the topic of diversity, especially racial and ethnic diversity, is addressed in the media, pundits and scholars often use negative terms rather than the positive terms that James Naisbitt used. Columnist George Will has criticized education's efforts to advocate for diversity, chastising institutions for engaging in "political correctness."

Skeptical of attempts to emphasize diversity, scholars such as Arthur Schlesinger, Jr. (1991), have argued that promoting multiculturalism would lead to the "balkanization" of the United States. Others refer to ethnic conflict in the former Yugoslavia as an example of the dangers of promoting ethnic affiliations. In the wake of the destruction of New York's World Trade Center, Americans assaulted and killed Arab Americans and vandalized mosques in several cities despite appeals from religious and

> It is well to remember that the entire universe,
> with on trifling exception, is composed of others.
>
> John Andrew Holmes (1789–1876)

political leaders. Misguided responses do not bode well for our future as the nation with the most diverse population on earth.

It is imperative that Americans understand how we benefit from diversity and that we learn more about previous and current contributions of diverse groups in our society because the real threat to our nation is not diversity but ignorance. Some Americans are choosing to focus on opportunities in a diverse society rather than on problems in areas such as business, community, and education. This issue does not simply affect the United States; rather, it is global. Naisbitt and Aburdene (1990) were among the first to describe global societies becoming culturally homogenized in the 1980s. Looking ahead to the twenty-first century, they predicted a "backlash against uniformity" as people struggled to "assert the uniqueness" of their culture in the global village: "As our outer worlds grow more similar, we will increasingly treasure the traditions that spring from within" (p. 120).

Attitudes About Diversity

Historians have long maintained that to understand the present, we must understand the past. In terms of diversity, the best way to understand historic attitudes toward societal diversity is to examine how Americans have responded to immigration, the primary source of our diversity. Although some Americans have been (and still are) guilty of anti-immigrant sentiments, many have expressed positive beliefs about immigrants assimilating into society. By reviewing past and present attitudes concerning immigration, Gordon (1964) described consistent ideological perspectives with regard to ethnic diversity: Anglo conformity, melting pot, and pluralism. Brooks (1996) and others have described a fourth perspective: separatism. Taken together, the four perspectives represent historic and contemporary American views on ethnic diversity. Curiously, despite the persistence of these ideological points of view, Anglo conformity has been and continues to be the dominant perspective on racial and ethnic diversity in the United States.

What does it mean to have an Anglo conformity perspective?

Cole and Cole (1954) first identified **Anglo conformity** as the efforts of English colonists to institute and maintain particular American values, norms, and standards. Anglo conformity is an extension of English culture and European civilization. It rejects diversity in favor of homogeneity, maintaining that everyone should conform to values, norms, and standards determined by the Anglo founders of the country and modified by a continuing white majority.

Anglo conformity requires that immigrants stop speaking native languages and use only English as soon as possible. Anglo conformity requires immigrants to abandon their ethnic heritages—the customs, ceremonies, clothing, and traditions of their former culture. Even if their native lands are European, immigrants have been expected to adopt American ways and to become similar to everyone else. Barrett and Roediger (2002) explained that people of color have found Anglo conformity to be a problem because it "took place in a nation obsessed by race. For new immigrant workers the processes of 'becoming white' and 'becoming American' were connected at every turn" (p. 30). Because immigrants of color could never become white, they could never completely achieve the goal of Anglo conformity: to look and act just like the members of the white majority.

FIGURE 7.1 Tom Torlino from Beinece Library

Anglo conformity is vividly illustrated in these two pictures of a Navajo student, Tom Torlino, before and after being enrolled in a BIA boarding school.

Source: Photo by J. N. Choate, Beinecke Rare Book and Manuscript Library, Yale University.

When referring to individuals assimilating into society, social scientists often use the term *Americanization*, yet it still refers to Anglo conformity. Early in our nation's history, Americanization was a process of assimilation applied even to children of indigenous people. In the late 1800s, as public schools were expected to be responsible for the Americanization of immigrant children, schools created by the Bureau of Indian Affairs (BIA) were expected to "Americanize" Native American children. Indians had long been viewed as an obstacle to U.S. expansion and occupation of new territories; Adams (1995) quoted a liberal reformer who argued that "We must either butcher them or civilize them, and what we do we must do quickly" (p. 2). The insistence on Americanizing Indian children led to the creation of BIA boarding schools. As illustrated in the photographs of Navajo student Tom Torlino (Figure 7.1), BIA boarding schools were a dramatic example of the Anglo conformity ideal.

How did the BIA boarding schools promote Anglo conformity with Indian children?

At first, Indian schools were established on reservations, but being close to parents meant Indian children would return home and go "back to the blanket"—back to Indian values and behaviors. Parental influence defeated one of the major purposes of BIA schools, which was, as Adams (1995) explained, to teach values: "to respect private property . . . to realize that the accumulation of personal wealth is a moral obligation" (p. 22). For the BIA to be more confident of success in its Americanization efforts, Indian children were

Two deer, two owls will behave differently from each other. I have studied many plants. The leaves of one plant, on the same stem, none is exactly alike. . . . If the Great Spirit likes the plants, the animals, even little mice and bugs to do this, how much more will he abhor people being alike, doing the same thing.

John Lame Deer (1903–1976)

taken to boarding schools away from reservations, where they were not allowed to return home even on weekends. Although years passed before anyone recognized the absurdity of trying to Americanize Native Americans, the boarding school experiment ultimately failed. Their emphasis on conformity, uniformity, and individual achievement were too contrary to intrinsic Indian values.

Which immigrant groups benefited from Anglo conformity?

Northern European ethnic immigrants to the United States could more easily achieve Anglo conformity. To insist that people Americanize—dress, talk, think, behave, and conform fully to the white majority—is an advantage for those with white skin. However, white advantage created frustration and anger for people of color, who rejected their heritage and native language and who imitated white behavior but could not overcome the disadvantage of skin color— they could not be as successful as their white peers. As Americans of color were denied rewards given to white ethnic groups, individuals with lighter skin sometimes opted to claim white skin—"passing for white"—although some who succeeded paid a psychological price. Their success illustrated the power of Anglo conformity and contradicted the concept of America as a melting pot.

What does it mean to describe America as a melting pot?

The **melting pot** perspective is that immigrants to America need not relinquish their entire racial or ethnic heritage. Instead, the idea was that ethnic differences would blend into the dominant culture

to create a new identity, an American identity, made up of cultures and customs carried to America by all immigrants (see Figure 7.2). This perspective was first articulated by eighteenth-century French immigrant Hector St. John de Crèvecoeur, who said of the United States: "Here individuals of all nations are melted into a new race of men" (Schlesinger, 1991, p. 12). Others such as Ralph Waldo Emerson also alluded to a melting pot concept, but Americans scarcely responded.

FIGURE 7.2

A political cartoon illustrating the idealistic image of the melting pot. Even though Japanese and blacks are included in the pot, anti-Irish prejudice is revealed in the caricature of an Irishman with a knife in one hand, the Irish flag in the other, and the caption that reads, "The Mortar of Assimilation—and the One Element That Won't Mix."

Courtesy of Michigan State University Museum.

THE MORTAR OF ASSIMILATION — AND THE ONE ELEMENT THAT WON'T MIX.

It was in 1908 when Israel Zangwill established this engaging and popular metaphor in the American imagination as his successful play, *The Melting Pot*, opened in Washington, D.C., during a tidal wave of immigration. The melting pot has been especially attractive in intellectual, artistic, and political circles with its compelling image of Americans as a blend of cultures. In the following excerpt, the character David, a Russian Jew, describes the metaphor but also defines the limits of the melting pot:

> America is God's Crucible, the great Melting Pot where all the races of Europe are melting and re-forming! Here you stand, good folk, think I, when I see them at Ellis Island, here you stand in your fifty groups, with your fifty languages and histories, and your fifty blood hatreds and rivalries. But you won't be long like that, brothers, for these are the fires of God you've come to—these are the fires of God. A fig for your feuds and vendettas! Germans and Frenchmen, Irishmen and Englishmen, Jews and Russians—into the Crucible with you all! God is making the American! (1915, p. 33)

Despite the rhapsodic oratory, notice the absence of references to people of color. Blacks, Latinos, Asians, and Native Americans are excluded. Only northern Europeans are invited to this highly selective melting pot; even members of certain white ethnic groups such as Greeks or Italians need not

> The energy of the Irish, Germans, Swedes, Poles, and Cossacks, and all the European tribes—and of the African, and of the Polynesians—will construct a new race, a new religion, a new state, a new literature.
>
> Ralph Waldo Emerson (1803–1882)

apply! As Laosa (1974) noted, the melting pot favored "the white Anglo-Saxon Protestant (WASP) group and . . . [neglected] certain 'culturally different' groups" (p. 136). Anglo conformity was actually reflected in government policy and educational programs, but the idea of America as a melting pot remained an idea—a belief about America embraced by some, rejected by others.

People of color first questioned the melting pot concept, criticizing it as a myth that had nothing to do with the reality of America's diversity. People of color were not only excluded from the melting pot, they weren't sure they wanted to be included. To them, melting meant giving up their ethnic identification, along with its history and traditions, to be accepted in America. Although the melting pot was supposed to be the combination of all subcultures into a new and superior culture, Laosa (1974) described the process as a "melting away of subcultures [and] the preponderance of the dominant group over the others" (p. 136). People could talk about a melting pot, but Anglo conformity was the reality.

The melting pot perspective deemphasized differences and emphasized instead the need to disregard diversity and accept immigrants as Americans as long as they learned to speak English and became citizens. The most common expression of the melting pot perspective today is the argument that people should be **color blind**; that is, we should ignore a person's skin color. Americans will often say, "When I look at you I don't see color, I just see an American (or a student or a neighbor)."

People of color often are offended by the color-blind approach, arguing that it implies a negative attitude about race. When white people say they don't notice the color of anyone's skin, people of color find it difficult to believe: White Americans seem to advocate being color blind only when it relates to skin color. People of color question why someone should be oblivious to skin color but not to other colors in the world—flowers, sunsets, animals, rainbows? Seldon (1996) believes the answer indicates a discomfort with those whose skin color is not white. To be color blind is to pretend that a person is white in order to be able to associate with them, work with them, or view them in a positive way.

Foner (2000) offers historical evidence that America has never been color blind, even before the passage of the 1790 naturalization law that limited citizenship to white immigrants; yet many Americans still lobby for a color blind society. Advocacy of a color blind approach in education is especially problematic. Nieto (2008) describes the U.S. Supreme Court's 1974 decision in *Lau v. Nichols*, in which the San Francisco schools were sued for not providing an equal education for Chinese students. The schools' lawyer argued that Chinese students had the same curriculum, teachers, and instruction as other students. The Supreme Court ruled that taking the same approach with diverse students, as if all of them had the same needs, did not fulfill the goal of providing an equal education since students whose first language was Chinese would not benefit from curriculum and instruction provided in English, as would students who were native speakers. And if being color blind results in problems at the institutional level, it is even more disastrous at the individual level. After describing teachers who took a color blind approach in teaching diverse children, Sleeter (1993) asked: "What does it mean to construct an interpretation of race

> We are not fighting for integration . . . We are fighting for recognition as human beings.
>
> Malcolm X (1925–1963)

that denies it?" (p. 161). The answer to this critical question illustrates why many people of color view a color blind attitude toward skin color as being just as negative as anything advocated by the people who represent a separatist perspective.

How is the separatist perspective negative?

Separatism is the most pessimistic of the four perspectives, yet it may also be the easiest to recognize. Separatists believe that different racial and ethnic groups ought to be apart; they should have their own places and "be with their own kind." The goal of separatism is for diverse groups to tolerate each other. Separatism is based on the premise that ineradicable differences exist between groups of people and that differences inevitably cause hostility. The logical outcome is to believe that different groups must have their own places separate from others and should interact only when necessary. The best a person can hope for is peaceful coexistence.

At various times, both majority and minority group members have advocated for the separatist perspective. Before the Civil War, white separatists advocated for African Americans being relocated to Africa, and some Americans assisted a number of former slaves in creating a new African nation called Liberia. Even President Lincoln considered the idea, but he abandoned the project after hearing a vehement rejection of the proposal at a White House meeting with a group of prominent African Americans including Frederick Douglass (Martin, 1984).

In the 1920s, Marcus Garvey promoted the goal of supporting black entrepreneurs in creating a self-reliant black society (Cronon, 1955). For a more contemporary example, Appleton (1983) described Switzerland as a "segregated pluralism where the country is divided into four distinct cultures" with four languages (p. 26). Although German speakers in the northern and eastern cantons constitute 70% of the population, 21% live in western cantons and speak French, 8% live in south-central cantons and speak Italian, and 1% living in the Alps speak Romansh.

Although there are separatist groups in the United States today, they attract few followers and most, such as the Aryan Nation or Black Muslims, are perceived as hate groups. Not all separatists advocate hatred, but they tend to subscribe to the pessimistic separatist premise. Some call for a separate state for African Americans; others reject the concept of integrated schools in favor of returning to the *Plessy v. Ferguson* principle of separate but equal education for white children and children of color. Contrasting views will continue to be part of the mix of voices reacting to diversity; however, pluralism is now challenging the dominance of Anglo conformity.

What attitudes about diversity does pluralism promote?

Pluralism (also known as **cultural pluralism**) refers to the equal coexistence of diverse cultures in a mutually supportive relationship within the boundaries of one nation (Pai & Adler, 1997). When Horace Kallen coined the term in 1906, his focus was on ethnic diversity, advocating that the cultural differences of immigrants were essential to American democratic life. Alain Locke advocated a pluralism that encompassed racial groups as well. In the 1920s, based on the work of Kallen and Locke, pluralists insisted that people in a diverse society such as the United States should have the right to preserve their cultural heritage and not be forced to abandon it to conform to a dominant culture (Hattam, 2004; Menand, 2001). Pluralism is based on the belief in "equality of opportunity for all people, respect for human dignity and the conviction that no single pattern of living is good for everyone" (Pai & Adler, 1997, p. 102). Beginning in the 1960s, the National Association for the Advancement of Colored People and professional organizations such as the National Education Association have actively promoted pluralism.

Advocates for pluralism believe that diversity is not a difficulty to be overcome but rather a positive attribute of a society. American pluralists do not refer to being tolerant of others; to pluralists, tolerance is an inadequate response in a nation as diverse as the United States. As Eck (2001) writes, "Tolerance can create a climate of restraint but not one of understanding. . . . It is far too fragile a foundation for a society . . . [as] complex as ours" (p. 72). In a society guided by pluralistic beliefs, people appreciate differences because everyone is enriched by a diverse society. To pluralists, individuals have the right to maintain and be proud of their racial, cultural, ethnic, or religious heritage.

Separatists say that human differences will always cause conflict and will never disappear. Melting pot advocates ignore differences to avoid problems arising from them. Anglo conformity advocates demand the elimination of differences based on the assumption that a homogeneous society will be a more harmonious one. By contrast, pluralism encourages individuals to identify themselves in terms of their heritage in addition to identifying themselves as American. Individuals who embrace pluralism tend to identify themselves as Italian American or Polish American, as African American or Arab American, as Mexican American or Cuban American, as Chinese American or Hmong American. The identification means they perceive their identity as being shaped by their racial or ethnic heritages as well as by a more homogeneous American culture. A recent adaptation in response to persistent criticisms of "hyphenated Americans" has been to refer to "Americans of Japanese (or other) descent." With regard to preserving one's cultural heritage, some have asked how Italian must an Italian American be? From a pluralist perspective, it is up to each individual to decide how much of the customs, traditions, and language of an ethnic heritage he or she wants to maintain.

Because pluralism promotes bilingual education and maintenance of one's native language, those in the English Only movement seem to misunderstand the pluralist position as a rejection of the need for English as a common language for all Americans. English Only groups in various states have organized to lobby for legislation establishing English as the official language of those states, with the ultimate goal of eliminating the use of all other languages. Of course, a society including diverse language groups needs a common language, and English has been and continues to be the common language for the United States. Can people become fluent in English without losing the language spoken in their home? Students the world over are taught to be fluent in more than one language. Should children and youth in America who are fluent in a language learned at home be taught English at school while maintaining their first-language fluency? Pluralists argue that speaking different languages is a fundamental part of a diversity that enriches our society: People who are proud of their heritage should not be forced to give up the language associated with that heritage. The concept of pluralism is consistent with American values about individuality and freedom, and as the diversity in our nation increases, it becomes increasingly necessary for Americans to reject Anglo conformity in favor of pluralism.

What are some arguments from people who are opposed to pluralism?

Opponents of cultural pluralism insist that promoting pluralistic attitudes contradicts the American emphasis on the individual by placing more importance on group membership in the creation of individual identity. They argue that emphasizing groups in a society will encourage identification with a group rather than with the nation, and that animosity will arise between individuals who identify with a group and those who simply perceive themselves as "American." But for a number of years, pluralist advocates have said that this criticism is a misinterpretation of pluralism (Appleton, 1983; Greeley, 1975; Pai & Adler, 1997). One of the goals of pluralism is to empower individuals to shape their own identity. Cultural pluralism does not require mindless adherence or conformity to a group's cultural heritage. Instead, pluralism fosters a dynamic process that allows individuals to decide the extent to which they choose to embrace their cultural heritage exclusively or to integrate certain aspects of other cultures or the dominant culture into that heritage. Pluralists would support both individuals who have chosen to maintain their heritage and those who choose to adopt other cultural ways while retaining important aspects of their cultural heritage.

Opponents maintain that there is still a problem with pluralism because it places so much emphasis on being proud of your cultural group. They argue that any level of individual identification with a cultural group inflates the importance of the group and exacerbates the potential for conflict between groups. They believe that the best way to avoid such conflicts is for all people living in the United States to identify themselves as Americans. Without this common bond, pluralism's critics believe that group conflicts are inevitable and will lead to the fragmentation and ultimate destruction of our society. Yet when Chua (2007) examined the historical record to understand the reasons for the achievements of the most successful nations, she discovered that a common thread connecting all of them was the promotion of pluralistic attitudes toward their diverse people. From the Roman empire to the Mongol dynasty to the British empire, the central government encouraged all of the people under its rule, including people they conquered, to maintain their culture and religion. In addition, the most gifted people from all groups were solicited and employed in ways that allowed the empire to benefit from their talents, and the government provided opportunities for diverse individuals to achieve, regardless of their background or their differences.

At the end of her book, Chua acknowledges that the United States is now a superpower, and she insists that "Tolerance played a critical role in every dimension of the United States' rise to superpower status" (p. 254). But tolerance is not enough; Chua argues that the United States will not benefit from its diverse population until it begins to promote pluralistic attitudes. For those critics who remain skeptical, pluralist advocates have tried to assure them that pluralism is consistent with both democratic principles and American values related to individuality and freedom. As diversity in the United States increases, it will become even more necessary for us to change our attitudes and our historic practice of demanding Anglo conformity in favor of promoting cultural pluralism.

Why should American society become pluralistic?

Anglo conformity remains the dominant perspective among Americans, even though numerous individuals and organizations advocate pluralism and question the appropriateness of Anglo conformity in a society as diverse as the United States. Although these advocates encounter resistance, they have articulated persuasive arguments in support of the practice and promotion of pluralism in America. Here are five of their compelling reasons:

1. *The failure of Anglo conformity* has been described by many social critics. Although a majority of Americans have historically endorsed Anglo conformity, this effort has been ineffective because its demand for conformity contradicts the historic identity of the United States. Eck (2001) observed, "America is a nation formed not by a race or a single people, but by the ideals articulated in the succession of founding documents, beginning with the Declaration of Independence" (p. 74). American immigrants have succeeded because they have accepted and embraced the civic culture of the United States as described by those founding documents; to require conformity based on race, religion, or other human differences in a society with such diversity is by nature unrealistic and illogical (Fuchs, 1990).

    Sociologists who note that Anglo conformity has failed in America argue that it is inherently unjust to those who cannot conform adequately because they are not white or Protestant (or at least Christian). People unable to conform have endured oppression, and many are still being oppressed today. Racial and ethnic minority groups are still disproportionately represented in the data on human suffering such as infant mortality rates, unemployment statistics, welfare rolls, inadequately funded schools, and unsafe neighborhoods. The availability of goods and services and accessibility to education and opportunity have been inequitable in the United States; distribution and access have been unfairly based on factors such as race, gender, social class, sexual orientation, and disability. Respect and self-respect have also been inequitably gained—an issue that goes beyond equity to raise an ethical question about a lack of human compassion.

2. *The impact on self-consciousness and self-determination* refers to the effect of being perceived as "different" on one's efforts to develop the kind of positive self-consciousness that is essential

for individuals to be confident in their ability to determine goals and to achieve them. If people consciously feel proud of who they are, it is easier to set goals and to believe they can be reached. Appleton (1983) argued that a primary purpose of democracy is to "provide an opportunity for individuals to choose who and what they will become" (p. 57). It is difficult for people to develop a sense of personal pride and to believe they can achieve their goals when they feel their abilities are constantly being doubted.

In one study, researchers reviewed the Graduate Record Examination (GRE) taken by undergraduates across the country as part of their applying for admission to graduate school. Twenty questions from the GRE were selected to create a "test" that was given to black and white undergraduate students. In testing sessions where they were asked to identify their race on a pretest questionnaire, black students only answered half as many questions correctly as compared to testing sessions where they were not asked to identify their race. After the test, African American students were asked if anything had happened that would interfere with their doing well on the test. They would typically say, "No." Even when asked specifically if identifying their race on the pretest questionnaire bothered them, they answered that it did not. Yet several African American students also admitted that they questioned their ability to achieve academic success at the graduate level (Gladwell, 2005). It is essential that people function in a context in which their abilities are clearly respected if they are to develop a positive consciousness of self and a belief that they can determine their own goals and achieve them.

3. *The necessity for human interdependence* concerns the extent to which people depend on others. Individuals interact in any society; as a society becomes more complex, people inevitably become more dependent on each other. A complex society relies on technology, cooperation, and division of labor. Some people grow food, some build homes and furniture, some sell and service cars, and so on. People rely on others to provide the goods and services needed in their daily lives. It is also essential that those in the workforce be paid well enough to support the social security system for retired workers. In any society, but especially in a democratic society, people rely on each other. According to Pai and Adler (1997), "a democratic society is necessarily pluralistic . . . because it is founded on a belief in the intrinsic worth of individuals and their unique capacities to become intelligent human beings" (p. 109); therefore, becoming a pluralistic society promotes positive relations

> Pluralism is the greatest philosophical ideal of our time.
>
> John Dewey (1859–1952)

between individuals in all areas and from all groups within that society.

The lack of a pluralistic perspective concerning racial and ethnic interdependence in the United States contributed to problems in the past. When drug use began to increase in urban ghettos and barrios in the 1950s and 1960s, the larger society ignored it. No one seemed to care what "those people" did to themselves because we did not understand that interdependence means that social problems cannot be confined. By the 1970s, drug use by urban and suburban white people increased significantly, and today, the entire society is confronted with an enormous health and economic problem because of the availability and use of illicit drugs. Drug use became a significant problem in the United States because the majority did not appreciate the interdependence of diverse groups in American society.

White people are not alone in misunderstanding social interdependence. When AIDS first appeared, most people, including people of color, ignored the disease because it seemed to affect only the gay community. Some people said—and some still say—that AIDS was a punishment from God on homosexuals. It was only when the virus spread to heterosexuals in highly publicized cases that the U.S. government began providing funds for research to find a cure. In the meantime, thousands of human beings died.

Human interdependence exists everywhere, but in a diverse, democratic society such as the United States, citizens must advocate for and practice pluralistic attitudes to ensure that our society functions as effectively as possible to be a good place for all (Locke, 1989). The Boy Scout study described in Chapter 3 illustrates this point. When boys competed with each other, hostility developed between groups, but hostility was eliminated when they cooperated to achieve a mutual goal. As Aronson (1999) concluded, "The key factor seems to be mutual interdependence—a situation wherein individuals need one another and are needed by one another in order to accomplish their goal" (p. 332). This is not a new insight. More than three centuries ago, poet John Donne wrote, "Any man's death diminishes me . . . therefore never send to know for whom the bell tolls; it tolls for thee" (Simpson, 1967, p. 101).

4. *The recognition of diversity as an ideal* implies that people must promote the idea that our diversity constitutes the best possible situation. We need only consider what has already occurred as a result of the diversity in the United States: Some of the best art, music, and literature ever created in America was a consequence of borrowing from different cultural traditions. Our modern English language has evolved by adopting words from languages of other cultures as diverse as those of Spain, Germany, France, Italy, and Mexico, as well as from African and Native American dialects (Claiborne, 1983). A major argument for promoting English as a world language is its ability to accommodate the infusion of words from other cultures—proving its flexibility and accessibility.

Diversity is regarded as an asset when people engage in solving problems. If we all examined problems the same way, we would generate similar solutions. Williams (2003) described a problem-solving conference in which a chemical company invited 50 employees who were women and people of color along with the company's top 125 predominantly white male managers. When divided into problem-solving teams, half of the groups consisted of white males only and half were diverse in both gender and race. Afterward, the company CEO said, "It was so obvious that the diverse teams

had the broader solutions. They had ideas I hadn't even thought of. . . . We realized that diversity is a strength as it relates to problem-solving" (pp. 442–443).

Diversity is also valued in the natural world: The more diversity there is in nature, the more likely it is that human life will adapt as new conditions arise. We have become concerned about endangered species and the destruction of rain forests: If diversity in nature is diminished, whatever potential usefulness we find in a species of plant or animal will be lost permanently. If diversity in nature can be appreciated and valued, should it be so difficult to appreciate diversity in human beings?

5. *The current existence of diversity* is perhaps the most compelling argument for promoting pluralism. If some quality is characteristic of a society, it makes sense that we value it rather than deny it or try to pretend that it doesn't exist.

> Commandment Number One of any truly civilized society is this: Let people be different.
>
> David Grayson (1870–1946)

If most of the players on a basketball team are tall, a coach will take advantage of their height to create offensive and defensive strategies. If the tall players graduate and next year's team is short and fast, the coach will take advantage of speed and quickness by creating new offensive and defensive strategies. As the most multicultural society in the world today, we must realize the advantages of diversity and embrace pluralism to capitalize on our advantages.

Other arguments for pluralism challenge us to think about how our society is changing and what sort of society it could become. To maintain Anglo conformity reinforces the current fear and hostility that certain groups have for each other and perpetuates conflicts between them. However, changing societal attitudes to a pluralistic perspective offers hope. Human beings have always encountered problems and conflicts, but in a diverse society, conflicts and problems are more likely to be resolved if everyone demonstrates pluralistic attitudes.

One of the ways to demonstrate pluralistic attitudes is to develop competencies in dealing with people from other cultures. In the fields of business and education, professionals have designed models to describe how individuals can develop cultural competence. For example, William Taylor has described a "Reflective Competence Model" that includes four stages of development (Jones, 2011):

1. Unconscious incompetence
2. Conscious incompetence
3. Conscious competence
4. Unconscious competence

Everyone starts at the first level, "unconscious incompetence," because schools do not typically provide enough information about diverse groups in our culture. Because of this inadequate education, white students may assume that they know what they need to know about people of color. Students of color learn a lot about white people in schools, but they don't learn much about people of color from groups other than their own. Yet they may also think they know what they need to know about other people of color. At this stage, the individuals are naïve; they are not aware of how much they don't know.

The first step toward cultural competence is to recognize your own ignorance—to become aware of what you don't know. At this stage you simply need to gain an understanding of the areas of your ignorance in preparation for addressing those knowledge deficiencies. This awareness leads to the second stage—identifying what you don't know and what you need to learn so that you can become more knowledgeable about other cultures. As a result of learning about other cultures, you move to stage three, which is to know that you have gained a lot of information about other cultures, creating a feeling of competence in dealing with people from these other cultures. To achieve the next stage, you must be engaged in interactions with people from other cultures on a regular basis to demonstrate that you have achieved a certain degree of competence while continuing to learn. This ongoing interaction and learning leads to the fourth stage, which is when the learning becomes intuitive. In other words, the knowledge gained is so deeply embedded in your inner consciousness that it is readily accessible without your having to think about it.

A person at this level demonstrates a value for diversity by virtue of the knowledge and skills shown in dealings with people from other cultures (Jones, 2011). Such models are useful to help Americans appreciate and value the nation's diversity, and in achieving that goal, they inevitably develop a deeper appreciation for individual differences.

Valuing Individual Differences

The evidence that Americans have already learned to value diversity on a basic level becomes most apparent when people are asked, "Would you want to live in a society where everyone was the same?" Most Americans reply that they would not want to live in such a society. It is an American belief that each person is unique, and most of us are proud of those factors that establish our individuality. The United States has always consisted of people from different races, cultures, and religions. If we value our own uniqueness, it is logical and consistent to value what is unique in others. Pluralists value human differences. Sooner or later, all Americans should embrace pluralism because no other perspective regards differences as an asset for a society. Still, to be a pluralist requires more than claiming to value diversity; pluralism must be practiced. As Eck (2001) noted, "diversity alone is not pluralism. Pluralism is not a given but must be created. Pluralism requires participation and attunement to the life and energies of one another" (p. 70). Individuals and organizations committed to pluralism are actively working to bring about social change in the United States and to transform social attitudes from our traditional acceptance of Anglo conformity to acceptance and promotion of pluralism.

Must one be actively involved in change to be a pluralist?

Terry (1975) has developed a matrix (see Figure 7.3) based on the idea that people can be either prejudiced against one or more groups (racist, sexist, homophobic) or they can demonstrate pluralistic attitudes toward diversity. According to Terry, people also can be active or passive in their prejudices or their acceptance of diversity. The matrix identifies

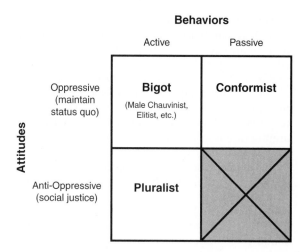

FIGURE 7.3 Matrix for Oppressive and Anti-Oppressive Behaviors

four different positions: (1) people may actively assert and promote their prejudices; those with such strong prejudices are typically perceived as extremists (such as a bigot or a male chauvinist). (2) People may be prejudiced without expressing those ideas or behaving in ways that obviously reflect prejudice; they do not disagree with bigots or chauvinists, but do not tend to articulate their ideas on behalf of causes. People in this group passively accept the status quo that has been shaped by past prejudice and thereby perpetuate injustice in our society. They are conformists. They like things as they are and they would like to see them stay that way.

In another position, (3) people may reject prejudiced ideas and sympathize with victims of social injustice but not express their views. Although opposed to prejudice and discrimination, they don't want to risk causing trouble or upsetting anyone, so they say nothing—and do nothing. Similar to those who are passive in their prejudice, people in this group conform to the status quo. By their conformity they help perpetuate problems that are known to be part of the status quo. There is little difference between prejudiced people and those opposed to prejudicial ideas and actions if they are both passive in their behavior. It is not possible to claim to have pluralistic attitudes and be passive, because passivity perpetuates social injustice.

Tatum (1997) describes the existence of prejudice and its benefits for the dominant group as similar to a moving walkway at an airport. People who actively engage in prejudice not only step on the walkway, but keep walking as well. People who are passive, whether their attitudes are prejudiced or opposed to prejudice, merely step on the walkway and let it carry them along. To be actively opposed to prejudice and the benefits it brings to the dominant group, people must step off the walkway as soon as they recognize its function. Using Tatum's metaphor, to escape the moving walkway means to be actively involved in promoting social justice.

To promote social justice, (4) people must reject prejudiced ideas, articulate pluralistic attitudes, and act on a new consciousness of human differences. To be a pluralist requires not only positive attitudes, but also a commitment to engage in activities to change social injustices in our society. Contrary to those who promote being color blind, pluralists argue that it is not consciousness of color that is the problem, but that people's consciousness of color and other differences has tended to be negative. Whites may feel uneasy around someone who is not white. Middle- or upper-class people may have contempt for welfare recipients. Nondisabled people feel pity for people with disabilities. Men may be condescending to women. What is needed is not to ignore differences but to consciously develop a positive attitude toward human differences. Put simply, unless we are part of the solution, we are part of the problem.

What kinds of activities can create social change?

If one has power to address a problem, one need only decide how to use that power to solve the problem. If individuals or groups do not have power to make a desired change, they may employ tactics to persuade those with power to implement the solutions they advocate. The tactics—deliberate and conscious strategies—employed to achieve social change in the United States are as old as the birth of our country, as illustrated in the Declaration of Independence and in the writing of John Adams, Thomas Jefferson, Thomas Paine, and others responsible for revolution against England and for eventual American independence. Terry (1975) identified six tactics historically employed to promote social change.

The most basic tactic is to engage in (1) a dialogue with those in power to convince them to implement a proposed change. If dialogue fails, people might organize (2) a confrontation of some kind: a march, a sit-down strike, or a rally. Confrontation dramatizes the need for change by public demonstration to show that people are concerned about an issue. The goal of confrontation is either to revive a dialogue that had been terminated or to pressure those in control to develop a greater sense of urgency about finding a solution.

If both dialogue and confrontation fail, those advocating change might (3) apply economic pressure to those individuals or organizations unwilling to change. Pressure usually takes the form of a **boycott** of products or services related to the issue in dispute. During the sit-ins at lunch counters in the 1960s, the youthful protestors were arrested and jailed, and their angry parents closed their charge accounts at these stores and encouraged others to do the same. In addition, white shoppers tended to avoid the stores because of the conflict. The economic hardship caused many store owners and managers to change their racist policies.

The best known example of this tactic was the Montgomery bus boycott that lasted more than a year and ended only when the courts ruled in favor of desegregation of public transportation. The bus boycott launched the career of Martin Luther King, Jr., and brought national attention to the civil rights movement (Williams, 1987; Wright, 1991). Nestlé Corporation was the target of a boycott based on concerns about the marketing strategies Nestlé had employed to sell infant formula in developing countries (Infact Canada, 2009).

In addition to boycotts, economic pressure can be applied through discrimination litigation calling for major economic penalties. In the 1990s, 1,300 African American employees at Coca-Cola brought a class-action lawsuit charging the corporation with discrimination in performance reviews, pay, and promotions. They won the case and were awarded $192 million. To improve the corporate image in the aftermath of the lawsuit, Coca-Cola committed additional resources to diversity issues including "increasing its use of minority suppliers, instituting a formal [diversity] mentoring program, and instituting days to celebrate diversity with its workforce" (Jones & George, 2003, p. 130).

People demanding change often initiate or support (4) research designed to examine data relevant to the issue being confronted. Research about a specific issue or problem might define the nature of the problem and perhaps identify its causes. Researchers may or may not recommend specific solutions to address problems, but the purpose of research is to provide information in support of a persuasive argument about changes being proposed to those in control.

Another tactic is to establish (5) an inside-outside alliance in which a member of a decision-making body (such as a board of directors, city council, or school board) collaborates with a group demanding change. This tactic may involve persuading someone who is already in the decision-making group of the benefits of the changes advocated, or it may mean working to elect a candidate or influence the appointment of someone who is sympathetic to the need for change. Once elected or appointed, the person selected can represent and articulate arguments for change advocated by outside groups. Jones and George (2003) provide the example of an insurance and annuity company committed to diversity that owned almost a

> A nation without the means of reform is without the means of survival.
>
> Edmund Burke (1729–1797)

million shares of Nucor Corporation; they exerted pressure on Nucor to add more women and people of color to its board of directors.

When all else fails, people resort to (6) violence to demonstrate their frustration and to dramatize the need for change. This tactic might involve destruction of property or an assault on people, or both. The use of violence is typically an unplanned and spontaneous reaction such as the Los Angeles riots of 1992 in response to the acquittal of the police officers who had been videotaped beating a black man, Rodney King. When violence is planned, most often it is meant primarily to be a symbolic gesture, such as the Boston Tea Party of 1773.

In the past, violence erupted when frustration over an issue reached a point where the people

TABLE 7.1 Riots in America: A Selected List of Riots in the United States Since the Nation Began

Year	Name/Location	Cause
1788	Doctors' Riot/New York City	Medical students digging up bodies
1834	Election Riots/Several cities	Allowing recent immigrants to vote
1835	Abolition Riots/Several cities	Opposing abolitionist efforts
1844	Bible Riots/Philadelphia	Use of Catholic Bible in public schools
1863	Draft Riots/New York City	Corruption and injustice in draft laws
1877	Railroad Riots/Baltimore, Pittsburgh, Chicago, others	Workers striking for fair pay riot in response to militia being called in
1885	Anti-Chinese Riots/Rock Springs, Wyoming	Opposing the railroad's use of Chinese labor
1908	Race Riot/Springfield (IL)	(False) allegation by a white woman of being raped by a black man
1917	Race Riot/East St. Louis	Blacks hired to replace white workers on strike
1921	Race Riot/Tulsa (OK)	(False) allegation by a white woman of an attempted rape by a black man
1942	Zoot Suit Riot/Los Angeles	Allegation that sailors were assaulted by *pachucas* in zoot suits leads to sailors attacking Mexican Americans
1965	Watts Riot/Los Angeles	"Routine" traffic stop sparks protest against unjust treatment by police and legal system
1967– 1968	Race Riots/Detroit, Newark, and other cities	Protesting police brutality against black suspects, other local racial injustices, and the assassination of Martin Luther King, Jr.
1992	Race Riot/Los Angeles	Protesting white jury acquitting white police officers caught on videotape beating a black man (Rodney King)

most affected could no longer control their rage, usually responding destructively to a specific incident. During the Civil War, if wealthy young men were drafted, they avoided military service by paying poor and often unemployed men to take their place. The poor knew that these young men were being exploited and that most of them would probably be killed in the war, and their anger resulted in the 1863 Draft Riot in New York City. More recently, riots occurred in several cities in 1968 following the assassination of Martin Luther King, Jr.,

and during the 1999 World Trade Organization protests in which some protesters smashed windows and vandalized businesses in response to police using pepper spray, tear gas, and stun guns against them. Violence rarely resolves problems, primarily because incidents igniting riots are typically only symptoms of larger problems. Even if symptoms are addressed following a riot, the causes of those symptoms will eventually create new problems.

In the last half of the twentieth century, people of color participated in riots, especially in urban areas. This has caused many Americans to associate violent tactics for change with people of color, but many groups have resorted to violence at one time or another. In fact, the history of riots in the United States reveals that white people have most often been the group causing riots (see Table 7.1). Jones (1997) reported on the historical record: "With few exceptions . . . previous racial riots had consisted of interracial fighting or the destruction of black communities by white mobs" (p. 46).

In identifying tactics, Terry noted that the first five not only represented nonviolent approaches but also illustrated the critical role education must play if individuals and groups are to engage in nonviolent change. The skills and means necessary to engage in nonviolent tactics are related to what we teach in our schools. To be persuasive in dialogue requires the kinds of communication and problem-solving skills students are taught in school. To engage successfully in confrontation, it is essential to understand how to work effectively in groups; from elementary school through college, students are provided opportunities to participate in collaborative activities and projects. In addition, students are taught how to deliver an effective public speech in school, and skillful confrontation requires one or more individuals with an ability to articulate the group's concerns to the public.

Although economic pressure may not seem to relate to schools but simply to the economic resources one controls, studies show that people earn higher salaries based on the level of education they have completed (Bonilla-Silva, 2001; U.S. Department of Labor, 2000). Organizing a successful boycott requires sufficient numbers of people in a community with economic resources to create pressure on those resisting change, and that largely depends on how much education the people have completed. The level of education an individual has completed is also a major factor in employing the tactic of an inside-outside alliance. The perception of an individual's credibility as a legitimate candidate for election or appointment to a decision-making body is typically influenced by his or her educational achievements.

> Be the change you want to see in the world.
>
> Mohandis K. Gandhi (1869–1948)

Finally, education also plays a pivotal role in research. Although studies can be conducted by anyone with a basic knowledge of principles of effective research, those results that are widely disseminated and that influence public and corporate policies tend to come from studies conducted

> We are all Americans who, because of our cultural heritage, contribute something unique to the fabric of American life. We are like the notes in a chord of music—if all the notes were the same, there would be no harmony, no real beauty, because harmony is based on differences, not similarities.
>
> Rosa Guerrero (1934–)

by people with college experience. Violence is the only tactic that does not require education; as Jefferson wrote in the Declaration of Independence, it is the approach people will choose when they believe no other options exist. It is essential that schools provide people with the skills and means for engaging in nonviolent tactics to address issues of social injustice.

AFTERWORD

The United States today is a society struggling with its internal diversity at the same time that it is attempting to understand and adjust to the external diversity of the global village. Americans have much to learn from other nations' experiences with diversity. Historically, societies dominated by Western Europeans have been intolerant of differences, persecuting those who did not think or act in accordance with what religious or political authorities deemed acceptable, causing conflicts between religions, ethnic groups, and countries. Even when tolerance was practiced, Zeldin (1994) argued that it was for the wrong reasons: "Not out of respect for other people's views, not out of deep knowledge of what they believe, but in despair of finding certainty. It meant closing one's eyes to what other people believed" (p. 272).

Being more diverse than all of Europe, the United States is engaged in a debate between maintaining Anglo conformity or promoting pluralism in response to diversity. Zeldin (1994) explained why advocating tolerance is inadequate: "The tolerated are increasingly demanding to be appreciated, not ignored, and becoming more sensitive to [the] contempt lurking behind the condescension. They do not want to be told that differences do not matter" (p. 272). Pluralism goes beyond tolerance, requiring understanding and acceptance of differences. Many American institutions are responding positively to diversity and taking public positions on the issue. Eck (2001) praised the following statement from the Girl Scouts:

> Pluralism means being inclusive and respectful of people or groups with different backgrounds, experiences, and cultures . . . although you can have diversity without pluralism, you cannot have pluralism without valuing diversity. (pp. 76–77)

If Americans are to demonstrate pluralistic attitudes, educators must teach all students about diversity and how individuals from diverse groups have contributed to our society. If the changes needed to improve and sustain this society are to come as a consequence of nonviolent tactics for change—from discussion and debate in the context of mutual respect—teachers must help students develop the abilities to use nonviolent tactics effectively. How schools can fulfill this role and what pluralistic policies and practices illustrate the changes happening in the United States will be the focus of the final section of this book, but first it is necessary to understand the problems experienced by diverse groups in our society.

TERMS AND DEFINITIONS

Anglo conformity Views the values, norms, and standards of the United States as an extension of English culture because the English were the dominant group during the colonial era and when the new nation was emerging

Boycott To abstain from using, buying, or associating with a group, organization, or nation to protest an injustice and to force the other to address this injustice

Color blind A response to race based on the belief that a person should not notice or consider the skin color of another

Melting pot The conceptual belief that when immigrants from diverse racial/ethnic backgrounds come to the United States they blend into the culture and, mixed together with those who have come before, develop into a new, distinctly American identity

Pluralism (cultural pluralism) The equal coexistence of diverse cultures in a mutually supportive relationship within the boundaries of one nation

Separatism The conceptual belief in the notion of establishing entirely separate societies for each distinct racial or ethnic group or other groups that exist within a society

DISCUSSION EXERCISES

Exercise #1 Differing Views: America's Ethnic Composition Activity

Directions: Have you heard or participated in conversations that reflect your perspectives about American racial and ethnic relationships? Identify each statement by its perspective on ethnic diversity.

_____ 1.   My parents decided not to teach us Laotian. They hoped that this would enable us to move more quickly through the process of becoming an American.

_____ 2.   More and more I think in family terms, less ambitiously, on a less than national scale. The differences involved in my being from an Italian family, and Catholic, and even growing up in a lower middle-class home seem more and more important to me.

_____ 3. The reliance of our race on the progress and achievements of others for a consideration in sympathy, justice, and rights is like a dependence on a broken stick: Resting on it will eventually consign you to the ground. The Negro needs a nation and a country of his own, where he can best show evidence of his own ability in the art of human progress.

_____ 4. Now listen to me, Nikki, you are beginning to understand our American ways, so the sooner you drop your Puerto Rican notions, the more successful you will be.

_____ 5. Our blood is as the flood of the Amazon, made up of a thousand noble currents all pouring into one. We are not a nation, so much as a world.

_____ 6. The Japanese race is an enemy race, and while many second- and third-generation Japanese born on United States soil possess U.S. citizenship and have become "Americanized," the racial strains are unchanged.

_____ 7. Outwardly I lived the life of the white man, yet all the while I kept in direct contact with tribal life. While I learned all that I could of the white man's culture, I never forgot that of my people. I kept the language, tribal manners and usages, sang the songs, and danced the dances.

_____ 8. A few years ago, these Greek immigrants had nothing, and now most of them have made it. They're all well off. Of course, the richest ones have left the Greek neighborhoods and live in the suburbs.

_____ 9. Teachers must teach our children what they need to know, but the teachers must also have a profound knowledge of our culture when they work with our children. This is of paramount importance to the preservation of the Cherokee nation.

_____ 10. The Amish keep to themselves. They are tied together by religion, by kinship, and by custom, and they want to keep it that way.

_____ 11. That's right, I was ashamed of my name. Not only that, I was ashamed of being a Jew. There you have it. Exit Abraham Isaac Arshawsky, Enter Art Shaw! You see, of course, how simple this little transformation was. Presto, Change-o! A new name, a new personality. As simple as that!

_____ 12. Indian children are taught to "be like a white man, and think like a white man." They completely lose their self-identity as Navajos.

_____ 13. What I should like to do is come to a better and more profound knowledge of who I am, whence my community came, and where my son and daughter, and their children's children, might wish to head in the future: I want to have a history.

_____ 14. I only ask of the government to be treated as all other men are treated. If I cannot go to my own home, let me have a home in some country where my people will not die so fast.

_____ 15. It makes no difference to me whether my students are black, white, brown, green, red, yellow, or purple. They are students, and I treat them all the same. After all, we are all human beings. Why can't we forget about color entirely and just treat each other like human beings?

Adapted from *Education in a Multicultural Society* by Fred Rodriguez, University Press of America (1983)

Exercise #2 Are You an Advocate for Gender Equality?

Directions: In our everyday language we make implicit comments that signal oppressive relationships. Read each of the following statements; then respond *Yes* or *No* and write a brief comment of explanation. Check for assumptions that are contained in the item before writing your response. What issues of culture, bias, stereotype, and prejudice arise?

1. Should a husband help his wife most of the time with homemaking and child care?
   Yes _____ No _____ Comment:

2. Should a husband usually ask his wife's opinion before making decisions about major purchases or investments?
   Yes _____ No _____ Comment:

3. Should a husband approve of his wife's working outside of the home, although it interferes with her homemaking and child-care duties?
   Yes _____ No _____ Comment:

4. Should a husband be willing to let his wife take the initiative sexually?
   Yes _____ No _____ Comment:

5. Should a husband be pleased when his wife expresses informal opinions about political or intellectual matters, even if her views differ from his?
   Yes _____ No _____ Comment:

6. Should a husband agree to baby-sit the children when his wife is unable to do so?
   Yes _____ No _____ Comment:

7. Do you rate yourself relatively liberated?
   Yes _____ No _____ Comment:

REFERENCES

Adams, D.W. (1995). *Education for extinction: American Indians and the boarding school experience, 1875–1928.* Lawrence: University Press of Kansas.

Appleton, N. (1983). *Cultural pluralism in education: Theoretical foundations.* New York, NY: Longman.

Aronson, E. (1999). *The social animal* (8th ed.). New York, NY: W. H. Freeman.

Barrett, J.R., & Roediger, D. (2002). How white people became white. In P. Rothenberg (Ed.), *White privilege: Essential readings on the other side of racism* (pp. 29–34). New York, NY: Worth.

Bonilla-Silva, E. (2001). *White supremacy and racism in the post-civil rights era.* Boulder, CO: Lynne Rienner.

Brooks, R.L. (1996). *Integration or separation?: A strategy for racial equality.* Cambridge, MA: Harvard University Press.

Chua, A. (2007). *Day of empire: How hyperpowers rise to global dominance—and why they fall.* New York, NY: Doubleday.

Claiborne, R. (1983). *Our marvelous native tongue: The life and times of the English language.* New York, NY: Times Books.

Cole, S.G., & Cole, M.W. (1954). *Minorities and American promise.* New York, NY: Harper Brothers.

Cronon, E.D. (1955). *The story of Marcus Garvey and the universal Negro Improvement Association.* Madison: University of Wisconsin Press.

Eck, D.L. (2001). *A new religious America: How a "Christian Country" has become the world's most religiously diverse nation.* New York, NY: HarperCollins.

Foner, E. (2000). Affirmative action and history. In J. Birnbaum & C. Taylor (Eds.), *Civil rights since 1787: A reader on the black struggle* (pp. 697–699). New York, NY: New York University Press.

Fuchs, L.H. (1990). *The American kaleidoscope: Race, ethnicity and the civic culture.* Hanover, NH: University Press of New England.

Gladwell, M. (2005). *Blink: The power of thinking without thinking.* New York, NY: Little, Brown.

Gordon, M. (1964). *Assimilation in America: The role of race, religion, and national origins.* New York, NY: Oxford University Press.

Greeley, A. (1975, summer). On ethnicity and cultural pluralism, *Change,* pp. 38–44.

Hattam, V. (2004). Ethnicity: An American genealogy. In N. Foner & G.M. Frederickson (Eds.), *Not just black and white: Historical and contemporary perspectives on immigration, race and ethnicity in the United States* (pp. 42–60). New York, NY: Russell Sage Foundation.

Infact Canada. (2009). *Nestle Boycott.* Retrieved June 12, 2008, from http://www.infactcanada.ca.

Jones, G.R., & George, J.M. (2003). Managing diverse employees in a diverse environment. In *Contemporary management* (3rd ed., pp. 112–149). New York, NY: McGraw-Hill.

Jones, S. (2011, April 15). *How to make the invisible visible?: Tools for pulling back the veil of privilege,* presented at the White Privilege Conference in Minneapolis, MN.

Laosa, L. (1974). Toward a research model of multicultural competency-based education. In W.A. Hunter (Ed.), *Multicultural education through competency-based education* (pp. 135–145). Washington, DC: American Association of Colleges for Teacher Education.

Locke, A. (1989). *The philosophy of Alain Locke: Harlem renaissance and beyond*, L. Harris (Ed.). Philadelphia, PA: Temple University Press.

Martin, W., Jr. (1984). *The mind of Frederick Douglass*. Chapel Hill: University of North Carolina Press.

Menand, L. (2001). *The metaphysical club*. New York, NY: Farrar, Straus, & Giroux.

Naisbitt, J., & Aburdene, P. (1990). Global lifestyles and cultural nationalism. In *Megatrends 2000* (pp. 118–153). New York, NY: William Morrow.

Nieto, S. (2008). *Affirming diversity: The sociopolitical context of multicultural education* (5th ed.). Boston, MA: Pearson.

Pai, Y., & Adler, S. (1997). *Cultural foundations of education* (2nd ed.). Upper Saddle River, NJ: Merrill/ Prentice Hall.

Pipher, M. (2002). *The middle of everywhere: The world's refugees come to our town*. New York, NY: Harcourt.

Schaefer, R.T. (2008). *Racial and ethnic groups* (11th ed.). Upper Saddle River, NJ: Pearson.

Schlesinger, A., Jr. (1991). *The disuniting of America: Reflections on a multicultural society*. Knoxville, TN: Whittle Books.

Seldon, H. (1996). On being color-blind. In J. Andrzejewski (Ed.), *Oppression and social justice: Critical frameworks* (5th ed., pp. 297–298). Needham, MA: Simon & Schuster.

Simpson, E. (Ed.). (1967). Meditation 17. *John Donne: Selected prose* (pp. 100–101). London: Oxford University Press.

Sleeter, C. (1993). How white teachers construct race. In C. McCarthy & W. Crichlow (Eds.), *Race identity and representation in education* (pp. 157–191). New York, NY: Routledge.

Tatum, B.D. (1997). *"Why are all the black kids sitting together in the cafeteria?" and other conversations about race*. New York, NY: Basic Books.

Terry, R.W. (1975). *For whites only* (2nd ed.). Grand Rapids, MI: William B. Eerdmans.

Terry, R.W. (1993). *Authentic leadership: Courage in action*. San Francisco, CA: Jossey-Bass.

U.S. Census Bureau. (2005). *Florida, California and Texas to dominate future population growth*. Retrieved July 10, 2006, from http://www.census.gov.

U.S. Department of Labor. (2009). *Education pays*. Retrieved April 10, 2009, from www.bls.gov/emp/ emptab7.htm.

Williams, C. (1968). *Manifesto*. Ann Arbor: Michigan Education Association.

Williams, C. (2003). Managing individuals and a diverse work force. In *Management* (2nd ed., pp. 343–371). Versailles, KY: Thomson Southwestern.

Williams, J. (1987). *Eyes on the prize: America's civil rights years, 1954–1965*. New York, NY: Viking Penguin.

Wright, R.H. (1991). *The birth of the Montgomery bus boycott*. Southfield, MI: Charro Press.

Zangwill, I. (1915). *The melting pot*. New York, NY: Macmillan.

Zeldin, T. (1994). An intimate history of humanity. New York, NY: HarperCollins.

Contemporary Dilemmas for Intergroup Relations

Section 3 examines oppression currently experienced by members of diverse groups based on differences of race, social class, gender, sexual orientation, and disability. Although institutional discrimination is emphasized, cultural biases and individual prejudices and negative behaviors also are addressed.

Even though the white supremacist attitudes described in Section 2 are no longer the cultural norm, Chapter 8 describes how white privilege continues to be reflected in American culture. Ongoing individual prejudices have resulted in increased racial segregation in neighborhoods and schools. Overt and covert institutional

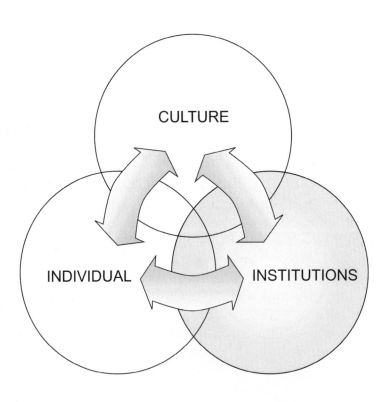

discrimination is revealed in such diverse practices as word-of-mouth hiring, tracking plans in schools, realtors steering clients to specific neighborhoods, and communities employing at-large elections to diminish or deny representation of racial minority groups.

Chapter 9 describes how American cultural values historically promulgate negative influences on individual perceptions of poor people in terms of their deficiencies and personal responsibility for their own poverty. American cultural influence was interrupted in the 1930s when the Great Depression forced many Americans to demand that the federal government become involved in addressing the widespread problems of poverty. Even though many of those 1930s poverty programs are still in place, negative attitudes have reappeared and have been reinforced by derogatory beliefs concerning the poor, including myths about the capability of welfare recipients. Institutions contribute to the exploitation of the poor through government economic policies that favor the wealthiest Americans, resulting in a growing disparity between rich and poor. Vulnerable low-income families are also subjected to economic manipulation by banks and merchants, as illustrated by redlining practices, high fees, rent-to-own stores, and pawnshops.

Chapter 10 examines the sexist messages inherent in everyday words and phrases and provides nonsexist alternatives to language that has historically promoted sexist cultural attitudes. Sexist attitudes in the United States are also manifested in violence against women ranging from domestic abuse to rape. Institutional sexist inequity is reflected in salary disparity between men and women, exploitation of women as part-time workers, and sexual harassment in the workplace.

Chapter 11 provides an overview of historical influences shaping the European and American cultural bias against homosexuality and the myths that have emerged from that bias. Although many of these myths are contradicted by scientific studies of sexuality, countless Americans maintain derogatory beliefs about gays and lesbians that justify their homophobia. Institutional discrimination is apparent in such areas as the workplace, the legal system, the military, and in schools; the campaign for "gay rights" represents the efforts of activists to demand equal legal status for all Americans regardless of sexual orientation.

Chapter 12 presents an overview of historical perceptions of people with disabilities, showing how they contributed to a cultural bias in America that resulted in the institutionalization of these individuals. Being kept apart from society reinforces negative perceptions of people with disabilities, especially the attitude that people with disabilities are unable to care for themselves, and results in discrimination against them even when they are living in one's community. Although many states have passed laws to reduce or eliminate these institutions today, people with disabilities encounter various forms of discrimination even when they require minimal accommodations for personal needs.

Chapter 8

Racism: Confronting a Legacy of White Domination in America

"The problem of race remains America's greatest moral dilemma. When one considers the impact it has upon the nation, its resolution might well determine our destiny."

Martin Luther King, Jr. (1929–1968)

According to Davis (2009), if we added the numbers of all people of color living in the United States, the total would be over 100 million. Comparing that number to population figures for nations around the world, this "nation" would be the twelfth most populous, occupying a rank between Mexico and the Philippines. The diversity of such a significant group of people could be an enormous asset for the United States, but racism causes many Americans to have a negative reaction to racial diversity. Although popular culture presents racism as something anyone of any race can engage in, for some time now scholars have described **racism** as a system of unequal power and privilege by which one racial group dominates others. David Wellman (1977) defined racism as a *system* of advantage based on race. In the United States, because the dominant group has historically been white, racism is a product of white racial prejudice and discrimination, reinforced intentionally or unintentionally by institutional power and authority, and used to the advantage of whites and the disadvantage of people of color (Hilliard, 1992). Even though individual whites may be "against" racism, they still benefit from a system that privileges whites as a group. Racism does not move back and forth, benefiting white people one day and people of color the next. The direction of power between whites and people of color is historic and has been normalized in ideology. People of color may hold prejudices and discriminate against whites, but they do not have the social, cultural, and institutional power backing their prejudice and discrimination that is necessary to be accurately labeled *racism*; the impact of their prejudice on whites is temporary and contextual. By contrast, white people hold social and institutional positions in society that empower them to infuse their racial prejudice into laws, policies, practices, and norms.

Cultural Racism

Cultural racism is the practice of recognizing the activities and contributions of one racial group in preference to others within a multiracial society; it often takes the form of **ethnocentrism**, the superimposition of the history and traditions of one racial group over others (Andrzejewski, 1996). From the beginning, America had a mix of races; however, a dominant culture emerged that did not reflect this diversity. Ever since, our society has continued to disseminate the message that it's better to be white than to be a person of color (DiAngelo, 2006; Dyer, 1997; Fine, 1997; Mills, 1997).

White people are presented as the dominant group in our culture in a variety of ways: in textbooks and other curricular materials; in media and advertising; in being the majority group among our teachers, role models, heroes, and heroines; in norms and standards of beauty that emphasize blonde (or at least straight) hair, blue eyes, slim hips, narrow noses, and round-shaped eyes; in popular television shows featuring friendships among individuals who are all white, even in racially diverse settings such as New York City; and in art, especially religious iconography that depicts God, Adam and Eve, and other ideal images as white.

> At the start of the twentieth century, over 98 percent of blacks in the United States were native-born, a much higher percentage than for whites. Blacks are as American as you can get.
>
> Marguerite Wright (Contemporary)

Holidays in the United States include the celebration of Columbus Day, honoring a man responsible for initiating the slavery and genocide of the indigenous people that would last for over three centuries and that history textbooks relegate to sidebars. Cultural racism is reflected in the return to pre-integration levels of segregation in schools and neighborhoods, and it is common in everyday discussions about what constitutes a good neighborhood. Ultimately, the most profound form of cultural racism may be the lack of a sense of loss about the absence of people of color in most white people's lives (DiAngelo, 2012).

Many of these examples illustrate implicit (indirect) rather than explicit (direct) messages reinforcing white superiority for all children and adults. While some may consciously reject the notion that whites are inherently better than people of color, it is impossible to avoid internalizing the message of white superiority because it is ubiquitous in mainstream culture and taught in our schools. George (2006) has argued: "Schools propagate and nurture whiteness by providing students with a steady diet of white ideology . . . [that] has resulted in a system that thinks, acts, and teaches 'white as right'" (p. 51). Consequently, white children are likely to unconsciously regard nonwhite people as less important. Decades of research have documented that feelings of white superiority appear to develop in white children as early as pre-school (Clark & Clark, 1950; Derman-Sparks, Ramsey, & Olsen, 2011), and Van Ausdale and Feagin (2001) even found racial hostility in white children as young as three years old.

Research over the past two decades has reported that children are much more aware of racial hierarchies than most people believe (Derman-Sparks, Ramsey, & Edwards, 2006; Quintana, 2008; Van Ausdale & Feagin, 2001). Even when race is not explicitly discussed, children internalize racial messages from their environment. For example, Monteiro, de Franca, and Rodrigues (2009) tested 283 white children aged 6 to 7 and 9 to 10 years. The children were asked to allocate money to white and black children, sometimes with a white adult in the room and sometimes without, to see if the presence of an adult impacted their behavior. They found that the 6- to 7-year-old children discriminated against black children in both conditions, but the 9- to 10-year-old children discriminated against black children only when the white adult was not present. The older children had not become less racially biased; rather, they had learned that they should hide their prejudice when adults could observe their behavior.

Cultural racism is reinforced by a racist socialization heavily influenced by media representations. For example, of the 50 top grossing films worldwide, all are American, and all were directed by men, 46 of whom are white. Consider the implications of a racially homogenous group empowered to tell our culture's stories. These implications aren't problematic because privileged white men are bad people; they are problematic because their worldview is necessarily limited, especially regarding race. Yet it is virtually the only worldview many of us see, and it unavoidably (and quite powerfully) shapes our worldview (Sensoy & DiAngelo, 2012). Those who decide which films to promote and award are also an extremely homogenous group. Of the 5,765 voting members of the Academy of Motion Picture Arts and Sciences, nearly 94% are white and 77% are male. Blacks represent about 2% of the Academy, and Latinos are less than 2%. Oscar voters have a median age of 62; people younger than 50 constitute just 14% of the membership (Horn, Sperling, & Smith, 2012).

The implicit messages of racism from the media and other sources are an example of what has been termed "new racism" (Bonilla-Silva, 2009). New racism refers to how racism has adapted over time so that modern norms, policies, and practices produce similarly discriminatory outcomes without appearing to be explicitly racist. For example, what is termed **colorblind racism** is an example of racism's ability to adapt to cultural changes (Bonilla-Silva, 2009).

This ideology asserts that by *ignoring* race we will end racism This idea was inspired by a misinterpretation of one line from Martin Luther King, Jr.'s 1963 "I Have a Dream" speech—a speech that was a turning point in the adaptation of racism. In the period before King gave this speech, many white people felt quite comfortable, even proud, to express their internalized sense of racial superiority and even to admit some of their racial prejudices. But one statement of King's speech—that one day he might be judged by the content of his character and not the color of his skin—struck a moral chord with the public. Seizing on this part of King's speech, the dominant culture began promoting the idea of "colorblindness" as a remedy for racism. However, King presented this speech at the "March on Washington for Jobs and Freedom"; its focus was economic justice, and King was advocating for the elimination of poverty. King did not mean that whites should deny that race mattered, but instead advocated that they should actively work to create a society in which it *actually* didn't matter. But once the civil rights movement became more mainstream and civil rights legislation was passed, there was a significant change in dominant culture; it was no longer as acceptable for white people to admit to racial prejudice (Picca & Feagin, 2007).

The civil rights movement didn't end racism; most whites just became more careful about how they spoke and acted in public spaces. Reducing King's work to the simplistic idea of "colorblindness" is an example of how racism adapts to cultural changes. People notice the race of others, and race has deep social meaning for us. Everyone receives value-laden racial messages daily that circulate in society. These messages did not end the day civil rights legislation was signed. While some messages are blatant (racist jokes, for example), most are subtle and often invisible, especially to whites; much of what is learned is below the level of one's conscious awareness (VanAusdale & Feagin, 2001). The idea of colorblindness may have started out as a well-intentioned strategy, but in practice it has served to deny the reality of racism and thus perpetuate it. Scholars have termed this *aversive racism*.

What is aversive racism?

Aversive racism refers to the type of racism that well-intentioned, educated, and progressive

people are more likely to enact (Hodson, Dovido, & Gaertner, 2004). As with colorblind racism, it often exists below the surface because it conflicts with consciously held beliefs of equality and justice among racial groups. Aversive racists act in ways that allow them to maintain a positive self-image ("I am not prejudiced"), and this is demonstrated in a variety of ways: rationalizing racial segregation as necessary in order to access "good schools"; explaining a lack of cross-racial friendships as a result of few people of color living in their neighborhood; avoiding direct racial language but using racially coded terms such as "underprivileged," "urban," "diverse," "sketchy," and "good neighborhoods"; denying that they have few cross-racial relationships by arguing how diverse their community or workplace is; and attributing inequality between whites and people of color to causes other than racism. Regardless of an individual white person's explicit racial beliefs, most are subjected to individual racism expressed by friends or family who will at least occasionally make direct comments and jokes about people of color. Despite the claims of many white young adults that racism is in the past and that they were taught to see everyone as equal, research on attitudes reflecting individual racism shows otherwise.

Individual Racism

Individual racism includes both racial prejudice and racist behavior. Racial prejudice refers to negative attitudes a person holds toward racial groups that are learned in many ways: from stereotypes in the media to myths and misconceptions passed on from one generation to the next. Racist behavior occurs when someone acts upon his or her racial prejudices by saying or doing something degrading or harmful toward a person or group. In a study by Picca and Feagin (2007), 626 white college students at 28 different colleges across the United States kept journals recording every instance related to racial issues, images, and understandings that they observed over the course of six to eight weeks. They recorded over 7,500 accounts of blatantly racist comments and actions by the white people in their lives (friends, family members, acquaintances, strangers). This study provided empirical evidence that racism continues to be explicitly expressed by whites, even those who are young and profess to be progressive, and it also described the difference between what has been termed *front* and *backstage* racism.

What are front and backstage racism?

In Picca and Feagin's study, *front* and *backstage racism* referred to a pattern in people's racist comments and actions. The majority of incidents occurred in what the researchers described as "backstage"—in all-white company. Whites often played predictable roles. There was a protagonist who initiated the racist act, a cheerleader who encouraged it through laughter or agreement, spectators who stood in silence, and (rarely) a dissenter who objected. Virtually all objectors were subjected to a form of peer pressure in which they were told it was "only a joke" and that they should "lighten up." The student journals documented that in "frontstage" settings (i.e., people of color were present), the white participants behaved differently and displayed racially conscious behaviors including: acting overly nice; avoiding contact (e.g., crossing a street or not going to a particular bar or club); using stereotypical black expressions in order to fit in with blacks; and avoiding racial terms or labels by using code words to talk negatively about people of color. In "backstage" settings (i.e., people of color were not present), white students often used humor to reinforce racial stereotypes about people of color, particularly blacks, and occasionally made blatantly racist comments. Picca and Feagin (2007) argue that the purpose of these backstage performances is to create white group solidarity and reinforce the ideology of white (and male) supremacy. This behavior reinforces individual racism in all people, albeit in less formal but perhaps more powerful ways than in the past.

In what ways are all people affected by individual racism?

The presence of racism in society means that all individuals will internalize it, including people of color, but these messages have a different impact on people of color than on whites. For people of color, these messages promote what is termed **internalized racial oppression**—the largely unconscious beliefs of racial inferiority and related behaviors that are accepted by people of color who have been raised in a white supremacist society. Conversely, the socialization of white people resulting in their acceptance of largely unconscious beliefs of racial superiority is termed **internalized racial dominance**. An internalized sense of racial dominance is evident in some white individuals by their blatant dislike for people of color, but for most white people, the feeling of racial superiority is more subtle; it is a sense of entitlement to white privileges, reinforced by the ideology of *individualism.*

How does the ideology of individualism reinforce individual racism?

The ideology of individualism emphasizes that we are each unique individuals and that categories such as race do not matter and have no relevance to our life outcomes. Many examples of **white privilege**, as described by McIntosh (2001), are in large part the result of the privilege of being perceived as an individual rather than as a member of a racial group (see Table 8.1). For example, Steven Spielberg is seen as a film director, but Spike Lee is seen as a *Black* film director; Joy Picoult and Emily Dickinson are writers, but Maya Angelou and Toni Morrison are *Black* writers. This tendency to name race only when it isn't white transforms the concept of being perceived as an individual into an advantage afforded only to whites. Suggesting that we are all just individuals may appear to represent everyone fairly and not function as a form of racism, but individualism is also applied on a macro level to explain persistent patterns in achievement and outcomes.

Individualism positions the group at the top of the social hierarchy (i.e., whites) as a collection of outstanding (and unraced) individuals who value hard work, education, and determination. Simultaneously, groups of color that have been consistently denied institutional access and have not had similar achievements are assumed to lack these values (Conley, 1999; Meizhu, Robles, & Leondar-Wright, 2006). If we believe that we are all individuals and that social categories such as race, class, and gender don't matter but are just "labels" that stereotype us, then logically it follows

TABLE 8.1 White Privilege

Because of white privilege, the following activities illustrate assumptions white people can make that people of color cannot make:

1. If I should need to move, I can be pretty sure of renting or purchasing housing in an area which I can afford and in which I would want to live.

2. I can be pretty sure that my neighbors in such a location will be neutral or pleasant to me.

3. I can go shopping alone most of the time, pretty well assured that I will not be followed or harassed.

4. When I am told about our national heritage or about "civilization," I am shown that people of my color made it what it is.

5. I can be sure that my children will be given curricular materials that testify to the existence of their race.

6. Whether I use checks, credit cards, or cash, I can count on my skin color not to work against the appearance of financial reliability.

7. I can swear, or dress in secondhand clothes, or not answer letters, without having people attribute these choices to the bad morals, the poverty, or the illiteracy of my race.

8. If a traffic cop pulls me over or if the IRS audits my tax return, I can be sure I haven't been singled out because of my race.

9. I can easily buy posters, postcards, picture books, greeting cards, dolls, toys, and children's magazines featuring people of my race.

10. I can choose blemish cover or bandages in "flesh" color and have them more or less match my skin.

Source: From "White Privilege: Unpacking the Invisible Knapsack" by Peggy McIntosh in *Race, Class, and Gender in the United States: An integrated study*, P. Rothenberg, Ed.

that we all end up in our appropriate place. Those at the top succeeded on their own individual merits, and those at the bottom failed because of individual shortcomings. Thus, individualism upholds the myth of meritocracy—that success is the result of ability and hard work—and the belief in the superiority of those at the top (Bonilla-Silva, 2009; Wise, 2005).

This belief in a "level playing field" where merit is rewarded crumbles before even a cursory examination of the American reality. Kozol (2005) cites research that in 86% of schools with primarily black and Latino students, more than half of the students qualify for free or reduced-price meals. Spriggs (2008) and Powell (2008) have documented that families of color overwhelmingly tend to live in racially segregated neighborhoods and send their children to schools that are often deteriorating.

A disproportionate number of people of color live in poverty, and even when people of color earn a college degree, they do not gain the same financial reward for that achievement as a white person. Rwehmeyer (2007) described a study demonstrating how economic forces arising from racial segregation created economic inequities even when there was no history of discrimination between two groups. He concluded: "even when social groups are economically equal, continued segregation may result in inequality over time" (p. 2).

Because so many whites choose to live racially segregated lives—another manifestation of racism—their sense of entitlement is seldom challenged, and when it is, lack of experience often leaves whites unsure of how to respond in constructive ways. One common way that racism is manifested toward people of Asian heritage is through the idea that they are not regarded as American but as *perpetual foreigners* (Howard, 2006). In 1998, American figure skater Tara Lipinski edged out Michelle Kwan, another American figure skater, for the Olympic gold medal. The MSNBC headline read, "American beats out Kwan." The assumption in this headline was that an Asian could not be American. Individuals of Asian heritage frequently encounter such sentiments when they are asked: "Where are you from?" If their answer is "Chicago," the next question often will be, "Okay, but where are you *really* from?" If the person responds by saying he or she has always lived in Chicago, the next question may be "Okay, but I mean, where did you come from?" In trying to ascertain the person's ethnicity, the questioner implies a perception that Asian Americans are foreigners. From there it's a small step to "You don't belong here." Most white Americans have not learned cognitive or affective skills that promote constructive engagement across racial divides. Instead, they tend to express cognitive rationalizations that prevent them from seeing, understanding, and challenging racism.

What are some examples of rationalizations justifying individual racism?

The 1954 *Brown v. Board of Education* decision said segregated schools were inherently unequal and ordered the desegregation of American schools. It was not until the 1960s that school desegregation plans were finally implemented, and then, in the 1980s, Supreme Court decisions backed away from the desegregation mandate. The resulting decline in aggressive political pressure brought desegregation efforts to a halt except in some urban schools. Few white students attended urban schools because their families had participated in the migration to segregated suburbs termed **white flight** (Thompson, 1999). Despite the presence of re-segregated schools, a common denial rationalization still used by many white Americans is to insist that schools are no longer segregated by race. However, when Massey (2003) analyzed multiracial societies around the world, he found that the only nation as segregated as the United States was South Africa under apartheid.

Another denial rationalization relates to affirmative action. Based on empirical evidence that

people of color were discriminated against in hiring, the Affirmative Action program was instituted in the 1960s to address this issue. Today, many white people use affirmative action to deny that racial discrimination exists; it is their misunderstanding that affirmative action requires an employer to give hiring preference to a person of color over a qualified white applicant even if the person of color is unqualified—in order to achieve a racial quota. But this is simply untrue. In reality, affirmative action was developed as a tool to ensure that qualified minority applicants are given the same opportunities for employment as white people, and the program has never mandated racial quotas in hiring decisions; no employer has ever been required to hire an unqualified person of color. In the elections that occurred 238 years after the first Congress was formed, only 86 members are people of color including only four senators. In the 112th Congress there are 44 African Americans, 26 Latinos, 11 Asian Americans (and still only one Native American). Of the nine members of the Supreme Court, only two are people of color. In addition, white people constitute the vast majority of CEOs, *Fortune* 500 executives, managers, lawyers, doctors, scientists, professors, and others who hold highly regarded positions of leadership. While whites are the majority of people in the United States, their overrepresentation in leadership roles is the result of over 300 years of white privilege and concrete discrimination against people of color in various institutions across our society. This discrimination against people of color continues today.

Another example of this preference for white applicants, whether conscious or unconscious, is the workplace concept of "fit," the tendency to prefer people whose cultural style matches the workplace culture. Since white people are still the dominant group in leadership positions in the workplace, they are more likely to view white applicants as a better "fit" with the workplace culture. In addition, despite the perception that affirmative action primarily benefits people of color, white women have actually been the greatest beneficiaries of affirmative action programs. Favoring white women over people of color in employment has contributed to the creation of what some have called a "persistent white ceiling." Reed (2011) has noted that when corporations demonstrate a concern for diversity in hiring executives, they tend to favor white women and those people of color who come from elite backgrounds outside the United States.

There are also victim-blaming rationalizations such as those identified in surveys conducted by scholars at the University of Chicago. At the National Opinion Research Center (1998), researchers randomly selected hundreds of households in 300 different communities and conducted surveys concerning white people's perceptions of African Americans. Their results revealed the persistence of stereotypes that blamed black people for their problems. For example, 56% of white people thought most blacks were lazy compared to whites, and 79% of white respondents perceived blacks as more violent than whites. Perceiving black people as violent has contributed to the demand for more prisons and tougher sentences for violent crimes; it has also reinforced racial profiling and affected how police officers respond to black suspects. Perhaps one of the most offensive victim-blaming rationalizations was the white response to a survey question about patriotism: 51% of white respondents said black people were less patriotic than white people, which is surprising since a conventional measure of patriotism in America is the willingness to risk one's life by enlisting in one of the military services to fight for our nation. Buckley (2001) described African

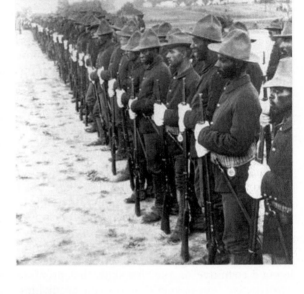

FIGURE 8.1

Members of the segregated 10th Calvary, called Buffalo soldiers, were part of the "Rough Riders" led by Teddy Roosevelt that took San Juan Hill during the Spanish-American War; African American soldiers are rarely acknowledged in films or in history books.

Source: Creative Commons

> Most of the people I meet in America are compassionate. Why is it that individually we can be so compassionate and collectively we can be so harsh? . . . I don't have an answer to that.
>
> Jonathan Kozol (1936–)

Americans who volunteered, fought, and died in every war in which the United States was involved: the Revolutionary War, Civil War, Spanish-American War, and all conflicts, large and small, in the twentieth century. (See Figure 8.1.) Black people enlisted in today's military services far outnumber their proportion of the population.

When white Americans acknowledge problems of discrimination against Americans of color, they often express no sense of responsibility. History provides numerous examples of the white majority in

the United States discussing "the Negro problem" as if it had nothing to do with whites. Novelist Richard Wright contradicted that assertion: "There isn't any Negro problem; there is only a white problem" (Lipsitz, 2008). Wright meant that the racial attitudes and behaviors of white people were the problem—that racism in America meant white racism. Saying that racism is only a problem for people of color allows white people to rationalize their unwillingness to do anything to address this issue.

Trainor (2005) discussed how white people reject or avoid racism by engaging in what she terms "White Talk" (see Table 8.2). These rationalizations illustrate many of the common white narratives that work to justify racism. Being aware of white talk can provide recognizable categories to conceptualize these narratives and can demonstrate how common and predictable they are. These examples also illustrate that opinions are not benign

TABLE 8.2 Examples of "White Talk"

Denial rationalizations	"You can't say that all white people are racist. They might have good reasons for how they feel." "Because of affirmative action, a lot of white people can't get into the college they want, and that's a kind of reverse racism."
Victim-blame rationalizations	"Minorities need to quit complaining; anyone can achieve any goal if they are willing to work hard." "In my neighborhood, Mexicans just had less respect for property."
Avoidance rationalizations	"Everybody faces struggles against prejudice and stereotypes toward their group." "I know there's some discrimination against racial minorities, but what can one person do?"

Adapted from Trainor (2005)

or merely uninformed; they are rooted in an unexamined ideology and perpetuate racism by rationalizing its reality. Rationalizing and denying racism may not be the conscious intention of those engaging in white talk, but such comments function to repudiate racism as an issue. If people are sincere about wanting to challenge racism and its inevitable

> As long as you keep a person down, some part of you has to be down there to hold him down, so it means you cannot soar as you otherwise might.
>
> Marian Anderson (1897–1993)

socializing power, they must be willing to challenge their worldviews. This requires not only an honest exploration of the ideology of individualism that perpetuates racism among the American people, but also an overhaul of the institutional policies and practices that continue to create unequal opportunity for people of color in our society.

Institutional Racism

Jones (1997) defined **institutional racism** as "established laws, customs, and practices that systematically reflect and produce racial inequities in American society" (p. 438). We rely on institutions in America. Although individual racism is damaging, institutional racism is far more devastating because of the broader impact institutions have on people.

Institutional racism can be intentional when it is a result of a prejudiced person making a conscious decision about a person or group based on their race. Williams (2007) described a study in which pairs of black and white males and pairs of Hispanic and white males applied for the same jobs. Identical qualifications were created on their résumés. The men were trained to present themselves in similar ways to minimize differences during interviews; still, white men received three times as many job offers as did black or Hispanic men. We also know that institutional racism can be unintentional. Although studies have reported that people of color pay more to purchase a car than white people, especially white men, representatives of car dealerships deny that they engage in discrimination, but perhaps they are simply not conscious of it. Gladwell (2005) cites a Chicago study in which 38 people dressed and identified themselves as professionals to purchase an automobile: fifteen white men, seven white women, eight black women, and five black men. They visited 242 car dealers and negotiated for a car according to strict instructions so that their behavior would be similar. The initial offers that sales representatives made to white men tended to be about $725 above dealer's invoice compared to initial offers of about $935 above invoice given to white women. The initial offers to black women tended to be $1,200 above invoice, and for black men it was $1,690.

Even after negotiating with the sales representatives, the average price of the car for black men was $1,550 above invoice, more than double what white men were offered without any bargaining.

Because most Americans seem to agree that it is wrong to discriminate based on race, ethnicity, gender, or other factors, it is important to understand how institutional racism occurs. Whether intentional or unintentional, institutional racism results in negative consequences for people of color. Unemployment statistics document how race makes a difference when decisions are made about hiring people.

> The sad truth is that most evil is done by people who never make up their minds to be either good or evil.
>
> Hannah Arendt (1898–1989)

How is institutional racism reflected in statistics on employment?

Disproportionate numbers of people of color work in low-paying, low-status jobs, and people of color tend to have significantly higher unemployment rates compared to whites. The data for black youth is staggering. Riley (2011) reported a 42% unemployment rate for black teenagers as compared to 21% for white teenagers and 24.5% for all teenagers. Black teenage unemployment is as high as 60% in some urban areas. According to Foster (2001), the employment discrepancy continues after graduation from high school. Higher percentages of African Americans are unemployed in the year after they graduate from high school than white graduates. It did not matter if the graduates were from rural or urban schools. The unemployment rate for black graduates was higher than whites regardless of socioeconomic status, the type of high school attended, or the type of academic program in which they were enrolled. In one study, white and black college graduates were given comparable résumés to submit with job application forms. After they were interviewed, three times as many white applicants were called back compared to black applicants, causing Aronson (2008)

to conclude: "Skin color, it seems, still outweighs character where hiring is concerned" (p. 307).

Despite affirmative action programs, studies by the U.S. Bureau of Labor Statistics (2001) document that disparity between unemployment rates for people of color compared to whites was slightly worse in 1990 (11% versus 4%) than it was in 1960 (10% versus 5%). In 2011, the disparity in unemployment continued with an 8% rate for whites, 11.3% for Latinos, and 16.0% for African Americans (U.S. Bureau of Labor Statistics, 2011). As for Native Americans, unemployment on some reservations is higher than 80%, and this group is three times more likely than whites to live in poverty (Jenkins, 2009). Urban areas showed even larger disparities in jobless rates for white and black workers. In a study by the Center for Economic Development at the University of Wisconsin-Milwaukee, Levine (2010) compared black and white jobless rates in Milwaukee with those in selected cities such as Chicago, Buffalo, Cleveland, and Detroit. Levine looked at jobless rates rather than unemployment rates because the latter does not include adult people in the workforce who have given up on finding a job, often because no jobs appear to be available. This is especially a problem in urban areas. Levine's data (see Table 8.3) reveals that urban black workers are almost twice as likely not to have a job as urban white workers. Milwaukee had the most significant problem with 53.3% of its black workers jobless, almost two and a half times the rate for white workers. Such data clearly suggests that race, whether intentional or unintentional, was a factor in hiring employees.

TABLE 8.3 Black/White Jobless Rates in Selected Metropolitan Areas

	Black	White	Black/White Ratio
1. Milwaukee	53.3	22.3	2.39
2. Chicago	50.3	23.9	2.10
3. Buffalo	52.3	26.0	2.01
4. Cleveland	52.3	26.3	1.99
5. Detroit	59.5	31.8	1.87

Source: Center for Economic Development, University of Wisconsin-Milwaukee (2010)

How does institutional racism influence hiring decisions?

To understand why disparities in black and white unemployment exist, examine how hiring decisions are made. Studies repeatedly show that one of the most important methods used to recruit and hire employees is **word-of-mouth hiring**. If job seekers have relatives or friends already working for the company to recommend them, those job seekers have a better chance of being hired. Research suggests that 60% to 90% of blue-collar workers were hired because of recommendations from family or friends—and the same pattern has been observed in hiring decisions for white-collar jobs.

Employers feel they benefit from the word-of-mouth approach. If a trusted employee recommends someone, the employers believe that the risk in determining the quality of the person being hired is greatly reduced. Another benefit is that hiring costs are minimal; jobs are filled without paying to advertise them. Because of word-of-mouth hiring, Lipsitz (2008) found that 86% of available jobs never appeared in the classified ads of local newspapers.

Word-of-mouth hiring disadvantages people of color because of the history of segregation and discrimination in the United States. In the past, white male employees were blatantly favored over applicants who were women or people of color. At one time the preference was so obvious that state and federal governments passed anti-discrimination laws to address the problem; still, white men constituted a disproportionate share of the workforce. Schaefer (2008) reviewed social distance studies indicating that people consistently indicate a preference for people most like themselves; therefore, white people may recommend other white people simply to make sure they will be with people with whom they are comfortable.

Furthermore, because of ongoing housing segregation, white Americans have not tended to become friends with people of color. When white workers recommend a friend or relative for a job, they may insist that they are not trying to prevent a person of color from being hired but instead are helping someone they know. Intentional or not, word-of-mouth job recruitment offers a distinct advantage to white job applicants and contributes to discrimination documented by statistics on unemployment disparities between black and white workers.

Another way to secure employment is to join a labor union. However, admission policies of many unions still discriminate against people of color, particularly in unions for skilled trades that are historically dominated by white workers and have records of past discrimination against people of color. Unions typically accept new members based primarily on recommendations of current members. As with word-of-mouth hiring, white union members may or may not recommend people of color, but they are more likely to know and recommend someone who is white (Feagin & Feagin, 1986; Lipsitz, 2008).

Discrimination also occurs in decisions regarding company location. Because neighborhoods in the United States still reveal a pattern of racial segregation, a company's decision to locate in a white suburb means that the employees hired will be primarily or exclusively white. Studies show that when a new company selects a location or an established company expands to a new location, employees who live within a 30- to 40-mile radius of the worksite tend to be hired.

In the 1990s, Wilson (1996) reported a trend toward the suburbanization of industry, especially among retail trade companies. The trend has continued. White suburbs are advantaged because they tend to be more affluent than urban areas and usually offer more incentives to influence a company's decision to relocate. Wilson reported that when a number of low-income blacks were placed in suburban apartments, they were significantly more likely to find work than the low-income blacks placed in apartments in the city; the reason was the higher availability of jobs in the suburbs. Leondar-Wright (2009) cites a study of 45 urban areas reporting that 25% to 50% of black unemployment was a result of jobs being shifted to the suburbs. A company's reasons for selecting a location may have more to do with economic incentives than with race, but the consequences of that decision have a racial impact.

How has institutional racism influenced the development of segregated neighborhoods?

Studies report that neighborhoods in the United States continue to reveal a pattern of racial segregation (Bonilla-Silva, 2001; Farley, 2010; Massey, 2001; Orser, 1990). Although there has been some improvement since the 1980s, Massey (2003) describes the level of black and white segregation in urban areas:

> The most common measure of residential segregation is an index that ranges from 0 to 100, where 0 indicates that blacks and whites are evenly distributed among neighborhoods and 100 means that blacks and whites share no neighborhood in common. Scores greater than 50 are considered to be "high"; those above 70 are "extreme." . . . The most segregated U.S. metropolitan area is Detroit, with an index of 85, followed by Milwaukee (82), New York (81), Newark, N.J. (80), and Chicago (80). Other areas with "extreme" segregation scores include Buffalo, Cincinnati, Cleveland, Kansas City, Philadelphia, and St. Louis. (p. 22)

Past practices of discrimination were overt, including the use of covenants by which homeowners guaranteed other homeowners in their neighborhood that if they sold their home it would not be sold to a family of color. Today such tactics are illegal, but other discriminatory practices still occur.

Some people believe American attitudes are changing. Foster (2001) cites a 1958 study in which white people were asked if they would leave their neighborhood if a black family moved in next to them: 44% of them said they would, but in a 1997 study, only 1% of white respondents said they would move. In the 1958 study, 80% of white respondents said they would leave their neighborhood if a large number of black families moved in, but in the 1997 study, only 18% said

> An illustration of the craving people have to attach favorable symbols to themselves is seen in the community where white people banded together to force out a Negro family that had moved in. They called themselves 'Neighborly Endeavor' and chose as their motto the Golden Rule.
>
> Gordon Allport (1897–1967)

they would leave. Yet Foster and others have cited studies documenting that white families will stay in a neighborhood as long as black families do not

exceed 7% or 8% of its residents. Once that percentage is exceeded, white families leave (Bonilla-Silva, 2001).

Neighborhood segregation is assured when realtors engage in a practice known as **steering**. The term refers to keeping files of homes for sale in white neighborhoods separate from those for sale in areas consisting predominantly or exclusively of families of color. Realtors show their clients homes in neighborhoods based on their race (Jenkins, 2007). Clients may be shown homes in integrated neighborhoods, if there are any, in response to a specific request. If accused of racism, realtors may claim that white homeowners who don't want people of color moving into their neighborhoods will not list their home with a realtor whom they believe will show their home to people of color. Realtors could insist that they are not being racist but are simply respecting the wishes of their clients.

Zoning ordinances might also contribute to racial segregation of neighborhoods. City councils often approve ordinances excluding multifamily dwellings in certain residential areas. The cost of homes in such areas is usually well beyond the means of many families of color, but the rental price of units in a multifamily dwelling might be affordable. So the passage of a zoning ordinance expressly prohibiting multifamily housing virtually eliminates the possibility of families of color moving into the neighborhood.

Segregation aside, it is often more difficult for people of color to finance the purchase of homes. A study of the Federal Reserve Bank of Boston reported almost three times as many mortgage loans in low-income neighborhoods consisting of white homeowners than in those consisting of African American homeowners. Home loan officers seem more willing to dismiss the credit record problems of white applicants. Lipsitz (2008) also cites a Los Angeles study that found different standards of eligibility for white and black loan applicants. A study of a Houston bank reported that 13% of middle-income white applicants were denied loans compared to 36% of middle-income black applicants; a study of home loan institutions in Atlanta found that they approved five times as many loans to whites as to blacks.

Between 1998 and 2008, banks and other lending institutions began to approve more home loans to people of color as part of the infamous sub-prime mortgage fiasco. During the financial collapse that took place in 2008, many critics blamed the lenders for making too many bad loans to people, especially people of color, whose finances were inadequate to pay off the home loans they received. Yet data was collected over the same ten-year period from the Community Advantage Program that facilitated loans to families with low incomes or single-headed households, and it reveals that even though these clients presented a greater risk, they were no more likely to default on conventional home mortgage loans than the rest of the population (Oliver & Shapiro, 2008). The problem with sub-prime mortgage loans was that they involved hidden costs, wildly adjustable rates, and severe pre-payment penalties. Adding insult to injury, African American families who qualified for conventional mortgages often were steered to the more profitable sub-prime home loans. As a consequence, three times more families of color were given sub-prime mortgages than white families, and twice as many African American and Latino homeowners ended up losing their homes because they defaulted on the sub-prime loans. One estimate of the loss of wealth to African American homeowners was somewhere between $72 and $93 billion (Oliver & Shapiro, 2008). These foreclosures not only harmed families who lost their homes, but also diminished the value of surrounding homes in the neighborhood. Since U.S. neighborhoods tend to be racially segregated, homeowners who were people of color were more likely to suffer a loss in the value of their homes because of foreclosures in their neighborhood. And reductions in home values result in fewer tax dollars to support the schools in these areas.

How does institutional racism occur in schools?

As the statistics given earlier in the chapter illustrate, American schools are racially segregated, in fact, more segregated than ever. According to Gary Orfield of the Harvard Civil Rights Project, schools in the United States were desegregating in compliance with court-ordered desegregation for slightly more than two decades, and data from that period show that the numbers of students of color graduating from high school increased significantly and the racial divide in test scores decreased substantially (Kozol, 2005). As schools began resegregating

in the 1990s, racial test scores widened once again. Orfield's research shows that this ongoing process of resegregation has resulted in 75% of African American and Latino students attending schools with predominantly minority populations, with more than 2 million attending "schools which we call apartheid schools" (Kozol, 2005, p. 19).

In response to the increasing presence of students of color, some schools, especially in urban areas, have implemented curricula more inclusive of the achievements of people of color, but few of them adequately address issues of prejudice or discrimination. Part of the problem is that textbooks have historically demonstrated a Eurocentric bias in history, literature, art, and music (Kirp, 1991; Loewen, 1995; Tobin and Ybarra, 2008). As Tobin and Ybarra (2008) state: "Bias plagues textbooks by choosing one group's narrative over another—when that narrative is historically wrong and the facts are not the facts" (p. 7). The prevalence of textbook bias necessitates that conscientious teachers develop supplementary materials to provide students with information about multicultural perspectives. This is a difficult task because the major function of teaching is delivering curriculum, and teachers have limited time and resources to develop new material.

Another significant issue in K–12 schools today involves racial disparities in the suspension of students. This is a critical issue because suspensions are a major factor in predicting students who will drop out of school. Losen (2011) reported that in 1973, suspensions for white, Hispanic, and Native American students were equal, with 3% of each group having been suspended at least once, while twice as many black students (6%) had been suspended. In 2007, suspensions of Hispanic and Native American students more than doubled to 7% and 8% respectively, with white students increasing only to 5%; however, three times as many black students (15%) had been suspended as white students. It was even worse for all groups in middle school, where 10% of white students were suspended, but approximately 16% of Hispanic and Native American students and over 28% of black students were suspended. Among middle school girls, four times as many black females had been suspended as white females. One study reported that white students were more likely to be suspended for offenses that could be objectively documented such as smoking, using profanity, and vandalism, but black students were more likely to be suspended for behaviors requiring a subjective judgment such as being disrespectful, being too loud, and loitering (Losen, 2011). The states with the largest disparities were Nebraska, which suspended almost 37% of its black students compared to 6.4% of white students, and Wisconsin, which suspended 34.4% of black students and only 7.2% of its white students. Losen (2011) referred to the conclusion from a study of 21 schools that found: "no evidence that African-American over-representation in school suspension is due to higher rates of misbehavior," but that "Black students were more likely to be sent to the office for disciplinary reasons" (pp. 6–7).

Another example of racism in schools is **tracking**—grouping students into categories by ability and assigning them to specific, ability-related classes. Most public elementary, middle, and high schools in America engage in some form of tracking. Based on supposedly objective tests of intellectual ability, children whose first language is not English have been inappropriately placed in remedial classes or even classes for cognitively disabled students (Fattah, 2001). Students of color tend to be overrepresented in classes for slow learners, underrepresented in accelerated classes, and placed in vocational or remedial classes in disproportionate numbers (Kershaw, 1992; Oakes, 2005; Oakes & Wells, 1996; Oakes et al., 2000). According to Callahan (2005), tracking is also harmful to English Language Learners (ELL) because teachers tend to regard these students as having cognitive deficits instead of realizing their difficulties may be related to their learning in another language. Rather than focusing on their strengths, teachers often avoided giving these students academically challenging tasks. These

> . . . if we were to select the most intelligent, imaginative, energetic, and stable third of all mankind, all races would be represented.
>
> Franz Boas (1858–1942)

practices decreased the chances that the ELL students would graduate from high school, and if they did graduate, they were not prepared for college.

Nieto (2008) described consequences established as early as middle school because tracking children who are still going through puberty influences economic and occupational outcomes when they become adults.

Research has found that tracking provides minimal value for accelerated learners, and it harms students tracked at lower levels, especially those at the lowest level. Because a large percentage of low-income students are racial minorities, tracking usually results in both race and class segregation because low-income students are typically placed in different tracks than middle- or upper-class students. Tracking has been justified by the argument that it improves education for all students, allowing teachers to provide instruction at the students' level so they learn more efficiently. Research does not support this assumption. Academic outcomes for high-achieving students do not appear to be compromised in heterogeneous classes. Middle- and low-achieving students appear to benefit by interacting with high-achieving students; scholastic development is curtailed significantly when they are stratified with other equally low-achieving students (Oakes, 2005; Oakes & Wells, 1996; Oakes et al., 2000).

It is difficult for people of color to confront institutional racism in jobs, housing, and schools because that requires political power at local, state, and federal levels. Institutional racism curtails opportunities to be elected to local governing bodies—school boards, city councils, county commissions—and makes it even more difficult to win party primaries or elections at the state and national levels.

How does institutional racism affect politics?

Although the situation is improving in some state legislatures, people of color still tend to be underrepresented in the House of Representatives and Senate at both state and federal levels (Bonilla-Silva, 1999). Although people of color constitute more than 35% of the U.S. population, in the 112th Congress there were only four (8%) in the Senate—two Latinos and two Asian Americans—and 82 (15%) in the House—44 African Americans, 26 Latinos, 11 Asian Americans, and one Native American. There are many problems for candidates of color to overcome.

> In a democracy, the majority of citizens is capable of exercising the most cruel oppression upon the minority.
>
> Edmund Burke (1729–1797)

In New Mexico, some Hispanic candidates have been successful emphasizing their Spanish (i.e., white) ancestry. Shorris (2001) noted that such candidates were elected to local and state offices "long before other Latinos could get past gerrymandering, ward politics, and at-large elections" (p. 167). The use of **at-large candidates** involves members of city councils or school boards being elected by the entire city, instead of by their respective districts or wards. If the majority of voters in a city are white, electing at-large candidates will assure all-white representation on councils or boards, despite having areas within the city consisting primarily or exclusively of people of color.

An Associated Press (2010) story described how the at-large issue was resolved in the wake of a discrimination lawsuit from Latinos living in Port Chester, New York. Port Chester is a community of 30,000 residents, half of whom are Latinos, but only one quarter of the Latino residents are voters. Every two years, Port Chester voters would elect two of the town's six trustees from a slate of at-large candidates, and even with the influx of Latino residents, all six trustees continued to be white. After reviewing the evidence, Judge Stephen Robinson ruled that Port Chester was in violation of the federal Voting Rights Act. The judge ordered the community to revise its electoral process so that Latino voters were not unfairly denied their political voice by "diluting" their votes. The village still wanted to elect trustees who were concerned for the entire community and not just one district within the community. Instead of creating districts, Port Chester approved an electoral process called "cumulative voting," in which each voter can vote for an at-large candidate more than one time. The plan called for all six trustees to be selected in a single election, and in casting their six votes, all voters were given the option of voting up to six times for the same candidate. In the first election implementing this new approach, Luis Marino,

a Peruvian immigrant, received the fourth highest number of votes, becoming Port Arthur's first Latino trustee.

In the 2008 presidential campaign, the Democratic Party exemplified the changing face of America by fielding three highly regarded candidates who were not white males. The Latino candidate, Governor Bill Richardson (New Mexico), dropped out of the race after the early primaries, but Hillary Rodham Clinton and Barack Obama competed for the nomination through the entire primary season. Perhaps the most significant achievement of Obama's campaign organization was its ability to overcome fundraising problems that have tended to disadvantage candidates of color at all levels in the past. For example, when Jesse Jackson ran for president in the Democratic primaries in 1984 and 1988, he used his celebrity status to compensate for his lack of funds because the national media gave extensive coverage to his campaign. Obama's phenomenal fundraising during the primaries was surpassed after he received the party's nomination for President, setting a record by raising $65 million in August and then shattering that record by raising $150 million in September. Much of the fundraising was done on the Internet as 3.1 million contributors gave an average of $86. Despite this fundraising success and Senator Obama's impressive oratory, pundits still wondered if white voters would vote for an African American candidate, but on election night, Barack Obama emerged as the first African American and the first openly biracial individual to become President of the United States.

Many Americans viewed President Obama's election as a major blow against racism in the United States, and they hoped that his victory would promote even more aggressive challenges to institutional racism in the years to come. However, in the period since the election, examples of both individual and institutional racism have demonstrated that neither can be expected to decline in the immediate future (see Figure 8.2). The evidence comes from the predatory lending practices that have disproportionately targeted families of color, employment data that has continued to document higher unemployment rates for workers of color, racial profiling implicitly endorsed in anti-immigrant statutes approved by state legislatures in Arizona and Alabama, and the continued growth and expansion of hate groups (Potok, 2011).

FIGURE 8.2

President Barack Obama's nomination of Judge Sonia Sotomayor meant that she would become the first Latina to serve on the Supreme Court. Although widely regarded as one of the best qualified nominees in recent years, Republican opponents demonstrated the persistence of historic prejudices as they questioned her abilities and even accused her of being "a racist" for arguing that her ethnicity provided a valuable perspective for her judicial decisions.

Source: Whitehouse.gov, Stacey Ilyse Photography

As Kurzban (2008) explained, negative attitudes among Americans have increased over the past three decades, perhaps related to the declining economic conditions for much of the middle class. Wages have been stagnant, some middle class neighborhoods are deteriorating, schools are consistently underfunded, and health care costs continue to increase significantly. These economic problems have been exacerbated by the recession that began prior to President Obama's election. Instead of confronting the economic and political issues behind this economic decline, it is easier to blame racial and ethnic groups, immigrants, and other scapegoats, but blaming others only makes it more difficult for Americans to discuss the real causes of our economic problems, and makes us less effective at promoting strategies that attempt to change the unfair policies and practices that represent institutional racism.

How can institutional racism be reduced in the United States?

Institutional racism involves complex problems that are not easily solved. In the 1970s, scholars began to emphasize that intent was not necessarily relevant to the issue of whether institutional policies and practices created advantages for white people and disadvantages for people of color. In the 1980s, however, the U.S. Supreme Court ruled that to prove a claim of discrimination, plaintiffs had to demonstrate that the intended purpose of institutional policies or practices was to discriminate against a particular group. Producing statistics documenting racial inequities was not enough; plaintiffs had to prove that those who developed policies or engaged in practices alleged as discriminatory were guilty of an evil intent. As Bonilla-Silva (1999) noted,

> The standards that the Supreme Court enacted . . . on discrimination (plaintiffs carrying the burden of proof in discrimination cases and the denial of statistical evidence as valid proof of discrimination) help to preserve intact contemporary forms for reproducing racial inequality in America. (p. 85)

The Supreme Court's ruling illustrates the difficulties involved in making much progress on institutional racism unless the people of the United States and the legal system acknowledge that evil intent is not always the cause of discrimination. When courts are willing to examine the issue of who is advantaged or disadvantaged by institutional policies or practices—regardless of the original goals that these policies or practices were intended to address—then we may see progress in the United States against subtle but widespread institutional practices of racism. In the meantime, people of color must rely on affirmative action programs and legal recourse to respond to blatant discrimination within American institutions. Affirmative action has been effective to a degree, but it also has produced vigorous criticisms.

How do advocates and critics assess the effectiveness of affirmative action programs?

Advocates of affirmative action cite studies beginning in the 1960s showing that the number of workers of color decreased in their traditional occupations and increased significantly in other occupations. For example, the percentage of African Americans employed as domestic servants or other service occupations decreased while their numbers have increased in the ranks of bank tellers, firefighters, electricians, and police officers. Professionals of color have moved into high-status positions in larger numbers than ever before. Critics of affirmative action argue that gains have primarily benefited people of color who were already middle class. They propose changing affirmative action

policies to focus on socioeconomic status rather than race, but Waller (2001) described extensive racism encountered by middle-class people of color despite their economic success.

Critics of affirmative action charge that these programs engender reverse discrimination by giving applicants of color preferential treatment over whites, especially white men. Studies do not support this allegation. Kivel (2002) summarizes a report reviewing opinions rendered by U.S. District Courts and Courts of Appeal for over four years. There were 3,000 discrimination cases, of which 100 alleged reverse discrimination. The courts found merit in only 6 of the 100 claims and ordered restitution. Kivel concluded that charges of reverse racism were part of a strategy "to counterattack attempts to promote racial justice" (p. 61). Affirmative action advocates agree, and they also argue that white men have benefited from preferential treatment, beginning with the U.S. Constitution and sustained in most policies and practices implemented since then. After describing the evolution of affirmative action and reviewing the arguments of its advocates and critics, Koppelman (2011) concluded that affirmative action programs were a major factor in the growth of the black middle class and in major gains in the employment of people of color in numerous occupations. In spite of these gains, ample evidence that racial discrimination persists requires that the United States maintain a commitment to affirmative action programs.

Critics of affirmative action insist that the most pernicious discrimination occurring today is **reverse discrimination** against white males. To support this allegation, they refer to studies showing that African Americans represented approximately 40% of new hires for police officers in U.S. cities from 1970 to 2000 (Reaves & Hickman, 2002). Because African Americans constitute only 12% of the population in the United States, this appears to justify the accusation that urban police departments are hiring an excessive number of African Americans.

African Americans actually constitute much more than 12% of the population in most urban areas, yet Jones (1997) reported that 95% of urban police officers in 1970 were white. To determine if hiring decisions by police departments have been fair, a useful measure would be to compare the percentage of officers of color with the percentage of people of color in an urban community. In police departments of many cities in the United States, the percentage of police officers of color still does not equal the percentage of the city's residents of color.

According to a Justice Department report, 63% of the police force in Detroit was African American, but African Americans comprise 82% of Detroit's population. Almost 39% of Baltimore's police officers were African American, but 65% of Baltimore's citizens are black. New York City's finest included 13.3% African American police officers, half of what it should be to equal the percentage of black people in New York City (Reaves & Hickman, 2002).

Such discrepancies do not just affect African Americans. Latinos represented 26% of New York City's population, but only 18% of the NYPD. San Diego's police force was 16% Hispanic, but Latinos constituted 26% of the population; 18% of Houston's police officers were Hispanic, less than half of the percentage of Latinos living in Houston; and 12% of Phoenix police officers were Hispanic, but a third of its citizens are Latino (Reaves & Hickman, 2002). Although people of color have constituted a significant percentage of the police officers hired over the past thirty years, claims of reverse discrimination can be countered by the argument that the hiring decisions were a justifiable effort to correct a history of discrimination.

What are some consequences of racial discrimination?

One consequence of racial discrimination can be seen in the asset inequalities based on race. Hollar (2010) cited a recent study that found the median net worth of white households to be over $143,000 compared to a median net worth of slightly more than $9,000 for African American and Latino

> Washing one's hands of the conflict between the powerful and the powerless means to side with the powerful, not to be neutral.
>
> Paolo Freire (1921–1997)

households. Even when researchers look at comparable households in terms of age, education, occupation, and income, black and Latino households typically have less than a quarter of the wealth of white households (Hamilton & Darity, Jr., 2009). In addition, Packer (2005) described the calculations of a Fannie Mae consultant to illustrate how life would be different for African Americans if the United States had achieved racial equality. In education, 2 million more African Americans would have graduated from high school, and another 2 million would have graduated from college. With regard to employment, almost 2 million more African Americans would have professional and managerial jobs, and they would have almost $200 billion more in income. In terms of housing, about 3 million more African Americans would own their own homes, with $760 billion more in home equity value. Finally, if racial equality existed in the United States, African Americans would have $120 billion more in their retirement accounts and $80 billion more in their bank accounts, and the wealth they controlled would be $1 trillion higher than it is today.

Another consequence of institutional racism is the incarceration of disproportionate numbers of African Americans, especially males. The Sentencing Project has calculated the racial disparity rates for each state (see Table 8.4). Many Americans still associate overt racism with southern states, but no southern state was included in the list of states with the most disproportionate number of blacks in prison. Rome (2008) argued that this disparity stems from racially biased penalties imposed

TABLE 8.4 Racial Disparities between Blacks and Whites in Prison

State	Disparity Index Rating*
1. New Jersey	13.15
2. Connecticut	12.77
3. Minnesota	12.63
4. Iowa	11.63
5. Wisconsin	11.59
6. Pennsylvania	10.53
7. New York	9.47
8. New Hampshire	9.26

Cited in Rome (2008); data came from the Sentencing Project in Washington, D.C.

*Index indicates the disparity between minorities and whites in prison as a percentage of their respective populations in the state.

during the judicial process, and institutional biases resulting in different outcomes for people of color. Rome asserted that police are given wide latitude in how they enforce the law and make arrests, that police are likely to spend far more time monitoring neighborhoods with low-income people of color, and that police are more likely to make an arrest if the complainant is white but less likely to make an arrest of someone who appears to be white and middle or upper class. Further, the FBI's Universal Crime Reports Index reflects societal biases by providing data on street crime but not white-collar crime that is largely committed by white people. In an analysis of criminal activity for one year, Arielly (2008) reported that the total cost of all robberies was $52 million compared to the cost of white-collar crimes such as employee theft and fraud ($600 billion) or income tax fraud ($350 billion).

Over two million African Americans are either in prison, jail, on parole, or on probation. Their number exceeds the number of blacks who were slaves in 1850, and upon their release from prison, they will encounter what Alexander (2010) has called a new "Jim Crow" system where the term "felon" is used to justify excluding them from juries, stripping them of voting rights, and discriminating against them in employment and housing. The refusal to allow felons to serve on juries has contributed to the resurgence of all-white juries in many states. In an effort to keep them away from their families, felons are not allowed to live in public housing for five years after their parole. Because so many states deny felons the right to vote, more black men are disenfranchised today than in the 1870s when such tactics as poll taxes and literacy tests were employed. Such draconian measures are surprising given that the majority of these "felons" are not violent criminals but were primarily arrested for using drugs, with only one out of five arrests for selling drugs (Alexander, 2010). According to a study of data from the 1990s, 80% of drug arrests were for using marijuana. Although national studies show that white people are more likely to smoke marijuana than black people, a study of marijuana arrests in New York City from 1998–2007 reported that 52% of those arrested were black, with another 33% Latino; whites accounted for only 15% (Philips & Roth, 2008).

Although crime rates have been declining since the 1990s, the prison population has increased dramatically, especially from 1985–2000 when drug arrests alone accounted for two-thirds of federal prisoners and one half of state prisoners. In some states, 80%–90% of all those sent to prison were African American (Ruiz, 2011). Once the prisoners are released, the recidivism rate is high; almost 70% will be arrested again within three years because of discrimination against ex-convicts. The discrimination not only encompasses jobs and housing, but even food. In most states, ex-convicts arrested on drug charges are legally ineligible to receive food stamps (Alexander, 2010). It is difficult for ex-convicts to find a job, especially if they are black. Aronson (2008) cited research that developed résumés and trained equal numbers of black and white male college graduates to apply for jobs, with half of each group saying they had served a year and a half in prison for a drug conviction. Of the applicants acknowledging a criminal record, white applicants were called back twice as often as blacks, and white applicants with criminal records were slightly preferred over blacks with no criminal record. Adding insult to injury, felons are not included in unemployment rates. To appreciate the real extent of black unemployment, an additional 14%–20% should be added to unemployment figures attributed to African Americans (Alexander, 2010). The problems caused by institutional racism cannot be resolved by piecemeal action, but will require aggressive proposals and actions targeting particular areas of concern such as unemployment, housing, and education.

What remedies have been proposed to address institutional racism?

To speak of remedies for problems as complex and widespread as those stemming from institutional racism is to speak of partial solutions and of good faith efforts. Ongoing research must be conducted on institutional racism because racist outcomes of policies and practices often are not easily identified and vary from one region and one institution to the next. Solutions will require cooperation and commitment, but whatever progress can be made represents a step forward. With each step, America comes closer to resolving race problems.

Remedies proposed to address problems stemming from racism have come from scholars such as Massey (2001); Bonilla-Silva (2009); Sensoy and DiAngelo (2012); and Feagin and Feagin (1986).

Among their proposed solutions for institutional racism are the following:

1. A national agency should be created that has regional offices to coordinate anti-discrimination activities across the nation. Such an agency would improve enforcement of anti-discrimination legislation and provide better documentation and dissemination of information. Most experts agree there are adequate laws against discrimination, but enforcement of those laws is not adequate because the responsibility for enforcement is currently assigned to the Justice Department, which has so many other areas of responsibility.

2. There must be a national and statewide commitment to stop the deterioration of inner cities in America. By providing resources, we could better address conditions that create misery and despair. Examples of resources include tax incentives to attract businesses to inner cities, federally funded jobs similar to the 1930s Works Progress Administration, training programs to give people skills related to available jobs, and day care subsidies to provide quality and affordable child care so that more people could work.

3. There must be active monitoring of real estate practices pertaining to advertising and marketing. Such oversight would ensure that practices are consistent with guidelines established in federal fair-housing legislation.

4. A commitment must be made to improve public elementary, middle, and high schools serving low-income students. Schools in low-income areas include many students of color who could be provided opportunities to develop the abilities and skills needed to function effectively in our highly technical, global economy. Resources will be required to remodel or build new schools, replacing the deteriorating buildings that low-income students often have to attend. Resources will also be required to develop and implement multicultural curriculum and to redesign teacher preparation programs.

5. Teachers must be taught how to work effectively with diverse student populations. They need to learn about the diversity of their students, not just students of color, but students with disabilities, low-income students, and students marginalized by the society or by other students.

Teachers must learn how to support positive intergroup relationships between students in their classrooms. They also must be able to identify bias in instructional materials and to teach students how to recognize bias. Until textbooks reflect multicultural content, schools must have resources to purchase multicultural instructional materials to supplement textbooks.

AFTERWORD

In *The Souls of Black Folk* published originally in 1903, W. E. B. Du Bois (1994) wrote that the problem of America was the problem of the "color line," that skin color divided America as if it were a line drawn in the sand, never to be crossed. The color line continues to prevent Americans from being united by a common vision, strengthened by an appreciation of diversity. Du Bois challenged Americans to solve the problem of the color line in the twentieth century. That challenge still has not been met at the beginning of the twenty-first century.

What must Americans do to confront the problem of the color line? For people of color, the challenge continues to be the same as it was for Du Bois, to overcome barriers created by racism. The challenge for white Americans is first to acknowledge the existence of racism, then to understand blatant and subtle ways it operates in society, and, finally, to join with Americans of goodwill to reduce racism in America's schools, neighborhoods, and institutions. If those of us who will commit to this goal are successful, we will bring this society closer to the ideals for which it stands: freedom, equality, and the opportunity for all people to pursue their vision

> [America is] a vast and quarrelsome family, a family rent by racial, social, political and class division, but a family nonetheless.
>
> Leonard Pitts (1957–)

of happiness. When we come closer to that goal, it will not just be a victory for Americans of color, it will be a victory for America.

TERMS AND DEFINITIONS

At-large candidates Refers to candidates for local offices being elected by an entire community rather than by districts or wards within that community

Aversive racism Forms of racism that allow well-meaning people to maintain a positive ("not racist") self-image while still perpetuating racism

Colorblind racism Pretending not to notice race or asserting that race has no meaning

Cultural racism The societal recognition and promotion of activities and contributions of one racial group in preference to others within a multiracial society; the superimposition of history and traditions of one racial group over other racial groups

Ethnocentrism The belief that one's race, nation, or culture is superior to all others; also individual actions or institutional practices based on that belief

Individual racism Prejudiced attitudes and behavior against others based on skin color demonstrated whenever someone responds by saying or doing something degrading or harmful about people of another race

Institutional racism Established laws, customs, and practices in a society that allow systematic discrimination between people or groups based on skin color

Internalized racial dominance The socialization of white people that results in their acceptance of these largely unconscious beliefs of racial superiority

Internalized racial oppression The largely unconscious racist beliefs and related behaviors that are accepted by people of color raised in a white supremacist society

Racism The creation of categories of human beings according to color, with one group establishing an artificial superiority to others; an attitude, action, or institutional structure that subordinates or limits a person on the basis of his or her race

Reverse discrimination The allegation that people of color are receiving preferential treatment with regard to decisions about hiring, promotion, participation, and admission to schools

Rightness of whiteness The belief that white people are the human norm against which all persons of color must be judged

Steering The practice of realtors of showing homes to prospective buyers in neighborhoods where residents are predominantly or exclusively of the same race

Tracking The process in which students are divided into categories so that they can be assigned in groups to various kinds of classes

White flight The migration of white families from an urban to a suburban location because of court rulings to desegregate urban schools

White privilege A set of options, opportunities, and opinions that are gained and maintained at the expense of people of color

Word-of-mouth hiring Employment of a job applicant based on the recommendation of current employees

DISCUSSION EXERCISES

Exercise #1 My Feelings About Race—A Personal Questionnaire

Directions: The twelve statements below could be a reaction that you might hear concerning another person's feelings about race. Create a response you think would be appropriate.

1. People should not be forced to integrate if they don't want to.

2. I don't believe I'm racist, but when it comes right down to it, I wouldn't marry a person of another race.

3. On the whole, the educated, the upper classes, the more sophisticated, or the more deeply religious people are much less racist.

4. I don't want to hear any more about the past and broken treaties; I should not be held responsible

for what white people did to Indians a hundred years ago.

5. When I am around angry blacks, it makes me feel defensive because it's as if they want me to feel guilty or something.

6. Other ethnic groups had to struggle, so why should it be any different for Mexican Americans? Why should they get bilingual education and other special accommodations?

7. These days, whenever a black man sneezes, 37 white people rush up to wipe his nose.

8. How can I be pro-Indian without being anti-white?

9. Don't tell me that blacks aren't more violent than whites. If you look at the statistics, you have to admit that there is a higher crime rate in the ghetto.

10. In many situations, minorities—especially Jews and blacks—are paranoid and oversensitive; they read more into a situation than is really there.

11. Because of the civil rights legislation passed in the mid-1960s, great opportunities are now available to racial minorities, and it is up to them to take more responsibility for exploiting those increased opportunities.

12. No, I'm not going to take the Understanding Diversity course because I'm not interested in learning about minorities; further, I've been told that it's a white-bashing course; male-bashing, too.

Exercise #2 My Experiences with Culture, Race, and Ethnicity

Directions: Reflect on at what age(s) over your life span you have had personal, direct contact with someone of a different culture, race, and ethnicity. Begin with the earliest recollection and move forward to the present.

1. Identify your first personal experiences with people different from you. What was the setting: home, school, family? What was the basis for the contact: dinner guest, classmate, playmate? What was your age at the time? Who was the person and how was he or she different?

2. Identify your earliest exposures to people who were different from you through movies or television shows, including newscasts. What was the story about? What was your age at the time? Who was the person and how was

he or she different? What impressions did you gain from each of these visual media experiences?

3. Identify your earliest exposure to others who were different from you through newspapers, storybooks, novels, or magazines. What was the story about? What was your age at the time? Who was the person and how was he or she different? What did you learn about people who are different from you because of these reading experiences?

Follow-up: Explain to others the impressions these experiences made on you at the time and your reactions to them then and now. Have your reactions changed over time?

REFERENCES

Alexander, M. (2010). *The new Jim Crow: Mass incarceration in the age of colorblindness*. New York, NY: The New Press.

Amer, M.L., & Manning, J.E. (2009). *Membership of the 11th Congress: A profile*. Retrieved September 21, 2009, from www.senate.gov.

Andrzejewski, J. (1996). Definitions for understanding oppression and social justice. In J. Andrzejewski (Ed.), *Oppression and social justice: Critical frameworks* (5th ed., pp. 52–58). Needham, MA: Simon & Schuster.

Arielly, D. (2008). *Predictably irrational: The hidden forces that shape our decisions*. New York, NY: HarperCollins.

Aronson, E. (2008). *The social animal* (10th ed.). New York, NY: Worth Publishers.

Associated Press. (2010, June 19). Vote system that elected NY Hispanic could expand. *La Crosse Tribune*, p. A5.

Bonilla-Silva, E. (1999). The new racism: Racial structure in the United States, 1960s–1990s. In P. Wong (Ed.), *Race, ethnicity, and nationality in the United States: Toward the twenty-first century* (pp. 55–101). Boulder, CO: Westview.

Bonilla-Silva, E. (2001). *White supremacy and racism in the post-civil rights era*. Boulder, CO: Lynne Rienner.

Bonilla-Silva, E. (2009). *Racism without racists: Color-blind racism and the persistence of racial inequality in America*. Lanham, MD: Rowman & Littlefield.

Buckley, G. (2001). *American patriots: The story of blacks in the military from the Revolution to Desert Storm.* New York, NY: Random House.

Callahan, R.M. (2005, Summer). Tracking and high school English learners: Limiting opportunity to learn. *American Educational Research Journal,* 42(2), 305–328.

Clark, K., & Clark, M. (1950). Emotional factors in racial identification and preference in Negro children. *The Journal of Negro Education,* 19(3), 341–350.

Conley, D. (1999). *Being black, Living in the red: Race, wealth and social policy in America.* Berkeley: University of California Press.

Davis, M. (2009, March/April). Editorial: Obama at Manassas. *New Left Review,* 56, 5–40.

Derman-Sparks, L., Ramsey, P., & Edwards, J. O. (2006). *What if all the kids are white?: Anti-bias multicultural education with young children and families.* New York: Teachers College Press.

Derman-Sparks, L., Ramsey, P., & Olsen, J. (2011). *What if the kids are all white? Anti-bias multicultural education with young children and families.* New York, NY: Teachers College Press.

DiAngelo, R. (2012). *What does it mean to be white? Developing white racial literacy.* New York, NY: Peter Lang.

DiAngelo, R. (2006). My class didn't trump my race: Using oppression to face privilege. *Multicultural Perspectives,* 8(1), 51–56.

Du Bois, W.E.B. (1994). *The souls of black folk.* New York, NY: Dover.

Dyer, R. (1997). *White.* New York, NY: Routledge.

Farley, J. (2010). *Majority-minority relations* (6th ed.). Upper Saddle River, NJ: Prentice-Hall.

Fattah, C. (2001, October). *Racial bias in special education.* FDCH Congressional Testimony, Washington, DC: eMediaMillWorks.

Feagin, J., & Feagin, C. (1986). *Discrimination American style* (2nd ed.). Malabar, FL: Krieger.

Feagin, J., & Sikes, M.P. (1994). *Living with racism: The black middle class experience.* Boston, MA: Beacon.

Fine, M. (1997a). Introduction. In M. Fine, L. Weis, C. Powell, & L. Wong (Eds.), *Off white: Readings on race, power and society* (pp. vii–xii). New York, NY: Routledge.

Foster, M. (2001). Education and socialization: A review of the literature. In W.H. Watkins, J.L. Lewis, & V. Chou (Eds.), *Race and education: The roles of history and society in educating African American students* (pp. 200–244). Boston, MA: Allyn & Bacon.

George, R.G. (2006). The race card: An interactive tool for teaching multiculturalism. *Multicultural Perspectives,* 8(3), 51–55.

Gladwell, M. (2005). *Blink: The power of thinking without thinking.* New York, NY: Little, Brown.

Hamilton, D., & Darity, W. Jr. (2009). Race, wealth, and intergenerational poverty. *The American Prospect,* 20(7), A10–A12.

Hilliard, A. (1992). *Racism: Its origins and how it works.* Paper presented at the meeting of the Mid-West Association for the Education of Young Children, Madison, WI.

Hodson, G., Dovido, J., & Gaertner, S. (2004). The aversive form of racism. In J. L. Chin (Ed.), *The psychology of prejudice and discrimination (Race and Ethnicity in Psychology)* (Vol. 1, pp. 119–136).Westport, CT: Praeger.

Hollar, J. (2010, June). Wealth gap yawns—and so do media. *Extra!* 23(6), 10–12.

Horn, J., Sperling, N., & Smith, D. (2012, February 19). Oscar voters overwhelmingly white, male. *Los Angeles Times.*

Howard, G.R. (2006). *We can't teach what we don't know: White teachers, multiracial schools.* New York, NY: Teachers College Press.

Hughes, R. (2004). The dwindling pool of qualified professors of color: Suburban legends. In D. Cleveland (Ed.), *A long way to go: Conversations about race by African American faculty and graduate students* (pp. 81–93). New York, NY: Peter Lang.

Jenkins, A. (2009). Recovering opportunity. *The American Prospect,* 20(7), A4–A7.

Jenkins, A. (2007, May). Inequality, race and remedy. *The American Prospect,* 18(5), A8–A11.

Jones, J. (1997). *Prejudice and racism* (2nd ed.). New York, NY: McGraw Hill.

Kershaw T. (1992). The effects of educational tracking on the social mobility of African Americans. *Journal of Black Studies,* 23(1), 152–170.

Kirp, D.L. (1991, Summer). Textbooks and tribalism in California. *Public Interest,* 104, 20–37.

Kivel, P. (2002). *Uprooting racism: How white people can work for racial justice* (Rev. ed.). Gabriola Island, British Columbia: New Society Publishers.

Koppelman, K. (2011). *The great diversity debate: Embracing pluralism in school and society.* New York, NY: Teachers College Press.

Kozol, J. (2005). *The shame of the nation: The restoration of apartheid schooling in America.* New York, NY: Crown.

Kurzban, I. (2008). Democracy and immigration. In D.C. Brotherton & P. Kretsedemas (Eds.), *Keeping out the other: A critical introduction to immigration enforcement today* (pp. 63–78). New York, NY: Columbia University Press.

Leondar-Wright, B. (2004). Black job loss deja vu. In C. Collins, A. Gluckman, M. Lui, B.L. Wright, & A. Scharf (Eds.), *The wealth inequality reader* (pp. 95–105). Cambridge, MA: Dollars & Sense.

Levine, M. (2010). *Research update: The crisis deepens: Black male joblessness in Milwaukee 2009.* Retrieved October 8, 2011, from www.uwm.edu/ced/publications.cfm.

Lipsitz, G. (2008). The possessive investment in whiteness. In P. Rothenberg (Ed.), *White privilege: Essential readings on the other side of racism* (pp. 61–84). New York, NY: Worth.

Loewen, J. (1995). *Lies my teacher told me: Everything your American history textbook got wrong.* New York, NY: The New Press.

Losen, D.J. (2011). *Discipline policies, successful schools, and racial justice.* Boulder, CO: National Education Policy Center. Retrieved October 25, 2011, from http://nepc.colorado.edu/publication/discipline-policies.

Massey, D.S. (2001). Residential segregation and neighborhood conditions in U.S. metropolitan areas. In N. Smelser, W. Wilson, & F. Mitchell (Eds.), *America becoming: Racial trends and their consequences.* East Lansing, MI: National Center for Research on Teacher Learning. (ERIC Document Reproduction Service No. ED449286)

Massey, D.S. (2003). The race case. *The American Prospect, 14*(3), 22.

McIntosh, P. (2001). White privilege: Unpacking the invisible knapsack. In P. Rothenberg (Ed.), *Race, class, and gender in the United States: An integrated study* (5th ed., pp. 163–168). New York, NY: Worth.

Meizhu, L., Robles, B., & Leondar-Wright, B. (2006). *The color of wealth: The story behind the U.S. racial wealth divide.* New York, NY: The New Press.

Mills, C.W. (1997). *The racial contract.* Ithaca, NY: Cornell University Press.

Monteiro, M.B., de França, D.X., & Rodrigues, R. (2009). The development of intergroup bias in childhood: How social norms can shape children's racial behaviors. *International Journal of Psychology, 44*(1), 29–39.

Morrison, T. (1993). *Playing in the dark.* New York, NY: Vintage Books.

National Opinion Research Center. (1998). *Race surveys.* University of Chicago. Retrieved October 4, 2012, from www.norc.uchicago.edu/projects/gensoc4.asp.

Nieto, S. (2008). *Affirming diversity: The sociopolitical context of multicultural education* (5th ed.). Boston, MA: Pearson.

Oakes, J. (2005). *Keeping track: How schools structure inequality.* New Haven, CT: Yale University Press.

Oakes, J., Quartz, K.H., Ryan, S., & Lipton, M. (2000). *Becoming good American schools: The struggle for civic virtue in school reform.* San Francisco, CA: Jossey-Bass.

Oakes, J., & Wells, A.S. (1996). *Beyond the technicalities of school reform: Policy lessons from detracking schools.* Los Angeles, CA: UCLA Graduate School of Education and Information Studies.

Oliver, M.L., & Shapiro, T.M. (2008, October). Subprime as a black catastrophe. *The American Prospect, 19*(10), A9–A11.

Orser, W.E. (1990). Secondhand suburbs. *Journal of Urban History, 16*(3), 227–263.

Packer, Z. (2005). Sorry, not buying. *The American Prospect, 16*(12), 46–48.

Phillips, P., & Roth, A. (Eds). Marijuana arrests set new record. *Project censored 2009* (pp. 99–103). New York, NY: Seven Stories Press.

Picca, L., & Feagin, J. (2007). *Two-faced racism: Whites in the backstage and frontstage.* New York, NY: Routledge.

Potok, M. (2011, Spring). The year in hate and extremism. *Intelligence Report, 141,* 41–44.

Powell, J.A. (2008, October). Race, place, and opportunity. *The American Prospect, 19*(10), A21–A23.

Quintana, S.M. (2008). Racial perspective taking ability: Developmental, theoretical, and empirical trends. In S.M. Quintana & C. McKown (Eds.), *Handbook of race, racism, and the developing child.* (pp. 1–15). Hoboken, NJ: John Wiley & Sons Inc.

Reaves, B.A., & Hickman, M.J. (2002). *Police departments in large cities, 1990–2000.* U.S. Department of Justice. Retrieved June 9, 2009, from http://www.ojp.usdoj.gov/bjs.

Reed, S. (2011). *The diversity index.* New York, NY: AMACOM.

Rehmeyer, J.J. (2007). Separate is never equal. *Science News.* Retrieved October 4, 2012, from: www.sciencenews.org/view/generic/id/8907/title/Math_Trek_Separate_Is_Never_Equal.

Riley, J.L. (2011, May 6). Race, politics and the minimum wage. *Wall Street Journal.* Retrieved October 10, 2011, from: http://online.wsj.com/article/SB10001424052748703859304576307201724065640.html.

Rome, D. (2008, Spring). *How stereotypes become acts of discrimination: A look at racial disparities in Wisconsin prisons.* Kaleidoscope II, The University of Wisconsin Institute on Race and Ethnicity, pp. 2–5.

Ruiz, R. (2011, January/February). Eyes on the prize. *The American Prospect,* 22(1), A3.

Schaefer, R.T. (2008). Prejudice. In *Racial and ethnic groups* (11th ed., pp. 37–65). Upper Saddle River, NJ: Pearson Education.

Sensoy, Ö. & DiAngelo, R. (2012). *Is everyone really equal? Key concepts in critical social justice education.* New York, NY: Teachers College Press.

Shorris, E. (2001). *Latinos: A biography of the people.* New York, NY: W.W. Norton.

Spriggs, W.E. (2008, October). The economic crisis in black and white. *The American Prospect,* 19(10), A2–A5.

Thompson, H.A. (1999). Rethinking the politics of white flight in the postwar city. *Journal of Urban History,* 25(2), 163–199.

Tobin, G.A., & Ybarra, D.R. (2008). Chapter one: Textbooks are in trouble. *The trouble with textbooks: Distorting history and religion.* Lanham, MD: Lexington Books.

Trainor, J. (2005). "My ancestors didn't own slaves": Understanding white talk about race. *Research in the Teaching of English,* 40(2), 140–167.

U.S. Bureau of Labor Statistics. (2011, September). *Employment situation summary.* Retrieved October 8, 2011, from www.bls.gov/news.release/empsit.nr0.htm.

U.S. Bureau of Labor Statistics. (2001). Counting minorities: A brief history and a look at the future. In *Report on the American Workforce.* Washington, DC: U.S. Department of Labor (www.bls.gov/opub).

VanAusdale, D., & Feagin, J. (2001). *The first R: How children learn race and racism.* New York, NY: Rowman & Littlefield.

Waller, J. (2001). *Face to face: The changing state of racism across America.* Cambridge, MA: Perseus Books Group.

Wellman, D. (1977). *Portraits of white racism.* New York, NY: Cambridge University Press.

Williams, C. (2003). Managing individuals in a diverse workforce. In *Management* (2nd ed., pp. 434–471). Versailles, KY: Thompson Southwestern.

Wilson, W.J. (1996). *When work disappears: The world of the new urban poor.* New York, NY: Knopf.

Wise, T. (2005). *Affirmative action: Racial preference in black and white.* Berkeley, CA: Soft Skull.

Chapter 9

Classism: Misperceptions and Myths About Income, Wealth, and Poverty

"The greatest of evils and the worst of crimes is poverty."

George Bernard Shaw (1856–1950)

Classism refers to attitudes and discriminatory actions toward others based on their low socio-economic status. It is nearly impossible to grow up in the United States without being affected by pervasive cultural messages that engender antagonism and sometimes contempt for poor people. In our American capitalist economic system, which emphasizes competition for opportunity and reward, there are winners and there are losers. Americans are encouraged to admire winners. Stories of winners are told daily in newspapers and magazines, and we applaud their success. Americans do not tend to identify with losers. Poor people are usually perceived as losers. Historically, our culture has produced many negative messages asserting that people living in poverty are deficient and inferior; these negative cultural messages represent **cultural classism**, and they constitute one factor influencing the process by which Americans have learned to devalue poor people.

Cultural Classism

When colonists came to the New World, they had a well-established tradition that caring for the poor was both a local responsibility and a religious obligation. Historically, the European Catholic Church provided food to the hungry, shelter for the homeless, and care for the sick; the legacy can still be found in Catholic and Protestant hospitals and social service agencies today. Problems of poverty remained local, affecting a small percentage of people, and church resources were adequate to the task. But in fourteenth- and fifteenth-century Europe, the number of poor people increased dramatically. Plagues, wars, and various economic changes dispossessed rural families of their livelihoods and land, forcing them to search for employment elsewhere, usually in major cities.

What was the response in England to people in poverty?

In England, the local response to poverty was termed *outdoor relief*, where food, funds, and other assistance were distributed to people as needed. However, because of the increasing numbers of people whose poverty did not seem temporary, vagrancy laws were created that proscribed punishment for beggars and vagrants: public whippings, then exile, forced labor, and, for people who persisted in being poor and making a nuisance of themselves, execution. Another strategy involved auctioning groups of poor people to the lowest bidder—the person who offered to care for the group for the fewest tax dollars. The purpose of punishment, banishment, auctions, and executions was not to address problems of poverty, but to be rid of the poor, and English colonists in particular brought these attitudes and strategies with them.

What was the response to poverty in America during the colonial period?

In the colonies, outdoor relief included sharing food, providing common grazing land (and "town cows"), building shelters for homeless families, and caring for sick persons in their homes when they had no family to help them. To reduce burdens of poverty in a community, potential settlers often were required to prove they could care for themselves. If they weren't convincing or if they failed to take care of their own needs as promised, they could be warned out—notified that they must leave the community. Komisar (1977) reported that in 1790, one Massachusetts community warned out almost a third of its population.

Meanwhile, English poorhouses providing food and shelter became an alternative to outdoor relief. People living in poorhouses were required to work to pay for their care, thereby reducing the need for local revenue. According to Katz (1986), Boston established the first colonial poorhouse in 1664; later, others were established in Philadelphia (1732), New York (1736), and Baltimore (1773). Although poorhouses were never intended to offer compassionate care, they were "the best means of frightening the able bodied into going to work and discouraging people from applying for aid" (Komisar, 1977, p. 21). The physical conditions in many poorhouses were atrocious: too many people crowded together, many with contagious diseases and often too little food or medical care. Poorhouses also included people with additional problems such as mental illness and alcoholism. Even when poorhouses had decent conditions, people were reluctant to live there because of the stigma associated with them. Because anyone applying for outdoor relief could be referred to a poorhouse, it was hoped that the threat of referral would reduce relief applications. For many years in both America and England, sending people to the poorhouse was a major strategy for dealing with poverty. (See Figure 9.1.)

FIGURE 9.1

If you were in a poorhouse, you might be able to let friends and family know where you were by sending a postcard like this one from the County Poor House in Burlington, Iowa, early 1900s.

Courtesy of the Poorhouse Lady.

County Poor House, Burlington, Iowa.

What happened to the "religious obligation" to help the poor?

Ironically, Christian faith in America was a major contributor to increasingly harsh attitudes toward the poor. Many colonial Protestants believed that poverty was a consequence of sin and slothfulness. They assumed the rich were rewarded for their thrift and virtue, whereas the poor were sinners needing reform. Americans often expressed their belief that anyone who wanted to work could find a job, as Matthew Carey noted in 1828:

> Many citizens entertain an idea that in the present state of society . . . every person able and willing to work may procure employment . . . [and that] the chief part of the distresses of the poor arises from idleness, dissipation, and worthlessness. (Katz, 1986, p. 7)

Carey believed that poverty was not a consequence of personal failure as much as it was low wages, poor working conditions resulting in accidents or illness, and the impact of economic downturns. Those who actually worked with poor people understood that many were industrious and virtuous, but still lived in poverty because of circumstances beyond their control. Despite the efforts of Carey and other advocates for poor people, negative attitudes prevailed, not only toward paupers but also toward the working poor who lived perilously on the brink of poverty.

Why were people who had jobs so close to poverty?

Komisar (1977) described an 1833 economic analysis of a construction worker's salary that concluded it was hardly sufficient to support a wife and two children. A continuing flow of immigrants exacerbated the problems of the poor by increasing competition for jobs; this allowed employers to keep wages low or even reduce them. Schwarz (2000) quotes social reformer Joseph Tuckerman explaining that wages in 1830 were so low "because the number of laborers [was] essentially greater than the demand for them" (p. 17). Because unemployment remained high, poorhouses never lacked occupants in spite of their deplorable conditions. Even so, Komisar provided an excerpt from a Massachusetts report in

1833 that complained of poor people who regarded poorhouses as their "inns":

> Here they find rest, when too much worn with fatigue to travel, and medical aid when they are sick. And as they choose not to labor, they leave these stopping places when they have regained strength to enable them to travel; and pass from town to town demanding their portion of the State's allowances for them as their right. (pp. 21–22)

In reality, poorhouses included so many children, elderly, and people with disabilities or illness that there were in fact few able-bodied residents. Komisar referred to an 1848 report of a Philadelphia poorhouse where only 12% of the residents were capable of working. In some communities, poorhouses were built on farmland in the hope that residents could pay for their care by operating the farm, yet "poor farms" often hired people to do the work because there were not enough healthy, able-bodied people in residence. Men who could work stayed out of poorhouses and tried to find employment, but it wasn't easy.

Why was it so difficult to find work?

The rapid development and use of machines throughout the second half of the nineteenth century contributed to unemployment, even in rural areas where hand threshing was eliminated by threshing machines. In urban areas, unskilled factory workers replaced skilled artisans, diminishing the satisfaction derived from work. Schwarz (2000) quoted a social reformer commenting on the dehumanizing aspect of factory jobs:

> [Factory work] tends to dwarf the intellectual powers, by confining the activity of the individual to a narrow range, to a few details, perhaps to the heading of pins, the pointing of nails, or the tying together of broken strings. (p. 15)

Although working wages were low for men, they were lower for women. Even children worked to help cover family expenses. If everyone in the family worked and everyone stayed healthy, it was possible to save money to be self-sufficient in old age. Retirement was rare: Workers didn't usually retire, but worked as long as they could. When they could no longer work, they typically lived with their adult children, who often could not afford to care for their parents without outdoor relief. Elderly who could not stay with children usually lived in poorhouses.

Why did people think poorhouses were the solution to poverty?

In the early 1800s, institutions were promoted as a solution to social problems: prisons for criminals, mental hospitals for the insane, orphanages for children, reform schools for juvenile delinquents, and poorhouses for the poor. In addition to rehabilitating inmates, these institutions were

> It is the function of religion to teach society to value human life more than property.
>
> Walter Rauschenbusch (1861–1918)

supposed to require minimal tax dollars from state and local governments. By 1850, many people had been placed in institutions; however, expenses proved more costly than anticipated. To make matters worse, Katz (1986) noted the realization that "Mental hospitals did not cure; prisons and reform schools did not rehabilitate; . . . and poorhouses did not check the growth of outdoor relief or promote industry" (p. 25). In fact, from the beginning, institutions tended to provide primarily custodial care to protect society from deviant individuals within.

Because of public opposition to providing relief to able-bodied men, the few men still in poorhouses in the late 1800s were expelled. They moved to cities to find work and often sought lodging with other poor families who were eager for the extra money lodgers would pay. Social activists were appalled because providing lodging to indigent men gave them sexual access to women in the home. Katz (1986) explains that the word *lodger* became a derisive term; still the housing need could not be ignored, and lodging houses, later nicknamed *flophouses*, evolved to provide inexpensive rooms for single itinerant men. Shortly after men were barred from poorhouses, children were removed as well, and poorhouses evolved into nursing homes for elderly people without families to care for them.

Why were children removed from poorhouses?

Social activists believed that poverty was caused in part by *hereditary pauperism*, as if being poor was a genetic defect. They argued that adult paupers were beyond help, but that children in poverty could be saved. In state after state, legislation was passed mandating the placement of children in orphanages if their parent or parents had been admitted to a poorhouse. By 1875, the majority of children in orphanages were not orphans; they had living parents who were poor.

Consequently, adoption patterns began to change. Low-income families had adopted children old enough to work outside the home or to assist with domestic chores, but middle- and upper-class families were increasingly adopting children based on the assumption that these infants would remember nothing of their impoverished origins and could be "saved" by being raised in good homes. Katz (1986) explains how social reformers defended the practice of taking children away from poor parents: "Only by snapping the bonds between pauper parents and their children could they prevent the transmission of dependence from one generation to another" (p. 106). Such negative attitudes were characteristic of this era, resulting in a minimal response to the needs of poor people.

What was the response to the needs of poor people?

In the late 1800s, charitable organizations including the Association for Improving the Condition of the Poor sent "friendly visitors" to homes of poor people to offer spiritual advice and to promote a Protestant work ethic, the notion that hard work is essential and that rewards come from one's willingness to work. Komisar (1977) reports that charitable organizations viewed a poor person asking for money to pay rent or purchase food as a "failure of character" (p. 33). Organizations provided minimal financial or material aid, believing people would work only if they were choosing between work and starvation. American society of the 1880s and 1890s tended to regard poverty as proof of moral misconduct; organizations denied aid to drunkards and would only help their families if the wife and children left the drunkard.

By the late 1890s, studies began to suggest that misconduct, especially alcohol abuse, was not a major cause of poverty. Data from one study suggested that alcohol abuse and other forms of misconduct affected only 10% to 30% of families living in poverty, but that circumstances beyond anyone's control accounted for 65% or more of families who were poor. Schwarz (2000) described social reformers such as Josephine Lowell defending poor people "who are not drunken and shiftless, but who lead lives of . . . heroic self-sacrifice and devotion" (p. 101). Social reformers began to challenge Christians to demonstrate a more altruistic attitude by helping people in poverty, and reformers often identified capitalists as the true cause of suffering among the poor.

By the early 1900s, attitudes had evolved to the point that social reformers no longer supported the practice of taking children from poor parents. Buttressed by new child development theories, they denounced orphanages as harmful to children and advocated foster parent placement and care as an alternative. They lobbied for outdoor relief to keep poor families together, reasoning that the presence of children was an incentive for parents to work. In response to studies, speeches, and arguments of social reformers, states began to initiate programs of financial assistance to single-parent mothers regardless of whether they had been abandoned by their husbands or had never married.

Financial support was necessary because it was hard for single women to make enough money to cover their own expenses, and even more difficult if they had children: Women were paid considerably less than male workers. Perhaps women's low pay was the reason they were the first to form unions and to initiate strikes demanding wage increases and better working conditions. Most early labor strikes were unsuccessful because impoverished women workers desperately needed money and could not afford to be out of work for long. Nevertheless, women workers—and men as well—continued to organize into unions throughout the 1800s as their best option to stop exploitation by employers.

What did workers do to protest employer exploitation?

In the early 1870s, 20,000 unemployed workers in Chicago marched to City Hall demanding food, clothing, and shelter; textile workers went on strike in Massachusetts; and coal miners struck in Pennsylvania. Despite union activism, railroad owners drastically cut worker wages in 1877, causing strikes in several states; the owners hired newly arrived immigrants to break many of the strikes, fueling anti-immigrant sentiments among workers. Local citizens often supported strikers, but railroad owners had the law on their side. As strikers barricaded buildings and blocked tracks, police and state militias were called in to drive striking workers away, with many injuries resulting from the violent confrontations.

Zinn (2003) described solidarity between local people and striking workers during the Pittsburgh strike against the Pennsylvania Railroad in 1877. Owners believed local militias would not fire at the strikers for fear of killing them and demanded that local officials call federal troops from Philadelphia. When troops arrived, the workers refused to be intimidated. In the first confrontation with strikers, the federal troops killed ten people; Pittsburgh residents responded angrily, surrounding the troops as they retreated to the nearest building, which was a railway roundhouse. Although the citizens surrounded the roundhouse and set fire to the building, the troops managed to escape and left the city.

How did unions ultimately help workers to gain higher salaries?

Despite union organizing and strikes, wages remained low. Komisar (1977) identified a 1904 economist who calculated that an annual salary of $460 was required to support a wife and three children. Most railroad workers made less than $375 a year. Out of all the jobs studied, the economist reported that a third of them paid less than $300 a year. If more than one person in the family worked and the family was frugal, they might manage to save money, but instead of receiving praise for being thrifty, their savings would often be used against them. Schwarz (2000) explained how: "When employers discovered that their workers earned enough to put something by, they concluded that they had been overpaying them" (p. 43).

In addition to low wages, laborers often toiled in dangerous workplaces. In 1908, the federal government reported that every year, over 35,000 workers were killed and 536,000 were injured on the job. The U.S. rates for worker injuries and deaths were much higher than those in most European countries. Although workers did not often convince employers to raise wages, they did persuade state legislators to address the issue of workplace risks. Katz (1986) reported that 43 of 45 states passed workers'

> The test of our progress is not whether we add more to the abundance of those who have much; it is whether we provide enough for those who have too little.
>
> Franklin Delano Roosevelt (1882–1945)

compensation laws between 1909 and 1920, over the objections of employers who complained of the financial burden of compensating workers for injuries sustained at work. Americans continued to debate what was fair for employees and employers until the Great Depression of the 1930s, when widespread unemployment demanded an aggressive response from the federal government.

How did the federal government address unemployment in the 1930s?

By the spring of 1931, Komisar estimated 5 million unemployed U.S. workers; for the following year, he estimated a total of 8 million. By 1933, when Franklin Roosevelt began his first presidential term, between 12 and 15 million workers were unemployed, a third of the U.S. labor force. Federal programs were installed as New Deal activities from Roosevelt's campaign pledge to offer a "new deal" for workers in America. When Roosevelt signed a Federal Emergency Relief Act (FERA) to provide assistance for people suffering from poverty, he ended a tradition of local and state governments having exclusive responsibility for the poor. FERA distributed $250 million to the states based on a formula of $1 of federal money for every $3 the state spent for relief or economic assistance to individuals; another $250 million was given to states with the most severe poverty problems. In some states, 40% of the people were on relief. As if to punish people for taking federal

funds, fourteen states passed laws preventing people on relief from voting.

In addition to providing money for relief, the federal government became an employer. The Civilian Conservation Corps recruited 250,000 young men (but no women) to work on projects to prevent floods, fires, and soil erosion, and to develop recreational areas. The Works Progress Administration (WPA) employed about 2 million men, a fourth of the workforce, to build roads or to construct bridges, public buildings, and parks. Some Americans did not support these actions; Komisar (1977) quoted a bank president who said, "I profoundly believe that society does not owe every man a living" (p. 56).

Although federal employment programs provided jobs, the numbers of unemployed continued to be significant, and employers took advantage of the oversupply of labor to keep wages low and (again) even reduce them, resulting in more worker protests and strikes. In response to this turmoil, the Wagner Act passed in 1935 created a National Labor Relations Board (NLRB) and granted unions legal status as collective bargaining agents for workers. The intent was that the NLRB would encourage peaceful resolutions of labor disputes by negotiation rather than through strikes and disruptive activities that often ended in violence. During World War II, the National War Labor Board supported unionization after getting a "no strike" agreement with the unions for the duration of the war. Ruling on a labor dispute with General Motors in 1942, the board mandated equal pay for equal work—a landmark decision that especially helped workers of color and women workers. Shortly after the end of the war, union membership had increased from 9 million to 15 million (Fraser, 2009).

What was the outcome of the New Deal?

Because of employment demands during World War II, the "make-work" New Deal programs were dismantled. Although European countries had been enacting social insurance programs since 1833, conservative critics had accused Roosevelt of aspiring to become a dictator and attacked his poverty programs, saying they would "threaten the integrity of our [capitalist] institutions" (Komisar, 1977, p. 62). Despite opposition, programs such as unemployment insurance and the social security and welfare programs that were created by the Economic Security Act of 1935 have been maintained to provide basic protection and support for people in need. A 1939 Gallup poll reported that 70% of Americans believed that the federal government should address the needs of unemployed people, and the same 70% approved the amount of relief available to the poor. Programs continue to function today because they have been successful, are still considered necessary, and enjoy widespread public support.

The legacy of Roosevelt's New Deal was not only social programs but also the principle of federal government involvement in poverty issues. The Civilian Conservation Corps, which is no longer in existence, was the forerunner of the Peace Corps and AmeriCorps and other programs that recruit young people to work on community projects locally and globally (see Figure 9.2). With regard to those opposed to involvement of the federal government in social programs, politicians may propose reform to welfare or schemes to privatize Social Security, but few would question the need for such programs or the appropriateness of the federal government providing them. Because of federal remedies to economic challenges of the 1930s, American culture developed new perceptions of poverty and the role of government in response to it. Unfortunately, some Americans cling to old attitudes and persist in accusing poor people of deficiencies as a cause of their poverty.

Individual Classism

Individual classism refers to attitudes and discriminatory actions stemming from prejudice against poor people (see Figure 9.3). According to a Harris poll, Taylor (2000) reports that 77% of Americans believe most unemployed people could find a job without much difficulty if they made an effort, an interesting assertion in a capitalist society. Unlike most Americans, economists understand that capitalism requires that a certain percentage of unemployed workers exist to keep wages low and to control inflation. Europeans seem to understand this economic principle better than Americans. In a 1990 survey of citizens from twelve European countries, 17% believed poverty was related to laziness or lack of willpower, but 66% said poverty

FIGURE 9.2

The Civilian Conservation Corps (CCC) gave young men jobs in the 1930s when jobs were scarce (top photo). The federal government continues to engage young adults to work on conservation projects (bottom photo), but unlike the CCC, the Student Conservation Association's diverse membership also includes women.

Courtesy of Franklin Delano Roosevelt Library (top photo) and Student Conservation Association (bottom photo).

resulted from social injustice, personal misfortune, or changes in the modern world (Wilson, 1996).

In contrast to European attitudes, Wilson also reported surveys finding Americans more likely to blame poor people for their poverty, assigning factors such as lack of effort, lack of ability, or loose morals. Ironically, our American penchant for

FIGURE 9.3

The Southern Poverty Law Center (SPLC) is dedicated to combating individual and institutional classicism by providing impoverished people with legal assistance. SPLC offices are located in Montgomery, Alabama, across the street from the Civil Rights Memorial designed by Maya Lin, visited by thousands each year.

Photo courtesy of Timothy Hursley, Southern Poverty Law Center.

blaming the victim overlooks the fact that children represent the largest percentage of poor people in the United States and that their numbers continue to increase. Further, a cross-cultural study found that the socioeconomic status of America's children was a better predictor of school performance than it was in European countries such as Denmark, the Netherlands, or France (Scott & Leonhardt, 2005). This would suggest that such countries are making an effort to address at least some of the needs of children living in poverty. Yet when Americans acknowledge poor children, all too often we blame them for not working harder in school to lift themselves out of poverty.

How are children from low-income families disadvantaged in schools?

Although Americans may argue that poor children should use free education provided in public schools to escape from poverty, Kozol (2005) and others have described the appalling conditions in schools attended by those living in poverty. Among the world's industrialized nations, the United States is the only one without universal preschool and child support programs. Wilson (1996) described an alternative approach: French child care programs of infant care, nursery schools, paid leave for parents of newborns, and medical care that includes a preventive care system for children and public health nurses to monitor children's health. The French support system sends a clear message that France values all children, not just middle- or upper-class children.

Over half of American children will experience poverty at some time in their lives—and poor children tend to have greater needs than middle- or upper-class children (McKernan, Ratcliffe, & Cellini, 2009). Anyon (2001) reported that 25% of U.S. urban school budgets are typically expended to respond to the psychological and social needs of

> For every talent that poverty has stimulated it has blighted a hundred.
>
> John Gardner (1912–2002)

students from low-income families, yet Americans often seem oblivious to the impact of poverty. Pipher (2002) provides this comment about American attitudes: "We were born on third base and we think we hit triples" (p. 21).

The consequences of educational advantages for children of the middle and upper classes can be ascertained by analyzing student SAT scores in relation to family income. According to multiple studies, higher family income in all races—socioeconomic standing—translates into higher scores on SAT tests (Berliner, 2005; Jairrels, 2008). Owen and Doerr (1999) argued that the power of socioeconomic standing should not be surprising because studies also report that low-income families seldom have computers in their homes and that students from low-income homes rarely can afford fees paid by other students for coaching sessions to improve SAT scores. Despite the obvious explanation for their children's higher scores on SAT tests, Owen and Doerr described how SAT scores provided middle- and upper-class families with:

> A scientific-sounding justification for the advantages they enjoyed. The wealthy lived in nice houses because they were smart; the poor were hungry because they were stupid. American society was just after all. (p. 175)

The most disadvantaged children are those who are homeless. Prior to 1980, homelessness was primarily a problem for people with alcohol or drug addictions or mental illness. In his first year in office, President Reagan slashed the budget for housing subsidies for low-income families by 50%, and made further reductions to this budget in subsequent years. Homelessness increased dramatically, and the population included many families with children. Near the end of Reagan's second term, the number of homeless people had doubled, with over a million Americans experiencing homelessness at some point during the year. In response, Congress passed the McKinney Act in 1987, and over the next decade the bill was amended to increase funding and expand its services (Drier, 2004). In its 2000 version, the renamed McKinney-Vento Act provided funds for various social service programs to assist homeless people, including the Education of Homeless Children and Youth Program administered by the Department of Education. This law mandated that homeless children should be given a "free and appropriate education," and required public schools to remove barriers to enrollment, attendance, and achievement of these students (National Coalition for the Homeless, 2006). The Department of Education provided funds to assist homeless children in such areas as transportation, school supplies, and academic assistance.

According to the National Center on Family Homelessness (2011), there are now over 1.3 million homeless children in the United States; they represent almost 40% of the homeless population. These children struggle with a multitude of problems including physical health issues, depression over being evicted from their home, anxiety about their family, and fears resulting from family instability and violence. Because homeless families move frequently, the children are often at one school for a brief period before transferring to another school. It is often difficult for teachers to determine whether a child has special needs such as a learning disability. The revised McKinney-Vento law required public schools to identify all homeless children at their school and to monitor them carefully for warning signs of a disability. When there appeared to be evidence of a possible disability in a child, the school was to initiate the diagnostic process, and if the child transferred to another school during the process, the school was directed to forward the paperwork to the new school so that the process could be completed (U.S. Department of Education, 2008).

Despite the good intentions of the McKinney-Vento Act, homeless children remain extremely vulnerable, and their numbers are increasing. Prior to the 2008 recession, 2.5 to 3.5 million Americans were homeless at some point during a given year, and these numbers included a million people employed full time or part time. Since 2008, family homelessness has increased by 9%, and during the 2008–2009 school year, almost one million homeless children and youth attended public schools, a 41% increase from the previous two school years. In response to this dramatic increase, President Obama included $4 billion in his stimulus plan, the American Recovery and Reinvestment Act, with $70 million representing additional funds for McKinney-Vento (National Law Center on Homelessness and Poverty, 2011). Critics argue that this level of funding was insufficient to address the problems of homeless people, especially the children, and further, that these programs tended to focus on the symptoms of homelessness while ignoring the causes. Yet advocates for homeless children insist that even insufficient funds can help schools make a difference in the lives of poor and homeless children.

How can schools make a difference in the lives of poor children?

In order to understand the importance of school in the lives of poor children, we must first recognize the consequences of doing nothing. A scholarly review of numerous studies concluded that brain development takes place over time, and that conditions associated with poverty are likely to have an adverse effect on a child's developing brain (Jairrels, 2008). For example, researchers in France tracked a group of children who had come from abusive homes, foster care, or institutional settings after the children were adopted by financially secure parents. At the time of the children's adoption, they were regarded as borderline for a diagnosis of mental retardation with an average IQ score of 77. Just nine years after their adoption, the IQ scores for all of these children had improved significantly, with the highest increases appearing in those children who were adopted into the most affluent families (Kirp, 2007). Although it is not feasible to place all poor children in affluent homes, they all have the opportunity to attend school, and

research on effective early childhood and preschool programs finds that these programs have an especially significant impact on low-income children. According to Webley (2011), a North Carolina study reported that low-income students participating in a state-funded preschool program had higher scores in math and reading than their low-income peers who were not enrolled in the program. In addition, several long-term studies have found that high-quality early-childhood education programs have resulted in lasting benefits for low-income children such as being less likely to repeat a grade, more likely to graduate from high school, more likely to earn more money as adults, and less likely to have ever been on welfare or incarcerated. For example, a Michigan study initiated in 1972 tracked two groups of low-income children with similar IQ scores—one group had attended preschool, but the other had not. At the age of 40, those participants in the study who had attended preschool had higher levels of education, earned higher incomes, were more likely to be homeowners, and were less likely to have spent time in jail (Webley, 2011).

Educational gains are not limited to programs for young children. Kahlenberg (2009) argues that when K–12 schools are segregated according to social class, they have an adverse effect on the academic achievement of students from low-income homes, and he asserts that reorganizing schools to eliminate such segregation benefits all students. He cites four decades of research concluding that the lives of low-income students are qualitatively better if they attend schools with predominantly middle-class students. Data from the 2007 National Assessment of Educational Progress (NAEP) reveals that low-income fourth grade students attending schools with a majority of middle-class students had math scores that were almost two years ahead of their low-income peers in high-poverty schools and were more than six months ahead of middle-class students attending high-poverty schools. This problem takes on a racial dimension because two-thirds of Latino and African American students attend public schools in which more than half of the students are eligible for subsidized meals; by comparison, only 20% of white students attend such schools. Across the nation, more than 60 school districts are trying to address this issue by limiting the numbers of students at any school who are eligible for free and reduced meals (Kahlenberg, 2009). Kahlenberg says the reasons that low-income students benefit from attending schools with a majority of middle-class students are not difficult to determine. Students who attend a largely middle-class school are more likely to have peers who are motivated for academic achievement and less likely to act out. In addition, they are more likely to have high-quality teachers with high expectations for students as well as parents who are willing to hold administrators and teachers accountable for the school's academic outcomes. Yet, the burden of addressing this issue should not fall on local and state governments alone; the federal government should also play a role in responding to the needs of low-income students.

How has the federal government addressed the disadvantages for low-income students?

For the 2003 renewal of the Elementary and Secondary Education Act, President George W. Bush promoted and signed the No Child Left Behind (NCLB) Act, which required rigorous testing of students and identification of those students not achieving designated test scores. Schools with student scores below the Adequate Yearly Progress (AYP) benchmarks for two consecutive years are labeled as "failing" (later softened to "in need of improvement"). In 2006, more than a fourth of all public schools failed to reach their AYP (Karp, 2006). If these schools fail to meet their benchmark in the following year, they are added to the list of schools in need of improvement and are in jeopardy of losing their federal funding. If schools remain on the list for four or five years, they must choose from drastic options such as (1) replacing all or most of their staff, (2) extending their school year or school day, or (3) contracting with an outside entity (or with the state) to operate the school (in violation of our long-standing principle of local control of schools).

Many educators have criticized NCLB for its reliance on standardized tests to determine student learning. Even makers of standardized tests admit that these tests measure only a portion of what a child learns, and that multiple measures are necessary for authentic assessment of learning. Yet the NCLB plan forces teachers to reduce their curriculum content to prepare students for the tests, including students learning English as a second language, at-risk students, and students in special education classes. In addition, NCLB makes no distinction between students attending underfunded, deteriorating schools with inadequate facilities in poverty areas and students attending well-maintained schools with state-of-the-art facilities. They all have to pass the same tests (Mathis, 2003).

If NCLB were achieving its goal, educators and parents would be applauding it; instead, all fifty states have introduced legislation rejecting all or parts of NCLB. According to a study by the Harvard Civil Rights project, NCLB has failed to improve student scores on reading and math achievement tests, and it has made no progress on reducing achievement gaps between students based on differences of income or race (Lee, 2006). Karp (2006) concluded that the primary lesson learned from NCLB was that "tests, more tests, and punitive sanctions that create a systematic and misleading impression of failure . . . (hurts) public education" (p. 13). In 2007, Congress was supposed to pass a reauthorization of NCLB, but perhaps because of the criticism, there was no agreement on how the program should be modified. In the absence of a new bill, the Obama administration provided almost $4.4 billion from stimulus funds for its "Race to the Top" initiative in an effort to promote innovation and reform. Critics point out that this initiative still emphasizes testing and proposes that test scores be included in teacher evaluations, a controversial suggestion since a student's test score is a product of many factors, not just the performance of the teacher (White, 2011). Also, education secretary Arne Duncan announced in 2009 that $5 billion will be committed to the promotion of charter schools, which has also prompted criticism because recent studies of charter schools have reported that the majority of their students do worse or about the same as students in public schools (Miners, 2009). With the majority of "failing" schools located in low-income neighborhoods, advocates for children living in poverty insist that any real effort to improve the lives of these children must include programs that address problems they encounter outside of school as well as in school.

Why should problems outside of school affect a child's performance in school?

Urban sociologist Pedro Noguera has argued that most public schools in the United States are doing a good job educating their students, and that the only crisis in education exists in schools where there is a concentration of children from low-income families. Further, he says: "we have asked (these) schools to solve problems that are not simply educational in nature. They are much deeper than that" (*Extra!*, 2011, p. 15). For example, in 2010, almost 49 million Americans experienced "food insecurity," including 17% of America's children. For almost half of these families, in any given month they have had to choose between paying for utilities and fuel or food, or between rent or food (Shepard, Setren, & Cooper, 2011). Inadequate nutrition is not only a health problem; it is an educational problem that affects children before they are born. If pregnant women aren't getting adequate nutrition, neither are the babies they are carrying; this often results in premature births and low-birth-weight babies. Low-birth-weight babies often have problems with cognitive development; they tend to have lower IQ scores and are more likely to be diagnosed with a learning disability or attention disorder. Low-income children enrolled in kindergarten tend to have lower test scores when their height and weight are below normal (Shepard, Setren, & Cooper, 2011). Further, Coles (2008-2009) cited studies finding that living in a food-insecure home not only affected academic performance as documented by lower test scores in reading and math, but these students had behavioral problems such as temper tantrums, fighting, anxiety, depression, and loneliness.

Berliner (2005) noted that there are: "thousands of studies showing correlation between poverty and (low) academic achievement" (p. 11). He suggested a number of reasons to explain the correlation including: (1) irregular and often inadequate nutrition impedes cognitive development; (2) children living in poverty are less likely to have stable home lives that promote a sense of personal security; and (3) children living in poverty are more likely to suffer from environmental deficiencies that often lead to health problems, and are less likely to receive appropriate medical care. For example, studies report that half of low-income children have vision problems that affect their academic performance; yet there is evidence that vision deficiencies can often be corrected with glasses or eye-exercise therapy. In one study involving two groups of low-income fourth grade children, the group receiving therapy or lenses earned significantly higher reading scores, but children in a comparison group who received no

treatment dropped even further behind their peers (Rothstein, 2009).

Another problem is asthma, which has reached epidemic proportions among poor children in America and is now the leading cause of chronic absenteeism in schools. Even when asthmatic children attend school, breathing problems may have kept them up at night so that they are sleepy and unable to focus on academic tasks. Middle-class children with asthma are typically treated for it so that their asthma is controlled, but low-income children are far less likely to receive such treatment. Further, having asthma makes children less likely to exercise so they become less physically fit and more irritable, leading to behavioral problems in school (Rothstein, 2009).

Low-income children are also more likely to suffer from lead poisoning. The Centers for Disease Control and Prevention (CDC) estimates that 450,000 American children between the ages of one and five have sufficient lead in their blood to impair cognitive development; lead poisoning also contributes to hearing impairment. Low-income children are reported to have dangerously high lead in their blood more than five times as often as middle-class children. Children referred by the CDC are usually poor, with the majority being children of color (Berliner, 2005; Rothstein, 2009). Other nations have made a far stronger commitment to address problems of poverty and the needs of children living in poverty than the United States. In 2005, all members of the United Nations signed a charter concerning the rights of children except for two nations—Somalia and the United States (Berliner, 2005).

According to the Census Bureau, there are over 46 million people living in poverty, the highest number for the entire 52 years that the Census Bureau has reported such data (Tavernise, 2011). Largely because of medical debts, one third of Americans slip in and out of poverty each year, and half of all Americans will live in poverty at some point before turning 65 (Foroohar, 2011; McKernan, Ratcliffe, & Cellini, 2009). Berliner (2005) noted that 14.5% of Americans are permanently poor, the highest rate of permanent poor of any industrialized nation. In addition, over 16 million children in the United States live in poverty (22%), the highest number since 1962, and the highest rate of child poverty of any industrialized nation (Tavernise, 2011). Shepard, Setren, and Cooper (2011) examined the costs of poverty related to inadequate education, illness, and charitable programs (many simply providing food), and reported that poverty costs each American household $1,410 annually. The authors concluded: "The nation pays far more by letting hunger exist than it would if our leaders took steps to eliminate it" (p. 17).

How do we know that addressing the social problems of children living in poverty will improve their academic achievement?

Berliner (2005) cites an IQ study that reported only 10% of the variation of IQ is related to genetic influence. According to Schwartz-Nobel (2002), the bodies of undernourished children use food energy first to maintain critical organs, next for growth, and then the remaining energy is for cognitive development. Even short-term nutritional deprivation diminishes the ability to learn. "Children who come to school hungry are known to have shorter attention spans. They are unable to perform as well as their peers" (p. 139). Although poor nutrition interferes with academic achievement, good nutrition enhances it. One study reported that children from food secure homes came to school performing well academically, but those who experienced food insecurity in later grades began to have declining reading scores. The study also reported that children from food insecure homes who fell behind their peers in reading performance during the first years of schooling were able to improve their reading scores if their homes became food secure by third grade (Coles, 2008-2009).

Rothstein (2009) affirms that: "Poor nutrition directly contributes to an achievement gap between lower- and middle-class children" (p. 45). Children in low-income families often have deficiencies in their diet related to certain vitamins and minerals; in experiments, such children were given vitamin and mineral supplements and researchers reported that children's test scores increased (Rothstein, 2009). Coles (2008-2009) described a study where middle-class children were given three options: eat no breakfast, eat a minimally nutritious breakfast, or eat a nutritious breakfast high in protein and fiber. Each child experienced each option, and one hour after breakfast, the children were given various cognitive assessments. When children ate a nutritious breakfast, they performed much better on assessments of skills related to complex visual processing, auditory attention, spatial memory, and short-term memory. Their scores were lower after eating the less nutritious breakfast, and lowest of all when they had no breakfast.

As for living in a stable home, several studies have reported that being poor places great psychological stress on adults as well as children, but escaping poverty can diminish psychological stress and lead to behavioral changes. Berliner (2005) describes a longitudinal study of families over a three-year period. When families identified as poor became less poor, their children's academic performance became similar to that of the children who had never been poor. This was true even when parents of children who were never poor earned significantly higher salaries than the parents who had been poor. The researchers concluded, "rising incomes provide families with dignity and hope" (p. 30). This is not new information; multiple studies over several decades have reported that environmental factors leading to health problems have adverse effects on learning, and that learning can be improved when social problems are addressed. In 1970, Stein and Susser engaged in a review of a considerable amount of data that included cross-cultural research and reported,

> Improvement in the social environment of groups at a marked social disadvantage can bring about a substantial improvement in IQ levels and a decline in the frequency of mild mental retardation . . . the greatest advantage will come from a serious attack on poverty . . . unemployment, deteriorated housing, physical environment, and poor and inappropriate schooling. (p. 64)

> Men in search of a myth will usually find one.
>
> Pueblo Indian Proverb

Schwartz-Nobel (2002) cites a projection that the U.S. labor force will lose "as much as $130 billion in future productive capacity . . . for every year that 14.5 million American children continue to live in poverty" (p. 224). Research suggests that to increase the academic achievement of low-income students, especially those living in poverty, school reform will be effective only if it occurs in the context of social programs that improve environmental factors for these children and youth. The stakes are high, not only for poor people but for our society as well because studies have found that low-achieving students are more likely to drop out of school—and studies of high school dropouts report that workers without a high school diploma are twice as likely to be poor as those who graduate from high school (Haskins & Sawhill, 2007). However, the effort to persuade Americans to make a serious commitment to addressing problems of the poor is persistently sabotaged by myths and misunderstandings about poverty, especially about welfare recipients.

What are some myths about welfare recipients?

There is confusion in the United States about who qualifies for welfare assistance. Americans have historically believed that it was possible for able-bodied men to receive welfare. Weaver (2000) explains that aside from programs for widows, orphans, and people with disabilities, over 90% of social support comes through Transitional Assistance for Needy Families (TANF), a program that replaced Aid to Families with Dependent Children (AFDC) in 1996. As with AFDC, TANF assists single-parent families, rarely including men but typically consisting of women with dependent children; children represent two thirds of recipients.

Johnson (1998) and others identify a variety of other myths about welfare; many have been around for a number of years. The following list includes examples of myths that have fostered negative or even hostile attitudes and actions toward recipients; further information is included to provide a more accurate picture about people receiving social assistance.

MYTH #1: Welfare rolls are increasing. This is a half-truth, and as the Yiddish proverb says, "A half truth is a whole lie." True, numbers of people on welfare are increasing, but so is the population. Since 1970, people receiving some form of social assistance as a percentage of overall population has been relatively stable, with increases or decreases reflecting economic conditions. Schorr (2001) explains that in good economic times,

women find available jobs and leave welfare; during economic downturns, unemployment increases, as do applications for social assistance.

MYTH #2: Welfare families are large. As the twentieth century ended, the average size of a family receiving social assistance included 2.9 children, down from 4.0 children thirty years earlier. Over 37% of all TANF families have one child; 27% have two children (U.S. Department of Health and Human Services, 2004). Weaver (2000) reports that the average size of families receiving assistance across the nation is about the same as the typical American family.

MYTH #3: People on welfare have a comfortable life by abusing the welfare system. In seven states offering the most generous social assistance, family income—including food stamps received—is raised to meet the poverty level. In more than half the states, combined forms of social assistance only raise a recipient's gross income to 75% of the poverty level, and to 60% of the poverty level in twelve southern states. Despite such inadequate support, less than 2% of recipients have been documented as being engaged in welfare fraud. Yet Allison and Lewis (2001) report Internal Revenue Service estimates revealing a considerably higher percentage of fraud in the tax returns of middle- and upper-class Americans, and Kivel (2002) reports that corporate fraud exceeds $200 billion each year.

MYTH #4: The government only helps people on welfare. The U.S. Congress has helped corporations in fiscal trouble such as Chrysler and Boeing, and it has offered assistance to corporations not in financial trouble. According to Kivel (2002), federal government policies in support of wealthy corporations amount to more than $160 billion each year, costing each taxpayer about $1,400 compared to $400 per taxpayer spent on welfare and food stamps for poor people. Critics of corporate welfare argue that U.S. government spending reduces competition by subsidizing a select few corporations, creating an uneven playing field by providing what they regard as unnecessary assistance for minimal economic benefits.

MYTH #5: Welfare recipients are too lazy to get a job. Two thirds of Americans receiving social assistance are children, half of whom are five years old or less. Before TANF, most state assistance programs penalized enrolled mothers who were employed, deducting one dollar from their welfare check for every dollar they earned, and yet almost half of welfare mothers held at least part-time jobs. Mead (2000) found that one of the most generous states paid benefits of $673 per month to a welfare mother—regardless of the number of children—and required that she work a minimum of thirty hours per week with child care paid for by the state. However, if that mother were employed at minimum wages for forty hours a week she would earn $824 each month, but because she is not on welfare she would not qualify for child care benefits. The additional $150 a month earned at her minimum wage job would not cover the cost of quality child care and work-related expenses such as clothing and transportation. Further, minimum wage jobs frequently lack health insurance, and if insurance is provided, it is likely restricted to employees only, not their families. Welfare assistance includes health care for families. It is not surprising that many mothers, forced to choose between such options, decide to swallow their pride and apply for assistance for the sake of their children.

MYTH #6: Welfare recipients stay on welfare forever. Because so many people believed this myth, the 1996 U.S. welfare reform placed time limits on assistance to recipients. Historically, the AFDC program provided few incentives to leave, yet recipients tended to require only temporary assistance. Studies showed that more than 30% of recipients left welfare each year, and 75% left within five years. Less than half returned to welfare. Of those who returned, 65% to 75% left the program again within a year, and most of those left permanently (Isaacs & Lyon, 2000; Sandefur & Cook, 1998). Even for families considered "highly dependent" because they were on welfare for over seven years, more than 80% of the daughters never became single mothers who required welfare assistance (Bray, 2000).

Myths about social assistance have shaped American attitudes and caused negative actions against welfare recipients. Although the negative actions illustrate individual classism, the inadequacies of American social assistance programs illustrate institutional classism.

Institutional Classism

Individual prejudice based on socioeconomic status and negative behaviors rooted in that prejudice are especially problematic in a society with as wide a disparity in wealth and income as exists in the United States. Yet **institutional classism**—institutional policies and practices that exploit low-income people and benefit middle- or upper-class individuals—has contributed even more to the wealth and income disparity. The increased economic disparity in the United States has made it more difficult for individuals from one class to move up to a higher class, contradicting the belief in social mobility that is still central to the American Dream. As reported in a *New York Times* poll in the spring of 2005, 35% of Americans believe that they have the same opportunity as has always existed in the United States to become successful enough to move from one social class to a higher one, and 40% of Americans believe that it is even easier to move up than it has ever been (Scott & Leonhardt, 2005). Yet Callahan (2007) reviewed studies on social mobility and concluded that "class status at birth largely determines life chances, and . . . this correlation has actually intensified in recent years" (p. A12). According to a study by the Federal Reserve Bank of Boston, social mobility declined during each of the last three decades of the twentieth century (Scott & Leonhardt, 2005), and that is reflected in cross-cultural studies that have reported less social mobility in the United States today than in Canada, Sweden, Australia, Denmark, Germany, Norway, France, Finland, and Great Britain (Foroohar, 2011). In fact, currently there is more social mobility downward in the United States than upward. Investigative reporter David Johnston found that from 1980 to 2005, the size of the American economy doubled, yet the incomes of the bottom 90% of Americans fell by an average of about $4,000 while the wealthiest

1% increased their incomes by 384% (Hightower & Frazer, 2010). According to a report from the Pew Charitable Trusts, 28% of American adults raised in middle-class homes have fallen from middle-class status (Acs, 2011). Considerable academic research finds that increased inequality and lack of social mobility causes problems not only for low-income people, but for the entire society by creating low levels of trust, high levels of anxiety, and increased health issues (Foroohar, 2011). As the middle class becomes smaller, the disparity between the rich and poor is becoming larger.

Why is the disparity between the richest and poorest Americans increasing?

Federal policies have played a major role in diverting resources to the richest Americans. Some Americans regard income redistribution as a socialist scheme, yet each year the U.S. Internal Revenue Service collects income taxes—scaled according to income—to fund programs and projects approved by our elected representatives. Phillips (1990) estimates that during the 1980s, $160 billion collected from middle- and low-income taxpayers replaced funds lost from capital gains tax cuts benefiting wealthy Americans and funded programs such as providing subsidies for overseas corporate advertising. Social economists term such effects a *redistribution of income*. Based on his analysis of global data, Massey (2007) reported that the United States ranks highest in the disparity of both income and wealth of families between the highest 20% and lowest 20% of our economy.

Income redistribution also occurs when federal and state governments offer tax breaks to wealthy individuals and corporations resulting in their taxes becoming a lower percentage of income than that of most Americans. Because of the tax cuts passed by Congress from 2001 to 2003, the top 1% of Americans kept an additional $79 billion from their tax payment. As Sheehan (2004) points out, that is enough money to fully fund NCLB, provide housing subsidies for a million working poor families, add 47 million low-income children to the Women, Infants and Children (WIC) nutrition program, add 11 million children to the Medicaid program, and fully fund Head Start so that the 40% of eligible children not being served could participate. The $79 billion could fund all of these improvements with money left over. Yet even such federal generosity to wealthy individuals and corporations is not sufficient; they are trying to reduce their tax payments even further.

According to the Internal Revenue Service (IRS), American corporations are supposed to pay 35% of their income in taxes, but the IRS estimates that over 400,000 businesses and individuals employ tax-dodging practices to avoid paying approximately $250 billion to $300 billion each year (Allen, 2004; Zuckerman, 2004a). The most popular tactic is to establish "headquarters" in a tax-free Caribbean island or another overseas location with few or no taxes assessed. In 1983, such tax havens accounted for $200 billion in wealth; in 2004, they accounted for $5 trillion. In the 1950s, corporate taxes constituted about 27% of income tax revenue, but the 2003 corporate tax payment was only 7.4%, the lowest percentage in over twenty years and second lowest since 1934 (Zuckerman, 2004a). Based on a study of tax receipts from 1996 to 2000, the General Accounting Office reported that over 60% of U.S. corporations paid no taxes at all. Noncompliant corporations that filed no tax reports and paid no taxes deprived the American people of $310 billion in 2004 alone (Allen, 2004).

Another indication of wealth and income disparity in the United States is the dramatic increase in billionaires. From the Reagan economic policies of the 1980s through the Internet expansion and economic boom of the 1990s, data document dramatic increases in wealth for the richest Americans and a contrasting decrease in resources for low-income Americans. Phillips (1990) reported two billionaires in the United States in 1980, but more than 50 by 1989, and *Forbes* (Sharma, 2012) identified 424 billionaires currently, representing over half of all the world's billionaires. As Sklar (2005) noted, someone could deposit $1 million a day, every day, for an entire year, but he or she would only have about half of what is necessary to be included in the Forbes 400. In the very near future only billionaires will be on this list. Bill Gates and Warren

> Wealth is a power usurped by the few to compel the many to labor for their benefit.
>
> Percy Bysshe Shelley (1792–1822)

Buffet are currently at the top of the Forbes 400, but four of the top ten families are heirs of Sam Walton, whose combined wealth is over $100 billion. While the rich have increased their wealth, thanks to federal tax cuts, 80% of working Americans earning $65,000 a year or less have seen their incomes stagnate (Zuckerman, 2004b).

How have salaries in the United States been affected by recent economic changes?

Based on data from the Department of Labor Statistics, beginning in 1950, hourly wages for workers increased each decade until the 1980s, then declined by almost $1 per hour in that decade. Wages dropped another 50 cents in the first five years of the 1990s, but the economy prospered in the late 1990s and the 50 cents was regained (Children's Defense Fund, 2001). By 2011, the weekly earning of full-time wage and salary workers as expressed in constant dollars was virtually the same as it was in 2002, almost ten years earlier (U.S. Department of Labor Statistics, 2011). The recent recession has made a bad situation worse. From 2007 to 2009, although new jobs were created, the United States economy lost a net total of 8.2 million jobs, and at the same time gained 3 million new workers (Hightower & Frazer, 2010). Further, 75% of the new jobs created since 2007 have salaries ranging from $7.50 to $13.50 an hour (Connell, 2011). A 2008 study of over 4,000 workers in such low-wage jobs described a variety of ways that workers were being exploited. More than 25% were paid less than minimum wage, and 75% worked overtime without receiving overtime pay despite labor law mandates. Further, 70% of these employees worked "off the clock," meaning they worked for additional hours and received no pay at all. Of the workers who complained or initiated efforts to form a union to gain better protection, 43% experienced retaliation ranging from being fired to having their hours cut, despite laws that forbid such retaliation (Bernhardt, Milkman, & Theodore, 2009).

Historically, white men have enjoyed an economic advantage resulting in their salaries being the highest in all worker categories, yet even wages for white men declined. In too many cases, having a full-time job no longer provides adequate financial support. Greenberg (2007) reports that 25% of the full-time jobs available in the United States do not provide compensation sufficient to keep a couple with two children above the poverty line. Of the people living in poverty in the United States, 11%—almost 3 million Americans—have full-time, year-round jobs, and among Asian American and Latino populations, 18% have such jobs (Spriggs, 2007). This situation is likely to become even worse. The Bureau of Labor Statistics has identified 30 jobs expected to experience the greatest future need for additional workers, but two thirds of those jobs pay either "low" or "very low" wages (Greenberg, 2007).

While wages for workers have declined, management has prospered. Sklar (1998) found that U.S. chief executive officer (CEO) salaries climbed astronomically since 1980 when the average CEO earned 42 times the average worker's salary, which is more than generous when compared to German CEOs, who make an average of 14 times the average worker salary. By 1995, U.S. CEOs were paid a corporate average of 224 times what the average worker earned, making their salaries the highest in the world. By 2010, American CEOs were making an average of 343 times the average worker's salary. Whereas German, Japanese, and British CEOs earned average annual salaries of about $500,000, the average CEO salary in the United States was $2 million; if you add their stock options, their average total compensation is $11.4 million, an increase of 23% over the previous year (American Federation of Labor, 2011).

How large is the disparity of wealth in the United States?

Income is generated by toil or investment; *wealth* refers to assets one already controls. Because wealth is an obvious means of designating upper class, that group controls much of our wealth. But what level of concentrated wealth results in excessive influence? Wealth controlled by the top 1% of U.S. families declined slightly in each of the four decades after 1940 until 1980. The slight decrease in assets, related in part to higher tax rates, helped fund valuable social programs such as the GI Bill, FHA loans, and college loans that provided economic assistance to middle- and low-income families, creating a larger and more robust middle class.

In 1959, the top 4% of Americans had as much wealth as the lowest 35%; but beginning in the 1980s, wealthy Americans amassed even more wealth. According to U.S. Census data, between 1979 and 2008, the income of the top 5%

of American families increased by 73%, while the lowest 20% experienced a decrease in wealth, and wealth for 90% of Americans was stagnant or increased only slightly; the 400 families in the Forbes list of wealthiest Americans hold as much wealth as the lowest 50% of all American families (Johnson, 2011). Schwartz-Nobel (2002) pointed out that the United States is currently the wealthiest nation in the world, and yet an American child is three times more likely to be poor than a French child, and six times more likely to be poor than a Danish or Swiss child. This is not merely because of wealth disparity but income disparity. According to a study by the Congressional Budget Office, the income disparity between the rich and poor at the end of the twentieth century was greater than at any time in the previous 250 years (Schwartz-Nobel, 2002).

Why has there been so little protest from Americans about the tax cuts for the wealthiest people in our society that have contributed to this upward redistribution of wealth and loss of wealth for the middle class? Perhaps Americans feel they lack the power needed to succeed in a confrontation with such a powerful group as the wealthy, or perhaps too many Americans see these tax cuts as benefiting them now or in the future. According to one poll, 19% of Americans identify themselves as being in the top 1% of incomes, and another 20% believe they will be in the top 1% in the near future (Collins, 2003). There is obviously considerable confusion in our society about how much wealth exists in America and who controls it.

How do income levels determine social class in the United States?

The nature of wealth in America makes it difficult to define who comprises the middle-income class. According to Heintz and Folbre (2000), middle-class wealth is overwhelmingly represented by two possessions: homes and cars. Historically, some American politicians lobbying for economic relief for their so-called middle-class constituents have argued for extending tax cuts to those with annual earnings of up to $200,000 or higher. Bonilla-Silva (2001) reported that a 1992 Congressional Budget Office study defined "middle class" as a family of four with an annual income of $19,000 to $78,000. More than 70% of Americans were middle class according to this definition. Wolfe (1998) conducted a survey asking Americans how large an annual income would have to be for someone to be considered too rich to be middle class. The answers were diverse, but ultimately it caused Wolfe to define **middle class** not as a specific income range but as a combination of attitudes, beliefs, and practices that characterize someone who is "not too poor to be considered dependent on others and not too rich to be so luxuriously ostentatious that one loses touch with common sense" (pp. 2–3).

It is not difficult to define "low income." The federal government established criteria for determining poverty, including earnings and number of people in a family (see Table 9.1). As of 2010, the federal definitions of **poverty levels** designate an

TABLE 9.1   Official Poverty Levels in the United States

Members in Family	Annual Income
Single	$11,344
Single 1 child	$15,030
Single 2 children	$17,552
Single 3 children	$22,113
Two adults 1 kid	$17,552
Two adults 2 kids	$22,859
Two adults 3 kids	$26,023
Annual Income for Minimum Wage Earner ($7.25/hr) = $15,080	

Source: United States Census Bureau 2010. Available at www.census.gov

income of $11,344 for a person (under 65) living alone; $15,030 for a single person with one child; and $17,522 for a single person with two children (U.S. Census Bureau, 2010). Keeping these poverty levels in mind, a full-time worker paid the minimum wage will earn $15,080 a year. Recognizing the inadequacy of the minimum wage, many U.S. communities are implementing a "living wage" to meet the needs of low-income families.

Who suffers most from poverty?

Studies indicate that gender becomes a significant factor since most single-parent families are headed by a female. A poverty rate of 31% has been reported for all female-headed households with no spouse present compared to a 13% poverty rate for male-headed households with no spouse. Even single women suffer the consequences of the gender gap in salaries as studies report that for single people living alone, 24% of the women fall below the poverty line, but only 18% of the men do so. Elderly women are also more likely than elderly men to live in poverty, in part from their greater reliance on Social Security. They were more likely to work in low-wage jobs, which results in less lifelong earnings and lower Social Security payments. These women were also less likely to have jobs offering pensions (Spriggs, 2007).

When mothers live in poverty, so do their children, and many social activists have argued that children are the group most adversely affected by poverty. In the United States, one out of five children lives in poverty; two out of three social assistance recipients are children; and one out of five newborns is born into poverty—the highest rate in the industrialized world (Children's Defense Fund, 2001, 2008). The problems these children face begin with inadequate or even nonexistent prenatal and postnatal care offered by the American health care system, causing the United States to rank twenty-second among industrialized nations in low birth weights and in infant mortality rates. Low birth weight means a baby is born weighing 5-1/2 pounds or less. In the United States, a low birth weight baby is born every two minutes and a very low birth weight baby (weighing 3 pounds, 4 ounces or less) is born every nine minutes. Since a newborn baby

in the United States dies every nineteen minutes, America ranks twenty-second in infant mortality rates. These babies tend to come from low-income families, and Americans pay a price for our neglect of these children. As Johnson (2007) reported, "More than one-third of the dollars spent in the U.S. on health care during the first year of life can be attributed to low birth weight, even though these infants account for less than 10 percent of all U.S. births" (p. A15). For the children from low-income homes who survive infancy despite inadequate health care and insufficient diets, their poor nutrition will affect brain development. Studies have found that these children will be more likely to drop out of high school and more likely to earn as much as 15% less than their normal birth weight peers (Johnson, 2007).

The U.S. federal government response to help children in poverty began with the Economic Security Act of 1935 that included Aid to Dependent Children (ADC), a program intended for mothers widowed or abandoned by their husband. In 1950, ADC was expanded to include any single parent with children and was termed Aid to Families with Dependent Children (AFDC). In 1964, food stamps were made available to low-income families. In 1996, Transitional Assistance for Needy Families (TANF) replaced AFDC. Rodgers (2006) notes, however, that the average value of TANF benefits in combination with food stamps was about the same as what low-income families received from AFDC alone in 1970.

In the late 1970s, studies assessed the impact of war-on-poverty programs initiated in the 1960s by President Lyndon Johnson, especially programs concerned with meeting nutritional needs of the poor. One study reported that hunger had been virtually eliminated (Edelman, 2001). However, the Children's Defense Fund (2011) estimated that in 2010, 16.4 million children (more than one in five of American children) were living in poverty and 7 million of them (one in ten) were living in "extreme poverty," meaning their family's annual income was less than half of the poverty level. A family of four would be living on less than $30 a day. For these children, not receiving proper nutrition is a regular feature of their lives. The presence of hungry children in the richest nation in the world illustrates a failure of our institutions to fulfill social obligations.

Despite social assistance programs such as TANF, Women, Infants and Children (WIC), food stamps, and Meals on Wheels, malnutrition exists primarily among the old and the young in the United States. Children who do not die from malnutrition may suffer brain damage related to protein-deficient diets and sometimes calorie-deficient diets. Brain damage resulting from malnutrition is just as devastating as physical violence because it is permanent; it cannot be reversed by free breakfasts or free lunches once a child starts school.

American health care systems also fail to provide adequate services to poor people because they are based on ability to pay. Poor people may visit free or low-cost clinics, yet these clinics are likely to be inadequately staffed and underfunded. Although the United States leads the world in medical technology, it is one of the worst among industrialized nations in health care delivery. The United States and South Africa are the only two developed nations without a universal health care program for all citizens. The United States ranks second to last among all developed nations (Mexico is last) in the percentage of children living in poverty, and twenty-sixth in the world in child mortality rates for children under twelve (Rifkin, 2004). The health care reform signed by President Obama in 2010 will add 30 million people to the ranks of the insured, reducing the number of uninsured Americans by 60%, and the Congressional Budget Office reported that the reform would reduce the federal deficit by as much as $138 billion by 2019 (Johnson, 2010). Yet, critics insist the reform will increase government spending significantly while the nation still struggles to come out of an economic recession. The Department of Health Care and Human Services has already announced that it will not be able to implement the part of the law calling for a program to help provide at-home care for elderly people and people with a disability because it could not provide a realistic plan for generating adequate revenue to fund the program for 75 years as stipulated by the law (Chaddock, 2011). The next few years will illustrate whether Americans have sufficient commitment to support even this relatively modest attempt to improve health care in America, especially for low-income Americans.

Another group of people significantly affected by poverty is the elderly. Many Americans believe that the United States effectively addressed the problem of poverty for elderly Americans with the establishment of the Social Security system in 1935, and there is some truth to this perception. Social Security is a major reason why only about 10% of people living in poverty in the United States are senior citizens (Spriggs, 2007), but elderly Americans continue to encounter serious problems related to poverty and to a form of prejudice that scholars have identified by the term "ageism."

Ageism

According to Macnicol (2006), anthropologists have reported that in all societies, age is one of the major factors for determining an individual's status. In the United States, status is primarily determined by age, race, class, and gender, and yet age has historically been the least acknowledged of the four. As scholars began investigating bias and prejudice against elderly people, they linked many negative attitudes to the fear of mortality. Nelson (2009) wrote: "Older people are a very poignant and salient reminder to younger people that they are mortal, that life is finite" (p. 436).

How do scholars define ageism?

Butler (2008) originally coined the term *ageism* in 1968, defining it as "a form of systematic stereotyping and discrimination against people because they are old" (p. 41). At first, social scientists were reluctant to accept this concept, but by 2000, the term *ageism* was widely viewed as a phenomenon that justified research to clarify its impact on elderly people (Levy & Banaji, 2002). An emerging view among some social scientists has been to argue for a broader definition of ageism, one that includes both the young and the elderly.

The trend toward a broader definition began in the 1980s with the formation of the Americans for Generational Equity (AGE). AGE focused on concerns related to the increasing use of resources to provide health care for elderly Americans, asserting that such an unbalanced distribution of resources was provided at the expense of the young, and that it represented prejudice against the young. Bytheway (2005) supported the idea of a broader definition of ageism that included all age groups: "We are all, throughout our lives, oppressed by ageism, by dominant expectations about age, expectations that dictate how we behave and relate to each other" (p. 338). Two prominent researchers in the field have offered a broader definition of **ageism** as "an alteration in feeling, belief, or behavior in response to an individual's or group's perceived chronological age" (Levy & Banaji, 2002, p. 50); nevertheless, most of the research on ageism pertains to the elderly more than any other age group. Studies of ageism have not only described current issues, but also explored how perceptions based on age have changed over time and influenced the creation of stereotypes and prejudices.

How has ageism manifested itself in American society?

During the colonial era, an elder was a highly respected member of the community, but as a sovereign nation, the United States became more industrialized, urban areas expanded dramatically, and attitudes toward the elderly began to change. The increased emphasis on a nuclear family resulted in parents living apart from their adult children, so that elderly people spent less time with their children and grandchildren. Further, with the growth of technology, younger workers were more likely to have the most highly valued skills and knowledge, transforming the historic ideal of the wise elder into the perception of older adults as out of touch, stuck in outdated ways of doing things, and yearning for the old days (Levin & Levin, 1980).

In addition, there has been a dramatic change in psychological views of the individual. According to Gullette (2011), American psychologists historically viewed mental ability in terms of an individual *mind* that was associated with personality, individuality, and moral or religious sentiments. In the twentieth century, the concept of mind gave way to an emphasis on the brain as the seat of mental activity, and scientists studied how the brain functioned. In recent years, this emphasis has been reduced further to memory, with considerable research being devoted to the study of memory loss. A decline in the ability to remember information, including nonsense syllables, has become the defining measure of mental decline. Ageism scholars have noted the increased use of the term *senility* in the medical profession and in society. Gullette (2011) observed

that in the past, senility "was available as a medical label, but it was much harder to apply to a particular old person when many valuable qualities were simultaneously observable" (p. 177).

Gullette (2004) has argued that ageism is a process of stripping someone of his or her identity and replacing it with a stereotypical image of an elderly person. In the United States, early stereotypes portrayed the old as frail and vulnerable, and although those stereotypes remain, more recent ones are likely to view the elderly as selfish and affluent individuals who demand resources to the detriment of other groups, especially young people. A Harris poll identified several stereotypical traits associated with elderly persons—moving slowly, thinking slowly, and not learning as well as younger adults. Other stereotypes suggest that elderly people dislike innovation and new ideas, are increasingly egocentric, make excessive demands on our nation's resources, and tend to be irritable and short-tempered. They are described as often repeating themselves in conversations, and more likely to reminisce about the past than to focus on the present or plan for the future. Finally, as they age, elderly people are expected to become more vulnerable to disease, mental deterioration, and perhaps recede into childishness. These stereotypical images are captured in such terms as *shrew, curmudgeon, blue hair, recluse, fossil, old-timer,* and *dinosaur* (Cuddy & Fiske, 2002; Levin & Levin, 1980). Many of the prejudices against the elderly are implicit rather than explicit. As Levy and Banaji (2002) noted: "One of the most insidious aspects of ageism is that it can operate without conscious awareness, control or intent to do harm" (p. 50). They argue that many Americans do not take ageism seriously because it is not characterized by explicit emotions such as the vitriolic bigotry directed against certain communities; instead, they describe a unique dimension to ageism:

> There are no hate groups that target the elderly as there are hate groups that target members of religious and racial and ethnic groups. . . . In contrast, social sanctions against expressions of negative attitudes and beliefs about the elderly are completely absent . . . This state of affairs stands in sharp contrast to other social groups.

Individuals who might be accused of ageism will not respond with the same sense of shame or defensiveness as would someone accused of racism or anti-Semitism or of harboring anti-gay attitudes. Ageism is so subtle and pervasive that it even affects the attitudes of elderly individuals. Whereas most groups reveal a bias favoring in-group members, in research using the Implicit Association Test to examine unconscious attitudes, subjects of all ages, including elderly subjects, demonstrated a bias in favor of young people and against elderly people (Levy & Banaji, 2002).

Ageist stereotypes and assumptions are part of our culture. Aging expert Steve Scrutton says: "Ageism surrounds us . . . but it is so engrained within the structure of social life that it is unlikely to be (noticed or) challenged" (Macnicol, 2006, p. 10). Children learn such stereotypes. Several studies have documented children's preference for young adults and their bias against elderly people (Montepare & Zebrowitz, 2002). When children describe older people, they tend to focus on physical aspects of aging such as baldness, wrinkles, and poor vision or hearing, and they use negative descriptive terms such as being sad, lonely, or boring. In one study, children who were 4, 6, or 8 years old were paired with an adult who was either 35 or 75 years old. The adults were all dressed according to current fashion, in good health, and instructed to act very friendly toward the children. Yet when paired with the 75-year-old adult, all three age groups of children tended to sit further away, to make less eye contact, and to engage in fewer interactions, including fewer requests for assistance. Although children do learn some positive stereotypes about older adults, several studies document that negative attitudes are predominant, and they intensify as children enter their adolescent years (Montepare & Zebrowitz, 2002). Macnicol (2006) described the cultural bias against aging and the elderly as revealed in a study in which researchers disguised themselves as elderly people and reported the range of responses from their encounters with younger people including "hostility, prejudice, contempt and patronizing sympathy" (p. 11).

As reported in studies of other minority groups, elderly people's view of themselves is affected by stereotypes. Levy and Banaji (2002) describe a stereotype threat study in which prior to a memory test, positive stereotypes about aging were presented to one elderly group, whereas another group was told negative stereotypes of elderly

people; the first group significantly outperformed the second group on the test. In another study, prior to being given a memory task to complete, a group of elderly subjects was given descriptions of negative traits associated with aging such as senility and another elderly group was presented with positive traits for elder people such as wisdom. The latter group did much better on memory tests than the former group (Kite & Wagner, 2002). In addition, studies have also demonstrated a physiological reaction from elderly subjects who were primed for an activity by the use of negative stereotypes. Groups of elderly people were given instructions in one room and then told to walk down the hallway to another room to take a test. The elderly people in groups that were presented positive traits associated with aging walked much faster down the hallway than elderly people given negative traits associated with aging (Kite & Wagner, 2002). Internalizing ageist stereotypes may even affect longevity. Gullette (2011) described the results of a longitudinal study of 660 people over the age of 50 in a small Ohio town in which individuals who had positive views about aging lived 7.5 years longer than those who had negative views about growing older. This represented a bigger increase in longevity than factors associated with exercise and the cessation of smoking.

In part because of the findings from ongoing research in medicine and gerontology, life expectancy in the United States has risen dramatically. Americans are not only living longer, but they are healthier and are living more vigorously into their 70s and 80s, with an increasing number holding full- or part-time jobs and a sizeable majority participating in volunteer work. Despite the stereotypes, 65% have no hearing problems and 90% have no vision problems. Of all adults over 85, only 25% require assistance with basic activities of daily life, and the majority of them are in nursing homes (Pasupathi & Lockenhoff, 2002). Yet, because elderly Americans live in a culture that emphasizes youth and beauty, aging is still regarded as a time of inevitable physical and mental decline and social marginality. Such perceptions and expectations can lead to discrimination in medical settings. Cuddy and Fiske (2002) described studies reporting that older people were denied psychiatric services offered to younger people who had similar symptoms. In addition, researchers have described how some physicians dismissed an elderly person's health complaint by attributing it to aging when the patient actually had a treatable health problem, and Pasupathi and Lockenhoff (2002) found that general practitioners tended to spend more time with younger patients than with elderly patients.

The institutionalization of ageist prejudices can be observed in something as simple as a birthday card. Cards created for older adults have often expressed sympathy for the person becoming another year older. Instead of presenting a positive sentiment, praising experience, knowledge, or wisdom, these birthday card messages state or imply a physical or mental decline. This is especially paradoxical since birthdays are ostensibly a celebration and ought to be a festive and joyful occasion. Nelson (2009) makes an apt comparison when he asks us to imagine the response if similar cards were sent to other groups saying "I'm so sorry that you are disabled" or "I was sorry to hear that you're gay." Institutional ageism may be further reinforced if the store selling birthday cards has shelves featuring anti-aging products such as skin creams, hair dyes, and other products intended to disguise the evidence of aging. On the other hand, youth advocates argue that ageism also includes negative attitudes toward young people.

Is there evidence to support claims of prejudiced attitudes toward youth?

In the media, terms like "Generation X," "Generation Y," or the "Millennial Generation" reinforce the use of generalizations about these cohort groups that are often stereotypical assumptions about the attitudes and behaviors of all members of each group. Specific negative stereotypes relate to perceptions of youth as drug users, irresponsible, sexually promiscuous, lacking ambition, and not valuing education. Macnicol (2006) discussed how these stereotypes are reinforced by the correlation between youth and higher crime rates, unemployment, homicides and other traumatic deaths, drug abuse, car accidents, and higher health costs. Much of this correlation is a consequence of economic and cultural factors, and of course, data about a few members of a group should never be used to characterize an entire group. Further, negative attitudes about youth have resulted in what some regard as institutionalized discrimination against

young people through what critics view as an arbitrary establishment of a minimum age for activities such as driving a car, serving on a jury, consuming alcohol, voting, running for public office, and attending adult films. In schools, some educators use the concept of "age-appropriate" curricula to avoid dealing with serious and controversial issues. Such discrimination against youth has been observed in other cultures. After he was elected President of South Africa, Nelson Mandela wanted to reward the country's youth for their participation in the struggle against Apartheid, but when he proposed lowering the voting age to 14, he encountered such vigorous resistance within his own political party that he withdrew the proposal (Mandela, 2010). Ultimately, the harshest impact of ageism on youth, as is true for elderly people, will always be found in the economic consequences stemming from their age. As most Americans struggle to survive one of the deepest recessions in the history of the global economy, it is important to understand the consequences of poverty in conjunction with ageism.

What are some economic consequences of ageism for both the elderly and youth?

Amendments to the 1967 Age Discrimination in Employment Act abolished mandatory retirement in almost all professions and outlawed employment discrimination based on age, but in 2000, the U.S. Supreme Court ruled that the state could use age "as a proxy for other qualities, abilities or characteristics" (Gullette, 2011, p. 4), implicitly approving the use of ageist stereotypes to discriminate based on age. Most Americans agree that age discrimination is a problem; several surveys found that about 80% of Americans believe employers have discriminated against older workers. Older Americans have been especially vulnerable in the recent recession. Gullette (2011) reported that the numbers of people over 55 filing for bankruptcy nearly tripled from a rate of 8% in the early 1990s to 22% in 2007; further, both men and women today are more likely than their parents were to still be working past retirement age. In addition, the intersection of poverty and gender should be recognized. Women make up 75% of the elderly poor, with the highest poverty rates existing among unmarried women. Women face additional stress and suffer economic consequences because of their traditional role in the culture as caregivers. Older women living in poverty often spend half of their income on health care; for that reason, proposals to ration health care or reduce Social Security implicitly have a sexist component. The margin for survival for women is already slim. Because of the gender gap in salaries, women receive an average of $200 less in monthly Social Security benefits compared to men (Calasanti & Slevin, 2001; Cawthorne, 2008).

Despite such minimal support, Social Security has been recognized as one of the most effective federal anti-poverty programs. In 1959, 35% of elderly people were living in poverty as compared to 10% today, a decrease that led Whitman and Purcell (2007) to conclude: "The reduction in poverty among older Americans is one of the most significant public policy successes of the past half century" (p. 194). According to Census Bureau data, Social Security payments constituted more than 90% of the income for almost 40% of elderly Americans. For more than two thirds of those past 65, Social Security payments provided half of their income, and for almost 25%, Social Security represented their only source of income (Whitman & Purcell, 2007). Without Social Security benefits, 44% of elderly people today would be living in poverty, but even with these benefits, almost 9% of elderly Americans live near the poverty level in addition to the 10% living below the poverty level (Cawthorne, 2008; Gullette, 2011).

The economic consequences of poverty for elderly Americans are likely to become even more significant in the next two decades. Demographers at the U.S. Census Bureau have predicted that from 2000 to 2030, the number of people over 65 will double (Nelson, 2009). In the workplace, policies and practices based on the ageist assumption that increased age brings a decline in mental capabilities may have a powerful negative impact, and the consequences are already being experienced. Barnett (2005) reported that an increasing number of workers cannot afford to retire under the present system. Those at the top of the economic hierarchy will never share the fate of the masses below them, yet they are likely to have a significant influence on what that fate may be. Wealthy and powerful people do not end up in nursing homes, nor do they rely on Social Security

checks to survive, but for the majority of Americans, fears about aging are largely related to the concern about what will happen after they have exhausted their financial resources.

As for the economic consequences of ageism for young people, it is especially significant for children and youth living in poverty, as described earlier, but other problems based on age have an adverse impact on young workers. The Age Discrimination in Employment Act of 1967 offered protection against job discrimination for people 40 years old and older, but there is no similar law for workers aged 18 to 24, even though media reports from the United States (*USA Today*, 2003) and Great Britain (*BBC News*, 2004) reflect a growing awareness that young workers experience various forms of job discrimination (Fletcher-Hackwood, 2010). A survey of 2,600 workers conducted by Mercer Resource Consulting in the United States revealed that only 44% of workers aged 18 to 24 felt they were treated fairly on the job as compared to 64% of the workers in the 45 to 55 age bracket (Lunn, 2005). In Great Britain, many younger workers believe that age discrimination stymied their job progression because of the perception by management that they were too young to take on extra responsibility (*Management Issues*, 2006). An increase in lawsuits filed by younger workers alleging reverse age discrimination is now part of the legal landscape in both countries.

The deepening worldwide economic recession holds potential for an increase in explicit and implicit ageism, with negative effects for both the young and the elderly, and the workplace is only one aspect of this problem. The problem of ageism should be important to everyone because each generation becomes the elderly population for a new generation. Complex problems facing citizens in the twenty-first century may require an alliance between young people and the elderly. An intergenerational union might be able to confront not only the failure of institutions to meet their needs, but also the institutional exploitation that affects all people living in poverty.

How do institutions exploit poor people?

Financial institutions exploit poor families simply by enforcing policies meant to protect them from losses. **Redlining** refers to banks and other

> Nobody talks more of free enterprise and competition and of the best man winning than the man who inherited his father's store or farm.
>
> C. Wright Mills (1916–1962)

lenders identifying a deteriorating portion of a city, and then refusing to lend money for mortgages or business loans in that area. For low-income workers, such areas are most likely to offer the best opportunity to purchase affordable homes, yet when they apply for mortgage loans, their applications may be denied. In such cases, denial is not based on bad credit ratings or lack of skills to maintain and improve property; it results from the age and/or current condition of properties in the redlined area and the average income levels of its residents.

In addition, minority entrepreneurs interested in opening a business in a largely minority neighborhood cannot get the bank loans needed if the area is redlined. Banks insist that it is just good business practice not to invest in declining areas, but refusing to lend money for purchase or improvement of property makes it inevitable that an area will continue to deteriorate. The bank's prediction becomes a self-fulfilling prophecy. The federal government has attempted to stop redlining practices, and some corporations have even offered low-interest loans to promote minority-owned businesses in redlined areas, but they have not been able to overcome the difficulties that banks have created by this practice. Although the reason for redlining is supposedly based on objective economic factors, this practice has had a significant impact on low-income people of color. As Shorris (2001) observed, "Redlining by the bank has taken the economic heart out of Latinos, as it did (for) blacks" (p. 323).

Another way financial agencies may discriminate against the poor is by insisting on a minimum balance of $150 or $200 for checking accounts, making it impossible for workers living from paycheck to paycheck to maintain checking accounts. Families are then forced to live on a cash-only basis—and most banks charge a fee for cashing payroll checks unless an individual has an account at the bank. Many workers find it more convenient to take their paychecks to a neighborhood check-cashing store, even though the convenience may cost them as much as 10% of the amount of the check. According to Barr (2004), over 8 million low-income workers with no checking or savings account pay over $1.5 billion annually in check-cashing fees. Over the course of a year, these fees can add up to two weeks of a worker's salary.

As banks have abandoned the central cities, check-cashing stores and payday lending outlets have proliferated. Ratcliffe (2009) reports that there are 4,000 more check-cashing and payday lending businesses in the United States today than the total combined retail stores for McDonald's, Burger King, Target, Sears, JCPenney, and Walmart. Barr (2004) observed that banks, thrifts, and credit unions are not as available in low-income areas as in higher-income areas. Based on an analysis of twelve cities, Kane (1996) reported that there were approximately equal numbers of banks per 1,000 residents in white and minority (primarily inner city) areas in 1970, but by the 1990s, there were three times as many banks in white areas as in minority areas. Fewer banks mean less money is available for businesses and homeowners. A decline in the number of banks has led to an increase in private financial companies that are legally allowed to charge interest rates higher than banks; Ratcliffe (2009) reported that a 400% annual interest rate is standard for payday lenders, and they make an annual profit of $4 billion. Some of this profit stems from the practice of payday lenders combining several high-interest loans and selling them to a bank for the interest owed. The bank owning the high-interest loans can then collect interest at a rate well above what it would normally be permitted to charge (Kane, 1996). But banks and private lenders are not the only businesses involved in the exploitation of low-income families and individuals.

How do businesses discriminate against poor people?

According to Feagin and Feagin (1986), retail businesses serving low-income people may charge higher prices for products than stores in suburban areas with similar merchandise. As described next, merchants engage in a variety of practices to exploit the poor:

Blank price tags Blank price tags on merchandise force the customer to ask for the price of an item. This allows merchants to quote higher prices to customers they feel may be particularly naïve.

Bait and switch Although the practice is illegal, stores may advertise a product at a low price to attract customers, who are then told that the product is of poor quality. Customers are encouraged to buy a similar product of better quality at a higher price. This tactic is increasingly being used by stores serving mainly middle-class customers.

Rent-to-own Customers rent a product that they can own by making weekly payments over a specified time. Rent-to-own customers may pay up to four times more for merchandise;

> Of course I believe in free enterprise, but in my system of free enterprise the democratic principle is that there never was, never has been, never will be, room for the ruthless exploitation of the many for the benefit of the few.
>
> Harry S. Truman (1884–1972)

only 25% eventually own the rented product. Store owners are exempt from laws limiting interest rates; they insist that they are not charging interest but renting a product. Ratcliffe (2009) gives the example of a computer that retails for $851 being rented for weekly payments of $49 for 91 weeks; in this arrangement the renter would own the computer after having made payments for 21 months totaling $4,449. Of course, if the renter missed a payment, the store could legally demand that the computer be returned with no obligation to return the payments already made.

Pawnshops An expensive option for low-income families is to surrender a possession as collateral for a loan. Pawnshops have proliferated in recent years, with interest rates up to 20%

a month—240% a year. Even when customers pay the interest and reclaim the property, the loan repayment does not go on their credit record, so the transaction does not improve their credit rating (Minutaglio, 1996).

Poor people are exploited in other ways in America, but the preceding examples illustrate that exploitation occurs. One must overcome numerous economic obstacles to escape poverty, and

> Governments exist to protect the rights of the poor and minorities; the loved and the rich need no protection.
>
> Wendell Phillips (1811–1884)

no simple solutions exist. As was demonstrated in the 1930s, federal and state governments must address issues of poverty if any progress is to be made concerning the exploitation of and discrimination against poor people.

What can federal and state governments do to assist families living in poverty?

Scholars Abelda, Drago, and Shulman (1997), Entwhistle, Alexander, and Olson (2001), and Haycock (2001) and social activist organizations such as the Children's Defense Fund (2001) have made suggestions regarding the role government must play in assisting people in poverty or in supporting those struggling to stay out of poverty:

1. Provide services to address critical needs; subsidies for battered women's shelters would provide options for women in abusive situations.
2. Subsidize child care services for low-income women who are enrolled in education or training programs. Because of child care expenses, the best financial option for a single mother working at minimum wage is to quit her job and receive support from social assistance programs.
3. Raise the minimum wage and strive for a living wage. It is difficult to take care of individual needs with the current minimum wage,

yet in many families both parents have minimum wage jobs. When the parents' combined salary is barely over $10 an hour, a family will still live in poverty. Jones and George (2003) concluded that for a couple earning $10 to $15 an hour, "it is often difficult, if not impossible, for them to meet their families' needs" (p. 123).

4. Restructure public school funding so that taxes to support schools are collected by the state and disbursed to schools according to a variable per pupil funding formula that takes into account factors such as: (a) number of low-income students in a given school; (b) amount of budget devoted to special learners; (c) mobility rate of students. In 1990, the New Jersey Supreme Court ruled that such plans are economically feasible and morally justified (*Abbott v. Burke*). Only by making a commitment to all children can we hope to nourish their talents and reap the benefits of these children becoming adults who know and use their abilities to the fullest.

5. Provide tax relief for low-income families. Tax relief for wealthy Americans exists as capital gains tax cuts and corporate exemptions from local property taxes for a specified number of years as an incentive to locate in an area. If tax relief is good for the wealthy, why not offer it to the poor? Some tax relief exists in the Earned Income Tax Credit (EITC) and child care allowances, although some politicians persist in proposing to eliminate these programs. Another form of tax relief for low-income workers might be to exempt home purchases to allow time to make improvements and save money in preparation for paying the resulting higher taxes assessed because of improvements.

6. Offer tax incentives for corporations to locate in inner cities, and tax incentives for corporations creating day care centers at the worksite if they allow low-income families in the area to place children in the centers. Wilson (1996) suggests that the reduction of businesses in inner cities has been a major factor in the increase of drug use and crime, and the general deterioration of those communities.

7. Strengthen educational opportunity by increasing support for Head Start programs and funding quality preschools and summer school programs for low-income children, especially during summers just before and after first grade, so children can experience educational gains similar to those made by middle- and upper-income children during the summer. For middle school and secondary school low-income students, high expectations reflected in clearly articulated standards must be accompanied by a challenging curriculum. Teacher salaries could be subsidized to ensure higher salaries for experienced, quality teachers willing to be assigned to schools in low-income areas.

8. Increase the opportunity for affordable housing. Almost 5 million families use over half their income to pay rent, often for substandard housing. The federal government could add 300,000 more housing vouchers each year for the next ten years. In addition, the Low-Income Home Energy Assistance Program could be expanded so low-income families can meet rising energy costs.

9. Maintain reasonable regulation of the private sector concerning job discrimination, possibly with affirmative action policies focused on socioeconomic status. State and federal governments could review policies pertaining to multinational corporations that relocate outside the United States. Although inevitable in a global economy, there could be incentives to keep those corporate jobs in the United States and disincentives for locating elsewhere. At the present time, American corporations have more incentives to locate overseas than to remain in this country.

AFTERWORD

Oppression is an inevitable consequence when power and resources are concentrated in one group. During the 1930s, U.S. Supreme Court justice Louis Brandeis expressed his concern for the future of democracy in America by proposing that the United States could continue to be a democracy or it could continue to allow great wealth to be accumulated by a few people, but that it was not possible to accomplish both. Equity and justice depend on transferring resources and power to oppressed groups. People suffer the misery of poverty not because they deserve it, but most likely as a consequence of birth. The consequences of poverty affect youth in their development toward adulthood and continue throughout their lives. As soon as they are perceived as "senior citizens," people may find themselves struggling against stereotypes and prejudices based simply on their age, affecting even those in the middle class.

If needs of adults living in poverty are neglected, we will perpetuate a despair that often produces drug abuse, crime, and violence. In America today, one of every five babies is born into poverty. If the needs of children living in poverty are neglected, we

> Until the great mass of the people shall be filled with the sense of responsibility for each other's welfare, social justice can never be attained.
>
> Helen Keller (1880–1968)

will be guilty of abandoning American ideals and betraying the decency and compassion Americans have long associated with those ideals. If Americans reject our social conscience, we make achievement of social justice impossible. When we look at faces of poor children, we are not only confronted with a moral dilemma in the present, but with a question about what kind of society America will be in the years to come.

TERMS AND DEFINITIONS

Ageism An alteration in feeling, belief, or behavior in response to an individual's or group's perceived age (Levy & Banaji, 2002)

Bait and switch An illegal strategy in which a merchant advertises a cheap product and when the customer comes in to purchase it, he or she is persuaded to buy a more expensive product

Classism An attitude, action, or institutional structure that subordinates or limits a person on the basis of his or her low socioeconomic status

Cultural classism The societal promotion of negative beliefs and practices that tend to portray poor, less educated, or socially unacceptable persons as deficient, inferior, and responsible for their own situation; the assumption of superiority by people or groups based on wealth, employment, education, or social standing

Individual classism Prejudiced attitudes and behavior against others based on the perception of level of income, education, or status as inferior, demonstrated whenever someone responds by saying or doing something degrading or harmful about persons whose income, education, or social standing is looked on as unacceptable

Institutional classism Established laws, customs, and practices in a society that allow systematic discrimination against low-income individuals or groups to the benefit of middle- or upper-class individuals or groups

Middle class A socioeconomic status determined partly by income and primarily by a cluster of attitudes, beliefs, and practices of someone not too poor to be considered dependent on others but not living in an ostentatious manner associated with being wealthy

Pawnshops Businesses that receive individual possessions as collateral for loans

Poverty levels Income levels established by the federal government based on earnings and the number of individuals in a family

Redlining The practice of banks and other lenders of designating certain areas, especially inner-city neighborhoods (ghettoes or barrios), as "deteriorating," which means they are viewed as bad risks for mortgage loans

Rent-to-own Businesses that offer merchandise on a rental basis to customers who cannot afford the purchase price of that merchandise, stipulating that at the end of the rental period the merchandise will become the property of the renter at an exorbitant cost

DISCUSSION EXERCISES

Exercise #1 Broadening the Wealth in America: Can We Avoid Economic Domination by the Wealthy?

The Proposal: Ideas for a more equitable distribution of economic resources in the United States have been implemented, including pension plans, profit sharing, the GI bill, FHA loans, and Social Security. Proponents argue that the money for the proposal below could be raised by increasing income tax on the wealthiest 40% of Americans (those making $80,000 or more) by 2%.

Directions: Review the plan. Does it seem to be a reasonable way to obtain funding to fulfill its objective? What special considerations might need to be made in its implementation?

Proposal

Every American would have a "wealth account" of $80,000 established for him or her at birth. Individuals could have access to this account upon turning twenty-one, but only upon graduation from high school. For the rest of their life, people could use this account to achieve desired goals, but anything taken from the account must be paid back. As an example of how the account could be used: eighteen-year-olds attending college would be permitted to access the account early to pay for college expenses (including the high school graduate trying to escape a violent and drug-ridden neighborhood); workers who are laid off from their job could live off the interest until they found a new job or they could pay for further training for a related or different occupation; a young couple who just had their first child and wanted to buy a house could use the money for a down payment; a truck driver could use the money to begin his or her own trucking company. Any of the interest or principal used from this "wealth account" would eventually be repaid so that when an individual died, the money plus interest from the wealth account would be reclaimed by the government and used to finance an account for another person. If an account did not have the full amount it

should have, the government would get to make the first claims on whatever assets the dead person left behind in order to get the full amount repaid.

(Adapted from Ackerman, B.A., & Alstott, A. (n.d.). $80,000 and a dream. The American Prospect Online. Retrieved December 22, 2003, from http://www.prospect.org/print/V11/16/ackerman-b.html)

Exercise #2 The Manager's Dilemma

Directions: The following dilemma is based on a true story. Read the description below and respond to the following questions: What would you do if you were the manager? What reasons would be primarily responsible for your decision?

You are the manager of a popular urban restaurant whose customers are primarily young professionals and office workers. The restaurant franchise has established strict rules for employee schedules with regard to how many hours an employee can work and what days and times employees must be available for work. These rules exist to reduce employees being paid to work overtime hours and to minimize the number of full-time employees eligible for benefits. Further, during their shift employees cannot leave work and then return, and they are not allowed to bring their children to the restaurant while they are working. All of your racially mixed wait staff are mothers (many are single parents) so the franchise rules create problems for taking care of their family obligations. To address their concerns, the women develop a plan and meet with you to discuss it.

They propose that employees commit to working for a minimum length of time during their shift—for example, four hours. Once those minimum hours are completed, they can leave if they need to take a child to the doctor, pick a child up from school, or meet some other obligation. The women have agreed to collaborate with each other to ensure that there will always be enough people working, especially during the busiest hours of the day. They ask that their children be allowed to come to the restaurant and eat lunch when their mother is getting off shortly after the lunch hour. Their proposal is based on the experience of a friend of one of your wait staff who works at another restaurant where they use this kind of flexible scheduling. The woman gives you the telephone number of that restaurant's manager.

When you call the manager, she says that the flexible scheduling has been in place for several years and it has worked well. In fact, she believes the schedule is the main reason why employee morale is high and turnover is low. She often sits with the children when they come to eat lunch, and even helps them with their homework. The manager admits that the franchise would probably not approve of the flexible scheduling if they knew about it, so she keeps two time sheets—one that she sends to the corporate office and another that she keeps with the actual hours that her employees have worked. The hours of work indicated for each employee on the official time sheet accurately reflect the hours actually worked according to the unofficial time sheet. The manager admits that she would probably be fired if her bosses discovered what she was doing, but she says the franchise is primarily interested in profit, and her restaurant has been even more profitable since she implemented the flexible schedule—largely because of low turnover. Asked why she has done this when it places her own job at risk, she said: "I just want to treat my employees as human beings; if I had to abide by the company rules, I would end up becoming a person I wouldn't like very much." Your employees ask you to think about their proposal and give them your decision in the next few days.

Adapted from Lisa Dodson (2009). *The Moral Underground: How Ordinary Americans Subvert an Unfair Economy.* New York, NY: The New Press.

REFERENCES

Abelda, R., Drago, R., & Shulman, S. (2004). *Unlevel playing fields*. New York, NY: McGraw-Hill.

Acs, G. (2011). *Downward mobility from the middle class: Waking up from the American Dream*. Washington, DC: The Pew Charitable Trusts.

Allen, J.T. (2004). Who lobbies for the cheaters? *U.S. News & World Report, 136*(14), 42.

Allison, L., & Lewis, C. (2001). *The cheating of America: How tax avoidance and evasion by the super rich are costing the country billions and what you can do about it*. New York, NY: Morrow.

American Federation of Labor. (2011). CEO pay: Feeding the 1%. *Executive Paywatch*. Retrieved October 30, 2011, from http://www.aflcio.org/corporatewatch/paywatch

Anyon, J. (2001). Inner cities, affluent suburbs, and unequal educational opportunity. In J.A. Banks & C.M. Banks (Eds.), *Multicultural education: Issues & perspectives* (4th ed., pp. 85–102). New York, NY: John Wiley.

Barnett, R. (2005, Fall). Ageism and sexism in the workplace. *Generations 29*: 25–30.

Barr, M.S. (2004). *Banking the poor: Policies to bring low-income Americans into the mainstream*. Washington, DC: The Brookings Institution.

BBC News. (2004, September 19). Work ageism affecting the young. Accessed January 3, 2009, from http://www.news.bbc.co.uk/1/hi/business/3668320.htm

Berliner, D.C. (2005, August). Our impoverished view of educational reform. *TCRecord*. Retrieved January 2, 2006, from http://www.tcrecord.org

Bernhardt, A., Milkman, R., & Theodore, N. (2009). Broken laws, unprotected workers. *The American Prospect*, 20(8), A3.

Bonilla-Silva, E. (2001). *White supremacy and racism in the post–civil rights era*. Boulder, CO: Lynne Rienner.

Bray, R. (2000). So how did I get here? In M. Adams, W.J. Blumenfeld, R. Castaneda, H.W. Hackman, M.L. Peters, & X. Zuniga (Eds.), *Readings for diversity and social justice* (pp. 425–429). New York, NY: Routledge.

Butler, R. (2008). *The longevity revolution: The benefits and challenges of living a long life*. New York, NY: Public Affairs.

Bytheway, B. (2005). Ageism. In M.L. Johnson (Ed.), *The Cambridge handbook of age and aging* (pp. 338–345). Cambridge, UK: Cambridge University Press.

Calasanti, T., & Slevin, K. (2001). *Gender, social inequalities, and aging*. New York, NY: Altamira Press, pp. 108–115.

Callahan, D. (2007, May). False choices on poverty. *The American Prospect, 18*(5), A12–A13.

Cawthorne, A. (2008). Elderly poverty: The challenge before us. *Center for American Progress*. Retrieved November 28, 2011, from www.americanprogress.org/issues/2008/07/elderly_poverty.html

Chaddock, G.R. (2011). Piece by piece, will Obama's health-care reform law be dismantled? *Christian Science Monitor*. Retrieved November 1, 2011, from www.csmonitor.com/USA/Politics/2011/1101/Piece-by-piece-will-Obama-s-health-care-reform-law-be-dismantled

Children's Defense Fund. (2011). *Child poverty in America 2010 fact sheet*. Retrieved October 30, 2011, from www.childrensdefense.org.child-research-data-publications

Children's Defense Fund. (2008). *Annual Report 2007*. Retrieved May 9, 2009, from http://www.childrendefensefund.org

Children's Defense Fund. (2001). *A Children's Defense Fund report: The state of America's children*. Boston, MA: Beacon.

Coles, G. (2008–2009, Winter). Hunger, academic success, and the hard bigotry of indifference. *Rethinking Schools, 23*(2), 34–37.

Collins, C. (2003). Tax wealth to broaden wealth. *The American Prospect, 14*(5), A6–A7.

Connection. (2011). *History of corporate executive wages*. Retrieved October 31, 2011, from http://connection.ebscohost.com/businessfinances/executive-pay

Connell, T. (2011). *Make work pay for us—CEO pay vs. the rest of us*. Retrieved October 31, 2011, from http://blog/aflcio.org/2011/10104

Cuddy, A.J., & Fiske, T. (2002). Doddering but dear: Process, content, and function in stereotyping of older persons. In T.D. Nelson (Ed.) *Ageism: Stereotyping and prejudice against older persons* (pp. 3–26). Cambridge, MA: A Bradford Book.

Dreier, P. (2004). *Reagan's legacy: Homelessness in America*. National Housing Institute. Retrieved November 9, 2011, from www.nhi.org/online/issues/135/reagan

Edelman, M.W. (2001). Introduction. *A Children's Defense Fund report: The state of America's children*. Boston, MA: Beacon.

Entwhistle, D., Alexander, K., & Olson, L.S. (2001, Fall). Keep the faucet flowing: Summer learning and home environment. *American Educator, 47*, 10–15, 47.

Extra! (2011) MisEducation Nation. *Extra!, 24*(11), 13–15.

Feagin, J., & Feagin, C.B. (1986). *Discrimination American style* (2nd ed.). Malabar, FL: Robert E. Krieger.

Fletcher-Hackwood, G. (2010). End financial discrimination against young people. Retrieved November 2, 2011, at www.thefword.org.uk/blog/2010/01/end_financial_d

Forbes. (2009). *The Forbes 400*. Retrieved May 10, 2009, from http://www.forbes.com

Foroohar, R. (2011). Whatever happened to upward mobility? *Time*, 178(19), 26–34.

Fraser, S. (2009). The good war and the workers. *The American Prospect, 20*(8), A18–A20.

Greenberg, M. (2007, May). Making poverty history. *The American Prospect, 18*(5), A3–A4.

Gullette, M.M. (2011). *Agewise: Fighting the new ageism in America*. Chicago, IL: The University of Chicago Press.

Gullette, M.M. (2004). *Aged by culture*. Chicago, IL: The University of Chicago Press.

Haskins, R., & Sawhill, I. (2007, May). Using carrots and sticks. *The American Prospect, 18*(5), A13–A15.

Haycock, K. (2001). Closing the achievement gap. *Educational Leadership, 58*(6), 6–11.

Heintz, J.S., & Folbre, N. (2000). Who owns how much? In M. Adams, W.J. Blumenfeld, R. Castaneda, H.W. Hackman, M.L. Peters, & X. Zuniga (Eds.), *Readings for diversity and social justice* (pp. 391–396). New York, NY: Routledge.

Hightower, J., & Frazer, P. (2010). Facts—not myths—about our economy. *The Hightower Lowdown, 12*(5), 1–4.

Hout, M., & Lucas, S.R. (2007). Narrowing the income gap between rich and poor. In P. Rothenberg (Ed.), *Race, class and gender in the United States: An integrated study* (7th ed.). New York, NY: Worth.

Isaacs, J.B., & Lyon, M.R. (2000). *A cross-state examination of families leaving welfare: Finding from the ASPE-funded leavers studies*. Presented at the National Association for Welfare Research and Statistics Workshop, August, Scottsdale, AZ. Available at http://www.dhhs.gov

Jairrels, V. (2008). *African Americans and standardized tests: The real reason for low test scores*. Sauk Village, IL: African American Images.

Johnson, D. (2011, February 14). *Nine pictures of the extreme income/wealth gap*. Retrieved October 31, 2011, from www.truth-out.org/nine-pictures-of-the-extreme-incomewealth-gap67743

Johnson, H.W. (1998). Public welfare and income maintenance. In *The social services: An introduction* (5th ed.). Itasca, IL: F. E. Peacock.

Johnson, R. (2007, December). From one generation to the next. *The American Prospect, 18*(12), A15–A16.

Johnson, T. (2010). Healthcare costs and U.S. competitiveness. *Council on Foreign Relations*. Retrieved October 31, 2011, from www.cfr.org/health-science-and-technology/healthcare-costs-us-competitiveness/p13325

Jones, G.R., & George, J.M. (2008). Managing diverse employees in a diverse environment. In *Contemporary management* (5th ed.). Boston, MA: McGraw-Hill.

Kahlenberg, R.D. (2009, Sept/Oct). Cutting class. *Washington Monthly, 4*(9/10), 83–85.

Kaiser Family Foundation. (2007). *Poverty rates by age, states (2006–2007), U.S. (2007)*. Accessed January 2, 2009, from http://www.statehealthfacts.org/comparebar.jsp?ind=10&cat=1

Kane, M. (1996). Fringe banks. In M. Hudson (Ed.), *Merchants of misery: How corporate America profits from poverty* (pp. 52–57). Monroe, ME: Common Courage Press.

Karp, S. (2006). Band-Aids or bulldozers: What's next for NCLB? *Rethinking Schools, 20*(3), 10–13.

Katz, M.B. (1986). *In the shadow of the poorhouse: A social history of welfare in America*. New York, NY: Basic Books.

Kirp, D.L. (2007, December). Nature, nurture, and destiny. *The American Prospect 18*(12), A19–A21.

Kite, M.E., & Wagner, L.S. (2002). Attitude toward older adults. In T.D. Nelson (Ed.), *Ageism: Stereotyping and prejudice against older persons* (pp. 129–161). Cambridge, MA: A Bradford Book.

Kivel, P. (2002). *Uprooting racism: How white people can work for racial justice* (rev. ed.). Gabriola Island, British Columbia: New Society Publishers.

Komisar, L. (1977). *Down and out in the USA: A history of public welfare* (rev. ed.). New York, NY: New Viewpoints.

Kozol, J. (2005). *The shame of the nation: The restoration of apartheid schooling in America*. New York, NY: Crown.

Lee, J. (2006). *Tracking achievement gaps and assessing the impact of NCLB on the gaps: An in-depth look into national and state reading and math outcomes*. Cambridge, MA: The Civil Rights Project at Harvard University.

Levin J., & Levin W.C. (1980). *Ageism: Prejudice and discrimination against the elderly*. Belmont, CA: Wadsworth Publishing Company.

Levy, B., & Banaji, M. (2002). Implicit ageism. In T. Nelson (Ed.), *Ageism*. London, England: MIT Press.

Lunn, E. (2005, January 11). Ageism affects young and old. *Hindu Times*, 1.

Macnicol, J. (2006). *Age discrimination: An historical and contemporary analysis*. Cambridge, UK: Cambridge University Press.

Management Issues. (2006, August 10). Younger workers more at risk of age discrimination, p. 4.

Mandela, N. (2010). *Conversations with myself*. New York, NY: Farrar, Straus and Giroux.

Massey, D.S. (2007). *Categorically unequal: The American stratification system*. New York, NY: The Russell Sage Foundation.

Mathis, W.J. (2003). No Child Left Behind: Costs and benefits. *Kappan*. Retrieved June 9, 2009, from http://www.pdkintl.org/kappan/k0305mat.htm, *Phi Delta Kappa International*.

McKernan, S., Ratcliffe, C., & Cellini, S.R. (2009). Understanding poverty. *The Urban Institute*. Retrieved November 8, 2009, from www.urban.org/uploaded-pdf/411956_transitioningpoverty.pdf

Mead, L. (2000). The twilight of liberal welfare reform. *Public Interest, 139*, 22–35.

Miners, Z. (2009). *Charter schools might not be better*. Retrieved November 8, 2011, from www.usnews.com/education/blogs/on-education/2009/06/17/charter-schools-might-not-be-better

Minutaglio, B. (1996). Prince of pawns. In M. Hudson (Ed.), *Merchants of misery: How corporate America profits from poverty* (pp. 58–70). Monroe, ME: Common Courage.

Montepare, J.M., & Zebrowitz, L.A. (2002). A social-developmental view of ageism. In T.D. Nelson (Ed.), *Ageism: Stereotyping and prejudice against older persons* (pp. 77–125). Cambridge, MA: A Bradford Book.

National Center on Family Homelessness. (2011). *Homeless children: America's new outcasts*. Retrieved November 10, 2011, from www.nhch.org/Shelter-Health/ToolKitA/A2HomelessChildren.pdf

National Coalition for the Homeless. (2006). *McKinney-Vento act*. Retrieved November 10, 2011, from www.nationalhomeless.org/publications/facts/Mckinney.pdf

National Law Center on Homelessness and Poverty. (2011). *"Simply unacceptable": Homelessness and the human right to housing in the United States*. Retrieved

November 18, 2011, from www.nlch.org/content/pubs/SimplyUnacceptableReport.pdf

Nelson, T.D. (2009). Ageism. In T.D. Nelson (Ed.), *Handbook of prejudice, stereotyping, and discrimination* (pp. 431–440). New York, NY: Psychology Press.

Owen, D., & Doerr, M. (1999). *None of the above: The truth behind the SATs* (rev. ed.). Lanham, MD: Rowman Littlefield.

Pasupathi, M., & Lockenhoff, C.E. (2002). Ageist behavior. In T.D. Nelson (Ed.), *Ageism: Stereotyping and prejudice against older persons* (pp. 201–246). Cambridge, MA: A Bradford Book.

Phillips, K. (1990). Wealth and favoritism. In *The politics of rich and poor: Wealth and the American electorate in the Reagan aftermath.* New York, NY: Random House.

Phillips, K. (2003). How wealth defines power. *The American Prospect, 14*(5), A8–A9.

Pipher, M. (2002). *The middle of everywhere: The world's refugees come to our town.* New York, NY: Harcourt.

Prosser, T. (2009). Executive compensation and the economic crisis. *International Training Center of the International Labor Organization.* Retrieved April 3, 2012, from http://forum2009.itcilo.org/en/thematical-papers/executive-compensation-and-the-economic-crisis/view.

Ratcliffe, J. (2009). A bridge to somewhere. *The American Prospect, 20*(6), A4–A6.

Rifkin, J. (2004). *The European dream: How Europe's vision of the future is quietly eclipsing the American dream.* New York, NY: Jeremy P. Tarcher/Penguin.

Rodgers, H. Jr. (2006). *American poverty in a new era of reform.* Armonk, NY: M.E. Sharpe.

Rothstein, R. (2009). Equalizing opportunity. *American Educator, 33* (2), 4–7, 45–46.

Sandefur, G.D., & Cook, S. (1998). Permanent exits from public assistance: The impact of duration, family and work. *Social Forces, 77*(2), 763–789.

Schorr, A.L. (2001). *Welfare reform: Failure and remedies.* Westport, CT: Praeger.

Schwartz-Nobel, L. (2002). *Growing up empty: The hunger epidemic in America.* New York, NY: HarperCollins.

Schwarz, J. (2000). *Fighting poverty with virtue: Moral reform and America's urban poor, 1825–2000.* Bloomington: Indiana University Press.

Scott, J., & Leonhardt, D. (2005). Shadowy lines that still divide. *Class Matters.* New York, NY: Times Books.

Sheehan, M. (2004). Tax breaks for the rich—or public programs for everyone? In *Dollars & Sense (Ed.), The Wealth Inequality Reader* (pp. 40–41). Cambridge, MA: Dollars & Sense—Economic Affairs Bureau.

Shepard, D.S., Setren, E., & Cooper, D. (2011). Hunger in America: Suffering we all pay for. *Center for American Progress.* Retrieved November 8, 2011, from www.americanprogress.org/issues/2011/10/hunger

Shorris, E. (2001). *Latinos: A biography of the people.* New York, NY: W.W. Norton.

Sklar, H. (2005, September). Growing gulf between rich and rest of America. *Raise the Floor.* Retrieved June 1, 2009, from http://www.ms.foundation.org

Sklar, H. (1998). CEO greed is out of control. *Z Magazine.* Retrieved June 10, 2009, from http://www.thirdworldtraveler.com

Spriggs, W.E. (2007, May). The changing face of poverty in America. *The American Prospect, 18*(5), A5–A7.

Stein, Z., & Susser, M. (1970). Mutability of intelligence and epidemiology of mild mental retardation. *Review of Educational Research, 40,* 29–68.

Tavernise, S. (2011, Sep. 13). Soaring poverty casts spotlight on "lost decade." *New York Times.* Retrieved November 7, 2011, from www.nytimes.com/2011/09/14/us/14census.html

Taylor, H. (2000, May 3). The public tends to blame the poor, the unemployed, and those on welfare for their problems. *Harris Poll #24.* Retrieved May 1, 2009, from http://www.harrisinteractive.com/harris_poll/index.asp?PID=87

USA Today. (2003, October 7). Young workers say their age holds them back, p. 3.

U.S. Bureau of Labor Statistics. (2008). Highlights of women's earnings in 2007. Retrieved June 12, 2009, from http://www.bls.gov

U.S. Census Bureau. (2010). *Poverty thresholds for 2010 by size of family and number of related children under 18 years.* Retrieved October 30, 2011, from http://www.census.gov

U.S. Department of Education. (2008). *Questions and answers on special education and homelessness.* Office of Special Education and Rehabilitative Services. Retrieved November 10, 2011, from www.doe.sd.gov/oess/documents/SPED_IEP_Homeless.pdf

U.S. Department of Health and Human Services. (2004, November). *6th annual report to Congress.* Office of Family Assistance. Retrieved May 15, 2009, from http:// acf.hhs.gov/programs/ofa/data-reports/

U.S. Department of Labor Statistics. (2011). *Economic news release: Table 1.* Retrieved October 30, 2011, from www.bls.gov/news/release/wkyeng/t01.htm

Weaver, R.K. (2000). *Ending welfare as we know it.* Washington, DC: Brookings Institution Press.

Webley, K. (2011, Oct. 10). The preschool wars. *Time, 178*(14), 47–49.

White, D. (2011). *Profile of Race to the Top.* Retrieved November 14, 2011, from http://usliberals.about .com/od/education/a/RacetotheTop.htm

Whitman, D., & Purcell, P. (2007). Topics in aging: Income and poverty among older Americans in 2004.

In L.O. Randal (Ed.), *Aging and the elderly: Psychology, sociology and health* (pp. 177–196). New York, NY: Nova Science Publishers.

Wilson, W.J. (1996). *When work disappears: The world of the new urban poor.* New York, NY: Knopf.

Wolfe, A. (1998). *One nation, after all: What middle-class Americans really think about God, country, family, racism, welfare, immigration, homosexuality, work, the right, the left, and each other.* New York, NY: Viking Penguin.

Zinn, H. (1999). *A people's history of the United States.* New York, NY: HarperCollins.

Zuckerman, M.B. (2004a). America's high anxiety. *U.S. News & World Report, 130*(9), 84.

Zuckerman, M.B. (2004b). An intolerable free ride. *U.S. News & World Report, 136*(17), 80.

Chapter 10

Sexism: Where the Personal Becomes Political

"Male supremacy has kept woman down. It has not knocked her out."

Claire Boothe Luce (1903–1987)

Segregation is the normal pattern for the relationship between dominant and oppressed groups. Most Americans have been segregated according to such differences as race, social class, and disabilities. Sexism, however, is a unique form of oppression because people who belong to the dominant and subordinate groups live together. Andrzejewski (1996) defines **sexism** as "an attitude, action, or institutional structure that subordinates or limits a person on the basis of sex" (p. 56). Although sexism is customarily regarded as the oppression and exploitation of women, the concept of sexism includes both men and women, and it is a type of oppression stemming from cultural norms for femininity and masculinity that prevent us from achieving our full potential as human beings. Racism and most other forms of oppression are influenced by the isolation and alienation of dominant and subordinate groups; yet because daily personal relationships exist between most women and men, we believe we have intrinsic, intimate knowledge about sexism.

How does daily interaction between men and women influence sexist attitudes?

Most people grow up in families in which they are likely to have close relationships with someone of the opposite sex—brother/sister, parent/child, grandparent/grandchild—and they often enjoy some degree of affection between males and females. Because they believe they genuinely like women, men are more likely to take gender issues lightly, to joke about them and discuss them without the fear and discomfort that usually affect discussions of racism or other forms of oppression. Men in our society are also more likely to make insensitive comments about women that they would never make about people of color.

To illustrate male insensitivity, consider the use of the *natural* argument. White Americans used to say people of color were naturally—meaning genetically—inferior to whites; this belief persisted through the first half of the twentieth century but is now mostly relegated to the ranks of white supremacy groups. Yet many white men in the United States have employed the natural argument in discussing male and female differences, usually to defend their beliefs about male superiority. To justify their argument, men may claim that "the male animal" is always larger than the female, illustrating nature's intent to make males the aggressive protector of females. Gould (1983) corrected this assumption by explaining that larger males are only true for mammals, and not all of them, whereas in the entire animal world—think of insects and fish—the more typical pattern is that females are larger than males.

In conversation, Americans are often more comfortable talking about gender issues than racial issues; men and women joke about the "war between the sexes" where any strategy is acceptable because "all's fair in love and war." When Virginia congressman Howard Smith amended the Civil Rights Act of 1964 by adding gender, he was not expressing concern about gender discrimination in this country; as a southerner, he wanted the bill defeated. Smith gambled that the "absurd" addition of women as a group whose civil rights needed protecting would appear so ridiculous that it would prevent or at least delay the bill's passage. Needless to say, the tactic backfired. The majority of members of the House of Representatives and the Senate were committed to voting for civil rights and the bill was passed (Branch, 1998).

Cultural Sexism

Cultural sexism in the United States originated in the gender roles brought by the English and other European colonists. Historically, men were expected to be in a superior role as head of the household while women were assigned the subordinate role as the person responsible for domestic chores, including child care. English law stipulated that any property a woman owned became her husband's property after marriage, and any money a wife earned had to be given to her husband. As Sir William Blackstone expressed it, "The husband and wife are one, and the husband is that one" (Collins, 2003, p. 12). These gender roles shaped our culture's ideals for masculine and feminine behavior in ways that have been modified but not radically changed since those early years. Perhaps these historical expectations help explain the results of a study reporting that when asked to estimate their IQ scores, men would consistently overestimate their scores while women consistently underestimated theirs (Hallinan, 2009). If history has played a role in creating such attitudes, it is important to understand that history.

What gender biases did women confront in the earliest years of the United States?

Although men were expected to provide for the family's needs, from the beginning women went beyond the limits of their gender role. To support the family, some women took in laundry or sewing, taught neighbor children, or made things to sell or barter. During the American Revolution—and all subsequent American wars—women assumed additional responsibilities while their husbands were away. Women joined together during the American Revolution to protest against certain merchants who were suspected of inflating prices. Angered by one exceptionally greedy merchant,

a group of women attacked the man, took his keys, and helped themselves to the coffee stored at his warehouse (Riley, 1986a).

Because of women's active involvement during the war, it is not surprising that Abigail Adams urged her husband John to make sure women's rights were protected in the Constitution then being written. Although an unmarried woman could own property and engage in business activities on her own, a married woman could not. She could not sign a contract or request a loan without her husband's approval. In the early 1800s, American women continued to earn extra money at home, producing four times

> And in the new code of laws . . . remember the ladies, and be more generous and favorable to them than your ancestors. Do not put such unlimited power into the hands of the husbands. Remember, all men would be tyrants if they could . . . [women] are determined to foment a rebellion and will not hold ourselves bound by any laws in which we have no voice or representation.
>
> Abigail Adams (1744–1818)

the textiles as were manufactured in textile factories. Women also began to protest against the common law stipulation that their property and earnings must be given to their husbands.

How and when did forms of discrimination change?

Activists such as Elizabeth Cady Stanton and Susan B. Anthony lobbied successfully in many states for women's property rights, but they were not as successful in their demand for women's right to vote. By the 1830s, individual states began to pass legislation to grant women the right to own property and keep their earnings. In 1848, in Seneca Falls, New York, women—and men supporting women's rights—met and signed a declaration of women's rights claiming full citizenship rights for all women, including the right to vote.

As more textile factories were built and more young women employed, factory owners exploited them, forcing workers into unions to strike for better pay and working conditions. With the number of schools increasing and so few men willing to take the low salary of a teacher, public schools reluctantly began to hire women, reducing the salary even further. One Ohio superintendent boasted that he was able to hire twice as many female teachers as other school districts that hired only men (Collins, 2003).

In addition to demanding gender equality, women became active in the anti-slavery movement. The Grimke sisters shocked those who felt it wasn't women's place to speak in public, especially not passionately about political issues. Women who defied society's norms provoked harsh criticism, as illustrated by this explanation of their "unladylike" behavior: "Some of them are old maids, whose personal charms were never very attractive and who have been sadly slighted by the masculine gender" (Evans, 1989, p. 102). These unladylike women continued to lobby for gender equality and against slavery as the Civil War approached.

What effect did the Civil War have on women's demands for gender equality?

During the Civil War, the wives of soldiers once again had to provide for themselves and their children. Women were hired to be office workers, government workers, factory workers, teachers, and nurses, yet they encountered a gauntlet of critics. Their morals were questioned and they were said to be a distraction to male workers. After the war, women continued to work and to be active politically, lobbying for such diverse causes as women's suffrage, immigrant issues, and temperance.

After the Civil War, many people migrated west, more men than women. In 1869, Wyoming became the first state to give women voting rights. The legislators also passed laws to guarantee married women's right to own property and to require equal pay for female teachers. With so few women in Wyoming, the passage of this legislation gave the *Cheyenne Leader* some hope of seeing "quite an immigration of ladies to Wyoming" (Collins, 2003, p. 235). Perhaps the need for women explains why the first twelve states giving women the right to vote were all in the West.

In the late 1800s, Congress passed a bill outlawing contraception, perhaps hoping that women with children would be too busy to be politically

active. American men usually did not appreciate women's political activities, especially those of college-educated women who provided much of the leadership. Studies warned women that only 28% of college-educated women would marry. A book by a professor at Harvard's medical school alleged that the rigors of a college education created a conflict between the brain and uterus, resulting in infertility (Faludi, 2006). Scientists like Paul Broca engaged in a study of brain size based on the theory that larger brains equaled greater intelligence. Not surprisingly, white male researchers reported that white males had the largest brains, with white women—and people of color—far behind. Based on his studies, Le Bon published his conclusions in 1879 about women's inferior intelligence:

> This inferiority is so obvious that no one can contest it for a moment; only its degree is worth discussion. All psychologists who have studied the intelligence of women . . . recognize today that they represent the most inferior forms of human evolution and that they are closer to children and savages than to an adult, civilized man. (Gould, 1981, pp. 104–105)

Still, new employment opportunities for women arose as the establishment of department stores required personnel who could assist predominantly female customers. By 1900, more than a third of all clerical workers were women; twenty years later, women would be the majority. Women already constituted the majority of teachers, and their numbers steadily increased among librarians, social workers, and nurses (Evans, 1989). But as women tried to redefine their "place" in the early twentieth century, they encountered strong resistance.

What progress and what resistance to women's rights occurred in the early twentieth century?

By 1910, 40% of college students were women, rising to 50% by 1920. Women held a third of all federal government jobs and pursued a greater variety of careers than ever before, but they tended to be unmarried. In the 1890s, only 3% of married women worked outside the home, increasing to 10% by the 1920s (Collins, 2003). Nevertheless, many women were politically active, especially for the cause of women's suffrage, and a few began to call themselves *feminists*. Using recently created psychological language, critics called them *lesbians*, accusing them of hating men. Yet women's efforts on behalf of suffrage succeeded after almost a century of struggle. Women cast their first votes for president in 1920; ironically, one year later, the first Miss America Beauty Pageant was held in Atlantic City, New Jersey, reminding women of their place and purpose.

With the trauma of World War I becoming a memory and the economy booming, Americans seemed uninterested in social issues. Members of the National Women's Party went to every state legislature to lobby for their proposed Equal Rights Amendment (ERA), stating, "Men and women shall have equal rights throughout the United States and every place subject to its jurisdiction" (Riley, 1986b, p. 81). In 1923, they even managed to get a congressional hearing on the ERA, but they seemed to encounter an unsympathetic audience wherever they went.

When the Great Depression of the 1930s arrived, men and women struggled simply to survive. With high unemployment and few jobs, employers preferred to hire men until World War II began.

As men left the workforce to join the military, women continued the pattern from earlier wars by doing the work that men were not available to do.

Did women workers during World War II prove their competence?

During the war, women became the majority (57%) of the workforce for the first time (Faludi, 2006). Several scientific studies from the 1930s and 1940s proved how research could be manipulated to support the prevailing needs in American society: When jobs were scarce during the Great Depression, studies concluded that menstruation reduced women's ability to be effective at work. One researcher even described the effects as debilitating; later, that same researcher conducted a study of working women during World War II and reported that menstruation caused no adverse effects on their ability to perform their jobs (Tavris, 1999).

Wartime women workers were praised for the quality of their work (see Figure 10.1), including

FIGURE 10.1

Advertisements like the one on the left glorified efforts of working women during World War II. Although the pictures such as the one below often depicted white women, a significant number of wartime workers were women of color.

Source: (left) N.S. National Archives; (right) Courtesy FDR Library, Hyde Park, New York.

advertising campaigns like the one celebrating "Rosie the Riveter," but no one expected them to stay in those jobs permanently—no one except the women. Seventy-five percent of women surveyed wanted to keep their jobs after the war. But industry had other ideas: Businesses that had praised the women's work during the war suddenly found them to have "bad attitudes" or to be incompetent. The aircraft industry was one of the first to act, firing over 800,000 women two months after the war ended (Faludi, 2006). The aggressive actions of the business community and the blatant bias of the media forced women out of the jobs they had proved they could do well.

What role did the media play in women being forced out of their jobs?

In 1945, a *Fortune* magazine poll reported that a majority of Americans believed that if a husband earned enough money to provide for his family, his wife should not work—even if she wanted to (Evans, 1989). The media was telling women to stop taking the jobs that men should have and go home where they belonged. By 1946, more than 3 million women were eliminated from well-paying industrial jobs. More than 80% did not quit working, but took jobs with lower salaries instead.

> I'm just a person trapped inside a woman's body.
>
> Elayne Boosler (Contemporary)

Three years after the war, the United States was the only nation in the Western Hemisphere that refused to sign a statement issued by the newly created United Nations supporting equal rights for women (Faludi, 2006).

From 1946 to 1952, there were huge increases in births, creating what is called the baby boomer generation. Women were reinforced in their role as wives and mothers. Evans (1989) described a 1950s *Look* magazine celebrating the "wondrous creature" who married young, had babies, and was still more feminine "than the emancipated girl of the 1920s" (p. 249). An additional factor that discouraged women from working was the growth of suburbs, which isolated them from cities, the site of most jobs. Still, women resisted these efforts to keep them in their place.

How did women respond to the pressure to stay home and not have a career?

After reaching a peak of 50% in 1930, the number of women college students decreased to 35%. In the 1950s, more women enrolled in college. Echoing research a half century earlier, a Cornell University study warned that 65% of college women were much more likely not to get married (Faludi, 2006). But women continued to enroll and continued to work, especially middle-class married women. Evans (1989) reported that middle-class married women "entered the labor force faster than any other group in the population through the 1950s and 1960s" (p. 254). By 1980, women represented 43% of the workforce and they were attending college in record numbers.

A 1986 Harvard–Yale study predicted that if women postponed marriage to get a college diploma, they would find few marriage partners available. According to the study, women had a 20% chance of marrying if they were thirty years old, a 5% chance at thirty-five, and a 1.3% chance at forty. But the prediction was based on an erroneous assumption: Earlier studies of marriage patterns had found that women tended to marry men two to three years older, and that assumption was used to produce the results of the Harvard–Yale study. By the 1980s, this pattern had changed as more women were marrying men closer to their age and even younger. Two other studies reported findings contradicting the conclusions of the Harvard–Yale study, but the popular press did not report on them (Faludi, 2006), once again revealing a sexist bias in our culture.

What sexist messages still exist in American culture and how are they being addressed?

For decades there have been (and continue to be) professions that are male dominated, and traditional terms such as *policemen, firemen,* and *mailmen* imply that these jobs are exclusively for men. Feminists have long recognized such gender prejudice in language, and they have been committed to changing the language by replacing sexist terms

> Culture is the medium through which children fashion their individual and collective identities.
>
> Henry A. Giroux (1943–)

with nonsexist alternatives (Arliss, 1991; Nilsen, 1977a, 1977b). Their efforts are reflected in language changes that have become common usage, such as *police officer, fire fighter,* and *letter carrier.* In addition to including women, this language is more descriptive of the job responsibilities. Since these examples show that language has changed, have attitudes and behaviors changed as well?

Studies suggest some evidence of changing attitudes among youth. In the past, American high school senior boys listed more than twice as many possible career options as did their female peers; few careers appeared on both lists. In a longitudinal study, Wulff and Steitz (1997) reported that junior high school students indicated interest in 45 careers—and 12 of them (26.7%) were identified by both girls and boys. Just before high school graduation, these same students expressed interest in 68 different careers, with 16 (23.5%) identified by both genders. According to data from the National Center for Educational Statistics, the number of women graduating with a master's degree or PhD in engineering has jumped from 1% in 1970 to 25% today. In addition, the number of women graduating with a bachelor's or master's degree in physical sciences and technology has gone from 14% to 41%, and women graduating with a bachelor's or master's degree in natural resources and agriculture increased from 9% to 50% (NCES, 2010).

Even with these impressive increases, traditional occupations continue to exert a strong attraction for both women and men. For example, women still constitute 80% or more of students graduating with bachelor's or master's degrees in education or health professions; therefore, even though high school graduates today, especially women, are more likely to pursue a nontraditional career than in the past, the numbers are still small—15% for women and 8% for men (Bernstein, 2004; NCES, 2010).

Increased use of nonsexist language may not be solely responsible for gender differences reported in career choice studies, but feminists continue to address changes in language that conveys a sexist perception that certain jobs are for men only or that men are more significant in our culture. Opponents question the impact of their efforts, insisting that changing sexist terms in our language is a trivial and ineffective way to change sexist attitudes. Yet there are examples of language being changed to accommodate men. After men won the right to work in the formerly all-female occupation of stewardess, airlines uniformly and rapidly revised the name to *flight attendant.* If it was so easy to change the language to be inclusive of men, why can't women be similarly accommodated?

To address sexism in our language, feminists have lobbied professional organizations, businesses, and institutions to promote the use of **inclusive language** (terms that include both men and women). In response, several organizations have changed the guidelines in their writing manuals to promote nonsexist language as preferred for their professional publications. The style manual of the American Psychological Association includes writing conventions employing language free of sexist implications (see Table 10.1). Despite such progress, feminist scholars continue to confront sexist language reflected in common words and phrases. Do we have a man-made product if it is manufactured in a factory employing only women? Can an organization "man the desk" with women? Does brotherly love include sisters? Does the opinion of the common man include women, or are women "uncommon"? Alternatives for sexist terms exist: a product is handmade, women can staff the desk, and the average person can give his or her opinion.

In addition to terms that exclude women, feminists also argue that sexist language often involves a distortion of reality. For example, using the common expression "founding fathers" denies the importance of women's historical role in the establishment of this country. The presence of immigrant families distinguished the settlements in what became the United States from New World settlements of the French (primarily men—trappers and hunters) and Spanish (primarily soldiers—conquistadores). Evans (1989) insists that compared to New World settlements of other nations, the presence of women and children in the English colonies had a definite impact on how American society evolved, and that an accurate picture of our nation's historical development is distorted by language denying

TABLE 10.1 Language Recommended by the American Psychological Association

Problematic	Gender Preferred
man a project	staff a project, hire personnel, employ staff
man-machine interface	user-system interface, person-system interface, human-computer interface
manpower	workforce, personnel, workers, human resources
man's search for knowledge	the search for knowledge
mothering	parenting, nurturing [or specify exact behavior]
The authors acknowledge the assistance of Mrs. John Smith	The authors acknowledge the assistance of Jane Smith.
cautious men and timid women	cautious women and men, cautious people, timid men and women, timid people

Source: APA Publication Manual (5th ed.), pp. 71–72, 74–75.

women's presence. Although feminists have made a good effort to eliminate negative terms, there is still much to be done to change sexist language.

For example, there is a pattern of condescending language toward women illustrated by the use of diminutive endings such as "poetess." Although the Academy Awards still has a "Best Actress" category, most women who receive the award refer to themselves as actors. American feminists have also explained that the term *coed* is a condescending reference from an era when men believed that women lacked the intelligence required for college studies—comparable to the condescending phrase *colored people* for African Americans. Colleges permitting women to attend were "coeducational"; therefore, the term *coed* reflects the historic perception of women as intellectually inferior to men. Oberlin College became the first coeducational campus in 1833. Although the college deserves credit for offering the opportunity, women admitted to Oberlin were required to meet one additional condition in order to attend: they had to agree to do the laundry for Oberlin's male students (Sadker & Sadker, 1994). This illustrates the reality that change is usually resisted, and rarely occurs without some sacrifice.

Another sexist pattern in American English is the consistent denigration of aging women, reinforcing the importance of female appearance: Women are valued only if they are beautiful. English novelist George Meredith argued that women die twice—their first death occurs when they lose their beauty.

Attractive young women are referred to as "kittenish," but with age they become "catty." The sexy young "chick" becomes the "old biddy" who "henpecks" her husband. And speaking of marriage, a man is considered a "good catch," but a woman is a "ball and chain." Our cultural history shows a persistent tendency to portray marriage as bad for men, whereas women should get married as soon as possible. Although such attitudes are not as intense today and many young women are waiting much later to get married, the perception persists that the unmarried woman is to be pitied, whereas the bachelor is envied. Women still have a bridal shower to celebrate the marriage while men traditionally have a stag

> The limits of my language are the limits of my world.
>
> Ludwig Wittgenstein (1889–1951)

party to mourn the groom's last night of freedom. Is there any evidence that marriage is such a desirable state for women and such a terrible burden for men?

What do studies say about who benefits from marriage in our culture?

Previously, studies found that married men tended to have fewer mental and physical health problems than single men; however, married women have more mental and physical health problems than single women (National Center for Health Statistics, 1999; Tavris & Wade, 1984). More women than men seek therapy for emotional problems, and the majority are married. Results from recent studies have challenged the previous studies, arguing that men and women both benefit from marriage. Simon (2002) reported that unmarried men and women were more likely to suffer from depression than men and women in stable marriages and that unmarried men were more likely to report alcohol abuse than married men. These studies would still seem to contradict the traditional belief that only women benefit from marriage.

Individual Sexism

As a result of learning sexist attitudes from our culture and from the sexist attitudes of others, people of both genders may engage in **individual sexism** involving prejudiced attitudes and actions against women or men because of rigid beliefs about gender and gender roles. Although both men and women can become "male chauvinists," they can also choose to be "feminists" in support of gender equality.

What does it mean to be a "male chauvinist" or a "feminist"?

The term "chauvinist" is reported to have originated with a Frenchman named Chauvin, a zealous soldier intensely loyal to Napoleon Bonaparte. To be a *chauvinist* has evolved to designate someone who believes in the superiority of someone or something (Partridge, 2009). In Chapter 3, Kimmel (2006) referred to people being chauvinistic about their culture. French scholars have been accused of being chauvinistic about their language, as demonstrated by their attempts to prevent foreign words, especially American phrases—"le hamburger" or "le week-end"—from polluting their native tongue. To call someone a male chauvinist is to accuse that person, who could be either male or female, of believing men are superior to women. A **male chauvinist** is a person who believes that men ought to be the leaders and decision makers and women should be subordinate. It is interesting that there are American men who publicly declare

themselves male chauvinists, yet they would bristle at being called racists or bigots.

Confusion exists also with the word *feminist* and with those labeled as *feminists*. Too many people perceive a feminist as an angry woman; our media has reinforced that view by focusing on feminists who represent radical perspectives. In reality, a **feminist** is a woman—or a man—who advocates for the personal, social, and economic equality of women. The goal of feminist activists is to increase the opportunities available for both men and women as part of the larger goal of eliminating traditional, stereotypical gender roles. To eliminate gender stereotypes, feminists have advocated an-

> People call me feminist whenever I express sentiments that differentiate me from a doormat or a prostitute.
>
> Dame Rebecca West (1892–1983)

drogyny, a concept that promotes interchangeability of female and male roles or responsibilities in all areas beyond fundamental biological ones.

What does it mean to be androgynous?

Androgyny has been confused with the unisex concept illustrated by unisex clothing, hair styling, and toilets, but the unisex concept denies differences between men and women and advocates treating members of both genders as if they were exactly the same. **Androgyny** is the belief that men and women share a variety of human traits that should be encouraged in both, as opposed to fostering certain traits in each gender based on traditional cultural stereotypes about masculinity and femininity (Tavris & Wade, 1984).

Androgynous people respond to situations as needed, without being limited by their gender. If a situation calls for aggressive behavior, an androgynous person responds aggressively; if the situation requires a nurturing response, the androgynous person is nurturing. The person's gender does not matter because aggression and nurturance are traits every human being possesses. Does each androgynous person respond the same way in a given situation? No, because each individual is different, but if everyone in a society were androgynous, the differences between people would derive from their individual abilities and preferences, not from artificial differences created by teaching children to conform to rigid stereotypes about being male or female. Many feminists believe that promoting androgyny from childhood could have a positive impact on the traditional ideas about gender roles that contribute to a serious problem for women in this society: aggressive and abusive behaviors of men that are often harmful to women physically, socially, and psychologically.

What kind of abuse do women encounter in the United States?

According to a Bureau of Justice study, almost 3.5 million adult women in the United States are stalked each year (75% of them are stalked by someone they know, with 30% of these women being stalked by a current or former intimate partner). In this study, 25% of the victims report stalkers using technology such as monitoring them with global positioning systems (GPS) or sending them unwanted messages via email or instant messaging (Stalking Resource Center, 2009). Almost 250,000 women in the United States are sexually assaulted annually, meaning that a sexual assault occurs every two minutes (525,600 minutes in a non-leap year divided by 250,000 victims; the math is simple). One out of six American women have been victims of sexual assault, and almost 75% of these assaults were committed by someone the victim knew. Approximately 44% of the victims of sexual assault are under the age of 18 (15% are younger than 12 years old), and 93% knew their attacker (RAINN, 2009).

As high as these numbers are, experts say the actual number of incidents is even higher. According to Gonnerman (2005), 73% of domestic violence incidents are not reported; more than 60% of women who did not report such an incident said they did not think the police would believe them. This is unfortunate because police officers are much more likely to arrest an abusive husband today. Responding to reports of domestic violence has proven to be a main source of injury to officers, especially when the abuser is a repeat offender, so many cities and states have passed laws calling for an aggressive police action in response to domestic violence. These laws typically call for the arrest and prosecution of the abuser based on evidence gathered by the police, and not on whether or not the victim presses charges (Catania, 2005).

Rape is a significant aspect of the violence against women in America; almost 90,000 women are victims of rape annually, which means a woman is raped every six minutes. Young women are especially vulnerable. One survey reported that almost 58% of rape victims were raped when they were 12 to 24 years old, and half of all date rapes occur among teenagers (American Bar Association, 2006; U.S. Department of Justice, 2009). There is often confusion when discussing rape because it has a history of being misrepresented. In 1927, the Federal Bureau of Investigation defined rape as "the carnal knowledge of a female, forcibly and against her will," but such a narrow definition excluded oral rape, anal rape, male rape, penetration by an object, and more. In 2012, the FBI finally issued a revised definition of **rape**: "The penetration, no matter how slight, of the vagina or anus with any body part or object, or oral penetration by a sex organ of another person, without the consent of the victim" (FBI, 2012). The new definition not only addresses some of the past misunderstandings

> There is no difference between being raped and being run over by a truck, except afterwards men ask if you liked it.
>
> Marge Piercy (1936–)

about rape, but also it should enhance the gathering of data with regard to this crime.

How has rape been misunderstood in the United States?

As the twentieth century was ending, *Newsweek* released a cover story on rape. Three fourths of the article was about "stranger rape"; the last section addressed the issue of "acquaintance rape," including date rape. The emphasis was the reverse of what really happens: Stranger rape accounts for about a third of all reported rapes and only 10% of college rapes (Sampson, 2003). It is important to recognize misperceptions about rape in order to understand the reality of that experience. Some generally conceded myths and realities about rape are listed in the box.

MYTH: Rape is an act of sexual arousal caused by an attractive, sexy woman who stimulated such sexual tension and passion that the man could not control himself.

REALITY: Rape is an act of power and humiliation, and any woman of any age is a potential victim regardless of her physical appearance.

MYTH: Rapes usually occur in dark alleys or poorly lit parking lots where the woman is isolated and therefore vulnerable.

REALITY: More than 60% of rapes occur in the victim's home or in a place where the woman would normally feel safe—the home of a friend, relative, or neighbor.

MYTH: Rapes are usually committed by violent strangers concealed somewhere usually at night waiting for an unwitting and unknown victim.

REALITY: Almost 66% of rapes are committed by someone the victim knows, such as a lover, a friend, a relative, or an acquaintance; other potential rapists may be trusted authority figures such as a teacher, a minister, a counselor, or a therapist.

MYTH: Because many women read and enjoy romance novels that typically include rape scenes, these women must fantasize about rape and secretly want to be raped.

REALITY: Romance novels are exciting fantasy adventures that tend to portray sex in terms of seduction. Although women may fantasize about being seduced by some handsome man, such fantasies bear no relationship to the brutality, violence, and violation associated with rape. It is well documented that boys and men enjoy reading novels and watching movies and television shows filled with murder and violence. Does that mean they secretly want to be murdered or assaulted?

Almost 18 million women have been the victims of rape or attempted rape in their lifetimes (RAINN, 2009). As high as that statistic is, as well as the other statistics cited earlier, law enforcement officials say this data would be even higher if all of the rapes and attempted rapes were reported.

Why do women choose not to report a rape or attempted rape?

Rape is an underreported crime, and feminists have argued that the one out of six rate that is reported for rape is conservative. Because of changes in police departments' processing of rape cases and new guidelines for rape trials, this crime is now more likely to be reported. Still, fear affects a woman's decision to report a rape. According to MacKinnon (1987, p. 82), victims have given four reasons for not reporting a rape:

Threats: Rapists often threaten to return and to inflict even more violence if victims go to the police. Some rapists even threaten to kill their victims, and just by reading newspapers, women know this has happened to others.

Reactions: Some victims fear the reactions of their significant others. Women have been verbally abused, beaten, and even abandoned by partners who would not believe that the woman did nothing to incite the rape.

Disbelief: Some women fear that if they report the rape, the police might not believe them. Even if the police are convinced, some women fear they may not be able to persuade a jury. There is no guarantee of justice from the legal system.

Publicity: Some women fear the loss of privacy, and the feeling of being exposed and vulnerable, as well as being subjected to embarrassing allegations about their personal lives in court. They are also reluctant to recall and relive (in front of an audience) a painful, humiliating incident they would rather forget.

The concerns of rape victims are the reason law enforcement officials and other experts have generally agreed with feminists that the number of reported rapes is probably much less than the number of incidents. Rape and domestic violence are painful consequences of sexism played, principally by men, as a power game in our culture.

Institutional Sexism

Institutional sexism is the consequence of established laws, customs, and practices that systematically discriminate against people or groups based on gender. Institutional sexism takes many forms, but a persistent problem is the ongoing gender discrimination in hiring. Jones and George (2003) describe a study in Philadelphia where men and women applied for well-paying restaurant jobs. Although their résumés were carefully constructed to make them equally qualified, men were called in for interviews twice as often as women, and five times as many men as women received job offers. Even though women now represent 49.9% of the workforce (excluding farm work), gender inequities persist. In 2009, women held 51.5% of high-paying management and professional positions, yet they were still a minority in the most highly paid positions, with only 25% being Chief Executive Officers and only 30% working as General Operations Managers. The numbers of women remain low in highly paid occupations such as lawyers, computer specialists, and engineers, while they dominate in professions that are less well paid such as teachers, nurses, social workers, and other service occupations. For example, only 32% of women are physicians, but 57% are physician's assistants (U.S. Bureau of Labor Statistics, 2010b).

Historically, there is ample evidence of inequities in the salaries of men and women, but attempts have been made to address this gender gap. There is disagreement about the extent to which gender salary inequities are being resolved, but most people concur that men earn more than women, even when they work in the same jobs (see Table 10.2).

Why are men earning more than women in the workforce?

Four arguments address the issue of salary inequity between men and women. The first argument is the claim that significant progress has been made in closing this income gap. According to the U.S. Bureau of Labor Statistics (2009), women earned approximately 60 cents for every dollar a man made from 1960 to 1980. Since then the gap narrowed, so that by 2008, American women were earning an average of 80 cents for every dollar a man earned.

> The Glass Ceiling hinders not only individuals but society as a whole. It effectively cuts our pool of potential corporate leaders by half. It deprives our economy of new leaders, new sources of creativity.
>
> Lynn M. Martin (1939–)

The answer to the salary inequity question would seem to be that men are still earning more, but that women must be getting more raises and promotions and are apparently catching up.

Careful analysis of salary data tells a different story: The primary reason for the decreasing gap is that the salaries of male workers have not been increasing; they have even been decreasing in some areas. The claim that women's salaries are becoming closer to men's salaries is based on the reality of salary stagnation for men. In addition, 80% of working women still earn less than $20,000 a year. It seems debatable to say that "progress" is being made concerning men's and women's salaries if closing the gender gap is based on women making small wage gains while men are receiving no wage increases.

A second argument regarding gender salary inequity is based on data showing that young women aged 16–24 entering the workforce are making 93% of what their male peers earn and women aged 25–34 are making 89% of what men in their age group earn (Catalyst, 2011). Such statistics have been used to argue that the gender inequity problem is being solved and to predict that the salary gap will eventually disappear as more highly paid young women pursue their careers. Although entry-level salaries are becoming more equal, feminists argue that women who stay in the workforce lose ground to their male peers because they are not promoted as readily as men. The term **glass ceiling** was coined to refer to an upper limit, usually middle management, beyond which women are not promoted. Studies have confirmed that women are not being promoted at the same rate as men; few are promoted to top leadership roles (U.S. Bureau of Labor Statistics, 2006).

According to a report from the White House Project's Corporate Council, no more than 20% of women function in leadership roles in fields as diverse as business, politics, and journalism, and even

TABLE 10.2 Median 2008 Earnings

Rank Earnings Gap	State	Men	Women	Female Earnings per Dollar of Male Earnings
1	Puerto Rico	$19,942	$20,165	101.1
2	District of Columbia	$57,393	$50,519	88.0
3	California	$47,758	$40,521	84.9
4	Arizona	$41,524	$34,556	83.2
5	Maryland	$53,189	$44,188	83.0
6	New York	$48,882	$40,490	82.8
7	Vermont	$41,778	$34,424	82.4
8	Georgia	$42,391	$34,513	81.4
9	Hawaii	$45,577	$36,709	80.5
10	Florida	$40,672	$32,506	79.9
11	Maine	$40,908	$32,613	79.7
12	North Carolina	$40,875	$32,397	79.3
13	New Jersey	$55,980	$44,343	79.2
14	Delaware	$46,898	$37,049	79.0
15	Oregon	$43,226	$33,959	78.6
16	Texas	$41,539	$32,530	78.3
17	Massachusetts	$55,555	$43,452	78.2
18	Colorado	$47,270	$36,618	77.5
19	Montana	$38,440	$29,634	77.1
20	Nevada	$45,178	$34,724	76.9
21	Tennessee	$40,458	$31,091	76.8
22	Minnesota	$48,637	$37,281	76.7
23	Iowa	$41,677	$31,903	76.5
24	Pennsylvania	$46,455	$35,265	75.9
25	Kentucky	$40,977	$31,089	75.9
26	Connecticut	$58,838	$44,625	75.9
27	New Mexico	$40,359	$30,623	75.9
28	South Dakota	$37,493	$28,431	75.8
29	South Carolina	$40,998	$31,063	75.8
30	Missouri	$42,106	$31,820	75.6
31	Oklahoma	$39,860	$31,123	75.6
32	Nebraska	$40,860	$30,885	75.6
33	Virginia	$50,023	$37,859	75.4

(continued)

Rank Earnings Gap	State	Men	Women	Female Earnings per Dollar of Male Earnings
34	Arkansas	$36,839	$27,487	74.6
35	Ohio	$45,214	$33,628	74.4
36	Wisconsin	$45,266	$33,640	74.3
37	Rhode Island	$49,265	$36,536	74.2
38	Alabama	$41,411	$30,681	74.1
39	Mississippi	$37,436	$27,697	74.0
40	Kansas	$43,346	$32,066	74.0
41	Washington	$51,272	$37,932	74.0
42	Illinois	$50,022	$36,968	73.9
43	Alaska	$51,500	$37,861	73.5
44	Michigan	$48,720	$35,260	72.4
45	North Dakota	$41,249	$29,589	71.7
46	Idaho	$41,461	$29,730	71.7
47	New Hampshire	$51,655	$36,946	71.5
48	Indiana	$44,906	$31,935	71.1
49	Utah	$45,028	$31,183	69.3
50	Louisiana	$43,326	$29,147	67.3
51	West Virginia	$40,941	$27,472	67.1
52	Wyoming	$48,555	$31,204	64.3

Source: U.S. Bureau of the Census, 2009

fewer are leaders in the military, large law firms, and Fortune 500 companies. Using a global comparison for women's political representation, the United States ranks 78th, lagging behind such nations as Rwanda, Angola, Belarus, and Turkmenistan" (Kim, 2012).

In addition, our dominant cultural expectation for women to perform housekeeping duties and raise children results in less opportunity for developing abilities, experience, contacts, and a reputation in their field. Businesses could do more to encourage women to maintain their careers while being a parent. According to Jeffery (2005), every industrialized nation except for the United States and Australia offers women paid parental leave and guarantees them a job when their leave is finished if they choose to return to work. The reduction of the gap between men's and women's salaries for entry-level jobs is important, but the economic penalty women pay for bearing and raising children still contributes significantly to the disparity between men's and women's salaries.

A third argument about gender salary disparity is based on the fact that more American women earn college diplomas than ever before. Because more education is assumed to mean more access to careers with higher salaries, gender disparity is predicted to decrease further, and eventually to disappear. Yet, according to 2008 Census Bureau data, the median annual income for a woman who had completed two years of college was $39,948 compared to $43,165 for a male with only a high school diploma. Reviewing median annual incomes related to earning college degrees, a bachelor's degree resulted in women making $54,204 compared to $82,197 for men. Women with doctorates made $83,762 compared to $129,773 for men, and women with a professional degree made $100,167 compared to $166,065 for men (Infoplease, 2011).

A fourth argument for gender salary inequity is that women tend to choose careers that pay lower salaries than the more highly paid professions men select. Although women account for 59% of low-paying jobs, including 70% of minimum-wage jobs, comparing the salaries of women and men within the same profession reveals that men are paid more—even in those professions where women constitute the majority of workers (Kim, 2000; U.S. Bureau of Labor Statistics, 2008).

What are economic consequences of institutional sexism for women?

Carnevale, Rose, and Cheah (2009) have analyzed the gender disparity in earnings, and they report significant gaps over a person's lifetime. Men with professional degrees will make over a million dollars more than a woman with a professional degree. A woman with a doctorate will earn about the same over her lifetime as a man with a bachelor's degree. A woman with a bachelor's degree will earn about the same as a man who only has some college credits, and she will make $654,000 less than a man with a bachelor's degree. A woman with a high school diploma will make $393,000 less than her male counterpart. The consequences are serious at all levels, but especially for the lower wage earners. One consequence of earning less money during their working years is that women over sixty-five are twice as likely as men to live in poverty.

For middle- and upper-class women, these economic disparities make it difficult for them to pursue political power by campaigning for national or state offices. Such campaigns are expensive and require personal funds as well as aggressive fundraising. Currently, women constitute only 17% of the U.S. Congress—91 of 435 seats in the House of Representatives and 17 Senate seats, a percentage exceeded by fifteen African nations. In the new government of Iraq, almost a third of the members of its parliament are women (Jeffery, 2005; Manning, 2011). In 2011, women constituted only 23.5% of state legislatures, 6 were governors, and 11 served as lieutenant governor. The states with the highest

percentage of women legislators included Colorado (41%), Vermont (38.9%), Arizona (34.4%), and Hawaii (34.2%). Among the 100 largest cities, 8 had female mayors including Houston, Baltimore, and Oakland (Center for American Women and Politics, 2011).

Part-time employment also illustrates the economic exploitation of women. For a variety of reasons, women constitute the majority of people working less than forty-hour weeks or working

> Whatever women do they must do twice as well as men to be thought half as good.
>
> Charlotte Whitton (1896–1975)

forty or more hours a week on a temporary basis. In either case, part-time workers are typically denied most or all fringe benefits provided to full-time employees, including day care, health insurance, life insurance, and employer contributions to retirement accounts.

Another economic consequence of institutional sexism concerns child support payments. When the family unit is broken, mothers are most often awarded custody of children and, as part of legal divorce settlements, fathers are almost always required to provide child support for children under the age of majority. In 2009, mothers represented almost 83% of all custodial parents, yet 64% of these mothers did not receive the full child support they were awarded, and more than 23% received no payments at all (U.S. Census Bureau, 2008). For mothers living below the poverty line, receiving full child support payments is critical as it constitutes nearly 50% of their annual income, yet 70% of these 3.5 million mothers received no child support, in part because half of the fathers were jobless (Mendel, 2009).

For low-income mothers, lack of child support often forces them to apply for public assistance, whereas middle-class mothers often return to college to upgrade their skills so they can compete for jobs in the labor market. If divorced custodial mothers applied for loans, they would likely be rejected not only because they may not have been able to establish a credit rating, but also because lenders are familiar with child support data and do not view child support payments as a reliable source of income. Lenders are familiar with the data on child support. Despite lower salaries, lack of child support, and other economic consequences, women often work for all the same reasons as men. And they do so regardless of discrimination in salaries and promotions, and despite another frustration encountered on the job: sexual harassment.

How is sexual harassment a significant problem for women in the workforce?

The behavior called *sexual harassment* is not new, but it wasn't until 1979 that Catherine MacKinnon created the term in her writings on workplace behaviors and gender discrimination (Wetzel & Brown, 2000). There were 11,364 sexual harassment complaints filed in 2011, and those making charges received $52.3 million. Sexual harassment in the workplace is not just a problem for women; men filed 16.3% of those complaints (EEOC, 2011). Typically, **sexual harassment** is defined as unwelcome deliberate and repeated behavior of a sexual nature that is neither requested nor returned. Men tend to be responsible for sexual harassment, even when men are the victims. Sexual harassment is an issue of power, not sex. Most men do not engage in sexual harassment at work; it is estimated that only 5% to 10% of the American male workforce engage in harassment. Men who do harass are being pressured to change their behavior.

What are the most common behaviors that women regard as sexual harassment?

There are two common reasons that women complain about sexual harassment. The behaviors described can be regarded as illustrating a "cultural" conflict between men and women. One complaint: Men make a nuisance of themselves by persistently asking women for dates. In response, the explanation is that during childhood and adolescence, every American male is taught some version of the cliché "if at first you don't succeed, try, try again." Men taught to view persistence as a positive attribute are encouraged to be persistent in anything they do. Accused of harassment, some men have yet to understand that persistently approaching women for dates may initially be regarded as obnoxious, but eventually becomes threatening. American women tend to regard

such harassment as a verbal form of stalking, and it is not surprising that many victims tend to describe harassers as disgusting, even ugly, regardless of the physical attractiveness of the harasser (Strauss & Espeland, 1992).

A second complaint has to do with men making unwelcome, sexually suggestive remarks to women, often in the form of sexual jokes sometimes told by men to each other. Now constituting almost half of the workforce, most women find this kind of humor unequivocally offensive. As our workforce continues to change, it is inevitable that some previously established norms and behaviors will also change. Men must recognize the need for reform and respond appropriately. Men must also recognize that respecting rather than resisting or criticizing reasons for reform demonstrates their respect for women.

Throughout the global economy, corporations are confronted with sexual harassment and must establish clear policies on what they consider acceptable and unacceptable behavior. The European Equal Opportunities Commission has ruled that flirting becomes harassment if it continues after the recipient has made it clear that it is offensive (Webb, 2000). How are employers at all levels supposed to monitor employee behavior in a way that is fair? The U.S. Equal Employment Opportunities Commission (EEOC) has established some reasonable guidelines.

What are the workplace guidelines for sexual harassment in the United States?

If sexual harassment is not severe—persistent requests for a date or telling sexual jokes—victims must tell the harasser that they regard this behavior as offensive. If the harasser continues the offensive behavior despite the victim's repeated objections, the victim can contact a supervisor to ask that he or she intervene or file a sexual harassment complaint. In cases where the behavior is not considered severe, it usually must be repeated a number of times before a sexual harassment complaint should be filed.

How many times must the victim be subjected to the behavior before filing a complaint? The courts use a "reasonable person" standard, meaning how long a reasonable person should have to tolerate such behavior before it is considered intolerable. Conversely, if the behavior is considered severe, such as demanding sexual favors from an employee in return for a raise or promotion, it only has to occur once for the victim, or an advocate aware of the behavior, to file a sexual harassment complaint (Webb, 2000).

In cases where the behavior is not severe, Carr-Ruffino (2007) has outlined clear steps to take in accordance with EEOC guidelines. Some of these steps include: (1) say something immediately to rebuke the harasser tactfully but clearly; (2) document each incident of harassment that occurs; (3) if harassment persists, confront the harasser with a demand to stop the inappropriate behavior, followed by a memo repeating this demand; (4) talk to witnesses who can attest to the unwanted behavior and ask them to jot down notes of what they saw; (5) talk to other colleagues who have worked with the harasser to find out if there has been a pattern of such behavior; (6) if the harassment continues, file a sexual harassment complaint. Most employers will find a sexual harassment complaint more credible if such steps have been taken.

Are American employers following sexual harassment guidelines?

Most American employers have demonstrated a willingness to take aggressive action against sexual harassment. This is probably because of a consistent pattern of court cases that have ruled for individuals making sexual harassment allegations. Business owners and managers cannot claim ignorance of the harassment because courts have ruled that they have a "vicarious liability" for what happens at their worksite. The main defense against sexual harassment allegations is to have sexual harassment policies in place and prove that the victim did not take advantage of them (Baker, 2006).

As employers become aware of research findings, they have even more reason to follow workplace guidelines. Studies report that one effect of sexual harassment in the workplace is a reduction of profits, which is reason enough for any employer to aggressively enforce policies against sexual harassment. According to research, when sexual harassment is not stopped at worksites, the consequences include increased worker absenteeism, lower worker productivity, and higher training costs from employee turnover (Knapp & Kustis, 1996). As American employers take aggressive actions to eliminate sexual harassment in the workplace, educators must take similar steps to eliminate sexual harassment from our schools and address other gender equity issues.

How much of a problem is sexual harassment in the schools?

In 1993, the American Association of University Women (AAUW) commissioned a Harris poll to examine sexual harassment in schools and reported that 81% of girls and 76% of boys had experienced sexual harassment, and that for 30% of girls and 18% of boys, it was a frequent occurrence. In 2011, the AAUW conducted another national survey (the third time since 1993) examining sexual harassment in America's schools. Nearly 2,000 students in grades 7 through 12 responded, with 56% of the girls and 40% of the boys indicating that they had experienced sexual harassment at least once during the past school year. Although these figures represent a significant decline from the first AAUW study in 1993, a new factor that could increase sexual harassment in the future is the use of technology. Almost one third of all students reported being sexually harassed by means such as email, Facebook, and text messaging, and 87% of students in the 2011 survey said that whether the sexual harassment was in person or via technology, the experience had negative consequences for them such as not wanting to go to school, skipping school, and not being able to focus on homework. The most common forms of sexual harassment involved nonverbal and verbal behaviors such as sexual comments, jokes, and gestures, but 13% of girls reported being touched in an inappropriate way. For 18% of both boys and girls, the harassment involved being called gays or lesbians. Perpetrators of sexual harassment were usually peers (96%) rather than adults, with 66% of sexual harassers being one or more male students, 19% one or more female students, and 11% involving a mixed group of male and female students. About 44% of students who admitted to engaging in harassment said it was "not a big deal," and 39% claimed they were just trying to be funny.

These findings may surprise many parents and teachers, because only about one fourth of the students discussed a sexual harassment incident with their parents, and only 9% of them reported the incident to school authorities. Yet the schools have both an ethical and a legal obligation to respond aggressively to such behavior. In 1999, the U.S. Supreme Court decision on *Davis v. Monroe County Board of Education* ruled that schools had a responsibility to take appropriate action to eliminate student sexual harassment and that they were legally liable if they did not take such action. The AAUW study and other studies have documented the impact of harassment, which reinforces the ethical obligation to address this problem. According to Meyer (2009) consequences have included declining academic performance, increased absenteeism, abuse of alcohol and drugs, and even some instances of suicidal behavior. To reduce sexual harassment, educators must confront sexist attitudes that encourage such behavior.

Some schools have responded to this issue by declaring any kind of harassment as a form of bullying behavior, but this is not likely to be effective because, as the AAUW noted in their 2011 report, calling harassment bullying tends to obscure the fact that gender is a major factor in selecting a victim. Meyer (2009) described major differences between harassment and bullying. Bullies tend to target a specific individual victim with the intent to cause harm, but the harm caused by harassers is sometimes unintended, and even if it is directed at a specific individual, harassment (and the school's response to it) has a more widespread impact that could potentially affect the entire school. In one case, a female student enrolled in a photography class was alone in the classroom when one of the male students walked in. She tried to leave, but he pushed her down on the floor and began groping her breasts. He must have heard someone was coming because he jumped up and ran out just before the teacher came in. Seeing the girl getting up from the floor, the teacher loudly asked what she was doing, and when she told him what had happened, he said it was her fault for wearing such short skirts to class. He sent her to the principal's office to serve detention (Meyer, 2009). This incident affects not only the victim, but the rest of the school as well. Both male and female students are going to hear about the incident and what happened to the victim, and this will likely encourage boys to engage in further harassment and discourage girls from reporting it. It is easy to predict the impact on female students feeling safe at school.

Technology has also given sexual harassers more tools to work with—cell phones, email, instant messaging, camera phones, personal Web sites and social-networking sites. School administrators have often been confused about how to deal with the abuse of technology and slow to respond to the sexual harassment that has occurred. At one high school, a female student allowed her boyfriend to take photos of her in the nude. When their relationship ended, the boyfriend posted these photos on the Internet. His intent was to embarrass her, but it resulted in sexual harassment in the form of unwanted sexual attention and even threats (Bissonette, 2009). Whether technology is being used for sexual harassment or for bullying others, teachers and other educators need to respond promptly and effectively to minimize the damage that can be inflicted. Many teachers complain that they aren't sure in some instances how to intervene because their school has no specific policies on this issue (Meyer, 2009). Schools need to develop such policies quickly because, as Bissonette (2009) reported, more students are willing to engage in bullying using technology than would have engaged in such activities in person. The probable reason is that bullying involves a direct confrontation with the victim, but cyberbullying can be done from a distance. This may also explain the findings from several studies that female students are as likely to engage in cyberbullying as male students (Bissonette, 2009). With or without the use of technology, sexual harassment is a major concern, but it is only one of several gender issues in our schools.

What are some other gender issues in schools?

Nonsexist educators have long advocated teaching strategies to confront sexist attitudes because gender problems in schools are not limited to sexual harassment. After collecting years of observational data on teacher–student interactions in K–12 classrooms, Sadker and Sadker (1994) reported consistent sexist patterns for both teacher and student behaviors. Boys were more likely to call out answers without raising their hands, and they interrupted when others gave answers. Because boys were more aggressive, teachers tended to call on them, praise them, and discipline them more often than girls. Teachers were more likely to challenge boys to finish their homework, whereas they would help girls finish theirs.

Are there gender equity issues for boys?

In recent years, the popular media has given attention to those who question whether schools have gone too far in promoting gender equity because boys are having more problems today. Gurian (2004) reports that girls are consistently earning higher grades than boys; they earn 60% of all A grades and boys are the recipients of 70% of all D and F grades. Approximately two thirds of all students in the top fifth of their class are girls, whereas boys constitute two thirds of all students diagnosed with a learning disability. Boys represent 90% of students with behaviors requiring disciplinary action in school and 80% of all dropouts. The federal government has considered modifying the Title IX act to permit single-sex schools, but when all-male schools have been tried previously, they did not produce the improved academic achievement they promised. As Sadker (2005) points out, they often became a "dumping ground" for boys with behavioral problems.

Gurian (2004) believes that schools need to provide teachers with a better background in recent findings from brain research so they can accommodate male ways of thinking and learning. He describes several specific teaching strategies stemming from the research that he believes will improve the academic achievement of boys. The central issue in this debate over gender equity in schools should be focused on whether both groups are being given the opportunity to learn and develop their talents and abilities so they can become confident and productive members of our rapidly changing society. Gender equity in education is not about winners and losers in a competition between boys and girls, but about the treatment of both boys and girls as they participate in school programs, both curricular and extracurricular. The goal of all educators should be to make that experience as fair and as equitable as possible for both boys and girls.

Many educators agree that there are gender equity issues for boys, but Sadker (2005) insists that most of these issues are not new. He believes the larger issue is that gender stereotypes for both boys and girls are still being reinforced in our schools and in society. For example, boys receive more math/science-related toys than girls, earn higher scores on most standardized achievement tests during high school and college, and continue to dominate high-paying occupations such as those in math- and science-related fields. We need to implement strategies both in schools and in society to address these ongoing gender equity issues.

What evidence indicates that gender equity issues are being addressed in schools and society?

One aspect of women's achievements that has evoked concern for males is access to higher education. Females are increasingly entering college, and they earn 57% or more of all bachelor's degrees, 60% of all master's degrees, and 52% of all doctorates (U.S. Census Bureau, 2010). In 2009, women constituted almost 60% of all biology/biomedical science majors, 85% of all majors in health professions and related clinical sciences, 49% of all business majors, and 62.5% of all communication/communication technology majors (Tulshyan, 2010). Although their numbers have declined slightly in recent years, women still constitute 47% of all students in law schools and in medical schools (Association of American Medical Colleges, 2010; Catalyst, 2010).

In addition to their academic achievements, girls and women are increasingly involved in athletics; one third of high school girls participate in sports, compared to almost half of boys. Since 1981, the number of college women's teams nearly doubled and the number of women participating in collegiate athletics increased by 81% (Parker-Pope, 2010; Tanner, 2002), and two studies have documented long-range benefits for women who participate in athletics. One study of women aged 25–34 concluded that participation in sports accounted for 20% of the increase in women's educational attainments and 40% of the increase in employment, and another study reported that participation in sports appeared to improve women's health in general and was responsible for a lower risk for obesity later in life (Parker-Pope, 2010).

As for the workplace, an ongoing problem for women workers is that so many of them are raising children; 65% of all families in the United States consist of either two parents or a single mother working full time. With so many working mothers, employers need to consider adopting changes such as flexible work hours to give these mothers the opportunity to respond to family needs. Companies such as Best Buy have implemented flexible work schedules in which individual workers can vary the time they come to work or leave work, and other companies such as J.C. Penney have experimented with online scheduling to allow workers to request certain hours or to trade shifts with other workers (Levin-Epstein, 2007). With these approaches, supervisors evaluate employee performance based on their productivity, and not simply by their hours at work. Early studies report that flexible scheduling reduces stress, increases productivity, and reduces the employee turnover rate. An article in the April 2006 issue of *The Economist* argued that women workers were the most underutilized segment of the workforce, and it recommended that governments work with businesses to address the difficulties preventing women with children from working (Williams, 2007). Some businesses have already implemented strategies such as offering child care at the worksite and paid family leave. According to Levin-Epstein (2007), one study reported that such strategies resulted in higher worker productivity and retention rates. Since the pattern of U.S. families with dual wage earners or a single working parent is likely to persist, businesses competing for quality workers will feel increasing pressure to develop and expand on such "family-friendly" practices. The pattern of women's increasing involvement in the workforce, politics, and other activities is reinforced by a 2010 White House report finding that women are marrying later in life and having fewer children than ever before, and more are choosing not to have children (White House Council on Women and Girls, 2010). Along with their significant gains in educational attainment, these changes suggest that women will be an increasingly important factor in decisions and changes that will evolve in the twenty-first century.

AFTERWORD

This description of cultural, individual, and institutional sexism is the tip of an iceberg. Gender discrimination occurs in our laws and in our court system, in the arts and in athletics, and in the images encountered in media and in school textbooks. Sexism permeates our institutions. Some men believe that sexism works to their advantage and resist efforts to promote gender equality, but sexism hurts men

and women, boys and girls. Anything that prevents people from using their talents and abilities results in

> What is enough? Enough is when somebody says, "Get me the best people you can find," and nobody notices when half of them turn out to be women.
>
> Louise Renne (1937–)

a loss for us all. When anyone is denied a chance to contribute to our society, the result is a nation that is less than it could have been. If Americans create a society that offers opportunities to all and receives the gifts each person has to offer, the male–female power game can cease—a victory for everyone.

TERMS AND DEFINITIONS

Androgyny The interchangeability of male and female roles and responsibilities in all areas beyond fundamental biological ones

Cultural sexism The societal promotion of negative beliefs and practices that reinforce rigid gender roles in which men are traditionally accorded a superior role in society while women are assigned to subordinate roles; the artificial superimposition of authority of one gender over another

Feminist A woman or man committed to the struggle for the social, economic, and personal rights of women and men; an advocate for equality between women and men

Glass ceiling An informal upper limit that keeps women and minorities from being promoted to positions of greatest responsibility in work organizations

Inclusive language Words or phrases that are not gender specific but inclusive of both genders

Individual sexism Prejudiced attitudes and behavior demeaning to women, or to men, because of beliefs about gender and gender roles, demonstrated whenever someone responds by saying or doing something degrading or harmful about persons of the other gender

Institutional sexism Established laws, customs, and practices in a society that allow systematic discrimination against people or groups based on gender

Male chauvinist A man or woman who believes that men ought to be the leaders and decision makers and women should be subordinate to them

Rape "The penetration, no matter how slight, of the vagina or anus with any body part or object, or oral penetration by a sex organ of another person, without the consent of the victim" (FBI, 2012)

Sexism An attitude, action, or institutional structure that subordinates or limits a person on the basis of sex (Andrzejewski, 1996)

Sexual harassment Deliberate and repeated behavior that has a sexual basis and is not welcomed, requested, or returned

DISCUSSION EXERCISES

Exercise #1 Find the Problem: Analyzing Sexist Language

Directions: Determine why the language in each statement has been termed "sexist." Write an appropriate nonsexist message to replace the sexist one. [Example: The average American drinks his coffee black. Nonsexist revision: The average American drinks black coffee.]

1. Dear Sir:
2. Any student who is not satisfied with his performance on the pretest may take the posttest.
3. Mr. McAllister runs the garage in partnership with his wife, a striking blonde who mans the pumps.
4. The English teacher developed a wonderful thematic unit on "Man and His World."
5. Housewives are feeling the pinch of higher food prices.
6. A writer can become so involved in his work that he neglects his family.
7. NCTE convention-goers and their wives are invited to attend the gala event.
8. One of our prehistoric ancestors was the Neanderthal man.
9. We are asking all the mothers to send cookies for our field trip tomorrow.
10. Blacks finally received the vote in 1870.
11. While lunch was delayed, the women gossiped about last night's meeting.
12. A slave could not claim his wife or children as his own because the laws did not recognize slave marriages.
13. The average student is worried about his grades.
14. The ancient Egyptians allowed women considerable control over property.
15. One of the political debates in the racial struggle taking place in South Africa is over the concept of "one man, one vote."

Exercise #2 Sexual Harassment: Case Studies from Higher Education

Directions: Sexual harassment may take several forms: innuendo or overt action toward either gender by those of the same or opposite sex, unwanted sexual advances, sexual assault, or sexual coercion (rape). In each situation, respond to the following three questions:

- Is this a case of sexual harassment? If yes, when did the harassment begin to occur?
- What are the harassing behaviors in this situation?
- What can the individual(s) involved in each situation do to address the harassment?

1. Kevin is taking an introductory English course. His first writing assignment dealt with his uncertainties about being a new student in college, on his own for the first time. When the essays are returned, his has no grade and only the comment, "Please see me." Kevin goes to the

teacher's office during the posted office hours. His teacher suggests that they go out for a drink to discuss the essay.

2. Connie is taking a math course that includes a unit on statistics. Connie has been having some difficulty understanding probability theory. She knows that this course is important to her career and a good grade in math can increase her chances of getting into graduate school. She contacts her teaching assistant and explains her concerns about the material and her wish to get a good grade to qualify for graduate school. They set up a series of tutoring sessions, and by the third session have not only become friends but have begun to date outside of the sessions.

3. Tamara, one of the few women in an engineering class, notices that her professor stares at her, especially while she takes quizzes. She is aware that the professor has a history of interrupting women students when they ask questions and even refusing to respond to their questions. In addition, during one class period the professor told a joke demeaning to women. Many of the men in the class laughed at the joke, which angered Tamara even more.

4. In her introductory psychology class, Sonia, a Latina, notices that her professor smiles and comments on her appearance as a greeting each morning, but that he does not greet any other student in that way. Before his lecture on contemporary sexual roles and behavior, he says to the class, "Sonia can probably help us understand this topic because she has to put up with macho types."

5. Near the entrance to the library, men using cards with the numbers one through ten "rate" the sexual attributes of women who enter the library, accompanied by much laughter and some ambiguous gestures. Their behavior causes many women to avoid going to the library.

6. In an undergraduate literature class, Professor Helmsley, who is also the director of Graduate Studies, expresses his opinion that courses in literature offered under the Women's Studies Program are useless preparation for graduate study. He has recommended that all such courses be dropped from the list of acceptable courses for the undergraduate major in literature.

Adapted from Sexual Harassment and the University: Seven Cases.

REFERENCES

American Association of University Women. (2011). *Crossing the line: Sexual harassment at school.* Washington, DC. Retrieved Nov. 6, 2011, at www.aauw.org

American Association of University Women. (1993). *Hostile hallways: The AAUW survey on sexual harassment in America's schools.* Washington, DC: Author.

American Bar Association. (2006). *Teenage dating violence facts.* Retrieved October 15, 2011, from www.clotheslineproject.org/teendatingviolencefacts.pdf.

Andrzejewski, J. (1996). Definitions for understanding oppression and social justice. In J. Andrzejewski (Ed.), *Oppression and social justice: Critical frameworks* (5th ed., pp. 52–58). Needham, MA: Simon & Schuster.

Arliss, L.P. (1991). *Gender communication.* Englewood Cliffs, NJ: Prentice Hall.

Association of American Medical Colleges. (2010). *U.S. medical school applicants and students 1982–1983 to 2010–2011.* Retrieved October 22, 2011, from www.aamc.org.

Baker, L.A. (2006). Sexual harassment by supervisors. *FBI Law Enforcement Bulletin, 75*(3), 25–33.

Bernstein, A. (2004). Women's pay: Why the gap remains a chasm. *Business Week, 3887,* 58–59.

Bissonette, A.M. (2009). *Cyber law: Maximizing safety and minimizing risk in classrooms.* Thousand Oaks, CA: Corwin.

Branch, T. (1998). *Pillar of fire: America in the King years 1963–65.* New York, NY: Simon & Schuster.

Carnevale, A.P., Rose, S J., & Cheah, B. (2009). *The college payoff: Education, occupations, lifetime earnings.* Washington, DC: The Georgetown University Center on Education and the Workforce.

Carr-Ruffino, N. (2007). *Managing diversity: People skills for a multicultural workplace* (7th ed.). Boston, MA: Pearson Custom Publishing.

Catalyst. (2011). *Women's earnings and income.* Retrieved from www.catalyst.org.

Catalyst. (2010). *Women in law in the U. S.* Retrieved from www.catalyst.org.

Catania, S. (2005). The counselor. *Mother Jones, 30*(4), 45–49, 88.

Center for American Women and Politics. (2011). *Women in elective office 2011.* Retrieved May 11, 2011, from www.cawp.rutgers.edu/fast_facts/index.php

Collins, G. (2003). *America's women: 400 years of dolls, drudges, helpmates, and heroines.* New York, NY: Harper Collins.

Daft, R.L. (2003). Managing diverse employees. In *Management* (6th ed., pp. 436–468). Versailles, KY: Thompson Southwestern.

Equal Employment Opportunity Commission (EEOC). (2011). Sexual harassment charges: FY19970FY2011. Retrieved October 11, 2012, from www.eeoc.gov/eeoc/statistics/enforcement/sexual_harassment.cfm

Equal Employment Opportunity Commission (EEOC). *Enforcement guidelines.* Retrieved September 24, 2009, at www.eeoc.gov

Evans, S. (1989). *Born for liberty: A history of women in America.* New York, NY: The Free Press.

Faludi, S. (2006). *Backlash: The undeclared war against American women.* New York, NY: Three Rivers Press.

FBI. (2012, January 6). *Attorney General Eric Holder announces revisions to the Uniform Crime Report's definition of rape.* Press release retrieved March 3, 2012, from http://www.fbi.gov/news/pressrel/press-releases

Gonnerman, J. (2005). The unforgiven. *Mother Jones, 30*(4), 38–43.

Gould, S.J. (1981). *The mismeasure of man.* New York, NY: W.W. Norton.

Gould, S.J. (1983). Big fish, little fish. In *Hen's teeth and horses toes* (pp. 21–31). New York, NY: W.W. Norton.

Grall, T. (2000, October). Child support for custodial mothers and fathers. *Current Population Reports.* Washington, DC: U.S. Department of Commerce.

Gurian, M. (2004). With boys and girls in mind. *Educational Leadership, 62*(3), 21–26.

Hallinan, J.T. (2009). *Why we make mistakes.* New York, NY: Broadway Books.

Infoplease. (2011). *Median annual income, by level of education.* Pearson Education. Retrieved October 22, 2011, from www.infoplease.com/ipa/AO883617.html.

Jeffery, C. (2005). Why women can't win for trying. *Mother Jones, 30*(4), 22–23.

Johnson, M.T. (2011). *The diversity code: Unlock the secrets to making differences work in the real world.* New York, NY: American Management Association.

Jones, G.R., & George, J.M. (2003). Managing diverse employees in a diverse environment. In *Contemporary management* (3rd ed., pp. 112–149). Boston, MA: McGraw Hill.

Kim, A. (2012). Where are the women wonks? *Washington Monthly, 44*(7/8), 5–6.

Kim, M. (2000, September). Women paid low wages: Who they are and where they work. *Monthly Labor Review,* pp. 26–31.

Kimmel, P.R. (2006). Culture and conflict. In M. Deutsch & P. Coleman (Eds.), *The handbook of conflict resolution.* San Francisco, CA: Jossey-Bass.

Knapp, D.E., & Kustis, G.A. (1996). The real "Disclosure": Sexual harassment and the bottom line. In M. Stockdale (Ed.), *Sexual harassment in the workplace: Perspectives, frontiers, and response strategies* (pp. 199–213). Thousand Oaks, CA: Sage.

Levin-Epstein, J. (2007, March). Responsive workplaces. *The American Prospect, 18*(3), A16–A18.

Luscombe, B. (2010, Nov. 22). The rise of the sheconomy. *Time, 176*(21), 58–61.

MacKinnon, C.A. (1987). A rally against rape. In *Feminism unmodified: Discourses on life and law* (pp. 81–84). Cambridge, MA: Harvard University Press.

Manning, J.E. (2011). *Membership of the 112th Congress: A profile.* Retrieved October 8, 2012, from http://fpc.state.gov/documents/organization/166794.pdf

Mendel, D. (2009). Don't forget the men. *The American Prospect, 20*(7), A18–A19.

Meyer, E.J. (2009). *Gender, bullying and harassment: Strategies to end sexism and homophobia in schools.* New York, NY: Teachers College Press.

National Center for Educational Statistics. (2010). *Digest of educational statistics.* Retrieved October 9, 2012, from http://nces.ed.gov/programs/digest/d11/tables/dt11_290.asp

National Center for Educational Statistics. (2004). *Trends in education equity of girls and women: 2004.* Retrieved October 14, 2008, from http://nces.ed.gov/pubs2005/equity/index.asp

National Center for Health Statistics. (1999). *National Vital Statistics 47*(21). Retrieved July 12, 2003, from http://www.cdc.gov/nchs

Nilsen, A.P. (1977a). Sexism as shown through the English vocabulary. In A.P. Nilsen, H. Bosmajian,

H.L. Gershuny, & J.P. Stanley (Eds.), *Sexism and language* (pp. 27–41). Urbana, IL: National Council of Teachers of English.

Nilsen, A.P. (1977b). Sexism in the language of marriage. In A.P. Nilsen, H. Bosmajian, H.L. Gershuny, & J.P. Stanley (Eds.), *Sexism and language* (pp. 131–140). Urbana, IL: National Council of Teachers of English.

Parker-Pope, T. (2010). As girls become women, sports pay dividends. *New York Times*. Retrieved October 22, 2011, from http:///well.blogs.nytimes.com/2010/02/15.

Partridge, E. (2009). *Origins: A short etymological dictionary of modern English* (p. 92). New York, NY: Routledge.

Quindlen, A. (2008, October 13). The leadership lid. *Newsweek*, 86.

RAINN. (2009). *Rape, Abuse, and Incest National Network*. Retrieved June 12, 2009, from http://www.rainn.org

Riley, G. (1986a). *Inventing the American woman: A perspective on women's history, 1607–1877: Vol. 1*. Arlington Heights, IL: Harlan Davidson.

Riley, G. (1986b). *Inventing the American woman: A perspective on women's history, 1865–present: Vol. 2*. Arlington Heights, IL: Harlan Davidson.

Sadker, D. (2005). Gender bias lives, for both sexes. *Education Digest, 70*(8), 27–30.

Sadker, D., & Sadker, M. (1994). *Failing at fairness: How America's schools cheat girls*. New York, NY: Charles Scribner.

Sampson, R. (2003). Acquaintance rape of college students. *Problem-Oriented Guides for Police, No 17*. Retrieved June 6, 2009, from www.cops.usdoj.gov.

Simon, R.W. (2002, January). Revisiting the relationships among gender, marital status, and mental health. *American Journal of Sociology, 107*(4), 1065–1097.

Stalking Resource Center. (2009). *Stalking Fact Sheet*. Retrieved October 10, 2011, at www.ncvc.org/src/main.aspx?dbID=DB_publications127

Strauss, S., & Espeland, P. (1992). *Sexual harassment and teens: A program for positive change*. Minneapolis, MN: Free Spirit.

Tanner, J. (2002). *Women in sports, issues in race, ethnicity and gender*. Washington, DC: CQ Press, 225–242.

Tavris, C. (1999). *The mismeasure of woman*. New York, NY: Peter Smith.

Tavris, C., & Wade, C. (1984). *The longest war: Sex differences in perspective* (2nd ed.). New York, NY: Harcourt Brace Jovanovich.

Tjaden, P., & Thoennes, N. (1998). *Prevalence, incidence, and consequences of violence against women: Findings from the National Violence Against Women Survey*. Washington, DC: United States Department of Justice. Retrieved June 10, 2009, from http://eric.ed.gov (ERIC # E0934980).

Trusty, J., Robinson, C.R., Plata, M., & Ng, K. (2000, Fall). Effects of gender, socioeconomic status, and early academic performance on postsecondary educational choice. i(4), 463–473.

Tulshyan, R. (2010, March 2). Top 10 college majors for women. Forbes.com. Retrieved October 23, 2012, from www.forbes.com/2010/03/03/top-10-college-majors-women-leadership-education.html.

U.S. Bureau of the Census. (2010). *Table 299: Earned degrees conferred by level and sex*. Retrieved October 22, 2011, from http://www.census.gov.

U.S. Bureau of the Census. (2008, April). *Custodial fathers and mothers and their child support: 2007*. Retrieved from www.census.gov/hhes/www/childsupport/cs07.html.

U.S. Bureau of Labor Statistics. (2010a). *Women's-to-men's earning ratio by age, 2009*. Retrieved October 22, 2011, from www.bls.gov/cps/demographics.htm#women.

U.S. Bureau of Labor Statistics. (2010b). *Women in the labor force: A databook* (2010 edition). Retrieved October 22, 2011, from www.bls.gov/cps/wof-databook2010.htm.

U.S. Bureau of Labor Statistics. (2008). *Highlights of women's earnings in 2007*. Retrieved June 11, 2009, from www.bls.gov

U.S. Bureau of Labor Statistics. (March 2006). Women still underrepresented among highest wage earners. *Issues in Labor Statistics*. Retrieved July 15, 2006, from www.bls.gov

U.S. Department of Justice. (2009). *Crime in the United States*. Retrieved October 15, 2011, from: www2.fbi .gov/ucr/cius2009/offenses/violent_crime/forcible_ rape.html.

Webb, S. (2000). *Step forward: Sexual harassment in the workplace* (2nd ed.). New York, NY: Master-media.

Wetzel, R., & Brown, N.W. (2000). *Student-generated sexual harassment in secondary schools*. Westport, CT: Bergin & Garvey.

White House Council on Women and Girls. (2010). *Women in America: Indicators of social and economic well-being*. Retrieved October 10, 2012, from: www .whitehouse.gov/administration/eop/cwg/data-on-women

Williams, J.C. (2007, March). The opt-out revolution revisited. *The American Prospect, 18*(3), A12–A15.

Wulff, M.B., & Steitz, J.A. (1997). Curricular track, career choice, and androgyny among adolescent females. *Adolescent, 32*(125), 43–50.

Chapter 11

Heterosexism: Transforming Homosexuality from Deviant to Different

"The only abnormality is the incapacity to love."

Anais Nin (1903–1977)

The word *homosexual* and the concept of homosexuality appear to have originated in the 1860s in the German medical writing of Dr. Karl Ulrichs. Homosexuality does not seem to enter into public discourse in a formal and explicit way until 1892, when scholars such as Havelock Ellis and Magnus Hirschfield published essays and books describing theories and research concerning human sexuality. In a highly regarded book published in 1886, Richard von Krafft-Ebing chose not to use "sexual inversion," the common term in America, but Ulrich's word, translated to English as *homosexuality*. Krafft-Ebing described a **homosexual** as someone sexually attracted to members of the same sex. Although same-sex liaisons had been documented throughout human history, the new term challenged the Western world's traditional heterosexual assumption.

What is the heterosexual assumption?

Non-Western cultures have a history of acknowledging and accepting sexual variation in human beings (Herdt, 1997; Williams, 2001). Western cultural attitudes about sexuality have been based on a **heterosexual assumption**: that all people were born **heterosexual** and that being attracted to opposite-sex partners was the natural condition of human beings. People who engaged in any sexual activity not conforming to heterosexual norms were assumed to be making deviant and unnatural choices, especially when sexual activity took place with a same-sex partner. The Bible was often used to justify beliefs about normal or deviant sexual behavior, and even twentieth-century psychologists reinforced the assumption by regarding homosexuality as a mental illness. Homosexuals were widely perceived as aberrations in need of correction (a cure) to bring them back to their true heterosexual nature (Duberman, Vicinus, & Chauncey, 1989).

When was the heterosexual assumption challenged?

Krafft-Ebing provided the term that challenged the heterosexual assumption. Although he still believed that homosexuality was immoral and unacceptable, he defined it as one of many forms of sexual desire. Krafft-Ebing argued that like fetishism or masochism, homosexuality was a condition, a mental defect that could be cured (Halperin, 1989).

Although the general public would not become familiar with the idea of homosexuality for another sixty years, Krafft-Ebing established the idea that there were various forms of sexual desire, and that one of these involved a desire for same-sex partners. His assertion was addressed by the evolving field of psychology as its practitioners searched for a way to remedy deviant behavior. The suggested "cures" included castration, sterilization, electric shock, and occasional lobotomies; however, none proved practically successful (Katz, 1985).

Although conventional wisdom among psychologists continued to regard homosexuality as deviant and unnatural—a mental defect—the failure of recommended remedies in the clinical setting caused a number of respected people in the field, including A.A. Brill, Magnus Hirschfield, and even Sigmund Freud, to conclude that homosexuality could not be cured and was probably a permanent condition. As psychologists became convinced that deviant sexual desires could not be redirected, they adopted approaches such as adjustment therapy to control homosexual behavior. These practices were the norm when the Kinsey Report was published in 1948.

How did the Kinsey Report challenge the heterosexual assumption?

With funding from the Rockefeller Foundation and Indiana University, a zoologist named Alfred Kinsey and his research staff engaged in a study of human sexual behavior from 1938 to 1956. The Kinsey Report issued in 1948 was controversial for many reasons, not the least of which was its proposition that **sexual orientation** was not a singular phenomenon, but a continuum of multiple possibilities ranging from exclusive heterosexuality to exclusive homosexuality, with a variety of bisexual orientations in between (see Figure 11.1). Based on self-reports of dreams and fantasies as well as behavior, Kinsey and his staff concluded that only a small percentage of their research subjects were exclusively heterosexual or exclusively homosexual (later a figure of 10% became widely used). Most appeared to have some potential for **bisexual** behavior—being sexually attracted to members of either gender—although sexual attraction might be biased more toward one gender than another.

The 1948 Kinsey Report (and the 1953 report focusing on women) challenged the general assumption that all human beings possessed a heterosexual orientation. Americans were confronted with the radical concept of sexual orientation: every human being is not heterosexual, and human sexuality encompasses categories of different sexual attractions and behaviors, including an attraction to and a desire for same-sex partners.

What was the impact of the Kinsey Report?

The term *homosexuality* provided a label for what Oscar Wilde's lover had called "the love that dare not speak its name," but most Americans were

FIGURE 11.1 The Kinsey Continuum of Sexual Orientation

The Kinsey Continuum of Sexual Orientation

0 = Exclusively heterosexual
1 = Predominantly heterosexual, only incidentally homosexual
2 = Predominantly heterosexual, but more than incidentally homosexual
3 = Equally heterosexual and homosexual
4 = Predominantly homosexual, but more than incidentally heterosexual
5 = Predominantly homosexual, only incidentally heterosexual
6 = Exclusively homosexual

uncomfortable with the subject and refused to discuss it. Most psychologists still regarded homosexuality as a defect, a form of mental illness, but homosexuals themselves began to reconsider their situation. There were, and always had been, same-sex–oriented people who were comfortable with their sexuality while being discreet in their behavior. These men and women became convinced that attitudes in America needed to change, but they weren't sure how that could happen.

Homosexual friends of psychologist Evelyn Hooker argued that psychologists persisted in regarding homosexuality as a mental illness because the homosexual patients who sought treatment were not comfortable with their own sexuality. These individuals were often filled with guilt and anxiety because of society's condemnation or their religious upbringing. One gay man urged Dr. Hooker to engage in research involving well-adjusted gay men, and he volunteered a number of such men for the research (Marcus, 1992).

Hooker subsequently conducted a study involving thirty homosexual men and thirty heterosexual men. She administered three different personality tests to each subject—Rorschach, Thematic Apperception, and Make a Picture Story—and submitted the results to a panel of internationally respected psychologists. None of the panelists could discern heterosexual from homosexual subjects, and they gave two thirds of the subjects from each group a score of average or higher, clearly refuting the belief that homosexuality was associated with inherent mental problems. Hooker presented the findings of the panel evaluations in her research at the national conference of the American Psychological Association (APA) in 1956. It would take another seventeen years for APA members to admit they had been wrong and take appropriate action.

In 1973, the American Psychological Association voted to remove homosexuality from its list of mental illnesses. The American Medical Association (AMA) would later join the APA in declaring that homosexuality was not a mental illness, affirming that gay men and lesbians could be just as healthy, competent, and capable of functioning effectively in society as heterosexuals. The decisions of the APA and AMA sent a clear message to people who believed they were justified in discriminating against individuals who were not heterosexual.

This resulted in the concept of **heterosexism**—the oppression or exploitation of human beings not biologically heterosexual.

> In my relationship with others, I have found that it does not help, in the long run, to act as if I am something I am not.
>
> Carl Rogers (1902–1987)

What has current research reported with regard to homosexuality?

Research on human sexuality has continued and, based on the studies, researchers seem to agree that sexual orientation has a significant biological basis. Using anthropological evidence and studies in child development, Pillard (1997) proposed that sexual orientation is an innate characteristic, a deeply embedded personality trait that can be observed in young children:

> There seems to be a fundamental bias toward either a heterosexual or a homosexual developmental path, prefigured early in life, neither taught nor learned, and profoundly resistant to modification. (p. 233)

Le Vay (1996) argued that the influence of sex hormones on brain functioning at the primary drive center, the hypothalamus, appears to be a significant biological factor. Although not denying the importance of biological factors, anthropologists have described cultural influences on behavior and attitudes concerning human sexuality (Herdt, 1997). In 2008, the world's largest study of twins affirmed what a number of studies have suggested, that "homosexual behavior is largely shaped by genetics and random environmental factors." The researchers noted that heterosexual behavior is also influenced by this same mix of environmental factors and genetics (Schlatter & Steinback, 2010, p. 32).

Reinforcing the idea of sexual variation among humans, studies of animal behavior have reported sexual activities between same-sex animals (Stein, 1999). Money (1988) described research that experimentally manipulated prenatal hormones affecting the sexual pathways of the brain to successfully influence animals (other than primates)

Research with an Agenda Is Not Research: The Story of Paul Cameron

In 1982, Dr. Paul Cameron, an assistant professor of Psychology at the University of Nebraska, opposed a change being considered by the Omaha city council to add lesbians and gay men to its civil rights ordinance. In a speech at a Lutheran church, Cameron claimed that a homosexual had recently kidnapped and castrated a local boy. The Omaha police and local hospitals had no record of the incident, but people were outraged. The proposal was defeated four to one.

In 1983, Cameron formed the Institute for the Scientific Investigation of Sexuality, announcing that he would conduct a national sex survey. Although it is considered unscientific for a researcher to predict results prior to conducting a study, Cameron said his study would show that sexually adventurous people contract more diseases, are less happy, and are more inclined to attempt suicide. Cameron's findings were consistent with his predictions, but legitimate researchers identified many flaws in his statistical analysis and research methodology. This study continues to be cited by Christian fundamentalist organizations and individuals who want research to justify their antigay attitudes.

Based on data from a 1978 study by Nicholas Groth, Cameron published a study in 1983 claiming that homosexuals are ten to twenty times more likely to molest children. Groth interviewed 175 convicted child molesters and reported that more boys than girls were victims; he also reported that the men either identified as heterosexual or had no interest in adult sex. Groth filed a complaint with the American Psychological Association (APA) accusing Cameron of misrepresenting data from his study. The APA stripped Cameron of his professional accreditation.

In 1992, as director of what he now called the Family Research Institute, Cameron moved to Colorado to assist supporters of a state constitutional amendment to ban civil rights protection for gay men and lesbians. Amendment supporters distributed thousands of copies of Cameron's antigay research a week before the election. A majority of the state's voters approved the proposed ban on civil rights protection for gays and lesbians.

In 1994, Cameron published his "Gay Obituary Study." Based on 6,000 newspaper obituaries of gay men, Cameron calculated the average life span of all gay men as 43. Because this figure was cited on radio and television talk shows, a Manhattan Institute scientist pointed out that the average age for AIDS victims was 40, so if the average life span for all gay men was 43, those without AIDS could not live past 46. The average age of 43 for gay men is a statistic still cited in antigay literature.

In a 2004 decision upholding a state law banning adoption by same-sex couples, the Florida Supreme Court cited a Cameron "study" as justification for their decision. After Cameron began claiming that his research was sociological, the American Sociological Association said he had misinterpreted sociological research and insisted that he cease claiming to be engaged in sociological study. Despite his "success," most scientists agree with Nicholas Groth's assessment of Cameron: "He disgraces his profession" (p. 14).

Source: **David Holthouse (2005), "The Fabulist,"** *Intelligence Report* to engage in exclusively homosexual or heterosexual behavior during mating. Money did not claim that scientists could have the same success with humans, explaining that prenatal hormones are thought to have a less absolute influence on primates, but he did conclude that manipulation of sex hormones can create a predisposition for sexual activity with same-sex or opposite-sex partners.

Research regarding human sexual variation would seem to parallel the role that variation plays throughout nature. Gould (1983) provides an illustration in his explanation of the variety in striping patterns for zebras. One striping pattern has numerous, narrow, parallel stripes configured relatively straight up and down the body. Another pattern has fewer, thicker stripes on the body and three broad slightly curved stripes on the haunch. A third pattern has even fewer and thicker stripes on the front of the body, and even broader stripes starting from the middle of the belly and curving back to the haunch (see Figure 11.2).

The three striping variations result from the striping mechanism being initiated at different times during fetal development. Because variation occurs in something as simple as the striping

pattern for zebras, it is difficult to maintain that all human beings possess the same heterosexual orientation, given the complexity of factors involved with the sexual development of the human fetus. It is far more logical to expect the kind of sexual variation described in the Kinsey Report, in the research conducted since 1948, and as recorded in human history.

Cultural Heterosexism

Cultural heterosexism refers to a dominant culture defining heterosexuality as the norm and anything else as deviant. The heterosexual assumption

> I can't understand any discussion of gays and lesbians as if they were something immoral or unsatisfactory. They're just doing what nature wants them to do.
>
> R. Buckminster Fuller (1895–1983)

FIGURE 11.2

A simple genetic striping mechanism occurring at different times during fetal development produces these three striping patterns.

Source: From *Hen's Teeth and Horse's Toes: Further Reflections in Natural History* by Stephen Jay Gould. Copyright © 1983 by Stephen Jay Gould. Used by permission of W. W. Norton & Company, Inc.

Equus burchelli (Burchell's zebra)

Equus zebra (mountain zebra)

Equus grevyi (Grevy's zebra)

is an example of cultural sexism. Although science has attempted to explain the complexity and variations in human sexual response, some people insist that the only acceptable way to love and make love is to be a heterosexual couple. History tells us, however, that homosexual feelings are not a contemporary aberration, but have been reflected in human behavior in all cultures, in every era.

What historical evidence has described the existence of homosexuality?

Love and sexual desire between men was accepted and widely practiced in ancient Greece. Greeks openly wrote about the love of one man for another. Although Sappho's poetry described women's love for other women, men were the primary authors of Greek literature that has been preserved. Approving of same-sex attraction wasn't an Athenian idiosyncrasy; it was also widely accepted in Sparta and other city-states. One of the most famous military units in Greek history was the Band of Thebes—150 pairs of lovers, a fighting force of 300 men; each pledged to stand by his lover in battle until death took one or both. The unit played a heroic part in Sparta's siege of Thebes: Fewer than 6,000 Theban defenders defeated more than 10,000 Spartan soldiers, a defeat from which Sparta never recovered, paving the way for the conquest of Greece by Philip of Macedonia. Philip's son, Alexander the Great, would become famous for conquering the known world during his lifetime and, according to contemporary accounts, was known to engage in sexual activity with male partners (Rowse, 1977).

One of the ironies of the history of homosexuality was recorded in nineteenth-century England. At a time when English society was extremely homophobic, wealthy families sent their sons to male-only boarding schools, where they learned to read Latin and Greek texts, some with homosexual themes. Many memoirs recall upper-class boarding school experiences where English boys are described as engaging in homosexual behavior that they called **Greek love**, a euphemism for homosexual activity (Crompton, 1998).

Anthropologists have observed that culture often determines societal attitudes toward homosexuality. Some Native American cultures believed that a homosexual is a special human being, possessing traits of both males and females, and thus endowed with great power. Katz (1976) provided historical and anthropological documentation as evidence of the acceptance of homosexuality in various Native American cultures.

Some Polynesian and Caribbean cultures also view same-sex attraction and homosexual behavior as acceptable. The Mediterranean region, including southern Italy and countries such as Greece, Morocco, and Turkey, has historically been a haven for European homosexuals because same-sex relationships were tolerated. Aristocratic homosexuals traveled there primarily to act on their sexual attraction to same-sex partners (Crompton, 1985; Williams, 2001). According to Zeldin (1994), homosexuality has been accepted at one time or another by about two thirds of human societies.

Early on, the Catholic Church played a major role in the denunciation of homosexuality in Europe. The church regarded homosexuality as a sin, yet in 1102, the Archbishop of Canterbury called for lenient punishments for people engaging in same-sex activity because, "this sin has been so public that hardly anyone has blushed for it" (Zeldin, 1994, p. 123). As part of investigations by the Inquisition, church persecution of homosexuals began in the thirteenth century as the Vatican sought to eliminate various heresies. The Inquisition lasted about 400 years, but homosexuals continued to be persecuted in Europe for the next 600 years (Boswell, 1994; Duberman, Vicinus, & Chauncey, 1989).

Medieval churchmen executed both male and female homosexuals, although women were equally likely to be executed as witches, also justified in the Bible. The persecution and execution of men has suggested the origin of the term *faggot* as derived from *fagot*, referring to sticks tied in a bundle for kindling. When medieval judges condemned men to death for engaging in sexual activity with another man, the executioner sometimes tied up and piled the men on top of one another like bundles of kindling and burned them (Kantor, 1998).

Even royalty were not immune from persecution. Kings and queens were permitted a variety of sins as long as they used discretion, but English monarch Edward II was not discreet. His coronation festivities were almost disrupted by public reaction to the king's obvious preference for his friend Piers Gaveston rather than his queen. Offended by the king's outrageous behavior, English nobles sent Gaveston back to

France. Edward could not bear to be separated from his lover and pleaded that Gaveston be allowed to come back. Shortly after Gaveston returned to England, he was murdered, which led to a civil war that ended with Edward's death at the hands of Queen Isabella and her lover, Mortimer (Rowse, 1977). Still, Edward II was the exception. For royalty or aristocrats, or perhaps an artist under their protection, it was possible to escape persecution for having homosexual feelings or behaviors.

Despite some degree of tolerance for occasional royal family and aristocratic dalliances, England continued to reflect homophobic attitudes that forced those with fame and fortune, like the poet Lord Byron, to seek sexual pleasure outside the boundaries of Britain for fear of punishment in the country. Indeed, popular playwright Oscar Wilde was tried and sent to prison (1895–1897) for his homosexual activity.

By the twentieth century, cultural attitudes about homosexuality in England had mellowed; this was true for most of Europe, but not for the United States. The contrast between European and American attitudes was illustrated by the appointment of James Hormel as U.S. ambassador to Luxembourg during the Clinton administration. Officials in Luxembourg raised no objection to Hormel, who was openly gay, but his appointment was stalled in the Senate for two years because of objections from influential conservative senators.

How have attitudes of the American people changed concerning homosexuality?

As it did with racial minorities, World War II had an impact on American homosexuals returning from the war. The 1948 Kinsey Report had refuted the heterosexual assumption, and many gay and lesbian

> Whenever I behold someone who possesses any talent or displays any dexterity of mind, who can do or say something more appropriately than the rest of the world, I am compelled to fall in love with him, and give myself away to him so entirely that I am no longer my own property but wholly his.
>
> Michelangelo [Buonarroti] (1475–1564)

veterans thought their military experience earned them the right to be accepted regardless of sexual orientation. Because California courts had upheld the right of openly gay men and lesbians to patronize certain bars and businesses, it seemed the safest place to live. San Francisco had been a major port of departure for men and women sent to the Pacific, and many returning gays and lesbians chose to remain there. As their numbers grew, so did their political activism; by the 1970s, mayoral candidates such as George Moscone were openly courting gay voters.

San Francisco was one of many cities across the United States to witness gay and lesbian political activism, yet when Harvey Milk, an openly gay candidate, was elected San Francisco city supervisor in 1977, national media reported the story. One year later, a city supervisor who objected to serving with a gay man murdered both Milk and Mayor Moscone. As an indication that anti-gay prejudice had not disappeared, the jury convicted Dan White of the minimal penalty possible in such a case, manslaughter. The White verdict sparked a riot that lasted more than two hours in gay areas of San Francisco; police responded by shouting homophobic slurs and brutally beating any gay man or lesbian they encountered (D'Emilio, 1989).

The San Francisco riot on the West Coast, like the Stonewall riot a decade earlier in New York City, were two of many events in the late twentieth century that would force Americans everywhere to acknowledge the presence of homosexuals (see Table 11.1). The word **gay** became accepted as the self-chosen label of the homosexual community, although usage eventually was limited to men. The identification of homosexuals in popular culture and the acceptance of gays and lesbians by prominent people were important factors in changing historical anti-gay attitudes. By the 1970s, columnist Abigail van Buren ("Dear Abby") responded to questions about homosexuality based on her understanding of scientific research, emphasizing the need to accept it. In 1975, David Kopay, a retired National Football League running back, published an autobiography in which he not only admitted his own homosexuality but also alleged that many professional athletes were gay. With the sexual identity of popular stars from the 1950s and 1960s such as Rock Hudson and Liberace being revealed to the public, gays and lesbians increasingly encountered more tolerant attitudes, especially in urban areas.

TABLE 11.1 A Timetable of Important Events in the Recognition of Gay Rights in the United States

1924	Formation of the first recognized activist group for gays and lesbians (Chicago).
1962	Illinois is the first state to repeal its sodomy laws.
1969	Police raid of the Stonewall Inn (a gay bar in New York City) results in riots that spark the beginning of the gay rights movement.
1970	First "Gay Pride" march (New York City) commemorates the Stonewall Riot.
1975	Retired NFL running back Dave Kopay is the first professional athlete to admit that he is gay.
1978	Harvey Milk, San Francisco's first openly gay City Supervisor, is assassinated.
1981	The Centers for Disease Control reports on the first case of what later becomes known as AIDS (initially called the "gay plague").
1982	Wisconsin is the first state to prohibit discrimination based on sexual orientation.
1982	Harvey Fierstein's play about a drag queen called "Torch Song Trilogy" opens on Broadway and wins the Tony Award for Best Play.
1984	Hollywood's legendary leading man Rock Hudson admits to being gay.
1987	Formation of ACT UP, which advocates for more funding for AIDS research.
1993	U.S. military adopts "don't ask, don't tell" policy as a compromise to address the problem of harassment of gay and lesbian soldiers.
1993	Hundreds of thousands participate in a march for equal rights for gays and lesbians (Washington, D.C.).
1996	U.S. Supreme Court declares equal rights for gays and lesbians.
1997	The popular television show *Ellen* is the first program to have a main character who admits to being gay (as does the actress, Ellen DeGeneres).
1998	The murder of Matthew Shepard gains national attention and is the catalyst in many states to include gays and lesbians in hate-crime legislation.
1999	Vermont's Supreme Court rules that same-sex couples have the same legal right to get married as heterosexual couples.
2003	U.S. Supreme Court rules that sodomy laws are unconstitutional, reversing its 1986 decision in *Hardwick v. Bowers*.

Most Americans tended to ignore the AIDS epidemic that arose in the early 1980s, although some radio and television ministers blamed homosexual behavior for causing this "gay disease." As Sontag (1989) explained, "The unsafe behavior that produces AIDS (was) judged to be more than just weakness. It is indulgence, delinquency—addiction to chemicals that are illegal and to sex regarded as deviant" (p. 25). As the epidemic continued, Americans were forced to confront the American historic cultural bias against gays; people increasingly recognized HIV as a virus, not a punishment from God. The fact that a young boy, Ryan White, could contract this fatal disease from a blood transfusion illustrated the point dramatically. (See Figure 11.3.) For seven of his eight years as president, Ronald Reagan never publicly acknowledged the spread of AIDS (Shilts, 1987). It took another presidential election before Congress passed the Ryan White Comprehensive AIDS Resources Emergency Act in 1990. But anti-gay attitudes in the United States have persisted, in part because of religious and cultural beliefs.

FIGURE 11.3

Ryan White returns to school after being sent home by school authorities who feared that having AIDS would make him a danger to the lives of the other students. Based on medical testimony, the courts disagreed.

Source: Bettmann/CORBIS.

What are some anti-gay cultural and religious beliefs?

Many Americans still cling to the cultural belief that homosexuality is unnatural, an accusation that calls for reasonable people to consider what it would mean for something to be natural. Some sexual activity, such as incest, is forbidden in every known culture, yet homosexual behavior is—or has been—accepted in most world cultures. Scientists have argued that anything observed and documented in nature should be considered natural. Stein (1999) found that scientific studies of animals in their natural habitat report occurrences of sexual activity between animals of the same sex in every group studied, suggesting that sexual activity between same-sex partners normally occurs in nature.

Although the Catholic Church accepts that homosexuality is a natural predisposition (that is, one is born with it), the Church continues to denounce homosexual activity as a sin—the only instance of the church forbidding something it admits to be natural. The struggle within the Catholic Church over this issue is reflected in a letter from American bishops urging Catholic parents to accept and love their gay and lesbian children regardless of whether they refrain from acting on their homosexuality (Christian Century Foundation, 1997).

Protestant churches are divided on the issue of accepting homosexuality. Some Protestant theologians continue to condemn homosexuality. Others argue that certain biblical passages have been mistranslated

> God loves homosexuals as much as he loves everybody else.
>
> Ryan White (1971–1990)

to justify regarding homosexual behavior as a sin—these passages actually denounce male and female prostitution, not homosexuality. Some feel biblical criticism of men engaging in homosexual acts was based on the biblical authors assuming everyone was heterosexual, and that anyone engaging in a homosexual act betrayed human nature (Doupe, 2001). Another argument that has arisen is that since biblical injunctions against eating pork or making clothes out of two types of material are now regarded as historic but no longer relevant, any biblical passage interpreted as an injunction against homosexual acts should also be regarded as an example of historic prejudice. Protestant debates about accepting homosexuality certainly will continue, as was apparent in the controversy in the Episcopal Church over the ordination of the first openly gay bishop. Time will tell if various Christian denominations will respond to research on sexual orientation and accept people who are not heterosexual.

Individual Heterosexism

Despite increasing acceptance of homosexuality in Western cultures outside the United States, as well as research findings discussed earlier, many Americans still regard homosexuality as unnatural and sinful. Sociological study confirms that **individual heterosexism**, negative attitudes and behaviors based on the belief that sexual orientations other than heterosexual are unnatural, is a major factor promoting one of the most common hate crimes in the United States—**gay bashing**, the physical assault of a person perceived to be gay. In a recent study, Herek (2009) reported that more than 63% of gay men have experienced verbal abuse, 35.5% have been subjected to violent threats, and 25% have been victims of physical assault. One of the most infamous gay bashing incidents occurred on October 7, 1998. Matthew Shepard, a 22-year-old University of Wyoming student, was savagely beaten, tied to a fence in a remote area, and left to die. (See Figure 11.4.) He suffered for 18 hours before he was found. At the hospital, doctors reported that his skull was fractured and there had been brain stem damage. He never regained consciousness and died just six days later. During the trial of the two young men who murdered

FIGURE 11.4

Matthew Shepard's legacy is not limited to his brutal and tragic murder, but to the expansion of the federal hate crimes law to include sexual orientation and gender identity.

Source: Photo courtesy of the Matthew Shepard Foundation.

Shepard, the prosecution argued that the crime resulted in large part because of the victim's sexual orientation. The killers could not be charged with a hate crime because sexual orientation was not included in the federal hate crimes law that had been passed in 1968 following the assassination of Dr. Martin Luther King, Jr. That law defined a hate crime as one motivated by the race, religion, or national origin of the victim. One response to Matthew Shepard's murder was an intense lobbying effort to expand the hate crimes act to include sexual orientation (ABCnews, 2004), but those trying to expand the law encountered considerable resistance from some members of Congress.

The effort to expand the hate crimes act began in 1997, and although the House of Representatives and the Senate each passed a version of the law over the next twelve years, both bodies could not agree on one version until 2008. The various versions of the bill had been supported by over 300 activist groups, over half of the state attorneys general, and almost all major national law enforcement agencies. As politicians in Washington delayed in taking action, 30 states amended their hate crime laws to include sexual orientation or disability, and 12 states added gender identity (Anti-Defamation League, 2009). Further, polls indicated growing public support. In a 2007 Gallup poll, 68% of Americans favored expanding the definition of hate crimes to include sexual orientation and gender identity. A 2007 Hart Research poll reported that even groups often viewed as not sympathetic toward gay causes expressed support for this change to hate crime laws—56% of Republican men and 63% of evangelical Christians (Human Rights Campaign, 2009). Finally, the House and Senate reached an agreement, and on October 28, 2009, President Barack Obama signed the bill that added sexual orientation, gender identity, and people with a disability to the groups identified under the Hate Crimes Prevention Act.

Although this act will assist law enforcement after a crime has been committed, it may not result in a reduction of anti-gay violence since personal prejudice is considered to be a major factor. Young men are the primary perpetrators of anti-gay violence, and studies of the motivations for anti-gay violence have revealed that young men often believe cultural myths about homosexuality and use them to justify their verbal abuse and physical attacks (Franklin, 1998). This finding suggests that an even more effective way to reduce gay bashing is for teachers in K–12 schools and postsecondary institutions to confront such myths in their classrooms, and provide more accurate information about sexual orientation to refute such myths. The stakes are high. In 2010, Rutgers student Tyler Clementi committed suicide after his roommate secretly filmed him kissing an older man in their dorm room and then put the video on social media for anyone to watch. In 2012, the jury found the roommate guilty of all charges, including the commission of a hate crime, but the judge disagreed and only sentenced him to thirty days in jail. One young man is dead and another will likely be haunted by the harm he inflicted on the Clementi family for the rest of his life.

What are some myths about homosexuality?

Myths regarding homosexuality contribute to individual prejudice and homophobia in the United States (Blumenfeld, 2001; Hollier, 2004). **Homophobia** is a stronger feeling than prejudice, usually defined as fear or hatred of homosexuals. Following are some examples of myths still perpetuated in American society about gays and lesbians along with refutations based on reality.

> **MYTH:** Anyone who has ever engaged in a homosexual act at any time is a homosexual.
>
> **REALITY:** To be identified as a homosexual means that a person demonstrates a persistent erotic attraction for people of the same sex. Gays and lesbians are not attracted to every same-sex person they see, but when they feel physically and emotionally attracted to someone, that person is consistently someone of the same sex.

Some people engage in sexual activity with a person of the same sex one time and never again. Some people have only engaged in homosexual acts during unusual and temporary circumstances, such as being in situations where there is no easy access to members of the opposite sex (such as in prison or in the military). Men or women who engage in sexual acts with a partner of the same sex in an unusual situation generally do not persist in this behavior when circumstances return to the more typical situation and thus should not be identified as homosexual.

> **MYTH:** Homosexuals tend to engage in criminal activity and are especially likely to prey on children and molest them.
>
> **REALITY:** Studies of criminal activity report that homosexuals are no more likely to engage in criminal activity than heterosexuals, and studies of child molesters reveal that over 99% are male and nearly 80% are white heterosexual men who are married or were formerly married (Abel & Harlow, 2001).

Child molesters are **pedophiles**—adults who desire sexual contact with children. There are heterosexual pedophiles who desire children of the opposite sex and homosexual pedophiles who desire children of the same sex. As the data show, children are at greater risk from heterosexuals than from gays and lesbians. Pedophilia has nothing to do with being homosexual.

> **MYTH:** Homosexuals attempt to seduce vulnerable adolescents and recruit them into their lifestyle.
>
> **REALITY:** Individuals who engage in homosexual behavior during adolescence tend to do so with other adolescents, not adults.

The accusation of corrupting the youth is an ancient one, as we know from the life of Socrates, who was accused of this crime (and others), found guilty, and ordered to drink a poisonous cup of hemlock for his punishment. Because the primary group responsible for gay bashing in the United States is adolescent males, gays are risking violence if they approach adolescents for sexual purposes.

> **MYTH:** Homosexuals do not have loving relationships but are only interested in sex and engage in sexually promiscuous behavior.
>
> **REALITY:** Americans have historically denied gay men and lesbians the right to marry and refused to recognize domestic partnerships; they have tolerated sexual activities of gays and lesbians who are discreet but have not sanctioned their activity.

This myth is especially egregious because American society has created conditions that promote the behavior being condemned. Gays and lesbians have been allowed to engage in sexual activity in

> If . . . marriage can keep you in touch with your past, your emotional self, and your humanity, the notion that this should be any less true for gay or lesbian couples than it is for heterosexuals is absurd.
>
> Derrick Bell (1930–2011)

gay bars and bathhouses, but they are not allowed to declare their affection publicly or to have their relationships acknowledged. Americans have vigorously resisted gays and lesbians who have sought public sanction for their relationships by demanding the right to marry or to be recognized in domestic partnerships. Although heterosexuals may engage in public displays of affection, gay men or lesbians are often verbally or physically assaulted for the same behavior.

Heterosexuals are encouraged to marry and be monogamous, yet the percentage engaging in premarital sex with many partners has increased, and it has been estimated that two thirds of all marriages in the United States will end in separation or divorce (Cushner, McClelland, & Safford, 2008). Given such projections, it is hypocritical for the heterosexual community to accuse gays and lesbians of promiscuity and to insist that marriage is sacred and should be reserved exclusively for heterosexual couples. According to psychologists, gays and lesbians have the same need as heterosexuals for long-term stable relationships. Because of the 2003 decision by the Massachusetts Supreme Court that gay and lesbian couples ought to have the same legal right to marry as heterosexuals, gay men and lesbians may have an opportunity to demonstrate their ability to have successful monogamous marital relationships. Other states where gay marriage is legal include: Iowa, Connecticut, Vermont, New Hampshire, New York, Washington, and Maryland, but 31 states have passed constitutional amendments banning gay marriage.

> **MYTH:** People become homosexual because they had a bad experience while involved in heterosexual activity; therefore gay men or lesbians could change their sexual behavior if they had a positive heterosexual experience.
>
> **REALITY:** Many gay men and lesbians have been involved in heterosexual relationships, including marriage, because of the hostility directed against homosexuality.

Many gays and lesbians have engaged in heterosexual activities in an effort to convince themselves of their normality, but sexual orientation is not a choice. Some people still refer to sexual preference as if lesbians and gays prefer to love same-sex partners. But human sexuality is not a matter of preference. Schlatter and Steinback (2010) report that evidence from "sexual reorientation" therapies clearly show that they have not been successful, and in a 2009 report, the American Psychological Association repudiated such therapies. One of the few studies that supported reparative therapy was conducted by noted psychiatrist Robert Spitzer in 2003, but in 2012, he recanted his findings, agreeing with his critics that the study was poorly designed and the conclusions were flawed, and he apologized to the gay community. Studies of human sexuality have concluded that sexual orientation is determined early in human development. Once we become aware of our sexual feelings, our only choice is to accept these feelings and act on them or to reject and repress them. Some gays and lesbians have accepted their sexual orientation but—as with some heterosexuals—have chosen to be chaste. Sexual abstinence is a choice any individual can make, but it is no more likely to lead to happiness for homosexuals than for heterosexuals.

Myth: Close personal relationships between adolescents or adults of the same sex could stimulate homosexual feelings and behavior, so intimate friendships should be avoided, especially between men.

Reality: It is perfectly normal for a man or a woman to feel and express love and affection for a person of the same sex as can be observed in other cultures.

Displays of affection between men and between women are common in many cultures. In American culture, women are allowed some degree of public intimacy with each other such as holding hands, dancing together, or even kissing (as long as they don't kiss on the lips). Men are not allowed to engage in similar public behaviors with other men without being perceived as homosexual; this creates a burden for American men who have the same human need for affection and intimacy as do women.

MYTH: People become homosexual because of negative childhood experiences such as being sexually abused or having parents who were not good heterosexual role models.

REALITY: Based on reviews of research, the American Psychiatric Association has stated that there is no evidence that parental deficiency is a cause of homosexuality. Further, the studies related to sexual abuse report that it is no more prevalent among children who identify as gay when they are adolescents or adults than among children who continue to identify as heterosexual during adolescence and when they become adults (Schlatter & Steinback, 2010).

In addition to having no foundation in reality, this myth attempts to demonize parents of gay men and lesbians. It is rooted in the past perception of homosexuality as a perversion of a person's normal sexual behavior; therefore, it must have been caused by someone or by some negative sexual experiences. This myth is also a denial of the conclusions that numerous studies have reached since the Kinsey Report was first published in 1948—that sexual orientation is a diverse human attribute, and that the influences shaping sexual orientation are complex, including both environmental and genetic factors.

Because of myths such as these, it should be easy to understand why most people would be reluctant to identify with such a reviled and persecuted group. Civil rights activists often claim that gays and lesbians encounter more blatant discrimination than any other group. In response to this discrimination, gays and lesbians have intensified their efforts to promote the concept of gay rights across America. (See Figure 11.5.)

Institutional Heterosexism

Although Kinsey suggested that the sexual orientation of approximately 10% of Americans is exclusively homosexual, surveys report approximately 3% of men identify themselves as gay and about 1.5% of women identify themselves as lesbian (Jones & George, 2009). It is impossible to

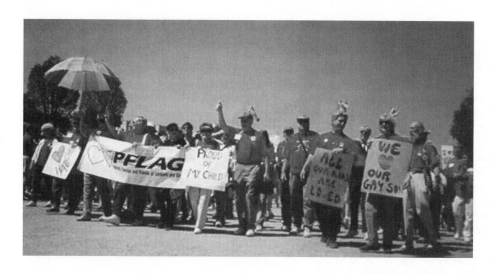

FIGURE 11.5

Parents, Families, and Friends of Lesbians and Gays (PFLAG) is an advocacy organization that started when the mother of a gay man participated in a 1972 gay pride march in New York City after her son had been assaulted because of his sexual orientation. Today PFLAG has a national office in Washington, D.C., with 500 affiliates that promote respect for human differences and the acceptance of all people regardless of sexual orientation or gender identity.

Source: Photo courtesy of PFLAG.

have a census of gay men and lesbians because of the number who conceal their sexual identity—or deny it—to protect themselves from other people's negative attitudes and behaviors. Hollier (2004) provides estimates of from 7 to 21 million gay and lesbian workers in the U.S. workforce, constituting anywhere from 3% to 12% of one's employees. **Institutional heterosexism**—established laws, customs, and practices that systematically discriminate against people who are not heterosexual—has been so prevalent and so blatant that activists have increased their efforts to combat discrimination across America. They are promoting **gay rights**, insisting that gays and lesbians should have the same rights and privileges as heterosexual Americans.

Is the demand for gay rights really a demand for special privileges?

The goal of gay rights is to make it possible for gays and lesbians to be honest about their sexual orientation without being deprived of civil rights. These rights do not entail special privileges, but rather the rights of citizens in our democracy. It is a question of tolerance: One can support civil rights for gays and lesbians without necessarily condoning homosexual behavior. It does require us to agree that if gays and lesbians identify their sexual orientation publicly, they should not be discriminated against in being hired for jobs, renting or purchasing a home, running for political office, enlisting in the military, attending their church of choice, or any other rights that heterosexuals take for granted. Gay rights means having the same—not special—rights and responsibilities as other

> Tolerance is the positive and cordial effort to understand another's beliefs, practices, and habits without necessarily sharing or accepting them.
>
> Joshua Liebman (1907–1948)

citizens of the United States. In most of the United States, gays and lesbians are often not extended the civil rights that heterosexuals enjoy unless they are **in the closet**, meaning they deny or disguise their sexual orientation.

According to Van Den Burgh (2003), one third of gay men and one fourth of lesbians surveyed said they had personally encountered discrimination at their work site. About 17% either were fired from a job or were denied employment when the employer became aware of their sexual orientation. When the research included the broad range of individuals included in the term **transgender**, discrimination remained at the same level, but a hostile work environment became more likely. A national study of lesbian, gay, and transgender employees reported that 17% had been fired or pressured to quit a job, and 25% had experienced harassment at work. For transgender people, the harassment could range from a co-worker not wanting to share a bathroom with them to being unfairly evaluated and denied a promotion. According to a study by the Transgender Law Center, half of all transgender employees have experienced some form of discrimination at work (Broadus, 2006). In the 1990s, only one state included gender identity in its nondiscrimination policies, but since the twenty-first century began, 16 additional states have revised or passed new nondiscrimination policies and 15 of them now include gender identity as well sexual orientation (see Table 11.2).

Only 21 states have laws against discrimination based on sexual orientation. In the other 29 states, it is legal for a business to refuse to hire or to be able to fire someone simply for being gay. Numerous examples exist of gays and lesbians who have been dismissed from jobs, not because they were inefficient or incompetent but because employers discovered their sexual orientation. A Baltimore civil rights advocate told the story of a lesbian manager of a diner who hired a gay dishwasher. When the owner of the diner realized the sexual orientation of the dishwasher, he insisted that the manager fire the man because he did not want gay employees on his payroll. The woman enjoyed a good relationship with her boss and had certainly proven her competence as a manager over the past ten years. She took a chance. She told the boss he already had a gay employee and he was looking at her. She also was fired. The civil rights advocate who related the

TABLE 11.2 States with Nondiscrimination Policies That Include Sexual Orientation

Wisconsin—1982
Massachusetts*—1989
Connecticut*—1991
Hawaii*—1991
New Jersey*—1992
Vermont*—1992
Minnesota*—1993
New Hampshire—1997
Nevada*—1999
Rhode Island*—2001
Maryland—2001
New York—2002
New Mexico*—2003
California*—2003
Illinois*—2005
Maine*—2005
Washington*—2006
Colorado*—2007
Iowa*—2007
Oregon*—2007
Delaware—2009

The asterisks identify those states that include gender identity as well as sexual orientation in their nondiscrimination policies.

Source: Transgender Law and Policy Institute (2012)

incident insisted the story was not unusual. The only way gays and lesbians can be certain of keeping their jobs is to stay in the closet. And so they do, but even then they do not avoid discrimination.

How can homosexuals be discriminated against if they don't reveal their identity?

If gay men and lesbians are in the closet—not perceived by their employers, supervisors, and co-workers as homosexual—it seems logical to assume that they should not experience discrimination, but that assumption is only accurate for blatant kinds of discrimination. Subtle forms of discrimination can affect such concerns as job advancement. According to a Harvard Business School study, gays and lesbians who did not identify themselves at work were not promoted as readily as their heterosexual peers. Because of the need to keep their personal lives secret, gay men and lesbians often maintained their personal privacy at work, not engaging frequently in casual conversations and not socializing with others after work or on weekends. The study concluded that social isolation in protection of one's identity is a major factor for gays and lesbians not being promoted (Badgett, 2001).

Another form of discrimination based on sexual orientation involves employee benefits. According to Hollier (2004), almost 40% of employee compensation is offered in benefits such as insurance (life, health, and dental), retirement (pension, health care), and leaves (bereavement, family). Employees who receive such benefits for their spouses are being compensated significantly more than co-workers who may be in committed domestic partnerships. A legal **domestic partnership** is defined as "An intimate, committed relationship between two individuals of legal age who are financially and emotionally interdependent, share the same residence, and intend to remain together indefinitely" (Badgett, 2001, p. 82).

Being unable to claim these benefits is a substantial financial loss for gay and lesbian employees who have a domestic partnership but are in the closet. In addition, openly gay and lesbian employees suffer the same loss when employers refuse to implement policies including domestic partners in employee benefits. According to the Bureau of Labor Statistics (2011), 50% of state and local employees who are in a domestic partnership receive survivor benefits compared to only 7% of those employed in private industry, and 33% of these state and local employees are eligible to be covered by their partner's health care benefits compared to 29% in private industry.

Why do homosexuals want legal recognition for domestic partnerships?

Many gays and lesbians are willing to let marriage remain an exclusively heterosexual arrangement as long as the law recognizes domestic partnerships. The purpose of legal recognition for domestic partnerships is to provide gay couples with the same legal rights married couples enjoy: having the right to make decisions for an incapacitated partner, being able to inherit a partner's property, or being eligible for a partner's survival benefits. Advocates for recognizing domestic partnerships emphasize the existence of such laws in Belgium, Denmark, Finland, France, Germany, Hungary, Iceland, the Netherlands, Norway, Portugal, Sweden, Argentina, Brazil, Canada, Croatia, Spain, and South Africa (The Pew Forum, 2009).

A dramatic example of the importance of recognizing domestic partnerships was illustrated in Minnesota. A head-on collision with a drunk driver left Sharon Kowalski paralyzed and unable to speak. Her long-term partner visited her at the hospital for as many as eight hours a day to read aloud to her, massage her, and make sure Sharon received rehabilitative therapy. At first appreciative, Sharon's parents began to question the behavior of Sharon's friend until they were finally told that their daughter was a lesbian and that the friend was actually her domestic partner. Sharon's father immediately took steps to prevent Sharon's partner from seeing his daughter, even though hospital personnel confirmed that Sharon was improving largely because of the therapy her partner had been providing (Griscom, 2009).

Sharon's father committed her to a nursing home, even though it offered minimal rehabilitation services. Sharon's partner pursued every possible course of action, and after eight years, the courts recognized that Sharon Kowalski was competent to make her own decisions and that it was her desire to be cared for by her partner. Since that incident, Minnesota legislators have added homosexuals to the list of protected groups in its civil rights law. With the U.S. Supreme Court's 2003 decision in *Lawrence v. Texas* that it is unconstitutional to criminalize gay sexual activity, opponents feared that the decision represents the first step toward sanctioning gay marriages.

> If what we think is right and wrong divides still further the human family, there must be something wrong with what we think is right.
>
> William Sloane Coffin (1924–2006)

If domestic partnerships were recognized, why would homosexuals wish to marry?

Gays and lesbians who desire a state-recognized marriage give reasons similar to those of heterosexuals: to make public statements about their commitment to each other, including the pledge to maintain a monogamous relationship. Rather than being a special privilege, marriage is a decision to participate in a legally and socially sanctioned activity. Church leaders may insist that marriage is a sacred rite reserved exclusively for people in heterosexual relationships; however, many gays and lesbians want to participate in a secular marriage ceremony performed in accordance with state law, not necessarily a religious ceremony. To assert that marriage is a legal contract available exclusively for heterosexual couples is to engage in discrimination based on sexual orientation. Even so, 31 states have passed constitutional amendments prohibiting same-sex marriage (ProCon, 2012).

In recent years, gays and lesbians have taken legal action to force the courts to rule on the legality of same-sex marriage. In 1996, a Hawaii Circuit Court found no legitimate legal basis for denying homosexuals the right to obtain marriage licenses, but the state court reversed that ruling three years later. In 1999, Vermont's Supreme Court ruled that denying gay and lesbian couples the opportunity to participate in legal, secular marriage violated the state constitution. In many states, the reaction to such rulings has been to pass legislation defining marriage as a legal contract between "a man and a woman," refusing to recognize same-sex marriages performed in other states. Yet eight states and the District of Columbia have legalized marriage (ProCon, 2012), and that has created a legal conflict for couples marrying in those states and moving to states where gay marriages are not recognized. The California Supreme Court decision in May of 2008 in support of gay marriage, followed by Californians voting for Proposition 8, which prohibits gay marriage, has made it even more likely that the U.S. Supreme Court will soon have to address the issue of whether gay men and lesbians have the legal right to get married. In the meantime, many gays and lesbians continue to enjoy stable, monogamous relationships, some choosing to have children, while they wait for state and federal law to acknowledge the reality of their relationships.

What harm is done to a child raised by gay parents?

It is harmful and immoral for a child to be abandoned, untouched, unloved, ridiculed, and physically or sexually abused. It is usually not harmful for a child to be cared for by his or her biological mother or father or to be adopted by loving parents, regardless of their sexual orientation. According to a 2011 study, the percent of Americans rejecting the right of gays to adopt and raise children has fallen from 50% in 2007 to 35% today. Almost half of Americans now feel that it doesn't make any difference if parents are gay or straight (Pew Research Center, 2011).

There are over 115,00 same-sex couples raising children. According to the 2010 census, 25% of all same sex households are raising children (U.S. Census Bureau, 2011). In the past, these children were from a previous marriage, before an individual understood and acknowledged his or her sexual orientation, and now with the use of reproductive technologies, about 84% of these children were being raised by a biological parent." (U.S. Census Bureau, 2011). Regardless of the reason for having children, studies suggest that same-sex couples are conscientious parents.

According to Schlatter and Steinback (2010), there is no research supporting the claim that children being raised by gay parents are being harmed. In fact, there is some evidence that they benefit from the experience. In evaluating children raised by gays or lesbians, studies have explored such factors as social interaction, intelligence, self-esteem, and ability to express feelings. Children of gays and lesbians not only appear to develop self-confidence and social skills, but also are more tolerant of differences than are other children (McLeod & Crawford, 1998). Research does not support the exclusion of gays and lesbians from any occupation or activity in which other U.S. citizens participate. In response to the research on parenting, the Child Welfare League, the American Academy of Pediatrics, and the American Psychological Association (APA) have released statements supporting the right of same-sex couples to be parents because, as the APA has stated, "parenting effectiveness and the adjustment development and psychological well-being of children is unrelated to parental sexual orientation" (Schlatter & Steinback, 2010, p. 32).

Why have homosexuals always been excluded from military service?

Historic evidence indicates that gays and lesbians have served in the military in the United States and in other countries. In addition to the Greek Band of Thebes, historic warriors such as Alexander the Great and Richard the Lion-Hearted had male lovers. As attitudes in the Western world became more negative toward homosexuality, same-sex behavior in the military also became more carefully concealed. Activities occasionally would be exposed, as in Germany's Eulenberg Affair where from 1907 to 1909, accusations of homosexual behavior were directed against officers in the German army, the diplomatic corps, and the cabinet of Kaiser Wilhelm (Steakley, 1989). Allegations were well documented, which led to several resignations by cabinet members and military officers.

In America, a navy investigation at Newport Naval Training Station following World War I similarly revealed widespread homosexual activity (Chauncey, 1989). During World War II, the army conducted an investigation of alleged lesbian activity in the Women's Army Corps (WAC) in which a WAC officer testified about a letter she received from the Surgeon General's Office that said "homosexual relationships should be tolerated" as long as they were discreet and did not lead to disruptions in the unit (Bérubé, 1989, p. 384).

Homosexual participation in the armed forces is not new. What is new is periodic blatant discrimination against gays and lesbians by the U.S. military. In 1981, the Pentagon instituted a policy banning all gays and lesbians from the armed forces because the leaders believed that homosexuality was incompatible with military service. Patriotic gay and lesbian soldiers serving their country could be discharged, not for incompetence or misbehavior, but because they were homosexual. The Clinton administration modified the policy in 1993, forbidding the military to inquire about a person's sexual orientation; neither recruits nor gays and lesbians already in the armed forces could be asked about their sexual orientation.

> You don't have to be straight to shoot straight.
>
> Barry Goldwater (1909–1998)

The "Don't Ask, Don't Tell" (DADT) policy was intended to discourage attempts to identify and remove homosexuals from the military. Under this policy, gay men and lesbians could be silent or they could lie about their sexual identity, but they could still be discharged if their identity was discovered or if they admitted to it. In a study of discharges over a ten-year period after DADT was implemented (1993–2003), the military discharged over 10,000 service members, including many with critical military skills or other highly important skills such as being fluent in Arabic, Korean, and Farsi. The case for repealing DADT gained strength over the years because of the need for quality recruits. The Pentagon found that 75% of young Americans were ineligible for military service because of issues such as weight problems, inadequate education, or having a criminal record (SLDF, 2010). It was becoming increasingly difficult to justify rejecting otherwise qualified soldiers or recruits simply on the basis of their sexual orientation. The repeal of DADT came in the wake of several polls in recent years documenting public support for its repeal. A 2010 CNN poll reported that 72% of Americans supported repealing DADT, and a 2009 Gallup poll reported that such support included 60% of people claiming to be "churchgoers," and 58% of people identifying as "conservative" (SLDF, 2010).

According to Bumiller (2011), U.S. military leaders asked President Obama to delay the repeal so that they would have time to prepare for the end of DADT by revising regulations and implementing new training programs. Also in anticipation of the end of DADT, the Pentagon began accepting applications from openly gay men and lesbians. Military leaders anticipated a smooth transition based on the largely tolerant attitudes of those currently serving in the military. A 2008 *Military Times* poll reported that only 10% of the soldiers surveyed said they would not re-enlist if DADT were repealed. In Canada and Great Britain, polls found that two thirds of those in the military expressed strong concerns about serving with openly gay soldiers, but once the policy was changed in both nations, not a single soldier who resigned or did not re-enlist said that the reason was related to the policy change (Schlatter & Steinback, 2010). The response from gays and lesbians currently in the military to the repeal of DADT has been largely muted and varied. One soldier stationed in Germany made two phone calls to

Alabama to come out to his father and mother. He videotaped the calls and posted them on YouTube. In Washington, D.C., several members of the military held a press conference to officially come out of the closet, and in Vermont, a Navy lieutenant and his partner celebrated the repeal of DADT by getting married (Lynch, 2011). With the repeal of DADT, the United States joined 35 other nations that allow openly gay men and lesbians to serve in their armed forces. Now gay activists are demanding that gays and lesbians be accepted in other professions as well, such as education, where they have been excluded because of prejudicial attitudes.

Why should homosexuals be allowed to become teachers?

During the early 1990s, the Republican governor of Massachusetts was concerned enough about the safety of gay youth to initiate an investigation. In its final report, the Governor's Commission described a disturbing pattern of abuse: Testimony from gay and lesbian youth and their parents described a constant barrage of taunts and slurs, being spit on, and physical attacks. One boy left all his classes late and arrived late to every class so he could walk through empty hallways to avoid constant harassment. Another student who was not gay was assaulted every day at school simply because other students thought he was homosexual. Having heard such painful testimony of widespread anti-gay violence, the commission's recommendations included implementing school policies to protect gay and lesbian youth from harassment and violence, establishing support groups for gay and lesbian students, and providing information in school curriculum and in school libraries on gay and lesbian issues (Massachusetts Governor's Commission on Gay and Lesbian Youth, 1994).

In the report issued by the Governor's Commission, more than 50% of the gay and lesbian students said that they had heard at least one teacher make a homophobic comment. When adults are in a position of authority, such as a teacher, and express prejudicial attitudes to children or youth, they are legitimizing those negative attitudes. To correct this problem, the Governor's Commission recommended hiring lesbian and gay teachers and providing additional training for teachers and counselors to be more accepting of gay and lesbian students.

The same issue occurs on college campuses. A national study by Rankin (2005) reported that more than one third of lesbian, gay, bisexual, and transgender (**LGBT**) undergraduate students experienced anti-gay behaviors—most often this took the form of derogatory remarks (89%), followed by threats (48%), derogatory graffiti (39%), and even physical assaults (11%). Almost 80% of the time, the harasser was another student. The most effective way to address this problem is for K–12 teachers and administrators at schools and college campuses to become more aggressive in defending both the safety and the rights of not just gay and lesbian students, but bisexual and transgender youth as well. Various studies report that the average age for gays and lesbians to identify themselves publicly, called **coming out**, dropped from 14 for males and 17 for females in the 1960s to 10 and 12, respectively, in the 1990s. According to a National School Climate Survey of LGBT youth, 72.4% of the students had heard homophobic remarks in school. Further, 90% experienced harassment at some time during the previous year related to their sexual orientation, with 84.6% subjected to verbal harassment, 40.1% being physically harassed, and 18.8% being physically assaulted (GLSEN, 2010). When homophobic remarks were made to them, students said that a teacher or other school staff member was present almost half of the time, and 41.4% of the time these adults did not say anything, 43.4% of them occasionally responded to the remarks, but only 15% of the time did teachers or school staff usually or always respond. The lack of intervention has negative consequences for LGBT students because the more frequently they were harassed, the more likely it was that their grade point average would decline (GLSEN, 2010).

Being confronted with such hostility while receiving little support from teachers or others can result in feelings of worthlessness and despair. According to a review of several studies by the Suicide Prevention Resource Center (2008), 30% to 47% of LBGT youth have considered committing suicide, and 30% to 40% have attempted to commit suicide at least once. These statistics are a measure of the homophobia LGBT students encounter in their everyday lives, including when they are at school. According to the National School Climate Survey, two thirds of LGBT students said they did not feel safe at school, and almost a third admit to staying home from school or skipping a class because they felt it was especially unsafe to attend on a particular day (GLSEN, 2010).

There was some good news from the National Survey; almost 47% of schools now report having a Gay-Straight Alliance (GSA) support group, and these groups appear to help. GSA groups consist of gay and lesbian students and gay-friendly straight students. LGBT students who attended schools with a GSA group were more likely to say that they felt safe in schools. In addition, LGBT students attending a school that enforced an anti-bullying policy reported feeling much safer in school, but only 18.2% of schools had such policies (GLSEN, 2010). It is important that schools hire not only gay and lesbian teachers but also straight teachers who are comfortable with and supportive of LGBT students. Such teachers can be role models for all of their students and can establish a more positive learning climate for everyone. LGBT youth deserve that as much as any other student.

> I believe all Americans who believe in freedom, tolerance and human rights have a responsibility to oppose bigotry and prejudice based on sexual orientation.
>
> Coretta Scott King (1927–2006)

Why are the terms *bisexual* and *transgender* being linked to gays and lesbians?

Both of these terms relate to the issue of sexual orientation, and although the terms are new, the issues are not. As Sullivan (2003) noted, "Although the terms *transsexual* and *transgender* have been coined only relatively recently, a variety of forms of gender ambiguity can be found throughout history" (p. 99). Introduced in 1949, *transsexual* was one of the first terms for a category eventually classified as "Gender Identity Disorder." A transsexual was someone who could not psychologically identify with his or her biological gender—a male identifying as a female or a female identifying as a male. By the 1960s and 1970s, the medical profession came to regard transsexuals as different from homosexuals as they established gender identity clinics and developed sex reassignment procedures.

In addition to transsexuals, there are also individuals who identify as transvestites (cross dressers) or drag queens/kings, so the term *transgender* evolved to encompass a broad range of gender identities. Based on the work of several scholars, Rankin (2005) defined *transgender* as "individuals whose gender identity conflicts with biological sex assignment or societal expectations for gender expression as male or female" (p. 29). Douglas (2008) describes how transgender people have slowly been accepted and included by people in gay and lesbian communities. Today, when scholars refer to this diverse group of people, they usually employ the LGBT acronym.

Another issue related to sexual orientation emerged for people who openly identified themselves as bisexual (attracted to sexual partners of either gender). Bisexual individuals appear to receive the least attention of all groups within the LGBT community, perhaps because their sexual orientation may be viewed as disconcertingly fluid and ambiguous. Young (2004) discusses how lesbian and gay activists resisted adding "bisexual" to the names of their organizations or to the titles of their conferences. Young interviewed a gay man who admitted that he used to identify himself as bisexual, but he felt that he had to make a choice because: "Nobody likes bisexuals" (2004, p. 394). For that reason, many bisexuals are in the closet, "passing" as a gay man or lesbian when interacting with homosexuals and as straight when interacting with heterosexuals.

AFTERWORD

One of the most important changes needed in the United States is to establish policies and practices that promote tolerance for people across the spectrum of sexual orientations, so that all LGBT people feel safe at school, at work, and in their neighborhoods. Some LGBT individuals are trying to change the language of hate by choosing the term **queer** to describe people with diverse gender identities, including those who are gay or lesbian, bisexual, transsexual, and transgender. They argue that the term helps to simplify a discussion of the issues affecting this diverse group. As one gay man said in an interview with the *New York Times*, "When you're trying to describe the community you have to list gays, lesbians, bisexuals, drag queens, transsexuals (post-op and pre), it gets unwieldy. Queer says it all" (Duggan, 2004, p. 59). On the other hand, Goldman (2004) articulates two opposing reactions to the term from LGBT people: ". . . many people employ the term *queer* because it blurs—and some would argue erases—boundaries" (p. 85). Despite the differences of opinion about the term, Queer Studies programs are appearing on many college campuses as scholars examine and disseminate information about issues in the lives of LGBT people.

Changing cultural attitudes will take a long time, but if it becomes more acceptable to be open about sexual identity, it is more likely that heterosexuals will find that they know someone who is homosexual. Simon (1998) has reported that when people know someone who is a gay man or a lesbian, they tend to be less homophobic and to have a more positive attitude about the issue of sexual orientation and homosexuality. Change is possible if conditions are created to allow it. Accepting homosexuality is an ethical challenge confronting nations around the world, and every American institution and individual must decide how to meet it.

TERMS AND DEFINITIONS

Bisexual A normative category of sexual identity referring to lifelong sexual desires and/or erotic relations with members of both genders

Coming out When gay and lesbian youth publicly announce their sexual orientation

Cultural heterosexism The societal promotion of negative beliefs and practices that reinforce dominant culture traits that define heterosexuality as the norm and anything else as deviant and unacceptable; the assumption of superiority of heterosexuals over those who are not heterosexual

Domestic partnership An intimate, committed relationship between two individuals of legal age who are financially and emotionally interdependent, share the same residence, and intend to remain together indefinitely (Badgett, 2001)

Gay, Gays A term in reference to homosexuality in general, but specifically to male homosexuals

Gay bashing Physical assault on an individual who is perceived as being gay, which is motivated by the individual's sexual orientation

Gay rights The demand that gay men and lesbians be able to openly identify their sexual orientation

and not be discriminated against with regard to the civil rights available to all other citizens

Greek love The nineteenth-century code phrase invented by boys at British boarding schools to describe their sexual activities with other boys

Heterosexism The systematic oppression and exploitation of bisexuals, lesbians, gay men, and transgender individuals, especially policies and practices reinforcing heterosexuality as the only option for relationships and families

Heterosexual A normative category of sexual identity referring to exclusive lifelong sexual desire and erotic relations with the opposite gender

Heterosexual assumption The assumption that every human being is born a heterosexual

Homophobia The culturally influenced fear and hatred of homosexual persons, acts, and events

Homosexual A normative moral category of sexual identity referring to exclusive lifelong sexual desire and erotic relations with the same gender

Individual heterosexism Prejudiced attitudes and behavior against others based on the assumption that sexual orientations other than heterosexual are unnatural; this is demonstrated whenever someone responds by saying or doing something degrading or harmful about persons who are not heterosexual

Institutional heterosexism Established laws, customs, and practices in a society that allow systematic discrimination against people or groups who are not heterosexual

In the closet The concealment of sexual orientation from colleagues, heterosexual friends, and/or family

LGBT An acronym identifying a group defined by sexual orientation and consisting of lesbians, gay men, bisexuals, and transgender people

Pedophiles Adults who desire sexual contact with children

Queer Generic term used to refer to people who are gay, lesbian, bisexual, transgender, and transsexual (LGBT)

Sexual orientation The sexual identity of an individual based on lifelong sexual fantasies, desires, and practices

Transgender A person whose gender identity or gender expression does not conform to concepts conventionally associated with his or her biological gender

DISCUSSION EXERCISES

Exercise #1 Testing Your Knowledge about Homosexuality

Directions: Misconception and myth typically contradict what is actually known about sexual orientation. Decide if each statement below is true or false.

1. Child development studies suggest that an individual's sexual orientation is established at an early age.
2. Gay men and lesbians are attracted to members of the same sex because they psychologically desire to be members of the opposite sex.
3. Most gay men and lesbians report being seduced during middle or high school years, usually by an older adult of the same sex.
4. If they undergo what is called "reparative therapy," gay men and lesbians can re-establish their original heterosexual orientation.
5. Researchers have documented same-sex sexual activity among most species of animals.
6. Beginning in the early 1970s, the American Psychological Association responded to research findings and removed homosexuality from its list of mental illnesses.
7. The majority of states in the United States maintain "sodomy laws" making it a crime for two people of the same sex to engage in sexual activity.
8. According to studies of men imprisoned for child molestation, heterosexual men are more likely to molest young girls than gay men are to molest young boys.
9. Despite claims about "gay bashing," gay men are no more likely to be victims of criminal violence than heterosexual men.
10. Some church denominations have welcomed gay men and lesbians into their congregations and have made public statements denouncing anti-gay discrimination.

Adapted from James T. Sears, *Coming Out of the Classroom Closet,* *1992, Harrington Park Press.*

Exercise #2 Integration in the Military

Directions: The statements below represent some original responses to the proposed U.S. military policy of racial integration. Rewrite each statement by substituting homosexual for racial or Negro, and heterosexual for white. Each statement will reflect a current argument concerning the integration of gay men and lesbians into the military. As you change the statements, decide whether the argument could be considered a legitimate concern with regard to integrating gay men and lesbians into the military today.

1. The opinion of soldiers: Army studies show that 80% of the white soldiers oppose racial integration in the armed forces.
2. The opinion of generals: Respected generals such as Dwight David Eisenhower and current military leaders have been and remain staunchly opposed to racial integration in the armed forces.
3. Objections based on unit cohesion: According to the Secretary of the Army, racial integration would undermine unit cohesion—"Effective comradeship in battle calls for a warm and close personal relationship within a unit"; an Army Report opposing racial integration argued—"The soldier on the battlefield deserves to have, and must have, utmost confidence in his fellow soldiers."
4. Objections based on opposition to using the military for social reforms: As one general has said, "the Army is not out to make any social reforms." It will change its policy on racial integration "when the Nation as a whole changes . . . experiments within the Army in the solution of social problems are fraught with danger to efficiency, discipline and morale."
5. Objections based on privacy: A Georgia Senator says racial integration in the armed forces would compromise the privacy rights of the white soldiers—"There is no more intimate relationship known to men than that of enlisted men serving together at the squad level. They eat and sleep together. They use the same facilities . . . They are compelled to stay together in the closest association."

6. Objections based on health concerns: The Senator from Georgia went on to say he had statistics "which will show that the incidence of (all venereal diseases) is appallingly higher among Negroes than among whites."

7. Objections based on religious beliefs: A Congressman from Alabama has argued that racial integration in the armed forces would lower not just the morale but the "morals" of soldiers.

8. Objections based on the will of the majority: The Department of Defense has taken the position that racial integration in the armed forces would erode public confidence in the military—"The Army can under no circumstances adopt a policy which is contrary to the dictates of a majority of people (because) to do so would alienate the people from the Army and lower their morale."

REFERENCES

ABCnews (2004). *New details emerge in Matthew Shepard murder.* Retrieved October 28, 2011, from http://abcnews.go.com/2020/story?id=277685&page=1

Abel, G., & Harlow, N. (2001). *The stop child molestation book.* Philadelphia, PA: Xlibris.

Anti-Defamation League. (2009). *What you need to know: The new federal hate crime law.* Retrieved October 28, 2011, from http://www.adl.org/combating_hate

Badgett, M.V.L. (2001). *Money, myths, and change: The economic lives of lesbians and gay men.* Chicago, IL: University of Chicago Press.

Bérbubé, A. (1989). Marching to a different drummer: Lesbian and gay GIs in World War II. In M. Duberman, M. Vicinus, & G. Chauncey, Jr. (Eds.), *Hidden from history: Reclaiming the gay and lesbian past* (pp. 456–476). New York, NY: Meridian.

Blumenfeld, W.J. (Ed.). (1992). *Homophobia: How we all pay the price.* Boston, MA: Beacon.

Boswell, J. (1994). *Same-sex unions in pre-modern Europe.* New York, NY: Villard.

Broadus, K.W. (2006). The evolution of employment discrimination protections for transgender people. In P. Currah, R.M. Juang, & S.P. Minter (Eds.), *Transgender rights* (pp. 93–101). Minneapolis, MN: University of Minnesota Press.

Bumiller, E. (2011). Obama ends "don't ask, don't tell" policy. *New York Times.* Retrieved October 27, 2011, from www.nytimescom/2011/07/23/us/23millitary.html

Chauncey, G., Jr. (1989). Christian brotherhood or sexual perversion? Homosexual identities and the construction of sexual boundaries in the World War I era. In M. Duberman, M. Vicinus, & G. Chauncey, Jr. (Eds.), *Hidden from history: Reclaiming the gay and lesbian past* (pp. 456–476). New York, NY: Meridian.

Christian Century Foundation. (1997). Accept gay orientation, say Catholic Bishops. *Christian Century, 114*(29), 936–937.

Crompton, L. (1998). *Byron and Greek love: Homophobia in 19th century England.* Swaffham, U.K.: Gay Men's Press.

Cushner, K., McClelland, A., & Safford, P. (2008). Education in a changing society. In *Human diversity in education: An integrative approach* (6th ed.). New York, NY: McGraw-Hill.

D'Emilio, J. (1989). Gay politics and community in San Francisco since World War II. In M. Duberman, M. Vicinus, & G. Chauncey, Jr. (Eds.), *Hidden from history: Reclaiming the gay and lesbian past* (pp. 456–476). New York, NY: Meridian.

Douglas, E. (2008, November). An uneasy alliance. *The American Prospect, 19*(11), 30–33.

Doupe, G.E. (1982). True to our tradition. In W. Blumenfeld (Ed.), *Homophobia: How we all pay the price* (pp. 187–204). Boston, MA: Beacon.

Duberman, M., Vicinus, M., & Chauncey, G. Jr. (Eds.). (1989). *Hidden from history: Reclaiming the gay and lesbian past.* New York, NY: Meridian.

Duggan, L. (2004). Making it perfectly queer. In D. Carlin & J. DiGrazia (Eds.), *Queer cultures* (pp. 51–67). Upper Saddle River, NJ: Pearson Prentice Hall.

Edwards, C. (2003, December 15). Coming out in corporate America. *Business Week,* p. 64.

Franklin, K. (1998). Unassuming motivations: Contextualizing the narratives of antigay assailants. In G. Herek (Ed.), *Stigma and sexual orientation: Understanding prejudice against lesbians, gay men and bisexuals* (pp. 339–363). Thousand Oaks, CA: Sage.

Galeano, E. (2004, January). The heresy of difference. *The Progressive, 68*(9), 16–17.

Gilgoff, D. (2004). The rise of the gay family: Special report. *U.S. News & World Report, 136*(18), 40–45.

GLSEN. (2010). *2009 national school climate survey.* The Gay, Lesbian and Straight Education Network. Retrieved October 28, 2011, from http://www .glsen.org

Goldman, R. (2004). Who is that queer queer? Exploring norms around sexuality, race, and class in queer theory. In D. Carlin & J. DiGrazia (Eds.), *Queer cultures* (pp. 83–98). Upper Saddle River, NJ: Pearson Prentice Hall.

Gould, S.J. (1983). How the zebra gets its stripes. In *Hen's teeth and horse's toes* (pp. 366–375). New York: W.W. Norton.

Griscom, J.L. (2009). The case of Sharon Kowalski and Karen Thompson: Ableism, heterosexism, and sexism. In P. Rothenberg (Ed.), *Race, class, and gender in the United States: An integrated study* (7th ed., pp. 496–504). New York, NY: Worth.

Halperin, D.M. (1989). Sex before sexuality: Pederasty, politics, and power in classical Athens. In M. Duberman, M. Vicinus, & G. Chauncey, Jr. (Eds.), *Hidden from history: Reclaiming the gay and lesbian past* (pp. 37–53). New York, NY: Meridian.

Herdt, G. (1997). *Same sex, different cultures. Exploring gay and lesbian lives.* Boulder, CO: Westview.

Herek, G.M. (2009, January). Hate crimes and stigma-related experiences among sexual minority groups in the United States: Prevalence estimates from a national probability sample. *Journal of Interpersonal Violence, 24*(1), 54–74.

Hollier, G.D. (2004, July). *Sexual orientation issues in today's workplace.* Paper presented at the International Diversity Conference at UCLA, Los Angeles, CA.

Holthouse, D. (2005, Winter). The fabulist. Intelligence Report, pp. 11–15.

Human Rights Campaign. (2009). *Issue: Hate Crimes Prevention Act.* Retrieved October 28, 2011, from www .hrc.org/issues/pages/hate-crimes-prevention-act.

Jones, G.R., & George, J.M. (2009). Managing diverse employees in a diverse environment. In *Contemporary management* (6th ed.). Hightstown, NJ: McGraw-Hill.

Kantor, M. (1998). *Homophobia: Description, development, and dynamics of gay bashing.* Westport, CT: Praeger.

Katz, J. (1985). *Gay American history: Lesbians and gay men in the U.S.A.* New York, NY: Harper Colophon.

Kinsey, A.C., Pomeroy, W.B., & Martin, C.E. (1948). *Sexual behavior in the human male.* Philadelphia, PA: W.B. Saunders.

LeVay, S. (1996). *Queer science: The use and abuse of research into homosexuality.* Cambridge, MA: University of Massachusetts Press.

Lynch, R. (2011). Don't ask, don't tell repeal lets gays, lesbians serve openly. *Los Angeles Times.* Retrieved October 27, 2011, from http://latimesblogs/ latimes.com/nationnow/2011/09/don't-ask-don't-tell-officially-repealed.html.

Marcus, E. (1992). *Making history: The struggle for gay and lesbian equal rights, 1945–1990.* New York, NY: HarperCollins.

Massachusetts Governor's Commission on Gay and Lesbian Youth. (1994). Making schools safe for gay and lesbian youth: Breaking the silence in schools and in families. In G. Remafedi (Ed.), *Death by denial: Studies of suicide in gay and lesbian teenagers* (pp. 151–205). Boston, MA: Alyson.

McLeod, A., & Crawford, I. (1998). The postmodern family: An examination of the psychosocial and legal perspectives of gay and lesbian parenting. In G. Herek (Ed.), *Stigma and sexual orientation: Understanding prejudice against lesbians, gay men and bisexuals* (pp. 211–222). Thousand Oaks, CA: Sage.

Money, J. (1988). *Gay, straight, and in-between: The sexology of erotic orientation.* New York, NY: Oxford.

Palmer, A. (1997). The military ban on gays and lesbians is based on prejudice. In T. Roleff (Ed.), *Gay rights* (pp. 126–131). San Diego, CA: Greenhaven.

Pillard, R.C. (1977). The search for a genetic influence on sexual orientation. In V. Rosairo (Ed.), *Science and homosexualities* (pp. 226–241). New York, NY: Routledge.

ProCon. (2012). *Gay marriage.* Retrieved October 12, 2012, from gaymarriage.procon.org.

Rankin, S.R. (2005, Fall). Campus climates for sexual minorities. In R. Sanlo (Ed.), *Gender identity and sexual orientation: Research, policy and personal perspectives,* No. 111 (pp. 17–23). San Francisco, CA: Jossey-Bass.

Rowse, A.L. (1977). *Homosexuals in history: A study of ambivalence in society, literature and the arts.* New York, NY: Dorset.

Schlatter, E., & Steinback, R. (2010, Winter). 10 myths. *Intelligence Report*, 140, 31–35.

Sears, J.T. (1992). Educators, homosexuality, and homosexual students: Are personal feelings related to professional beliefs? In K. Harbeck, *Coming out of the classroom closet: Gay and lesbian students, teachers and curricula*. Binghamton, NY: Harrington Park Press.

Shilts, R. (1987). *And the band played on: Politics, people and the AIDS epidemic*. New York, NY: St. Martin's Press.

Simon, A. (1998). The relationship between stereotypes of and attitudes toward lesbians and gays. In G. Herek (Ed.), *Stigma and sexual orientation: Understanding prejudice against lesbians, gay men and bisexuals* (pp. 62–81). Thousand Oaks, CA: Sage.

SLDF. (2010). *About "don't ask, don't tell."* Servicemembers Legal Defense Fund. Retrieved from www.sldn.org/pages/about-dadt.

Sontag, S. (1989). *AIDS and its metaphors*. New York, NY: Farrar, Straus, and Giroux.

Steakley, J.D. (1989). Iconography of a scandal: Political cartoons and the Eulenberg affair in Wilhelmine Germany. In M. Duberman, M. Vicinus, & G. Chauncey, Jr. (Eds.), *Hidden from history: Reclaiming the gay and lesbian past* (pp. 233–263). New York, NY: Meridian.

Stein, E. (1999). *The mismeasure of desire: The science, theory, and ethics of sexual orientation*. Oxford, England: Oxford University Press.

Suicide Prevention Resource Center. (2008). *Suicide risk and prevention for lesbian, gay, bisexual, and transgender youth*. Newton, MA: Education Development Center, Inc. Retrieved October 27, 2011, from www.sprc.org/library/SPRC_LGBT_Youth.pdf

Sullivan, N. (2003). *A critical introduction to queer theory*. Washington Square, NY: New York University Press.

Transgender Law and Policy Institute. (2012). *Nondiscrimination laws that include gender identity and expression*. Retrieved from www.transgenderlaw.org/ndlaws/index

U.S. Census Bureau. (2011). *Same-sex couple households*. Retrieved October 15, 2012, from: www.census.gov/prod/2011pubs/acsbr10-03.pdf

Van Den Bergh, N. (2003). Getting a piece of the pie: Cultural competence for GLBT employees at the workplace. In M. Sullivan (Ed.), *Sexual minorities: Discrimination, challenges, and development in America* (pp. 55–73). New York, NY: The Haworth Press.

Williams, W.L. (2001). Benefits for non-homophobic societies: An anthropological perspective. In W. Blumenfeld (Ed.), *Homophobia: How we all pay the price* (pp. 258–274). Boston, MA: Beacon.

Young, S. (2004). Dichotomies and displacement: Bisexuality in queer theory and politics. In D. Carlin & J. DiGrazia (Eds.), *Queer cultures* (pp. 83–98). Upper Saddle River, NJ: Pearson Prentice Hall.

Zeldin, T. (1994). *An intimate history of humanity*. New York, NY: HarperCollins.

Zemsky, B., & Sanlo, R.L. (2005). Do policies matter? In R. Sanlo (Ed.), *Gender identity and sexual orientation: Research, policy and personal perspectives*, No. 111 (pp. 7–15). San Francisco, CA: Jossey-Bass.

Chapter 12

Ableism: Disability Does Not Mean Inability

"All governments treat disabled people badly. They all see us as a burden. All governments, whether capitalist or socialist, have separated us from the rest of society. . . . Until we are businessmen, politicians, community leaders, people at all levels of society, we will be marginalized and segregated."

Joshua Malinga (Contemporary)

In 1993, members of the United Nations declared people with disabilities an oppressed minority group. Writers of the UN Human Rights and Disabled Persons Report documented that around the world, people with disabilities were being treated as outcasts and that the situation was getting worse as their numbers increased. The 1995 representatives at the World Summit on Social Development in Copenhagen described people with disabilities as "one of the world's largest minority groups facing poverty and unemployment as well as social and cultural isolation" (Ervelles, 2001, p. 93). Despite the statements of these global organizations, the concept of *ableism* (sometimes erroneously called *handicapism*) has yet to be accepted by many people in the United States and around the world.

Ableism has been defined by Linton (1998) as the negative determination of an individual's abilities based on his or her disabilities. Ableism promotes the belief that people with disabilities are inferior to able-bodied persons in order to justify discrimination against them. Linton's definition asserts that the dominant group oppresses people with disabilities, as do other minority groups. Many people, including some people with disabilities, reject that assumption. Hahn (1988) observed,

> Unlike other minorities . . . disabled men and women have not yet been able to refute the implicit and direct accusations of biological inferiority that have often been invoked to rationalize the oppression of groups whose appearance differs from the standards of the dominant majority. (p. 26)

Why should people with disabilities be considered a minority group?

In 1973, the passage of the Rehabilitation Act was perhaps the first public acknowledgment that people with disabilities could be considered a minority group in need of civil rights protections. Section 504 of that act prohibited discrimination against people with a disability who had appropriate qualifications for jobs in federally funded programs (Longmore, 2003). In 1990, Congress acknowledged discrimination against disabled people by passing the Americans with Disabilities Act (ADA) to provide a legal recourse against discrimination. Hahn (1994) argued that in a democratic society, policies and practices reflected people's attitudes, and that American social attitudes were a major source of problems for people with disabilities. Nevertheless, some people still question the appropriateness of viewing persons with disabilities as a minority group.

The Fall 2001 issue of the *Journal of Disability Policy Studies* addressed the question of whether people with disabilities could be regarded as an oppressed minority. Although the contributors agreed that people with disabilities were oppressed, guest editor Andrew Batavia strongly disagreed. Although acknowledging problems in the past, Batavia argued that people with disabilities in the United States live in conditions "dramatically better" than those in other countries. Reacting to the high rate of unemployment for individuals with disabilities in the United States, Batavia said employers had the right to hire the most qualified person for a job regardless of disability, implying that applicants with disabilities were often not the most qualified.

Because of the efforts of disability rights advocates and with the passage of the Americans with Disabilities Act (ADA) in 1990, Batavia argued that people with disabilities no longer experience the regrettable discrimination that occurred in the past and therefore do not qualify as an "oppressed minority." Apparently Batavia had not reviewed recent statistics: A survey of people with disabilities reported that the percentage of unemployed adults had increased since the ADA became law, as had the percentage of people living in poverty (Wilson & Lewicki-Wilson, 2001). And the problem has continued: The U.S. Census Bureau (2012) reports that almost half of people who have a disability were living in poverty. Batavia's denial rationalization that discrimination no longer affects people with disabilities today is unusual because such arguments are more likely to be expressed by a nondisabled person than someone like Batavia who has a disability.

Another argument denies that people with disabilities are oppressed because having a disability makes one part of the majority. According to the rationale of this argument, having a disability places a person on a continuum where mild physical disabilities, such as poor eyesight, can be corrected by wearing glasses, whereas a more severe physical disability may require someone to use a wheelchair. The logic continues that whether minimal or severe, almost all of us are disabled in one way or another and must learn to live with the condition. In response, Gill (1994) argues that to be a person with a disability means the disability has a significant impact on daily life: For example, the disability influences an individual's sense of identity, or others' perceptions of the disability have a significant influence on their reactions to the person, including the likelihood of negative attitudes of rejection or even discrimination. Our reactions reflect a similar rejection of or discrimination toward people from other minority groups.

Putnam (2005) argues that identifying people with a disability as a minority group is consistent with other acceptable models for disability because it defines the problems associated with disabilities as stemming from an inappropriate "fit" between the environment and the persons with disabilities and not emanating from the individual. Having a disability would not present a problem "if a particular environment offered all of the resources a particular individual required to perform a task or activity" (p. 189). Putnam also cites research concluding that persons with disabilities share certain characteristics with other minority groups: "stigma, social distance, nonacceptance, negative stereotypes, prejudice, and discrimination" (p. 189).

Disability rights advocates argue that the concept of people with disabilities being an oppressed group would be more readily accepted if disability studies were included in secondary and higher education courses that examine women's issues, racial and ethnic problems, and negative social, cultural, and institutional experiences of other minority groups. Understanding experiences of people with disabilities requires recognition of dominant group privileges and power not shared. Linton (1998) suggests that such recognition could parallel that afforded other minority groups in viewing the dominant nondisabled group as "not the neutral, universal position from which disabled people deviate, rather, it is a category of people whose power and cultural capital keep them at the center" (p. 32).

> The disability rights approach views disability as a natural phenomenon which occurs in every generation, and always will. It recognizes people with disabilities as a distinct minority group, subject at times to discrimination and segregation . . . but also capable of taking our rightful place in society.
>
> Laura Hershey (1962–2010)

Cultural Ableism

Negative attitudes toward people with disabilities are not recent phenomena. Whether perceived as wicked, violent, or merely foolish, people with physical, emotional, or mental disabilities have been identified consistently as **deviant** because they were not normal, leading to negative and sometimes hostile behaviors. In the early 1900s, the U.S. Public Health Service categorized people with retardation as "defectives" along with criminals and delinquents, later labeling them "mental defectives" to distinguish them from the prostitutes, pimps, pickpockets, and paupers. But all such human beings were frequently placed together in institutions because they were nevertheless deviants, different from the norm, requiring their removal from communities. The historical record reveals a pattern of **cultural ableism**, images and beliefs perpetuated in society that promote the perception of people with disabilities as deviant or incompetent. It is a pattern that people with disabilities continue to confront. (See Figure 12.1.)

FIGURE 12.1

To confront negative attitudes toward people with a disability, many states have sponsored pageants since 1972 to select Ms. Wheelchair America; pictured here is Tamika Citchen, Ms. Wheelchair Michigan.

Source: Ms. Wheelchair Michigan promotional photo.

What are the historical perceptions of people with disabilities?

Understanding how societies have regarded people with various kinds of disabilities can explain not only negative individual attitudes, but also why different societies institutionalized people with disabilities. Wolfensberger (1970) explained some of the major historical perceptions of people with disabilities in the following categories.

A subhuman organism.   Although other groups (such as African Americans, Native Americans, and Jews) historically have been regarded as subhuman, the perception is still associated with people with disabilities, especially those labeled "mentally retarded" who have been occasionally referred to as "vegetables," alluding to medical terminology for performance of vital functions (heart rate, blood pressure) as vegetative functions. Logical thinking and other higher brain activity were assumed impossible for persons with retardation. As late as the nineteenth century, "mental defectives" were housed in rooms not heated in winter nor cooled in summer because it was assumed that they were not sensitive to heat or cold like "normal" people. Even in the last half of the twentieth century, caregivers for institutionalized people with mental disabilities have been known to use cattle prods for control. Once we dehumanize a group to subhuman status, there are few limitations to what can be done. Another example of the subhuman perception was articulated in a 1960s *Atlantic Monthly* article suggesting that organs should be harvested from severely and profoundly retarded people, referred to by the author as "human vegetables," and donated to those on organ waiting lists to "increase the intellectual betterment of mankind" (Wolfensberger, 1970, p. 17).

Menace to society.   This perception regards people with disabilities as evil. It is fostered in children's literature with villains such as Captain Hook and Long John Silver and in fairy tales by an array of wicked goblins, giants, and other weird, frightening characters who are ultimately subjugated or eliminated (Fiedler, 1993). Winzer (1997) described how adult literature continues the pattern, portraying disabled people as criminal, homicidal, or maladjusted monsters who are often sexual deviants as well. Charles Dickens created a dwarf called Quilp to be the evil villain in pursuit of the innocent Nell in *The Old Curiosity Shop*. Popular literature is often made into popular films, and there are several versions of *The Hunchback of Notre Dame* and *The Phantom of the Opera* to remind us that a person with a disability is a "monster" whose fearful features suggest "a disfigurement of personality and deformity of soul" (Longmore, 2003).

Object of dread. The origin of this perception is the medieval myth of the changeling in which people believed that upon the birth of a normal child, evil spirits came in the night and stole the child, replacing it with a defective child such as one who had mental retardation or cerebral palsy. In Grimm's fairy tale "The Elves," a changeling with "fixed staring eyes" is substituted for the original baby. The belief that evil spirits were the source of changelings may have influenced Martin Luther's perception of defective children as spawn of Satan, denouncing them as a "mass of flesh" without a soul (Winzer, 1997). Today, some Christians regard deformity or disability as a sign of "moral failure" or as a visible stigma of sinfulness (Pelka, 1994). Some parents of children with disabilities regard the child as punishment from God; some mothers experience enough depression to seek therapy following the birth of such a child.

Object of pity. This perception may not seem negative because it appears to include compassion for individuals with disabilities, but it is a compassion seldom accompanied by respect. Fundraising campaigns by well-meaning organizations work to arouse pity with poster children or by having telethons that parade children with disabilities to stimulate viewers to make contributions. According to Charlton (1998), surveys conducted in the United States have concluded that more people form their attitudes about people with disabilities from telethons than from any other source. Because telethons tend to reinforce images of people with disabilities as helpless or dependent, the disability community in America has voiced objections to them, with some organizations responding by agreeing not to participate in telethons for fundraising purposes.

Diseased organism. This perception views a person's physical or mental disability as a temporary condition that can be cured by chemical or psychological treatments. Ancient Egyptians often regarded disability as a condition for which medical "cures" were prescribed. Egyptian doctors hoped to restore eyesight to blind people by applying a solution to their eyes made of copper, myrrh, Cyprus seeds, and other ingredients. Although many Greeks believed that supernatural forces caused disabilities, physicians including Hippocrates rejected superstition and attempted to identify physiological causes (Winzer, 1997). In the United States today, national fund drives solicit money for research to find cures for disabilities, presenting people with that disability not only as an object of pity, but also as a diseased organism: The disability is perceived as "unhealthy" and the person is portrayed as needing to be cured. This medical view of people with disabilities is pessimistic because until a cure can be found, people with disabilities are regarded as having "incurable diseases." Because of such perceptions, people with disabilities have been placed in institutions, which penalize them for the crime of being disabled.

Holy innocent/eternal child. This perception is normally identified with one group: people labeled "mentally retarded." Viewed as incapable of sin, the Holy Innocent image can be found in most countries, religions, and cultures, and is often regarded as a benign view. The perception suggests that people with mental retardation need to be protected and sheltered, isolated from the outside world to perpetuate their innocent, childlike qualities. But encouraging people with mental retardation to maintain childish behaviors rather than learn adult behaviors is a barrier to empowering them to live independently. Linton (1998) observed that when people with disabilities are viewed as "living in the body, not in the mind, [they] are configured as childlike, even infant like, acting on primary drives rather than engaging in purposeful behavior" (pp. 95–96). This perception can become a self-fulfilling prophecy, illustrated in reports of people with mental retardation who have been constantly treated as children even during adolescence and who persist in childlike behaviors as adults, requiring constant care (Wehmeyer, 2000).

Object of ridicule. In literature, folk stories, and jokes, people with disabilities are subject to humiliation for the sake of humor. People with mental retardation have been portrayed as village idiots and ridiculed in moron jokes. According to Fiedler (1993), pagan practices of displaying freaks for public entertainment were revived in the Middle Ages by the Catholic Church, which displayed disabled or deformed "monsters" on feast days. In the nineteenth century, carnival side shows with magicians and sword swallowers also featured freaks: giants, dwarves, human skeletons, and other physically malformed or disabled people. Legendary showman P.T. Barnum popularized the freak show in the United States, exhibiting Chang and Eng (the original Siamese twins) and General Tom Thumb (a midget), along with anonymous pinheads and armless or legless wonders, now immortalized in wax at

> The point is, we are all one great big family, and any one of us can get hurt at any moment. . . . We should never walk by somebody who's in a wheelchair and be afraid of them or think of them as a stranger.
>
> Christopher Reeve (1951–2004)

the Circus World Museum in Baraboo, Wisconsin. Living or dead, people with deformities or disabilities are still often perceived as odd, ridiculous, or bizarre—anything but human. (See Figure 12.2.)

Each of these historical perceptions has stigmatized various disabilities and dehumanized people who had them. Today, many disability advocates in the United States (and elsewhere) are combating such negative images by insisting that people with disabilities are simply one cultural group among many others in a diverse society, that they have a disability culture that influences their development in different ways from the experiences that affect nondisabled Americans. According to Johnson and Nieto (2007), these arguments are being supported by an emerging discipline called Disability Studies, in which scholars examine "disability as an area of study in a manner similar to ethnic, linguistic, and women's studies" (p. 40). These scholars have identified characteristics that describe what advocates mean when they talk about a disability culture.

How do scholars describe a disability culture?

Because of past rejection, many people with similar disabilities have come together to support each other in their efforts to achieve the goal of living

FIGURE 12.2

In the 1800s, people reacted to James Merrick with dread, pity, and ridicule and as if he were subhuman. But Merrick worked at normal jobs until his tumors made that impossible, and only then did he put himself on display as the "Elephant Man" to earn a living. His story was told with compassion in the 1980 film *The Elephant Man*, nominated for several Academy Awards.

Source: Royal London Hospital Archives.

a normal life that includes a job, a home, a family, and so on. As a result of this collaboration, they have had similar experiences and developed cohesiveness based on common needs and shared aspirations. As Pai and Adler (1997) point out, a traditional concept of culture suggests that a group's historical experience together will create a "pattern of knowledge, skills, behaviors, attitudes and beliefs, as well as material artifacts" (p. 23). Using this kind of conventional definition for culture, Reagan (2005) argues that people with disabilities have created and continue to be influenced by a unique disability culture in the same way that individuals from racial and ethnic groups are shaped by their unique cultures.

Perhaps the clearest example of a disability culture is the deaf culture since it represents both cultural and linguistic diversity. Reagan (2005) agrees with scholars who describe many components of culture, but he identified four that must be shared by all members of a culture: (1) historical knowledge and awareness, (2) a common language, (3) awareness of a cultural identity supported by cultural artifacts and identified by distinctive norms and patterns of behavior, and (4) a network of voluntary, in-group social organizations.

Scholars have provided evidence that deaf culture includes these components. With regard to the first component, much has been written in disability studies research about the shared historical experience that has shaped the deaf community and individual identities. As Padden and Humphries (1998) have noted: "(The) knowledge of Deaf people is not simply a camaraderie with others who have a similar physical condition, but is, like many other cultures . . . historically created and actively transmitted across generations" (p. 2). The issue of transmitting the culture leads to perhaps the most compelling argument for a deaf culture in the United States: the existence of American Sign Language (ASL). In the early 1970s, linguistic research concluded that ASL was a language characterized by its unique grammar and syntax, and that "manual language developed naturally in deaf children similarly to the way oral language developed in hearing children" (Hehir, 2005, p. 21). Deaf children usually become fluent in ASL early in their lives, and information being transmitted by this language becomes what Padden and Humphries (1998) describe as "the heart of the culture" (p. 5). This is the reason many deaf people advocate for a bilingual/bicultural approach in classrooms educating deaf children and youth. In addition to recognizing deaf culture, this pedagogical approach should challenge the historic perspective of deafness as a deficit

and enhance the goal of helping deaf children learn Standard English. Deaf advocates also argue that hearing students could benefit from learning about historical events that have affected the deaf community as well as some of the issues confronting deaf people today. These arguments are the same ones made by other cultural groups who advocate for bilingual/bicultural education for their children.

As for the two remaining components for culture, deaf people frequently express their sense of a shared cultural identity. Padden and Humphries (1998) and Reagan (2005) have reported about their distinctive cultural artifacts in communications with the Telecommunications Device for the Deaf (TDD) combined with a Teletypewriter (TTY)—a computer with a keyboard input and printer or display output; in television (closed-caption programming); and other personal devices such as doorbells connected to lights in their homes. These cultural artifacts exist to assist deaf people in functioning more effectively in their everyday lives. As for patterns of behavior, Reagan (2005) identified cultural patterns among deaf people such as a high rate of endogamous (in-group) marriage, and behavioral differences such as establishing eye contact or the acceptability of physical contact. These cultural norms for deaf people have sometimes created misunderstandings similar to what has been experienced by ethnic groups during cross-cultural interactions. Finally, the deaf community has established numerous social organizations related to sports, theater and the arts, and social clubs, as well as state and national organizations.

Many deaf people and disability advocates are working to remove the stigma historically associated with disabilities. In the United States, they are challenging people to reject the assumption that regards any disability as a deficit, and to understand disability as one more example of human diversity. Since 20% of Americans have some form of disability (Russell, 1998), it is surprising that so many

> Before I was paralyzed, there were 10,000 things I could do. Now there are 9,000. I could dwell on the 1,000 I lost or focus on the 9,000 I have left.
>
> Walter Mitchell (Contemporary)

individuals persist in maintaining negative attitudes about people with physical or mental disabilities. To understand this phenomenon, it is necessary to examine some factors that contribute to the perpetuation of these negative attitudes.

Individual Ableism

Negative attitudes are reflected in the language we employ to identify disabled people. The word *disabled* implies inability; the prefix *dis* is generally regarded as signifying *not* or *no*. Derived from Latin, the prefix actually means *apart* or *asunder*, which is consistent with the historic practice of keeping people with disabilities apart from society.

People with disabilities are described as being "afflicted with" or a "victim of" a disability. Affliction is associated with disease, as is being a victim, so this language relates to the cultural image of the person with a disability as a diseased organism. Using words or phrases like *crippled, handicapped, impaired,* or *confined to a wheelchair* foster the belief that people with disabilities are incompetent or damaged, not capable of being independent. The term *confined to a wheelchair* is especially absurd. People in wheelchairs are not confined, but liberated by them. The wheelchair provides mobility to people who might be "confined" to their apartment or home if they did not have a wheelchair. Physical barriers can be identified easily, but it is much more difficult in America today to identify and overcome barriers created by **individual ableism**— prejudiced attitudes and actions toward people with a disability based on our assumptions about them.

What assumptions are made about people with disabilities?

Fine and Asch (2000) discussed five erroneous assumptions commonly made about persons with disabilities:

1. **Disability is a biological problem of a particular individual.** This assumption is related to the medical model of disability, which views the disability as a problem and the solution is to find a cure for it. The assumption overlooks the influence of prejudices, stereotypes, and discrimination about disabilities. Individuals with disabilities react to their environmental circumstances. Putnam (2005) commented that the absence of disability accommodations by architects, urban planners, and public officials suggests to people with disabilities that they are not being recognized nor included as part of a community. That is not a problem created by their disability but by the thoughts and decisions of others.

2. **Any problems for a person with a disability must stem from the disability.** People with disabilities may have health problems like anyone else, but they are not "unhealthy," nor is a disability a cause of disease. If a man with a disability is upset because he feels he has been discriminated against, it is discrimination and not the disability that is the cause of his anger. Being in a wheelchair is not necessarily frustrating, but a woman in a wheelchair may be frustrated when confronted with no curb cuts, no ramps for her to enter a building, or inaccessible restrooms within the building.

3. **A person with a disability is a "victim."** This assumption may suggest a humane and even compassionate attitude, but it is steeped in pity and lacks respect for the person with a disability. Studies of people with disabilities often report that the participants do not feel that they are victims but are more concerned about how to function effectively in their environment. In one study cited by Fine and Asch (2000), when people with disabilities were questioned about their disability, a consistent response was "it could be worse" (p. 323). Human beings want to live full, productive lives, and people with a disability are no different.

4. **Being disabled is central to self-concept and social comparisons for a person with a disability.** Although having a disability is usually a factor in shaping a person's sense of identity, self-concept refers to how a person feels about himself or herself. A person with a disability will develop his or her self-concept in ways similar to others who tend to rely on factors such as academic achievement, honors and awards, aesthetic interests, good relationships with family and friends, demonstrating competence at work, and so on. As for social comparisons, people with a disability who have a

job are likely to compare their job performance with that of *all* of their co-workers, not just others with disabilities. Fine and Asch (2000) explain that a paraplegic woman "may be as likely to compare herself with other women her age, others of her occupation, others of her family, class, race or a host of other people and groups who function as (her) reference group" (p. 334).

5. **Having a disability means a person will need assistance.** This assumption comes from the historical notion of "handicapped people" as helpless and dependent on others. In the 1930s, people with a disability were classified as "unemployable," preventing them from being considered for jobs in federal and local work relief programs (Longmore, 2003). Based on this assumption, individuals with disabilities are not viewed as responsible for their disability, nor are they perceived as capable of resolving difficulties created by their disability. Yet people with disabilities are only as dependent as the environment makes them. The blind person on the elevator may ask someone to push the button for the right floor unless the elevator panel also has floor numbers in Braille. A wheelchair user will have to bring friends or ask strangers for help getting past a flight of steps if there is no ramp allowing wheelchair access. People with severe cerebral palsy may have trouble communicating with others if they are not given access to a computer or assistive device and trained to use it. Because of assumptions like these, advocates for people with disabilities have had to aggressively demand that they be given opportunities to achieve their goals.

For example, a young woman who was born without arms chose to attend a large Midwestern university and enrolled in the nursing program. Although she had an excellent academic record, the nursing faculty was opposed to accepting her based on concerns that she would not be able to perform the physical tasks required of nurses. When a campus disability advocate became involved, a compromise was reached. The young woman was admitted to the nursing program but would not be allowed to take licensure exams. This resolution was acceptable to her; she had hoped

to earn a nursing degree because of her interest in the subject matter. After graduation, she wrote articles for nursing journals, based on her research and observations, and eventually became an editor. Nursing faculty had not focused on what the young woman could do, nor had they anticipated this outcome; their focus had been on tasks the disability would prevent her from doing.

One more example: Sharisa Kochmeister was born with severe cerebral palsy. As a child she was also diagnosed as having severe mental retardation before she learned to use a computer. Initially someone held her hand while she hunted for letters on the keyboard; eventually, she could operate a computer independently. When she turned fifteen, her IQ was retested and her score was measured at 142. In a similar case, a teenager who had been diagnosed as mentally retarded was asked what it felt like before she learned to communicate with a computer. She replied, "(As if) I was a clown in a world that was not a circus" (Kliewer & Biklin, 1996, p. 90). These examples of change do not reflect a transformation in the ability of the people being labeled; rather, they reflect a change in opportunities they received and in the assumptions of those responsible for the labeling.

What labels represent legitimate ways of identifying people?

Most Americans appear to believe that the "mentally retarded" label is a well-defined, scientifically determined, unambiguous way to categorize human beings: It is not. In the early 1900s, people with Down syndrome were considered profoundly retarded; today, it is estimated that 20% to 50% of people with Down syndrome are mildly retarded. In 1952, the American Psychological Association (APA) recommended institutionalization of people with IQs less than 50 who were considered severely retarded (Adelman, 1996). The current conclusion of the APA is that half of those with IQs of less than 50 can be considered moderately retarded and that neither moderate nor severely retarded individuals require continuous custodial care.

Another disability that professionals have been forced to reevaluate is cerebral palsy. In 1960, experts assumed that 75% of people with cerebral palsy were retarded. After some alternative methods of communication and assessment were developed, from adaptations for typewriters to special computers, assumptions of mental retardation diminished significantly (Kliewer & Biklin, 1996). These examples demonstrate why disability advocates are concerned about the labels given to people, especially children, and the consequences of such labeling.

What are some current controversies about labeling children?

Over the past fifty years, studies have reported an overrepresentation of children of color among those labeled as needing special education services (Losen & Orfield, 2002; U.S. Commission on Civil Rights, 2009). Overrepresentation means that children from a particular racial group are at least twice as likely to be labeled as white students are. For example, as we began the twenty-first century, African American children were still the most overrepresented racial group in diagnoses of mental retardation. According to Losen & Orfield (2002), black children were three times more likely to be given that label than white children. Parrish (2002) found that "In at least 45 states, black children in special education are extensively overrepresented in some categories" (p. 15). Parrish reported that American Indian children also tend to be overrepresented in special education, while Latino children are overrepresented in some states but underrepresented in others. As a further clarification, Parrish noted that when a racial group represents a significant part of a state's population, it is even more likely that children from this group will be overrepresented in special education classes. For example, although Asian American/Pacific Islander children tend to be underrepresented in all special education categories in the United States as a whole, in Hawaii, where these children comprise 59% of all K–12 students, Asian American/Pacific Islander children are almost three and a half times more likely to be labeled mentally retarded (Parrish, 2002).

In addition to the negative attitudes fostered by such labels, there is some evidence of significant differences by race in how these labeled children are treated in schools. According to Fierros and Conroy (2002), in school districts with a large number of racial minority students, among the population of students identified as needing special education services, black students were more likely than white

students to be placed in restrictive settings rather than in regular classrooms. In addition, Losen and Gillespie (2012) report that all students of color with disabilities are far more likely to be suspended, expelled, or removed from schools, but especially black students. In one school year, 25% of black K–12 students with a disability were suspended at least once compared to 9% for white students with a disability, and they were suspended two or more times twice as often as students without a disability. This disparity betrays the schools' fundamental purpose of providing a safe and appropriate setting for all students to learn. Students should come to school expecting to find an environment in which they are encouraged to develop their abilities and receive support services when necessary to help them achieve academic success. When schools reinforce negative attitudes toward students with a disability, they reinforce the negative perceptions of those who continue to view disabled people as "not able."

How can negative attitudes be changed?

The first thing that can be done is to create labels that promote a more positive image. The use of *people with disabilities* began to be widely accepted in the 1970s as a substitute for *the disabled* and *the handicapped* (Linton, 1998). The term places people first

> It is not the fact that [a person] cannot walk that is disabling but that society is organized for walking and not wheelchair-using individuals. [A person's] disability is not paraplegia but steps, pavement kerbs, buses and prejudiced shopkeepers.
>
> Victor Finkelstein (Contemporary)

to emphasize the humanity of the group and retains the word "disability" to acknowledge an existing mental or physical problem. Linton (1998) defined **people with disabilities** as referring to "people with behavioral or anatomical characteristics marked as deviant . . . that makes them targets of discrimination" (p. 12).

Although there is no agreement regarding the acceptability of alternative terms, there is agreement on the offensiveness of negative terms such as *impaired, crippled,* and *handicapped.* These are words that contribute to the perception of people with disabilities being not just "disabled" but "unable," implying an inability to manage for themselves or to contribute to society. According to the World Health Organization, a disability is not a handicap. **Disability** refers to "a restriction of functional ability and activity caused by an impairment (e.g., hearing loss, reduced mobility)," whereas **handicap** generally is employed as a reference to "an environmental or attitudinal barrier that limits the opportunity for a person to participate fully in a role that is normal (depending on age, sex, and social and cultural factors) for that individual" (Bernell, 2003, p. 41).

Imagine a woman in a wheelchair approaching a building. Her legs do not function well enough for her to walk; the wheelchair provides mobility. As she nears the steps of the building, she discovers it has no access ramp. Now she is handicapped. She has found a way to be mobile, but because of the insensitivity or prejudice of the architect or building owners, the lack of a ramp is a barrier that denies her and any wheelchair user access to the building.

Institutional Ableism

Institutional ableism is a consequence of established laws, customs, and practices that systematically discriminate against people with disabilities. A unique consequence for this minority group has been their placement in institutions in the United States, comparable only to nineteenth-century poorhouses for paupers. Poorhouses and poor farms have come and gone; yet institutions for people who have mental or physical disabilities remain, despite efforts in recent years to close them and to place people with disabilities into communities.

Why were people with disabilities placed in institutions?

The first institutions charged with caring for people with disabilities were hospices built within monasteries. An early reported example comes in the fourth century: a hospice for the blind at a monastery in Caesarea, now Turkey. According to the legend of St. Nicholas, as bishop of Mya in

southwestern Turkey, he provided care for "idiots and imbeciles." For his efforts he was named the patron saint of the mentally retarded, although that part of his history was lost in his transformation into the American Santa Claus (Winzer, 1997). As monasteries were built in Europe, many included hospices to care for poor, homeless, or disabled people. Using hospices to satisfy Christian mandates to care for "the least of these" continued into the sixteenth century, when turmoil over church reforms created a schism termed the Reformation, resulting in Protestant churches as alternatives to the Catholic Church.

Even before the Reformation, the Catholic Church contributed to an increasingly negative attitude toward people with disabilities. St. Augustine sowed seeds for religious rejection when he refused to allow deaf people to become church members because of his literal interpretation of St. Paul (Romans 10:17): "Faith comes by hearing." During the Middle Ages, as Europe was devastated by plague and pestilence, especially the Black Death, fear fostered a growing hostility toward people exhibiting strange appearances or odd behavior (Barzun, 2000).

With the Reformation, monasteries were abandoned or forcibly closed and inhabitants evacuated. Communities were confronted with the problem of disabled people and beggars wandering the streets. Not surprisingly, attitudes toward the newly released people became increasingly negative. Laws were passed that vagrants were to be whipped (Ribton-Turner, 1972). By the fifteenth century, the Catholic Church declared a virtual war on witches, which resulted in the arrests, torture, and deaths of a great many people who in some way were considered unusual or deviant. Evidence suggests that people who were mentally ill and people with disabilities were among the unfortunates serving as scapegoats.

The association with witchcraft often stemmed from people with mental retardation making odd comments or from mutterings of the mentally ill. Some citizens believed the strange talk was dialogue with the devil; others regarded the conversations as divinely inspired. Whether they talked with God or the devil, deviants were not tolerated on the streets. Some communities placed mentally retarded vagrants in the old city wall guard towers, which came to be called a "Fool's Tower" or "Idiot's Cage" (Winzer, 1997). In other communities, homeless people were charged with vagrancy, tortured, and expelled, or if they could work, they were forced into slavery (Ribton-Turner, 1972).

Reformation leaders John Calvin and Martin Luther did not question the prejudices behind this behavior; in fact, they contributed to them. According to Calvin, Satan possessed mentally retarded people; Luther believed Satan was responsible for fathering all mentally retarded children, and urged the parents of one mentally retarded child to drown it in a nearby river (Winzer, 1997).

When the centuries-old scourge of leprosy ended as the seventeenth century began, buildings used to quarantine lepers (leprosaria) became vacant. Communities found a solution to their dilemma of what to do with deviants: Europe initiated *the great confinement* to these newly christened "lunatic hospitals" (Foucault, 1989). Although the hospitals were initially used to house mentally ill people, they accepted "mental defectives," including people with various physical and mental disabilities, and eventually amassed a wide assortment of "defectives." Before long, only about 10% of inmates were considered insane in the average lunatic hospital. In addition to people with disabilities, other inmates included prostitutes, beggars, alcoholics, social dissidents, and people with syphilis (Winzer, 1997). Whereas hospices had protected disabled people from the wickedness of the world, lunatic hospitals protected the world from the wickedness of such morally, mentally, and physically deviant human beings.

It was apparent early on that hospitals could not provide treatment to rehabilitate inmates. The purpose of institutions was to remove defective people from society. Not surprisingly, the quality of "care" in such places was not good; rumors often circulated of inhumane treatment. In England, the Hospital of St. Mary of Bethlehem was referred to as "Bethlehem," which reduced to "Bedlam," coining a word to describe chaotic conditions there. By the nineteenth century, reformers visiting lunatic hospitals were appalled by the horrible conditions: some inmates wandering around naked and shivering, others chained to beds, some sitting in their own excrement, many bitten by rats or other vermin roaming the grounds. Reformers advocated for "moral treatment" of people in the institutions: eliminating chains, giving patients work, and treating patients with respect to develop self-esteem (Foucault, 1989).

Moral treatment involved not defining patients as deviant so much as regarding their defects as conditions requiring accommodations for them to function more effectively. Foucault (1989) tells the story of a mentally ill man who refused to eat because he thought he was dead and he was certain that dead people did not eat. One night, institutional staff came to the patient's bed looking pale, ashen, and dressed in clothing to simulate the look of a corpse. They brought in a table and some food, then sat down and began eating. When the patient asked why they were eating when they appeared to be dead, they replied that dead people had to eat like anyone else. They finished their meal and left. The next day the patient resumed eating. This approach was taken with patients who had mental or physical disabilities as well.

Instead of being defined as insurmountable deviance, *disability* gradually came to be regarded as a human condition; institutional staff began to provide accommodations to help individuals take better care of themselves and to function effectively with others. Although reforms were not universally applied, they constituted a practical alternative to the punitive treatment that had characterized previous institutional practices.

How were institutions for people with disabilities established in the United States?

When the United States entered the global community as a new nation, people with disabilities simply lived in communities and were cared for primarily by their families, although some religious facilities also provided assistance. Their situations varied widely—from being employed to being the town fool or even a pariah whom the family hid from the community. In nineteenth-century America, attitudes toward people with disabilities were challenged. Americans no longer could view people's disabilities as an act of God but instead in a

> Progress, far from consisting in change, depends on retentiveness. . . . Those who cannot remember the past are condemned to repeat it.
>
> George Santayana (1863–1952)

biological context: Rehabilitation was emphasized as the appropriate response.

Following the Civil War, a transformation of public attitudes seemed to be demonstrated by the construction of numerous institutions and residential schools that were often dedicated to a particular kind of disability. Institutionalizing people with disabilities was especially popular in urban areas, indicating a shift in responsibility for care from families and communities to the state as the nation moved into the twentieth century. Based on a biological view of human disability, the institutions were usually administered by people with medical training who claimed to use rehabilitative strategies. In reality, the function of institutions was usually custodial care—monitoring and restraining patients—reflecting ongoing negative American attitudes toward disabled people.

What evidence exists that negative attitudes prevailed in institutions and in society?

The negative attitude toward institutionalized patients is documented legal history. A 1913 Wisconsin law mandated the institutionalization of disabled people who constituted a "menace to society." A similar law passed the following year in Texas stated that people with disabilities mingling freely in the community was "a most baneful evil," describing people with disabilities as "defect(s) . . . [that] wound our citizenry a thousand times more than any plague . . . [they are] a blight on mankind" (Garrett History Brief, 2001, p. 72). Encouraged by the **eugenics** movement following World War I, every state in the United States passed laws singling out for institutionalization people with mental or physical disabilities. Some states went so far as to authorize the removal of children with disabilities from their homes, even against the wishes of parents.

With most disabled people confined to institutions, continuing prejudice was demonstrated in the 1930s when over thirty states enacted laws permitting involuntary sterilization of people in state-funded institutions. Among the targets of this law were those identified as feeble minded, idiots, morons, and mental defectives. States justified their actions by claiming the need to eradicate the possibility of procreation for people who were such burdens on society (Garrett History Brief, 2001; Russell, 1998).

In Europe, German Nazis implemented a program of involuntary sterilization that was continued until the end of World War II. Subsequently, allies identified forced sterilization of people with disabilities for inclusion on the list of Nazi war crimes. Russell (1998) explained why it was deleted: "Allied authorities were unable to classify the sterilizations as war crimes, because similar laws had . . . recently been upheld in the United States" (p. 22).

People with disabilities who were institutionalized in the United States were largely ignored until 1972, when Geraldo Rivera exposed the appalling conditions at New York's Willowbrook State School where "one hundred percent of all residents contracted hepatitis within six months of entering the institution. . . . Many lay on dayroom floors (naked) in their own feces" (Linton, 1998, p. 40). The description parallels conditions denounced by "moral treatment" reformers a century earlier, yet ten years after the Willowbrook scandal, problems persisted in American institutions. Linton (1998) cites a 1984 *New York Times* article about a community facility for people with physical and mental disabilities in California that described staff serving spoiled food, not repairing malfunctioning toilets, and physically and sexually abusing patients.

Are institutions for people with disabilities providing good care today?

Although reduced in number, institutions for physically and mentally disabled people still exist despite the fact that national and state political leaders know they are harmful to the people in them. In 1996, a federal General Accounting Office (GAO) investigation of public institutions for mentally retarded people warned Congress of serious deficiencies in quality of care: "insufficient staffing, lack of active treatment and deficient medical and psychiatric care" (Garrett History Brief, 2001, p. 72). The GAO report described harm to residents including injuries, unnecessary illnesses, and physical degeneration—in a few instances the institutional "care" contributed to a resident's death.

Some states attempted to eliminate institutions by passing "deinstitutionalization" laws, but this has not solved the problem. When institutions have closed, residents have often been relocated not to communities but to another form of institutional care—nursing homes. Care provided in nursing homes reportedly is no better, and is sometimes worse, than the care residents experienced in institutions (Russell, 1998).

What is the alternative to placing people with disabilities in institutions?

Instead of being placed in institutions, people with disabilities prefer to live in family homes or group homes in their communities. A 1996 federal court ruling found that some city zoning ordinances had limited or prevented the establishment of group homes in neighborhoods by including "density laws" restricting the number of "unrelated persons" in a house or the number of group homes within a certain area. Some cities have even passed so-called ugly laws that forbid people with an unsightly appearance from appearing in public (Garrett History Brief, 2001, p. 72). The irony of such ordinances is that placing disabled people in communities to receive care not only increases their quality of life, but it is also more cost effective for taxpayers than providing care in nursing homes or institutions.

What is the cost of care for people with disabilities?

Taxpayers fund over 60% of the expenses for people with disabilities in nursing homes and institutions. Although people with disabilities overwhelmingly prefer to be cared for at home and require only minimal assistance, almost 2 million Americans with disabilities live in nursing homes at a cost of over $40,000 per person per year (La Fleur, 2009). According to Russell (1998), costs could total less than $10,000 per year to provide an individual with personal assistance services at home. State institutions are even more expensive: More than 75,000 people with developmental disabilities still live in state institutions at an average annual cost of more than $80,000 per person, whereas the average cost to provide adequate care for someone living in their own home within their own community was about $37,800 (Institute for Community Living, 2004).

Charlton (1998) reviewed numerous studies that consistently reported benefits for people with disabilities living in communities: "living at home, in a house or an apartment, is better psychologically,

> If our brothers are oppressed, then we are oppressed. If they hunger, we hunger. If their freedom is taken away, our freedom is not secure.
>
> Stephen Vincent Benet (1898–1943)

more fulfilling, and cheaper than living in nursing homes" (p. 47). By contrast, critics point out that nursing homes and institutions make substantial profits as private corporations while providing primarily low-wage jobs. As quoted in *Business First*, one private corporation providing "health care" said their three primary objectives were: "1. increase net profit, 2. increase net profit, and 3. increase net profit" (Russell, 1998, p. 103).

Advocates for **normalization** oppose confining disabled people in institutions. The concept refers to the implementation of policies and practices to help create life conditions and opportunities for disabled people that are at least as good as those of average citizens. Normalization promotes strategies for disabled people to live and work in communities, and it challenges nondisabled people to eliminate barriers that prevent disabled people from being involved in community life. Based on the concept of normalization, disability advocates help people with disabilities move out of institutions and into communities, and they have lobbied for legislation to protect the civil rights of disabled people living in communities. (See Figure 12.3.)

How do other countries respond to the needs of people with disabilities?

In 1995, the House of Representatives Ways and Means Committee reported that the United States spent less on long-term disability benefits than several European countries (Russell, 1998). Germany and Austria both provide cash benefits to disabled people regardless of their financial resources. Those receiving benefits can spend the money however they wish, including hiring family members to provide care. In Germany, cash benefits are half of the total that can be obtained in service benefits, but it is at the discretion of the recipient to determine which kind of benefits to accept. Human services personnel pay random visits to recipients to assess the

FIGURE 12.3

Today people with a disability are just as likely to protest discrimination and demand their rights as any other minority group.

Photo by Tom Olin

adequacy of their care. Austria's disability benefits are funded by general tax revenues, but Germany's benefits are funded by a 1.7% tax on salaries and pensions, a cost shared by employers, employees, and retired workers (Batavia, 2002).

Austrian legislation has promoted hiring workers with disabilities, stipulating that for every twenty-five workers employed, one worker must be a person with a disability. If the company fails to meet this standard, it is assessed a fine of approximately $155 a month that it must continue to pay until it meets the requirement. Money collected from fines is retained in an account from which employers can receive funds to make physical modifications necessary to employ workers with disabilities (Koppelman, 2001; National Disability Authority, 2012).

In France, benefits to people with disabilities are not as generous as in Austria and Germany, but they exceed those of the United States. Benefits are based on financial resources of recipients, with a maximum national benefit. Local French governments responsible for providing benefits

are funded from general tax revenues that supported approximately 86,000 people in 2000. Local agency representatives make annual home visits to recipients to ensure that adequate services are being provided (Batavia, 2002).

How does the U.S. government provide support for people with disabilities?

European countries began providing social insurance and welfare assistance in the eighteenth and nineteenth centuries. In the United States, the federal Social Security program was established in 1935, although it did not include disabled people until the 1950s (Stone, 1984). Whereas European countries seem to have accepted their responsibility to provide care for individuals with disabilities, the United States has continually questioned its obligation. In 1996, Congress voted to add $320 million to the Social Security Administration, doubling the budget, but not with the purpose of assisting more disabled people. The budget increase was designated to fund reviews of recipients to determine if they could be removed from the list of those eligible for disability benefits. Ironically, that same year, Congress provided approximately $32 million for programs to protect disabled people from being discriminated against in hiring decisions (Russell, 1998).

The 1990 Americans with Disabilities Act (ADA) was enacted to prevent discrimination against people with disabilities. In the first four years after the law was passed, 3,600 complaints were filed, charging employer hiring practices with discrimination against workers with disabilities: The Equal Employment Opportunities Commission (EEOC) approved 28 to be pursued in court. In 2011, the EEOC reported that people with a disability had filed 25,742 discrimination complaints, of which about 10% were resolved with monetary compensation of over $100 million (EEOC, 2012).

How does the United States support people with disabilities who want to live independently?

In 1973, the Supplemental Security Income (SSI) program was created to assist people with disabilities. The means-tested program offers a range of $400 to $700 per month, but recipients must remain without other means of support to receive SSI funds. If recipients make extra money to be more financially secure, they are likely to lose the benefit.

In one case that exemplifies SSI policy, Lynn Thompson, a quadriplegic, was attempting to live on SSI payments of about $600 a month when she began earning extra income at home stuffing envelopes. After she reported her earnings, Social Security officials declared her income in excess of allowable limits and ordered her to return $10,000 of the benefits received or, if she couldn't pay the money, her benefits would be terminated until that amount was withheld. Termination of her benefits meant Thompson could no longer afford to hire a personal care attendant and she would need to leave her home and enter a nursing home. Thompson fought to overturn this decision, but the legal battle dragged on. Ms. Thompson committed suicide rather than be forced into a nursing home (Russell, 1998). Today there is controversy over a proposal to reduce or eliminate SSI payments for family members who have a diagnosed mental illness, including children (Gamble, 2012).

Is there discrimination against people with disabilities living in communities?

People with disabilities who are fortunate enough not to be institutionalized also encounter discrimination in the community. Hahn (1988) described the problems:

> Disabled persons have not only exhibited one of the highest rates of unemployment, welfare dependency, and poverty in the United States; but they also have experienced a more pervasive form of segregation in education, housing, transportation, and public accommodations than the most rigid policies of apartheid enacted by racist governments. (p. 26)

In addition to housing, already discussed, disabled people experience discrimination in four critical areas: jobs, mobility/accessibility, health care, and education.

Jobs.   Because of the shortage of men, women were hired for traditional male jobs during World War II; employment of people with disabilities also increased during the war. As was true for women workers, unemployment rates for disabled people increased after the war, as jobs were assigned to returning soldiers. The work performance of people with disabilities during the war proved that they not only wanted jobs, but they could perform their tasks competently. This lesson has apparently been lost on employers: Ongoing documentation reveals that people with disabilities continue to be discriminated against in hiring decisions.

According to the U.S. Census Bureau, people with a disability constitute almost 20% of the population of the United States (Bernstein, 2008), yet a Harris poll reports that only 21% of those between the ages of 18 and 64 are employed full or part time compared to 59% of nondisabled Americans. Further, 42% of unemployed people with a disability say that employers are not willing to provide the accommodations they need to perform the job successfully (Orkis, 2010). A survey by the National Organization on Disability reported that 66% of working-age disabled adults want to work rather than rely on SSI benefits. Of people with a disability who have jobs, a majority are employed in sheltered workshops that hire only disabled workers for as little as 10% to 20% of the minimum wage, often earning as little as $44 a week compared to $456 a week for people working in traditional jobs (National Disability Rights

> I am not broken! I am not broken! I am a representative of the diversity of the human race.
>
> Norman Kunc (1957–)

Network, 2011). Although the unemployment rate was less than 4% in the late 1990s, unemployment for working-age disabled adults maintained the same range—from 65% to 71%. A 2010 Harris poll reported that only 21% of adults with a disability were employed (Taylor, Krane, & Orkis, 2010).

In a case illustrating the difficulties of finding work, a disabled man in Maine with a PhD in chemistry asked the state agency for assistance in finding a job. The agency sent him to the Goodwill store to be trained to sort socks. Another case occurred in Rhode Island where the vocational rehabilitation agency refused to provide further education to a quadriplegic man, arguing that he was adequately taken care of by SSI benefits (Garrett History Brief, 2001). Longmore (2003) cited a study in which 40% of people with a disability who were unemployed or working only part time identified "employer bias" as a major factor in their difficulty finding full-time employment. Even when they are employed full time, people with disabilities may still encounter discrimination by being paid less than their co-workers who have similar responsibilities or by being hired for a position with few responsibilities and little

chance for promotion. Given this kind of discrimination, it should come as no surprise that in the United States, almost a third of working-age adults with disabilities are living in poverty.

Mobility/accessibility. The ability of people in wheelchairs to function effectively in the community is affected by the existence of ramps, elevators, curb cuts, and wheelchair lifts on public buses. According to a Harris survey, 60% of people with disabilities report that their social, recreational, and employment opportunities are substantially limited due to lack of accessible public transportation. Accessibility problems have been cited as the reason why 40% of disabled people say they cannot participate in community activities such as attending church. Even buildings with ramps are not necessarily accessible. Many ramps are too narrow, too steep, or lack handrails. Theaters, sports facilities and other public settings may provide wheelchair accessible spaces that are segregated from the other seats, not allowing wheelchair users to sit with friends or colleagues (Longmore, 2003). Most wheelchair users do not insist that they be treated any different from someone who is mobile, but they do demand that they be given the same opportunities (see Figure 12.4).

Accessibility problems can also impede a disabled citizen's right to vote. Although the Voting Accessibility for Elderly and Handicapped Act of 1984 mandated accessible voting facilities, there are still polling

---

FIGURE 12.4

In the 1980s, Berke Breathed's "Bloom County" was one of the first comic strips to feature a character using a wheelchair.

©1982, The Washington Post Writer's Group. Reprinted with permission.

places that interfere with a disabled citizen's right to vote. In a study of 100 randomly selected counties across the United States, researchers found that 84% of voter registration offices and polling places had at least one impediment. None of the polling places made an effort to accommodate people with disabilities by providing special ballots or technology to assist people with vision problems or with difficulties in their fine motor skills. A recent election year study reported that out of 35 million voters who had a disability, only 14 million voted (Tokaji & Colker, 2007). People with a disability have tried to overcome voting difficulties by using absentee ballots; one study reported that they were the only group of voters who were less likely to vote in person and more likely to use absentee ballots. Some disability advocates argue that people with a disability should be given permanent absentee status so that they do not have to apply for an absentee ballot prior to every election, but would automatically receive absentee ballots (Tokaji & Colker, 2007).

Although the passage of the Americans with Disabilities Act (ADA) required public buildings to be accessible, most are still not, and the ADA did not require accessibility for nonpublic buildings. A concept promoting accessibility to all buildings is termed "visitability"; advocates encourage the construction of homes, businesses, and other non-public buildings to accommodate people with disabilities. The primary accommodations required are level entryways, wide doorways, and an accessible bathroom. This concept not only benefits people with disabilities but their family, friends, and neighbors who want to interact with them (Kaminski et al., 2006). This idea is not new. In 1985, Mace proposed the **universal design** concept that advocates creating products capable of being used by all people and constructing environments that are accessible to everyone. A ramp instead of steps leading to the entrance of a building provides access for people with disabilities but also makes access easier for parents with baby strollers or workers carrying heavy items. The concept of universal design is a means of improving a community for everyone.

Health care. According to Sulewski, Gilmore, and Foley (2006), people with disabilities spend more on health care than people without disabilities; therefore, access to health care is a major concern. People with disabilities often encounter difficulties in obtaining health insurance. The insurance industry openly uses personal health and genetic data in its review of potential clients. Russell (1998) cited one study reporting that 47% of applicants identified to be screened for "defects" were ultimately denied health insurance—even though no defects were found. The Americans with Disabilities Act (ADA) made such actions illegal, but the National Council on Disability (2009) reports that the ADA has been ineffective in addressing health care delivery for people with a disability. In addition, a Harris poll found that compared to nondisabled Americans, almost twice as many people with a disability reported that they had not received needed medical services, for both physical and mental health problems, at least once in the preceding year (Orkis, 2010). With the implementation of the Affordable Care Act, having a disability should be considered a pre-existing condition and cannot be used to deny health insurance.

Because some people with disabilities need services and equipment not provided by private insurance, access to Medicaid is essential. Medicaid is the primary provider of health care for nearly 7 million people under age 65 who have disabilities (Sulewski, Gilmore, & Foley, 2006). People with disabilities often report that one of the main obstacles to seeking employment is the fear of losing Medicaid because taking a full-time job can jeopardize their eligibility. Once they are covered by an employer's health care plan, they can lose their federally funded medical benefits. Often, it takes up to two years to reclaim and receive federally funded health care if an individual with a disability loses his or her job. Many choose to not work or to only work part time for a salary that keeps them eligible for Medicaid. According to a 2010 Harris poll, one third of all disabled people who are unemployed chose not to work rather than risk violating their eligibility for Medicaid (Taylor, Krane, & Orkis, 2010).

Education   Since the United States began, children with disabilities were kept at home or sent to segregated institutions. From 1930 to 1960, the number of children and youth with a disability increased significantly, and so did research on their needs. By the 1950s, public schools were allowed to establish special education programs for these students, and from 1948 to 1956, schools providing such programs increased by 83% (Osgood, 2005).

Even so, the assumption persisted that a segregated setting was the best way to teach these students. In the 1960s, researchers coined the term "learning disability" and identified various conditions that interfered with a child's ability to learn, and the ranks of disability activists grew. Following several court decisions and state legislation, the federal government passed the Education for All Handicapped Children Act (EAHC) in 1975, requiring public schools to educate students with a disability in the "least restrictive environment." Although the Act did not use the term **mainstreaming**, the idea that students with disabilities should be educated in the least restrictive and most acceptable available environment had become the law of the land.

Analyzing School Curricula Regarding Portrayals of People with a Disability

1. **Absence of people with a disability**

   Inclusion is an issue for all minority groups in fiction and nonfiction texts. The omission of any group suggests that they are not part of the diverse human family. This is especially important for people whose disabilities aren't obvious (visible).

2. **Use of stereotypes to represent people with a disability**

   In the text or in illustrations, people with a disability may be portrayed with stereotypical attributes such as being helpless, child like, or with little emotional range (e.g., always happy). People with disabilities should be portrayed as people with diverse personalities, and when they are included they should be one of the main characters in some books rather than always being minor characters.

3. **Content that promotes ableism**

   Curricula may intentionally or unintentionally reinforce negative cultural attitudes and actions toward people with a disability. Are the problems faced by a character with a disability (CWD) presented as personal challenges to be overcome, or do the problems stem from societal prejudice and discrimination against people with a disability? Is the CWD presented as a resourceful problem solver (for self or others) or are the problems of a CWD resolved through the intervention of a nondisabled character? Does a person with a disability have to be an extraordinary person (i.e., "supercrip") to be accepted or admired?

4. **Use of words with negative messages about disability**

   Derogatory views of people with disabilities are promoted by the use of loaded words such as lame, suffer from, confined to a wheelchair (or wheelchair-bound), victim, and, of course, crippled, and also by culturally derisive phrases such as blind as a bat, deaf as a post, lame joke, blind drunk, and idiot proof. If such words are included, teachers should use them as a "teachable moment" and have students analyze the negative perceptions such language promotes.

5. **People with disabilities presented in passive roles**

   Every person with a disability should not be presented as heroic since that would simply be a positive stereotype and not a realistic portrayal; nevertheless, people with a disability should be portrayed as often as possible as people who play a significant role in the development of a story. They should be rescuers as well as rescued, leaders as well as supporters, problem solvers as well as people with problems. People with disabilities encounter many problems in daily life related to transportation, housing, education, employment and self-determination, so it is important for students to be provided with realistic accounts of such problems. It is also important that people with disabilities are shown responding actively to their problems whether they are able to resolve them or not, including their efforts to reach out to allies to work with them in solving problems as opposed to simply being "rescued" by others.

NOTE: In reviewing curricular materials, make sure the text includes "People First" language (e.g., using "people with epilepsy" instead of "an epileptic"; for more examples, go to www.disabilityisnatural.com/explore/pfl), and always check the copyright dates of books and curricular materials because portrayals of people with disabilities have improved significantly in more recent publications.

Adapted from: Myers, C., & Bersani, H., Jr. (2008–2009).

Ten quick ways to analyze children's books for ableism. *Rethinking Schools, 23*(2), 52–54.

The problem that quickly emerged was that the concept of mainstreaming had different meanings for different people, including parents, teachers, and administrators. Some viewed mainstreaming as promoting the placement of students with disabilities into regular classes with support services to help them become academically successful; others argued that the "least restrictive environment" for academic achievement was occasionally a regular classroom, but more often a special education classroom where special accommodations could be made (Osgood, 2005). Research studies tended to support the position of disability advocates, who insisted that students with physical and mental disabilities learned more when they were integrated into regular classes than when they were taught in separate classes (Hines, 2001; Kochhar, West, & Taymans, 2000). Yet the pace of change was slow, and the degree of ongoing segregation for special education students was documented in a 1987 Massachusetts report that included a comment from a student with a disability who had graduated from high school. Reflecting on his school experience, he stated that he and his disabled peers were "completely unprepared for the real world. . . . Believe me, a segregated environment just will not do as preparation for an integrated life" (Osgood, 2005, p. 162).

In 1988, the U.S. Supreme Court made a decision affirming the rights of students with an emotional disability in the *Honig v. Doe* decision. In two separate incidents, two students with emotional disabilities had been suspended from the San Francisco Unified School District (SFUSD) for disruptive and violent behavior and eventually they were expelled. The parents sued on the basis of a provision in the 1975 EAHC Act that stated schools could not change a student's placement without the parents' consent. SFUSD and State School Superintendent Bill Honig justified their actions by arguing that both students represented a danger to other students. The court sided with the parents since the nature of each student's emotional disturbance made them prone to exactly the kind of violent and disruptive behavior that resulted in their expulsion (U.S. Supreme Court, 1988).

In 1990, the EAHC was renamed the Individuals with Disabilities Education Act (IDEA) and legislators included a provision that a student could be suspended for up to 45 days for coming to school or a school function with a weapon, with drugs, or if he or she physically assaulted someone. Despite these exceptions, IDEA continued to reinforce the rights of all students, even those who are emotionally disturbed, to have a "free and appropriate public education" (Whitted, Cleary, & Takiff, 2011), but the *Honig v. Doe* decision was perhaps a major factor encouraging parents and advocates for students with disabilities to become more assertive in promoting their vision of an "appropriate" education for these students.

In the 1990s, disability advocates began arguing for the merger of regular education and special education both in schools and in teacher preparation programs. They had abandoned mainstreaming to lobby for **inclusion** or "full inclusion"—calling for a total integration of students with disabilities in regular education classrooms (Kavale & Forness, 2005). Their efforts were assisted by a series of court decisions, influenced by civil rights laws, that ruled in favor of families with disabled children and ordered schools to adapt regular classrooms to meet the needs of students with a disability (Osgood, 2005). Despite these rulings, the debate has continued to the present. Opponents argue that students with disabilities demand too much time from teachers and that it is unfair to other students (Morse, 2005). Advocates counter that teachers can utilize aides, peers, and classroom strategies to ensure that all students receive appropriate educational experiences. Although Gliona, Gonzales, and Jacobson (2005) argue that alternate placements (i.e., segregation) may provide a better learning environment to meet the needs of some disabled students, Linton (1998) insists that inclusion is more than a teaching approach, and that it is not just "an educational plan to benefit disabled children. It is a model for educating all children equitably" (p. 61). Despite these arguments, the reality is that serious problems persist in educating students with a disability. A Harris poll reported that 17% of students with a disability are not graduating from high school compared to an 11% rate for those students without disabilities. Although the gap is still too large, significant progress has been made since 1986 when almost 40% of students with a disability did not graduate from high school (Orkis, 2010). Osgood (2005) assessed the issue:

> Most of this progress has been recorded with children who have mild disabilities. Representing almost 90 percent of the overall special education population, children identified as mildly disabled have been the foot soldiers in efforts to integrate regular classrooms, as their academic needs and classroom behavior supposedly demanded less in the way of classroom adaptations, classroom disruption, or teacher time. (p. 194)

Studies report that children are curious and interested in human differences and that they do not demonstrate a fear of differences unless they are taught to do so (Coleman, 2006). Even so, disability activists contend that most problems for people with disabilities stem from the attitudes of the nondisabled. When they advocate for inclusion, they argue not only that integration benefits students with disabilities by confronting stereotypes and stigmatizing labels, but also that the presence of students with disabilities can benefit other students by providing opportunities to develop attitudes and skills that will enable them to work with people who may be different from themselves (Sapon-Shevin, 1999). Although the Americans with Disabilities Act (ADA) provided legal recourse against discrimination, disability advocates have argued that it is more effective to address the negative attitudes causing discrimination. For that reason, many believe that inclusion is the best strategy to improve attitudes and increase opportunities for people with disabilities.

How difficult is it to change people's attitudes?

As Fiedler (2008) wrote, "Perhaps the greatest obstacle to school change efforts is the attitudes of the individuals who must implement the change" (p. 258). The effectiveness of school change efforts has varied according to the attitudes of the teachers and administrators involved; this is true for community change efforts as well. Posner (1979) described an incident from Israel illustrating the difficulties involved in changing attitudes. Two villages did not have enough orange pickers at harvest time, so they arranged for young men at a nearby institution for the mentally retarded to help with the harvest. Before the young men arrived, researchers came to the villages and conducted an attitude survey. The researchers reported that 66% of villagers said there should be no contact between retarded people and children; 68% thought retarded people should be permitted to work only in sheltered workshops; 95% said institutions were the best place for retarded people; and 58% believed that retarded people should be forbidden to marry.

When the retarded workers came, they picked oranges with great care and an enthusiasm not often displayed by other workers. Workers were told that if fallen oranges had not been bruised they could be used; only the retarded men inspected oranges that had fallen or been dropped. The retarded men climbed to the tops of ladders to pick oranges from high branches; no other workers were willing to climb so high. As the days passed, townspeople invited the workers to join them for lunch and the retarded men played with the children from the village. When the harvest was over, the young men returned to their institution.

The researchers returned to conduct a second attitude survey to see if changes had occurred in the attitudes of village residents. They found that the same 66% still believed there should be no contact between retarded people and children; the

> But in the ideal world, my differences, though noted, would not be devalued. Nor would I. Society would accept my experience as "disability culture," which would in turn be accepted as part of "human diversity." . . . In such a world, no one would mind being called Disabled.
>
> Carol Gill (Contemporary)

same 68% still thought retarded people should not work alongside others; the same 95% said retarded people should be in institutions; and the same 58% believed they should not marry. But please, all the villagers asked, will you make sure they send those nice young men back again next year?

AFTERWORD

Our attitudes are resistant to change: Change occurs only when we first examine our attitudes for myths, misperceptions, or stereotypes. It is especially important for aspiring teachers to reflect on their attitudes because every teacher will teach children or youth with disabilities. Assessing personal attitudes is not only appropriate for teachers but for others as well: It is equally important for employers who have the choice of hiring a person with a disability and for employees who may work with that disabled person. According to the Census Bureau (2010), nearly one out of five Americans—almost 57 million people—has a disability. Those who do not have a disability could be regarded as "nondisabled," a term used throughout this chapter because it acknowledges the possibility that anyone can become disabled as a consequence of an accident or an unexpected health problem. Since all of us could become a person with a disability at any point in our lives, for reasons of self-interest alone we should be committed to a just society that provides opportunities for people with disabilities to live full, engaging, and productive lives. We should advocate for a society that opens doors to opportunities for education and employment for those with disabilities rather than creating obstacles for them. Working together as allies, we could be a force for change that has a positive impact on the people with disabilities who live in our communities.

TERMS AND DEFINITIONS

Ableism The determination of an individual's abilities based on his or her disabilities; any policy or practice promoting the belief that disabled people are inferior to able-bodied persons to justify discrimination against people with disabilities

Cultural ableism The societal promotion of negative beliefs and images concerning people with disabilities that tend to portray the less able as deviant or incompetent; an assumption of superiority by people or groups based upon physical, mental, and emotional attributes

Deviant/Deviancy Someone whose appearance or behavior differs from the norm, from acceptable standards, in society

Disability A restriction of functional ability and activity caused by an impairment (such as hearing loss or reduced mobility) (Bernell, 2003)

Eugenics The study of agencies under social control that may improve or repair the racial qualities of future generations, either physically or mentally

Handicap An environmental or attitudinal barrier that limits the opportunity for a person to participate fully in a role that is normal (depending on age, sex, and social and cultural factors) for that individual (Bernell, 2003)

Inclusion Integration of all students with a disability into regular education classrooms

Individual ableism Prejudiced attitudes and behavior against others based on the assumption that one's level of ability is deviant from the norm, demonstrated whenever someone responds by saying or doing something degrading or harmful about persons whose ability is looked on as unacceptable

Institutional ableism Established laws, customs, and practices in a society that allow systematic discrimination against people with disabilities

Mainstreaming The responsibility of schools to educate all students, regardless of disability, in the least restrictive and most normally acceptable environment

Normalization Policies and practices that help create life conditions and opportunities for disabled people that are at least as good as those of average citizens

People with disabilities People with behavioral or anatomical characteristics marked as deviant, which identify them as targets for discrimination (Linton, 1998)

Universal design Designing and creating products and constructing environments that are accessible to everyone

DISCUSSION EXERCISES

Exercise #1 Group Home Discussion Activity

Directions: Imagine that you are a supervisor for people with various disabilities living in a group home. Identify activities listed below that a mentally retarded (MR), cerebral palsied (CP), epileptic (E), or physically disabled (PD) person should be permitted to do. Write the abbreviation for the particular disability next to each activity. If you feel that all people with the disabilities listed here should or should not be allowed to do the particular activity write "all."

Category/Activity

  I. Interpersonal Relationships
    1. Date
    2. Engage in safe sex
    3. Marry
    4. Have and raise children

 II. Lifestyle Concerns
    1. Choose their own clothing
    2. Dress the way they want
    3. Participate actively in the church of their choice
    4. Plan their own leisure time
    5. Engage in recreational activities of their choice

III. Economic Issues
    1. Choose the job they want
    2. Support themselves
    3. Be financially independent
    4. Enter into contracts
    5. Live where they choose

IV. Rights and Responsibilities
    1. Vote in political elections
    2. Drive a car
    3. Drink beer or liquor
    4. Have medical insurance
    5. Be educated to their fullest potential
    6. Be held responsible for their actions

Exercise #2 Disability Awareness Activity

What is a disability? How much do we know about disabilities? How prevalent are our disabilities?

Part One: List all the disabilities that you can think of; you will be reminded of additional disabilities as you listen to the suggestions of others. Attempt to identify at least 50 different disabilities. ("Paraplegic" may be combined with "quadriplegic" for example, in order for there to be room for a wide representation.)

Part Two: Sort your disabilities list into three principal groups: physical, emotional, or physiological. (For example, multiple sclerosis is a physical degeneration of one's muscular system; schizophrenia is commonly identified as a brain chemistry imbalance.) If you are uncertain of the category of a disability, discuss it with others. Recall from the chapter that disabilities may be permanent or temporary, evident and observable, or invisible.

Personal Insight Builder: Make three generalizations regarding how humans are different according to disability. Can you identify instances of unjustifiable discrimination against persons with disabilities? What attitudinal adjustments might be made within the general U.S. population regarding our attitudes toward persons with disabilities?

REFERENCES

Adelman, H.S. (1996). The classification problem. In W. Stainback & S. Stainback (Eds.), *Controversial issues confronting special education: Divergent perspectives* (pp. 29–44). Boston, MA: Allyn & Bacon.

Barzun, J. (2000). *From dawn to decadence: 500 years of Western cultural life (1500 to the present)*. New York, NY: HarperCollins.

Batavia, A. (2001). The new paternalism: Portraying people with disabilities as an oppressed minority. *Journal of Disability Policy Studies, 12*(2), 107–113.

Batavia, A. (2002). Consumer direction, consumer choice, and the future of long-term care. In L. Powers (Ed.), *Journal of Disability Policy Studies, 13*(2), 67–73.

Bernell, S. (2003). Theoretical and applied issues in defining disability in labor market research. *Journal of Disability Policy Studies, 14*(1), 36–45.

Bernstein, R. (2008, December 18). *Number of Americans with a disability reaches 54.4 million.* Retrieved June 10, 2009, from www.census.gov/newsroom/releases/archives/income_wealth/

Charlton, J.I. (1998). *Nothing about us without us.* Berkeley: University of California Press.

Coleman, L.M. (2006). Stigma. In L. Davis (Ed.), *The disability studies reader* (pp. 216–233). New York, NY: Routledge.

EEOC. (2012). *Americans with Disabilities Act of 1990 (ADA) Changes FY 1997–FY2011.* Retrieved October 17, 2012, from www.eeoc.gov/eeoc/statistics/enforcement/ada-charges.cfm

EEOC. (2009). *Disability discrimination.* Retrieved September 28, 2009, from http://www.eeoc.gov/types/ada.html.

Ervelles, N. (2001). In search of the disabled subject. In J.C. Wilson & C. Lewicki-Wilson (Eds.), *Embodied rhetorics: Disability in language and culture* (pp. 92–111). Carbondale: Southern Illinois University Press.

Fiedler, C. (2008). *Making a difference: Advocacy competencies for special education professionals.* Austin, TX: Pro Ed.

Fiedler, C., & Rylance, B. (Eds.). (2001, Fall). *Journal of Disability Policy Studies, 12*(2).

Fiedler, L. (1993). *Freaks: Myths and images of the secret self.* New York, NY: Anchor Books.

Fierros, E.G., & Conroy, J.W. (2002). Double jeopardy: An exploration of restrictiveness and race in special education. In D.J. Losen & G. Orfield (Eds.), *Racial inequity in special education* (pp. 39–70). Cambridge, MA: Harvard Education Press.

Fine, M., & Asch, A. (2000). Disability beyond stigma: Social interaction, discrimination, and activism. In M. Adams, W.J. Blumenfeld, R. Castaneda, H.W. Hackman, M.L. Peters, & X. Zuniga (Eds.), *Readings for diversity and social justice* (pp. 330–339). New York, NY: Routledge.

Foucault, M. (1989). *Madness and civilization: A history of insanity in the age of reason.* London, England: Routledge.

Gamble, A. (2012). *Cutting supplementary income (SSI) hurts mentally ill children.* Retrieved October 17, 2012, from Natashatracy.com/mental-illness-issues/cutting-supplemental-security-income-ssi-hurts-mentally-ill/

Garrett History Brief. (2001). *Journal of Disability Policy Studies, 12*(2), 70–78.

Gill, C.J. (1994). Questioning continuum. In B. Shaw (Ed.), *The ragged edge: The disability experience from the pages of the first fifteen years of "The Disability Rag"* (pp. 42–49). Louisville, KY: The Advocado Press.

Gliona, M.F., Gonzales, A.K., & Jacobson, E.S. (2005). Dedicated, not segregated: Suggested changes in thinking about instructional environments and in the language of special education. In J.M. Kauffman & D.P. Hallahan (Eds.), *The illusion of full inclusion: A comprehensive critique of a current special education bandwagon* (pp. 136–146). Austin, TX: Pro-ed.

Hahn, H. (1988, Winter). Can disability be beautiful? *Social Policy, 18,* 26–32.

Hahn, H. (1994). The minority group model of disability: Implications for medical sociology. *Research in the Sociology of Health Care, 11,* 3–24.

Hehir, T. (2005). *New directions in special education.* Cambridge, MA: Harvard Education Press.

Hines, R.A. (2001). *Inclusion in middle schools.* (Report No. EDO-PS-01-13). Champaign, IL: ERIC Clearinghouse on Elementary and Early Childhood Education, Children's Research Center, University of Illinois. (ERIC Document Reproduction Service No. 459000)

Institute for Community Living. (2004). *Policy research brief: Costs and outcomes of community services for persons with intellectual and developmental disabilities.* Retrieved October 16, 2012, from http://ici.umn.edu/products/prb/151/default.html

Johnson, J.R., & Nieto, J. (2007). Towards a cultural understanding of the disability and deaf experience: A content analysis of introductory multicultural education textbooks. *Multicultural Perspectives, 9*(3), 33–43.

Kaminski, S.E., Mazumdar, S., DiMento, J.F.C., & Geis, G. (2006). The viability of voluntary visitability. *Journal of Disability Policy Studies, 17*(1), 49–56.

Kavale, K.A., & Forness, S.R. (2005). History, rhetoric, and reality: Analysis of the inclusion debate. In J.M. Kauffman and D.P. Hallahan (Eds.), *The illusion of full inclusion: A comprehensive critique of a current special education bandwagon* (pp. 235–278). Austin, TX: Pro-ed.

Kliewer, C., & Biklin, D. (1996). Labeling: Who wants to be called retarded? In J. Stainbeck & S. Stainbeck (Eds.), *Controversial issues confronting special education: Divergent perspectives* (pp. 83–95). Baltimore, MD: Brookes.

Kochhar, C.A., West, L.L., & Taymans, J.M. (2000). *Successful inclusion: Practical strategies for a shared responsibility*. Upper Saddle River, NJ: Prentice-Hall.

Koppelman, K. (2001). *The only thing we have to fear. Values in the key of life: Making harmony in the human community* (pp. 24–28). Amityville, NY: Baywood.

La Fleur, J. (2009, June 22). *Nursing homes get old for many with disabilities*. Retrieved September 28, 2009, from www.propublicorg/feature/nursing-homes-get-old-for-many-with-disabilities-621

Linton, S. (1998). *Claiming disability: Knowledge and identity*. New York, NY: New York University Press.

Longmore, P.K. (2003). *Why I burned my book and other essays on disability*. Philadelphia, PA: Temple University Press.

Losen, D.J., & Orfield, G. (2002). Introduction. In D.J. Losen & G. Orfield (Eds.), *Racial inequity in special education*. Cambridge, MA: Harvard Education Press.

Morse, W.C. (2005). Comments from a biased viewpoint. In J.M. Kauffman & D.P. Hallahan (Eds.), *The illusion of full inclusion: A comprehensive critique of a current special education bandwagon* (pp. 79–95). Austin, TX: Pro-ed.

Myers, C., & Bersani H., Jr. (2008–2009). Ten quick ways to analyze children's books for ableism. *Rethinking Schools, 23*(2), 52–54.

National Council on Disability. (2009). *The current state of health care for people with disabilities*. Retrieved October 17, 2012, from www.ncd.gov/publications/2009/Sept302009#exesum

National Disability Authority. (2012). *International practice in quote monitoring*. Retrieved October 16, 2012, from www.nda.ie/cntmgmtnew.nsf/0/84AA79B029E870AE8025729D0046CAED/$File/people_with_disabilities_in-public_sector_04.htm

National Disability Rights Network. (2011). *Segregated and exploited: A call to action*. Retrieved October 17, 2012, from www.drcme/org/uploads/Beyond_Segregated_and_exploited.pdf

Orkis, K. (2010). *The ADA, 20 years later. A Harris interactive poll sponsored by the Kessler Foundation/National Organization on Disability*. Retrieved December 2, 2011, from http://kesslerfoundation.org/researchcenter/sci/files/surveyresults_sad.pdf

Osgood, R.L. (2005). *The history of inclusion in the United States*. Washington, DC: Gallaudet University Press.

Osher, D., Woodruff, D., & Sims, A.E. (2002). Schools make a difference: The overrepresentation of African American youth in special education and the juvenile justice system. In D.J. Losen & G. Orfield (Eds.), *Racial inequity in special education*. Cambridge, MA: Harvard Education Press.

Padden, C., & Humphries, T. (1998). *Deaf in America: Voices from a culture*. Cambridge, MA: Harvard University Press.

Pai, Y., & Adler, S. (1997). *Cultural foundations of education*. Upper Saddle River, NJ: Merrill/Prentice Hall.

Parrish, T. (2002). Racial disparities in the identification, funding, and provision of special education. In D.J. Losen & G. Orfield (Eds.), *Racial inequity in special education* (pp. 15–37). Cambridge, MA: Harvard Education Press.

Pelka, F. (1994, July/August). Hating the sick: Health chauvinism and its cure. *Humanist, 54*(4), 17–21.

Posner, B. (1979). Israel: A tale of two people. *Disabled USA, 2*(8), 16–17.

Putnam, M. (2005). Conceptualizing disability. *Journal of Disability Policy Studies, 16*(3), 188–198.

Reagan, T. (2005). A case study in cultural and linguistic difference: The DEAF-WORLD. In T. Osborn (Ed.), *Language and cultural diversity in U.S. schools* (pp. 53–64). Westport, CT: Praeger.

Ribton-Turner, C.J. (1972). *A history of vagrants and vagrancy*. Montclair, NJ: Patterson Smith.

Russell, M. (1998). *Beyond ramps: Disability at the end of the social contract*. Monroe, ME: Common Courage Press.

Sapon-Shevin, M. (1999). *Because we can change the world: A practical guide to building cooperative, inclusive classroom communities*. Boston, MA: Allyn & Bacon.

Sowers, J., McLean, D., & Owens, C. (2002). Self-directed employment for people with developmental disabilities: Issues, characteristics, and illustrations. *Journal of Disability Policy Studies, 13*(2), 96–103.

Stone, D.A. (1984). *The disabled state.* Philadelphia, PA: Temple University Press.

Sulewski, J.S., Gilmore, D.S., & Foley, S.M. (2006, Winter). Medicaid and employment of people with disabilities. *Journal of Disability Policy Studies, 17*(3), 158–165.

Taylor, H., Krane, D., & Orkis, K. (2010). *The ADA, 20 years later.* Retrieved October 17, 2012, from www.2010disabilitysurveys.org

Tokaji, D.P., & Colker, R. (2007). Absentee voting by people with disabilities: Promoting access and integrity. *McGeorge Law Review*, 38, 1015–1064.

U.S. Census Bureau. (2012). Anniversary of Americans with Disabilities Act: July 26. Retrieved October 16 2012, from www.census.gov/newsroom/releases/archives/facts)_for_features_special_editions/cb12-ff16.html

U.S. Commission on Civil Rights. (2009). Minorities in special education. Retrieved October 16, 2012, from www.usccr.gov/pubs/MinoritiesinSpecialEducation.pdf

U.S. Supreme Court (1988). *Honig v. Doe,* et. al. Retrieved December 1, 2011, from www.wrightslaw.com/case/caselaw/ussupct/honig.doe.htm

Wehmeyer, M. (2000, Summer). Riding the third wave. *Focus on Autism & Other Developmental Disabilities, 15*(2), 106–116.

Whitted, B.R., Cleary, L.A., & Takiff, N.E. (2011). *Educational mandates for children with disabilities: School policies, case law, and the school social worker.* Retrieved December 1, 2011, from www.wct-law.com/CM/Publications/publications17.asp

Williams, C. (2003). Managing individuals in a diverse work force. In *Management* (2nd ed., pp. 434–471). Versailles, KY: Thompson Southwestern.

Wilson, J.C., & Lewicki-Wilson, C. (2001). Disability, rhetoric, and the body. In J.C. Wilson & C. Lewicki-Wilson (Eds.), *Embodied rhetorics: Disability in language and culture* (pp. 1–24). Carbondale: Southern Illinois University Press.

Winzer, M.A. (1997). Disability and society before the eighteenth century: Dread and despair. In L. Davis (Ed.), *The disability studies reader* (pp. 75–109). London, England: Routledge.

Wolfensberger, W. (1970). *The principle of normalization in human services.* Toronto: National Institute on Mental Retardation.

The Challenge of Diversity to American Institutions

This section describes the changes in the United States that take advantage of American population diversity.

Elementary, middle, and secondary schools have historically been considered the vehicle by which we transmit our cultural values and knowledge to future generations, and Chapter 13 describes the philosophy and practices of school multicultural education curriculums. Following a brief review of America's traditional educational philosophy known as "essentialism," this chapter describes the changes necessary to create schools and classrooms where policies, practices, curriculum, and instruction reflect the purposes

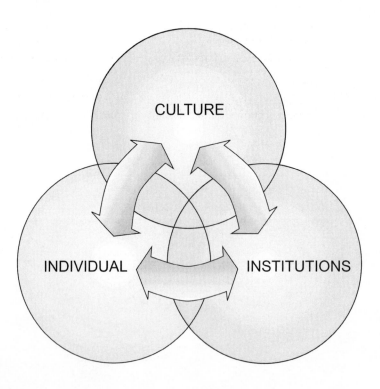

and goals of multicultural education. The chapter concludes with an explanation of why multicultural education represents an educational reform that needs to be pursued for the benefit of all our students and for the future of our diverse society.

Currently, considerable effort is being made to instill in the American workforce a more inclusive attitude toward diversity. Chapter 14 describes changes occurring in major institutions of our society that reflect the growing influence of pluralism as the preferred perspective in response to the increasing diversity of the American people. Our government continues to require affirmative action plans to ensure that opportunities are provided to members of groups that were discriminated against in the past and continue to experience discrimination. Higher education administrators have embraced the value of affirmative plans to broaden the diversity of faculty as well as student populations and to argue that such diversity enhances the education of all students.

In the corporate world, business leaders have recognized the growing diversity of the workforce and consumers, and they are increasingly implementing diversity training to take advantage of both. Mass media organizations have promoted diversity by placing more women and people of color in positions that have high public visibility, and the diversity in this profession is likely to increase, given the significantly increasing numbers of women and people of color currently majoring in journalism or mass communication on college campuses. In addition, the dramatic growth of digital media has created new concerns from racial stereotypes in video games and on Web sites to the creation and dissemination of deliberate distortions of reality by bloggers and vloggers. The military has taken aggressive action to promote gender and racial equality in its recruitment, promotion policies and practices, and diversity training programs.

Change occurring in institutions across the United States reinforces the need to prepare new generations to appreciate and participate effectively in the unique and increasing diversity that defines our American society in the twenty-first century.

Chapter 13

Pluralism in Schools: The Promise of Multicultural Education

"Learning to read was, for slaves, not an immediate passport to freedom but rather a way of gaining access to one of the powerful instruments of their oppressors: the book."

Alberto Manguel (1948–)

Learning and schooling are critical for every person in any society. The future of our diverse society will depend on how schools educate the coming generations, and pluralism must be a significant factor in that education. During an interview for a college administrative position, an African American candidate asked about his views on diversity responded, "First, let me say that I'm a pluralist. After all, we had a diverse society when we had slaves." This is an important distinction. Many people refer to *diversity* and *pluralism* as if the two terms were synonymous, but **diversity** simply describes the existence of many different groups of people within a society, whereas **pluralism** describes a society in which diversity is accepted and supported. In a pluralistic society, diverse groups function together effectively, with mutual respect. In a society that is diverse but not pluralistic, schools tend to teach principally about the dominant group—its influence on the evolution of society, and its literature, art, and music. In a diverse society committed to pluralism, schools teach about all groups within the society, from most ancient to most recent.

Misunderstanding of terms occurs when we fail to clarify meanings and intentions. No study of human differences is complete without special terms, and precise communication exists only when everyone involved is clear about their meaning. So we must begin by clarifying our definition of multicultural education and explaining our vision of its importance for the future of our diverse society.

Defining Multicultural Education

Multicultural education is based on a commitment to pluralism; its guiding purpose is to prepare students to be active participants in a diverse, democratic society. There is confusion and considerable debate about multicultural education, even among educators who advocate for it. Some people regard multicultural education simply as the process of integrating issues and information about race and ethnicity into school curricula, but that describes what Banks (2006) defines as **multiethnic education**. In a study cited by Gayle-Evans and Michael (2006), some teachers regarded multicultural education as a curriculum for teaching about cultures around the world, but that is usually called **global (or international) education**. Others say multicultural education includes recognition of women, gays and lesbians, people with disabilities, and other minority groups; opponents to this idea argue that such groups do not constitute distinct cultures and therefore should not be included. This confusion raises many questions that must be answered before we can understand what multicultural education is and recognize schools that are engaged in an authentic form of this educational approach.

In addition to conflicting opinions about the definition of the term *multicultural education* and about who should be included, there are numerous perceptions about who benefits from it. Americans seem to agree that students of color benefit from multicultural education, especially in urban multiracial and multiethnic classrooms; yet many educators and parents in suburban or rural school districts consisting predominantly or exclusively of white students appear to believe that multicultural education provides no benefits. Gayle-Evans and Michael (2006) review several studies reporting that many teachers were uncomfortable incorporating multicultural issues into their content because they felt that the topics were "too sensitive"; educators also said they did not feel that their teacher education programs adequately prepared them to implement multicultural education practices. Kumashiro (2010) has argued that much of the reluctance to implement multicultural education stems from the social justice issues that are addressed. For white students in particular, multicultural education challenges what students think they know—assumptions that seem "natural" or just "common sense." Hines (2007) has argued that students in multicultural education classes must be taught to rethink their assumptions by asking questions such as "What are the alternatives?" and "Who benefits from this (policy/practice/outcome)?" Kumashiro (2010) also asserts that concepts learned in multicultural education often require that students unlearn some of their assumptions first, a process that may make them uncomfortable, so uncomfortable that they begin to resist the theories and research presented to them. In their classrooms, teachers who choose to avoid this issue simply include the contributions of a few people of color in their curriculum, but this does not adequately provide an education that can be called *multicultural* in any meaningful way.

What does it mean for education to be called *multicultural*?

As early as 1974, Hilliard wrote that **multicultural** refers to a society "made up of a number of cultural groups based upon race, ethnicity, religion, language, nationality, income, etc." (p. 41). Because income level is not usually regarded as representing a different culture—rich or poor, we're all Americans—Hilliard's comment is assumed to mean that the term *multicultural* includes other subordinate groups that he did not specifically identify, such as women, gays and lesbians, and people with disabilities.

As for the term *education*, we must distinguish between *education* and *training*. Some dictionaries suggest that education and training are synonyms, but people take classes to train them in a particular skill. A person can be trained to drive or cook, or even be trained to train a dog. Education is a broader concept. Partridge (1983) explained that *educate* derives from the Latin word *ducere*, which means to lead; *educere* means to lead out or bring forth (p. 169). By extrapolation, *education* means to bring forth the potential of an individual. In addition to developing cognitive skill and affective sensitivity, education entails developing an understanding of previous achievements in subjects such as history, literature, and science as a basis for making individual and societal choices in the future. Carse (1986) distinguished education from training:

> Education discovers an increasing richness in the past because it sees what is unfinished there. Training regards the past as finished and the future to be finished. Education leads toward a continuing self-discovery; training leads toward a final self-definition. (p. 23)

Multicultural education integrates information about past issues with achievements of diverse groups to describe how they have influenced our society. Children and youth from all groups are thereby provided with a sense of belonging to our society by understanding how their group has helped to shape what our society is and by appreciating the potential they have for influencing what it will become.

What is an appropriate definition for multicultural education?

Multicultural education is a journey that leads students to self-discovery and to a sense of personal efficacy. Nieto (2008) provides a comprehensive definition and description of multicultural education that includes the components to be addressed in this chapter:

> **Multicultural education** is a process of comprehensive school reform and basic education for all students. It challenges and rejects racism and other forms of discrimination in schools and society and accepts and affirms the pluralism (ethnic, racial, linguistic, religious, economic, and gender, among others) that students, their communities, and teachers reflect. Multicultural education permeates the

Frank and Ernest

FIGURE 13.1

©1998 Thaves/Reprinted with permission.

schools' curriculum and instructional strategies, as well as the interactions among teachers, students, and families, and the very way that schools conceptualize the nature of teaching and learning. Because it uses critical pedagogy as its underlying philosophy . . . multicultural education promotes democratic principles of social justice. (p. 44)

Nieto's definition and description of multicultural education emphasizes that it is not a "business-as-usual" approach to schooling. It requires changes in teaching methods and perspectives on learning because of critical philosophical differences between traditional education and multicultural education (see Figure 13.1).

Traditional Assumptions in American Education

The development of American schools has been based on a conservative philosophy that was eventually labeled *essentialism*, and essentialist assumptions are still in place. The term stems from the belief that an essential body of knowledge and essential human values that have stood the test of time can be identified and transmitted to students. Essentialists describe the purpose of schools as the transmission of the most significant accumulated knowledge and values from previous generations to the coming generation.

What body of knowledge have essentialists identified?

Essentialist scholars maintain that knowledge from four disciplines is essential: social studies, science, mathematics, and English language and literature; therefore these four subjects are emphasized in elementary, middle, and high school. Graduation requirements for high school students usually include a minimum of two years of course work, often three or even four, in social studies, science, mathematics, and English. To essentialists, subjects such as art, music, and physical education are accepted principally to make school more enjoyable, but they are regarded as additional rather than essential. When administrators consider budget reductions, programs in art, music, and physical education are scrutinized and are most likely to be reduced or eliminated. Similar assumptions continue into college, where general education programs often require students to choose among a selection of courses in social studies, science, math, and English literature and composition.

What essential human values do schools teach?

As indicated in Chapter 1, Myrdal (1944) identified core American values embraced by most citizens and taught in most schools. In addition, Americans presume that certain values represent the

American middle class: promptness, honesty, hard work, competitiveness, and efficiency. Teachers implement traditional approaches to teaching values (see Chapter 1) to convince children and youth that the core values are worthwhile and should be adopted. Students may say they believe in these values because it's expected of them, even though their behavior often does not suggest that they have a genuine commitment to them.

How do essentialists define or describe learning?

Essentialists define learning as the acquisition of essential knowledge and values. Metaphors used by essentialists to describe learning portray knowledge as water and students as empty vessels to be filled or as sponges ready to absorb. To assess learning, essentialists favor objective tests with

> Teachers open the door, but you must enter by yourself.
>
> Chinese Proverb

questions about factual information to ascertain if students absorbed the information. (If not, teachers may review the information and test students again.) In extreme cases, students may repeat a grade to have a second chance to learn material in the hope that the teacher, perhaps a different teacher, will be more successful helping them acquire the information. Maturity and readiness are considered secondary in this process.

What is the role of the essentialist teacher in helping students learn?

An essentialist teacher is supposed to be a skillful transmitter of information and an advocate for American values. Teachers are expected to be role models for our society's values—both inside and outside the classroom. As transmitters of information, teachers are expected to use technology to make information interesting and thereby promote acquisition of knowledge. Although teachers may

select from a variety of pedagogical techniques, the goal is to motivate students to remember information provided in textbooks, lectures, and media. The problem is that few students can demonstrate that they are learning what teachers are teaching.

Why are students not learning in essentialist schools?

The first problem has to do with what has been considered essential. During the past several decades, research in various fields, especially the sciences, has generated what scholars have called a *knowledge explosion*. Given so much new knowledge, how is one to determine which facts are most important? Feminists and scholars of color have developed alternative interpretations of historical events that challenge conventional views; they believe their perspectives should be included in school curricula. Whereas women and writers of color were minimally represented in previous literature anthologies, advocates are increasingly demanding that their voices and ideas be acknowledged. Curriculum reformers suggest that most students regard traditional essentialist curriculum as inaccurate, irrelevant, and not at all motivational.

Another problem is that we know students learn at different rates. If teachers transmit information at the same rate, some students learn all of it, some learn most of it, and some retain very little of it; yet teachers often must proceed as if all students learned equally. The solution essentialists have developed to address incomplete learning is to group students according to ability, which is known as *tracking*. Studies of tracking have found that excellent students learn just as well in heterogeneous groups as in homogeneous groups where they are grouped by ability, but that the achievement of moderate and slow learners improves significantly when they are in mixed groups rather than when they are grouped according to academic ability (Kershaw, 1992; Oakes, 2005; Oakes & Wells, 1996; Oakes et al., 2000). Despite these consistent research conclusions, essentialist schools tend to continue to group students according to ability.

Perhaps the most significant obstacle to learning in essentialist schools is the problem of retention and transfer. **Retention** refers to student recall of knowledge; **transfer** is the ability of students to apply that knowledge both inside and outside the classroom. Students have long complained about cramming before taking exams that require them to memorize material. Studies have consistently found that when tested for retention of information, students tend to recall no more than 20% of what they had supposedly learned the first time they took the exam.

The learning problems attributed to an essentialist approach may explain the results of a charter school study conducted by the Center for Research on Educational Outcomes (CREDO) at Stanford University. More than 4,000 charter schools enrolling over a million students have been established primarily in urban school districts. These schools were intended to be publicly funded experiments in innovative educational practices that would promote changes in public schools to foster more effective ways of teaching diverse students, but it hasn't worked out that way (Dingerson, Miner, Peterson, & Walters, 2008). The CREDO study involved a longitudinal assessment of charter schools nationwide. Researchers reviewed student academic achievements in more than 2,400 charter schools in 15 states and the District of Columbia. The study found that the academic achievement of 50% of charter school students was comparable to their public school peers, but 37% had even lower achievement scores (Jackson, 2009). Despite the assumption that non-unionized teachers and less bureaucracy would promote innovative approaches and improved student performance, charter schools have largely followed an essentialist model of education that is ineffective according to multiple studies. As an alternative to the failed charter school approach, many educators advocate multicultural education, which requires a transformation of the assumptions essentialist schools have made about schools, teaching, and learning.

Assumptions of Multicultural Education

To resolve problems related to student learning, as parents or educators, we must change our assumptions about curriculum content, learning, teaching, and the purpose of schools. As described by Nieto (2008), Banks (2008), Sleeter (1996), and others,

multicultural education challenges us to change those assumptions.

What assumptions do multicultural educators make about curriculum?

Nieto's widely accepted definition of multicultural education includes an affirmation of diversity that must permeate the curriculum to provide honest representations of diversity in American society. At present, textbooks continue to be dominated by the art, music, history, literature, perspectives, and images of white Americans. Sleeter and Grant (2003) reviewed forty-seven textbooks in social studies, reading, language arts, science, and mathematics for elementary and middle-level students. They reported that whites were featured predominantly in all of them. Although some improvements have been found in more recent textbooks, when people of color are included, the textbooks typically have provided:

> A sketchy account of Black history and little sense of contemporary Black life. Asian Americans appear mainly as figures on the landscape with virtually no history or contemporary ethnic experience. . . . Native Americans appear mainly as historical figures. (p. 22)

American elementary, middle, and secondary textbooks also tend to omit or provide only minimal representation of other groups: women, gays and lesbians, people with disabilities, and low-income families. School textbooks not only represent a problem for minority children but also are apt to teach white children a dishonest perspective of their society. As Baker (1994) explained, "Non-minority children are led to believe that their behavior, the ways they are taught to respond, are the only accepted ways of behaving" (p. 8). To present a realistic understanding of our multicultural society and the influence of diverse groups on our society, advocates support a multicultural curriculum for all students, not just for students of color.

A multicultural curriculum examines the influences of diverse groups on historical events, literary developments, musical styles, artistic expression, athletic achievements, and other facets of American society—but the goal is not simply to memorize facts. Appleton (1983) described multicultural curriculum as "a conceptual approach that provides a

> It is probably never really wise, or even necessary, or anything better than harmful, to educate a human being toward a good end by telling him lies.
>
> James Agee (1910–1955)

framework for understanding the experience and perspectives of all the groups" (p. 211). The need for a conceptual approach is another assumption about curriculum by multicultural educators.

Why is it necessary to take a conceptual approach to curriculum?

Because of the knowledge explosion, it is impractical to emphasize memorization. It is not possible for us to remember all available information in every subject; we also know that much information soon will be obsolete or supplanted by new knowledge. In a multicultural curriculum, understanding broad concepts is preferable to memorizing facts. Gay (1977) described a multicultural curriculum design based on a thematic approach and a conceptual framework. In the thematic approach, students employ information from different disciplines to explore universal themes such as the search for identity, communication and conflict resolution, human interdependence, economics and exploitation, or the struggle for a just society (see also Gay, 2010).

Curriculum based on a conceptual framework also requires an interdisciplinary approach. Beginning with a concept such as power, alienation, or socialization, students could collect data from various sources addressing the concept, leading them to the identification and exploration of related concepts. Gay (1977) argued that both curriculum designs must be interdisciplinary because they require "the use of knowledge, concepts, and principles from many different disciplines" (p. 101). In either a thematic or a conceptual framework approach, students examine past and present experiences to develop an integrated understanding of principles and relationships between concepts.

Because multicultural curriculum is based on concepts rather than on specific content, students are involved in an ongoing and dynamic search for knowledge that is never finished, whereas the monocultural curriculum traditionally presented in schools is a finished product. As Nieto (2008) wrote,

> When reality is presented in schools as static, finished, and flat, the underlying tensions, controversies, passions and problems faced by people throughout history and today disappear. (p. 55)

Identifying concepts for students to analyze and discuss to clarify their understanding is the foundation of multicultural curriculum; to be effective, it is critical that the curriculum not be sabotaged by the hidden curriculum in school.

What is the hidden curriculum?

Pai and Adler (1997) define **hidden curriculum** as the indirect means by which schools teach students "the norms and values of their society" (p. 148). They describe the hidden curriculum as subtle messages learned from pictures displayed on bulletin boards or from school policies such as tardy slips and tracking. Messages may be intentional or unintentional; still, they have an impact on learners. Through the hidden curriculum, schools can promote such values as punctuality, assertiveness, or competitiveness. Pai and Adler suggest that the hidden curriculum may vary according to socioeconomic status, with upper-class children being taught leadership skills and having opportunities for creativity and problem solving in contrast to low-income students being taught to respect authority and receiving rewards for compliance and conformity.

Everyday situations reveal a hidden curriculum in school policies and practices, and subtle messages can even be found in formal curriculum. An education professor entered a Los Angeles high school English classroom, where 80% of the students were Hispanic; she noticed that only white authors were featured on wall posters. An unmarried high school student was expelled from the local chapter of the National Honor Society because she was pregnant. A student teacher in a fourth-grade classroom of predominantly white students wanted to make a "Black History Month" bulletin board for February, but her supervising teacher rejected the idea because she believed that the students were "too young" for that (Koppelman, 2001).

Teaching that Columbus discovered America tells children that Native Americans were irrelevant and can be ignored; perhaps it is no coincidence that the white majority ignores Native Americans who protest Indian mascots for school sports teams. Brigham Young took his followers to Mexican territory because of the oppression and violence Mormons had encountered in the United States. Teaching that Mormons settled in Utah instead of Mexican territory implies that religious groups have always been able to practice their beliefs

> The wise person can see a question from all sides without bias. The foolish person is biased and can see a question only from one side.
>
> Confucius (551–479 BCE)

freely in the United States and ignores the difficulty America has experienced living up to the principle of religious freedom. Teaching that Old World art refers only to ancient Greek and Roman cultures denies the artistic heritage of many—especially non-Western—countries. Nieto (2008) argued that presenting history only from the perspective of the dominant group teaches a skewed version of the truth. Educators implementing multicultural curricula must be especially sensitive to subtle messages provided by the hidden curriculum.

Why have schools implemented multicultural curriculum?

Many schools across the United States, especially in urban areas, have developed their own multicultural materials to supplement inadequate textbooks. Banks (2008) categorized the efforts into four approaches: the contributions approach, the additive approach, the transformation approach, and the social action approach. The first two approaches address multicultural education minimally by including heroes, holidays, and other cultural information (*contributions*), and then adding some multicultural concepts and perspectives to the curriculum (*additive*), but leaving its basic structure unchanged. The last two approaches come much closer to satisfying Nieto's definition of

what it means to implement multicultural education in a school.

A *transformation* approach to multicultural curriculum design emphasizes concepts and themes. Students are presented with multiple perspectives on issues, and the goal is not to identify a "right perspective," but to understand how each perspective contributes to a richer understanding of issues. Critical thinking skills are emphasized as students develop their own insights and conclusions and logically justify them.

A *social action* approach to multicultural curriculum design encourages students to take action based on their ideas and conclusions. Students–individually or collectively—pursue projects at school and in their community to address problems they identify and study. The goal of a social action approach is to empower students and to demonstrate that learning is not a game of *Trivial Pursuit*. Knowledge can lead to social action and create positive change. By encouraging critical thinking and active learning, multicultural educators combine theory and practice about conditions necessary to promote effective learning.

How do multicultural educators describe learning?

Advocates for multicultural education rely on cognitive development theory to describe how people learn. In essence, learning is a process of meaning making. Learners organize ideas, information, and experiences they encounter in order to make sense of them. They may categorize, seek relationships, and simplify complex issues to achieve understanding. According to Sleeter and Grant (2003), "Learning is a process of constructing knowledge through the interaction of mind and experience" (p. 196). Piaget (1974) observed that children learn by interacting physically and intellectually with their environment. If students are provided information through lecture, they may attempt to extract relevant meaning from it, but if they perceive no relevance in the information, they are not likely to make the effort.

Learning results from the active interaction of individuals with information. Learning also requires meaningfulness. Information regarded as meaningless will not be learned. Being an active learner promotes the development of competence and confidence, the basis for Dewey's insistence that children "learn by doing." Feeling competent and gaining self-confidence leads to a sense of power. As Hilliard (1974) wrote, "Learning is related to a sense of power over some of the forces

> In every child who is born, under no matter what circumstances, and of no matter what parents, the potentiality of the human race is born again; and in [that child] . . . and in each of us, our terrific responsibility towards human life; toward the utmost idea of goodness.
>
> James Agee (1910–1955)

which impinge upon our lives" (p. 47). If students feel powerless, they have little motivation to learn; when students are active, they develop skills and demonstrate abilities that reinforce self-confidence and give a sense of personal competence, and they acquire an enthusiasm for learning.

With regard to skill development, learning must not be limited to basic academic skills—reading, writing, computing—but must include a multitude of skills related to critical thinking, creativity, decision making, problem solving, information accessing, interpersonal and cross-cultural communication, conflict resolution, visual literacy, and self-analysis. Gay (1977) argued that an education that "does not include the development of skills that will increase and enhance students' capabilities to live and function in a culturally pluralistic setting is incomplete" (p. 98). Although they may develop skills, an obstacle to facilitating skill development is that students have multiple ways of learning; therefore a single teaching strategy may be inadequate. Teachers committed to multicultural education must believe that all children can learn—if learning activities are designed to accommodate each child.

In what different ways do individuals learn?

Considerable research has been conducted to identify and explain styles of learning, but the result has been to categorize learning as a complex assortment

of more than a dozen different learning styles. In more recent years, multicultural educators have been attracted to the work of Gardner (1993), whose theory of multiple intelligences is regarded by many as one of the best explanations of the diversity in learning. Gardner defines intelligence as the ability to process information and to generate solutions or products of value within a particular context.

Gardner (1993) originally identified seven distinct ways that people demonstrate intelligence, but since then he has added an eighth category of intelligence (Gardner, 1999). According to Gardner, each person has the potential to engage in all eight means of processing information, although an individual is likely to be more competent in certain dimensions based on personal idiosyncrasies or the influence of his or her culture. (See Table 13.1.) The theory rejects the educational practice of recognizing and rewarding primarily two intelligences: logical-mathematical and linguistic. Gardner's theory describes a more complete means of understanding intelligence and identifying intellectual abilities. The challenge for teachers is to create instructional strategies and assessment procedures that accommodate more than one kind of intelligence. If teachers can meet this challenge, more students will have successful learning experiences, which will promote self-confidence.

Why is self-confidence necessary for learning?

Attitudes affect learning. It is generally understood that if students think they cannot learn something, they aren't likely to learn it. Combs (1979) claimed, "People behave in terms of what they believe about themselves. Whether we feel adequate or inadequate greatly affects how we approach a task" (p. 108). Research studies have confirmed that attitudes of teachers (and others) can positively or negatively affect student self-confidence. Research cited by Baker (1994) concluded, "There appears to be a high correlation between achievement in school and students' self-concept of academic ability as determined by the expectations and evaluations of significant others" (p. 9). By "significant others" Baker meant teachers and other school personnel. Although expectations should not be unrealistic, teachers must express high expectations for students to facilitate learning.

TABLE 13.1 Descriptions of Multiple Intelligences

1. *Logical-Mathematical*: Ability to understand and solve logical problems, especially involving the use and manipulation of numbers.

2. *Linguistic:* Ability to understand nuances of meanings and multiple meanings of words, including a special appreciation for the sounds and rhythms of language.

3. *Bodily-Kinesthetic*: Ability to learn and master physical tasks involving motion and balance, and including manual manipulation of objects.

4. *Musical*: Ability to understand, reproduce and appreciate musical sounds and rhythms in a range of musical expressions.

5. *Spatial:* Ability to understand spatial relationships in the environment and to cognitively modify those relationships for particular purposes.

6. *Interpersonal*: Sensitivity to nonverbal expressions of feelings and desires of other people and the ability to respond appropriately to them.

7. *Intrapersonal:* Ability for self-analysis, to understand clearly one's own feelings and desires and to apply that knowledge in one's choices and behaviors.

8. *Naturalist:* Ability to discern similarities and differences in plants and animals that leads to an enhanced understanding of established classifications.

Source: Gardner (1999).

What must teachers do to implement a multicultural education approach?

Educators must determine which multicultural education approach they will implement. Sleeter and Grant (2003) identified five distinct approaches, two of which also satisfy the criteria included in Nieto's description: multicultural education and education that is multicultural *and* social reconstructionist (see Table 13.2). For purposes of clarity, the latter is referred to here as the *social reconstructionist approach.*

Principles underlying a multicultural education approach are reflected in a statement entitled "No One Model American" issued by the Commission on Multicultural Education (Hunter, 1974):

> Multicultural education values cultural pluralism. Multicultural education rejects the view that schools should seek to melt away cultural differences or the view that schools should merely tolerate cultural pluralism. Instead, multicultural education affirms that schools should be oriented toward the cultural enrichment of all children and youth through programs rooted to the preservation and extension of cultural diversity as a fact of life in American society. (p. 21)

A *multicultural education approach* insists that a diverse society can achieve unity through diversity; it need not eliminate cultural differences. Although some advocates of this approach focus on racial and ethnic groups, most promote an inclusive view of diversity by incorporating information on women, gays and lesbians, low-income families, and people with disabilities.

Multicultural education advocates support integration, inclusion, and "de-tracking" to create heterogeneous classrooms emphasizing skill development to gain knowledge and a better understanding of diverse groups in American society. Further, a multicultural education approach calls for curricular reform to correct omissions and distortions in textbooks concerning diverse groups, and provides multiple perspectives on important historical or contemporary events. Advocates have criticized visual images in textbooks for not representing diversity in American society adequately and for continuing to depict certain groups in stereotypical ways. They urge teachers to use bulletin boards and media to provide accurate representations of diverse groups.

TABLE 13.2 Approaches to Multicultural Education

Teaching the Exceptional and the Culturally Different

GOALS: To help low-achieving students succeed within traditional education by building bridges between them and the curriculum, and providing special assistance.

CURRICULUM: Based on the traditional curriculum but incorporates students' experiences (especially those who are culturally different). Uses classroom materials that include meaningful contexts for the students.

INSTRUCTION: Implements English as a Second Language or transitional bilingual education for language minority students and culturally relevant teaching for culturally different students; provides remedial classes including special education placement for temporary but intensive remediation; displays images relevant to students on wall posters and bulletin boards.

Human Relations

GOALS: To maintain traditional educational assumptions but with an emphasis on reducing prejudice, developing positive student self-concepts, and promoting acceptance of individual diversity.

CURRICULUM: Based on the traditional curriculum but including content on prejudice and stereotypes, similarities and differences among groups and individuals, and societal contributions from members of diverse groups in society, especially those groups represented by the students in the school.

INSTRUCTION: Uses strategies that build student-student relationships such as conflict mediation, role playing, simulations that address interpersonal relationships, and cooperative learning; displays student work on walls and bulletin boards.

Single Group Studies

GOALS: To provide knowledge about a particular group (Women's Studies, Chicano Studies, etc.) including an examination of structural inequalities affecting members of this group and encouraging students to work for social change.

CURRICULUM: Provides information (for a unit or course) about cultural characteristics and historical experiences of a group with emphasis on perspectives of group members and how this group has been and still is oppressed.

INSTRUCTION: Responds to learning style differences of the group with accommodations for individual learning styles; incorporates media, music, performances, and guest speakers to address aspects of the culture or issues related to the group; wall displays and bulletin boards emphasize societal contributions from individual members of the group.

Multicultural Education

GOALS: To promote cultural pluralism by emphasizing respect for human differences, including individual lifestyles, equal opportunity for all in school and society, and the need for power equity among diverse groups in society.

CURRICULUM: Provides content on diverse groups and their contributions to society with emphasis on perspectives from members of each group; incorporates student experiences to enhance curriculum relevance, and emphasizes the need to be aware of and understand alternative

(continues)

TABLE 13.2 *(Continued)*

perspectives on issues; addresses "hidden curriculum" by including diversity in special events, holidays, school menus, etc.

INSTRUCTION: Responds to student learning styles and skill levels with emphasis on an analysis of curriculum content and critical thinking activities; promotes respect for and use of other languages and dialects while learning standard English; displays wall posters and bulletin boards that reflect human diversity represented by race, ethnicity, gender, disability, religion, and other diverse groups, as well as issues reflecting individual student interests.

Education That Is Multicultural and Social Reconstructionist

GOALS: To promote cultural pluralism and structural equality for diverse groups in our society, to prepare students to be active participants in our democratic society by understanding structural inequalities and promoting equal opportunity.

CURRICULUM: Provides content on current social issues of oppression and structural inequalities for diverse groups using perspectives of members of those groups including the perspectives of students and community members; emphasizes historic and contemporary life experiences for self-reflection, for analyzing oppression, and for understanding alternative perspectives; addresses "hidden curriculum" by including diversity in special events, holidays, school menus, etc.

INSTRUCTION: Responds to student learning styles and skill levels with emphasis on active student involvement in democratic decision making in the school; engages students in critical thinking and in problem solving to promote the development of social action skills that empower students; employs cooperative learning and group projects, especially those involving the community; avoids testing and tracking procedures that represent narrow views of student learning that label some students as failures; displays wall posters and bulletin boards that reflect cultural diversity, social action themes, and student interests.

Source: Sleeter and Grant (2003). Used with the approval of the author.

Advocates for the multicultural education approach challenge teachers to be sensitive to language that is derogatory toward any group and to model use of inclusive language. Teachers must study and understand diverse ways of learning and design or modify lessons to accommodate differences. In addition to having high expectations for students, multicultural teachers encourage cooperation between students in the classroom through group activities. Teachers need not strive to treat students equally—treating all students the same—but to address students equitably with responses based on the diverse needs of individual students.

A *social reconstructionist approach* shares many principles and practices of a multicultural education approach. Four major differences include:

(1) attention to structural inequalities in America; (2) emphasis on democratic decision making in the classroom; (3) development of social action skills to empower students; and (4) use of an activist curriculum with student projects addressing problems in schools and communities.

Social reconstructionism has roots in the Progressive Education movement and in Dewey's 1920 book *Reconstruction in Philosophy* that inspired the term. In the early 1930s, Counts and Rugg, leaders of a group called "Frontier Thinkers," were concerned about inequities in American society and urged that schools play a more active role in creating a more equitable society (Kneller, 1971). In his 1956 book, *Toward a Reconstructed Philosophy of Education,* Brameld became an influential advocate for reconstructionism, suggesting that schools create a new social order by fostering democratic principles and demanding more citizen control over major institutions and resources.

A social reconstructionist approach to multicultural education focuses less on awareness of cultural diversity and more on the ongoing struggles of diverse groups against oppression. The curriculum includes examples of successful resistance to oppression by subordinate groups and actions against injustice by individuals from the dominant group. This approach emphasizes specific classroom practices to develop student decision-making skills and to encourage social action projects.

What specific instructional strategies are recommended for teachers?

Sleeter (1996) insisted that implementing multicultural education effectively requires that teaching not be regarded as merely experimenting with a variety of classroom strategies; instead she described the importance of "listening to oppressed people, including scholars, with the aim of learning to hear and understand what is being said" (p. 134). By listening to students and their parents, teachers will develop appreciation for and understanding of their students, and will genuinely project high regard and high expectations for all students. As Nieto (2008) described it, "Becoming a multicultural teacher . . . means first becoming a multicultural person" (p. 424). Becoming a multicultural person means knowing about human differences and desiring to learn more; examining attitudes for biases, stereotypes, and prejudices; and understanding the need to look at issues from more than one perspective.

Advocates for either of the two multicultural education approaches just described agree that to create a multicultural curriculum, teachers must employ **critical pedagogy**. Nieto (2008) describes critical pedagogy as a liberating experience that "encourages students to take risks, to be curious, and to question. Rather than expecting students to repeat teachers' words, it expects them to seek their own answers" (p. 56). Critical pedagogy is also illustrated by Sleeter's (1996) description of *Why? Papers*: In this activity students are assigned the task of asking a question about some issue involving race, social class, or gender. In doing research and

writing their responses to the questions, students are asked to take the perspective of the oppressed group identified in the question. Examples of "Why?" questions include:

- Why are Mexican American children frequently absent from school?
- Why do Native American students drop out of school?
- Why are many African American males in prison? (p. 120)

According to Sleeter (1996), taking the minority perspective has been effective because students talk with members of oppressed groups as they search for answers; this provides them with unique insights on the group's past experiences and their perspectives on the problems being addressed. Multiple insights and perspectives influence the analysis and conclusions students present in their papers:

> They framed concrete observations of inequality in terms of institutional discrimination and uncovered strategies oppressed groups use to cope with or attempt to advance from a minority position. (p. 123)

Appleton (1983) recommended process-oriented teaching strategies such as role playing, simulation games, using students as discussion leaders, and assigning individual or group projects based on student interests. Using the community to create learning experiences is essential for social action activities, but communities also have human resources—such as students' parents—who can be invited to the classroom to discuss the impact of past or current issues on the community. For students who struggle with nonstructured tasks, teachers might provide a mastery learning activity in which learning is partitioned into a series of sequential tasks and students can periodically evaluate themselves to determine when they achieve mastery. Effective multicultural teaching must allow for the flexibility to modify learning activities so that students will have the opportunity to be successful learners.

Maintaining such flexibility illustrates the point that the goal of multicultural teachers is not to think "I am fair because I treat all students equally." Cymrot (2002) argues that "equally" in this context usually means "the same," but each student is a unique person, in part because of lessons learned from his or her culture. Diller and Moule (2005) emphasize the need for teachers to be culturally competent. Although the dominant culture in the United States emphasizes individual achievement, other cultures place more value on the collective needs of the group. A teacher should avoid making assumptions about a student's behavior based on the norms of the teacher's culture. For example, it is easy to misinterpret the behavior of a child whose culture has taught him that possessions are to be shared and not used exclusively by one person. Having many different cultures represented in classrooms should not be viewed as a challenge but as a learning opportunity for teachers as well as students. In culturally diverse classrooms, Cymrot (2002) argues, "good teaching is about an exchange of cultures" (p. 17).

Because tracking practices have tended to diminish diversity in classrooms as well as academic achievement, multicultural educators deplore tracking and encourage the use of learning centers or cooperative groups as effective strategies in heterogeneous classrooms. Tiedt and Tiedt (2009) describe a learning center as a part of the classroom set aside for the study of a specific topic or for the purpose of developing a specific set of skills; it may be devoted to studying the issue of prejudice or filled with exercises requiring critical thinking. Before using a learning center, students are given directions concerning the center's activities and instructions for using equipment or materials. Students involved in learning center activities can proceed as individuals learning at their own pace or they can be organized into teams.

Cooperative learning strategies are especially attractive to advocates of multicultural education because they involve students of mixed abilities in learning tasks that have clearly defined responsibilities for each group member. Each person must complete his or her task in order for the group to complete the project. According to Sleeter and Grant (2003), research findings suggest that this strategy works well with children from diverse racial and ethnic groups, in terms of not only academic achievement but also the development of positive interpersonal relationships. In reviewing research on cooperative learning, Kagan (2006) cites studies documenting that young children in schools with diverse student populations initially

interact with others and choose their friends without regard to race, but by the end of their second grade year, self-segregation by race has begun and is dramatically apparent by the end of elementary school. Yet, research studies have also found that in classrooms that have implemented cooperative learning strategies, self-segregation was virtually eliminated. Based on his review of four decades of research, Kagan concluded: "Cooperative learning, when it includes heterogeneous teams and team-building, is the single most powerful tool this nation has for improving race relations" (2006, p. 53).

How can multicultural education help to reduce student prejudice?

Reducing prejudice and developing conflict resolution skills are important objectives in multicultural education. Referring to a review of prejudice reduction programs, Nieto (2008) reported that activities designed to reduce prejudice were more effective if students viewed cognitive learning as the primary objective. When prejudice reduction was the primary objective of an activity, students tended to feel as if they were being manipulated to "say the right thing," and they became defensive or resentful. The success of indirect approaches emphasizing cognitive tasks for reducing student prejudice may explain why studies have found cooperative learning strategies to be effective in this area.

Prejudice is not simply a black and white issue. Sheets (2005) cited a study of a school with diverse students in which African American children expressed negative attitudes toward children who were Asian American or Hispanic American, and there have been numerous incidents of interracial conflict between youth from diverse groups in schools and in communities. Based on the results of several studies, Stephan (1999) concluded that teaching conflict resolution skills can reduce the influence of prejudice on intergroup relations in schools. One study reported that helping students develop conflict resolution skills "improved students' abilities to manage conflicts, increased their social support from other students, and decreased victimization by others" (p. 70). Stephan added that teaching conflict resolution skills to students had a positive effect on decreasing student anxiety, increasing self-esteem, and improving intergroup relations. Engaging students in prejudice reduction activities and developing their skills in conflict resolution to improve intergroup relationships is a persuasive rationale for all educators. In addition, teachers are increasingly being challenged to

> Prejudices, it is well known, are most difficult to eradicate from the heart whose soil has never been loosened or fertilized by education; they grow there, firm as weeds among stones.
>
> Charlotte Bronte (1816–1855)

teach in ways that take into account the diverse cultures from which their students come. This approach has been called "culturally responsive teaching" (Gay, 2010).

Multicultural Education as a Context for Culturally Responsive Teaching

Multicultural education incorporates the idea that all students—regardless of their gender, social class, ethnic, racial, or cultural differences—should have an equal opportunity to learn in school (Banks & Banks, 2003). However, the public school system in the United States is plagued with vast inequalities, and on virtually every measure, students of color and students from lower economic classes achieve below the level of their white and middle-class counterparts. This disparity in outcomes is called "the achievement gap." Mainstream explanations tend to blame the achievement gap on uninformed assumptions about families and communities (i.e., "they just don't value education"), but advocates for multicultural education have examined the ways schools are structured, and they report that institutional characteristics of schools systematically deny some groups of students equal educational opportunities (Banks & Banks, 2003). For example, in the early grades, the academic achievement of students of color is nearly the same as that of white middle-class students, but the longer students of color stay in school, the more the achievement gap

widens (Banks, 2004). Students in high-poverty, high-minority schools are routinely provided fewer resources, fewer qualified teachers, fewer advanced level courses, and higher levels of policing in their schools than their more affluent white peers. As a result, they experience lower academic achievement, lower rates of high school graduation, and more interaction with the criminal justice system (Orfield, Losen, Wald, & Swanson, 2004). Thus, a major goal of multicultural education is to improve the academic achievement of students who are traditionally marginalized in school by considering several interconnected aspects of schooling itself. Many multicultural educators advocate culturally responsive teaching as a key strategy to achieve some of their major goals.

How does culturally responsive teaching address multicultural education goals?

Culturally responsive teaching addresses the goal of changing school practices that marginalize nontraditional students. Culturally responsive teaching is grounded in the perception of schooling as linked to social forces in the broader society. Schooling is a primary site of socialization, and, as such, schools play a key role in sorting students into predetermined places within a society that is hierarchical and socially stratified. Schools prepare students to occupy roles that have unequal value in society; for example, vocational training versus college preparation or special education versus honors courses (Anyon, 2003; Oakes, Wells, Jones, & Datnow, 1997). Because schools are such a powerful site of social reproduction, all aspects of schools are inherently political. Knowledge is never neutral; it is infused with the implicit cultural assumptions, frames of reference, biases, and interests of those who hold the power to determine which aspects of knowledge are valid and how they will be measured. Yet schools present the cultural norms, styles, and perspectives of dominant social groups as objective, and they reward those who fit these norms and penalize those who don't.

Other aspects of schooling that contribute to the achievement gap include standardized testing, culturally biased curriculum, ability tracking, unequal funding between urban and suburban schools, low expectations for students of color, and zero tolerance policies that criminalize minority students and

FIGURE 13.2

With the increasing diversity of children and youth in the United States, there is a growing interest in and advocacy for culturally responsive teaching.

---

channel them from school into the prison system (Clark, 2007). As defined and promoted by multicultural education advocates, culturally responsive teaching seeks to interrupt these inequitable aspects of schooling (Banks & Banks, 2003; Ladson-Billings, 1995). While challenging these structural inequities will take time and society-wide effort, multicultural education advocates argue that individual teachers can make an immediate difference in their classrooms by infusing culturally responsive teaching. (See Figure 13.2.)

Gay (2000) defines culturally responsive teaching as using the cultural knowledge, prior experiences, and performance styles of diverse students to make learning more appropriate and effective for them. Rather than viewing these students as deficient, culturally responsive pedagogy teaches to their specific strengths. According to Gay (2000), culturally responsive teaching has the following characteristics:

- It acknowledges the legitimacy of the cultural heritages of different ethnic groups, both as legacies that affect students' dispositions, attitudes, and approaches to learning and as worthy content to be taught in the formal curriculum.
- It builds bridges of meaningfulness between home and school experiences as well as between academic abstractions and lived sociocultural realities.

- It uses a wide variety of instructional strategies that are connected to different learning styles.
- It teaches students to know and praise their own and each others' cultural heritages.
- It incorporates multicultural information, resources, and materials in all the subjects and skills routinely taught in schools (p. 29).

Culturally responsive teaching is an all-encompassing and ever-present "lens" through which teachers view their practice; at its core is the expectation that all students can experience academic success while developing the critical consciousness to challenge the inequity of the status quo.

What are some current issues that make culturally responsive teaching difficult?

Despite the common belief that racial segregation is a practice of the past, our schools are more segregated than ever before (Kozol, 2005; Villegas & Lucas, 2002). Most students of color and lower income students are concentrated in urban areas, whereas most middle-class and white students attend suburban schools in which they have very little authentic interaction with students who are different from them. In addition, the teaching force is getting more, not less, homogeneous. Trends continue to indicate that the teaching force is becoming increasingly white and middle class (Gordon, 2005), while at the same time, the student population is getting more diverse. Fewer than 16% of teachers are educators of color (Kearney, 2008; Stevens, Hamman, & Olivarez, 2007). Further, 80%–93% of teacher education students are white and 88% of teacher education professors are white (DiAngelo, 2012). The vast majority of teachers are not only white, but they also tend to come from segregated suburban schools and neighborhoods. In addition, they are challenged in their understanding of children whose backgrounds differ from their own. Howard (2003) states that "Teachers need to understand that racially diverse students frequently bring cultural capital to the classroom that is oftentimes drastically different from mainstream norms and worldviews" (p. 197). Because teachers and students often come from dissimilar backgrounds, teachers must "construct pedagogical practices in ways that are culturally relevant, racially affirming, and socially meaningful for their students" (p. 187).

Although urban schools may indeed be located in cities and be composed predominantly of low-income students and students of color, "urban" does not necessarily indicate location. In more affluent cities such as Seattle, San Francisco, and Boston, schools located inside the city limits that are primarily white are not labeled "urban"; the term *urban* is used as the dominant culture's code for indicating the existence of a percentage of students of color that is "too high" for white families to feel comfortable with. Johnson and Shapiro (2003) found that perceptions of white parents regarding "good schools" were often based on the racial demographics of the school; the whiter the student body, the better the school was perceived to be. They concluded that race may be not just a factor in school choice for white families, but rather the primary factor. Schools that are not perceived as "good" because of the presence of a percentage of students of color are labeled "urban" (or "inner-city"). In turn, these schools are abandoned by white families and have unequal funding and resources, which perpetuates the cycle (Kozol, 1991; Kozol, 2005). Although these factors complicate the efforts of teachers to engage in culturally responsive teaching, they also provide reasons for engaging in such practices to help students.

Which students benefit from culturally responsive teaching?

Because race appears to be a key issue in decisions white people make when choosing schools and neighborhoods, one could easily argue that all students and all teachers could benefit from culturally responsive teaching, regardless of the overall racial demographics of their schools or neighborhoods. White children attending segregated schools need to be prepared, perhaps more so than any other group, to interact in a culturally diverse society (DiAngelo, 2006). Culturally responsive teaching builds a foundation for all students to engage in the critical tasks of empathetic and equitable engagement with the diversity that is so often lacking in their immediate world because of pervasive segregation in our schools

and neighborhoods (Derman-Sparks & Ramsey, 2004). The bigger question is not who benefits from culturally responsive teaching, but what is required for an individual teacher to successfully implement culturally responsive teaching.

What characteristics are necessary to be a culturally responsive teacher?

The following characteristics of culturally responsive teachers are adapted from Villegas and Lucas (2002) and Gay (2000). Culturally responsive teachers are those who:

- Understand teaching as a contextual and situational process in which students' prior experiences, community settings, cultural backgrounds, and ethnic identities are acknowledged and infused into the curriculum.
- Are familiar with their students' prior knowledge and beliefs, derived from both personal and cultural experiences and well-designed instruction that builds on what students already know while stretching them beyond the familiar.
- Have sociocultural consciousness; they recognize that the ways people perceive the world, interact with one another, and approach learning are deeply influenced by such factors as race/ethnicity, social class, and language.
- Are aware that they also are sociocultural beings, with a particular and limited cultural viewpoint: They know that no human is objective and they consistently engage in self-reflection and self-examination of their beliefs, values, and assumptions about those who are different from them.
- Have a positive perspective on students and families who are from diverse backgrounds, seeing resources for learning in all students rather than viewing differences as deficiencies, or problems to be solved.
- Communicate high expectations for all children.
- Have a sense that they are capable of and responsible for bringing about educational change that will make schooling more responsive to students from diverse backgrounds.

The characteristics outlined above involve ongoing education and self-awareness, particularly for those who have not grown up in environments that offered consistent and sustained opportunities to build relationships with people different from themselves in key social areas, such as race and class. Because culturally responsive teaching challenges our conventional worldviews and our sense of self in relation to others, it develops over a lifetime and is not achieved in the short term. At the same time, educators can't grow into culturally responsive teachers without practice, trial and error, and risk taking. Although a school-wide commitment is necessary for authentic transformation in education (Villegas & Lucas, 2002), individual teachers may infuse culturally responsive teaching into their classroom practice without waiting for support or encouragement from outside of their classroom.

What actual classroom experiences illustrate culturally responsive teaching?

A social studies teacher with the non-Western first name of Özlem begins her class by explaining how her name is written and pronounced, and what it means in her first language, Turkish. She has students practice writing and saying her name. She explains how in North America the "dots" are often absent from the "O," and then tells her name's "story." She talks about the script change from Turkish to English and wonders aloud how the change in the spelling of her name affects her cultural identity. She shares why the Turkish spelling of her name is significant to her as someone whose family immigrated to Canada from Turkey. After this brief discussion, she invites each student to teach the class how to pronounce and spell his or her name and to "tell us the story of your name." If needed, she provides prompts such as "Who named you? What does your name mean? Do you have a nickname you prefer to be called? If so, how did you get it? Do you know the roots of your name?" She doesn't move on to the next student until the last student to share his or her name is satisfied that everyone has learned to pronounce it correctly. This exercise builds community by affirming cultural diversity as represented by the names of students in her class, allowing students to claim their names and tell their stories, and providing a culturally relevant framework for issues that will be discussed in the class, such as the following:

- *The cultural dimensions of names and the connections between religion and culture.* Students will find that many names are influenced by religion; for example, the middle names "Kaur" (for girls) and "Singh" (for boys) indicate Sikh heritage, just as Paul and John have religious significance for families of Christian heritage.
- *The cultural connections that have been lost by institutional practices that shortened or "corrected" immigrants' names.* Upon arrival in the United States, an immigrant with a name such as *Yih-Shue* could be changed to *Sherry*. The inability to make or represent certain sounds in different languages; the power relations imbedded in which individuals' names are adapted or modified upon immigration; and the politics of who decides how that will be done are some of the issues students could discuss.
- *The impact of marriage on names, and the norms for patriarchal versus matriarchal societies.* Students could discuss who changes their surname when they get married and why. Further, how are naming norms changing over time, with gender roles evolving and the legalization of same-sex marriages in some states in the United States and Canada?

This activity also illustrates a key tenet in multicultural education: recognition of the individual as well as the society in which the individual is embedded. Following this exercise, students make decorative nameplates for their desks. As new students join the class, the sharing of names is repeated to include the newcomers (adapted from Sensoy, 2009).

Another teacher, Ms. Walker, infuses culturally responsive teaching into a history lesson on heroes. Instead of asking students to stand outside of their own lives and write in the third person about people chosen for them by their textbooks, she asks her students to select and interview a "hero" from their community who works for social justice. If a student is having trouble identifying a hero, Ms. Walker offers a range of possibilities based on her knowledge of leaders in the child's community and the interests of the child. The students generate questions that might include: What accomplishments are you proud of? What challenges did you face in achieving your goals? What methods did you use to affect change? What do you regret? What advice do you have for others? The students' community heroes are then invited to be guest speakers in the class so that all students may meet and learn from them. If students' heroes are not available for interviews, the students write essays as if they were the hero reflecting on the same questions at the end of his or her life. This lesson humanizes heroes, and, rather than presenting overwhelmingly white and male figures from the dominant culture with the same few sanitized exceptions of Susan B. Anthony, Martin Luther King, Jr., and Rosa Parks, it affirms the range of communities from which the students come. The students' communities are brought directly into the classroom and utilized as a resource for everyone, and mainstream definitions of what makes a hero are challenged.

It is commonly assumed that culturally responsive teaching is only relevant to some subjects, such as social studies or reading, but not applicable to others such as science and math. This assumption rests on a belief that the sciences are objective. But no subject is objective or value-free; the sciences are as laden with cultural assumptions as any other field. Indeed, much of the early rationale for racist practices in the United States was founded in what is termed "scientific racism"—using racially biased questions, methods, and interpretations of data to justify the lower social and institutional positions of people of color.

Some of the ways we see bias in math and science today are through the corporate interests behind which research gets funded, the questions being asked, the interpretations being made, the cultural assumptions and biases in story problems, the biased assumptions about which students will succeed in math and science, and the homogenous representations of historical and current leaders in the fields. In sum, no field of study—including math and science—is objective and value free because humans are not objective and value free. Sandra Harding (1998), a philosopher of science, has made this point, arguing that the closer we come to acknowledging how social positions shape our perspective, the closer we may come to objectivity. Not acknowledging the cultural biases that inform individual perspectives keeps them hidden and intact, making it more likely that the dominant perspective is presented as neutral and universal, and that dominant interests will continue to be reinforced. By engaging in culturally responsive

practices, we actually expand our view rather than limit it. Thus it is imperative to integrate culturally responsive perspectives and practices throughout the entire curriculum.

Jana Dean (2007) has demonstrated how a math teacher can incorporate culturally responsive teaching. She teaches a math lesson by using typical wages in her students' community to build a bridge between her students' lives and algebra. Her students calculate and graph daily and monthly incomes in service sector jobs, using a day's wages and a month's wages for four full-time service industry occupations that many in their community hold—for example, a retail clerk at Walmart a security guard, a fast food restaurant cook, and a home nursing aide. Her students graph four linear relationships on the same coordinate grid and write equations for each. Along the way, they discuss questions such as: "What is a minimum wage, and who gets to set it?" She says, "Following an example that I had prepared in advance, students worked together to draw an x- and y-axis on 11-by-17–inch graph paper. I told them that they would be graphing one day's wages, or eight hours, and that the size of one's paycheck depends on the number of hours worked; therefore, money—the dependent variable—belongs on the y-axis. The independent variable, however, will be the same for everyone: You are all going to work an eight-hour day."

After students complete the graphs, she introduces the variables x and y. In this case, y represents the paycheck and x stands for the number of hours worked. Ms. Dean also challenges her students to write an equation for each line that would show the relationship between time and earnings, and they arrive at equations to represent the lines on their graphs. She then asks her students to respond in writing to the following prompt: "How does the rate of pay affect the shape and steepness of the lines on your coordinate grid? Describe the shape of a graph for the wage of a job at $20 per hour. Describe the shape of a graph for the wage of a job at the federal minimum of $5.15 per hour." The prompt leads students to observe that the steeper the line, the higher the wage, and that each of the situations produces a straight line. Both observations pave the way for introducing the term "slope," meaning the rate of increase, and "linear," meaning a relationship that graphs as a straight line. This prompt also serves to identify the coefficient of x

or the number that multiplies *x* as the value that determines the steepness of the line. Once students recognize linear relationships, Ms. Dean introduces the concept of *y*-intercept by having students make a table showing pay minus expenses for the first ten hours of work. This gives students a real-world context for operating with negative numbers. Other dimensions of her "living algebra" lesson include calculating the cost of housing and other expenses, comparing state and national minimum wages, and learning about the activism and organizing effort behind her state's highest-in-the-nation minimum wage (adapted from Dean, 2007). The math and the pedagogy of this lesson are clearly culturally relevant.

As these examples illustrate, culturally responsive teaching can be an effective pedagogical approach, but it is also a challenging one. Sleeter (2010) identified four problems that teachers are likely to encounter and how they can be resolved to use this approach successfully:

1. The tendency to define students in terms of their membership in sociocultural groups and to engage in practices and activities with students associated with these groups. The best way to avoid this problem is for teachers to learn about your students and their communities.
2. The assumption that culturally responsive teaching simply means teaching culturally diverse students about their respective cultures. Culturally responsive teachers regard students as a cultural resource, and that their cultural knowledge can help them apply what they already know to new academic knowledge.
3. The "silver bullet" fallacy—believing there is only one approach that will improve student learning. Teachers must explore alternative approaches, innovative strategies, and new uses of traditional approaches, creating a classroom that combines pedagogical strategies. Successful teachers are lifelong learners who keep searching for what works best for their students.
4. The perception that culturally responsive teaching is only necessary when teaching students of color, an especially harmful perception because it transforms students into "the other." Culturally responsive teaching should transform teachers by requiring a rigorous

self-examination of how they have been influenced by their culture, and how they teach and interact with their students.

Sleeter (2010) argues that culturally responsive teaching is a "starting point" for productive dialogues between teachers and students, teachers and parents, teachers with other teachers, and that the effectiveness of a culturally responsive teaching approach will depend on: "A teacher's willingness to spend time as a learner in the community of his or her students" (p. 117).

What other strategies for culturally responsible teaching have been advocated?

The problems that Sleeter described offer some useful guidelines for considering specific classroom strategies. At Brown University, a consortium of educators called the Education Alliance is committed to enhancing the ability of teachers to work effectively and equitably with English language learners. They have identified numerous culturally responsive teaching strategies, and some examples are provided below (2006):

1. Learn about students' cultures
   - Have students share artifacts from home that reflect their culture
   - Have students write about traditions shared by their families
   - Have students research different aspects of their culture
   - Have members of the community speak to students on various subjects
   - Ask members of the community to teach a lesson or give a demonstration (in their field of expertise) to the students
2. Promote positive perspectives on parents and families
   - Conduct home visits in which parents are able to speak freely about their expectations and concerns for their children
   - Send weekly/monthly newsletters (in the home language) informing parents of school activities
   - Host family nights at school to introduce parents to concepts and ideas children are learning in their classes and to share interactive journals

- Research the cultural background of students' families
- Visit local community centers to find out about cultural activities and beliefs of the students

3. Bridge cultural differences through effective communication
   - Teach and talk to students about differences between individuals
   - Show how differences among the students make for better learning
   - Attend community events important to the students and discuss the events with the students
   - See your classroom as a community of learners, rather than as individuals learning separately from one another
   - Use cooperative learning strategies

4. Promote student engagement
   - Have students generate lists of topics they wish to study and/or research
   - Allow students to select their own reading material
   - Share responsibility of instruction with students and community members
   - Have students lead discussion groups or re-teach concepts
   - Create classroom projects that involve the community

5. Provide culturally mediated instruction using diverse teaching strategies
   - Use role-playing strategies
   - Assign students research projects that focus on issues that apply to their own community or cultural group
   - Ask educators who come from the same cultural background as the students about effective ways to teach them
   - Allow the use of the student's first language to enhance learning
   - Use classroom management techniques that are culturally familiar to students

6. Reshape the curriculum
   - Use resources other than textbooks for study
   - Have students research aspects of a topic within their community
   - Encourage students to interview members of their community who have knowledge of the topic they are studying

- Provide information to the students on alternative viewpoints or beliefs about a topic
- Allow students to set their own goals for a project

Although culturally responsive teaching requires extra effort and may even seem daunting, it is no more difficult than any strategy promoting successful classroom practices that are effective with diverse students. Good teaching is never easy, but in the history of education, including our current era, there have always been numerous teachers who have been effective in the classroom, so we know it's not impossible. This should be the response to the complaints from some critics who feel that culturally responsive teaching in particular and multicultural education in general are too idealistic to work in the "real world" of challenges inherent in the everyday task of classroom teaching.

What other educational reforms are being implemented?

Many educational reforms are being promoted today, but two are especially interesting because of their results and the fact that they could easily accommodate principles and practices of multicultural education. Pearson Learning Teams, a unit of Pearson Education North America, is a consulting firm in California specializing in education services. The firm has worked with many school districts to create a "professional learning community" that promotes collaboration among the teaching staff. In observing such a community, Burns (2011) noted: "The best teachers become coaches, sharing their skills and shifting the drive for change to the front lines" (p. 41). This approach is supported by a global study of schools focusing on how the schools became more successful in their work with students. The study found that the amount of money spent made little impact, even in cases where funding was doubled or tripled, but a common theme among schools that caused significant improvement was that teachers were given opportunities to work together (Burns, 2011).

With assistance from staff at Pearson Learning Teams, Wilmington Middle School in the Los Angeles Unified School District (LAUSD) implemented collaborative teaching. Wilmington's 1,900 students were a diverse population with a significant number of students living in poverty. In 2000, none of Wilmington's eighth grade students received *proficient* or *advanced* scores in algebra. The Pearson consultants trained certain teachers to be facilitators so they could provide leadership for teams of teachers. The teams collaborated on creating and implementing lesson plans, and on analyzing the results so they could brainstorm better teaching strategies. By 2010, almost 40% of the eighth grade students had achieved *proficient* or *advanced* scores in algebra compared to 34% of all California eighth graders. Students not only had improved academically, but also were demonstrating a more positive attitude toward school. In the 2009–2010 academic year, Wilmington had the best attendance record of all schools in the LAUSD. Another middle school near Los Angeles with 500 Latino students from largely high-poverty homes also implemented reforms based on teacher collaboration. Student test scores began to improve, and by 2010, 64% of their student scores in algebra were *proficient* or *advanced*—the highest scores of any school in their school district (Burns, 2011).

Another education reform movement promotes a "community school" concept. Blank, Jacobson, and Pearson (2009) describe a community school as a place that "integrates academic, health and social services, youth and community development and civic engagement to improve student learning, develop stronger families, and create healthier communities" (p. 31). A community school forms partnerships with community agencies and organizations that are responsible for programs involving health care, youth development, and social services. In order to manage the expanded activities, the school must have a full-time community school coordinator who cultivates organizational partnerships, pursues grants and other funding sources, and coordinates services provided at the school to inform and connect various service providers. There are 194 schools in 27 states that have established the partnerships necessary to become community schools, including 21 in New York City alone. The services that a community school may provide are based on the needs of the residents in that particular community; in the New York schools the services include educational enrichment programs before and after school (and on weekends and during the summer), medical and dental services, mental health counseling, adult education, early childhood education, and parental involvement programs.

Early research studies report that students in community schools are demonstrating increased academic achievement in reading and math, and they have had a significant increase in their graduation rates (Blank, Jacobson, & Pearson, 2009).

For both of these reform movements, the principles and practices of multicultural education could be easily integrated into the pedagogical and philosophical approach being implemented. Both movements tend to be focused on urban schools attended primarily by students of color, with a significant percentage coming from low-income families. Multicultural education provides a framework for addressing the needs of these students in terms of a relevant curriculum, pedagogy emphasizing collaboration and active learning, and a school environment that is positive and supportive toward students and their families. Further, multicultural education already has a history of support from educational organizations. The largest teacher union, the National Education Association (NEA), has promoted multicultural education since the 1960s, and the National Council for Accreditation of Teacher Education (NCATE) requires teacher education programs to address diversity issues and to include principles and practices of multicultural education in order to receive accreditation for the preparation of teachers. NEA and NCATE have promoted multicultural education because of its

> The role of the teacher remains the highest calling of a free people. To the teacher, America entrusts her most precious resource, her children; and asks that they be prepared, in all their glorious diversity, to face the rigors of individual participation in a democratic society.
>
> Shirley Hufstedler (1925–)

emphasis on respecting the diversity represented by the students attending schools in the United States, especially urban schools. For any major reform effort, it would be logical to collaborate with multicultural education advocates to achieve the goal of improving education today so that tomorrow our schools will provide a better education for all students. As George Lipsitz (2007) has written: "More than anything else, teaching is an act of faith for the future" (p. 261).

AFTERWORD

Diversity is not just an issue for K–12 schools; most universities and colleges mandate diversity courses in their general education programs, and corporations implement policies promoting diversity and provide diversity training for managers and employees. Churches, community organizations, and civic groups already articulate pluralistic mission statements about the value of diversity in our society. Idealistic or not, multicultural education is likely to become increasingly influential in American schools in the twenty-first century. Fortunately, we have many excellent resources that describe teaching strategies based on principles of multicultural education (Derman-Sparks & Ramsey, 2004; Ladson-Billings, 2001; Pasternak, 1986; Sapon-Shevin, 1999; Shade, Kelly, & Oberg, 1997; Sleeter & Grant, 2009; Tiedt & Tiedt, 2009).

The challenge confronting us today is how to become multicultural individuals. In the teaching profession, that question will be answered primarily by white middle-class people—primarily women. As our schools increasingly consist of students from subordinate groups—students of color, students from low-income families, children and youth who are not Christian, gay and lesbian youth, learners with disabilities—teachers continue to enter the profession from our dominant societal group. Orfield, Kucsera, and Siegel-Hawley (2012) report that students of color are nearly half of our K–12 school population today, yet Cochran-Smith (2003) reports that 86% of all teachers are white. Although the percentage of white teachers is predicted to remain stable in the coming decades, the percentage of students of color is predicted to be 57% by 2035 (see Table 13.3).

Pang (2005) has urged white teachers to engage in self-analysis to understand how being white has shaped their identity, and to study how oppression has affected and shaped the identities of members of subordinate groups in our society. Self-analysis is part of the journey toward becoming a multicultural teacher; it may often feel uncomfortable, but if pursued, it can also be

TABLE 13.3   U.S. Public School Teachers

Category	Percentage
Gender	
Female	79
Male	21
Race	
White	84.3
Black	7.6
Hispanic	5.6
Other	2.5
Highest Degree	
Bachelor's	61.9
Master's	23.1
Years of Experience	
Less than 10	41.7
10–20	28.5
More than 20	29.8

Source: U.S. Department of Education (2006) National Center for Education Statistics

liberating. In the end, white teachers can develop a profound appreciation for both diversity and democracy—and the need to be pluralistic in order to promote and sustain both in our schools and in our society.

TERMS AND DEFINITIONS

Critical pedagogy Providing opportunities for students to analyze perspectives and use their analysis to understand and act on perceived inconsistencies

Diversity The presence of human beings with perceived or actual differences based on a variety of human characteristics

Global (international) education Teaching about the cultures of nations around the world

Hidden curriculum Indirect means by which schools teach the norms and values of a society

Multicultural Any society composed of a number of subordinate groups based on race, ethnicity, religion, language, nationality, income, gender, sexual orientation, and degree of physical, mental, or emotional ability

Multicultural education A process of comprehensive school reform that rejects discrimination in schools and society and accepts and affirms pluralism

Multiethnic education Integrating issues and information about race and ethnicity into school curricula

Pluralism The equal coexistence of diverse cultures, institutions, and/or individuals within a mutually supportive relationship within the boundaries of one nation

Retention The ability of students to recall knowledge they have been taught

Transfer The ability of students to apply retained knowledge to situations occurring inside and outside the classroom

DISCUSSION EXERCISES

Exercise #1 The Hidden Curriculum: American Indians

Directions: Might children and youth be learning lessons that we aren't aware they are being taught? Through misunderstanding or lack of adequate knowledge of facts, curriculums may be teaching American children to be biased or to stereotype others. The statements below were originally developed as an elementary punctuation exercise [which is why they have no punctuation marks at the end of each statement].

Explain in what way each phrase or sentence is biased. Underline the word or words that you judge need replacement.

Other than learning correct punctuation, what else might children completing this exercise have learned that wasn't intended?

1. Indians lived in our country many years before the white man
2. Have you ever seen an Indian
3. Indians belong to the red race
4. Their skin is of a copper color
5. Most of the men are called warriors
6. The women are called squaws
7. Do they live in wigwams and tepees
8. The red man's name for corn was maize
9. Were bows and arrows used for hunting by the Indians
10. A group of Indians living together is called a "tribe"
11. Do little Indian girls and boys play games
12. The squaws carried their babies on their backs
13. What does each Indian tribe call its "leader"
14. The leader of each tribe is called a "chief"
15. A few Indian tribes still live in the western part of our country

Exercise #2 Whom Would You Hire? Selecting Elementary Teachers

Introduction: Being fair to schoolchildren and youth involves providing the best teachers to help them. Imagine that you are a committee member with responsibility for hiring new teachers. You have four positions open in grades 1 to 3 and eight applicants from whom to choose. You have interviewed all eight, and each has impressed you favorably.

Directions: Read the brief descriptions below and select the four you would hire.

Candidate 1: Forty-year-old woman, single, lives alone, with eighteen years of outstanding experience; highly successful with typically unsuccessful children. Possibly in a lesbian relationship.

Candidate 2: Twenty-four-year-old man, single, two years of experience in a ghetto school. A near genius, he brings outstanding recommendations. Leader of local black power group; his students use African names and openly reject "slave" names.

Candidate 3: Thirty-five-year-old man, married, father of six. Community minded, interested in Cub Scouts. Known for having very well-organized planned lessons and classes. Ten years of experience. Native American heritage.

Candidate 4: Forty-year-old man, single, living with elderly parents. The candidate has extensive experience from being a local business entrepreneur before returning to college for credentials. Just completed requirements and received a $20,000 grant to work with junior high school students in distributive education. Native of India; practicing Catholic.

Candidate 5: Twenty-six-year-old woman, divorced, supports self and three small children. Highly creative; three years of experience; outstanding recommendations on professional capability. Native of Puerto Rico.

Candidate 6: Fifty-eight-year-old man, highly respected former Episcopal minister who left pulpit to work full time with children. Has just completed teaching credentials.

Candidate 7: Forty-eight-year-old woman, widowed. Twenty-five years of experience, including three years in the Infants School of England. Wants to incorporate Infant School concepts here. Independently wealthy through both her own and her spouse's families.

Candidate 8: Twenty-two-year-old woman, single, a year of experience, excellent recommendations. Voluntarily tutored all four years in college, including full time in summers. Living openly in the community with a man of another race.

Follow-up: Discuss the qualifications of each committee member. When your group has selected four teacher candidates for the jobs, post your selections and compare your choices with those of other groups.

REFERENCES

Anyon, J. (2003). Inner cities, affluent suburbs, and unequal educational opportunity. In J.A. Banks & C.M. Banks (Eds.), *Multicultural education: Issues & perspectives* (4th ed., pp. 85–102). New York, NY: John Wiley & Sons.

Appleton, N. (1983). *Cultural pluralism in education: Theoretical foundations.* New York, NY: Longman.

Baker, G.C. (1994). *Planning and organizing for multicultural instruction.* Reading, MA: Addison Wesley.

Banks, J.A. (2008). *An introduction to multicultural education* (4th ed.). Boston, MA: Pearson Allyn & Bacon.

Banks, J.A. (2006). *Cultural diversity and education: Foundations, curriculum and teaching* (5th ed.). Boston, MA: Allyn & Bacon.

Banks, J.A. (2004). Multicultural education: Characteristics and goals. In J.A. Banks & C.M. Banks, (Eds.), *Multicultural education: Issues & perspectives* (5th ed., pp. 3–27). New York, NY: John Wiley & Sons.

Banks, J.A. (2003). Multicultural education: Characteristics and goals. In J.A. Banks, & C.M. Banks (Eds.), *Multicultural education: Issues & perspectives* (4th ed., pp. 3–30). New York, NY: John Wiley & Sons.

Banks, J.A., & Banks, C.M. (Eds.). (2003). *Multicultural education: Issues & perspectives* (4th ed.). New York, NY: John Wiley & Sons.

Blank, M., Jacobson, R., & Pearson, S.S. (2009). A coordinated effort. *American Educator, 33*(2), 30–36.

Brameld, T.B.H. (1956). *Toward a reconstructed philosophy of education.* New York, NY: Dryden Press.

Burns, M. (2011, September/October). Teachers get better by getting together. *Miller-McCune,* 38–45.

Carse, J. (1986). *Finite and infinite games: A vision of life as play and possibility.* New York, NY: Free Press.

Clark, C. (2007). *Understanding neoliberalism and its impact on education.* NAME Conference, Baltimore, November 2007.

Cochran-Smith, M. (2003). Standing at the crossroads: Multicultural teacher education at the beginning of the 21st century. *Multicultural Perspectives, 5*(3), 3–11.

Combs, A.W. (1979). *Myths in education: Beliefs that hinder progress and their alternatives.* Boston, MA: Allyn & Bacon.

Cymrot, T.Z. (2002). What is diversity? In L. Darling-Hammond, J. French, & S.P. Garcia Lopez (Eds.), *Learning to teach for social justice* (pp. 13–17). New York, NY: Teachers College Press.

Dean, J. (2007). Living algebra, living wage. *Rethinking Schools, 21*(4), 31–35.

Derman-Sparks, L., & Ramsey, P. (2004). *What if all the kids are white?: Anti-bias multicultural education with young children and families.* New York, NY: Teachers College Press.

DiAngelo, R. (2012). *What does it mean to be white? Developing white racial literacy.* New York, NY: Peter Lang.

DiAngelo, R. (2006). "I'm leaving!": White fragility in racial dialogue. In B. McMahon & D. Armstrong (Eds.),

Chapter 14

Pluralism in Society: Creating Unity in a Diverse America

"How many goodly creatures are there here! How beauteous mankind is! O brave new world, That has such people in't."

William Shakespeare (1564–1616)

All around us, a brave new world is indeed taking shape in America. Despite a wealth of **diversity**, America has not yet become a pluralistic society. **Pluralism** entails perceiving human differences as enriching, and valuing that diversity in our society. Yet Americans are still wary of one another, and fearful when conflicts occur between groups. Nevertheless, changes are taking place that encourage us to become more accepting of others and more pluralistic. It is obvious that students in K–12 schools and colleges today will shape our society in the future; yet many Americans don't realize that almost 50% of all K–12 children and youth are students of color (Orfield, Kucsera, & Siegel-Hawley, 2012). According to 2000 census data, students of color in California, Florida, and Texas already comprise 50% of the K–12 population. Immigrants constitute 12% of the American workforce, and 20% of all K–12 students are foreign-born or have foreign-born parents (Orfield & Lee, 2007). U.S. trade agreements guarantee that these figures will increase.

The diversity and location of racial and ethnic groups have changed dramatically. For example, more than 600 Somali refugees live in Owatonna, Minnesota. And although our media still tend to present U.S. diversity as principally African American, Hispanic Americans have become the largest ethnic minority group. As these societal changes occur, they are reflected in organizations such as the American military: More than 3,400 Muslims and 5,200 Buddhists serve in the U.S. Armed Forces (Brady, 2009; Dreazen, 2009). In 2011, 31%

of women in the military were black (twice their percentage of the population) compared to 16% of the men (Dao, 2011).

To capitalize on these unprecedented demographic changes, Americans must realize the need for new approaches to living and working together and must create new partnerships with people in their communities. In Billings, Montana, a Jewish family decorated their home for Hanukkah and placed a menorah by their front window. After a vandal threw a cinder block through their window, thousands of Christian families put pictures of menorahs in their windows so vandals could not identify for certain which homes in their community had Jewish families (Eck, 2001).

America is the most diverse society in our diverse world: The global presence of major U.S. corporations requires that we cultivate sensitivity to countless global issues and cultures. Americans come from almost every country on the planet; our diversity is represented by differences not only in geographical origins (ethnicity) but also in religion, social class, disabilities, gender, sexual orientation, age, region, and dialect, as well as individuals who fit into multiple categories.

Psychologist Howard Gardner (2006) identified five categories of mental abilities that will be increasingly necessary in the future, not just in the United States but globally, and he argues that schools and professional training programs need to be cultivating these skills now. He calls one of these categories "The Respectful Mind," and it is characterized by a person's ability to encounter others without being threatened by their individual or cultural differences, but rather to respond to them with acceptance and respect. Gardner believes this mental ability can be taught, especially when teachers successfully model this behavior, but the lessons cannot come from teachers alone: "Messages of respect or disrespect, tolerance or intolerance, are signaled throughout a society" (p. 111). Gardner insists

> For each age is a dream that is dying. Or one that is coming to birth.
>
> Arthur O'Shaughnessy (1844–1881)

that simply tolerating differences is an inadequate response to the human diversity that is increasing in societies around the world; he rejects the idea of ignoring differences such as pretending to be "colorblind," but advocates for fostering pluralistic attitudes that enable people to interact and collaborate more effectively with the diverse individuals they will inevitably encounter in schools, while shopping, at recreational activities, at work, and even in neighborhoods as intolerance and old patterns of racial segregation finally begin to break down.

Forces at work in all areas of society increasingly recognize pluralism as a preferred alternative to the Anglo conformity demanded in the past. Although the transformation from America's preference for conformity to an unequivocal acceptance of human differences will not be resolved for decades to come, we must be aware of recent changes and prepare for future challenges. This chapter reports on five major societal areas—the federal government, higher education, business, mass media, and the military—and how each is making conscious and deliberate efforts to respond positively to diversity in the United States. The information provided is based on these three questions:

How do advocates promote pluralism?
How do detractors oppose pluralism?
What changes illustrate progress toward pluralism?

Regardless of the profession chosen, most individuals starting their careers are likely to encounter some form of the challenges and changes described in this chapter.

Federal Government

President John F. Kennedy first used the phrase **affirmative action** when he issued Executive Order 10025 mandating that the federal government aggressively recruit and hire African Americans (Painter, 2005). Title VII of the 1964 Civil Rights Act expanded this concept to include people of color and women being employed by private companies contracted to do work for the federal government. Companies had to file affirmative action plans with hiring goals and timetables for those goals. By mandating affirmative action, the federal government began a major initiative to promote pluralism by reducing acts of discrimination and providing opportunity for women and people of color. Title VII stated that if a court rules a finding of discrimination is justified, the court might order an employer "to take such affirmative action as may be appropriate." A 1972 Title VII amendment added "or any other equitable relief as the courts deem appropriate" (Greene, 1989, p. 15). Title VII has been controversial from the moment the Civil Rights Act became law, consistently keeping the issue of equal opportunity for all Americans in the public eye.

According to the Civil Rights Act, affirmative action plans represent voluntary programs unless a court orders that an affirmative action plan be designed and implemented. Determining the need for an affirmative action plan begins by analyzing the diversity of employees at a business or agency, or the student population at a university. If population variation is similar to that of available applicants, there is said to be no equity problem. If disparities exist, however, each phase of the application and selection process is evaluated for bias that may advantage some applicants and disadvantage others.

The Affirmative Action Debate

Debate concerning affirmative action has resonated from the public square to the U.S. Supreme Court. The crux of the debate concerns whether affirmative action was intended only to redress victims of intentional discrimination or if it mandates that programs create a more just distribution of women and minorities in the workforce and in higher education. In the business community, the principal emphasis has been on compensating victims of discrimination; institutions of higher education have implemented admissions policies designed to increase the numbers of women and minorities admitted.

Affirmative action advocates argue that aggressive action is required to address inequities in hiring and college admissions. Proponents insist our society must guarantee equal opportunity to every citizen, and they argue that ample evidence demonstrates our failure to achieve this goal. Because a college education is required to become qualified for certain jobs, policies and practices of college admission are scrutinized, just as businesses and corporations are monitored to ensure that women and minorities have the same opportunity as white men to work and to receive promotions. Affirmative action advocates explain that monitoring is not intended as punitive, but rather that it meets a broader goal of strengthening our society by creating racial, gender, and ethnic unity. Greene (1989) argued that if white men "continue to hold positions of power and prestige to the exclusion of other groups . . . divisions will continue to exist" (p. 10).

Affirmative action opponents counter that equal opportunity programs have created greater American disunity. They denounce affirmative action plans as racist when race is emphasized to create quotas, establishing what they term "preferential treatment." Opponents also claim that businesses and schools have often been forced to accept women and minorities who are less qualified than the rejected white men. They say it is ironic that affirmative action—with a goal of reducing discrimination—is engaging in "reverse discrimination"—decreasing opportunity for qualified white men. Eastland (2000) expressed gratitude for reverse discrimination lawsuits because they remind us of the principle "that no one in America should be discriminated against on account of race" (p. 175). Opponents also suggest that affirmative action plans have an adverse effect on society because quality and competence are being compromised, making the "solution" worse than the problem.

Judicial Limitations on Affirmative Action

Quality and competence were the focus of the *Griggs v. Duke Power* case heard by the U.S. Supreme Court in 1971. Job applicants at the Duke Power Company were required to have a high school diploma or passing scores on a specific standardized test. Lawyers argued that the requirement excluded a higher percentage of blacks than whites because unequal educational opportunities and other inequities prevented more black than white youth from earning high school diplomas. The U.S. Supreme Court ruled that any hiring practice that was intended to select the most qualified candidates was legitimate. Companies could not be held accountable for past discrimination that adversely affected individuals in the present. As long as job requirements were related to work performance, they could not be labeled discriminatory, even if they did advantage some job applicants.

Based on the same concept, the U.S. Supreme Court also upheld the seniority system to determine layoffs during economic downturns. Because of past discrimination against women and minorities, adhering to **seniority system** priorities required employers to lay off people with least seniority: "last hired is the first fired." Although the procedure seemed race neutral, lawyers provided evidence that the majority of women and minority employees had low seniority and were most likely to be dismissed. Supreme Court justices acknowledged the problem but consistently have found the seniority system constitutional because it does not represent intentional discrimination. The Court has ruled with the same consistency on cases in which the affirmative action plan appears to include a racial quota, that is, a specific number of people hired or accepted based on race.

Affirmative Action and Quotas

Whenever **racial quotas** have been employed, the U.S. Supreme Court has always ruled against them, declaring that Title VII never mandated racial (or other) quotas. Indeed, the justices are correct. There is no mention of quotas in Title VII, nor anything to suggest that employers must hire unqualified applicants; as Greene (1989) noted, section 703 (j) of Title VII states:

> Nothing contained in this title shall be interpreted to require any employer, employment agency, labor organization, or joint labor-management committee subject to this title to grant preferential treatment to any individual or group. (p. 60)

One of the clearest judgments against racial quotas was the Supreme Court's ruling in the case of *Regents of California v. Bakke*. In 1970, 80% of the 800 students of color attending medical school in the United States were enrolled in programs at two historically black universities. Because minorities were never more than 3% of students at the University of California–Davis Medical School, the

> One who gains strength by overcoming obstacles possesses the only strength which can overcome adversity.
>
> Albert Schweitzer (1875–1965)

university decided to reserve eight of their admissions places (16%) for minority applicants. For two consecutive years, Alan Bakke was rejected by UC despite having a grade-point average and Medical College Admissions Test scores higher than those of several minority applicants admitted. Ball (2000) explained the strategy of Bakke's lawyers in arguing relentlessly against the concept of racial quotas while UC–Davis lawyers argued that the university only accepted academically qualified applicants to their medical school and that preferential treatment of minorities was necessary to increase the numbers of minorities in professions "from which minorities were long excluded because of generations of pervasive racial discrimination" (p. 92).

The final decision on *Bakke* in 1978 fragmented the Court. Four justices approved UC–Davis affirmative action procedures, and four justices rejected them, arguing that race should play no role whatsoever on admission decisions. Justice Powell cast the deciding vote. In his written opinion, Powell declared that racial quotas were an unconstitutional strategy for achieving affirmative action goals, but that race could be used as one factor among others in considerations of college applicants.

Affirmative Action for Minority-Owned Businesses

Another affirmative action strategy rejected by the courts was the practice of setting aside a certain percentage of tax-funded projects for minority-owned businesses. In 1983, the city of Richmond,

Virginia, was 50% African American, but in the previous five years, less than 1% of funds spent on city projects had been paid to minority-owned businesses. The Richmond city council approved an affirmative action plan to require recipients of city construction projects to subcontract at least 30% of the dollar value of these projects to minority-owned businesses. When J.A. Croson Company insisted it could not find any suitable minority-owned businesses and asked for a waiver of the subcontracting requirement, the city refused and informed the company that it would resubmit their part of the project for new bids. The company brought the case to federal court, and the Supreme Court ruled on the case in 1989.

Writing for the majority in the *City of Richmond v. J.A. Croson Co.*, Sandra Day O'Connor criticized Richmond's **set-aside program** for its apparently arbitrary determination of the 30% figure and for not providing evidence demonstrating that previous major contractors had intentionally discriminated against minority-owned businesses. O'Connor said the Richmond City Council could have implemented effective, race-neutral strategies rather than establishing set-aside quotas. The court affirmed the right to remedy past discrimination, but again rejected racial quotas as a legitimate constitutional strategy (Crosby & VanDeVeer, 2000).

The Future of Affirmative Action

In 1995, the National Employment Lawyers Association issued a position paper citing a number of studies in support of affirmative action to substantiate their contention that affirmative action had "significantly reduced job discrimination and improved occupational status and mobility for minorities and women" (2000, p. 711). Yet because of ongoing criticism of affirmative action, during that same year, President Clinton appointed a task force to review all federal affirmative action programs. Although some changes were recommended, the task force concluded that the programs reviewed did not include quotas, did not mandate preferences for unqualified individuals, and did not engage in reverse discrimination. Instead, the programs were designed to remedy past discrimination and "lead the nation toward the goal of equal opportunity" (Ball, 2000, p. 163).

California voters did not agree. In 1996, they voted to approve **Proposition 209**, prohibiting preferential treatment to individuals or groups in hiring, awarding public contracts, and college admissions. According to Ball (2000), African American admissions to California law schools dropped 72% the year after the proposition was approved, and admission of all students of color to UC–Berkeley dropped 50%. The following year, UCLA and Berkeley reported continuing decreases in numbers of students of color. In response to complaints of increased segregation on state university campuses, California legislators voted to guarantee admission to any California university campus to all high school students graduating in the top 4% of their class. Critics said the vote represented a cynical recognition of racial segregation in California high schools. Although other states such as Oregon have passed propositions similar to Proposition 209, advocates argued that eliminating affirmative action was premature, and most would agree with the perspective expressed by Clayton and Crosby (2000):

> When the goals of true equality have been reached . . . affirmative action will be unnecessary. We have not yet reached such a happy state of being. Sexism and racism are still strong forces in American society, and both hostility toward and stereotypes about women and people of color influence decisions. (p. 88)

Higher Education

Since the 1960s, colleges and universities have implemented affirmative action plans to increase the numbers of students of color on their campuses. Although many administrators initially viewed affirmative action as unnecessary interference, in recent years administrators have displayed a pluralistic attitude, arguing that diversity of all kinds benefits the entire student population. Administrators, faculty, and student leaders on college campuses have consistently supported setting diversity goals. Musil (1996) summarized their perspective:

> To invite that diversity onto campus is not simply an act of charity. It is an act of raw self-interest. . . . it will make higher education better than it is. It expands

our notion of learning. It widens what we study and how we study it. It improves our pedagogy. It adds to our resources in human capital. (p. 225)

Criticism of Diversity Goals in Higher Education

Affirmative action plans in higher education and the increased diversity they have helped produce have been the subject of much criticism. Even some people of color say affirmative action has stigmatized students of color, as white students question their academic ability and believe they are admitted through lower standards. Some faculty blame affirmative action for a perceived decline in academic standards and for promoting a multicultural curriculum that has caused a decline in the rigor of traditional college education.

Critics persist in denouncing changes in traditional curriculum, accusing faculty who are creating a more inclusive curriculum of having a "political agenda" rather than purely academic objectives. However, it would seem equally appropriate to accuse advocates for the preservation of a curriculum that emphasizes white people as having a political agenda as well. It is true that traditional Western civilization classes in college and high schools that used to emphasize Western achievements and ignore controversial issues have declined, but they have often been replaced by courses in world history with a more objective presentation of content. Even so, a study of high school classes on world history reported that 67% of content focused on Western history (Stearns, 2006).

The critics are correct in insisting that feminists and people of color are challenging the lack of relevance and inclusiveness in college curricula. Duncan (2002) noted that women and students of color in college courses encounter minimal information written by or about their groups, and often the information provided misrepresents or distorts the group being described. Even worse, Duncan claimed that students of color find "both explicit and subtle racist themes in what they . . . study" (p. 45). What is included in college curricula is a critical issue, as Groff and Cain explained: "Curriculum is a microcosm of the culture: its inclusions and exclusions are an index of what the culture deems important" (Yamane, 2001, p. 6).

FIGURE 14.1

Source: Courtesy of *The Daily Cardinal*, University of Wisconsin.

Diversity in College Faculty and Course Content

In addition to the omission of people of color in curriculum, few faculty of color are represented at most universities. Tusmith and Reddy (2002) reported that people of color constitute less than 15% of higher education faculty, and that the majority were nontenured lecturers or instructors. Browne-Miller (1996) quoted an Asian American student observing that the teaching styles of her white professors were "geared to white middle-class males, overlooking the fact that this may not be the most effective . . . with non-white students and women" (p. 90). Courses taught by faculty of color would benefit all students, including white students, by presenting perspectives they are not likely to have encountered. Reddy (2002) noted,

> Students—especially but not exclusively white students—arrive in our college classrooms with predictable baggage. Prepared by virtually every element of the society in which we live, they come ready to accept white authority, intelligence and rightness while discounting the views and experiences of people of color. (p. 54)

Because of Reddy's "predictable baggage," it is not inevitable that positive outcomes will occur if white students and students of color are brought together on a college campus; they may or may not enjoy each other or learn from each other. (See Figure 14.1.) Almost a century ago, journalist John Reed observed that participating in a diverse community may bring "pain, isolation of separateness, [or] intellectual exhilaration, greater self-knowledge and . . . human reconciliation" (Lowe, 1999, p. 22). To ensure productive interactions between members of diverse groups, colleges sponsor frequent diversity workshops and seminars, require all students to take at least one course on diversity, encourage relevant academic departments to include at least one course with significant content on diversity issues in their majors and minors, and encourage all faculty to integrate content about diversity issues into the courses they teach.

Since the 1960s, professors in numerous institutions of higher education have created scholarly courses focusing on one or more diverse groups. As these professors have grappled with diversity issues, their efforts have been learning experiences for themselves as well as their students. To struggle with diversity issues is to engage in an evolutionary process of change. According to Musil (1996), colleges cannot assume that they can "simply add diversity and stir and think the recipe will not be fundamentally altered" (p. 224). To illustrate, Musil went on to describe the limitations of initial courses developed to examine diversity issues, and what professors and students involved in those courses learned:

> Black studies were typically about only men. Women's studies were typically only about white women. Gay and lesbian studies had no practicing Christians or Jews. And none of the three paid much attention to those in the group who were old, working class or disabled. Today it is largely commonplace in the most influential texts . . . in these kinds of courses to recognize the reality of our multiple identities. (p. 228)

Unfortunately, enrollment figures indicate that only a few white students take ethnic studies courses, and there have been few men enrolled in women's studies courses. Duncan (2002) believes that most white students, especially white males, are so accustomed to white experience being the focus of curriculum that they feel strange, defensive, and uncomfortable as they struggle to understand information that focuses on experiences of women or people of color. Despite these difficulties, colleges and universities continue to promote the goal of students gaining knowledge about diverse groups. Although designed to heighten student acceptance of diverse populations, courses on diversity have tended to be an addition to rather than a replacement for traditional curriculum. Kolodny (1998) addressed the importance of adding diversity content to the traditional curriculum:

> We are expanding our students' repertoire of reading and interpretive strategies, teaching them to comprehend and appreciate the aesthetic rules and cultural practices governing the Zuni story of emergence as well as those governing the composition of a Shakespeare play. (p. 49)

In 1989, the University of Wisconsin System—consisting of 13 four-year and 12 two-year institutions of higher education—implemented a **Design for Diversity** plan mandating changes in policies and practices on all campuses to make them more welcoming places for students of color. Across America, universities have instituted changes to create positive environments for the increasingly diverse college student population. Humphreys (2000) presented results of a survey finding that 63% of colleges and universities either have at least one diversity course as a graduation requirement or they are developing such a course; 42% require more than one course; and 25% have had such a requirement for more than ten years.

Results and Possibilities

Diversity courses not only provide greater understanding of diverse groups, but they also help students appreciate the benefits of diversity. According to Browne-Miller (1996), one student learned "More diversity allows for more possibilities, be it knowledge, friends, understanding between people" (p. 83). In a society as diverse and democratic as the United States, colleges and universities must actively facilitate understanding between diverse groups. Ball (2000) commented, "For democracy to flourish, college students have to be able to interact with other students who are different from them" (p. 13). In a series of diversity reports, the American Association of Colleges and Universities (AACU) argued that diversity challenges democratic commitments: "instead of creating fragmentation and alienation . . . [AACU] asserts that only through diversity can we achieve a deeper and lasting national unity" (Musil, 1996, p. 226).

Diversity does not just refer to obvious differences of race, ethnicity, gender, or disabilities. Diversity includes other changes taking place in students attending college today: Almost 50% of all college students are over twenty-four years old, more than 50% are the first in their family to attend college, and students with learning disabilities are the fastest growing category of students with disabilities on our campuses. Individuals accepted today may require modifications of and accommodations within traditional policies and practices governing campuses. Yet as demographic developments and affirmative action plans change the face of our campuses, opponents struggle to maintain the status quo. White students filed suit against both graduate and undergraduate admissions programs at the University of Michigan for including race in their admissions procedures. In 2003, the Supreme Court's ruling on this case maintained its consistent position of allowing race to be used as a factor in admissions procedures while rejecting approaches

> Democracy is a way of life . . . a vibrant, living sweep of hope and progress which constantly strives for the fulfillment of its objective in life—the search for truth, justice, and human dignity.
>
> Saul Alinsky (1909–1972)

that appear to establish racial quotas. In response to the accusation that less qualified minority students were being admitted to the University of Michigan law school, a study was conducted of Michigan's law school graduates in terms of their job status, salaries, awards, and community contributions. The study reported that minority graduates were just as successful on these measures as their white peers (Johnson, 2011). Yet affirmative action continues to be challenged in court as illustrated by the 2012 *Fisher v. University of Texas* case.

Corporate and Small Business

It surprised some opponents of affirmative action to discover that several Fortune 500 corporations filed amicus briefs in support of Michigan's program; for the past two decades, the private sector has been in support of affirmative action. In the early 1980s, many corporations opposed the Reagan administration's efforts to reduce the demand for contractor compliance on federal projects. According to responses from Corporate Executive Officers (CEOs) reported by Reskin (2000), 122 of 128 major corporations would "retain their affirmative action plans [even] if the Federal government ended [required] affirmative action" (p. 111). On surveys, CEOs tend to agree that affirmative action has improved hiring,

marketing, and productivity. According to Harvard business professor David Thomas, a diverse workforce is an "inescapable reality" for any corporation with over 100 employees no matter where it is located (Hymowitz, 2005).

In recent years, American businesses have become more attentive to diversity. They have to be. White men and people of color each represent one third of the workforce today, and 83% of the new workers between now and 2050 will be immigrants and their children (Burns, Barton, & Kerby, 2012). In a 2005 article for the *Wall Street Journal*, Hymowitz stated, "If companies are going to sell products and services globally, they will need a rich mix of employees with varied perspectives and experiences" (p. R1). Business leaders understand that responding positively to diversity by implementing pluralistic policies and practices is necessary because not only is the workforce becoming more diverse, but so are the customers. Mor-Barak (2005) rejects the old workplace model requiring workers to conform to established organizational values and norms reflecting the dominant culture; instead, she argues for promoting a respect for "all cultural perspectives represented among its employees" (p. 8).

The growing numbers of women and people of color in the workforce mirror the increasing percentage they represent as consumers, and their numbers are going to continue to grow. Experts are predicting that the population of the United States will increase by 50% over the next 50 years, and that almost 90% of that increase will be occurring in communities of color (Williams, 2003, p. 442). According to the U.S. Department of Commerce, even if the income gap between white workers and workers of color persists over the next 30 years, the increasing numbers of people of color means that their purchasing power will still expand to about 32% of disposable income (Carr-Ruffino, 2007). When people have money to spend, they command attention from American businesses. According to recent data, people of color represent $1.5 trillion of purchasing power, and 144 million women have at least $1.1 trillion of purchasing power, but that is certainly an underestimate because woman often choose clothes for men and recommend other items that men purchase—but their influence would not be reflected in data on women's purchases (see Table 14.1). Luscombe (2010) cites a Pew study of 30- to 44-year-old consumers, which found that

TABLE 14.1 Diversity and Purchasing Power Among U.S. Consumers

Group	Population Numbers	Purchasing Power
LGBT people	(10–20 million)	$743 billion
People with disabilities	54 million	$408 billion
African Americans	42 million	$957 billion
Asian Americans	12 million	$544 billion
Hispanic Americans	50.5 million	$1 trillion
Women	157 million	$5 trillion

Sources: Purchasing power data for race/ethnic groups from Catalyst (2011); for people with disabilities from Imparato, A.J., Houtenville, A.J., & Shaffert, R.L. (2010); for women from Bennett, J., & Ellison, J. (2010). Population data from the Census Bureau.

even when the husband's income is the primary or sole financial support for a family, both spouses play an equal role in making decisions about spending, and for 22% of households in which the woman's income exceeded that of her husband, wives made more than twice as many decisions about spending to address family needs. Women are major customers in the $200 billion consumer electronics field, where they account for $90 billion, and of the $256 billion home-improvement field, women spend $105 billion (Luscombe, 2010). One corporate executive has argued that more corporations need to appoint women to their boards of directors because: "Women either control or influence nearly all consumer purchases" (Jones & George, 2003, p. 118).

Corporate Litigation

American demographic changes represent compelling reasons for corporate America to value diversity. Discrimination litigation has also provided motivation. In the 1980s and early 1990s, Denny's Restaurants were the sites of several alleged racist incidents, including one involving 21 Secret Service agents en route to Annapolis to make security preparations for a presidential visit. When they stopped at a Denny's restaurant to eat supper, the white agents were given what they ordered, but the black Secret Service agents were never served any food. Despite being one of the largest restaurant chains in the United States, Denny's hired few minority employees, and none of its major suppliers was a minority-owned firm. At the time of its

purchase by Advantica Corporation, Denny's had just paid $54 million out of court to settle discrimination claims. According to Williams (2003), Advantica's CEO said the lawsuits had turned Denny's into "a poster child for racism" (p. 467).

Advantica took aggressive action to change the Denny's image. As the twenty-first century began, 42% of Denny's employees were minorities, as were 33% of its managers. Nearly 20% of its suppliers were minority-owned firms, and 35% of its franchises were minority owned. Denny's commitment to diversity was recognized by *Fortune* magazine, which identified it as one of the top ten companies in its support of minorities. Although Denny's is no longer in *Fortune*'s top ten list, it is still praised for its dramatic effort to transform its racist image.

In 1998, Arab American workers and managers alleged discrimination in decisions on promotions and pay raises in a class action lawsuit filed against Detroit Edison, the largest electric utility in Michigan. Detroit Edison representatives began negotiations immediately and promised changes. They kept their promises. They recruited and hired an Arab American widely known throughout the state to serve as vice president, and their contracts with suppliers included an increased number of businesses owned by people of Middle Eastern descent. In response, the Arab American community commended Detroit Edison, and its CEO accepted an invitation to serve on the advisory board of the Michigan chapter's Arab-American Anti-Discrimination committee (Millman, 2005).

Denny's and Detroit Edison's experiences are not isolated incidents. Shoney's Restaurants paid $132.8 million to settle a claim of racial discrimination in hiring; Edison International paid $11 million for the same offense. Bell Atlantic Telephone paid $500 million for discrimination against blacks in employee promotions. After making significant changes in policies and practices, all three companies are now listed among *Fortune* magazine's top 50 companies for their support of minorities (Williams, 2003). Corporations appear to be learning the lesson that discrimination must be eliminated. In 2008, the Equal Employment Opportunity Commission reported that the fines that all businesses paid to resolve discrimination complaints (largely based on race and gender) totaled only $102 million (Johnson, 2011). Further, global corporations such as Nike have also changed their policies and practices in response to accusations of discrimination or exploitation (see the box on page 353).

Workplace Diversity

Most businesses do not address diversity issues in response to legal action, but rather because they recognize the advantages of promoting workplace diversity. In areas with significant Hispanic populations, Sears and Target Stores have profited by accommodating Hispanic consumers, as have Darden's Restaurants by providing Spanish menus (Jones & George, 2003). Furthermore, having diverse managers and employees increases the likelihood of appropriate responses to customer needs. In a study comparing sales of businesses that had little, some, or considerable racial diversity in their workforce,

> This country will not be a good place for any of us to live in unless we make it a good place for all of us to live in.
>
> Theodore Roosevelt (1858–1919)

researchers reported the following average sales for these businesses: $3.1 million for those with little diversity, $3.7 million for those with some diversity, and $5.7 million for those with considerable diversity (Johnson, 2011). Businesses that want a diverse

workforce employ strategies such as (1) providing college scholarships and workplace mentors, (2) disseminating information on available jobs to local churches and Spanish-language radio and television stations, (3) sponsoring seminars on diversity for managers, (4) establishing a full-time position as diversity coordinator, or (5) sponsoring community events such as Cinco de Mayo or a Gay Pride march (Hymowitz, 2005).

Having a positive work environment to accommodate diversity improves productivity and reduces turnover costs. Depending on whether the job is low wage or high wage, the cost in the private sector for hiring a new employee ranges from $3,500 to $24,000 (Sasha, 2007). According to Griffin (2002), one pharmaceutical corporation saved $50,000 by lowering its turnover rate among women and minorities. The creation of positive work environments for diverse employees may be one reason why 62% of job seekers said they would prefer to work for organizations demonstrating a commitment to diversity (Daft, 2003).

According to Carr-Ruffino (2007), businesses taking a multicultural approach to diversity in their workplaces will experience numerous benefits, including: (1) attracting and retaining the most talented workers, (2) attracting and retaining diverse customers and suppliers, (3) reducing costs, (4) enhancing innovation and problem-solving capabilities, and (5) increasing productivity. All of these factors contribute to having a more profitable business, but it also requires employers to create a positive work environment for diverse employees. Many even attend to subtle differences such as being a single parent or part of a dual-career couple. Some companies have established day care centers at their worksites or have instituted flexible working hours. Benefits packages have been structured to address the diverse needs of employees. Being flexible does not have to be expensive, even when providing accommodations for people with disabilities. According to Williams (2003), the average cost of accommodating workers with disabilities was $250; 20% of accommodations involved no direct cost.

Diversity Training Programs

Diversity training programs are not new, but older programs have been considered largely ineffective

FIGURE 14.2

The cartoon illustrates why many corporations and businesses believe it is necessary to engage in diversity training for employees.

because they tended to use one of two approaches: sensitivity training, which appeared to have little practical value, or a confrontational approach that antagonized white men. Current diversity training covers a broader range of topics, focuses on a pragmatic business rationale for promoting diversity, and develops specific skills in communication and management. Many businesses are implementing intensive diversity training programs not only to improve work relations between diverse employees and managers, but also to ensure that employees will interact effectively with diverse customers. At the conclusion of diversity training, some businesses engage in evaluations of how employees and managers respond to diversity (Egodigwe, 2005). A quarterly survey of Allstate Insurance employees included a "diversity index" for evaluating managers on diversity issues: 25% of a manager's bonus pay was determined by that score (Daft, 2003).

To promote a positive environment for diversity at the worksite, some U.S. companies have instituted **diversity training** programs for managers and employees. Training programs may include **diversity pairing**, where people from diverse backgrounds are paired to provide them with opportunities to interact and become better acquainted. Such pairs may be combined with mentoring as when a white male manager is paired with an employee of color or a woman. Many businesses create multicultural teams for more effective problem solving; these "teams" also provide an opportunity for workers to learn more about their colleagues. (See Figure 14.2.)

Jones and George (2003) described the diversity training program at United Parcel Service (UPS) that requires upper-level managers to participate in community programs for a full month. Approximately 40 managers per year work in organizations

From Exploitation to Exemplary Practice

Critics of America's involvement in the global economy have expressed concerns not just about outsourcing jobs to other countries but also about the exploitation of workers of color in those countries. When Nike Corporation was founded in the 1960s, executives wanted to experiment with the idea of marketing shoes but not manufacturing them. Nike designed the shoes, but purchased the product from independent contractors in Asian or Southeast Asian countries where wages were low. This innovative approach became so profitable that it soon became the norm for American corporations.

Beginning in the 1990s, national and local media published news reports about inhumane labor conditions at Nike's overseas factories. When consumers expressed outrage, Nike executives insisted that it was not their responsibility to tell factory owners how to run their businesses, but news coverage continued to make disturbing allegations, especially concerning child labor abuses. As Nike's stock value dropped, Nike executives finally began to implement programs to improve monitoring of labor conditions at factories making Nike products.

Today, Nike pre-screens factories before signing contracts with suppliers, and it has become a role model for other corporations because of its careful monitoring of worksite conditions. Nike publishes the names and addresses of all factories producing its products and publicly discloses its workplace monitoring activities. Nike's Web site (www.nikebiz.com) has been acknowledged as an excellent resource on international labor standards (Frank, 2008).

---

such as homeless shelters, Head Start centers, migrant farm worker assistance groups, and detention centers. Since 1968, over 800 managers have been involved in the program, and UPS believes it has had a positive impact on the abilities of its managers to respond more effectively to diversity issues.

Some U.S. corporations have been especially aggressive in their commitment to diversity. In 1995, the CEO at International Business Machines (IBM) was concerned that his senior executive team had minimal diversity, despite IBM's affirmative action efforts. He implemented a new diversity initiative, which over a ten-year period resulted in an increase of five times the number of female senior executives and tripled the number of those who were U.S.-born minorities. In 2000, IBM had no women as country managers for its overseas operations, but by 2005, the company had hired nine women general managers for such countries as France, Spain, Thailand, New Zealand, and Peru.

IBM's Web site (2012) notes that 28% of its employees are women, as are 24% of its managers, 19% of its executive managers, and two senior vice presidents. In addition, IBM's current CEO is a woman—Virginia Rometty. IBM's efforts illustrate a comment from a CEO of another multinational corporation: "Affirmative action brings people in the door, and the inclusion piece brings people to the table. You really need both to be successful" (Egodigwe, 2005, p. R4).

Lingering Problems

Diversity problems still arise in the business community. Jones and George report that women and minorities continue to be disadvantaged because of the way they are regarded by white colleagues, especially at worksites where they are a numerical minority. Daft (2003) cited two studies, with one reporting that 59% of minority managers believed there was a "racially motivated double standard in the delegation of assignments" (p. 443). Another study found that employees of color believed they had to work longer hours and make extra efforts to be given the same respect as white co-workers. Salary data documents that women and minorities still earn substantially less money than white men and that minorities are still underrepresented in management. Although African Americans and Hispanics constitute 36% of the U.S. population, they represent only 15.9% of managers—8.4% and 7.5% respectively (Catalyst, 2012).

Women hold 41.4% of managerial positions (Catalyst, 2012) and appear to be fairly represented, but the **glass ceiling** prevents them from rising as high as their abilities should permit. Jones and George (2003) reported on evidence of women's managerial ability, with one study concluding that female executives outperformed males on listening, motivating others, communicating effectively, and producing high-quality work. Another study of 425 top executives assessed 52 skills and found that women received higher ratings than men on 42 of them; yet women remain underrepresented in top executive positions. Williams (2003) reported that 90% of women executives said the glass ceiling had restricted their career growth; 80% indicated that they left their last job because the glass ceiling hurt their chances for promotion. Studies show that women are increasingly leaving organizations to start their own businesses because of their perception of a glass ceiling at work.

Corporate leaders know that problems arising from human differences must be resolved if U.S. businesses are to remain competitive in the global economy. Multinational corporations with headquarters in nations other than the United States have openly promoted diversity and implemented policies to assure that diverse workers receive fair treatment in the workplace. As Mor-Barak (2005) has written: "The second half of the twentieth century witnessed an unprecedented global trend in antidiscrimination and equal opportunity legislation" (p. 17). To match the efforts of their global counterparts, corporate leaders in the United States are likely to continue to publicly promote diversity, hire job seekers who appreciate corporate commitments to diversity, and provide diversity training to create a positive work environment for diverse employees. Williams (2003) stated,

> The general purpose of diversity programs is to create a positive work environment where no one is advantaged or disadvantaged, where "we" is everyone, where everyone can do their best work, where differences are respected and not ignored, where everyone feels comfortable. (pp. 438–439)

Mass Media

Kawamoto (2003) has written that traditional definitions of mass media have addressed various means of sending information to a mass audience, and these definitions have traditionally focused on such vehicles as books, newspapers, magazines, radio, and television—what some scholars now refer to as "legacy media." The continuing growth of digital media has challenged these traditional definitions of mass media along with many of the conventional assumptions about how messages and images are created and delivered. Although it is important to address how diversity is represented and how people from diverse groups are involved in conventional forms of mass media, it is critical to look at what is happening in digital media.

Diversity and Representations of Diversity in Conventional Mass Media

In conventional mass media, the best evidence of the acceptance of diversity and the promotion of the concept of pluralism is the increasing numbers of women and people of color entering media-related professions. McQueen (2002) reported that 61% of college students majoring in journalism and mass communication were female and 27% were students of color; further, experts predict that students of color will increase to 40% by 2035. The greatest barrier currently to increasing diversity in the mass media is the recession. According to a 2010 survey, full-time employment dropped by 10% in 2008 and another 5% in 2009—an unprecedented decline in employment. According to one survey, two thirds of journalism students receiving a bachelor's degree were only able to find jobs writing or editing for Internet outlets.

The survey also noted that women graduates have been more successful than men at finding employment, but people of color have encountered more difficulty being hired than white applicants (Becker et al., 2010).

This racial disparity is reflected in job distributions in mass media organizations. According to the American Society of Newspaper Editors, if the percentage of people of color in the U.S. population were reflected in newsrooms, they would be 30% of the journalists; instead, journalists of color constitute only 13% of newsroom staff. Many journalists of color report an interest in being a sports reporter, yet in a survey of over 300 newspapers, 79% of sports reporters were white males, 10.3% were white females, 6.6% were black males, and only 1% were black women; of 300 sports editors, only five were black (Lee, 2006). Because of the 2008 recession, the numbers are declining further; journalists of color are increasingly writing for online news outlets and now represent almost 20% of online journalists. Yet even online journalism continues to be dominated by white males (Wilson & Costanza-Chock, 2012).

Although there are more women and people of color appearing on television news and entertainment programs, the majority of jobs are behind the camera—writers, producers, camera operators, and technicians—where the numbers of women and people of color are low. For example, Stanhope (2009) reported that minority writers in television declined from 10% to 9% with black writers having the biggest decline. Further, Johnson (2000) found only one black writer employed by a white-themed show while 80% of black writers were writing for black-themed shows, a trend that appears to be ongoing (Hunt, 2007). This disparity documents a seemingly blatant form of racism, suggesting that black writers can't write scripts for white actors even though white writers have written for black actors for many years. Popper (2000) made this observation about the future for women and people of color in television and films: "Most industry people expect on-air staff to remain diverse, since that's what the audience sees. What happens behind the scenes is less clear" (p. 67).

Another concern in conventional mass media is not just the inclusion of diversity but how diversity is being presented. Media scholars examine whether

groups are being portrayed in stereotypical ways or if characters presented from a group illustrate diversity within that group and if multiple voices are included rather than a dominant perspective. Although omission is not usually a problem today, it can still occur. In *Time* magazine's 2011 commemorative issue of the tragic events of 9/11, not one African American was included in the photographs (largely of Ground Zero in New York City) or in the content. Given the historic and significant presence of African Americans in New York City, this is a glaring oversight. More typical was a Los Angeles study of television news in which researchers found that although blacks accounted for only 21% of arrests according to police records, they were identified in 37% of the arrests reported on air; by contrast, white people constituted 28% of arrests, but only 21% of those reported on the news (Luther, Lepre, & Clark, 2012). Ferguson (1998) discussed a study of television news programming in twenty-nine North American cities that described a tendency for newscasts to engage in both positive and negative stereotypes by covering successful black athletes and entertainers, yet providing frequent images of blacks as criminals and welfare mothers, and other images representing a range of antisocial behaviors. Fourteen years later, another study found that when television news reports addressed poverty, they tended to present images of black women living in poverty, even though the number of whites and blacks living in poverty are roughly equal (Luther, Lepre, & Clark, 2012). As the numbers of people of color increase, such omissions and distortions of reality may generate more criticism. As one California journalism professor observed: "In a multicultural society, people pay attention to media that pay attention to them" (Chuang, 2010, p. 1).

Media has the power to provide positive images of people and to promote social change. In 1984, Levi Jeans aired the first advertisement providing a positive portrayal of a person with a disability. The energetic wheelchair user "popped a wheelie" to demonstrate his enthusiasm for Levi Jeans. The positive response to this advertisement caused a few more businesses to use people with disabilities in their advertisements. Although their presence remains minimal, people with disabilities are no longer completely absent from television, and there is other evidence that advertisers began to include people with a disability in planning their ads. In the six years following the Levi Jeans commercial, more than 200 businesses produced over 2,600 advertisements with closed captions for hard-of-hearing people (Riley, 2005). Such changes are not simply altruistic; people with disabilities have $408 billion of purchasing power (Imparato, Houtenville, & Shaffert, 2010), and their inclusion in corporate advertising may influence not only their personal consumer choices but also those of their family and friends.

The Impact of Digital Media

As the twenty-first century began, over half of American households had personal computers and 72% said computers had improved their lives (Kawamoto, 2003). Although men were initially the dominant users of digital media, by 2000 more women than men were going online. One of the first demonstrations of the power of digital media came in 1999 when the World Trade Organization (WTO) met in Seattle in late November. People worldwide had become critical about the policies and practices of the WTO, and for almost a year before the Seattle meeting, activists had been planning for a protest in Seattle when the WTO met. Using digital media, these organizers formed coalitions and alliances, and created a Web site to disseminate information to an international audience. Protestors planning to come to Seattle were linked to Seattle residents who were willing to provide lodging. When the protests began, conventional corporate media largely tried to ignore the activities and continued to show little interest even as police used tear gas and pepper spray on the crowds and arrested hundreds of protestors. Because so many people in the U.S. and across the globe who wanted to know more about the protests were compelled to use Internet sources to get information, conventional media finally began providing some coverage of the protest activities (Kawamoto, 2003). The Seattle protest demonstrated the observation from Everett (2012) that digital media: "have enabled media consumers and political activists to become savvy media producers as well as informed consumers, which has made bloggers and vloggers major competitors for traditional media companies and powers" (p. 147).

Another example of the impact of digital media was its role during the 2008 U.S. presidential campaign. The election was historic not only because Americans chose the nation's first black President, but also for the brilliant use of digital media by the Obama campaign staff. Everett (2012) described how the campaign used digital media to engage in fundraising, connect supporters, disseminate campaign themes, and respond to "attack ads." On the other hand, digital media was also used against Obama; the video clip of his pastor from Chicago, Jeremiah Wright, damning America was replayed constantly on television and digital media, forcing Obama to give a major address on the issue of race. Lost in the controversy was the minister's actual message, his criticism of America's indifference to the drug problems in minority communities. Another example of manipulating digital media occurred when conservative blogger Andrew Breitbart edited a videotape of a speech by Shirley Sherrod, a black woman in the Obama administration. In the edited clip she appeared to be making racist comments; the Obama administration immediately asked for her resignation. When people looked at the unedited video of Sherrod's speech, they discovered that she was talking about how we can overcome racism, both individually and as a nation. Another misuse of digital media involved an Internet rumor spread by right wing bloggers that President Obama had provided funds to pay for free cell phones for people of color living in poverty, arousing widespread anger among conservatives who believed this falsehood (Everett, 2012). These examples underscore an additional concern, that people can avoid information they don't want to receive by selectively going only to those Web sites that affirm their view of reality—a technological illustration of the confirmation bias. Political experts speculate that such uses of the Internet may be a major factor in the increasing political polarization in the United States.

Whether it is put to good or bad uses, the Internet has become a permanent part of American society, especially among youth. Instead of being inundated with images and messages from conventional corporate-controlled media, young people today are increasingly likely to be viewing user-generated content on venues such as YouTube or Facebook. According to the Federal Communications Commission, in 2010 about two thirds of

American homes had broadband Internet (Sandvig, 2012), but this raises the question of the extent and nature of diversity among Internet users. A 2010 study of households to identify the presence of computers with an Internet connection found that the percentage of American households with access to the Internet varied by race: 65% of whites, 65% of Asian Americans, 46% of African Americans, 43% of American Indians, and 40% of Hispanics/Latinos. There was also a class divide as 84% of college-educated households had broadband, but only 28% of households where parents did not graduate from high school did (Wilson & Costanza-Chock, 2012). A footnote is necessary to clarify the data on the Internet access for American Indians. On most reservations, estimates of Internet access drops to well below 10%; the main exceptions are those reservations connected to the Tribal Digital Village (TDV), a solar wireless Internet distribution network in Southern California. Funded by a grant from Hewlett Packard, 100% of households on the TDV reservations have broadband Internet, and residents report that they use it daily. Their growing competency has occurred largely because of their cultural value of cooperation. The people living on these reservations willingly ask for and receive assistance and advice from their neighbors on how to use their computers. With the help of TDV, these reservations are now proposing to establish a digital record of their history and culture, including old photographs, songs, stories, and the spoken language, as well as creating Web-based tools for teaching the language. This reflects the efforts of many other Indian tribal councils across the United States that have established Web sites such as nativevillage.org and nativeweb.org to preserve their culture and to serve as a resource for others (Luther, Lepre, & Clark, 2012).

American Indians are not the only racial or ethnic group exploring the possibilities of digital media. Luther, Lepre, and Clark (2012) identified a successful African American social networking site, and described Black Planet, a popular news and entertainment Web site. Although Latinos are currently the least likely group to have computers in their homes, this is partly an economic issue. Media scholars predict that as K–12 Latino students become more familiar with the Internet from using computers at school, their use of digital media will increase significantly, especially the use of Spanish-language Web sites. Based on the marketing potential of this growing population, Sony Electronics began selling computers in 2006 with a Spanish-language operating system and keyboard. In that same year, advertisers increased their spending on Spanish language Web sites by 32% (Luther, Lepre, & Clark, 2012).

Some media critics worry about racism being promoted in digital media. Galloway (2012) argued that race coding is a feature of many video games, especially when they are based on fantasy worlds, since fantasy characters can avoid the criticism that their characters are ascribed obvious stereotypical traits associated with certain racial or ethnic groups. Further, race is a fixed quality in these games, whereas social status is fluid. Other media critics such as Boyd (2012) worry that social networking sites are beginning to reflect race and class divisions in society, especially among teenage users. A more blatant example of racism in digital media is the creation of numerous Web sites by neo-Nazis and other hate groups. Many have simply transferred their virulent, bigoted rhetoric from printed newsletters, but others have created sophisticated sites that even include racist activities and games for children. The use of digital media to promote racism prompted Everett (2012) to comment: "We may well lament the compelling nature of America's racial scripts that endure and threaten to undermine . . . progressive gains (from) media technologies" (p. 163).

Even so, there is ample evidence that digital media can be used to draw attention to important issues and mobilize people to work on them. As with the 1999 Seattle demonstrations, the "Occupy Wall Street" protests were largely ignored for the first two weeks by conventional corporate media until they were finally compelled to pay attention because "Independent mediamakers, citizen journalists, everyday people with camera phones were capturing the voices and faces of this burgeoning movement and uploading them to YouTube, Facebook and Twitter" (Yu, 2011, p. 8). The early corporate media coverage tended to describe the protesters as aimless hippies using drugs until a New York City police officer was caught on tape using pepper spray on peaceful women protesters. That tape was viewed on YouTube over two million times, and then corporate media began covering the story with heightened interest in what the protest was about, and reporters began paying attention to other "Occupy" protests around the nation (Yu, 2011). Based on what has happened during the Seattle, Wall Street, and other "Occupy" protest activities, digital media appears to be empowering average Americans by making it easier

> We are now at the point where we must decide whether we are to honor the concept of a plural society which gains strength through diversity or whether we are to have bitter fragmentation that will result in perpetual tension and strife.
>
> Justice Earl Warren (1891–1974)

for people who are communicating electronically to sign petitions, organize boycotts, and promote other collective activities that address social justice concerns—and many would argue that the most dramatic examples have occurred outside the United States. Digital media played a major role in the "Arab Spring" movement that challenged oppressive regimes in the Middle East in 2011, bringing down the governments of Hosni Mubarek in Egypt and Muammar Gaddafi in Libya. It is too early yet to tell what direction those nations will take, but the power of digital media clearly has global implications.

Military Services

Diversity in the armed forces of the United States is not a new issue; it is only the nature of the diversity that has changed. Although the military kept no records in its earliest years, there is anecdotal evidence that ethnic diversity in society was reflected in its military, and we know of at least one woman—Deborah Sampson—who disguised herself as a man and engaged in combat during the Revolutionary War (Craft-Fairchild, 1997).

Starting in 1856, records exist showing a significant percentage of ethnic immigrants serving in the army—a shortcut to being granted citizenship—but they also reveal problems. During the Mexican-American War, many Irish Catholic soldiers were reluctant to kill Mexican Catholics, and a number of them deserted to avoid doing so (Johnson, 1999). Nevertheless, diversity continued to exist in the U.S. Army. According to Buckley (2001), at the end of the Civil War there were 140 black regiments with over 100,000 soldiers, and the army continued to recruit blacks and immigrants. Johnson (1999) cited an 1896 army report documenting that 7% of that year's recruits were black and 33% were ethnic immigrants.

Significant differences concerning diversity in the military today include racial desegregation, inclusion of women, and exclusive reliance on volunteers. Each difference has created unique problems for military leadership to address, parallel to similar problems stemming from race and gender in the larger society. Dansby, Stewart, and Webb (2001) wrote, "In many ways the military has always been a mirror of American society, reflecting back the scars and blemishes as well as the face of the nation" (p. xvii). Although diversity problems have not yet been resolved, the U.S. military has made substantial progress, even more than society in general has made, according to sociologists Moskos and Butler (1996).

Military Desegregation

Desegregation in the military began with a research project during World War II. Black army platoons were integrated into white infantry companies and the social experiment was carefully monitored. The research team found that no unusual problems occurred and that all soldiers functioned effectively. Despite positive results, military leaders continued to oppose racial desegregation, even after President Truman issued an executive order mandating military racial desegregation. Because of racist attitudes among military leaders, the executive order was not fulfilled until the Korean War when desegregation became necessary for the sake of efficiency.

Dansby, Stewart, and Webb (2001) described problems with desegregation that came to the forefront during the Vietnam War. African Americans protesting against unequal treatment rioted at Fort Dix, Fort Bragg, on two aircraft carriers, and at Travis Air Force base. As the Vietnam War was ending in the early 1970s, General Creighton Abrams testified that poor race relations had had a negative impact on combat effectiveness. Complicating matters further, in 1973, Congress ended the draft and established an all-volunteer army. Recruiting and retaining quality soldiers would be affected by how the army addressed issues of race relations.

The army's response was to create a Defense Race Relations Institute charged with the responsibility of creating a race relations training program. The initial program lasted for six weeks; it was later expanded to include sexual harassment and discrimination, and now has become one of the army's most ambitious programs. Dansby and Landis (2001) report that the current training program lasts 16 weeks and, according to the American Council on Education, is equivalent to 23 undergraduate semester college credits. A major objective is "To create an environment that values diversity and fosters mutual respect and cooperation" (p. 9). The diversity training has continued, but today it includes cultural and language training to prepare soldiers for dealing with people from a different culture (e.g., in Afghanistan) to create a more positive relationship with the people they must interact with where they are deployed (Abbe & Gouge, 2012).

Integration Problems

Johnson (2001) evaluated the Defense Race Relations program and concluded that the training had an immediate positive effect on participant attitudes and improved subsequent work performance. Even so, problems with race relations in the U.S. military persist. Katzenstein and Reppy (1999) referred to a 1996 task force that found evidence of racism at 4 of 19 military facilities evaluated. Individual soldiers have been involved in incidents of racial violence; some continue to be members of extremist groups promoting racism or white supremacy, even though military policy prohibits active participation in such groups. Waldman (1996) explained the reason for that policy: "The nature of the military means that anything that gets in the way of mission accomplishment is unacceptable. Racism gets in the way" (p. 27).

Sexism gets in the way as well. Prior to the establishment of the all-volunteer army, fewer than 2% of recruits were women, with 90% of them receiving medical or administrative assignments (Katzenstein & Reppy, 1999); to maintain

This Coast Guard rescue swimmer saved a drowning fisherman 35 miles at sea.

(Her boyfriend just stopped by to bring her lunch.)

FIGURE 14.3

recruitment standards, however, the pool of candidates was expanded (see Figure 14.3). Peterson (1999) found that female recruits tended to be better educated, to have higher scores on aptitude tests, and to be less likely to cause disciplinary problems. According to Patten and Parker (2011), in only four decades women have increased from 4% to 14% of enlisted personnel and they are 16% of officers. Peterson (1999) concluded, "The Army fields the highest quality force in its history owing to the gains brought about by the all-volunteer force" (p. 100).

Increasing the role of minorities and women in the military has challenged male recruits because of cultural messages some men have internalized about masculinity. Katzenstein and Reppy (1999) explain, "Cultural ideas of masculinity encourage recruits to prove their fitness for military life by flaunting their masculine prowess in bigoted and sexist behavior" (p. 2). Military leaders did not understand this cultural influence at first. Defense directives about **sexual harassment** had been in place for many years before the 1991 Tailhook incident, in which drunken navy pilots forced female

> Injustice anywhere is a threat to justice everywhere. We are caught in an inescapable network of mutuality, tied in a single garment of destiny. Whatever affects one directly affects all indirectly.
>
> Martin Luther King, Jr. (1929–1968)

officers to walk through a gauntlet while they were groped and verbally humiliated. The chief of naval operations said later, "Until Tailhook we dealt too often with sexual harassment . . . one case at a time, rather than understanding it as a cultural issue" (Katzenstein & Reppy, 1999, p. 2). The problem was intensified five years later when rape charges were brought against drill sergeants at the Aberdeen Army base. In 2002, cadet women of the Air Force Academy reported allegations of sexual assault, indicating the ongoing challenge for the U.S. military to address male concepts of power and gender superiority.

Diversity Policy and Gender

As military leaders study the gender problem, they realize that rules are not always being observed. Kier (1999) reported that no action was taken for 56% of all sexual harassment complaints. Women had reported sexual harassment for years but had been ignored or encouraged to drop their complaint; some encountered hostile reactions from their male superiors. Katzenstein and Reppy (1999) conclude, "It was not a failure to have rules; [these] are problems emerging out of a culture at odds with [military] institutional policy" (p. 3). The 2002 and 2003 allegations of sexual harassment and even sexual assault at the Air Force Academy (AFA) demonstrated that more must be done to resolve these problems. Almost half of female AFA cadets reported that they had

personally experienced sexual harassment, 64% heard derogatory remarks based on gender, and 66% reported being discriminated against because of their gender. Despite this evidence, AFA leaders denied that there were any serious gender issues at the Academy, causing the authors of the 2003 report to conclude that gender problems at the AFA were a consequence of "a lack of leadership at the Academy and at the highest levels of the Air Force itself" (Zeigler & Gunderson, 2005, p. 121).

Some people opposed to women in the military argue that sexual harassment is a reaction to double standards that allow women to perform at lower levels of competence. The army's response is that levels are adjusted to take account of physiological differences for men as well as for women. Roush (1999) pointed out that for soldiers of the same height, men are allowed to weigh 30 pounds more than women before being required to enter weight control programs. In areas where no weight adjustment is necessary, women and men compete on an equal basis. Women soldiers have demonstrated excellent marksmanship by winning the army's highest awards, and have participated on marksmanship teams at the Olympics (Carter, 2002). Shooting skills are only part of women's impressive record of achievement that has opened doors to new responsibilities.

During the 1970s and 1980s, the U.S. Army employed a **risk rule** that measured how close certain roles would bring a participant to battle and did not assign women to roles that would bring them into combat. Carter (2002) observed that the 1989 Panama invasion altered the rules when women soldiers engaged in battle while working in support units that were fired on. Women driving convoy trucks and flying helicopters to transport wounded men to safety were fired on and women in military police units assisted with cordoning off neighborhoods in search of guerrillas. Some women would have earned medals if their assignments had officially listed them as combatants.

In 1991, Desert Storm provided another opportunity for women to prove their combat readiness. Despite predictions of critics, mixed-gender units displayed as much cohesiveness as single-gender units. Because of their performance in the Gulf War, women are now assigned to command military police companies, pilot helicopters, and serve in artillery units. The 2003 Iraq war placed thousands of women in battle zones, and actual combat assignments no longer seem unthinkable. Perhaps the performance of women soldiers under fire is one reason why a survey of Reserve Officer Training Corps (ROTC) cadets conducted by Zeigler and Gunderson (2005) found that almost 60% of ROTC cadets said that women should be allowed to volunteer for combat and should be assigned to combat roles just as men are.

In a survey of civilians, 53% agreed that women should be permitted to serve in combat, but a survey of military leaders revealed that 62% of them did not favor using women in diverse combat roles (Zeigler & Gunderson, 2005). Guenther-Schlesinger (2001) reported that 70% of women want to be assigned to combat roles because major promotions are more likely to be given to those who prove themselves on the battlefield. In recognition that more than 130 women soldiers have died and over 800 have been wounded in the two recent wars, the Pentagon is opening up more positions for women while still not permitting them a combat role. Two women soldiers have filed a discrimination lawsuit, and Congress has issued reports recommending that the Department of Defense allow women to compete for any job for which they are qualified, including combat roles (*New York Times*, 2012). Kier (1999) believes women will never be treated as equals in the military culture as long as their names are "missing from the rostrum of heroes, stories, and myths" arising from combat (p. 49).

Having studied demographic predictions, military leaders expect the percentage of women and minorities in the armed forces to increase; they are prepared to do much more recruiting from the growing pool of Hispanic American and Asian American candidates. Although there will be twice as many African Americans in the candidate pool by 2050, half of the U.S. population growth from 2000 to 2050 will occur among Latinos, with a smaller yet significant growth of Southeast Asians. Recruiters are encouraged by 1997 data showing that more Hispanics joined the military than any other ethnic group, but a major concern is the high dropout rate: Army policy requires that 90% of all recruits must have high school diplomas. According to the National Center for Educational Statistics, 20% of Hispanic students drop out of high school, the highest rate of groups included in their study (Fuller, 2011).

Religion and Sexual Orientation

Racial, ethnic, and gender diversity is only the beginning. The American military also has procedures for accommodating religious differences. The military accepts recruits of all faiths, including more obscure faiths such as Wicca. As for sexual orientation, gay Americans have always fought in this country's wars, but their sexual orientation was not an issue until World War I, when military regulations excluded openly gay men from military service. Yet there were closeted gay men in uniform when World War II began, including gay sergeants responsible for training the massive numbers of new soldiers enlisted after the attack on Pearl Harbor (Estes, 2007). Psychiatrists involved in screening procedures during the war rejected fewer than 5,000 recruits for being gay, but it is estimated that as many as 650,000 of the 16 million American troops were gay men (Estes, 2007). With the repeal of the "Don't Ask, Don't Tell" (DADT) policy, the armed forces are now recruiting openly gay men and lesbians into the military.

The history of lesbians entering the military is different since women were segregated from the beginning. The formation of the Women's Army Corps (WACs), the Women Accepted for Volunteer Emergency Service (WAVES), and the admission of women into the Marines in 1943 brought lesbians as well as straight women into military service. The presence of lesbians was well known to military leaders, who waited until the war was over before purging lesbians from the ranks by giving them dishonorable discharges. Female soldiers continued to play traditional support roles in the military until the early 1970s when Congress ended the draft. Military leaders recognized that there were many roles that women could play, and it was simply a pragmatic decision to recruit women as well as men. Some men initially expressed their reluctance to serve with women soldiers, but attitudes have changed as both lesbians and straight women have proven their abilities. Even before the repeal of the DADT policy, there was evidence that attitudes toward serving with openly gay soldiers was changing.

Matthews (1999) reported results of a survey of 270 male soldiers, finding only 36% strongly opposed to serving with gay soldiers; twice as many women soldiers said they would serve with lesbians as those who said they would not. Opponents to gays and lesbians serving in the military say the army is not the place for social experiments, but Katzenstein and Reppy (1999) note that the army and other units of America's armed forces have always been affected by societal changes: "The American military has at different times trailed, led or simply mirrored efforts to combat prejudice, but it has never been isolated from those prejudices" (p. 10). Although it is too early to tell, military leaders have been pleased with how smoothly the transition has gone since the DADT policy was terminated. The increased acceptance of gay men and lesbians as soldiers may stem from a growing recognition that serving in the military is actually a fundamental civil rights issue. As Segal, Segal, and Booth (1999) argued: "To be denied the right to serve is to have one's citizenship denied" (p. 225).

Military Leadership

As military recruiters make contact with an increasingly diverse pool of candidates, they must offer evidence that advancement is possible. According to Stewart and Firestone (2001), minorities are underrepresented at the general officer level. Jones (1999) recommended that military services immediately identify and attract more minority officer candidates to function as a "source of inspiration" for minority soldiers. Sayles (1999) discussed the importance of women and minority role models at all levels in the military organizational structure to provide women and minorities proof of genuine opportunity for advancement in the military—rather than a glass ceiling. All branches of the service have been asked to address the need for minority officers in their affirmative action plans; as an example, the Navy goal is to commission at least 7% black and 4% Hispanic officers each year. According to a Department of Defense (2010) report, the Navy has exceeded these goals: Blacks constitute 7.8% of its officers and Hispanics are

> One of the most successful institutions in American society in dealing with racial integration has been the United States Army. At the other extreme . . . [public] schools are among the most segregated associations in the country.
>
> Eugene Y. Lowe, Jr. (1949–)

6.2%. Jones (1999) stated, "Commitment to diversity and equal opportunity is the keystone to our entire value structure" (p. 62).

AFTERWORD

In his discussion of diversity issues in the military, Jones (1999) commented, "Americans tend to be ignorant about other societies and even about subcultures within their own society" (p. 62). His comment echoes a concern multicultural education advocates have expressed for several years: that too many K–12 schools do not address diversity issues adequately. This book was written to address diversity issues with college students, but the issues need to be addressed in K–12 classrooms as well. Schools in rural or suburban areas with predominantly white students tend to offer too little information about diversity. White teachers are often uncomfortable with controversies related to diverse groups; some insist that they don't need to address diversity because there are no—or few—students of color in their schools!

If white students rarely encounter people of color, it is even more important for teachers to provide accurate cognitive information about history, contributions, and issues affecting diverse populations in this country both historically and today. Further, this is not just a need for white students: Jones's comment referred to American recruits from diverse groups. African American students may know little about cultures or experiences of Native Americans; Native American students may only know about the "model minority" and have little knowledge of the past oppression, achievements, and current barriers of Asian Americans. Latino students may not understand why Somali students are in their school, and Somali students may have learned negative stereotypes about Latinos. Middle-class students need to understand the realities for low-income families; nondisabled students must confront misperceptions about people with disabilities; heterosexual students can unlearn myths they have been taught about gays and lesbians. In a diverse society, everyone needs to learn more about the diverse groups of people calling themselves Americans.

During the debate over ratifying the U.S. Constitution, some state leaders focused on the many differences dividing the states and argued that they could never be melded into a single union, but should instead remain independent states. Alexander Hamilton rejected the argument, insisting that a unified nation encompassing those diverse cultures had already formed, and the Constitution would simply reflect the shared values and vision of that union (Chernow, 2004).

Today, people living in our fifty states are not defined as much by the state where they live as by their membership in social groups determined by race, gender, disability, social class, and sexual orientation; yet we are all Americans. We live in a nation that adopted the motto "E Pluribus Unum" in 1782, originally meaning: "from many states, one nation." The motto has also been a metaphor for the people in a nation built on foundations established by Native Americans,

> When we dream alone, we are merely dreaming; but when we dream together, that's the beginning of reality.
>
> Brazilian Proverb

profiting from import of Africans, and exploiting the labor of immigrants and women: Each group has struggled to find its place in the kaleidoscope of changing images and altered realities. Their achievements were based on an American dream of a good life for themselves and their families, of a nation where they had freedom to work, worship, and live as they pleased among diverse people who were also guaranteed equal rights and equal opportunities.

That American dream has always been an ideal. Some groups were granted this ideal more readily than others, but all have sought it. America's history is a history of that struggle. We are farther along than ever today, yet we still have much to do to bring the dream closer to reality for all Americans. Pluralism represents a vehicle to move us forward. Committing ourselves to being pluralistic represents a commitment to the American dream, a commitment to make our nation's motto—"out of the many, one"—a description of the nation we are becoming. That is a dream worth dreaming.

TERMS AND DEFINITIONS

Affirmative action A written plan required of businesses and institutions of higher education to reduce discrimination in hiring, public contracting, and college admissions

Design for Diversity A Wisconsin program that mandates changes in policies and practices on all thirteen UW System campuses to make them more welcoming places for diverse students

Diversity The presence of human beings with perceived or actual differences based on a variety of human characteristics

Diversity pairing A diversity training strategy in which two people from diverse backgrounds are paired to provide them with opportunities to interact and become better acquainted

Diversity training Programs designed by businesses to promote a positive environment for diverse employees and managers at the worksite

Glass ceiling An informal upper limit that keeps women and minorities from being promoted to positions of greatest responsibility in work organizations

Pluralism The equal coexistence of diverse cultures in a mutually supportive relationship within the boundaries of one nation

Proposition 209 A California statute prohibiting preferential treatment to individuals or groups in hiring, awarding public contracts, and college admissions

Racial quota Designation of a specific number of applicants to be hired or admitted based on their race

Risk rule An army practice of measuring how close certain roles would bring a participant to combat and not assigning women to any role that would bring them too close

Seniority system Requires employees with least seniority to be laid off work if the employer needs to release a certain number of employees

Set-aside program Requiring contractors to hire a certain percentage of minority subcontractors if they are awarded a project funded by tax dollars

Sexual harassment Deliberate and repeated behavior that has a sexual basis and is not welcomed, requested, or returned

DISCUSSION EXERCISES

Exercise #1 Enhancing Unity in America Discussion: What Should We Do Next?

Directions: America today demonstrates its diversity in our military, marketplace, and manufacturing, in our media, and in federal, state, and local governments. The following questions ask for your speculation to resolve current issues for our future well-being.

1. Should our federal government eliminate, or modify, the current affirmative action program?
   - If you believe it should be eliminated, explain why.
   - If you believe it should be modified, explain how and why.
2. Do you agree that increased diversity among students on a college campus strengthens the education of all students?
   - How many—or what type—of diversity-related courses should all students be required to take?
   - What should be the outcome of any study of American cultural, racial, and societal human differences?
3. Assume that you have majored and matriculated in some aspect of business; following graduation, you receive two job offers: one with a company that has a good reputation for having a positive environment for diversity; the other, which offers a higher salary with better benefits, has little or no record of attention to attracting a diverse workforce.
   - Which one would you choose, and why?
   - How can a diverse workforce create unity in America?
4. Now that women are approximately half of all managers, why are women still being excluded from a proportional share of top management positions?
   - What will it take to eliminate this glass ceiling?
   - How might business and industry change if women were adequately represented in leadership roles?
5. If the predictions are correct and twenty years from now print and broadcast media employ significantly greater numbers of women and people of color, how will it make a difference in the following areas:
   - Which news stories are covered by print and broadcast journalists
   - How new stories are covered
   - Which stories are presented by news programs (e.g., *20/20* and *Dateline*)
   - Which images and text are presented in advertisements
   - What content and diversity of characters are available in prime-time programming
6. Simply requiring that American societal institutions establish policies against sexual harassment has not been effective.
   - What must the military services do to eliminate the problem of sexual harassment?
   - Business and manufacturing?
   - Nonprofit and religious institutions?

Exercise #2 Creating a More Just Society for the 99%

Directions: Below are ten recommendations to make the United States a more just society for all of its citizens. Discuss each one in terms of whether or not you would like to see it enacted, and your reasons for supporting or rejecting it.

1. Eliminate for-profit schools that have saddled college students with huge debts and have failed to provide jobs to most of their graduates. Increase funds to make low-interest loans available to college students, especially those students from low-income homes.
2. Pass legislation to make banking practices (e.g., credit card charges to both consumers and merchants) more transparent; the federal government must discontinue underwriting questionable financial practices by banks (e.g., derivative transactions).
3. Establish government programs that encourage low-income and middle-income Americans to open savings accounts. Government incentives could include matching grants or an

expansion of current programs that assist first-time homeowners.

4. Reduce corporate welfare by eliminating the loopholes, exceptions, and exemptions in the tax code that provide hidden subsidies for corporations.

5. Establish election day as a federal holiday and make voting a requirement for all American citizens (including fines for failing to vote). This has been done successfully in other nations such as Australia, where the percentage of people voting in elections exceeds 90%.

6. Establish incentives for American corporations to locate within the United States, keeping jobs in this country rather than exporting them overseas.

7. Strengthen affirmative action legislation to provide better enforcement in order to ensure that workers with comparable qualifications from diverse minority groups (e.g., women, people of color, people with a disability) are receiving fair treatment in terms of hiring and promotion decisions.

8. Increase federal government investment in infrastructure, education, and technology based on the studies reporting that these investments were the basis for much of the financial success experienced in the twentieth century.

9. Reaffirm the estate taxes collected from people inheriting $5 million or more so that inheritances do not create a class of wealthy people who can exercise enormous power over the rest of society from one generation to the next.

10. Eliminate practices such as gerrymandering and the filibuster that are used primarily to manipulate the political system for the benefit of a political party rather than for the good of the nation as a whole.

Source: Adapted from: United for a Fair Economy (www.faireconomy.org) and Stiglitz, J. E. (2012). *The price of inequality.* New York: W. W. Norton & Co.

REFERENCES

Abbe, A. & Gouge, M. (2012). *Cultural training for military personnel.* 90(4), pp. 9–17.

Ball, H. (2000). *The Bakke case: Race, education, and affirmative action.* Lawrence: University Press of Kansas.

Becker, L.B., Vlad, T., Kazragis, W., Toledo, C., & Desnoes, P. (2010). *Annual survey of journalism and mass communication graduates.* Retrieved December 4, 2011, from www.grady.uga.edu/annualsurveys/

Bennett, J., & Ellison, J. (2010, July 5). Women will rule the world. *Newsweek.* Retrieved April 3, 2012, from The Daily Beast at www.thedailybeast.com/newsweek/2010/07/06/women-will-rule-the-world.html.

Boyd, D. (2012). White flight in networked publics: How race and class shaped American teen engagement with MySpace and Facebook. In L. Nakamura & P.A. Chow-White (Eds.), *Race after the Internet* (pp. 203–222). New York, NY: Routledge.

Brady, J. (2009). *Military Buddhist chapel represents tolerance.* NPR. Retrieved October 24, 2012, from www.npr.org/templates/story/story.php?storyid=113501618

Browne-Miller, A. (1996). *Shameful admissions: The losing battle to serve everyone in our universities.* San Francisco, CA: Jossey-Bass.

Buckley, G. (2001). *American patriots: The story of blacks in the military from the Revolution to Desert Storm.* New York, NY: Random House.

Burns, C., Barton, K., & Kirby, S. (2012). *The state of diversity in today's workforce.* Center for American Progress. Retrieved October 25, 2012, from www.americanprogress.org/issues/labor/report/2012/07/12/11938

Carr-Ruffino, N. (2007). *Managing diversity: People skills for a multicultural workplace.* Boston, MA: Pearson Custom.

Carter, P. (2002). War dames. *The Washington Monthly, 34*(12), 32–37.

Catalyst (2012). *People of color in the U.S.* Retrieved October 25, 2012, from www.catalyst.org/publication/356/people-of-color-in-the-us

Catalyst. (2012). *Statistical overview of women in the workplace.* Retrieved October 25, 2012, from www.catalyst.org/publication/219/statistical-overview-of-women-in-the-workplace

Chernow, R. (2004). *Alexander Hamilton.* New York, NY: Penguin.

Chuang, A (2010). *The future of ethnic media depends on generation that sees color differently.* Retrieved December 5, 2011, from www.poynter.org/404 (select diversity at work).

Clayton, S.D., & Crosby, F.J. (2000). Justice, gender, and affirmative action. In F.J. Crosby & C. VanDeVeer (Eds.), *Sex, race, and merit: Debating affirmative action in education and employment* (pp. 81–88). Ann Arbor: University of Michigan Press.

Cochran-Smith, M. (2003). Standing at the crossroads: Multicultural teacher education at the beginning of the 21st century. *Multicultural Perspectives, 5*(3), 3–11.

Craft-Fairchild, C. (1997, Fall). Women warriors in the 18th century. *St. Thomas,* 32–35.

Crosby, F.J., & VanDeVeer, C. (Eds.). (2000). *City of Richmond v. J.A. Croson Co.* In *Sex, race, and merit: Debating affirmative action in education and employment* (pp. 280–293). Ann Arbor: University of Michigan Press.

Daft, R.L. (2003). Managing diverse employees. In *Management* (4th ed., pp. 436–468). Versailles, KY: Thompson Southwestern.

Dansby, M.R., & Landis, D. (2001). Intercultural training in the United States military. In M.R. Dansby, J.B. Stewart, & S.C. Webb (Eds.), *Managing diversity in the military: Research perspectives from the Defense Equal Opportunity Management Institute* (pp. 9–28). New Brunswick, NJ: Transaction.

Dansby, M.R., Stewart, J.B., & Webb, S.C. (Eds.). (2001). Overview. In *Managing diversity in the military: Research perspectives from the Defense Equal Opportunity Management Institute* (pp. xvii–xxxii). New Brunswick, NJ: Transaction.

Dao, J. (2011). Black women enlisting at higher rates in U.S. military. *New York Times.* Retrieved October 24, 2012, from www.nytimes.com/2011/12/23/us/black-women-enlist-at-higher-rates-in-us-military.html

Department of Defense. (2010). *Population representation in the military services.* Retrieved http://prhome.defense.gov/RFM/MPP/ACCESSIONPOLICY/PopRep2010/contents/contents.html

Diaz, R.F. (1999). The Hispanic market: An overview. In L.J. Matthews & T. Pavri (Eds.), *Population diversity and the U.S. Army* (pp. 87–98). Carlisle, PA: Strategic Studies Institute.

Dreazen, Y. (2009). Muslim population in the military raises difficult issues. *Wall Street Journal.* Retrieved October 24, 2012, from wsj.com/article/SB125755853525335343.html

Duncan, P. (2002). Decentering whiteness: Resisting racism in the women's studies classroom. In B. Tusmith & M.T. Reddy (Eds.), *Race in the college classroom: Pedagogy and politics* (pp. 40–50). New Brunswick, NJ: Rutgers University Press.

Eastland, T. (2000). Ending affirmative action: The case for colorblind justice. In F.J. Crosby & C. VanDeVeer (Eds.), *Sex, race, and merit: Debating affirmative action in education and employment* (pp. 174–175). Ann Arbor: University of Michigan Press.

Eck, D.L. (2001). *A new religious America: How a "Christian country" has become the world's most religiously diverse nation.* New York, NY: HarperCollins.

Egodigwe, L. (2005, November 14). Back to class. *Wall Street Journal,* p. R4.

Estes, S. (2007). *Ask & tell: Gay and lesbian veterans speak out.* Chapel Hill, NC: The University of North Carolina Press.

Everett, A. (2012). Have we become postracial yet? Race and media technology in the age of President Obama. In L. Nakamura & P.A. Chow-White (Eds.), *Race after the Internet* (pp. 146–167). New York, NY: Routledge.

Ferguson, R. (1998). *Representing "race": Ideology, identity and the media.* London, England: Arnold.

Frank, T.A. (2008, April). Confessions of a sweatshop inspector. *The Washington Monthly, 40*(4), 34–37.

Fuller, L. (2011). The "silent crisis" of the Latino dropout rate. neatoday. Retrieved on November 11, 2012 from http://neatoday/org/2011/06/21/the-silent-crisis-of-the-latino-dropout-rate/

Galloway, A.R. (2012). Does the whatever speak? In L. Nakamura & P.A. Chow-White (Eds.), *Race after the Internet* (pp. 111–127). New York, NY: Routledge.

Gardner, H. (2006). *Five minds for the future.* Boston, MA: Harvard Business School Press.

Greene, K.W. (1989). *Affirmative action and principles of justice.* New York, NY: Greenwood.

Griffin, R. (2002). The cultural and multicultural environment. In *Management* (7th ed., pp. 162–191). Boston, MA: Houghton Mifflin.

Guenther-Schlesinger, S. (2001). Persistence of sexual harassment: The impact of military culture on policy implementation. In M.F. Katzenstein & J. Reppy (Eds.), *Beyond zero tolerance: Discrimination in military culture* (pp. 195–212). Lanham, MD: Rowman & Littlefield.

Humphreys, D. (Ed.). (2000, Fall). National survey finds diversity requirements common around the country. *Diversity Digest,* pp. 1–2.

Hunt, D.M. (2007). Whose stories are we telling? *Writers Guild of America.* Retrieved October 25, 2012, from www.wga.org/uploadedFiles/who_we_are/HWR07.pdf

Hymowitz, C. (2005, November 14). The new diversity. *Wall Street Journal*, pp. R1, R3.

IBM. (2012). *IBM named a top company where women succeed.* Retrieved October 25, 2012, from http://www-03.ibm.com/employment/us/diverse/feature_nafe.shtml

Imparato, A.J., Houtenville, A.J., & Shaffert, R.L. (2010). *Increasing the employment rate of people with disabilities.* Retrieved April 4, 2012, from https://www.google.com/search?q=Increasing+the+employment+rate+of+people+with+disabilities&ie=utf-8&oe=utf-8&aq=t&rls=org.mozilla:en-US:official&client=firefox-a

Johnson, D. (1999). The U.S. Army and ethnic diversity: A historical overview. In L.J. Matthews & T. Pavri (Eds.), *Population diversity and the U.S. Army* (pp. 45–56). Carlisle, PA: Strategic Studies Institute.

Johnson, J.L. (2001). Local effects and global impact of Defense Equal Opportunity Management Institute Training. In M.R. Dansby, J.B. Stewart, & S.C. Webb (Eds.), *Managing diversity in the military: Research perspectives from the Defense Equal Opportunity Management Institute* (pp. 178–188). New Brunswick, NJ: Trans action.

Johnson, M.T. (2011). *The diversity code.* New York, NY: AMACOM.

Johnson, S.D. (2000, June). Keep the pressure on. *Essence, 1*(2), 184.

Jones, G.R., & George, J.M. (2003). Managing diverse employees in a diverse environment. *Contemporary management* (3rd ed., pp. 112–149). New York, NY: McGraw-Hill.

Jones, J.C. (1999). Diversity in the 21st century: Leadership issues. In L.J. Matthews & T. Pavri (Eds.), *Population diversity and the U.S. Army* (pp. 57–68). Carlisle, PA: Strategic Studies Institute.

Katzenstein, M.F., & Reppy, J. (Eds.). (1999). Introduction: Rethinking military culture. In *Beyond zero tolerance: Discrimination in military culture* (pp. 1–21). Lanham, MD: Rowman & Littlefield.

Kawamoto, K. (2003). *Media and society in the digital age.* Boston, MA: Allyn & Bacon.

Kier, E. (1999). Discrimination and military cohesion: An organizational perspective. In M.F. Katzenstein & J. Reppy (Eds.), *Beyond zero tolerance: Discrimination in military culture* (pp. 25–32). Lanham, MD: Rowman & Littlefield.

Kolodny, A. (1998). *Failing the future: A dean looks at higher education in the twenty-first century.* Durham, NC: Duke University Press.

Lee, G.H., Jr. (2006, November/December) Sporting news. *The Crisis, 113*(6), 22–23.

Lowe, E.Y., Jr. (Ed.). (1999). Promise and dilemma: Incorporating racial diversity in selective higher education. In *Promise and dilemma: Perspectives on racial diversity and higher education* (pp. 3–43). Princeton, NJ: Princeton University Press.

Luscombe, B. (2010). The rise of the sheconomy. *Time, 176*(21), pp. 58–61.

Luther, C.A., Lepre, C.R., & Clark, N. (2012). *Diversity in U.S. mass media.* Malden, MA: Wiley-Blackwell.

Matthews, L. (1999). Introduction: Primer on future recruitment of diversity. In L.J. Matthews & T. Pavri (Eds.), *Population diversity and the U.S. Army* (p. 116). Carlisle, PA: Strategic Studies Institute.

McQueen, M. (2002, July/August). What about diverse faculty? *Quill, 90*(6), 19–22.

Millman, J. (2005, November 14). Delayed recognition. *Wall Street Journal*, p. R8.

Mor-Barak, M.E. (2005). *Managing diversity: Toward a globally inclusive workplace.* Thousand Oaks, CA: Sage Publications.

Moskos, C.C., & Butler, J.S. (1996). *All that we can be: Black leadership and racial integration in the army.* New York, NY: Basic Books.

Musil, C.M. (1996, November/December). The maturing diversity initiatives on American campuses. *American Behavioral Scientist, 40*(2), 222–232.

National Employment Lawyers Association. (2000). Position paper on affirmative action. In J. Birnbaum & C. Taylor (Eds.), *Civil Rights since 1787: A reader on the black struggle* (pp. 708–713). New York, NY: New York University Press.

New York Times. (2012, June 4). Women in combat. A24.

Orfield, G., Kucsera, J., & Siegel-Hawley, G. (2012). Civil Rights Project. Retrieved October 24, 2012, from www.civilrightsproject.ucla.edu/research

Orfield, G., & Lee, C. (2007). *Historic reversals, accelerating resegregation, and the need for new integration strategies.* Civil Rights Project. Retrieved

October 17, 2012, from www.civilrightsproject.ucla .edu/research

Painter, N.I. (2005). *Creating Black Americans: African-American history and its meaning, 1619 to the present.* Oxford, England: Oxford University Press.

Patten, E., & Parker, K. (2011). *Women in the U.S Military: Growing share, distinctive profile.* Retrieved October 25, 2012, from www.pewsocialtrends .org/2011/12/222/women-in-th-u-s-military-growing-share-distinctive-profile/2/#active-duty-women

Peterson, M.J. (1999). Women in the U.S. military. In L.J. Matthews & T. Pavri (Eds.), *Population diversity and the U.S. Army* (pp. 99–106). Carlisle, PA: Strategic Studies Institute.

Pipher, M. (2002). *The middle of everywhere: The world's refugees come to our town.* New York, NY: Harcourt.

Popper, B. (2000). Minority hiring may be facing retrenchment. *USA Today Magazine, 128*(2658), 66–67.

Reddy, M.T. (2002). Smashing the rules of racial standing. In B. Tusmith & M.T. Reddy (Eds.), *Race in the college classroom: Pedagogy and politics* (pp. 51–61). New Brunswick, NJ: Rutgers University Press.

Reskin, B.F. (2000). The realities of affirmative action in employment. In F.J. Crosby & C. VanDeVeer (Eds.), *Sex, race, and merit: Debating affirmative action in education and employment* (pp. 103–113). Ann Arbor: University of Michigan Press.

Riley, C.A. II. (2005). *Disability and the media: Prescriptions for change.* Lebanon, NH: University Press of New England.

Roush, P.E. (1999). A tangled Webb the Navy can't afford. In M.F. Katzenstein & J. Reppy (Eds.), *Beyond zero tolerance: Discrimination in military culture* (pp. 81–100). Lanham, MD: Rowman & Littlefield.

Sandvig, C. (2012). Connection at Ewiiaapaayp Mountain: Indigenous Internet infrastructure. In L. Nakamura & P.A. Chow-White (Eds.), *Race after the Internet* (pp. 168–200). New York, NY: Routledge.

Sasha Corporation. (2007). *Compilation of turnover cost studies.* Retrieved October 25, 2012, from www .sashacorp.com/turnframe.html

Sayles, A.H. (1999). Person to person: The diversity challenge for the Army after next. In L.J. Matthews & T. Pavri (Eds.), *Population diversity and the U.S. Army* (pp. 107–124). Carlisle, PA: Strategic Studies Institute.

Segal, D.R., Segal, M.W., & Booth, B. (1999). Gender and sexual orientation diversity in modern military forces: Cross-national patterns. In M.F. Katzenstein & J. Reppy (Eds.), *Beyond zero tolerance: Discrimination in military culture* (pp. 225–250). Lanham, MD: Rowman & Littlefield.

Stanhope, K. (2009). *Report: Minority, female writers in TV still underrepresented.* Retrieved October 25, 2012, from www.tvguide.com/News/Report-Minority-Female-1012279.aspx

Stearns, P. (2006). *World history: Curriculum and controversy.* Retrieved October 24, 2012, from http:// worldhistoryconnected.press.illinois.edu/3.3/stearns .html

Stewart, J.B., & Firestone, J.M. (2001). Looking for a few good men: Predicting patterns of retention, promotion, and accession of minority and women officers. In M.R. Dansby, J.B. Stewart, & S.C. Webb (Eds.), *Managing diversity in the military: Research perspectives from the defense equal opportunity management institute* (pp. 231–256). New Brunswick, NJ: Transaction.

Tusmith, B., & Reddy, M.T. (2002). Introduction: Race in the college classroom. In B. Tusmith & M.T. Reddy (Eds.), *Race in the college classroom: Pedagogy and politics* (pp. 1–3). New Brunswick, NJ: Rutgers University Press.

Waldman, A. (1996, November). GIs: Not your average Joes: What the military can teach us about race, class, and citizenship. *The Washington Monthly*, 26–33.

Williams, C. (2003). Managing individuals and a diverse work force. In *Management* (2nd ed., pp. 434–471). Versailles, KY: Thompson Southwestern.

Wilson, E.J., III, & Costanza-Chock, S. (2012). New voices on the Net? The digital journalism and the costs of network exclusion. In L. Nakamura & P.A. Chow-White (Eds.), *Race after the Internet* (pp. 246–268). New York, NY: Routledge.

Yamane, D. (2001). *Student movements for multiculturalism: Challenging the curricular color line in higher education.* Baltimore, MD: Johns Hopkins University Press.

Yu, B. (2011). Media justice and the 99 percent movement. *Extra!, 24*(12), 8–9.

Zeigler, S.L., & Gunderson, G.G. (2005). *Moving beyond G. I. Jane: Women and the U.S. military.* Lanham, MD: University Press of America.

Index